Cruising **FRENCH** WATERWAYS

THIRD EDITION

Winner of the Thomas Cook
Guide Book Award

SHERIDAN HOUSE

Cruising **FRENCH** WATERWAYS

Hugh McKnight

Third edition published 1999 by Sheridan House Inc.
145 Palisade Street, Dobbs Ferry, New York 10522

First published in Great Britain by
Stanford Maritime in 1984
Second edition published by
Adlard Coles Nautical 1991

Library of Congress Cataloging-in-Publication Data

McKnight, Hugh.
Cruising French waterways / Hugh McKnight. – 3rd. ed. p. cm.
Previously published under title: Cruising French canals and rivers.
Includes bibliographical references and index.
1. Boats and boating—France guidebooks. 2. Inland navigation—France Guidebooks. 3. Canals—France Guidebooks. 4. Rivers—France Guidebooks. 5. France Guidebooks. I. McKnight, Hugh. Cruising French canals and Rivers. II. Title.
GV776.48.A2M4 1999
914.404'839—dc21 99-22891
CIP

Printed in Great Britain

ISBN 1-57409-087-9

Winner of the Thomas Cook Guide Book Award

TITLE PAGE: Laval on the River Mayenne
PAGE 5: Detail of the fine Belle Époque metalwork at the base of a lamp standard on the Briare Aqueduct on the Canal Latéral à la Loire
PAGE 6: The 12th century fortified village of Châteauneuf overlooking the Canal de Bourgogne

To my Mother
1904–1999
That she was christened Grace Darling
may possibly account for a long-standing
family interest in *inland* boating.

FOREWORD *by The Earl of Snowdon*

In 1977 my family and I enjoyed a wonderful holiday on the Canal du Midi, joining it at Castelnaudary and ending up at Marseillan. I had no idea at the time that my great grandfather Linley Sambourne, the political cartoonist on "Punch", had experienced the same pleasure 104 years before. His sketches were published shortly afterwards in a book called "Our Autumn Holiday on French Rivers". Although I too spent most of the time sketching the views, bridges and locks, mine were of such an inferior quality, they remain in a bottom drawer.

Like him, I was excited to discover this amazing survival of 17th century engineering and architecture. Water transport pre-dates the age of steam: yet in France inland waterways are still used by commerce. They are not just a reconstruction job for tourists, but are very much used for industry as well as for pleasure.

The speed is slow and ideal for sketch book or camera. You stop when and where you want. And if you take off on the boat's bicycles for shopping or sight seeing, the towpaths and quiet lanes have none of the fumes and dangers of the main roads.

Among my companions on that journey was the author, Hugh McKnight. With this book to guide them, I am sure that many more people will be encouraged to discover these hidden highways.

Snowdon

Contents

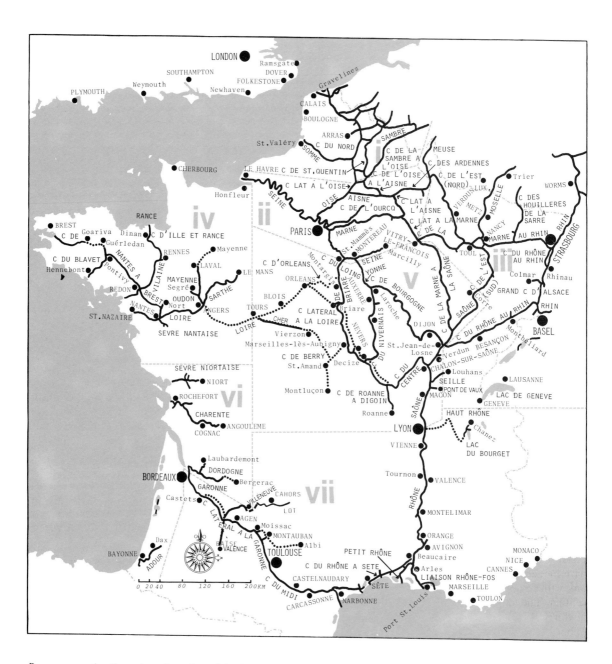

Roman numerals refer to the main sections of this book

INTRODUCTION

'Madame reminded her husband of an Englishman who had come up this canal in a steamer.

"'Perhaps Mr Moens in the *Ytene*,'" I suggested.

"'That's it,'" assented the husband. "He had his wife and family with him, and servants. He came ashore at all the locks and asked the name of the villages, whether from boatmen or lock keepers; and then he wrote, wrote them down. Oh, he wrote enormously! I suppose it was a wager.'"

Robert Louis Stevenson, *An Inland Voyage*, 1878

Equipped with camera and tape recorder, I have often felt like William Moens, attempting to describe waterways in a foreign land whose language he could speak only with difficulty. It all began more than forty years ago, when as a fourteen-year-old I travelled abroad for the first time to stay with a French family in Lyon. Already an enthusiastic Thames boater, I would watch barges gliding peacefully down the Saône to the confluence with a then untamed Rhône. There, the green and wild water picked them up and hurled them out of sight on their voyage to the South and the Mediterranean. Some day, I thought, it would make a great adventure to explore the canals and rivers of France.

But Britain came first. For the next decade the waterways of England, Scotland, Wales and Ireland absorbed all my spare time. Then, in the autumn of 1968, I accepted an invitation from John Liley of *Motor Boat & Yachting* magazine to join a party of friends on a Saint Line cruiser, making a circuit from the Canal du Nivernais. It was pure magic! Horse barges were not quite extinct and we must have met all that remained in service, an evocative link with freight transport as practised in the 19th century. The following spring I was among a group of thirty British people who took part in a five-day publicity cruise from Bordeaux to Toulouse at the inauguration of France's second hire boat company, Blue Line Cruisers. Since then I have returned to the French waterways annually (often many times in a single year) discovering new routes in everything from an inflatable dinghy to passenger vessels, hire cruisers and private motor yachts.

There are about 8,500km of navigable canals and rivers in France (compared with 12,467km in 1879), enabling the aquatic tourist to penetrate almost every region: from the Ardennes to Picardy, Provence to the Île de France, Burgundy to the Vosges. Developed over many centuries, the network has regularly been modernised and extended. Recent years have seen new lines opened up for 2,000 tonne barges; many older canals are now fitted with automated locks and swing bridges controlled by radar beams, switches suspended from pylons or *télécommandes* (portable push button devices); flights of locks have been replaced by boat lifts, reducing several hours of effort to a matter of minutes.

However, in spite of massive investment, commercial freight carriage continues to decline, largely because of extremely unfair subsidies available to alternative transport systems. That the waterways of France manage to prosper is increasingly due to a massive growth in pleasure traffic.

Pleasure cruising is relatively new. Sea-going craft have long used inland routes between the English Channel, the Rhine and the Mediterranean, or taken a short-cut from the Atlantic across the sun-drenched country of Languedoc. But now inland boating is firmly established as an activity in its own right. For the solitary traveller or family alike, there can be no more peaceful way to explore this beautiful land, seeking out ancient towns and villages, drinking local wines and eating in waterside *auberges*. The key to fullest enjoyment is to avoid being hurried: 30km and 10 locks each day is a target ambitious enough for anyone. Yachtsmen's stories of dawn to dusk navigation, through flights of tiring locks, leaving a mob of angry canal staff astern of their wash, all too often suggests a totally wrong approach to the subject.

Safety and peace are prime characteristics of French inland boating. In thousands of kilometres of cruising I have had few anxious moments, with the possible exception of the time when the yacht on which I was a guest caught fire in a lock near St-Dizier. By comparison, the world of dry land is infinitely more dangerous and long-remembered hazards include my being thrown from the pillion of the ship's motorcycle into the path of a lorry on the hilly approach to Langres; being surrounded by gangs of hostile youths in the early hours of the morning as I tried to sleep in a tent on the banks of the Marne; and having my car broken into twice in one year while boating by inflatable: parking sites were subsequently chosen with a greater regard for security. Coastal cruising can also introduce elements of danger from which canals and rivers are generally free. After travelling the Lower Seine from Paris to Honfleur, I agreed to stay aboard the boat for a further day's run by sea to Cherbourg. Many hours after our estimated arrival time we were enveloped in a dense fog with faulty steering, one of the two engines defunct and a rapidly dwindling fuel supply. Thanks to the radio telephone, a rescue tug from the *Affaires Maritimes* pulled us into the safety of the harbour in the early hours of the morning. I then decided that inland waters were more trustworthy.

Waterways are a constant state of change. Information which is accurate at the time of writing may well have altered. Shops come and go, restaurants experience changes of ownership, lock opening times are adjusted and even the physical layout of some canals may alter. This third edition is mainly updated to early-1999. I strongly suggest that it is used in conjunction with the appropriate *Carte Guides*, in which it is possible to note revisions with greater frequency. I freely admit that, given the sheer size of the task, there are some areas that I have not been able to check with the accuracy I would have wished. My greatest concern - one that has provided considerable pleasure - was to add new entries for those routes recently brought back into full use from utter dereliction. These include the River Baïse, River Cher and connected portion of the Canal du Berry and a series of small arms and branches. There are some references to Customs posts in the book, but of course they are now unmanned and there is no requirement to visit those in EU countries. While every effort has been made to ensure that matter in this book was correct when it went to press, neither I nor my publishers can accept responsibility for any consequential difficulties arising from statements contained in it.

Cruising French Waterways was the first and remains the only descriptive account of the entire French network. It is designed to inform readers exactly what they can expect of each waterway in terms of historical development, scenery, places to visit, suitable moorings and (to a more limited extent, for here the *Carte Guides* are designed to provide the fullest information) other facilities. One quandary was to decide which end of a canal or river should start the description. Inevitably, some users will be making their journey in the opposite direction. But, where possible, through routes or circuits have been dealt with as a continuous sequence. **Rather than adopt the convention of making references to the left bank or right bank when moving downstream (this works with rivers but is most confusing on canals), left and right refer to the direction of travel.**

I hope that English-speaking readers will accept my use of metric measurements throughout. For many years Britain has been on the verge of conversion and kilometres and metres have been the accepted units in schools for a long while. Perhaps in time we shall doubtless all be able to reject miles and yards in mental calculations: for the present, it is helpful to remember that metres and yards are roughly interchangeable. A kilometre is five-eighths of a mile (50 miles = 80km). For practical purposes, I find that conversion from kilometres to miles is easily achieved by dividing by 2 and adding 'a bit'. Use of a dual system in this book would have complicated the issue. In any event, France has been metric for two hundred years and all publications such as the *Carte Guides* quote the native units. For those used to thinking in miles, the kilometre is a surprisingly optimistic form of measurement, 30km being a reasonable day's cruising distance while 30 miles could constitute a daunting prospect.

This book has been designed to be used in conjunction with the excellent series of *Carte Guides* listed in the Bibliography. The appropriate volume is identified at the start of each chapter. These map/guides, regularly updated, contain text in French, English and German and include full details of facilities en route such as fuel, water points, moorings, repairs, shopping and restaurants. For planning purposes, a large-scale map of the waterways system is also very useful. Signals for traffic control and between vessels, navigational and other marks are published either in the *Carte Guides* or on a small self-adhesive poster which can be placed alongside the steering position for instant reference (see Bibliography).

Many friends have assisted me with compilation and I am extremely grateful to them. First, June and John Humphries, whose enthusiasm for French boating has been boundless. I began exploring waterways with them and their four daughters thirty years ago. That we acquired in 1983 the jointly-owned sea-going motor yacht *Avonbay* for Continental use was an indication of our combined involvement with the subject. Since 1997, *Avonbay* has been in my sole ownership, but I hope to welcome them aboard for many years to come. Their assistance has taken numerous practical forms, not least the encouragement I have received throughout the life of this book. The late Lord and Lady Harvington regularly invited me aboard their charming motor cruisers *Melita* and *Melitina*. These voyages generally featured a rapid and sometimes exciting progress through France. There were few yachtsmen who explored Continental waterways so extensively and with such perennial enthusiasm: Grant Harvington was to take delivery of his final vessel when well into his eighties.

John Liley, subsequently a hotel barge proprietor, was responsible for my very first French canal trav-els. The cruiser was owned by Pierre Zivy, then of Saint Line: it was he who introduced hire craft to France and as a result saved the Canal du Nivernais (and quite possibly many other routes) from certain closure. By launching Blue Line Cruisers (France) Ltd., the late Michael Streat instigated many of my fluvial forays and on one memorable occasion was a guest aboard *Avonbay*. The company's original president, Gerald Norman, francophile, was a source of great inspiration, instilling in me a love of France, its history and people. The late Professor David Horsfall, wit, world expert on coal washing and fellow collector of waterways literature, shared a small but invaluable portion of the practical cruising research. The executives, base managers and staff of Blue Line Cruisers (now Crown Blue Line) past and present and especially Charles Gérard (now of H$_2$O, St-Jean de Losne) and Keith

Specially selected for French waterways: the author's steel twin-engined motor cruiser Avonbay.

Gregory, all provided services, facilities and hospitality. So did Jimmy Hoseason and his colleagues of Hoseason's Holidays, Messrs Blake's Holidays, Andrew Brock of French Country Cruises, Messrs Locoboat Plaisance and the staff of the French Government Tourist Office in London.

In recent years, Mig and Jim Macdonald have regularly cruised with me on Avonbay and other 'research' vessels, providing reassuring confidence and the necessary expertise for coastal voyages. Jim has also offered much appreciated engineering support, necessary to maintain my boat in a suitable condition for the rigorous adventures demanded of her.

Many readers of the first two editions were kind enough to write to me saying how much this book had added to their cruising enjoyment. A number of them went to considerable trouble to provide additional information, all of which I have tried to incorporate into the present updated version. These include Denise Closier, Robert Cowley, John Cruse, Mike and Tania Herniman, Carrie and Mike Hofman, J. R. Liney, Marshall Long, Vernon Marchant, Jim Marshall, D. C. Minett, the late Tony Paris, Karen and Morvyn Phillips, Bob van Gulik, the Rev. Ricky Yates and Sefton Sandford.

Two fellow waterways authors deserve credit: David Edwards-May for answering questions and for keeping me up to date with new developments, and Dr Roger Pilkington whose *Small Boat* books have long been a source of inspiration. My original editor, Phoebe Mason, viewed the gestation of this book with remarkable patience and good humour - a rare combination in a publisher. This excellent relationship continues under Janet Murphy. Lastly, I salute the lock keepers and people of France who have accepted my invasion of their country with real kindness. Thank you to all.

Unless otherwise acknowledged, all photographs are my own, with historical material drawn from the Hugh McKnight Photography Collection.

If, during the course of their French cruises, readers should discover information which might enhance future editions of this book, I shall be delighted to hear from them.

HUGH McKNIGHT
The Swan House
Priory Terrace
St. Neots
Cambs. PE19 2BH
England

AFLOAT IN FRANCE

Some years ago, France, in common with a number of other European nations, decided that those in charge of private pleasure craft should be examined in the theory and practice of boating techniques. When it was realised that such legislation would bring the fast-growing and economically important hire cruiser industry to its abrupt destruction, it was decreed that hire customers could be exempted on the grounds of a few minutes of basic instruction at the start of their holidays. This was a typically Gallic solution! Private boat owners, whose skills are almost invariably superior, would still be subjected to an official test. This situation remains.

In Britain, there is no such requirement, but if we are to use French inland waters in our own craft, we must have an acceptable qualification. Thus, it is necessary to hold an International Certificate of Competence (ICC) or equivalent, issued by the Royal Yachting Association, RYA House, Romsey Road, Eastleigh, Hampshire SO5 4YA. Tel. 01703 627400. The RYA will, on application, provide the syllabus, together with a list of approved boating school test centres. All the information needed for this test is contained in *The RYA Book of EuroRegs for Inland Waterways* by Marian Martin published by Adlard Coles Nautical. Fees are charged both by the Association and the examiners. The ICC is now only available to British subjects, meaning that Americans, Australians and other English-speaking yachtsmen must either obtain equivalent qualifications in their own countries or opt to take a test in France, where use of an interpreter is permitted.

While the test for inland waters is not especially difficult, the fact that it is required at all is, to say the least, irksome, in view of the situation relating to boat hirers.

As a British subject, you are entitled to use and keep your boat on French waters with exactly the same freedom that you can cruise in your home country, although it is necessary to have proof that Value Added Tax has been paid on your boat. It would be wise to check all regulations that may be in force with the RYA. The situation is more complicated for non-European Community nationals, where, if they are to avoid payment of 18.6% French tax on the estimated value of their boat, it may only be used in France for a total of six months in each year, its registration papers being lodged with a local customs office as proof of non use. This arrangement can last for three consecutive years, after which documentary evidence must record that the vessel has been exported from France, if only for a brief period. Then, another three year cycle can start. That is my understanding of the situation, although non-European private boat owners are recommended to check the current situation with the French Embassy in their own country. For regulations relating to larger, heavier vessels such as converted barges, it would be wise to consult either The Barge Cruising Association. (Beverley Stainer, Honorary Secretary, Good Shelter, Spade Oak Reach, Bourne End SL8 5RQ. Tel. 01753 648112) or the Dutch Barge Association Ltd. (Carl Walters, Membership Secretary, 'De Hoop', Ryepeck Meadow, Chertsey Road, Shepperton, Middlesex, TW17 9NU. Tel. 01932 569112). Much useful information including traffic signals, rule of the road, navigation lights etc is contained *European Waterways* and *The RYA Book of EuroRegs for Inland Waterways* both by Marian Martin published by Adlard Coles Nautical.

The intention of this book is to describe the waterways themselves rather than such matters as what equipment to take, working through locks, or organizing shopping expeditions in unknown towns. In many respects, inland cruising in France is much the same as anywhere: provided your boat is well fendered, furnished with adequate lines and preferably has one or more bicycles aboard (useful for sight-seeing, shopping and travelling up canal towpath to help keepers prepare manual locks), you should encounter few difficulties.

Most, but not quite all, locks are manned by resident or mobile lock keepers. You are expected to help them, under their direction. Locks on larger waterways may be contacted in advance of your boat's arrival via VHF radio telephone. Appropriate channel numbers appear in the *Carte Guides*. In this

A young crew member lifts up the rod to operate the switch gear to work an automatic lock. The blue rod on the left controls gates and paddles; the red one on the right halts all activity in the event of an emergency. If a hard push fails to produce any action, advice can be sought on the telephone alongside, though the keeper who answers may be several locks away.

way, the keeper may well be able to prepare the chamber before you reach it.

Until 1991, French waterways were available to pleasure craft free of charge. Since then, a licence (*vignette*) has been necessary for each boat. Currently, these may be purchased for one day, or 16 days use, start and finishing dates to be specified; 30 days (not necessarily consecutive, a 'day' being counted only when the boat is moving); or for a year, terminating 31 December following date of purchase. Various price categories depend on the total area of the vessel (length x beam). Very small and low-powered craft are exempt, while no charge is made for using certain routes which are under local rather than national control: these include the Canal du Nivernais, rivers and canals in Brittany and the French canalised Rhine.

It is preferable to buy a *vignette* by post, well in advance of the start of a cruise, as the various regional offices of the navigation authority appear to

open at irregular hours. The completed application form should be accompanied by payment in French francs and photocopies of your personal helmsman's certificate and the boat's registration document. Details are available from Voies Navigables de la France (VNF), rue Ludovic Boutleux, BP 820, 62408 Béthune, France. Tel. 21 63 24 24.

Other necessary paperwork to carry on the boat includes passports for all on board, insurance certificate for the vessel and licences (a) for the installation and (b) for the use of VHF radio.

Lock opening hours vary with the time of year and between one navigation and another. Broadly speaking, keepers are on duty from 6.00–19.30h in the summer, with a break for the midday meal. Occasionally, some routes are closed on a particular day of the week. Stoppages (chômages) for routine repairs generally avoid peak pleasure boating periods. A list, compiled around late March each year, is available from VNF (see above) or the French Government Tourist Office, 178, Piccadilly, London, W1V 0AL.

Many locks are these days worked automatically by radar or electronic sensors or manually operated switches suspended over the waterways. Printed instructions are dispensed to boat crews before entering such a section. A small number of routes are worked by boaters, either manually (Rivers Charente and Upper Lot) or by special 'smart card' (River Baïse).

Boatyards and marinas are moderately prolific in many areas, but they are rarely as common as in the UK. Drinking water supplies are sometimes few and far between, so it is best to top up whenever possible, especially if your boat's tank capacity is limited. The same applies to diesel supplies, where it should be noted that red (tax-free) fuel bought in France may not be used to propel craft, although it is permitted for central heating purposes. Imported red diesel may be used, but you are strongly advised to keep accurate details of consumption/distances travelled etc as French Customs are known to carry out spot checks and their penalties are severe. Waterside petrol pumps, chiefly of interest to users of outboard motors, are virtually non-existent: here, fuel must be carried in cans from roadside garages.

Bottled gas (propane or butane, often used for cooking, water heating and refrigeration) is widely available throughout France from marinas, garages and supermarkets. Empty 'foreign' cylinders are not exchangable for French brands. It is best to utilise the two types that are distributed in most regions: Primagaz and Butagaz. Note that the fittings differ from those used in the UK: French chandleries and hardware shops stock suitable replacements.

At the present time, living costs for British holiday-maker in France represent excellent value. Most food products, with the possible exception of meat, are considerably cheaper than at home. Wine and beer are a fraction of the price. Careful research will reveal restaurants where a four-course meal, inclusive of house wine, can still be bought for £5! As a rule, by selecting the more ambitious menu at an inexpensive village restaurant, you will always obtain better value than by attempting to economise at a smart establishment. Watch where the lock keepers, *pénichiers*, and lorry drivers are eating and do likewise. Supermarket shopping provides really fresh food without any language barrier. Otherwise, country lock keepers may sell you their own produce, from fruit and vegetables to eggs, rabbits, chicken or wine. I tend to buy from such places rather than offer tips, which can appear a little patronising and, on a long journey become very expensive.

Try not to antagonise the people who make their living on the waterways. Earn the respect of barge families who are using the waterways for twelve months of the year. Never race working boats to a lock unless you are certain you will be out of their way before they are ready to pass through. It can be infuriating to have the same barge stern in view, lock after lock, as when I once crawled up the Canal de l'Est for three days behind a convoy of slow-moving laden *péniches*, none of the pounds being long enough to allow overtaking. But in compensation we had ample opportunity to really get to know these working-boat people, exchanged bottles of wine and finally ended up enjoying an open-air dinner with them under the towpath plane trees. Equally, while almost all of lock keepers are charming, the odd sour example will be enountered. Always reflect that you are a foreigner in someone else's territory and remain patient.

Speed limits are imposed for the safey of other craft and to protect canal banks from erosion. These are usually 6kph on small canals, 8–10kph on larger artificial waterways and 20–25kph on river navigations. But if, even within these speeds, you are creating a breaking wave on the banks, you should slow down. Never endanger those in canoes or rowing boats and try to be considerate to fishermen (this is sometimes impossible to achieve, judging from the comments you will receive). Noticeboards inform where reduced speed is demanded. Certain river reaches are classified for water-skiing, with limits as high as 40kph. Never be tempted to emulate the disgraceful behaviour of certain power boaters, whose passage can cause far more disturbance than a 1,350-tonne barge. Sadly, not everyone afloat is blessed with either common sense or good manners! Almost nothing annoys waterways authorities and lock keepers as much as boats tearing along a canal creating a massive bow wave with wash breaking on the banks. If the boat happens to be capable of being described as a floating gin palace, the offence is compounded! It is no excuse to claim urgent business elsewhere, or that your vessel handles badly at slow speeds. The worst offenders are generally sea-going yachts using the waterways as a coast-to-coast shortcut. They can give a bad name to all pleasure craft. Unless you are willing to slow down to conventional canal and river speeds and enjoy waterways boating as an experience in its own right, it is better to stick to the sea.

You should be familiar with all forms of navigation markers, signals and instruction noticeboards: these are explained in the *Carte Guides*, in colour. All but the shortest tunnels (where a strong torch is adequate) require a powerful search light, with one or more handheld torches ready for use. Many tunnels are now illuminated. Additional illumination can be provided by turning the cabin lights on, but not so as to impair the helmsman's vision. Other necessary equipment to take includes a loud horn to alert lock keepers of your approach; portable devices working on a can of compressed gas are excellent and will not be confused with car hooters. Acquire a really long (25m or more) water hose: mine folds flat on a reel and occupies far less space than the conventional type. French taps with threaded outlets occur in several diameters. Most French hardware stores stock necessary adaptors, although a rubber compression fitting adjusted with a jubilee clip is the best solution. A French courtesy flag to fly in addition to your national ensign, clothes pegs for securing washing, plastic rubbish sacks, large fuel can for emergency use where bankside pumps are not available and a medical kit are all items to take.

Where a trans-France passage with a substantial motor sailing boat is proposed, mast and spars will need to be unstepped and stored on deck in order to clear bridges. If the mast greatly overhangs the hull, there will be anxious moments when passing through locks. Some owners prefer to have the mast sent ahead by road on a passage between the Rhône Delta and Le Havre or vice-versa. One firm who will undertake this service is Port Napoléon, 13230 Port Saint Louis du Rhône, tel. 04 42 48 41 21; fax 04 42 86 06 63.

Choosing a Boat

There is no such thing a the ideal vessel for exploring French rivers and canals. Even if money is no object, what is suitable for you may be quite wrong for someone else. I know from experience that given good company, an outfit costing less than £1,000 may provide more pleasure than a luxury cruiser priced at over £100,000.

Starting at the lowest end of the scale: in order to carry out research for part of this book, I spent six thoroughly enjoyable weeks mainly in a quality 9ft (2.70m) inflatable dinghy with a low-powered outboard motor with clutch. This took me safely down the Upper Seine to Paris, along much of the Saône, the Seille, part of the Canal du Midi and Canal Latéral à la Garonne, the Charente and the Sèvre Niortaise. Some of the time I was singlehanded, but elsewhere I was joined by a friend. Our combined weights left space for little beyond fuel, tent, stove, bedding and cameras. We survived superbly in mainly brilliant May sunshine, buying food as required or eating ashore. The huge advantage of using tiny craft like this is that one-way boating becomes possible. Leaving equipment in safekeeping, it is easy to recover the car by public transport and drive on to the next waterway location. Twice, we resorted to packing the whole outfit into taxis: to return from the head of navigation on the Seille to the Saône, and to overcome a series of locks near Toulouse, which were closed by an emergency stoppage. On another occasion, having arrived at a lock just on closing time, we spent 20 minutes portaging everything from one end to the other and enjoyed a further two hours of evening boating on the long pound that followed. Disadvantages were susceptibility to wash – not from commercial traffic but from thoughtless speedboats. But here we no more than shipped some water. Another problem was that nobody would believe we had come farther than the last town: after all, it did look a frail and insignificant little boat.

Similar considerations apply to canoes, especially collapsible versions that can be carried by train; and the range of usable waters is greatly increased. However, even going with the current, I regard canoeing as something too much like hard work. Many of the 19th century explorers of French canals travelled by rowing boat. George Waring and his wife drifted 200 miles (321km) down the Moselle, employing an oarsman for much of the time. Rather later, in the 1920s, Mr and Mrs C. S. Forester spent three months in a camping dinghy fitted with an outboard which they never managed to fully understand. Their contempories may have lived on steam yachts with paid hands, but it is evident from their respective narratives which form of transport was the more pleasurable.

Still remembering that small can be beautiful, in 1998, one of my friends bought a very cheap, elderly and frankly wornout timber motorised sailing cruiser in Cornwall, took her to France by car ferry, and spent an enjoyable summer slowly travelling down to the Mediterranean. On reaching the port of Sète, he literally gave the boat to the first local who showed any interest. (I must emphasise that this vessel's condition was such that it represented no danger to either user or other craft.) Once, I spent three days on the Canal de l'Est, locking in company with a Dutch carpenter who had put a cabin on his little wooden lifeboat and had passed an entire season voyaging on the cheap from the Netherlands to the Mediterranean and back. He wore the most colourful hand-knotted socks ever seen and was accompanied by a young lady who generally declined to appear except at dusk, when she exercised her black cat on the towpath.

One of my favourite waterways stories is Weston's Martyr's *The £200 Millionaire*, first published in 1932. It tells of an English doctor who retired early with £4,000 capital of which he spent £200 on a small cabin cruiser fitted with sails and an engine. Investing the remainder brought him an annual income of just £200, then more than sufficient to live aboard for 12 months of the year, wintering in the warmer climes of the Mediterranean and ranging throughout Europe's rivers and canals for the rest of the time. He had seen waterways in Denmark, Sweden, Germany, France, the Netherlands and down the Danube to the Black Sea. He would stock up with cheap wine where prices were low in French villages, find free wood for the stove, and buy food from lock keepers – all at trifling expense: this wandering life continued for 10 years at an average cost of £150 a year. Seventy years later, the finances have changed but the principle remains good. Waterway travel is not the sole preserve of the rich.

One advance in the quest for mobility is the trailed cruiser. Here, you are restricted to a boat no more than about 20ft (6m) long, which can be towed by a moderate-size car. Often, there need be no winter mooring fees: you park at home in the front garden. Driving from England (or wherever) the boat becomes a private hotel, parked overnight in camping sites or at the excellent French *autoroute* service areas, where showers, loos and restaurants are at hand. Arriving at your chosen waterway, you merely consult the appropriate *Carte Guide* for a suitable slipway or boatyard with lifting facilities – and the voyage begins. As with an inflatable, there is no necessity to return by water to the starting points: public transport to collect car and trailer solves that problem.

So much for the really mobile rig, which in the view of some people involves a degree of discomfort. If you have a large family, like to sleep in real beds and hate to sever your links with civilization, something bigger is called for. Many choose to hire, a more convenient and cheaper approach unless you intend to go boating often. I was involved with the establishment of the second hire cruiser company in France in 1969: much has changed since. Now, most parts of the French network – and all the beautiful lengths – are well served by self-drive cabin boats, sleeping from two to ten passengers. For a long time British firms led the market, drawing on experience gained in the UK over several decades; many of their boats remain among the best in terms of looks and equipment. But today most French-owned cruisers are quite as good, with full-sized cookers, refrigerators and engines as standard fitments. One of the nicest types, aesthetically, is the fibreglass *pénichette*, produced by a French company in the form of a scaled-down working barge.

GRP (glass reinforced plastic) is now an almost ubiquitous material for hulls and superstructures of inland craft and, thanks to mass production techniques, generally offers the best value. Maintenance is negligible and most repairs can be carried out without much difficulty if you are unlucky enough to suffer damage. I have owned too many elderly wooden boats to be able to recommend them to anyone but a real enthusiast or a very wealthy man. This is a personal opinion, and I am the first to agree that a timber-built cruiser can be an object of great beauty.

Another suitable material is steel. Properly protected against rust, it is strong: indeed an inland boat needs to be. There will be frequent contact with lock walls, quays and even commercial barges at moorings. Visit a marina in the Netherlands, and you will find many of the best-looking craft are made of steel.

Anything primarily designed for inland boating should be capable of ranging throughout the whole network (with the possible exception of certain less important sub-standard sections). Sizes must be within the dimensions that are listed on page 21.

Routes used by large freight-carriers are not ideal boating territory for very tiny craft. Yet I have used an inflatable successfully on the quite busy Upper Seine, it would not take much to persuade me to do the same on the now tamed Rhône, and I have witnessed canoes taking their chances with 2,000-tonne ships on the fast-flowing French Rhine near Strasbourg. But a degree of caution must be wise: do not be tempted to tackle waters for which your boat is not fitted.

If you buy an inland boat in the UK, it will normally have to travel to France via car ferry on a trailer or low-loader; the latter can be expensive (Perhaps around £1,500 in 1999 for a 14m narrow boat, London to one of the mainland European ports). One firm with considerable experience in such operations is Ray Bowern, Streethay Wharf, Streethay, Lichfield, Staffs., England. Tel. 01543 414808, or mobile 0860 729522. Little craft regularly cross the Channel under their own power. My own 11m twin-engined motor yacht has done so without difficulty on several occasions. You will know, or should take expert advice, whether this course is open to you. If your boat is suitable, but you do not feel competent at marine navigation, a professional delivery skipper can take it across.

Outboard motors are ideal for the very smallest craft. My own British Seagull performed on the back of the inflatable for six weeks without even a hint of temperamental behaviour. But they do tend to be less reliable than inboard diesels, and power for power, are very considerably more expensive to run. I would always follow the practice of the better hire companies and install a diesel in any cruiser over 20ft (6m). These days, petrol (gasoline) inboard engines are best avoided on safety grounds, although I have noted that the American boating industry appears to disagree.

So far, I have considered inland cruisers to the exclusion of sea-going boats or converted barges. Normally, the bigger the vessel the greater the expense of initial purchase and running. However, this is not invariably true. Rarely does anything smaller than the 38m/350-tonne capacity *péniche* carry cargo today. But many lesser working boats remain in service as holiday boats. The smaller they are (and consequently the easier to handle and maintain), the higher the value. The traditional hunting ground is the Netherlands, where the authorities offered cash benefits to encourage owners to withdraw small capacity barges from freight use. Enter this world warily; although good examples upwards of 100 years old can be found, there are obvious pitfalls. Equipped with a single engine and boatman's accommodation, but otherwise unconverted, an 80-footer (24m) might cost £25,000. Add at least as much again for necessary conversion and you should have a potentially luxurious vessel, able to roam throughout Europe and capable of making short sea passages under ideal conditions. Fully converted barges are advertised in the British and French boating press at prices from around £35,000 upwards. Probably nothing is better suited or looks so well on river or canal, but you should not underestimate the responsibilities that barge ownership entails. Running costs, maintenance, mooring charges and ease of handling are all rather different than with a cruiser. Often, when travelling, marinas will be encountered where barges are not welcome and you will have to utilise public quays used by working craft. As an initial step, arrange to look over as many privately owned examples as possible and book a cabin for a week aboard one of the many hotel boats of this type so as to get an accurate impression of what is involved. Better still, from boating magazine classified advertisements, locate a barge that offers practical handling courses in France.

Boats of all types, suitable for the French waterways, are regularly advertised in the British *Boats & Planes for Sale, Canal Boat, Motor Boat & Yachting, Motor Boats Monthly* and *Waterways World*. Try also the journals of The Barge Cruising Association (details on page 15). The 6-times-a-year French *Fluvial* is well worth study.

Recommended barge brokers/builders include Bowcrest Marine (SE England), tel./fax 01634 255729. Delta Marine Services (Midlands), tel. 01926 499337. Enkhuizen Maritiem (Netherlands), tel. 02280 17279; fax 02280 18297. Friesland Boating (Netherlands), tel. 05142 2607; fax 05142 2620. H2O (Central France), tel. 03 80 39 23 00; fax 03 80 29 04 67. The London Tideway Harbour Company Ltd (West London), tel. 0181 748 2715; fax 0181 748 5237. Sagar Marine (Yorkshire), tel. 01484 714541. Virginia Currer Marine (West London), tel. 01753 832312; fax 01753 830130. Staff at all these companies speak English.

It is very ill-advised to buy any boat without using the services of a qualified specialist surveyor. Two gentlemen with wide experience of all types of inland vessel (who both regularly travel on European waterways and are based in the UK but also conduct surveys elsewhere) are Balliol Fowden, tel. 01788 541020; fax 01788 543517. And James Macdonald, tel. 01923 248145; mobile 0860 613449.

A few words are in order about using the very popular variety of English 'barge' on French waterways: the narrow boat, either converted from freight vessels or purpose-built for pleasure. In earlier editions of this book, I advised against their use in mainland Europe on grounds of the restricted accommodation offered by their 7ft (2.10m) beam and a possible lack of stability resulting from their length:beam ratio. In recent years, many such vessels have been transported to the French waterways – a few have even made the journey by sea. I have since felt it necessary to revise my views. In the hands of competent users, narrow boats are well suited to French inland waters. If you already own one and do not wish to part with it, I now see no reason why they should not be used successfully. But I continue to maintain that a narrow boat is not ideal if purchased specifically for France. Fitted with a suitably powerful engine and provided your insurer is happy to give cover, there is no reason why narrow boats in the hands of experienced skippers should not navigate all French waterways, the Rhine included.

Now to sea-going craft: if you live outside France, this may be the ultimate answer. I admit to being slightly biased. Having previously possessed a 12ft (3.7m) motorised camping dinghy, 20ft (6m) gaff sloop and 40ft (12m) vintage narrow-beam ice-breaker (all for use on British inland waters), since 1983 I have owned the twin-engined steel motor yacht *Avonbay*. She is 37ft (11.3m) long x 11ft (3.40m) beam x 4ft 3ins (1.30m) draft x 7ft 10ins (2.40m) air draft, and was specifically chosen for her ability to travel *almost* everywhere in France while being able to put to sea for coastal or cross-Channel passages. Some of my French cruising had already been on this type of vessel, in the late Lord Harvington's 58ft (17.70m) *Melita* and his subsequent 42ft (12.80m) Nelson *Melitina*. Only on rare occasions did the ample draft or headroom present problems.

Craft Dimensions

French rivers and canals are generously proportioned compared with most in the UK. Equally, there are many large motor cruisers or sailing vessels whose excessive draft or air draft restricts use to the larger river navigations: in these cases coast-to-coast voyages across France will not be possible. Nevertheless, dimensions are only as great as they

Freycinet waterways	Length	Beam	Draft	Height above water:	centre	sides
	38.5m	5.0m	1.8m	3.5m		
Smaller waterways						
Canal de Berry (Noyers-Selles)	42.2m	5.2m	0.8m	3.0m		
River Baïse (Ec. St.-Leger)	40.5m	5.2m	1.5m	3.5m		
(Buzet Branch)	30.65m	6.0m	1.5m	3.75m		
(Buzet-Ec. Lavardac)	32.0m	5.2m	1.5m	3.5m		
(Ec. St Crabary-Ec. Nérac)	30.8m	4.15m	1.0m	3.5m		
(Ec. Nazareth-Valence)	30.8m	4.15m	1.0m	3.0m		
River Blavet	26.3m	4.7m	1.6m	2.6m		
Canal de Bourgogne	39.0m	5.0m	1.8m		3.0m	2.2m
River Boutonne	34.8m	5.5m	0.8m	2.3m		
River Charente	34.0m	6.0m	0.8m	3.5m		
River Cher (Vallet-Noyers)	34.0m	5.0m	0.7m	4.0m	(Barrage	
River Ill	34.5m	5.1m	1.4m	2.25m	Vauban — Port du Quai des Pêcheurs)	
			1.8m	3.4m	(Port du Quai des Pêcheurs –	
Canal d'Ille et Rance	27.1m	4.7m	1.35m	2.5m	Barrage de la Robertsau)	
River Lot (isolated 64km, Luzech-St-Cirq-Lapopie	30.0m	5.0m	1.0m	3.7m		
River Mayenne	30.0m	5.0m	1.1m	3.4m		
Canal du Midi (W of the Grand Bief)	30.0m	5.25m	1.6m		3.4m	2.0m
Canal de Nantes à Brest:						
Nantes—Redon	26.5m	4.7m	1.5m	3.9m		
N of Redon	25.7m	4.65m	1.5m	3.15m		
Rohan—Pontivy			0.8m			
Canal du Nivernais:						
Cercy-la-Tour to Sardy-les-Epiry	30.15m	5.1m	1.3m	2.71m		
(Sardy-Clamecy)	38.5m	5.2m	1.3m	2.97m		
River Oudon	30.0m	5.0m	1.5m	4.1m		
Canal de l'Ourcq, smaller section	58.8m	3.2m	0.8m	2.4m		
River Sarthe	30.0m	5.0m	1.1m	3.4m		
River Seille	30.4m	5.2m	1.3m	4.7m		
River Sèvre Nantaise	31.5m	5.5m	1.2m	5.5m		
River Sèvre Niortaise	31.5m	5.2m	1.2m	2.2m		
Canal Transaquitain	18.0m	3.0m	1.2m	2.0m	(approx)	
River Vilaine	25.87m	4.52m	1.1m	3.2m		

Drafts on the Bourgogne, Midi, Nantes à Brest, Nivernais and Vilaine are officially 2.2, 1.8, 1.6, 1.6 and 1.2m respectively. Latest information suggests that the figures given in the table are more realistic.

are thanks to the enlightened decision taken by Charles Louis de Saulces de Freycinet, Minister of Public Works 1877–9. The Freycinet Act of 1879 classified waterways as (a) principal lines and (b) routes of secondary importance. At that time only 1,467km of a total of 12,467km were sufficiently large to admit Flemish barges loading 300 tonnes. Enlarging the principal lines to this size involved a massive programme of deepening channels, increasing the capacity of locks and raising bridges. Certain navigations such as the Canal de Briare were almost totally reconstructed and other quite recently opened waterways like the Canal de la Marne à la Saône were subjected to far-reaching structural changes. By 1892, no fewer than 4,123km had been improved to the Freycinet standard. Certain routes have remained where infrequent use made enlargement hardly worthwhile: details of these sub-standard waterways appear on page 21. Many other little-used waterways became derelict during the first half of the 20th century, although in recent years substantial portions have been returned to navigation. More are expected to follow over the next two decades as a result of the spectacular growth of pleasure boating. Some navigations are of course able to pass craft very considerably larger than the standard *péniche*, although it is doubtful if many more waterways will in future be enlarged for the benefit of the declining commercial freight traffic. For fullest details, consult the *Carte Guides* or the latest edition of *Inland Waterways of France* by David Edwards-May. Headroom on rivers may be reduced in times of flood. If your boat appears to be close to the limits, check with local canal authority offices (addresses in the above publications), enclosing a dimensioned sketch of the boat's superstructure. Remember that boats with upperworks that are nearly square in cross section will have greater difficulties at arched bridges than those whose maximum air draft rapidly reduces towards the vessel's sides.

Hire Craft, Hotel Boats and Tripping Boats

Until 1969 there was just a single hire cruiser company on French inland waters: now most regions are well served, with numerous vessels on the most popular rivers and canals (Midi, Nivernais, Bourgogne, Brittany, Alsace etc). Owned both by French and British firms, cruisers range from two-berth cabin boats to large craft sleeping ten people. English-speaking readers may prefer to book direct with one of the main operators or agencies, after studying their annual brochures. These are Blakes International Travel Ltd., Wroxham, Norfolk NR12 8DH England. Tel. 01603 739400; Connoisseur Cruisers, Halte Nautique, Ile Sauzay, 70100 Gray. France. Tel. 3 84 64 95 20. Crown Blue Line, Le Grand Bassin, BP21, 11401 Castelnaudary Cedex France. Tel. 3 68 94 52 72. French Country Cruises, 54 High Street, Uppingham, Rutland LE15 9PZ England. Tel. 01572 821330. Hoseasons Holidays, Sunway House, Lowestoft, Suffolk. NR32 2LW. Tel. 01502 502 602. Otherwise, request a list of cruiser hirers from Maison de la France, 178, Piccadilly, London W1V 0AL. England. Tel. 0891 244123. Details of many smaller French-owned hire cruiser companies, including those offering boats on less-frequented routes, can be gleaned from advertisements in *Fluvial* magazine (see Appendix.) Other possibilities exist, such as hiring a canoe on the fast-flowing River Ardèche (make local enquiries).

Many waterways are served by luxury hotel boats, purpose-built or using converted *péniches*. These are fully crewed, usually provide catering of a very high standard and frequently attract American clients. Such luxury is only available at a high price. Rather larger vessels, the size of the small ships, also operate hotel-style cruises on rivers such as the Seine, Saône, Rhône and Rhine. Details from Maison de la France, above. Less pretentious alternatives, often aboard owner/operator barges, can also be found among the classified advertisements of British and French waterways magazines.

A large number of passenger vessels provide excursions on canals and rivers throughout the summer season. Journey times range from an hour to a full day. Information and timetables will gladly be supplied by tourist offices serving main towns in any chosen area.

Waterways Museums

There is, as yet, no collection of inland vessels and other historical relics of the French waterways which can compare with the British canal museums of Gloucester and Ellesmere Port. During the 1970s and 1980s, numerous French craft, especially those of timber construction, were broken up or allowed to decay. Other waterways 'antiques', among them a variety of bank towing locomotives, similarly deserve rescue and preservation. A start to reverse this trend seems likely at the Alsation Navigation Museum, currently being created in Strasbourg. However, establishment of a truly national boat collection is urgently required while potential exhibits are still capable of restoration.

For opening times local enquiry is advised, as information is subject to change.

River Adour Display of local river vessels. Musée Basque, 1 rue Marengo, 64100 Bayonne, tel. (59) 59.08.98.

Canal de Berry Museum at Reugny, near Montluçon. Various items. including a complete *berrichon* barge. Times of opening restricted. Normally afternoons, late July – mid-Sept. Details, tel. (70) 06.70.92.

Canal be Bourgogne Various ancient offerings recovered from the headwaters of the Seine are displayed in the former Abbaye Sainte-Bénigne, 5 rue du Docteur Maret, 21000 Dijon, tel. (80) 30.88.54.

Canal du Centre Documents and objects relevant to the development of the canal and its effect on the economics of the area. Eco-Musée de la

Eighteenth century French barge traffic depicted on a hand-painted faïence dish in the Musée de la Batellerie, Conflans-Ste-Honorine.

Communauté Urbaine Le Creusot/Montceau-les-Mines, Maison Écluse No 6, 71860 Ecuisses, tel. (85) 55.01.11.

River Dordogne Relics of transport by water of wine, timber for barrels, gravel extraction and salmon-fishing boats. Musée Municipal, 5–7 rue des Conférences, 24100 Bergerac, tel. (53) 57.60.22.

Étang de Thau A good collection devoted to jousting boats, both from France and elsewhere. Musée Paul Valéry, 75 Voie Communale, 34200 Sète, tel. (67) 74.88.30.

River Gironde Musée de la Marine, 33000 Bordeaux. Includes some material relating to river craft.

Liaison au Grand Gabarit More than 50 waterways objects, including barge models, locks and bridges can be seen in the Musée des Arts et Traditions Populaires, 6 rue du Tribunal, 62400 Béthune, tel. (21) 68.40.74.

River Loire Many artefacts connected with Loire barges are displayed in the Musée Municipal, Le Château, 45110 Châteauneuf-sur-Loire, tel. (38) 58.43.35. Similar relics can be seen in the Musée du Vieux Chinon, 47 rue Haute St-Maurice, 37500 Chinon, tel. (47) 93.06.77. Another equally good collection is in the Musée Municipal, Bibliothèque Palais de Justice, 58200 Cosne-sur-Loire, tel. (96) 28.06.01. Freshwater fishing has its own exhibition in the Musée de la Pêche, Château de la Bussière,

45500 Gien, tel. (38) 35.93.35 (10km from Gien). Material relating to the lower river and its estuary is conserved in the Musée des Salorges, Château des Ducs de Bretagne, 44000 Nantes, tel. (40) 47.88.37. The life of the Loire boatmen is commemorated in the Musée Municipal, 16 rue St-Genest, 58000 Nantes, tel. (86) 57.35.31. Another similar collection will be found in the Musée du Prieuré, 42170 St-Just/St-Rambert, tel. (77) 51.33.11.

Canal de la Marne au Rhin Exhibition aboard a dry-land *péniche*, by the Arzvillers Inclined Plane.

Canal Marseille-Rhône Relics of barges and fishing boats. Musée Municipal du Vieux Martigues à Ferrières, rue du Colonel Denfert-Rochereau, 13500 Martigues.

Canal du Midi A splendid complex of modern buildings, on an island site, house an exhibition devoted to Riquet and his canal; between Écluses 16 and 17 (west of the summit pound) and also reached via the *Autoroute* A61 service area. Centre Cultural Riquet à Port Lauragais, 32190 Villefranche du Lauragais, tel. (61) 75.62.81.

Canal du Nivernais Relics of *flottage* (timber rafting) on the River Yonne. Musée Municipal, Hôtel de Bellegarde, 58500 Clamecy, tel. (86) 27.17.99.

River Rhine Plans were announced in 1987 for the establishment of the Musée Alsacien de la Navigation on a site in the Strasbourg Docks. L'ancienne commanderie de St-Jean, on the water's edge, provides 1,600 square metres of covered display space. Numerous historic boats and other exhibits have been gathered together. Costs of the project vary from 2.8 – 7.6 million francs.

River Rhône Relics of barge traffic at the Musée Vivarois César Filhol, 15 rue Bechetoile, 07100 Annonay, tel. (75) 67.67.93. Religious crosses of Rhône bargemen can be seen in the Musée Théodore Aubanel, Quartier St-Pierre, Avignon. Objects associated with the Great Fair of Beaucaire, which attracted large numbers of barges, are on view in the Musée du Vieux Beaucaire, 30300 Beaucaire, tel. (66) 59.47.61. L'Association des Amis de la Batellerie du Rhône is attempting to preserve the steam tug *Ardèche* as the centre of an open-air museum; details from M. Tracol, 5 rue Pasteur, 26000 Valence. Religious barge crosses, boatmen's costumes and models are included in the collection of the Ancienne Chapelle St-Sornin, Quartier St-Sornin, 07340 Serrières, tel. (75) 34.05.03. (Between Tournon and Vienne.) The construction of the first large suspension bridge (1825) over the Rhône at Tournon, designed by engineer Marc Seguin, is recalled in a display at the Château de Tournon, quai Marc Seguin, 07300 Tournon.

River Saône An exhibit on river freight traffic will be found in the Musée Municipal Denon, Place de l'Hôtel de Ville, 71100 Chalon-sur-Saône, tel. (85) 48.01.70. A waterways display in a lockside *péniche* is established at the Écluse de Couzon, upstream of Lyon.

River Seine The leading French waterways collection is the Musée de la Batellerie, Place Gévelot, 78700 Conflans-Ste-Honorine, tel. (3) 972.58.05. Included are portions of actual vessels, models, various artefacts and a huge number of prints, photographs and old postcards.

River Vilaine Marine and inland boat traditions can be studied at Le Musée de la Vilaine Maritime, La Roche Bernard, tel. (99) 90.83.47.

I·PAS-DE-CALAIS, SOMME AND THE NORTH

1 · La Liaison au Grand Gabarit – Dunkerque to Belgium via Valenciennes

Carte Guide: *Nord Pas-de-Calais*
Composed of a series of individual waterways, recently much enlarged to carry massive barges, the Canal au Grand Gabarit comprises the Canal de Bourbourg, River Aa, Canal de Neuffossé, Canal d'Aire, Canal de la Deûle, Canal de la Sensée and River Escaut. Through distance, Dunkerque to Belgium, is 187km with 14 locks. The many connections with other waterways are indicated on the accompanying map.

Before attempting even to plan a route, it is essential to study the *Carte Guide Nord Pas-de-Calais* (see Bibliography) and battle with the maze of interconnecting navigations of this northern corner of France until they begin to make some sort of sense. In practice, full comprehension is much easier when actually cruising.

It is important to appreciate that this is not among the most attractive regions of France. Further, widespread and continuing canal improvements have introduced much concrete into a fairly bleak area. The *Carte Guide* claims that 'industry and extensive agriculture co-exist in complete harmony': I detect a note of wishful thinking. Having accepted this warning, these waterways will be found by no means lacking in interest, derived both from frequent encounters with large cargo vessels and from a series of historic towns and villages. It really is most heartening to see modern canal transport alive and flourishing.

At present, opportunities for hiring pleasure cruisers in the Nord – Pas-de-Calais are rather limited. The route is, however, heavily used by sea-going motor yachts and similar craft, especially from SE England and the Thames. The London – Ramsgate – Dover – Calais crossing is quite the quickest route to reach the French inland waterways; and (while never wishing to advocate that unsuitable boats should attempt a Channel crossing) this short hop may well be practicable where the longer run from England across to the Somme or Seine Estuary at Le Havre is not. For information on how we tackled a voyage from London to Calais, see my *Slow Boat Through France* (David & Charles, 1991).

As implied by its ponderous name, all this route is big-gauge, accepting push-tows up to 3,000 tonnes capacity. Nevertheless, standard 38m *péniches* are widespread. This is the Frank country, dreadfully damaged in both world wars but now rebuilt in a blend of old and new. Buildings are mostly of brick with distinct Flemish influences in the architecture of town squares and *Hôtels de Ville*. Flanders (Flandre) is a name synonymous with World War I trench fighting, but in places there is an unexpected quiet beauty. Coming inland from the sea, the first region with its own identity is the Audomarais, 3,400 hectares of marshland near St-Omer, intersected by many watercourses and intensively cultivated with vegetables. Around Valenciennes is France's first regional and natural park of St-Amand-Raismes, designated in 1968 and devoted to a carefully managed blend of sporting activities and wildlife conservation. Festivals such as the Fisherman's Carnival of Dunkerque are held in most of the leading towns. Food owes much to immigrants from other parts of Europe and so do not be surprised to find that classic French *cuisine* and wines are sometimes replaced by black pudding and beer!

Brief history The region is well served by natural rivers flowing through flat country. From the 12th century the Counts of Flanders began to make them suitable for barge traffic and cities started to develop along the banks of the new transport medium. Thus, towns like St-Omer, Béthune, La Bassée, Lille, Douai, Valenciennes, Dunkerque and Calais were able to grow with a trading advantage and direct access to the coast. Mainly artificial parts of the through route include the Canal de Bourbourg, Dunkerque to the River Aa, built in the 17th century under Louis XIV; the Canal de Neuffossé, St-Omer to Aire, started by Vauban and finished shortly before the Revolution, it largely followed the line of a 13th century defensive channel, dividing Flanders and the Artois; the Canal d'Aire, connecting the River Lys and Canal de Neuffossé with the Canal de la Deûle, 40km SE: opened in 1825 and a direct link from the River Escaut to the ports of Calais and Dunkerque; the Canal de la Deûle, joining the River Lys with the River Scarpe and originally rendered navigable in the 13th century; and the 25km Canal de la Sensée, from the River Scarpe to the River Escaut and finished in 1819.

Some of the earliest efforts to replace the barge horse appeared in this area, with 77km of steam railway laid on the towpaths of the Aire, Neuffossé and Deûle (Fontinettes to Douai) between about 1880 and 1886. It was not judged a great success, partly because of interference with traditional towpath users and also as the locomotive drivers could not be persuaded to work the long hours generally associated with horse towage. After trials on the Canal de Bourgogne, Denefle et Cie introduced electric bank traction on the Aire and Deûle canals in the 1890s. By 1900 there were 120 towing units, steered rather than being mounted on rails. Four years later a similar electric horse using 1m gauge rails was successfully put through trials on the Canal de la Sensée and by 1907 the track had grown to 76km, Béthune to Le Bassin Rond, junction with the Sensée and the Escaut. All lengths were absorbed into the system of the *Compagnie Générale de Traction sur les Voies Navigables* (CGTVN) in 1940. This type of haulage lasted until the 1960s, at which time new track was laid on the Canal de la Deûle; diesel engines had then taken over from electric ones in most cases. To the end, the CGTVN maintained that one horsepower on the bank was worth four in a barge.

A significant development on the line was the erection of the great vertical boat lift at Les Fontinettes in 1888: it replaced five locks. Although itself now replaced by a single deep lock, it is preserved as a marvel of 19th century engineering.

After World War II barge traffic had reached saturation point and industry in the locality was under serious threat. Far-reaching improvements were begun in 1959, converting a *péniche*-sized navigation into one fit for 1,350-tonners and 3,000 tonne push-tows. New locks 144.6m × 12m were made, each with intermediate sets of gates resulting in a 45m chamber for two *péniches* side by side; or alternatively, one 91.6m long for four *péniches* or one 1,350-tonner. The full-length locks pass six *péniches* or a single 3,000 tonne push-tow unit. Each Liaison lock has one pair of closely-spaced

bollards, suitable for pleasure craft. More than 25 new high-level bridges were necessary with extensive bank protection and deepening and straightening of the channel. At the time of writing further rebuilding is in progress to increase still more an annual tonnage which as long ago as the early 1960s stood at 13 million.

For entry to the network from the English Channel at **Dunkerque**, use Marine Chart 1010 (Éditions Cartographiques Maritimes). Here is a maze of dockland waterways, with fuel, water, showers and lifting facilities at the Yacht Club de la Mer du Nord situated in an arm SE of the Outer Harbour. Non-tidal waters are gained by working through the nearly Écluse Trystram; otherwise, through either Écluse Maritime Wattier or Écluse Maritime Charles de Gaulle, both of which lead directly from the Outer Harbour. The normal route inland is along the Bassin Maritime, running westwards parallel with the coast, and then via the huge Bassin de Mardyke which links with the Canal de Bourbourg, start of La Liaison au Grand Gabarit. Dunkerque (Dunkirk) has its origins in a little fishing port near a church: over the centuries, French ships would leave here on raiding expeditions into the Channel. More than three-quarters of the town was destroyed early in World War II and the beaches witnessed perhaps the biggest rescue operation of the 20th century, when 500,000 British and Allied troops were ferried to the safety of England in a flotilla of small craft. It has since grown into the third largest port in France, with car ferry connections to Dover, Ramsgate and Harwich.

Two additional waterways may be joined in the centre of Dunkerque: the **Canal de Furnes** follows a 13.2km course parallel with the coast and crosses the Belgian border, destination **Furnes (Veurne)**. Opened in 1638, it has a lock at each end. That in Dunkerque and several swing bridges are closed on Sundays and public holidays unless advance notice is given by telephoning (28) 66.80.46 on the day before holidays or up to 12.00h on Saturdays (for Sunday use). 8.1km of the lock-free **Canal de Bergues** connect Dunkerque with **Bergues**, a place of Flemish buildings and a notable star-shaped fortress built by Vauban. It was of great use during the French defence of Dunkerque in 1940. The canal, originally in use in the 9th century and repaired in the 18th, is now a dead end; but until closure of the **Canal de la Haute Colme** and the **Canal de Bergues à Furnes** there were links with the Canal de Bourbourg (at Lynck, providing a more agreeable way through to La Liaison au Grand Gabarit, avoiding the docks and industrial zone of Dunkerque) and with Furnes, to the east.

At Dunkerque's Bassin de **Mardyke**, we enter the start of the Liaison au Grand Gabarit, via Écluse de Mardyke (K143, distances being measured from Le Bassin Rond, junction with the River Escaut). Railway sidings, fuel storage depots and barge wharves (K140) are followed by a junction, left, with a Freycinet gauge section of the **Canal de Bourbourg** (K137.5) leading back into the centre of Dunkerque and providing access to the Canal de Furnes and the Canal de Bergues, mentioned above: there is one lock on this length, Écluse Jeu-de-Mail, with water point and fuelling station. At K135.2 we leave a short section of shared Canal de Bourbourg, which itself continues SW for 8.3km, through one lock at **Bourbourg** (two lift bridges, good shopping and garage) to join the River Aa at Écluse **le Guindal** (Chapter 3).

One general characteristic of La Liaison is that widening and improvement with consequent concrete-sided banks and a fairly violent wash from passing traffic makes for uncomfortable moorings. In some cases town centres have poor access from the new route. Where possible, moor (subject to hazards from barges) near lock approaches or better still in the various side arms that better serve points of civilization.

After a left-hand junction with the closed **Canal de la Haute Colme** at **Lynck** (K127.9) there is little of note until Écluse 1, **Watten** (K121.5). A little beyond, the River Aa can be entered on the right, providing access to the coast at Gravelines (see Chapter 3); this in turn has a connection with the Canal de Calais, perhaps the most convenient of all routes from the English Channel (see Chapter 2). Shopping, restaurants and garages may be visited in Watten village, where broad views over the *Forêt d'Eperlecques* are obtained from a hill. 6km SW, via the D207, is a World War II blockhouse (open to the public Easter–11 Nov from 14.30h, or 10.30h in July and Aug). This massive structure was designed as a launching site from which to rain V2 rockets on England, although it was never put into service. 500m beyond the road bridge that follows the Aa junction, a dock on the left is the headquarters of the Club Nautique de l'Aa, with slipway, crane and the possibility of quiet moorings. Alternatively, escape from the hectic turmoil of the large canal lies in the little **River Houlle**, fully navigable for about 4km. Restaurant and butcher are located near the entrance in **Cité des Tuileries**, with another restaurant near the head of navigation at **Houlle**.

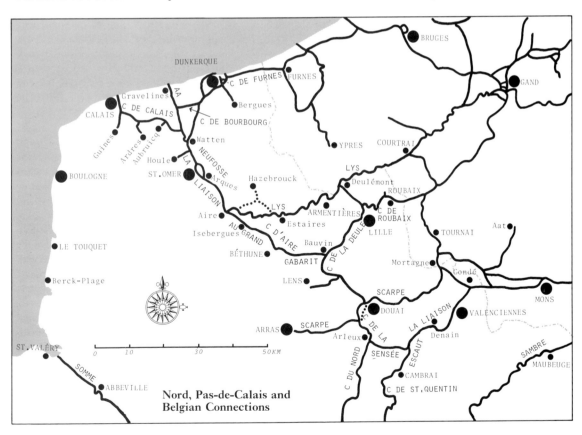

Nord, Pas-de-Calais and Belgian Connections

Starting first on the right and then spreading like veins on both sides of the waterway is an astonishingly complex network of small canals, known as the Audomarais. Total distance could be several hundred km. Some portions are navigable by motor craft and offer excellent prospects for peaceful overnight moorings. Elsewhere powered boats will not be welcomed, although no one is likely to object to a random exploration by dinghy. On the SW fringe is the fine old city of **St-Omer**, with a first-rate pedestrianized shopping street and huge 12–15th century Basilica. A road runs eastwards from the railway station towards **Clairmarais**, lined for several km by vendors of fresh local vegetables (especially cauliflowers), brought in from the marshland market gardens in small boats. Marzipan vegetables are widely available in the cake shops. Two points for waterways enthusiasts travelling by car: small-craft trips are run in the summer (watch for signs on the vegetable sellers' road); and 6km NW of the town on the N43 at **Tilques** is a superbly different hotel, Le Château Tilques established in a 19th century mansion with excellent restaurant in the stable block. As it is a short drive from the Channel Ports, I have often spent my first or last night in France there. A special welcome seems to be reserved for British clients: at any rate the proprietor radiates happiness when our elderly green Bentley sweeps up his gravel drive! Another equally attractive and less commercialized *château-hôtel* is the beautiful 18th century Château de Cocove at Recques-sur-Hem, a little north of the A26 Calais *autoroute* (junction 2). Approaching St-Omer, the waterway passes along a new course from K112 and avoids the town altogether. One original channel from this point and via Écluse du Haut Pont should provide access to the town centre, but latest information suggests a through route is not to be relied on. Instead, remain on the Liaison, noting a public mooring basin immediately before Écluse Flandre (K108, water point). After locking, take the first turning on the right which leads via Écluse St-Bertin into the middle of St-Omer. This intricate layout of waterways is shown clearly in the *Carte Guide*.

Arques (K107) is situated just beyond the St-Omer junction on the right bank and is useful for shopping. Local industries include glass, metal, paper and cement products. On the left bank is the splendid twin-caisson vertical boat lift of **Les Fontinettes**, which replaced a series of five 18th century locks. These could be negotiated in 1hr 10min by a descending boat, while uphill craft took 1hr 35min. In order to pass the maximum number of vessels, three days of each week were devoted to downhillers and four to uphillers, enabling between 40 and 50 craft to work through every day.

Waiting time sometimes amounted to five or six days. In 1875 it was decided to duplicate the flight: the scheme was abandoned when in 1879 the Freycinet Act established 38.5m locks on all principal navigations; the old Fontinettes locks were only 35m long. Relying on experience gained with the Anderton vertical lift in England, which since 1875 had provided communication between the River Weaver and the Trent & Mersey Canal, vertical lift designs were prepared by Edwin Clark (engineer of Anderton) and Sidengham Duer. Clark's less expensive hydraulic machinery was selected in 1881, although following an accident at Anderton it was subsequently modified. There can be few other instances of French waterways being based on British engineering principles! Building took place during 1883–7, with official inauguration in July 1888. Working as a double hydraulic press, one caisson virtually balanced the other, regardless of whether both chambers were occupied by barges or not. Six men were employed to work the machinery and control the safety gates at the upper end. Difference in levels is 13.13m.

When in 1959 it was determined to enlarge the canal for much bigger vessels, the working days of the lift were numbered. A new single lock, 13.13m rise and fall, Écluse des Fontinettes (K106, water point) was constructed a little farther down the canal. When it was completed in August 1967 both vertical lift and the old locks of 1760 (which had remained in occasional use) were worked for the last time. While able to pass 3,000 tonnes of freight, the new lock uses no less than $25,000m^3$ of water, compared with $400m^3$ consumed during operation of the lift.

For several years after its closure the lift was derelict. It has since been refurbished as an outstanding example of industrial archaeology and is open for public inspection. Spikily elegant, with green-painted ironwork and towers of brick and stone, one raised tank is permanently occupied by a *péniche*. The design is unique although similar structures continue to operate in Belgium, Germany, England and Canada.

Quiet moorings will be found in the truncated arm once leading to the lift's upper level and entered from above the Écluse de Fontinettes. The same freedom from wash is rarely to be obtained in the next section, where you might wish to stop for shopping in **Wardrecques** (K102.5, right bank) or at a public mooring by the bridge of **Pont d'Asquin** (K101.2, right bank, baker, butcher, grocer and restaurant). Similar shopping facilities are located in **Blaringhem** (K98.3) with a public quay immediately before the bridge (right bank). A complicated junction of watercourses at **Aire** (K93) includes a left-hand turn into the canalized

Nineteenth century splendour in the vertical boat lift of Les Fontinettes.

Replacing the old lift is this 13.13m deep single lock at Arques. The barge is a 1,350-tonner.

River Lys, leading via Armentières to the Belgian border and Gent (Gand). (See Chapter 4.) Pleasure boats may moor just before the first of two bridges spanning La Liaison; otherwise, continue under the second bridge and turn back along a channel serving quays in the town. Aire was an important city during the Spanish occupation of the 16th and 17th centuries and has a notable large square, surrounded mainly by 18th century buildings. Its Église Collégiale St-Pierre is among the best examples of the Renaissance style in Flanders. Navigation continues via the Canal d'Aire.

In order to visit **Isbergues** (K89), it is advised to pass under a road, railway and two further road bridges before reaching a *port public* on the right. All facilities are within a moderate distance. The leading local industry is a steelworks. Pilgrims come to visit the shrine of Sainte-Isbergues, sister of Charlemagne, in the 15th century church. Several villages with facilities in the next reach include **Busnes** (butcher, grocer, baker and garage) 1.8km south of a bridge at K83.7; **Robecq** (K81, grocer and baker); and **Hinges**, right of bridges at K75.7 or K74.5 (all shops within 1km). We have now entered a thickly populated belt noted for its coal mines and heavy industry. **Béthune** is effectively bypassed by the new waterway and there are no suitable moorings close to the centre. It is, however, a stylish town with a lovely central square surrounded by Flemish-type buildings mostly constructed after the holocaust of World War I. Among them is an art deco *Hôtel de Ville* of 1928, while at the centre rises a 14th century bell-tower with carillon. Excellent food is

served with unaccustomed speed in a large restaurant opposite. Moorings off the main line will be found in a dead-end arm (K72.5) running away to the right just before the bridge preceding an aqueduct over the River Lawe. While there is a public mooring at **Gorre** (K68, left bank), it is preferable to continue for 1km to the right-hand junction with the 2.5km **Canal de Beuvry**, leading back into the town of that name (shopping). Garage and all shops are encountered in **Cuinchy** (K64.2), not long before the Écluse de Cuinchy (water point). Alternative places to buy food are **Auchy-les-Mines** (K61.3, right bank) and **La Bassée** (K60), where a 4.2km *péniche*-sized remnant of the former waterway offers a detour. Here are pontoon moorings for visitors, close to a supermarket, shops and restaurants. Useful moorings will also be found in a basin on the downstream side of the railway bridge with a barge repair works opposite (baker, butcher, restaurant and garage).

Transfer to the Canal de la Deûle takes place at a triangular junction with an island, near **Bauvin** (K54). At K50 is a *Relais Nautique*, with further moorings possible on a quay a short distance up the Deûle. The left fork, of Freycinet gauge, leads to Lille, the Canal de Roubaix and on to Belgium (see Chapters 5 and 6). The through route of La Liaison runs due south through a succession of small towns of limited interest. At least it can be said the facilities are widespread. **Meurchin** (K51, left bank) has a public mooring on the opposite side of the canal. After the Dambrain barge works in a basin (K49.6), shops will be found in

Pont à Vendin (K48.4) with public mooring opposite, right bank. Restaurant and barge yard in **Estevelles** (K47) are followed by safe moorings (K46, right bank). **Carvin**, reached from a road bridge (K44.2), is perhaps rather far to be of much use at 3km. A righthand junction (K43.8) marks a confluence with the **Canal de Lens**. Of an original 11.3km about 8km remains in service, one lock and the terminal basin at Lens being closed. Opened in 1886, it utilized the bed of the River Souchez and was designed primarily as a coal carrier. Unless you are intent on exploring every part of the network there is little purpose in making this detour. Shopping is possible from the public quay in **Harnes**; grocer, baker and restaurant may be reached from the penultimate bridge at **Loison-sous-Lens**. Lens itself, beyond the terminus, will hold few attractions for the boater.

Dreary scenery continues past **Dourges** (K38.8, grocer, butcher) and **Noyelle Godault** (K36.1), with a useful escape from working boats in a 'leisure basin', right bank, at **Courcelles** (K35.4). While there are pleasant wooded banks, K36–34, elsewhere there is much evidence of coal traffic in the form of loading basins and spoil tips. Commercial traffic intensifies at **Dorignies** (K30.6) where La Liaison skirts the city of **Douai** by 'borrowing' a portion of the River Scarpe navigation. Three waterside fuel pumps enable diesel tanks to be replenished near the junction with the eastern part of the Scarpe: this offers communication with Belgium and the Haut Escaut near Tournai (see Chapter 7). Twin locks (Écluses Douai, K28, water point) are the closest approach to the city centre, with moorings on quays. Until completion of the Scarpe *dérivation*, the waterway followed a course through three locks in the heart of Douai. This is now closed but intact and features pleasant quays lined with old houses in the manner of Utrecht or Amsterdam, a bascule bridge, and paddle gear comprising giant spoked wheels. Local coal mines (now in decline) have inspired several original souvenirs, including miners' lamps and rich chocolates wrapped in shiny black cellophane and packed in tiny hessian coal sacks. Douai's most celebrated feature is the bell-tower, an imposing 64m Gothic structure built at the end of the 14th century. Topped by pinnacles, it can be climbed via 192 steps to obtain a memorable view (open every Sun 14.30–17.30h, and on other days April 1–Aug 31, 10.00–12.00h and 14.30–17.00h). An assortment of good stores surrounds a large modernized square.

Beyond the southern city limits a further pair of locks, Écluses de **Courchelettes** (K24, water point), mark the junction (restaurant) with the Upper Scarpe: this continues to a terminus in Arras (see Chapter 7).

Shopping and garage can easily be reached in Courchelettes, perhaps mooring in the entrance to the abandoned old course of the Scarpe. We now join the Canal de la Sensée and negotiate Écluses de **Goeulzin**, with duplicated chambers (K20.3; water point). Water, canalside diesel and basic shopping can all be obtained at the **Arleux** bridge (K15.4) near a junction with the Canal du Nord (see Chapter 8). At this very wide intersection is an excellent barge chandlery, providing moorings, supermarket, bar, fuel and water. Part of the Sensée is bordered by a chain of marshland lakes, bringing a much needed impression of real countryside. Beyond the Marais de **Brunémont** (K12.3) is a village grocer and restaurant, while the next lake, Marais d'Aubigny-au-Bac, close to the canal bank, has been landscaped with swimming beach and other recreational features. Restaurant, garage, grocer and baker are in **Aubencheu-au-Bac** (K11, righthand side), while full shopping is to be found opposite in Aubigny-au-Bac, **Fressies** (K8, right), **Féchain**, reached from bridges at K8 or K6.2, and **Hem-Lenglet** (K6.2, public mooring); with grocer, baker and restaurant in **Wasnes-au-Bac** (K3.5) beyond another water-based leisure park.

A choice of routes now presents itself: you can either stay with La Liaison for 2.5km or take a slightly longer and much more pleasant course to the right through **Paillencourt** (all shops) and **Le Bassin Rond**. Note a rare selection of pleasure craft facilities either at Nord Croisière (hire cruisers) or in a basin opposite **Étrun** where Escaut Yachting provide moorings, water, fuel,

Near the heart of Douai: this original part of the Scarpe is now closed to boats.

On the Sensée at Bassin Rond: an early 20th century tow-path tractor designed for utility rather than beauty. From an old postcard.

showers, crane and repairs. Surroundings are very agreeable, with a length of waterway up to 100m in width. Surprisingly, in 1990, this route featured signs warning of a water draft of only 0.8m. We passed through with a 1.3m draft and experienced no difficulty. Beyond the next bridge, turn left to rejoin La Liaison and the River Escaut, large-gauge section, with water point at Écluse Port Malin (K0), or right into the Upper Escaut (Freycinet gauge) connecting with the Canal de St-Quentin.

The **Upper Escaut**, 12km from Le Bassin Rond to Cambrai, has five locks, each with duplicated and mechanized chambers. These are 5, Iwuy (K2.1 from the Canal de la Sensée); 4, **Tun-l'Evêque** (K4.2); 3, Erre (K8.3, water point); 2, Selles (K11.1); and 1, Camtimpré (K11.9, water point). Although quite heavily used by commercial traffic, the wooded fringes of the waterway, passing through a region of cornfields, is much more intimate than the main line of La Liaison. Lock cottages are of brownish brick and many of the keepers sell garden produce. **Cambrai** is a busy port with barge repair yards, diesel pump at the far end of a basin entered from below Écluse 2, and a pleasure craft harbour reached from the lower end of Écluse 1 near the junction with the Canal de St-Quentin (see Chapter 10). In spite of the infamous pounding received during World War I, Cambrai still possesses many old buildings, not least the early 18th century Cathedral of Notre-Dame. In the church of St-Géry is an Entombment painted by Rubens. Traditionally and still a centre of linen manufacture (*cambric*), the city boasts an important art museum and there are traces of Vauban fortifications in public gardens. Food specialities are *andouillettes* (sausages made from pork or veal

tripe), *tripes* (mainly ox tripe), *friandises à la menthe* 'betises de Cambrai' (mint sweetmeats) and *boulette de Cambrai* (a white farm cheese, flavoured with herbs).

Returning to the Escaut section of La Liaison, Écluse 6, Port Malin (K0, distances now being measured between here and the Belgian frontier), we gradually return to industrial surroundings. Both the River Sambre and the River Meuse provide more agreeable ways of reaching Belgium. **Bouchain** (K1) makes a useful halt for garage and shopping, while there are similar facilities in **Lourches** (K5) and **Denain** (K7). Just before Écluse 8, Denain (K8), is a chandlery with diesel and water points. Petrol refineries and factories abound. Hurrying past **Wavrechain-sous-Denain**, shops can be visited in either **Thiant** or **Prouvy** (K13), close to an airport and A2 *autoroute*. Now follow the right-hand channel for Écluse 10, **Trith-St-Léger** (K15, shopping). Not long after, we arrive in the city of **Valenciennes**, with Écluse 12, Folien (K22) near the centre. One place to seek moorings out of the way of passing traffic is to enter the upper end of the weir stream. Once known as the 'Athens of the North' on account of the artistic talent which flourished, Valenciennes is a thriving industrial town with an impressive and bustling modern square at its heart. Two educational visits might be planned: for culture, to the huge Musée des Beaux-Arts on the far side of town. It has outstanding collections of the Flemish School as well as paintings by leading French artists of the 18th and 19th centuries. Another, more prosaic, tour would be to the Musée des Charbonnages et de la Métallurgie on the opposite side of the waterway in **Anzin**.

Scenery is reminiscent of the more squalid regions of Yorkshire's Aire & Calder Navigation. Écluse 13, La Folie (K26), lies between Valenciennes and a junction with the **Canal de Pommeroeul à Condé** at **Fresnes-sur-Escaut** (K32, shopping). Considerable works, completed in 1983, involved resiting Écluse 14 and cutting a more convenient channel. By turning right along the Canal de Pommeroeul the Belgian border is reached within 5km, with connections thereafter to Mons and Brussels via the Ronquières inclined plane.

Condé-sur-l'Escaut (K33), west of the junction, has all facilities with the remains of Vauban fortifications, an 18th century *Hôtel de Ville* and a 15th century *château*. Further recent improvements to the channel of the Escaut have been undertaken at **Odomez** (K35). Good shopping will be found in **Hergnies** (K37). Écluse 16, **Rodignies** (K42), was removed in 1983, and there is now a level run through a drawbridge at **Flines-les-Mortagne** (K44) to a junction with the River Scarpe from Douai (see Chapter 7). Shops and restaurants are near this point on the right bank with grocer, butcher and restaurant on the opposite bank in Maulde. Ahead, lies the Belgian border and routes to the Haut Escaut (Schelde), Tournai and Gent.

2 · Canal de Calais

Carte Guide: *Nord Pas-de-Calais*
From the English Channel at Calais to the canalized River Aa near Watten, 29.5km with 1 lock. There are three lock-free branches: the Canal de Guînes, from the main line near Coulogne to a terminus in Guînes, 6.2km; the Canal d'Ardres, from the main line at Le Pont d'Ardres to Ardres, 4.8km; and the Audruicq branch, from the main line near Hennuin to Audruicq, 2.3km. The latter pair are available to non-motorized craft only.

Calais harbour is quite the easiest entry to French inland waterways for sea-going pleasure craft from England. The canal, although regularly navigated by *péniches*, is something of a backwater, in stark contrast to many km of large-tonnage waterway that must be followed once La Liaison is joined at Watten. Many of the typical elements of French canals are present, but with fairly undemanding conditions the Canal de Calais provides an easy introduction.

One problem, however, that has affected the waterway in recent years is the build-up of large quantities of duckweed, especially towards the end of summer. It is sometimes sufficiently bad to choke propellers, or worse, to block the inlets of water-cooled engines. If encountered, keep a close eye on temperature gauges.

Mainly completed under Louis XIV in 1681, the canal is fed by water supplies at Ardres and Guînes. In addition to linking Calais with the interior, it served a useful land drainage function.

For many British visitors France starts at **Calais**, a town I have tried hard to like, fully aware that the inhabitants doubtless judge all visitors from the UK by the behaviour of day-trippers. Closeness to England accounts for an atmosphere rather less than totally French. But as a refuge from the open

sea or a place to await settled weather before venturing out, the safe, still water of Calais can seem like paradise. There is a choice of three good restaurants facing the Bassin de l'Ouest, of which Le Channel is excellent.

At the harbour entrance the Bassin de l'Ouest, on the right coming in and opposite the car ferry terminal, provides moorings, clubhouse, water, fuel, crane and repairs. This is easily the safest place to leave a boat after or before a Channel crossing; gates provide access for a short period at high water. Otherwise, buoys in the (tidal) outer harbour offer (very disturbed) moorings. For the Canal de Calais route, continue up the harbour to lock gates into the non-tidal Bassin Carnot. Locks into both basins are operated 1½hr before HW, at HW and 30 min after HW (Mon-Fri inclusive); 2hr before HW, and HW and 2hr after HW (Sat, Sun). As wharves may well be occupied by shipping within the Bassin Carnot, it is preferable to pass through the Écluse de la Batellerie at the far end (open 8.00–12.00 and 14.00–18.00h, closed Sat afternoons and all Sun) and use moorings on the right, beyond the next bridge. This is a convenient point from which to visit the town.

Calais has recovered well from extensive damage suffered in World War II. Its most memorable building is the red brick and stone *Hôtel de Ville* with 75m high bell-tower. A stained glass window depicts the departure of the English in 1558 after the town had been occupied for 210 years. Nearby beaches such as **Blériot Plage** are agreeable sandy resorts.

One peculiarity of the canal is that surplus water is sometimes drained off to the sea via sluices, with a strong attendant current. Red flashing lights warn of this operation. A useful restaurant will be found on the right by the **Coulogne** lift bridge (K4) with shopping and garage in the town (left bank). Soon afterwards the **Guînes** branch forks away to the right. It is spanned by three opening bridges whose keepers should be informed of your expected time of arrival (closed Sun). Facilities include a garage after the first bridge at **La Planche Tournoire**; restaurant by the second bridge, Pont de l'Écluse Carrée; and a good range of shops at the end of the line in Guînes. Nearby was the setting for the Field of the Cloth of Gold where in 1520 François I of France and Henry VIII of England vied with each other, displaying a magnificent court and entourage.

Returning to the main line, shops and garage will be found in **Les Attaques** (K9) by a lift bridge. At the intersection of the Canal de Calais, Canal des Trois Cornets and Canal d'Ardres (K12), the through route is spanned by the Pont Sans Pareil, a curious X-shaped bridge which prevented craft longer than 28m from turning into the Ardres branch: this is now closed to motor boats but is well worth exploration by rowing dinghy for 4.8km past several lakes to the once fortified market town of **Ardres**. Grocer, baker and restaurant are at the junction and all services in Ardres itself, although access by water is difficult beyond a lift bridge some distance before the town.

The Canal de Calais continues through marshland with few features until the short branch to **Audruicq** (K22, closed to motorized boats). Grocer and restaurant are alongside a lift bridge just before the canal's only lock at **Hennuin** (K24, water point, restaurant). Loneliness of the surroundings is correctly suggested by the name of a waterside hamlet – **Le Coin Perdu** or 'The Lost Corner'. Shops, garage and restaurant are on the right bank at **Ruminghem** (K27.5). Several curious red-brick structures, seen here and elsewhere along the canal, are not (as might initially be supposed) old fortifications: they are houses for the forcing of chicory. The River Aa is reached at an isolated junction by the Pont-du-West (K29.5): turn right for Watten and La Liaison au Grand Gabarit, leading to a series of important connections (see Chapter 1). The other direction heads back to the English Channel via Gravelines.

3 · River Aa

Carte Guide: *Nord Pas-de-Calais*
From the English Channel near Gravelines to St-Omer, junction with the Canal de Neuffossé. 28.7km with 1 lock and a sea lock at the estuary. 10km between Watten and St-Omer form part of La Liaison au Grand Gabarit and are described in Chapter 1. Junctions with the canal de Bourbourg and the Canal de Calais.

A less well known approach to the French waterways network from the coast, the River Aa follows a straight course through one-time marshland which was drained by creating a complex series of channels in the 18th century. Scenery is very flat and rather lacking in features. The Gravelines lock and several opening bridges are normally closed to boats on Sunday and public holidays, unless advance notice is given to the keeper at Le Guindal before 12.00h on a Saturday (for Sunday use) or up to a similar time on the day before a holiday:

tel. (28) 22.21.03. All navigation is banned when flood prevention measures entail pumping water out of the river: under these circumstances flashing lights provide a warning at Le Guindal and the La Bistade bridge. From the sea to Watten is of standard Freycinet gauge; Watten to St-Omer is much larger.

Originally made navigable under Philip III of Spain in the 16th century, the Aa was further improved in 1737 during the reign of Louis XV with more work carried out twelve years later. The uppermost 10km were substantially enlarged in recent years as part of creation of La Liaison au Grand Gabarit.

Approach from the English Channel is via a tideway guarded at the entrance by fortifications known as **Grand Fort Philippe** and **Petit Fort Philippe**. The latter is now both fishing port and small holiday resort, with a slipway. Still water is reached after passing through the Écluse Maritime at **Gravelines** (K0) which is available for $1\frac{1}{2}$hr either side of HW. Adequate pontoon moorings will be found in the tideway with a range of facilities located in the basin upstream of the tidal lock (boatyards, chandleries, moorings, crane, repairs and water point). Shopping is also close at hand in the town, where extensive fortifications remain, encircled by a moat. They played a leading rôle in the defence of Dunkerque early in World War II. Between the lock and an opening railway bridge is a commercial barge repair yard. From here to St-Omer is a lock-free run. Main points of interest are a junction with the Canal de Bourbourg (K5.9, see Chapter 1) at **Le Guindal**, providing a link with La Liaison au Grand Gabarit and Dunkerque; a restaurant (right bank) beyond the next opening bridge at **St-Nicholas** (K8.2); grocer and baker in **St-Pierre-Brouck** (K11.2); and a right-hand junction with the Canal de Calais (K13.5, see Chapter 2) at **Pont-du-West**. La Liaison au Grand Gabarit is joined near **Watten** (K18.4). This route continues in Chapter 1.

4 · River Lys

Carte Guide: *Nord Pas-de-Calais*
From La Liaison au Grand Gabarit at Aire to the Belgian frontier at Halluin, 65km with 7 locks. At Deûlémont connects with the Canal de la Deûle.

The canalized Lys runs for the greater part through quite agreeable farming country, its valley littered with cemeteries recalling the slaughter of World War I. About 24km onwards from Armentières it forms the boundary with Belgium, and it eventually flows into the River Escaut (Schelde) at Ghent (Gand). Although lacking the attractions of waterways in other parts of France, the Lys is sufficiently interesting to support a hire cruiser base at Armentières, one of very few currently established in the North/Pas-de-Calais region.

Used by freight craft over many centuries, the Lys was canalized and straightened in the 1870s. By 1936 fifty per cent of the annual 773,000 tonnes carried consisted of coal. Currently of *péniche* gauge, consideration is now being given to its enlargement to *grand gabarit*, making it suitable for 1,350 tonne barges.

Aire-sur-la-Lys (K0, see Chapter 1) marks the junction of the Liaison au Grand Gabarit and the canalized River Lys. We soon pass through Écluse 1, Fort Gassion (K0.6). After a mobile bridge at **Thiennes** (K3.7) the disused Canal de la Nieppe will be seen beyond a lock on the left. This provided an alternative route to Merville farther down the Lys, with a branch line to Hazebrouck. Together the Nieppe, Hazebrouck and Préaven Canals and the canalized River Bourre totalled 25km with 5 locks but were only sufficiently large for 27m barges loading 90 tonnes. Closure took place at some date after 1965. Écluse 2, Cense à Witz, follows at K6.7 with the third lock near the centre of **St-Venant** (K12.6, shops close by). Mobile bridges span each end of Écluse 4 at **Merville** (K19.3) by a junction with the disused canalized Bourre. Water point and shopping.

Few changes of level are required in the flat landscape and there are no more locks until Écluse 5, **Bac de St-Maur** (K32.5), convenient shopping places en route including **La Gorge** and **Estaires** (K25.7), and **Sailly-sur-la-Lys** (K30.2). **Armentières** (K41.6), a name well known from the World War I British song, saw repeated action between 1914 and 1917. During an early bombardment the *Hôtel de Ville* clock was damaged, giving rise to the popular name 'Eleven o'Clock Square'. Completely rebuilt, Armentières now flourishes with brewing and linen interests. Lakes on the old course of the Lys have been landscaped as the Base des Pres du Hem. On the NE side of this attractive water park a pleasure boat harbour, entered via a channel on the left of the navigation, offers slipway, fuel, moorings, electricity and water; small cruisers can be hired. Nearby activities include dinghy sailing and windsurfing, sandy beach with a long water-filled children's slide known as a *toboggan nautique*, miniature farm and bird sanctuary. A Customs post is located on the right bank a little above Écluse 6 (K42.7, water point). For a short distance the river lies entirely in Belgium, then briefly returns to France and for the next 24km acts as the frontier between the two countries.

Deûlémont (K48.9, shopping) stands by a right-hand junction with the Canal de la Deûle, connecting with Lille and the Liaison au Grand Gabarit at Bauvin. The final French lock, No. 7 at **Comines** (K56.2), actually lies within Belgium. There are shopping facilities here in **Wervick-Sud** (K59.8) and at **Halluin** (K65). Onwards from here, the Lys flows entirely through Belgium.

5 · Canal de la Deûle

Carte Guide: *Nord Pas-de-Calais*
Part of this waterway, from the River Scarpe at Douai to Bauvin, forms a portion of La Liaison au Grand Gabarit and is described in Chapter 1. The remainder runs from La Liaison at Bauvin to a junction with the River Lys at Deûlémont, on the Belgian border. 36km with 4 locks. A junction is made with the Canal de Roubaix at Marquette-lez-Lille.

This section of the Deûle is mainly notable for serving the great industrial region centred on Lille, capital of French Flanders. Scenically, the waterway holds few

Fun on the toboggan nautique *at the Base des Pres du Hem water park.*

attractions for the pleasure boater and its chief interest lies in providing a rapid transit between Ghent (Gent) and the Belgian Schelde and the main network of Northern France.

Portions of the River Deûle were first made navigable for barges as long ago as the 13th century; it was linked with the Scarpe in the 17th century and with the Lys in the middle of the 18th century. Widespread use of electric tractors to haul *péniches*, using vehicles both on rails and running on pneumatic tyres, lasted into the 1960s; one of the final developments in this field was the introduction of lengths of welded rail, each more than 1km.

Conversion of the Freycinet waterway into a *grand gabarit* route for 1,350 tonne barges from Bauvin to Lille is now complete.

A triangular island marks the start of the Canal de la Deûle at **Bauvin** (moorings at a gravel barge quay). The first feature is the new 144.6m Écluse de **Don** (K3.5), with water point a short distance into a parallel channel leading to the disused Freycinet lock. Most town facilities will be found in nearby **Sainghin-en-Weppes**. If you stop at the bridge following a power station on the left bank, the town of **Wavrin** is within 2.5km. More limited supplies can be obtained at a grocer by the next bridge at **Bac-de-Wavrin**. This is situated a little before a 4.5km branch (right bank, K8) leading to **Seclin**, noted for its *Hôpital* founded in the 13th century and mainly built in a Flemish Baroque style.

The waterway now passes through the heart of a heavily industrialized region with many commercial barge quays. Suburbs include **Hambourdin Emmerin, Sequedin** and **Loos** before one arrives at the busy wharves of **Lille** (K19). Various channels serve the harbour areas. Most promising city moorings are likely to be located by turning out of the through navigation after a large island and heading towards a disused Freycinet lock, Écluse de la Barre. Lille's massive *Citadelle*, built in the 17th century by Vauban and constructed of 60 million bricks, occupies an island site. It is the most impressive and best preserved of all such structures in France. (No public visits to the interior.) Although Lille is not the kind of industrial complex that would normally attract tourists, it does have one of the country's best art collections in its Musée and a fascinating Old Quarter near the Place Général de Gaulle; the leading historical building is the 17th century Flemish Baroque *Bourse*, with a magnificent galleried courtyard. By keeping the *Citadelle* on your right the Écluse du Grand Carré will be seen

ahead (K19.7, water point). Soon afterwards the canal ceases to be of 1,350 tonne standard and the remainder of the route is currently being enlarged from 300 tonne gauge to 600–800 tonnes.

Shortly before a right-hand junction with the Canal de Roubaix at **Marquette-lez-Lille** (K24), there is a waterside fuel point on the left. Extensive new works have seen removal of a lock at **Wambrechies** (K26), with a replacement substituted in **Quesnoy-sur-Deûle** (K30). One final lock must be negotiated in **Deûlémont** (K35.5, water point, butcher, baker and restaurant) before reaching the River Lys which marks the border between France and Belgium (see Chapter 4).

6 · Canal de Roubaix

Carte Guide: *Nord Pas-de-Calais*
From a junction with the Canal de la Deûle at Marquette-lez-Lille to Roubaix, border with Belgium and start of the Canal de l'Espierre. 20km with 12 locks. There are two navigable branches: Embranchement de Croix, 2.3km, 1 lock; and Embranchement de Tourcoing, 1.5km no locks.

Industrial from end to end, this link with Belgium's Haut Escaut and the Bovenschelde climbs from each terminus to a summit level at Roubaix/Tourcoing. Locks and opening bridges are normally closed on Sundays and Public Holidays; special arrangements for a passage can, however, be made by contacting Écluse du Plomeux, before midday on the day before the closure.

Although planned in 1825, the Canal de Roubaix was not opened to traffic until 1877. It passes Freycinet-sized barges.

Écluse 1, de **Marquette-lez-Lille** (K0.4) and Écluse 2, **Marcq-en-Barœul** (K3.7) both have water points. Thereafter the navigation winds considerably up to the start of the **Croix** branch (K7.6) at **Wasquehal**. Then comes a flight of locks (Écluses 3, Trieste: 3 *bis*, Wasquehal; 4, Plomeux; 5, Noir Bonnet; 6, Cotigny; and 7, Masure), leading to the **Roubaix** summit. Best shopping stop for the city is after an opening bridge well beyond the first descending lock, Écluse 8, Union (K12.9). Roubaix is a flourishing centre for textiles and engineering. 5km south is an outstanding modern chapel at **Hem**, finished in 1958. On the canal's left bank **Tourcoing** specializes in woollen thread, producing 40 per cent of French output. Both towns are well served by shops and other urban facilities.

Écluses 9, Nouveau Monde (K14.7); 10, Calvaire (K15); 11, Galon-d'Eau (K15.2); and 12, Sartel (K16.5) lead past **Wattrelos**, with a Customs post on the right of the last bridge in the French section (the Grimonpont lift bridge, K18.8).

7 · River Scarpe

Carte Guide: *Nord Pas-de-Calais*
From a terminus in Arras to the Belgian frontier at Mortagne-du-Nord, junction with the Escaut. 66km with 17 locks. 8km of the line near Douai has been replaced by the Scarpe *dérivation* and forms part of La Liaison au Grand Gabarit (see Chapter 1).

The navigable River Scarpe passes through a densely populated area but, with the exception of Douai, generally manages to avoid centres of thickest industry. Much of the course is set in very pleasing countryside, with meadows and woodland. With the exception of the enlarged portion near Douai, the waterway is designed for 38m *péniches*, the five locks nearest Arras being arranged as an automatic series. Full instructions for their operation appear in the relevant *Carte Guide*.

Information on the development of the Scarpe is infuriatingly elusive. It would appear that parts have been used by barges over many centuries, while most of the present infrastructure is 19th century.

Navigation starts at an agreeable landscaped basin 600m from the centre of **Arras**, with good moorings on a floating pontoon. Although minimal use by *péniches* or pleasure craft encouraged thick duckweed in many sections during our 1990 Scarpe cruise, it is an exceptionally pleasant navigation. Many towns now have basic mooring facilities. Remember that being a river navigation there is sometimes a strong flow. Keep clear of weirs when coming downstream. In spite of dreadful destruction during World War I the city has recovered magnificently, the twin squares of the Place des Heros and the Grand Place being almost without equal in France. Although dating from the 11th century, they are now surrounded by extremely fine gabled buildings

in the Flemish style, erected in the 17th and 18th centuries. Here, there is a remarkable absence of inappropriate street furniture, even the telephone boxes being placed underground and out of sight. From the Middle Ages tapestry was produced, and in English 'arras' was once used to describe woven pictures. The great 15th century *Hôtel de Ville* with 75m belfry overlooks a colourful Saturday market. This region was fiercely fought over throughout the Great War. Nowhere are the battles more eloquently recalled than at **Vimy Ridge**, 11km to the north. Parkland planted with 75,000 trees in memory of the same number of Canadian soldiers who died here in 1917 fails to mask the tortured landscape, where bomb craters and trenches have been preserved in such a way as to provide graphic understanding of just what happened. Visits are possible to underground tunnels wriggling throughout the front line. To go there is a moving yet fascinating experience.

Écluse 28, St-Nicholas (K0.5) is the first of a sequence of automatic locks on the edge of Arras. Beware of bad silting below the lock, where the river enters the navigation for the first time. Soon comes another lock, No. 29, **St-Laurent-Blangy** (K2.3, good shopping in the village). Onwards from this point is a series of further villages, mostly at lock sites, and all offering nearby shopping. These include **Athies** (K4.9, Écluse 30); **Fampoux** (K7.3, Écluse 31); **Roeux** (K10.1, fishing lakes); **Pelvès** (K11.1); and **Biache-St-Vaast**, (K14.2), Écluse 32. Two locks in **Brébières** are Écluse 34, Haute-Tenue (K20.1) and 35, Basse-Tenue (K20.6) with all shops and a garage. Although intended to be radar-controlled, we found few of the locks worked automatically, even when we held a sheet of aluminium (a locker door from the boat) over the sensor. We then resorted to calling up the Liaison's Écluses de Courchelettes on our VHF radio telephone (see *Carte Guide* for channel number) and arranged for personal lock keepers. Considerable commercial traffic was noted at factories on the lowest part of the Scarpe Supérieure. After Écluse 36, very sharp bend below, **Corbehem** (K22.4, all shops) we reach La Liaison. Turn right for Cambrai and Valenciennes, or left along the *dérivation de la Scarpe* past Douai (described in Chapter 1). The river assumes its own true identity close to a boatmen's chapel at **Dorignies** junction (K29), a hectic place with big barges constantly manoeuvring between the two waterways.

Once clear of Douai the river takes on more of a village character, even if these villages have grown as a result of coal mining. Always, food and fuel supplies are never far away. Locks are renumbered from Écluse 1, de Fort de Scarpe (K30), with adequate shopping by a mobile bridge either in **Frais-Marais** or **Râches** (K33.3). Equally convenient is **Lallaing**, near Écluse 2 (K36.8). Four bridges on at **Vred** (K41.5, baker, butcher, grocer and garage) lies the former abbey of Anchin, a Benedictine house of great antiquity and partly ruined during the Revolution. During an early August heatwave in 1990, the Vred swing bridge had become inoperable through heat expansion (it was 33°C!); we were requested to wait overnight and pass through in the early morning. *Halte nautique* with water and electricity. **Marchiennes-Ville** (K45.3) at Écluse 3 has water point, shopping and fuel station. Remains of an abbey founded in the 7th century may be visited on summer Sundays, 11.00–13.00h and 15.00–17.00h. 2km north is the 800 hectare Forêt de Marchiennes, a popular area for walks, picnics, riding and fishing. Baker and grocer are near Écluse 4, **Warlaing** (K49.7).

A long pound now extends to **St-Amand-les-Eaux** and Écluse 5 (K59.3), well known for a 7th century abbey founded by St Amand. Most of the buildings now remaining date from the 17th century. These include an impressive Baroque façade, an 82m tower with carillon (concerts at 12.00h and 12.30h, with additional performances on Saturdays and Sundays, June–September 19.00–20.00h) and a museum. The final lock, Écluse 6, Thun (K64.8), is near shops in **Mortagne-du-Nord**, with a commercial barge yard and the possibility of diesel delivery by tanker. Extensive dredging carried out in 1990 and the total rebuilding of the lock are indicative of a desire to encourage pleasure boats to use this underpublicized but very pleasant route. Beyond, the Scarpe flows into the Escaut near the Belgian border.

8 · Canal du Nord

Carte Guide: *Nord Pas-de-Calais or Picardie*
From a junction with the Canal Latéral à l'Oise near Pont-l'Evêque to a junction with the Canal de la Sensée (Liaison au Grand Gabarit) at Arleux, 95km with 19 locks. There are two tunnels: Ruyaulcourt, 4,350m and Panneterie, 1,061m. 20km of the central part of the canal shares an improved channel with the older Canal de la Somme (Béthencourt-sur-Somme to Biaches, near Péronne), described in Chapter 9.

Much the more convenient and quickest route between the Seine and the Channel Ports, the Canal du Nord is

perhaps the most important totally new navigation opened in recent years. Locks are 91.9m long by 6m wide and were designed to take a pair of pushed *péniches* with a 700 tonne payload. Operated by hydraulics from a central control cabin, chambers are equipped with lifting tail gates and side ponds which save one-third of the quantity of water used at each locking. Two new locks on the improved central section, shared with the Canal de la Somme, are of a different design. With the exception of this pair, all have pumping stations enabling more than 100,000m^3 of water to be lifted to the two summit levels each day.

Both tunnels are worked one-way with the aid of traffic lights, closed circuit television and microphones allowing communication between barge crews and keeper. Barges normally enter the longer one, Ruyaulcourt, in groups of four starting simultaneously from each end. At the centre there is a two-way 1,000m long passing point. This was the first canal tunnel in France to be equipped with a mechanical ventilation system.

Large, modern waterways obviously lack the intimacy of older, smaller navigations and the Canal du Nord is in parts rather bleak with severe concrete sides. But devotees of commercial water transport will enjoy a journey along this highly efficient route before they too start to pine for more bucolic byways such as the Canal de Bourgogne. The engineering is, however, impressive, while a landscape of expansive cornfields is not without its own attractions.

Brief history Heavy congestion on the Canal de St-Quentin, then the sole water link between the Seine Basin and the North, prompted the government to launch the Flamant Project in 1878, creating a totally new waterway. A start was made at the northern, Arleux, end just before the turn of the century and in spite of widespread disquiet at the costs involved, a four month emergency stoppage on the Canal de St-Quentin at Jussy in 1900 with consequent disruption of all traffic was a major factor in starting construction in earnest in 1908. Three-quarters of the excavations, 11 locks and all the bridges were finished and work well advanced on each tunnel when war broke out in 1914. The canal found itself in the heart of the battlefields and destruction was widespread. Nothing came of attempts to resume building before World War II.

Under the Third Plan of 1959 it was decided to begin again, following substantially the same design but increasing the length of locks from 85m to 91.9m. Work started in 1960 and the new waterway was opened to traffic late in 1965. Banks almost throughout are of concrete or concrete and bitumen. Two new ports were laid out at Péronne and Noyon with numerous unloading quays at other locations. The Canal du Nord was used by no fewer than 7,000 craft in the first six months of operations and traffic has been heavy ever since.

Leaving the Canal latéral à l'Oise at **Pont-l'Evêque**, whose facilities are listed in Chapter 17, the Nord passes through two locks, Écluses 19, Pont-l'Evêque (K0.6) and 18, **Noyon** (K1.6), with recommended public moorings beyond the centre of Noyon on the right bank. The city supports varied industries from brewing to printing and furniture making; as an ecclesiastical town it has an ancient history. Charlemagne was crowned King of Normandy here in 768 and Hugues Capet King of France in 987. Fully restored after severe World War I damage, the 12th–13th century cathedral is a splendid example of the early Gothic. Calvin was born in the town in 1509 and his entirely rebuilt birthplace house is now a museum of his work (open Feb 15–Nov 30 10.00–11.30h and 14.30–17.00h; the remainder of the year by special request; closed Tues). Naturally there are good shopping and eating possibilities.

Between Noyon and Péronne are no nearby towns of any great size but the majority of villages will be able to supply basic food needs. After **Beaurains-lès-Noyon** (K6) we pass through Écluse 17, **Sermaize-Haudival** (K7.3) followed in turn by **Catigny** (K11) and Écluse 16, **Campagne** (K13.1). Panneterie tunnel, one-way and controlled by lights, presents no great problems. This is the first of two summit levels, as the waterway crosses the divide between Rivers Oise and Somme. Shortly before a bridge (K20), public moorings will be seen in a small basin on the right. Such sites are of greater importance to pleasure craft than on most canals, as the banks of sloping concrete are generally unsuitable as well as being subject to wash from passing barges. Through the bridge at **Breuil** (K24), the *port public de* **Languevoisin** is established on the left. Then comes Écluse 15 (K29), dropping the canal to the level of the Canal de la Somme beyond the prosperous farming villages of **Rouy-le-Grand** and **Roy-le-Petit** (K30, no facilities). From here to **Biaches** (K50), beyond **Péronne** (K47), see the description of the Canal de la Somme (Chapter 9). In order, from junction to junction, through distances on the Canal du Nord are as follows: **Béthencourt-sur-Somme** (K31); **Pargny** (K34); Écluse 14, **Epénancourt** (K35); **St-Christ** (K39); **Eterpigny** (K42); Écluse 13, **Péronne** (K46).

Climbing away from the Somme valley, the Canal du Nord ascends a series of locks: 12, **Cléry-sur-Somme** (K52); 11, **Feuillaucourt** (K53); 10, **Allaines** (K56, café, grocer); and Écluses 9 (K57) and 8 (K58), **Moislains**. Frankly, the waterway provides somewhat dull scenery: as an alternative to pressing on a welcome break can be made by visiting shops in Moislains. There is a water point on the public quay, right bank. Now on the second summit level, the next point of interest, north of **Manancourt** and **Etricourt**, is the beginning of the impressively large **Ruyaulcourt** tunnel (K66) at the end of a deep cutting. (See beginning of this chapter.) Beyond are isolated locks in the open and windswept cornfields: Écluses 7 (K78) and 6 (K80), **Graincourt-lès-Havrincourt** and Écluse 5, **Mœuvres** (K81). Within walking distance are all basic food shops. Otherwise, a larger range of facilities is found in **Inchy-en-Artois** (K84), reached from a bridge in the middle of the pound between Écluses 4 and 3, **Sains-lès-Marquion**. This is a small town of rusty brick courtyards and massive grain barns.

A noticeable softening of the countryside brings with it more attractive villages including **Marquion** (K88), with public mooring north of Écluse 2, through the bridge on the right bank (garage, restaurant and shopping). The next bridge serves **Sauchy-Cauchy** (K90, grocer, bar). Last of the Canal du Nord locks is Écluse 1, **Palluel** (K94, garage, grocer). To the west is a pleasant region of lakes along the course of the River Sensée, which at some stage in the past was navigable. Remains of a very small lock fitted with single gates at each end can be found alongside the Palluel–Arleux road, while one village a little upstream bears the suggestive name of **l'Écluse**. Immediately before the junction with the Canal de la Sensée, **Arleux** (K95) has a quay with water point and fuel pump (see Chapter 1). Turn left into the series of waterways collectively known as La Liaison au Grand Gabarit, leading to Calais and Dunkerque, or right for the River Escaut, Valenciennes and the Belgian border.

9 · Canal de la Somme

Carte Guide: *Picardie*

From a junction with the Canal de St-Quentin at St-Simon to the English Channel at St-Valéry-sur-Somme, 156.5km with 25 locks. Some 20.5km of the route from near Voyennes to near Péronne is shared by the Canal du Nord. The lower section is known as the Canal Maritime d'Abbeville à St-Valéry.

Though virtually inseparable from associations with the appalling slaughter of the Battle of the Somme which claimed about one million dead or wounded during four months in 1916, the River Somme is a remarkably pleasant waterway, at times quite equalling the very best of French navigations in its bucolic charm. That its attractions have rarely been described in print is only partly accounted for by the fact that Calais offers an easier and more rapid entry to France from the Thames Estuary and SE coast of England. Yet many of the British craft that choose to join the network at either Calais or via the Seine at Le Havre would undoubtedly come this way if it were better known and publicized.

Rising in Picardy near Fonsommes, 245km from the sea, the waterway consists of a lateral canal between St-Simon and Bray-sur-Somme and thereafter mostly follows the natural bed of the river to the coast. Throughout much of the course there are numerous lakes alongside: these were formed from flooded peat workings begun many centuries ago and closely recalling the origin of the Norfolk and Suffolk Broads in England. Peat was still dug and burned as a domestic fuel in Amiens early in this century. Teeming with fish, exceptionally noisy frogs and carpets of water lilies, these poplar-shaded pools have become one of France's leading angling areas. The shooting of swans ceased to be a local sport around the beginning of the 18th century. But many other forms of wildlife are keenly persecuted with Gallic fervour and quite tiny towns and villages frequently support emporia filled with sophisticated apparatus to trap creatures that swim, fly or run along the ground.

Commercial traffic, while regular, is quite light, largely because of the absence of any effective seaport for coastal shipping at St-Valéry. At the time of writing, mechanization of locks and bascule bridges is being undertaken but is far from complete.

All locks are closed on Sundays, September 1–May 9 with the exception of the length shared with the Canal du Nord. Short conducted tours of the fascinating Amiens *Hortillonnages*, a complex of small waterways intersecting the city's market gardens, are available in open *barques*. Day-long cruises in a 65-seater vessel *Rose de Picardie* are made up and downstream of Amiens.

Brief history There is published evidence of the Somme being navigable for small craft upstream to St-Quentin in the Middle Ages, but construction of a locked waterway was not mooted until 1725. Following a survey by M. Laurent in 1768 and 1769 plans were agreed the next year and work on the upper end started almost immediately. Early progress saw the route open to traffic between St-Simon and Bray (a distance of 54km) by 1772. Meanwhile, obstructions in the sandbanked estuary at St-Valéry had resulted in discussions to reopen navigation between the sea and Abbeville in 1740. Numerous delays were to prevent completion of the whole through route until 1843.

Intended for the transport of salt, grain, wool, wood, coal and wine, traffic was never destined to be very busy. In the 19th century barges known as *gribannes* traded on the length downstream of Amiens, later assisted by a few steam-powered craft. Such boats as continue to carry cargo today are standard motorized *péniches*, but the waterway can hardly be described as busy.

Our journey starts in the marshy valley of the Somme at **St-Simon**. Having risen to the NE of St-Quentin, the river has already served as a feeder for the Canal de St-Quentin for a considerable distance, but it will still be a long while before it becomes navigable in its own right. Here, the village has a café, grocer and baker. A lock is virtually at the junction, with Écluse 2 in **Ham** (K6.6), a town best known for having the biggest sugar silo in Europe, with a capacity of 26,000 tonnes. Until destruction by the Germans in 1917 there was a massive fortress built between the 13th and 15th centuries, with walls 11m thick. Intended as a place for holding political prisoners, its most notable captive was Louis-Napoléon Bonaparte. After six years he was able to escape to safety in England in 1846. The church of Nôtre-Dame is a splendid 12th and 13th century abbey, well restored. In a pleasant town centre, all facilities will be found. Écluse 3 (K7.2) leads to open country with great fields of wheat, potatoes and beet reaching to the horizon. Patches of woodland shelter numerous wild deer and rabbits.

Le Domaine des Îles at **Offoy** (Écluse 4, K12.4) is a combination of water park and leisure centre, with fishing punts and pedalos, riding and a miniature train arranged round a series of lakes (open mid-Feb–mid-Nov). Grocer, restaurant and banker are in the village, while at the next bridge (K14.8) **Buny** (right bank) has a café and grocer and **Voyennes** (left bank) a butcher, garage and seller of farm-made goat cheese. Near **Rouy-le-Petit** (K16.4, no facilities) the Canal du Nord enters on the left; from this point to Péronne, the same route is common to each waterway and technically the improved Canal de la Somme is also known as the Canal du Nord, 2nd Section. Prosperous farming villages follow in succession, but facilities are very sparse. They include **Béthencourt-sur-Somme**

(K18.5; 3km NE lies the stunningly-named village of **Y**, whose entry sign makes an amusing photograph, **Fontaine-les-Pargny**, **Pargny** (K20.6) and **Epénancourt** (K22.1), site of Écluse 5. A useful restaurant, La Clé des Champs, together with basic shops will be found in **St-Christ** (K25.7) at the head of a chain of canalside lakes. Écluse 6 (K32.9) appears on the south outskirts of **Péronne**, an ancient fortified city built by the confluence of the Rivers Somme and Cologne which suffered almost total destruction during 1916 and 1917. Relics have been saved from the onslaught, such as an early 17th century gateway, the Porte de Bretagne, a 13th century *château* (open Sunday afternoons) and a Renaissance *Hôtel de Ville*. Fish-filled ponds are a famed centre for eels, eaten smoked or as *paté*, and there are canal-intersected market gardens known as *hardines*, similar to those in Amiens and St-Omer. Modern the city certainly is, but it does offer the pleasure boater all services. Commercial traffic gathers at a freight port and a wash-free basin has been expertly converted into a small marina with facilities ranging from hire cruisers to water, electricity, slipway, chandlery and long-term moorings. Within 100m are a restaurant and garage. At K36.7 the Canal du Nord branches off on its journey to the Canal de la Sensée and the River Scarpe, and the Somme resumes its sleepy existence, rarely disturbed by the passage of craft either commercial or pleasure.

We are now approaching the start of a long and quite exciting passage through peat bogs and lakes that can justifiably boast the title 'Fishing Capital of France'. Many of the towns and villages have developed as inland holiday centres with little weekend homes at the waterside and an assortment of restaurants such as is rarely encountered along inland waterways. Écluse 7, Sormont (K39.1) within reach of **Cléry-sur-Somme** is followed by an A1 *autoroute* crossing, and then at **Feuillères** a swing bridge (K41.3) close to which are restaurant, garage and good moorings. Chalk cliffs begin to dominate the valley on the left, providing views down to the old course of the Somme, now a complicated pattern of reedy pools teeming with wildlife. Frogs are so numerous (and vocal) that their croaking can cause a sleepless night unless moorings are selected with care! Écluses 8 (K43.6) and 9 in **Frise** are mechanized. Aptly named **Éclusier** (K46.9) turns out to have no lock, merely a manned bascule bridge with village shopping and restaurants. 2km N up the road towards **Maricourt** is the **Belvédère de Vaux**, a notable viewpoint from which to look down on the patchwork of willow-fringed ponds.

Cappy (K50.2), left of the next road bridge and a little before Écluse 10, is served by a charming little steam railway (60cm gauge) running for 7km between **Froissy** and **Dompierre**. Designed as a World War I military line, it carried up to 1,500 tonnes of munitions a day in 1916; when the war was over it served a vital rôle in the great rebuilding programme of the district. For many years its continued purpose was the transport of minerals; and from 1972 the line was restored as a passenger carrying tourist attraction through outstandingly pleasant scenery. Locomotives and rolling stock represent an amazingly varied collection dating from 1914 to 1946. One part of the track is arranged as a zig-zag switchback, enabling a sudden change in levels to be overcome within limited space, similar to a practice widespread in the Andes and Himalayas. Passengers board at Froissy (K52.9) near Écluse 11, scheduled services running on Sundays and public holidays from Easter to end Sept every $\frac{3}{4}$hr from 14.15–18.00. An additional Wed and Sat service operates on afternoons in June, July and Aug. Updated timetables from the Association Picarde pour la Préservation et l'Entretien des Véhicules Anciens, BP 106, 80001 Amiens. Eating and limited shopping is possible in Cappy, although much more extensive town facilities will be found at **Bray-sur-Somme**, the 'capital' of nearby fishing resorts about 2km north of the canal at Écluse 11, although in former times it was a river port and is still served by a short navigable branch line, (max. draft 1.0m).

Etinehem (where there is another branch leading to a 'port') is followed by Écluse 12 at **Méricourt-sur-Somme** (K58.6). Caravans and chalets are concealed in the waterside undergrowth and the little River Somme chuckles along close to the canal adding to the charms of this outstandingly lovely navigation. Most of the villages now encountered remain pleasingly rural with huge ancient hay barns and sufficient shops to keep pleasure boaters well stocked with food. In **Chipilly** (K62.3) is the small Oasis restaurant, while the Auberge des Pêcheurs provides meals throughout the summer in **Sailly-Laurette** (K65.2) near Écluse 13.

Between the Somme and the River Ancre at Écluse 14, **Corbie** (K74.4) is a sizeable town (all facilities) once famous for its Benedictine abbey, founded in the mid-7th century by St-Bathilde, Queen of Clovis II. Little now remains of the great establishment. One notable building is the elaborate *Hôtel de Ville*, a *château*-like fantasy in stone and brick with a series of carved horses' heads over the doorways on the original stable block. There are several restaurants. War graves proliferate throughout the area, for there was very heavy fighting here during World War I; 11,000 Australians who died between 1916 and 1918 are remembered by a National Memorial 3km south of the waterway, on the road connecting **Fouilloy** and **Villers-Bretonneux**.

Locks 15, **Daours** (K79.7) and 16, **Lamotte-Brébière** (K84.3) lead to **Camon** (K90.1), a suburb with restaurant and boat chandlery. Soon afterwards **Amiens** (K93.3) is reached: capital of Picardy and long associated with the English from the days when Edward VI signed a peace treaty with France's Henry II (1550). Although there was widespread destruction in both world wars the outstanding Gothic cathedral survived intact. A comprehensive rebuilding scheme has resulted in much 1950s concrete architecture, varying from the uninspired to the unpleasant. For a time the real river serves as the navigation channel, lined by charming tumbledown brick cottages and a range of central moorings. Although not as widely used as earlier in the 20th century, curious flat-bottomed punts (*cornets*), treated with tar and featuring elegant upturned bows, bring garden produce to market from the *Hortillonages*. This fascinating area comprises 300 hectares of fertile plots known as *aires*, intersected by numerous tiny canals (*rieux*) that resulted from medieval peat workings. Agreeable conducted tours by open boat provide the tourist with root-level views of cabbages and onions: several embarkation points are associated with restaurants just off the main waterway. Throughout the length and breadth of France rivers and lakes are lined with wooden fishing punts, and although plastic versions have also begun to appear, the traditional pattern persists. It is surprisingly rare to encounter such craft being built, but Amiens does possess one of these normally hidden boatyards where heaps of newly cut timber are being formed into elegant little vessels. Speciality foods to search for include *tuiles au chocolat*, almond biscuits shaped like curved 'tiles', *ficelles Picardes*, a pancake filled with cream, ham and cheese or mushrooms, *pâté de canard en croûte*, duck pâté in a pastry case and macaroons. Past Écluse 17 (K94) open country is soon reached once more with a continued string of peat lakes, called *Chés Intailles* in the Picardy dialect: if anything, the valley becomes even more beautiful than upstream of Amiens, while fishing attracts hoards of ardent devotees.

Écluse 18, **Montiéres** (K97.7) is followed by Écluse 19 in **Ailly-sur-Somme** (K102.5): this latter chamber is one of several on the canal built almost in the form of a two-rise, the lower part having sloping sides and seemingly used as a kind of flood lock or perhaps to pass unusually deep-draft craft. Ailly's church is an unusual modernistic structure, its roof looking like a ship's sail. Having passed further small lakes, the most interesting little town of **Picquigny** appears on the left

(K108) rising from the riverfront around a thickly wooded hill. Here ended the Hundred Years War when Louis IX signed a treaty with Edward IV of England in 1475. In order to prevent any possibility of a murderous attack such as had taken place during a similar meeting on the bridge in Montereau some 56 years earlier (see Chapter 13), the monarchs approached each other on the Île de la Trève in the centre of the river separated by iron bars! High above the town and commanding a fine view of the Somme are the remains of a once massive fortified *château* with a pair of gateways and a magnificent Renaissance kitchen with vaulted ceiling. It is also possible to see a range of underground tunnels with *graffiti* carved by prisoners of long ago. Cherry trees and wild roses tumble down the grey walls towards the rooftops of houses below. Directly alongside is the collegiate church of St-Martin (13th–15th centuries). A cemetery opposite the Pavillon Sévigné contains a number of graves of British World War I soldiers, regimental comrades of the author's father. At the request of his mother, John McKnight had attended church in London one Sunday in 1916. While the service was in progress most of his colleagues were suddenly despatched to France, few of them ever to return. It will thus be appreciated that but for the religious wishes of my grandmother, this book might never have been written! The two-rise Écluse 20 is mechanized. There are ample shops and a choice of restaurants. To the SE, across the river at **La Chaussée-Tirancourt**, can be seen ditches of a Roman town covering about 20 hectares and known as Caesar's Camp.

NW from Picquigny, **Belloy-sur-Somme** has two *châteaux*, from the 18th and 19th centuries. In the next reach, 3km downstream on the left, the ruins of the 12th century Abbaye du Gard may be visited by the public.

Rarely does a waterway present such a rich collection of pleasing villages and small towns. The next, **Hangest-sur-Somme** (K114.5), is known for its watercress beds. German troops under Rommel crossed the Somme here in 1940. Good meals may be obtained at the Hôtel du Canard, with a number of shops near by. Écluse 21, Labreilloire (K117.5) marks a point where most left bank villages become rather remote from the waterway, with green and lily-filled lakes intervening between the river and the D218 highway. Several features in **Long**, Écluse 22 (K124.8) add to the enjoyment of exploration. While only a small place, it has a spectacular town hall crowned with an extraordinary 19th century Gothic bell tower recalling the railway station at Abbeville. Nor is the adjacent bar-café what you would expect, for it is filled with expensive and sophisticated angling equipment with which to capture the giant carp and pike of the vicinity. There are several shops and an opportunity to hire bicycles for tours through the lakeland. A Louis XV *château* is constructed in white stone and pink brick. At **Fontaine-sur-Somme**, across the ponds to the SW, a boatbuilder sells wooden punts: filled with water, they are stacked at the edge of the main road.

Even after a moderate summer rain the Somme flows fast through **Pont-Rémy** (K130.6), a village with delightful waterfront, brick and stone church containing mid-16th century stained glass windows and a 15th century *château* on an island, reconstructed about 1837 in the Gothic troubadour style. Shopping is good. Écluse 23 (K131.2) will be found here. **Epagne** (K136) has a jewel of a small *château* and soon afterwards we arrive in **Abbeville** (K141), now an industrial town with dejected outskirts but considerable charm in its centre. From the 13th–15th centuries it was possessed in turn by the English, Burgundians and the French, but it was not to become a true part of France until the marriage in 1514 of Louis XII to Mary of England. He was 53 and she just 16. It appears that the strain was too much for Louis, for he died the following year of 'consumption'. The British army established a headquarters in the town in World War I and it was very severely damaged in 1940, more than 2,000 houses being bombed with the loss of hundreds of civilians. Waterway banks are well landscaped with moorings among greenery close to shops and restaurants (doubtless it is possible to eat well ashore, but I have to admit I suffered a memorably poor meal in a restaurant that was suspiciously empty, the only customers – as I later learned – being tourists like myself). Abbeville's great treasure is not a cathedral or *château* but the railway station, a wonderful symphony in pink brick and elaborate barge-boarding, dating, astonishingly, only from 1912. Note the monument next to a nearby bridge, to a nineteen-year-old youth who suffered severe torture for failing to salute a procession in 1766! As the town is partly built on an island, watercourses are an essential feature. Navigation follows the left channel, terminating at Écluse 24 (K141.7).

After many outstandingly pretty reaches the remainder of the Somme is disappointing, running quite straight and level to the coast. There are several swing bridges, that at **Petit-Port** (K148.2) being alongside a bar/grocer. While these final 15km are lacking in scenic attraction, it is well worth pressing on to the ancient little seaport of **St Valéry-sur-Somme** (K156.5), whether you are planning to travel out to the coast or not. Floating pontoon well upstream of the first set of tidal gates is the most convenient

Abbeville's extravagant railway station.

overnight halt. The non-tidal canal ceases at Écluse 25, where there are two installations about 200m apart: the upstream one comprises a guillotine with set of mitre gates at the bottom, while that at the beginning of the tideway has a guillotine with pairs of mitre gates facing in each direction. Water level throughout this reach changes during operation, effectively creating a 'flash lock'. Entry is normally at high water, or alternatively by giving three blasts on the horn having previously contacted the keeper (see Carte Guide for tel. no.). At low water the marked sea channel across the Somme Bay dries out completely. An updated maritime chart is strongly recommended if you intend to continue your cruise along the coast. Mooring is possible both above and below the lock, within easy reach of the town. Visitors' berths are reserved on the tideway and can be approached for about 2hr either side of high water.

Slipway, 6 tonne crane, fuelling and other services are available, with a chandlery by the bascule bridge. Coasters used to navigate upriver to Abbeville, while many picturesque fishing craft will be seen in the marine channel at St-Valéry. If coming in from the English Channel, it is recommended to arrive at the lead-in buoy and wait well off the coast until about 1hr before high water. The incoming tide rushes in at considerable speed, providing an exciting 'slalom course' up the marked approach channel. William the Conqueror sailed from here to England in 1066, and Joan of Arc passed through before her brief imprisonment at the hands of the English in nearby **Le Crotoy** (1430). The town is divided into the Ville Basse, along the seafront, and the Ville Haute, over-looking the coast with remnants of fortifications.

Shellfish and fish are leading local industries, along with tourism for there are excellent sandy beaches and dunes on all parts of the coast (the sea retreats a great distance at low tide in the Bay itself). Splendid summertime excursions can be made aboard a little railway serving locations around the Bay: **Cayeux-sur-Mer**, St-Valéry, **Noyelles** and Le Crotoy. Opened in 1887, it operates only in July and August (timetables available locally). Diesel and steam locomotives are used on a track totalling 27km. Passage of trains over the lock bridge in St-Valéry is accompanied by much hooting, ringing bells and waving red flags, as the jolly little outfit momentarily joins road traffic. Some 2,000 hectares of marshes in the NE part of the Bay are set aside as a nature reserve where over 300 varieties of migratory birds have been sighted.

Approaching the estuary of the Somme at St-Valéry-sur-Somme.

10 · Canal de St-Quentin

Carte Guide: *Picardie*

From the River Escaut (Scheldt) at Cambrai to a junction with the Canal latéral à l'Oise at Chauny, 92.5km with 35 duplicated locks. There are tunnels at Bony 5,670m and at Lesdins 1,300m. Branches connect the main line with a short length of navigable River Oise at Chauny, 270m with 1 lock; and from Point Y, near Tergnier with the Canal de la Sambre à l'Oise at La Fère, 3.8km with no locks. Additionally there is a link with the start of the Canal de la Somme near St-Simon.

Until the opening of the Canal du Nord in 1965, the Canal de St-Quentin provided to sole water connection between the Channel ports and the River Escaut with Paris and the rest of the French network. Traffic has declined very considerably in the last decade although until very recent times it was undisputedly the busiest artificial navigation in the country. Rising to a 20.4km summit level, it is provided with duplicated and mechanized locks throughout. One notable feature is the series of iron and glass lock control cabins.

In spite of a widespread belief that this corner of Northern France is both flat and scenically dull, the Canal de St-Quentin is often most attractive, passing through vast plains of rolling cornfields with leafy cuttings along the summit pound. Bankside facilities are generally good. All craft are required to pay for being towed in a *rame* through the longer of the two tunnels. At the time of writing, pleasure craft use their own engines to negotiate the cutting between the tunnels and the shorter tunnel itself. The entire summit level operates on a one-way control system. You are advised to seek local information on towing times, which tend to vary.

Brief history The canal is composed of two parts: the King's ministers Colbert and Mazarin had both proposed linking the Rivers Oise and Somme in the 17th century and the resulting Canal Crozat, or Canal de Picardie, was opened between Chauny and St-Simon in 1738. Construction of the remainder, connecting the Seine Basin with the Escaut, was an extended process, having first been designed by an engineer named Devicq in 1727 who died in combat near Prague in 1742. A revised plan was produced by Laurent de Lyonne, Director-General of Canal Works, and begun in 1768 with the object of passing 1,500 boats a year. There were numerous objections to the great cost, especially that of boring a single bricked tunnel 14km in length at Bony. Building ground to a halt in 1774, pending discovery of a line that would avoid the expensive tunnel. But the urgency of opening up a route to the coast was becoming ever more vital, for the Somme Bay was progressively silting at St-Valéry. Therefore, in 1781 M. de la Fitte de Clavé was charged to dig a navigation from the Oise at Landrecies to the Escaut: this route would have been considerably shorter. Nothing came of this alternative. Wars with England intervened and after endless arguments in favour of different approaches to the problem, Napoléon himself insisted in 1801 that work should begin once more, using the design advanced by Devicq 74 years earlier. Greatest effort was devoted to the two tunnels and their approach cuttings. In the longer one at Bony, shafts were cut at 100m intervals and up to 83m deep; after the canal had been in service for a few years only twelve of these remained open to the sky, the others having been sealed up. Osiers were planted to stabilize the cutting sides which were up to 35m high. Generous underground water supplies were tapped in the workings. The Emperor's demand that building should proceed without delay was obviously heeded, for he was able to open the navigation in April 1810.

The canal was an immediate success, with traffic levels building up to the extent that later there was a need to duplicate locks, deepen the channel, enlarge each tunnel and provide better water supplies. Improvements in the 20th century involved electric barge traction on rails, installed during World War I, mechanizing locks and lighting the most heavily used sections. By 1878 the waterway had reached saturation point, with up to 110 barges crossing the summit daily. It was therefore determined to duplicate the route by constructing the Canal du Nord, which was not finally completed until 1965 (see Chapter 8). Even though coal traffic from Belgium had started to decline in the early 1950s, the Canal de St-Quentin had more freight than any other man-made waterway in France, 8 million tonnes of goods being carried in 1964 alone. In order of importance these were construction materials, petroleum products, agricultural produce, minerals and chemicals. In the long term there is a possibility that the Canal de St-Quentin may be duplicated by a new 3,000 tonne capacity Seine-Nord Canal. Meanwhile, it offers a more interesting and agreeable route than the Canal du Nord.

Navigation passes from the River Escaut to the canal with no change in levels at **Cambrai** (see Chapter 1).

The city is soon left astern. Although the countryside is well populated, it is unexpectedly pleasant. Locks tell of punishingly hard use, with battered timber piers guiding craft into one or other of the duplicated chambers. Locks are moderately frequent on the fairly steep climb to the canal's watershed, beginning with Écluse 1, **Proville** (K2.2), soon to be followed by Écluse 2, Cantigneul (K3.8); Écluse 3, **Novelles** (K4.4); Écluse 4, Talma (K7.3) and Écluse 5, **Marcoing** (K7.8). Shopping and other facilities are not difficult to find, especially in Marcoing. Fierce battles raged throughout the district during the Battle of Cambrai in November 1917, with almost 11,000 German prisoners and 140 guns being taken by British divisions. But it was not until September of the following year that the Allies gained full control of the area. Beyond Écluse 6, Bracheux (K9.4), a bridge in **Masnièrs** (K10.7) replaces one which collapsed under the weight of a British tank late in 1917 after it had been damaged by German mines. More shopping can be attended to here or, after Écluse 8, St-Waast (K12.7), in **Crèvecœur-sur-l'Escaut** (K14, Écluse 9). Écluse 10, baker, with a butcher on the right between Écluses 10 and 11.

East of the bridge at Écluse 12 (K17.8, café) lies the 12th century Cistercian Abbaye de Nôtre-Dame de Vaucelles. Its foundation stone was laid by St Bernard. Magnificent buildings were encircled by 7km of walls. Guided tours are possible on the last Sunday of each month, April–October. Between Écluses 12 and 13, an island creates a one-way section at the Pont des Grenouillères; southbound boats should take the righthand channel. The route is regularly punctuated by locks: Écluse 13, **Bantouzelle** (K20); Écluse 14, **Banteux** (K20.5) and Écluse 15, **Honnecourt** (K23.2) with food shops in each village. Écluses 16, Moulin-Lafosse (K24.2) and 17, Bosquet (K24.7) complete the ascent to the summit level and the waterway heads south into hills, away from the Escaut valley. There is a large basin in **Vendhuille** (K26.6) reserved for cereal barges and an ever-deepening cutting leads to the north portal of the great **Bony** tunnel (K29). This point is easily reached by car-bound waterway enthusiasts from a small road running east out of **Le Catelet**.

Until the early 1980s, all craft, commercial and pleasure, were marshalled into a *rame* and drawn by electric tug along the whole of the summit (both tunnels included). Now, the tug is obligatory only in the longer tunnel. The procedure is extremely slow, depending on the number of working boats in line ahead of cruisers: the record is said to be 74! Elsewhere in France, tunnel towage has often been superseded by arrangements enabling craft to proceed under their own power: the narrow channels and heavy traffic indicate that this is not likely to occur at Bony. Lighting relieves the gloom at intervals. In spite of laden barges being placed ahead of empty ones with all 'yachts' attached to the tail, one is expected to resume original positions in the queue for locks at the far end. William Moens had a nocturnal adventure while waiting at the southern portal (*Through France and Belgium by River and Canal in the Steam Yacht 'Ytene'*, 1876); in those days, the tug was steam powered and he resolved to jump the queue to avoid its fumes and the smoke of thirty cabin stoves on the barges waiting to pass. 'Suddenly, at about nine o'clock, we heard a great outcry in the tunnel, and men came running along the towing path, asking if we had a pump. We said yes, several, but not moveable; and they explained that one of the barges had struck violently against a stone in the side of the tunnel and had been stove in, and there was great fear lest she should sink in the tunnel itself with the 270 tons of coal with which she was laden. This was a pretty state of things, and we soon thought that our route to Belgium would be barred for weeks and that we might have to retrace our way back again. The tug steamer soon, however, emerged from the arch, and came to a standstill when three or four barges were out of the tunnel. It was the first that was injured, and she was already sunk to within three or four inches of the gunwale.

'Long planks were soon put out to the shore, and a crowd of excited Frenchmen assembled, each with a large galvanized iron pump borrowed from the barges behind us. They were all soon at work pumping, and I returned to the *Ytene* to fetch A… [Mrs Anne Moens] to endeavour to comfort the poor women and children that had been landed with bundles of clothes, &c. as they were afraid that the barge might go down. It was a curious and exciting sight, all those collected together having large lanterns with them; loud and hurried orders being heard from those in charge; the poor women and children, with their cat, huddled together on the bank of the canal, crying and lamenting bitterly as the sinking barge, with all its furniture, was their home and property.

'I ordered my men to go on board and assist at the work, and at last, after great exertions, it was found that the vessel did not sink deeper in the canal, and after some time the pumps, increased in number, began to gain on the water, and the hole was discovered on her starboard bow. There had been formerly a towing path on each side of the tunnel; but it being found that the water space was not wide enough, that on the left hand was cut away, but leaving rough stones and projections; against one of which the unfortunate vessel had struck

being towed at too rapid a pace by the tug. Some planks and nails were obtained, and I contributed some cotton waste, and after some work the leak was stopped. We remained on the scene of action until the women returned to their vessel; their bedding, however, having got quite soaked with the water. After the danger had passed, to cheer themselves, they began to tell fearful stories of accidents on the canal, and of various friends of theirs having been drowned.'

During World War I both tunnels were used by the Germans as defences in the Hindenburg Line, with shafts dug to connect with other fortifications. Virtually impregnable, these underground vaults were fitted with electric lighting and served as stabling, hospitals and command centres. The southern entrance (K34.7) has been made into a tourist attraction with signboards and steps leading down from the N44 road between **Bellicourt** and **Riqueval**. A crumbling stone plaque records the tunnel's completion in 1810. 600m south down the road is a restaurant, with a *Bar du Souterrain* conveniently close. The canal continues southwards through Riqueval (K36), where a bridge over the cutting was the scene of one of the most remarkable photographs of World War I. After **Bellenglise** (K38.2) and **Le Haucourt** (K41.1), the **Lesdins** (or Tronquoy) tunnel appears (K41.9). Being quite straight and less than one quarter as long, its passage is tame compared with Bony! Pleasure craft pass through under their own power.

Downhill locks start with Écluse 18, Lesdins (K45.2), with further changes in level at Écluse 19, Pascal (K45.5); Écluse 20 (baker), **Omissy** (K46.7, shopping) and Écluse 21, Moulin Brûlé (K48.7). Entry to the city of **St-Quentin** is near Écluse 22 (K50.9) where moorings can be found in a large basin to the right (K52.8, about 600m to the town centre). Tales of the World War I destruction might suggest that the rebuilt St-Quentin is an unappealing town, but it has a surprisingly elegant main square surrounded by flourishing shops and restaurants. Notable buildings are the early 16th century Gothic *Hôtel de Ville* (37-bell carillon and magnificent Renaissance chimneypiece); the massive Basilica whose 9th century crypt is said to con-

British troops on the banks of the canal at Riqueval during World War I. Rebuilt, the bridge is recognizable today. (Photograph courtesy Imperial War Museum, London.)

tain the remains of Caius Quintinus, a young Christian nobleman who was martyred in the 4th century and gives his name to the town; and the Musée Antoine Lécuyer, mainly devoted to portraits of 18th century celebrities. St-Quentin lies on the Somme which broadens into a pleasant lake with bathing *plage* (near the railway station). But memories of war refuse to disappear. Montmorency's army was soundly beaten by Spanish troops in the Battle of St-Quentin (1557). Further hardships followed a defeat by the Germans in the Franco-Prussian troubles of 1870. And once more the town was in German hands from August 1914 until October 1, 1918: by the time it was retaken by the Allies much had been destroyed and the already ruined Basilica was on the point of being blown up. Holes in the stonework show where demolition charges were to be laid.

A level pound extends as far as Écluse 23, **Fontaine-lès-Clercs** (K58.3), with full shopping and garage beyond the River Somme in **Seraucourt-le-Grand** (K61.1), site of a British war cemetery. Past Écluse 24 (K62.7), **Artemps** (K64.4) offers grass bank moorings by the bridge near a bar and grocer. Now deep in real country, the canal is accompanied by the infant Somme through **Pont-Tugny** (K66.3, café/ *tabac*) where a former lock is out of service: take the left channel. Shortly before **St-Simon** (see Chapter 9) a tiny island marks the start of the Canal de la Somme, which branches away towards the coast on the right.

Marshland and lakes characterize the waterway through pastoral surroundings with few signs of habitation to **Jussy** (K74.1, most services) with little of note apart from Écluses 26, Jussy (K77); 27, **Mennessis** (K79.6) and 28, Voyaux (K80.2, grocer, bar). **Ternier** (K84.2) and its neighbouring town of **Fargniers** are scruffy ironworking centres, the former being a kind of Crewe Junction for the railway network of this part of France. As your boat negotiates Écluses 29–31, Fargniers, there will be opportunities for some of the ship's complement to buy galley supplies. But it is decidedly not an area for unnecessary lingering! At prosaically named Point Y, after Écluse 31, you can turn left along the La Fère branch and reach the Canal de la Sambre à l'Oise near **La Fère** (see Chapter 11). This involves 3.8km of level cruising. If, on the other hand, you are bound for the Oise and the Seine or wish to travel eastwards to the Canal des Ardennes, it is preferable to remain on the main line of the Canal de St-Quentin and work through Écluses 32, Ternier (K85.8); 33, **Viry** (K88.4); 34, **Senicourt** (K90.8) and 35, **Chauny** (K92.3) before emerging on the Canal latéral à l'Oise. For facilities in Chauny, see Chapter 17.

11 · Canal de la Sambre à l'Oise

Carte Guide: *Picardie*
From a junction with the La Fère branch of the Canal de St-Quentin at La Fère to a junction with the River Sambre in Landrecies, 67.2km with 38 locks.

Providing a route to Belgium which is continued via the River Sambre, the canal climbs to a summit level and leaves the Oise valley to cross a chalk divide near Oisy before dropping down the valley of the Sambre. This is a country of brick buildings, gravel pits, sometimes scruffy towns and pleasant reaches of countryside through meadows. Locks are presently at a stage of transition, some remaining manual while others are mechanized or arranged in automatic groups. Robert Louis Stevenson canoed this way through flood and rainstorm (*An Inland Voyage*, 1878) but recorded few impressions of the waterway itself: he was more concerned with overnight quarters at small inns, where he and his companion Sir Walter Grindlay Simpson, Bart. were not infrequently taken for pedlars of the roughest kind.

Proposed by an Irishman named Shée (Shea?) in 1749, who saw the route as being useful for transport of arms from Landrecies, the canal was built as a private enterprise by the Compagnie du Canal de la Sambre à l'Oise. It opened in 1839 and was taken over by the State in 1949. As it connected the Belgian coalfields in the Mons–Charleroi area with the Seine Basin, coal was a major freight. In the final years of the 19th century mechanical bank traction began to replace horse haulage in the north of France and tractors running on inflated tyres provided a service throughout the Sambre à l'Oise until unpowered craft were totally phased out in the late 1960s.

La Fère, where the canal leaves a branch of the Canal de St-Quentin (see Chapter 10), provides useful shopping facilities. It has long been a place of strategic importance, guarding the Oise valley and the approaches to the Île de France from the fortress *château*, erected in the 15th and 16th centuries. The town fell to the Prussians after a hard-fought battle in 1870 and during World War I was on the Hindenburg Line. Attractions include the Musée Jeanne d'Aboville (paintings and archaeology: open daily 14.00–18.00h except Tuesdays). After passing through Écluse 35,

Travecy (K2.2), best approach to the town on the left bank, we arrive at a manned swing bridge (K3.5). Then comes Écluse 34, **Vendeuil** (K4.8) with an aqueduct over the River Oise. Vendeuil itself lies 1.7km west of the next bridge. Among the attractions here are a small zoo in the ruins of an 1875 fort and a pleasant water park established close to the canal in former gravel workings with swimming and sailing.

Midway between Écluses 33, **Brissy** (K8.8) and 32, **Hamégicourt** (K10.3), a bridge leads into **Brissy-Hamégicourt**, a small town surrounded by gravel pits with a range of shops and a church with a curious 'hooded' spire. **Berthenicourt** near Écluse 31 (K12.7, automatically operated) is agreeably situated by the river. Alongside Écluse 30, **Mézières-sur-Oise** (K14.2) is a restaurant with adequate shops not far away. **Châtillon-sur-Oise** lies west of Écluse 29 (K15.7) with another aqueduct in the pound above. Clues as to one of the canal's freight traffics are given by a large grain silo near Écluse 28, **Sissay** (K17.6), where the charming ruined church was replaced by one with a concrete spire in the 1930s.

While involving a walk of 2km from Écluse 27 (K19.2), **Ribemont** is a sizeable town with a good selection of shops; it was the birthplace of 18th century mathematician and revolutionary Marquis de Condorcet. Much of a hillside has been excavated for cement at **Origny-Ste-Benoite** (K23.3). Here will be found a café by the bridge, overlooking an extensive and busy barge basin. Shops, restaurants and garage are all easily accessible. West of the waterway at Écluse 24 (K26.3) is the charming brick-built village of **Bernot**, very rural and offering café, baker and grocer. Locks in this area are hand worked and mostly have a dejected appearance with poorly cultivated gardens. In 1983 the café/grocer at **Hauteville**, Écluse 23 (K28.6), was closed down and advertised for sale. There are no alternative facilities either here or, café excepted, in **Noyales**, a superb backwater settlement of brick houses SW of Écluse 21 (K32.1). Note the iron water pumps in the streets. Another pleasant village is **Vadencourt**, NW of Écluse 19 (K35.6), where groups of poplars line the banks of the flood-prone Oise. Several houses display exceptionally fine decorative stonework and the 12th century church has an unusually crooked slate spire and intricate carved column heads. Shopping includes bar, grocer and farm milk with fuel available at a garage. A swing bridge is followed by Écluse 18, **Grand-Verly** (K37.2). In the next 11km 18 locks indicate the extent to which the canal is climbing to its summit level. We pass through the centre of **Tupigny** (K39.9), perhaps the most pleasant small town on this route; a pair of swing bridges enhance excitingly varied architecture, complemented by tubs of flowers. Café and butcher. Scenery begins to improve dramatically in hilly country at **Hannappes**, Écluse 12 (K42.2, swing bridge), where there is a café. The Oise is left behind and from time to time the Sambre is incorporated into the navigation.

Three locks at **Vénérolles** (K43.4) lead to the moderate sized town of **Étreux** (K45.5) at the confluence of the River Noirrieu. Shops and all other facilities are excellent. A concrete bridge replaces the former swing span. Further basic shops exist in the summit level village of **Oisy** (K51.2) with another brief meeting with the Sambre. Our descent towards Belgium starts at Écluse 1, Bois l'Abbaye (K55.2). Quite soon the canal arrives close to the middle of **Catillon-sur-Sambre** (K58.6) whose vast church square is within a short distance of the lift bridge (extensive shopping). **Ors**, by Écluse 2 (K61.5), has nothing more exciting than a *café/dépôt de pain*. The canal merges with the canalized River Sambre beyond Écluse 3 (K66.9) in the busy market town of **Landrecies**. While visiting the bustling Saturday morning market, I got into conversation with the lady owner of a large hardware shop and she told me she had a copy of a most unusual 19th century book describing an Englishman's travels on the waterways of France. Intrigued at the prospect of a hitherto 'unknown' work, I accompanied her to her place of business where she produced with a flourish a translation of Robert Louis Stevenson's *An Inland Voyage*. The discovery was almost as disappointing as the canal content of the book itself! Stevenson did not care for Landrecies: in addition to 'simply bedlamite' weather, he found that 'it consists almost entirely of fortifications. Within the ramparts, a few blocks of houses, a long row of barracks, and a church, figure, with what countenance they may, as the town. There seems to be no trade; and a shopkeeper from whom I bought a sixpenny flint-and-steel was so much affected that he filled my pockets with spare flints into the bargain.' Exactly a century before, de La Lande had commented that the garrison town of Landrecies 'is poor, peopled by retired soldiers, without trade, without manufacture and without commerce'. Matters have since improved.

12 · River Sambre

Carte Guide: *Picardie* (ECM)
From a junction with the Canal de la Sambre à l'Oise at Landrecies to the Belgian border beyond Jeumont.

(Navigation continues through Belgium to Charleroi and the Meuse at Namur.) 54.3km with 9 locks.

The Sambre rises near Le Nouvion-en-Thiérache and runs for about 193km before reaching the Meuse. The navigation is quite attractive in its upper reaches, but suffers from urban development from Maubeuge to the Belgian frontier, where it is still only a moderate-sized river.

It was used for the *flottage* of logs from the latter part of the 17th century, and barges are recorded as using the Sambre in 1712 after the army had built a series of 33 locks on the Landrecies – Maubeuge length. These works were not well designed; half a century later locks were considered to be too few in number to enable boats to carry a fully economic load. Present locks date from the 19th century. Traditionally, trade mainly served the metallurgical district around Maubeuge with coal from Belgium and return loads of French pit-props.

After **Landrecies** (see Chapter 11), the River Sambre flows past the SE borders of the Forêt de Mormal, soon to find itself in pleasant wooded pastures. Beyond Écluse 1, **Étoquies** (K3), with a lift bridge, we enter the hamlet of **Hachette**, where the Café des Pecheurs is a popular weekend resort for anglers by Écluse 2 (K7.7, water point). This and several other locks are manually worked but feature an ingenious overhead lever, enabling both gates to be opened by winding on one side only. Note another café by the railway level crossing at Écluse 3, **Sassegnies** (K11.1), and a grocer in the village itself, a cluster of appealing rusty-red brick buildings (approached from a flat steel bridge, K13).

Berlaimont, mainly hidden from the river by a belt of trees, has a full range of facilities and is easily reached from Écluse 4 (K17.8). Having taken in the waters of the River Sambrette, the stream then swings round two great curves. At the start of the first is **Pont-sur-Sambre** and Écluse 5 (K21.7). This is a most handsome small town, consisting of a long and wide main street where houses display a fascinating variety of architectural styles. At the centre is a tall brick tower, built on a square plan. Seeking overnight lodgings, Robert Louis Stevenson and his canoeing companion were taken for pedlars in a Pont-sur-Sambre labourers' alehouse: this was intended as a compliment, judging from the superior class of fare put before them at the communal dining table! The town is now more updated and welcoming, with shops and garage to cater for most needs of travelling *plaisanciers*.

Écluse 6, Quartes (K26.2), marks the end of agreeable countryside. Not long after, we reach **Hautmont** and Écluse 7 (K35.4), a positively industrial place where the utility of its shops is in no way matched by its beauty. These dejected surroundings stay with us for most of the remaining journey to Belgium. One is apt to regard **Maubeuge** in a more kindly light on learning that it was mostly destroyed during air raids in 1940. Much of what we now see is a symphony of 1950s and 1960s concrete in an already outdated 1930s cinema style of architecture. Steel works have replaced one-time arms manufacture. For 12 days in July there is a beer festival (a concept rather more Belgian than French) with a folklore carnival and procession each Easter Monday. Roger Pilkington was trapped by flood water for a week in Maubeuge and was treated royally when news of his arrival spread through the district (*Small Boat to Luxembourg*, 1967). Earlier in the 20th century, Dr Pilkington's family had operated a French subsidiary of their St Helens-based glassworks in the town, and although long closed down it was well remembered by former employees. Fortifications were raised by Vauban and traces remain. Moor near Écluse 8 (K41.4) and a host of shops will be found within shouting distance.

All the adjuncts of industrialized civilization are present through **Assevent** (K45.3) and **Boussois** (K47.7). Although not notably suitable boating country, a number of cruisers will be seen at a *club nautique* upstream of Écluse 9, **Marpent** (K51.8). The frontier town of **Jeumont** (K53.3) offers a convenient quayside mooring with bollards (by a multi-coloured block of flats) and well placed for the shopping centre. Craft intent on crossing the border should call at a Customs quay (K53.1) a little before the main road bridge.

II·SEINE AND CHAMPAGNE

13 · River Seine

Carte Guides: *Seine, Paris – Marcilly; Seine, Paris – Le Havre*

From Marcilly-sur-Seine to the English Channel at Le Havre. 535km with 25 locks. There are two additional locks on the 25km Canal du Havre à Tancarville, which duplicates the lowest portion of the estuary. Travelling downstream, the following junctions are made: with the River Yonne at Montereau; the Canal du Loing at St-Mammès; the River Marne in Paris (Alfortville); the Canal St-Martin (leading to the Canal St-Denis and the Canal de l'Ourcq) in Paris near the Pont d'Austerlitz; the Canal St-Denis at St-Denis (29km below Paris, Île de la Cité); and the River Oise at Conflans-Ste-Honorine.

Not only is the Seine the longest inland navigation in France but it carries easily more commercial freight than any other waterway. A glance at the map immediately reveals the reason for its Latin name *Sequana* – the snake. As an obvious and convenient entry to the canal and river network from the English Channel, all long-distance cruises through France are likely to include part of the Seine, while a journey from one end to the other is a fascinating experience.

Personal research suggests that the river can be safely navigated by very small craft between Marcilly and the upstream side of Paris. Below this point, exceptionally busy commercial traffic makes the use of low-powered pleasure boats unwise and hire cruiser companies would be unlikely to sanction a passage. But few problems will be encountered by experienced owners of private craft. Numerous regulations apply to the use of pleasure boats and these together with a wealth of other practical information are contained in the *Carte Guides*. They are quite indispensable.

Lock-keepers aim to pass pleasure craft through in company with other vessels and are entitled to keep them waiting for up to 20 minutes; if no other craft have arrived within that time you will be worked through alone. For seasonal changes in lock opening times, closures for public holidays and out-of-hours passage through locks (on payment of a substantial fee), consult the *Carte Guides*. In simplified form, the hours are as follows: Conflans to Ablon, April–Sept inclusive, 6.30–19.30h. (Conflans to Jaulnes, inclusive, there is a lunch break between 12.00 and 12.30h.) Port-à-Anglais to Amfreville, inclusive, 7.00–19.00h, throughout the year.

The entire river is provided with excellent navigation markers, although there is sometimes a lack of kilometre posts. Distances are calculated from Marcilly to Île de la Cité, Paris (K0–K170) and then begin again from Paris to Le Havre (K0–K365). Night navigation is forbidden in all pleasure craft below Rouen. With an adequately powered vessel about four days should be reserved for the passage Paris to Le Havre and three days for Marcilly to Paris: these are, of course, minimum times and the attractions of the Seine are such that many weeks could be spent making a thorough exploration. Almost throughout the whole waterway, smaller cruisers may find the wash produced by commercial traffic and passenger boats rather uncomfortable when moored at night. I have known otherwise good sailors to be overcome by seasickness within 15 minutes of lying on the river in Paris. In my view, the only central Paris berth worth consideration is the excellent Bassin de l'Arsenal (lowest pound of the Canal St-Martin, near the Place de la Bastille). In certain locations, it is possible to seek protection offered by an island (where commercial vessels take an alternative route), the approach channel of a former lock, or (best of all) off the river altogether in one of the numerous connected gravel workings. This last solution is naturally subject to avoiding pits still being used by barges or where entry is prohibited by notice boards.

Rising in Burgundy, 776km from the sea, the Seine becomes navigable in Champagne and flows through the Île de France and Normandy before eventually reaching the coast. Often, the surroundings are pleasant rather than spectacular and the appeal of a voyage is derived largely from a wealth of historical towns on the banks, the movement of other boats and the leisure activities of the many people who relax by the side of this great waterway. The finest scenery is found in the

28km between Les Andelys and the Amfreville Locks, where tall chalk cliffs restrict its valley. In this book it is possible to mention only a selection of the attractions. Probably the most useful additional volumes are the Green Michelin Guides *Nord de la France*, *Environs de Paris*, *Paris* (English edition) and *Normandy* (English edition).

Many would claim that there is no city in Europe to match the beauty of Paris and the highlight of any Seine cruise must be to be able to arrive by water and moor for as long as you wish within walking distance of the leading sights. Until recently, this was an uncomfortable prospect for smaller craft on account of the almost ceaseless wash from passing traffic. But since 1983 calm berths have been available for visitors in the Port de Plaisance de Paris-Arsenal on the Canal St-Martin. This facility, much needed, deserves to be popular: advance booking is advised to the Capitainerie du Port de Plaisance de Paris-Arsenal, 11 Boulevard de la Bastille, 75012 Paris.

Those who come to Paris without a boat have ample opportunity for getting afloat by *bateau-mouche*. One of the most pleasant ways of passing a summer evening is to take a dinner cruise, where powerful ship-mounted floodlights illuminate the bankside buildings.

The Seine means many different things to different people: river of history, commercial lifeblood of the capital, inspiration of great artists from Turner to Monet and the French Impressionists. But, emphatically downstream of Paris, it is not a suitable training ground for the novice boatman.

Brief history Rouen is the fourth largest port in France, handling an annual 20 million tonnes of freight; Paris is the fifth with over 15 million tonnes. How this has been achieved on a river that was often reduced to 0.23m depth well below the capital as recently as the first half of the 19th century is a fascinating tale of French tenacity.

About 4,500 years ago, in the Bronze Age, the Seine was used for transport in tiny boats. Rather later, in Gallo-Roman times, it became a somewhat primitive artery of commerce. When the Vikings arrived from northern waters in their longships (*drakkars*) propelled by sail and oar, they found rich pickings as they plundered the abbeys and monasteries which lined the banks. Peace with the invaders was negotiated in the year 911, when Charles the Simple granted Normandy and his daughter in marriage to the Viking King Rollo. This proved to have a decidedly stabilizing effect on the Viking, who energetically started Seine training

works by building dykes, dredging the channel and draining marshland. Over the centuries that followed, traffic increased as Paris grew in size and importance: firewood was floated down the Yonne from the Morvan to heat the city's houses. Grain arrived from Brie and wine from Burgundy. Passengers made long and sometimes dangerous journeys by *coche-d'eau*, hauled by men or horses or powered by sail. Freight movements were encouraged by the opening of early canals like the 17th century Briare, linking the Loire valley with that of the Seine. But transport on the river was a hazardous undertaking and the boats were of tiny capacity.

As recently as the 1830s substantial sections of the route downstream of Paris were reduced to a depth of 0.80m for a third of the year. The only lock above Paris, at Nogent, had been built in 1677. Not infrequently, between 40 and 60 horses were required to haul a single barge up a shallow reach. Sailing vessels often took four days to reach Rouen from the sea. Paddle steamers had been successful from their introduction on the Seine in 1825, both on freight hauls and with passengers, but something was urgently required to be done to improve the channel. In 1827 a scheme was suggested that would have largely transferred boats from the Seine to a lateral canal running much of the way between Paris and the sea: its then cost was put at about £6 million, and before work could begin the project was shelved in favour of the newly arriving railways.

The Upper Seine was canalized between 1848 and 1899, with 13 locks and five diversions between Montereau and Marcilly. A further 44km of totally artificial canal with 20 locks continued navigation up the valley to Troyes: this Canal de la Haute-Seine had been withdrawn from service by the 1970s. Nine locks were installed on the middle river between Montereau and Argenteuil from 1860 onwards, with improvements in 1912 and again in the 1920s and 1930s. More locks arrived on the lower reaches, with eight in service between Paris and Rouen by the 1870s, by which time a depth of almost 2m could be relied upon for much of the year. The breakthrough which brought sophisticated control to water levels was the invention of a new form of adjustable weir sluice. 1850 saw completion of steam haulage by submerged chain all the way from Le Havre to Montereau. In 1887, 25km of the Canal de Tancarville enabled smaller vessels to avoid the most difficult part of the estuary down to Le Havre.

Serious flooding in the Seine in 1910 prompted more improvements and, although all traffic was halted for a period during World War II, work has continued apace after the river was restored in 1944. Apart from the uppermost nine locks, all chambers are mechanized and enlarged to accommodate 3,000 tonne push-tows.

New ports have opened or are scheduled; every year winding lengths of the river are bypassed by new cuts. The Seine can look with confidence to the future as one of Europe's busiest inland navigations.

Some sources of famous rivers are disappointing locations: but thanks to the City of Paris which purchased the site in the 19th century, the Seine's origins are suitably grand. In a copse of pines off the N71 and 34km NW of Dijon, a reclining statue of the goddess Sequana has lived in a grotto since 1865. The waters are variously claimed to possess healing or aphrodisiac properties. Numerous Gallo-Roman votive offerings and a magnificent bronze image of Sequana riding in a duck-shaped boat have been discovered here and may be seen in the Dijon Archaeological Museum. Another priceless treasure of the Seine's headwaters is the Vase of Vix, a huge decorated bronze urn standing 1.64m high and found in a burial mound near **Châtillon** in 1953. Believed to date from the 6th century BC, it is on show in the local museum.

When Robert Gibbings explored the Seine (*Coming Down the Seine*, 1953) he launched his little rowing boat into floods at **Barberey**, on the outskirts of **Troyes**. Then, he could just as well have selected the safer but more prosaic **Canal de la Haute-Seine** which connected the city with the waterway at **Marcilly-sur-Seine** (K0). The canal is now closed and a boating journey must commence instead where the river receives a tributary larger than itself – the Aube. Marcilly is a truly charming village on the right bank, providing most basic requirements including fuel. As if to emphasize that the Seine acts as a magnet for leisure seekers throughout its long course, there are already camping grounds and a sandy bathing beach. Extensive windings of the river are bypassed by sections of tree-lined canal, starting at Écluse 1, **Conflans** (K3.4), the first of nine manual locks whose gate and paddle gear requires considerable effort. Water points are installed at virtually all of the Seine locks. The canal runs very straight through **Crancey** (K8, butcher, baker and grocer), **Pont-sur-Seine** (K11, most shops), **Marnay-sur-Seine** (K14), Écluse 2, and re-emerges into the river below Écluse 3, Bernières, where the chamber has inconveniently sloping sides.

Nogent-sur-Seine (K19.5) is the first sizeable town on the navigable waterway, with Écluse 4 at the head of an island. Old half-timbered houses contrast with vast modern flour mills served by *péniches*. There is a rail link with Paris and Troyes: rarely is the Seine far from convenient stations, a useful factor when collecting crew or for recovering a car at the end of a trip. Designed in a blend of gothic and Renaissance styles, the 16th-century church of St-Laurent is a fine structure in grey stone. An ivy-clad vault is all that remains of the convent of *Le Paraclet* where 12th century lovers Héloïse and Abélard were united in death. Peter Abélard was a brilliant 36-year-old poet and teacher hired by Canon Fulbert of Notre Dame as tutor for his 17-year-old niece Héloïse. Inevitably, they fell in love and secretly married. This action turned out to be ill-advised, for Uncle Fulbert was enraged. Sensing his folly, Abélard placed his wife with the safe-keeping of the Abbess of Argenteuil; but Fulbert was not satisfied and sent a band of men to castrate him. When Abélard died many years later, Héloïse, by then Abbess of Nogent, had his body brought to the town for burial. Twenty-two years afterwards she too died and when her husband's tomb was opened it is said that he rose to

PARIS. — LA GRANDE CRUE DE LA SEINE (Janvier 1910)
Inondation du quai des Grands-Augustins, service de sauvetage et de ravitaillement. — ND Phot

An old postcard view of the Great Flood of January 1910, when the Seine poured into the streets of Paris and numerous small craft were pressed into service for rescue and food distribution.

embrace the Héloïse from whom he had been separated for much of a lifetime. Their remains were reinterred in the Père Lachaise Cemetery in Paris after the Revolution.

Winding reaches below Nogent through open country and poplar plantations are bypassed by a new cut leading directly into a long, wide and rather tedious canal beginning at guard lock Beaulieu, No. 5 (K23.5). Peaceful moorings exist on both upper and lower sections of the original river. Écluse 6, **Metz** (K27.2), and 7, **Villiers-sur-Seine** (K31.9) intervene before joining the river again above **Le Port Montain** (K34.4). A slipway is used by owners of high speed craft which will be encountered in the *bassin de vitesse*, downstream. It is an extraordinary characteristic of many French rivers (and of the Seine in particular) that speeds of up to 60km per hour are permitted in specified reaches! All other users from canoeists and oarsmen upwards are expected to fend for themselves. This policy reaches extremes in the 24-hour powerboat race through the bridges of Paris, an event to be avoided by sane and sedate pleasure craft. Food shops and restaurant will be found in **Noyen**, 1km SE of the bridge.

All your skills of lockmanship will be tested by the sloping-sided chamber of Écluse 8, Vezoult (K37.1). **Grisy-sur-Seine** (K38) follows on the left bank, a village of grey houses with beach and launching ramp suitable for small cruisers (grocer). Timber summer houses are dotted about on both sides. Écluse 9, **Jaunes** (K43), has a weir alongside, with no prospect of easy access to the village opposite. In any event, most needs can be found in **Bray-sur-Seine** (K46), with swimming pool and beach, a tree-shaded riverside walk and good public moorings just above the bridge. St Nicholas, patron saint of boat people and often to be encountered on the French waterways, is represented by a statue in the church. Half-timbered buildings with stucco walls are a foretaste of Normandy farmhouses of the lower river. Many *péniches* trade to the prominent flour mills. Navigation continues along the recently improved course of the original river, Écluses 10, 11 and 12 on the Bray – La Tombe Canal all being disused. We are now entering a region of gravel pits connected with the waterway: those that are no longer worked provide tranquil moorings, but take care to avoid those marked with 'No Entry' signs.

From now onwards, commercial traffic becomes increasingly brisk and the Seine is dedicated wholeheartedly to transport of freight. Écluse La Grand Bosse (K49.2) is the first of the giant lock chambers, electrically worked by a keeper comfortably installed in an ultra modern control cabin. It was completed in 1979. If working through alone, you will marvel at having your boat penned in such a vast space! Beyond, 8km of concrete-sided channel produces decidedly rough water in a strong wind: there are no possibilities of mooring safely unless you chance slipping into one of the adjoining gravel pits. Pusher tugs manoeuvre their sand barges almost without cease. Surroundings improve by the village of **La Tombe** (K57), where further grain silos appear above a bridge. Facilities include slipway, grocer and garage.

Another cut begins at K60, leading to **Marolles-sur-Seine** (K61.5), where all traffic uses the right-hand, mechanized lock chamber. Old *péniches* and houseboats line the approaches to the smaller lock where temporary moorings should be available. This is an agreeable little town, providing fuel and shopping and typically good value in the inexpensive *Lion d'Or* restaurant. Expansive sand pits off the right bank (K62.5) provide an ideal, quiet overnight stopping place – at least until a projected harbour is built. Ahead, in the distance, tower blocks announce the approach of the major town of **Montereau-faut-Yonne** (K68), entered after passing under a new bridge carrying the exciting high speed Paris–Marseilles express trains (*TGV*). To the left is a commercial port serving the city's *zone industrielle* and a little beyond it the remains of a former lock house and wall of the chamber itself. Yet another case of a tributary being more important than the river it joins is the Yonne entering from the left. Montereau is very much a barge town: *péniches* line the quays three or four abreast, frequently making the discovery of pleasure boat moorings rather difficult. Seek permission to come alongside vessels not wishing to move off before your own departure. Alternatively, try a short distance up the Yonne, on the right hand bank. Really rather drab and industrialized, Montereau does not live up to the promise of its historical associations. John the Good, Duke of Burgundy, met the Dauphin, the future Charles VII of France, on the Yonne bridge in 1419; they were to discuss an alliance against the English. But one of Charles' knights suddenly attacked the Duke, killing him in retaliation for the assassination of the Duke of Orléans twelve years earlier. Now, the Duke's son Philip the Fearless took Montereau and signed the Treaty of Troyes, disinheriting the Dauphin and establishing Henry V of England as King of France. Here, also, Napoléon won practically his last victory over the Allies in February 1814. His bronze statue can be seen on a peninsula between the Seine and Yonne bridges, bearing his statement: 'The bullet that will kill me is yet to be made'. Fuelling facilities and two launching slips may be used by pleasure boaters: otherwise the yards are more accustomed to building and repairing commercial vessels. Facing the junction, on the right, the new town of **Surville** is a typical product of the 1960s, its tower blocks rising 25 storeys.

Having left the Petite-Seine, the Haute-Seine now follows to Paris, locks being renumbered from Écluse 1, **Varennes** (K71.5). Banks are mostly well wooded past gravel workings and several dominant power stations issuing a tangle of pylon lines. Just upstream of one, moorings can be found on the right bank at the former Madelaine Lock (K76.5). **St-Mammès** (K81), at the junction of the Canal du Loing, is a famous barge town where dozens of *péniches* lie in the shade of pollarded limes. Moor either at the Base Nautique du Touring Club de France (left bank, K79.6, opposite the village of **La Celle**) or more centrally on the Loing near the disused Écluse 20. Fuel points and a selection of village shops are here joined by exciting establishments stocking working boat requirements – everything from tar to rope and powerful brass horns. Where suitable for pleasure craft, items bought in such places offer much better value than from yacht chandlers. Sunday mornings see a quayside market. St-Mammès (the 's' is silent) is the best (and only convenient) point from which to visit the medieval town of **Moret-sur-Loing** and it is decidedly well worth cruising almost 2km up the Loing to lie below the first lock (see Chapter 39). While here, an excursion can be made by public transport to the Palace and Gardens of **Fontainebleau** (12km), whose forest borders both Seine and Loing. The magnificent structure originated as a royal hunting lodge and was mainly designed under Louis XIV, XV and XVI. English guide books are readily obtained locally, although it would be difficult to better the *Green Michelin Guide: Environs de Paris* (in French). Louis XV imported gondolas from Venice in order to convey his packs of hounds over the Seine when hunting: a charming, if eccentric, idea.

Champagne-sur-Seine (K83) offers little in the way of attractions, but if a shopping expedition is planned there is a public quay, waterside fuelling point and reasonably quiet moorings in the approaches of the disused lock on the right bank. Écluse 2 is alongside: a modern device with an upper gate that sinks below water level to admit traffic. Situated on the edge of the Fontainebleau Forest, **Thomery** (K85.5) introduces a pleasingly wooded section of river. There is a quay, adequate shops and dessert grapes in springtime, thanks to the custom of cutting them nearly ripe from the vine in the autumn and placing them in carefully controlled *chambres des raisins* in vases of water where they preserve their freshness until the following April or May. By now sufficiently close to Paris for daily

Early 20th century view, showing steam tugs and barges in the lock at Suresnes, River Seine.

commuters or the convenient use of weekend residences, the Seine is lined with spectacular and fantastic creations in *fin de siècle* Gothic, each cast-iron decorated turret, pinnacle or lavish coursing of patterned brick attempting to outshine those of its neighbour. Trees and lawns exude affluence. Day cruisers and rowing boats may be hired in **Valvins** (K89.5), for all the world as if this was Henley-on-Thames and not the busiest waterway in France with commercial traffic surging past almost ceaselessly! (Restaurant, mooring jetties and slipway, left bank, above the bridge.) A really unusual restaurant is Plaisance-sur-Seine at **Vulaines-sur-Seine** (K90, right bank). Here, you may moor alongside the charming thatched building, where a waiter will offer you a rod and line in order to catch disgracefully tame trout and salmon-trout from a series of streams in the grounds. These will be prepared and cooked over a charcoal grill. On the riverside at **Samois-sur-Seine** (K93) another elegant restaurant beckons: as often is the case, there are difficulties in mooring safely and a good site below a small island (keep to the right channel) at a former lock is said to be for short duration only. Shops of most kinds are here and in **Héricy** opposite (slipway). **Chartrettes** (K101) boasts a real *port de plaisance*, right bank above Écluse 3, La Cave. Shopping can be attended to in the very extended town, while a restaurant can be reached by crossing the weir and lock chambers into the village of **Bois-le-Roi**. 10km SW on the edge of the forest,

Barbizon was a famous gathering place for artists and writers in the 19th century. Millet, Corot, Rousseau and many others are still remembered; some of their houses are open to the public.

More fantasy mansions are scattered over a long distance on the left bank until the approach of the city of **Melun** (K110) whose riverbanks are grassed and tree-covered or lined with a pleasing jumble of houseboats. One deep-water mooring is on the left bank, directly under a road bridge (K109.5). Like Paris, the city grew from beginnings on a river island. There is now some industry, but its origin as a market for the surrounding farmland is not forgotten. Melun eels are celebrated and so is the *Brie de Melun*, a famous soft white cheese, distinguishable by gourmets from the *bries* of Meaux, Coulommiers and Montereau. All commercial traffic takes the channel to the left of the island: smaller pleasure cruisers should therefore discover quiet moorings with sufficient water depth on the other stream. But do avoid setting up camp for the night on the upper part of the island itself: I once did after a day of unremitting rain in an open boat. Just as I had completed erecting the tent and arranged my bedding within, a stern voice from the trees above my head ordered me to remove myself without delay, adding that the police would be there within minutes if I failed to comply. In the gathering dusk I realized that the 'old fortifications' alongside were the perimeter walls of the city prison and that the disembodied voice belonged to an armed guard in a watchtower. Abandoning a brief attempt at gentle persuasion, I dismantled the soaking tent in fury, getting completely wet in the process, and made for the noisier roadside bank opposite. That night I would gladly have exchanged my quarters for a centrally heated prison cell!

Once clear of Melun, the Seine again becomes quite countrified, although its villages are now mostly residential suburbs of Paris and much visited by city dwellers at weekends. This is so of **Boissettes** (K114), **Vosves** (K115) and the little town of **Boissise-la-Bertrand** (K116.3) opposite Écluse 4, Vives Eaux. Grocer's shop and restaurant are within easy reach if you moor on the right bank, immediately below the weir. Coming to the outskirts of **St-Fargeau-Ponthierry**, another excellent mooring is found at the old lock, left bank (K123). From here to Paris shore facilities become increasingly frequent, with shops, restaurants and fuelling points readily seen from the river or located in the *Carte Guide*.

Vertical stone quays in St-Fargeau (K125) may be used if not occupied by *péniches*. A modern and very select housing estate has been created around disused gravel pits, each garden having a lake or river side fron-

tage. Lock numbering is no longer consecutive, some weirs having been removed, so that the next is Écluse 7, Coudray (K129.5), with a boat club on the right bank, upstream. Ahead, tower blocks are a reminder of the considerable expansion of Greater Paris since World War II. Pleasure craft can expect a welcome at Port-Saintry (K131.2), with good overnight moorings and a convenient restaurant.

From now onwards, the sights and sounds of the metropolis crowd in on each bank: mills, factories, power stations and increasing barge traffic combine to create a vibrant impression of urban life. **Corbeil-Essonnes** (K134) is the grain store of Paris, with day cruisers for hire and a landing stage (left bank, K133.4). Slipway and moorings will be found just upstream of the bridge at **Evry-Petit-Bourg** (K137.7), with duplicated Écluse 8, Evry (K138.9). Greenery on the right bank is the expanse of the Forest of Sénart, popular with Parisians for walks and picnics. Romantic school painter Ferdinand Victor Eugène Delacroix (1798–1863) lived on the edge of the forest at **Champrosay** (K141.5), as did writer Alphonse Daudet (1840–97), whose stories included the canal barge tale *La Belle-Nivernaise*. Rather wasted countryside lingers on around **Vigneux-sur-Seine** (K148.5) but increasingly, gravel extraction and industry are more profitable than raising cattle or growing corn. After Écluse 9, **Ablon** (K150), a halt can be made at the nautical centre, left bank (slipway, fuel and shopping). **Orly Airport** lies to the NW: if you can tolerate the noise, the moorings of the Touring Club de France (K154.6) at **Villeneuve St-Georges** provide fuel, crane, water and restaurant. A similar opportunity for coming alongside is at the GDF Harbour (K158.6) in **Choisy-le-Roi**. Power stations and railway tracks lead to the last lock before Paris, Écluse 10, Port-à-l'Anglais (K161). Much of the city's household refuse is burned in a massive incinerator at **Ivry-sur-Seine** (K163), the heat produced being used for central heating, an admirable example of energy conservation.

The Seine is shortly joined on the right by the River Marne (K163.4) and soon thereafter a long vista opens through numerous bridges to the heart of **Paris**. Few of the Seine crossings lack interest. One of the most unusual is the Pont de Bercy (K167), a stone road bridge of 1863–4 to which a Métro viaduct was added on top in 1909: the many rounded arches recall the Roman Pont-du-Gard aqueduct in Provence. A mobile fuelling barge is based upstream of the bridge, left

Sharing the Écluse Vives Eaux, near Melun, with an assortment of large freight barges.

bank: make sure that you are served with tax-paid diesel, not the cheaper variety which is for commercial craft and central heating only! Beyond the Pont d'Austerlitz, the best city moorings of all lie inside the Canal St-Martin (see Chapter 16). Now in sight is the Île St-Louis and the Île de la Cité, the original nucleus of Paris. Here, the Cathedral of Notre Dame is so symbolic of the capital that one learns with surprise that it was reduced to ruins during the Revolution; its present state was not achieved until Viollet-le-Duc's restoration between 1844 and 1864, the window glass, lacy spire and gargoyles dating from this period.

River traffic is routed on one-way systems past the islands and, of course, through the bridges. To avoid confrontations with barges or tripping boats it is vital to follow the directions indicated in the *Carte Guide* and note the times when one-way traffic operates.

To arrive in the centre of Paris by water is a great thrill – more so if the voyage has been a long one. The Seine is unquestionably the city's chief street and many of the leading buildings and monuments lie alongside a 10km stretch between the Pont de Tolbiac (K166) and the Pont de Grenelle (K176/K6.6, distances being renumbered downstream of the Île St-Louis, K0). There is no better or more relaxing way of seeing Paris than from the deck of a cruiser, with a *bateau-mouche* as a very fair substitute. The scene changes with the time of day and season of the year. Take an afternoon in high summer, and it seems as if the whole population is afloat in water buses or relaxing on the quays. By night, huge restaurant cruisers bearing banks of floodlights surge backwards and forwards in defiance of every regulation relating to navigation after dark. In winter, the bare branches of plane trees and the greyness of buildings seen against a grey sky bring a feeling of melancholy: but spring is never far away and there is nothing quite like spring in Paris.

Paris is frequently the subject of a complete book: here, there is space only to hint at a selection of personal highlights likely to interest the waterway enthusiast. Armed with a copy of the *Green Michelin Guide to Paris* (in English), the best way to explore is to start walking. Along the waterside quays, past groups of converted *péniches* and other houseboats – living afloat is widespread; over the bridges, more than 30 of them in the central area alone; down the banks of the Canal St-Martin with its charming iron footbridges and locks (see Chapter 16); looking at antique, flower and animal markets; browsing in second-hand bookshops or the open-air stalls of the *bouquinistes* by the river (especially near Notre Dame). Of all the many museums and galleries, it would be hard to better the superb Musée d'Orsay, lately established in a turn-of-the-century

railway station as a showcase for 19th century paintings, sculpture and decorative arts. For bird's eye views, ascend the Eiffel Tower or visit the terrace outside the Sacré Cœur at Montmartre. Watch life pass by from the table of a café. Off-beat visits include the Père-Lachaise Cemetery, NE of the river, containing the tombs of celebrities as diverse as Abélard and Héloïse, Edith Piaf, Oscar Wilde, Chopin, Proust and Molière. With a vast choice of restaurants in the city, none has a décor more amazing and splendid than the superb *fin de siècle* Le Train Bleu at the Gare de Lyon. It is highly recommended if you enjoy good food in an astonishingly lavish interior. It is not impossibly expensive and quite unlike what you might expect of dining at a railway station!

The river water is decidedly unfit for swimming; you might consider visiting a pool situated in a large floating structure, the Piscine Deligny on the Quai Anatole France. Clients wear costumes graphically described in French as *le minimum*, a phenomenon that will also be noticed along the Quai des Tuileries where hot weather attracts sun-worshippers who are frequently outnumbered by the throngs of *voyeurs* looking down from the street above! Paris has a justified reputation for vibrant night life and for sheer lavish spectacle it would be difficult to beat the magnificently dressed (or undressed?) Lido Cabaret in the *Champs-Elysées*: we took two eleven-year-olds who were totally accepted, even if the show does not conform to the Anglo-Saxon notion of 'family entertainment'. Advance booking for the dinner/dancing/show is recommended. The newly-found freedom of modern Paris is such that when dusk falls on the riverside quays, lovers are no longer content to merely hold hands.

In a city of surprises, it nevertheless comes as a shock to discover an English bookshop in an elegant building near Notre Dame where the proprietor (the illegitimate grandson of a well-known American poet) offers *free* accommodation to any *bona fide* author who introduces himself – patronage of literature indeed!

No brief description of Paris would be complete without mentioning the superb underground railway network, Le Métro. Bright, clean and efficient with trains that glide on rubber wheels, nowhere is more than 500m from a station. Be sure to pass through the Louvre, where the platforms are adorned with reproductions from the vast collection of artworks above. Tourists may purchase special tickets for unlimited travel, first class, for periods of 2, 4 or 7 days (available on production of a passport at larger stations or the RATP, 53 *bis* Quai des Grands Augustins, 6°).

Oldest of the Parisian bridges, perversely, is the

Pont-Neuf (K1.2), crossing the tail of the Île de la Cité; it was opened by Henry IV in 1607 and was then unique in that it carried no buildings. The most elegant and elaborate is the Pont Alexandre III (K3.5), a flamboyant structure completed in 1900. Everlasting gratitude must be expressed that a mid-1960s scheme to replace the waterside quays by fast motor roads was largely discarded. Marshy fringes of the Seine were first embanked in this way under Henry IV. Americans will note with delight a quarter-scale version of New York's Statue of Liberty at the tail of the Allées des Cygnes island (K6.6). The larger model was presented by France to the USA as a token of friendship in 1886. A Viking longship was discovered here in 1903.

The Seine is reluctant to leave Paris, making one huge loop after another as it winds through the western suburbs, with the Bois de Boulogne appearing to starboard at K8 only to be seen once more at K16. These 900 hectares of former royal hunting forest were given to the people by Napoléon III and modelled on London's Hyde Park. **Versailles** and its great palace of Louis XIV lies about 12km SW. Surroundings are heavily built up past **Boulogne-Billancourt** (K10, fuel), **St-Cloud** (K14.5) and **Suresnes** (K16.5), with Écluse de Suresnes (K17) at the head of the Île de Puteaux. Motor cruisers of under 10hp will find sheltered waters safe from the wash of passing traffic, by turning into the weir stream reached from the downstream end of the island. All larger craft are banned. Over 40,000 pet dogs, cats and horses are buried in the world's first animal cemetery on the Île des Ravageurs (K23.5) at **Clichy**; opened in 1899, it contains the grave of a St Bernard named Barry who saved 41 lives in the Alps. He was sadly killed by the 41st who mistook his snow-covered shape for a bear and attacked him with an ice-axe: Barry staggered off to alert rescuers and expired. Film star Rin-Tin-Tin is also to be found here. A little downstream is the *Port de Plaisance* Van Gogh.

Île St-Denis, an island more than 7km in length, extends downstream of **St-Ouen** (K25.5). The left-hand channel past **Villeneuve-la-Garenne** (K29) is available throughout for upstream-bound craft, but contains a central section closed to downhillers. Many commercial barge yards will be of interest to students of commercial transport: *péniches* and other vessels are to be seen hauled out of the water, under construction, repair or being converted into houseboats or floating restaurants. Possibilities for robust mechanical aid to pleasure craft exist. Taking the alternative right-hand channel, you pass **St-Denis** (K27). Legend claims that after his decapitation in Montmartre in the 3rd century, Denis walked on, head in hands, until he collap-

sed at this spot. During the late 5th century St Geneviève, patron saint of Paris, had a church built on the site. This was later replaced by the present 12th century Gothic basilica. During 12 centuries most French monarchs from Dagobert (629–39) to Louis XVIII (1814–24) were buried here, although the corpses were disposed of during the Revolution.

On the right bank, K28.8, the Canal St-Denis enters the Seine, offering the prospect of a return to Paris, where it joins the Canal St-Martin and the Canal de l'Ourcq (see Chapter 16). Still in urban surroundings, the river divides again (K40.2) below **Bezons** and there is a choice of routes for a little over 8km, separated by an island first known as Chatou, then du Chiard and finally de la Chaussée. The left branch is closed in times of flood and passes through **Nanterre** (K42), known for a miraculous well, *charcuterie* (cold meat products) and *madeleine* cakes. This is followed in turn by **Rueil-Malmaison** (K45), with Empress Josephine's favourite residence where she died in 1814. It is now devoted to a Napoléonic museum. **Bougival** (K47.5) was a haunt of Impressionist painters Monet, Sisley, Degas and Renoir: many of their best works feature river traffic. There are quayside moorings above the lock. Below Écluse de Bougival (K48.5) the Seine unites once more. The other, right-hand section, Bras de Rivière Neuve, flows past **Carrières-sur-Seine** (K43) to a lock at **Chatou** (K44.5).

Three sides of the great forest of **St-Germain** are encircled by the waterway. Many kings of France and England are associated with the magnificent *château*, easily reached from the Pont de Pecq (K52) if a suitable mooring can be located. Downstream traffic must pass to the right of the Île Corbière (K52.5), leaving the other channel for up-going boats. Numerous pleasure craft occupy an arm on the left (K58.3), below the **Maisons-Laffite** railway bridge. Flocks of seagulls cluster round a massive sewage works opposite **La Frette-sur-Seine** (K63), a sure sign that the Paris conurbation is at last astern. Moorings at the *halte nautique*.

'Home' to inland boat people from many parts of Northern France, **Conflans-Ste-Honorine** (K70) takes its name in part from its situation at the junction with the River Oise and secondly as the final resting place of the relics of a 3rd century martyr. The quays are animated, with many *péniches* hung with lines of washing and undergoing the ceaseless painting and polishing which seems to fill every idle moment of a boatman's life. A white-hulled barge, *Je Sers*, has been converted into a chapel. On the weekend of the last Sunday in June dozens of working boats, decorated from end to end with flags and paper flowers, congregate at Conflans for the Pardon National de la Batellerie, a form of *péniche* rally established in 1960. The hilly little town joins in with enthusiasm, attractions including a large fair, fireworks and *son et lumière*. By a terrace overlooking the Seine, the Château du Prieuré houses a National Waterways Museum. Its various displays, models and huge store of historical photographs all relating to the history of French inland navigations is the country's leading collection and well worth making a special trip. (Details appear under 'Waterways Museums'.) On the opposite side of the river, the shady verges of the N184 through the Forest of St-Germain were, until recently, a notorious haunt of extremely blatant 'ladies of easy virtue'. The presence of numbers of police cars resulted, however, from a tendency of distracted drivers to swerve off the carriageways! Then, rather than attempt to impose a direct prohibition on the 'trade', the authorities introduced a rigorously enforced parking ban causing an immediate end to the practice!

Below the wide junction with the Oise (K71.2), the navigation divides: normally you must follow the left

Freight craft under repair at a barge yard near St-Denis.

channel through the Écluse d'Andrésy (K72.7). However, the alternative route is used when this lock is under repair, the Écluse de **Carrières-sous-Poissy** (K76) operating instead. In either event, all the facilities of **Andrésy** (shops, restaurants, water, refuse disposal, electricity) may be reached by running for 1km down the right arm with quayside moorings at K73. Fully rural once more, with willows along its banks, the Seine flows to **Poissy** (K78), site of a large Talbot car works. By entering a backwater on the left bank you may escape the effects of passing traffic. A pleasure boat yard, Nautis, lies at the far end, K80.1. On the right bank, K81.1, the Nauti-Méchanique marina provides moorings, slipway and other services in a protected basin. Waterside houses with trees and lawns recall the Upper Thames. Pass either side of the Île de **Médan** (K81.8) and through the little town where Émile Zola wrote his most important books between 1879 and 1902. **Médan Plage** is an agreeable inland swimming and boating resort on the island, reached by ferry from the left bank. A notice board informs, enigmatically, *Naturisme Tolérée avec Sexe Cachée* (it should not be translated too literally!). Clients may moor to the jetty of the Moulin Rouge Restaurant or at

Péniches await cargoes at Conflans-Ste-Honorine, junction with the Oise.

quays on the mainland. **Triel-sur-Seine** (K85.2), right bank, has a 13–16th century church. Many gravel pits now line the left shore, resulting in frequent push-tows of barges.

Through traffic keeps to the left side of the water-way, past **Vaux-sur-Seine** (K89.5) and on to **Les Mureaux** (K93.5). Shore facilities are numerous here, with moorings downstream (K94.1) or, sheltered by Belle Île along an arm, right bank, at **Meulan** (K93). The island fortress which once controlled the fortunes of freight craft passing up and down the Seine was

taken by the English and liberated by du Guesclin in 1364. If you stay in the left channel you will notice a disused lock at K95. The other route, down the Bras de Mézy, provides an opportunity for shopping in **Juziers** (K98.3). Products of the massive Renault car works at **Flins** (K97–98) will be seen plying the Seine in double-decked transporter barges, each holding several hundred vehicles. Some are conveyed between here and another factory on the outskirts of Paris at Billancourt, while others run downstream for export from the docks at Le Havre: a thoroughly civilized and economic method of transportation.

Rouen-bound craft leave the Île de Rangiport (K101) on the left, the other channel being reserved for vessels working upriver. Beyond, numerous power lines are seen spreading from the power station at **Porcheville** (K105), to which coal supplies are brought by water. Providing a mooring can be located, all shops are found in the town (K103.6). River width increases very considerably by the new commercial port (K106.8) upstream of **Mantes-la-Jolie** (K108.5), situated to the left of the Île de Limay and Île l'Aumône. Best moorings in the area are on the right bank below the Pont de **Limay** (K109.4), to a quay and close to most shops; alternatively, continue to a yacht harbour opposite the junction of the two islands (K109.9). Here mooring, water and electricity are free for a 48 hours stay. Mantes is the more important and attractive of these two towns, easily reached from the right bank by bridges. Heavily bombed in World War II, it was demanded by William the Conqueror in 1087. Philip I of France refused and went so far as to make insulting remarks about William's famous bloated stomach. This was too much for William and he reduced the place to smoking ruins. Sadly for him, in his moment of triumph he fell from his horse, dying from stomach wounds only six weeks later! Mantes' greatest treasure is its massive 12–13th century cathedral of Notre Dame; it stands close to the river and bears comparison with its better known namesake in Paris.

From here onwards the river is wide and most attractive. Patches of white chalk cliffs protrude from woodland, a characteristic of the Seine for much of the journey to Rouen. Port Maria is a yacht harbour on the right bank at **Dennemont** (K112.1). **Rosny-sur-Seine**, left bank (K117), is noted for the Château de Sully built during the early 17th century. It is open to the public from July 21 to Aug 31, afternoons. The town makes a pretty picture from the water and has useful shops. A fuel point (K119) is just upstream of **Rolleboise**, where the river swings to the NE and then south again in a great loop. Until the advent of the railway a passenger boat service (*galiote*) made regular runs upstream to Poissy. Drawn by four horses, the vessels carried 90 people. Three chambers are built side by side at the Écluse de Méricourt (K120.7). During one cruise between Paris and the estuary, I lay above the locks for the night, following the first pusher-tug/barge combination downriver at dawn the next day. For more than two hours the September fog was so thick that we caught only occasional glimpses of the banks for the next 20km. Navigating by radar and expert local knowledge, the working craft ahead rarely slackened speed as it surged into the swirling whiteness: grimly we followed his tail, sometimes losing sight of him altogether. In spite of having radar ourselves, it was not an experience I hope to repeat!

Keeping right around the island of St-Martin-la-Garenne (K125), the next town of interest is **La Roche Guyon** (K133). In the shadow of chalk cliffs, a 16–18th century *château* is the property of the Rochfoucault family, whose ancestor François compiled his pithy *Maxims* here in 1665: a typical example: 'True love is like ghosts – everyone talks about them, but they have been experienced by few.' Towards the end of World War II, German Field Marshal Rommel set up a command post in the castle. Take care if mooring, for there is little depth. Similarly, choose any stopping point judiciously in **Bonnières-sur-Seine** (K139.8); one possibility is at a yacht club on the upstream end of Grande Île. But apart from shops, there are few attractions, its main claim to fame being the Singer sewing machine factory. Some protection from the wash of passing vessels is offered by the approach channels to a former lock opposite **Villez** (K144.9): there are many worse places to spend the night. Increasingly on the lower Seine, the small boat owner will realize that convenient stopping places are few and far between, resulting in a high level of anxiety as dusk approaches with nothing better than rock-strewn walls in sight. Advance planning is vital.

As if to celebrate entry into the province of Normandy, several typical half-timbered houses will be seen near **Vernon** (K150), a town with much of interest and well worth making a halt. Even more so because of the charming moorings by the remains of a 12th century bridge on the right-hand **Vernonnet** bank, just downstream of the modern Pont de Vernon. A pontoon of the sailing club is reserved for visitors (free of charge), with showers ashore by the Château des Tourelles. Vernon was founded in the 9th century by Rollo the Dane, first Duke of Normandy. The usual eating and shopping facilities are waiting ashore. 4km upstream on the north bank is the village of **Giverny** where the founder of the French Impressionists, Claude Monet, created his beautiful garden with Japanese bridge and lily pond. He lived here from 1883 until his death in 1926. The Monet house and grounds are open throughout the summer, little changed since the great painter's time.

Chalk cliffs with dense woodland lead to Écluse de **Notre Dame de la Garenne** (K161.1), with no fewer than four chambers and a massive weir. At K171, tail of the Île de la Tour, a mooring quay is situated on the outskirts of **Bouafles**. Shortly thereafter the Seine's finest spectacle comes into view – the ruins of Château Gaillard, 'the Gallant Castle', perched on rocks above **Les Andelys** (K173.4). It was erected in the late 12th century by Richard Coeur de Lion to prevent the King of France passing down the Seine to Rouen. After a

Château Gaillard with bow-hauliers. Engraving from the early 19th century painting by J. M. W. Turner.

long siege it fell to the French in 1204, Bayeux and Rouen following soon after. England withdrew from Normandy, but failed to recognize the fact until the end of the Hundred Years War in 1453. Nicholas Poussin the painter (1593–1665) was born here. Most boaters will want to linger in this lovely area and it is worth trying to enter the small public marina shortly below the Pont de Port Morin and almost in the shadow of the *château* itself. Superb river views from the cliffs. While there is little of individual note as the Seine continues past villages and islands, these last reaches of non-tidal water are certainly the most attractive on the whole river, flanked by the white cliffs with fine houses in brick and half-timbering. Frequently all this recalls the Thames, but here the scale is larger and pleasure craft are mainly replaced by a ceaseless stream of commercial vessels.

One more lock, Écluse d'**Amfreville** (K202), offers the chance of mooring at the upstream approach (but well clear of barge traffic) or, more peacefully, on the south bank by a village quay in **Poses**. This is reached by passing to the left of the lock island. From now on there are tidal considerations, which increase progressively towards Rouen. Here, the rise and fall is little

more than 1m. Although still far from the sea, the Seine is no longer a typical inland waterway: tide tables must be studied before making the passage, bearing in mind that safe moorings are rare. Pleasure craft venturing into these waters will be adequately powered sea-going vessels, able to cope with strong streams and in the charge of people conversant with shipping practice. It is not a place for beginners. Much useful navigational information will be gleaned from the *Carte Guide*. Steep cliffs above the locks are known as La Côte des Deux Amants, 'the Hillside of the Two Lovers'. Here, legend says, a young squire named Edmond saved Calixte, his childhood friend and daughter of the Comte Rulph, from certain death by a wild boar. The irascible Comte asked the young man what reward he wished: 'The hand of your daughter', he replied. Considering Edmond too lowly, Comte Rulph set him the task of climbing the hillside with Calixte on his back. If he so much as paused for breath, he would be unworthy of the prize. A great crowd gathered to witness the attempt. Either Edmond was in poor shape or his beloved was a big girl, for at the very moment he reached the summit he fell dead on the ground! Horrified, Calixte picked up the corpse (yes, she was a big girl) and the two plunged down the precipice in a tight embrace. Next day, they were buried in a single tomb: he in the clothes of a knight, she in a bridal gown. Shades of Abélard and Héloïse.

In the 19th century there was a lock at **Pont de l'Arche** (K208); long disused, there is no possibility of stopping. Once, this had been the site of the bridge nearest the sea. Beaches of sand and shingle with willow trees look best when the river is brimful at high water. The Seine increases in size after a junction with the River Eure near **Elbeuf**, with a splendid quayside mooring, left bank, between the two bridges (K219.1). Be sure to adjust the boat's lines if staying for any length of time. Excellent shops are within 300m, together with fine old half-timbered buildings and the church of St-Étienne, with 16th century stained glass. Wooded cliffs accompany the river as it winds in a series of tight loops, especially fine around **Orival** (K221.5). Fuelling points – a choice of three – appear on the right bank at **Amfreville** (K238.5), shortly before the great city and port of **Rouen** (K241). Municipal moorings on floating pontoons have been established on the very convenient Île Lacroix (K241.6), reached by taking the right-hand channel and passing under a railway viaduct and the Pont Mathilde. Supervised for 24 hours a day, they are reasonably quiet, supplied with water and electricity and always remaining afloat and are totally free from any tidal problems, which will endear Rouen to all true

Turner's view of river passengers in Rouen.

inland boaters! Fuel is available at a boatyard and chandlery immediately downstream. Four more bridges intervene before sailing boats may raise their masts. A crane is available for this purpose by the yacht pontoon in the Bassin St-Gervais (K246), right bank.

Although badly damaged during bombing raids in World War II, Rouen has been extensively restored: this applies particularly to over 700 half-timbered buildings in the old quarter along the right bank of the Seine. The English are not likely to forget the fate of Joan of Arc, burned at the stake in the Place du Vieux Marché in 1431. She was not canonized until 1920 and is now Patron Saint of France. Much of the atmosphere of the city is best absorbed by walking down the bustling pedestrianized Rue du Gros-Horloge and into the market area by the exciting modern church of Joan of Arc, whose curving slate roof recalls the hull of an upturned ship; 16th century stained glass of considerable magnificence creates a successful blend between old and new. The huge Cathedral of Notre Dame was begun in the 12th century and is one of the finest examples of the French Gothic style. Its cast-iron spire was a

19th century addition. Writers Pierre Corneille (1606–84) and Gustave Flaubert (1821–80) were born in the city and are both commemorated by museums. For further information on the many sights of Rouen, consult the *Green Michelin Guide to Normandy* (in English).

Rouen to the coast at Le Havre and Honfleur is 114km. Depending on tides the run is perfectly possible in a single day, although it may be necessary to lie at anchor in the tideway for several hours to avoid punching against the stream, which can flow very strongly – up to 6 knots near Tancarville. Bankside moorings with certain qualified exceptions, do not exist between Rouen and Tancarville. Because of the near-impossibility of going ashore, these reaches will be described in less detail. The Seine's tidal bore, Le Mascaret, is a shadow of its former self thanks to training works in the estuary and presents no dangers. First-rate buoyage and navigation beacons are installed onwards from Rouen, but all passage of pleasure craft is strictly banned at night. Boats which accidentally find themselves in the river after dark will be pounced upon by patrol launches, and even in daylight your progress is constantly monitored by radar. These measures are for the protection of many ocean-going ships from all parts of the world: they proceed upriver on the tide as far as Rouen in the charge of pilots and frequently have little clearance under their keels. So stay well clear!

It takes a considerable time to cruise beyond Rouen's dockland, where ships from such diverse places as Scotland, Casablanca and Singapore are seen exchanging cargoes with swarms of dwarfed *péniches*. Now that there are just two more (high level) bridges, small car ferries will be noticed: without them, water-side villages would be totally isolated from the opposite bank. Further chalk cliffs and wooded scenery provide a pleasant prospect with sandy beaches and weed-covered rocks at low water. **Duclair** (K278) with a riverside promenade, seems a pleasant town, but moor-ing is forbidden. Even at slack low tide, the echo-sounder measures more than 9m depth. Provided you are able to see over the banks, there is generally a lovely vista of little half-timbered farmhouses and apple orchards, particularly in the reaches above **Jumièges** (K296).

The Belgian writer and mystic Maurice Maeterlinck (1862–1949), author of *The Blue Bird*, lived in the Abbey of **St-Wandrille** (K308). These ruins of a 6th century foundation must have made an unusual setting for performances of Shakespeare and Maeterlinck's own works: rather than change scenery, he moved actors and audience from one location to another and was fond of gliding through the cloisters on roller skates. The Abbey was returned to a religious order in 1931. Beyond the high-level Brotonne suspension bridge, note a monument (K308.7) in the form of a concrete aeroplane, erected in memory of some aviators lost in the Arctic in 1929. **Caudebec** (K309.5) was formerly a well known place for watching (or being engulfed by) the Seine tidal bore. Henry IV described the 15–16th century Gothic church of Notre Dame as 'the most beautiful chapel in my kingdom'. Anchoring is possible – with normal precautions – near the right bank, just below the ferry crossing. A brief stay would enable a visit to be made to shops and restaurants. Buoys off **Villequier** (K313.3) could provide a chance of stopping, perhaps making an expedition to the town shops by dinghy. A museum recalls a tragedy when Victor Hugo's newly married 19-year-old daughter Léopoldine and her husband Charles were drowned, their sailing boat being overturned by the Mascaret. We enter salt water at **Aizier** (K323). Anchoring is satisfactory inside the ship mooring buoys at **Quillebeuf-sur-Seine** (K331.9).

Getting ever wider, the Seine is now fast-flowing and laden with mud; as the tide drains out huge sandbanks appear on the shores. Ahead is the highly impressive **Tancarville** Bridge (K338.2), a span of 1,400m with a height above high water of 48m which was opened in 1959. It has transformed the local economy, connecting lands south of the river with the conurbation of Le Havre. Yachts may moor between projecting dolphins and a quayside near **Les Alluvions** (K337.9), on the right bank just upriver of the bridge. 25km of the Tancarville Canal were opened in 1887 between here and the Havre docks. Entry to the Tancarville lock is from 4hr before to $3\frac{1}{4}$hr after HW at Le Havre. For full details of the waterway, opening arrangements for the bridges and the operation of the locks at the seaward end, consult the *Carte Guide*. Partially rendered obsolete by the increased dimensions of ships, the canal is only of use to pleasure craft if conditions in the estuary are rough. Being tideless, it adds several hours to a journey.

To all intents and purposes, the remaining Seine is a seaway and hardly within the scope of this book. On the north shore, **Le Havre** is the second largest port in France, with first-rate marina facilities for pleasure craft (see the *Carte Guide*). One further location does, however, merit mention: this is the superb little port of **Honfleur**, without question one of the most attractive towns in the whole of France. Situated on the south shore of the Seine estuary, it is approached via a short channel that dries out at low water. If necessary, a jetty at the entrance by a prominent radar control tower makes a convenient place to wait for the tide. In the 16th century French discoverers set sail for the new lands of Canada from here, numerous settlers following in their wake. Trade has long since crossed the estuary to Le Havre, leaving the little town to brightly painted fishing boats, tourists, artists and yachtsmen. At the centre is the Vieux Bassin, filled with pleasure craft and lined on three sides by tall houses, partly faced with slates, the windows decorated with colourful sun-

The great Tancarville road bridge.

Shipping in the lower Seine between Quillebeuf and Ville-quier, engraved from the picture by Turner.

blinds. La Lieutenance, the former house of the Governor of Honfleur, is a 16th century structure alongside the entrance lock; the latter opens to admit boats from 1hr before to 1hr after HW at Le Havre. St-Catherine's church was built entirely in timber by shipwrights. Within walking distance along the Côte de Grâce towards fashionable **Deauville** are agreeable beaches on the Channel coast.

14 · Canal Latéral à la Marne

Carte Guide: *La Marne*

From Vitry-le-François, junction with the Canal de la Marne à la Saône and the Canal de la Marne au Rhin to a junction with the River Marne at Dizy, near Épernay: 66.7km with 15 locks. A connection with the Canal de l'Aisne à la Marne is made at Condé-sur-Marne.

This is an unexceptional waterway, closely following the unnavigable course of the Marne but featuring long and straight sections with limited scenic interest. Passing through a mainly rural chalky region giving rise to dust-producing cement works, it provides a well used route for *péniches* from Vitry-le-François, a leading canal centre of NE France, to the Paris area via the Marne. The major industry at its NW end is the world-famous champagne trade, based on Épernay. Most locks are electrically operated.

Designed to offer a more reliable navigation than that provided by the Upper Marne, the canal was completed in 1845. As well as making possible freight transport of agricultural goods in its densely populated valley, it soon became widely used for carrying coal, coke and building materials.

All facilities including water, fuel and commercial craft engineers are to be found in the large town of **Vitry-le-François** (see Chapter 27), meeting place of three canals. Beyond an aqueduct spanning the River Saulx upstream of its confluence with the Marne and on the outskirts of the city is Écluse 1 (K2.3). Écluse 2, l'Ermite (K3.7), is a charming area, with bargemen's café where bottled gas and basic chandlery are available. The diesel fuel sold here is, however, taxfree and can be sold only to commercial barges. Note on the left a branch which originally led into the river via one lock. On the right bank, between a road bridge and Écluse 3 (K4.8), **Couvrot** offers basic food shops. The nearby River Marne is here a wild and fast-flowing stream, tumbling over gravel beds and littered with the branches of trees. Ahead, the large cement works of the Societé des Ciments Français dominates the landscape, casting a thin layer of white dust over buildings and canalside shrubs. This situation affects the waterway for a considerable distance, through **Soulanges**, Écluse 4 (K9.2), where there is a small port (*halte nautique*), grocer and restaurant and a little grey stone church with slated spire, and on to the pleasant little town of **La Chaussée-sur-Marne** (K14.2), with shops and restaurant.

Another substantial cement works is passed in **Omey** (K16.5). The next town, **Pogny** (K17.9, a good quay if not occupied by barges), is very convenient for all shops but followed by an utterly straight and rather dull run past **Vésigneul-sur-Marne** (K20.4), **St-Germain-la-Ville**, Écluse 7 (food shops and restaurant, K21.8) and **Sarry**, Écluse 8 (baker, grocer and restaurant, K27). Suburban development intervenes at the approach to the city of **Châlons-sur-Marne** (K32). Pass to the left of a wooded island shortly before Écluse 9; the alternative channel is not navigable. Central quayside moorings, at the upstream end of the lock. This was the Gallo-Roman town of Catalaunum and was the scene of a fierce battle against Attila the Hun in the 5th century. Early in World War I the Germans held Châlons briefly, before launching into the Battle of the Marne. All the attractions of the city centre will be found close to the canal, which is generally animated by numerous *péniches* of particularly smart appearance. As capital of the Marne *département* there are many fine municipal buildings, with a modern and stylish quarter near the massive Gothic cathedral of St-Étienne. In recent years a number of ancient half-timbered houses have been expertly restored, their structure revealed by stripping off stucco cladding. Two small rivers, the Nau and the Mau, wind through the centre with attractive planting schemes. The 12th century church of Notre-Dame en Vaux is noted for fine stained glass and a 56-bell carillon. As would be expected, shopping is of a high quality. Industries include brewing and champagne production.

Shortly before **St-Martin-sur-le-Pré** (K34.8), an aqueduct carries the canal over a feeder bringing water supplies from the Marne and the two run in close com-pany almost to Condé-sur-Marne. The waterway continues very straight through **Recy** (K37), Écluse 10; **Juvigny** (K39.3); **Vraux** and Écluse 11 (grocer, K44.3), and **Aigny** (K46.4) with a mixture of waterside woodlands and large, open, flat fields of chalky soil. At K48.4 a junction on the right marks the start of the Canal de l'Aisne à la Marne (Chapter 21) with food shops, fuel and restaurant in the nearby town of **Condé-sur-Marne**. With the River Marne now alongside the canal, the true champagne country is entered at **Tours-sur-Marne** (Écluse 12, K53), the self-styled 'Crossroads of Champagne' where the advertising signs of sparkling wine producers vie with each other. This is a charming little town, all shops being within a short distance of the lock. Soon the first vineyards are visible at the approach to **Bisseuil** (K55.4, swing bridge), spreading far over the hillsides. The village has a baker and grocer.

After Écluse 13 (K58.1), the waterway widens through **Mareuil-sur-Ay** (K59.4), a convenient shopping stop with a garage on the far side of town (K60). An 18th century *château* has long been associated with champagne production. When calling at the Champagne house of Marc Hébrart to replenish the ship's supplies in September 1990, we found the *vendange* reaching a crescendo. With scarcely a glance in our direction, a young man commanded that we should stack over a hundred heavy plastic crates in which the grapes had just arrived from the vineyards for pressing. This task completed, Madame was able to spare a moment from feeding the workers to process our not insubstantial order. This was duly delivered to our boat, lying on pontoons near the town centre. 3km north lies **Avenay-Val-d'Or**, well worth a visit to see the ornate 13–16th century church of St-Trésain with its grand organ dating from the 16th century. **Ay**, just before Écluse 14 (K62.6), is a leading town of wine *maisons*, grapes having been cultivated here in Roman times. Its wines were highly prized by François I, Henry VIII of England and Henri IV. A wide range of shops will be found here. All the atmosphere of pre-World War II horseboats in this very location is admirably portrayed in Georges Simenon's 1931 novel *Le Charretier de la 'Providence'*, published in English as *Maigret Meets a Milord*. Fuel can be obtained from a garage on the left bank at the N51 road bridge at **Dizy** (K64.7), with limited shopping in the village. **Épernay** offers a full range of requirements, its centre being about 3km south of the canal at this point (see Chapter 15). A more convenient approach by water would be to work through the last lock, Écluse 15 (K66.6), join the River Marne and run upstream for 5km to moor in the *port de plaisance* at the head of navigation.

15 · River Marne

Carte Guide: *La Marne*

From a junction with the Canal Latéral à la Marne at Dizy, near Épernay to the River Seine at Alfortville, a short distance upstream of central Paris. The official length of 178.4km has been slightly shortened by improvements, but the former kilometre marks continue in use. There are 18 locks with tunnels on canal sections at Chalifert (290m) and St-Maur (600m). A former inclined plane connection (the *transbordeur*) with the Canal de l'Ourcq near Meaux is long disused, but there is a possibility that some new form of link may be made in the future, so opening up a most appealing pleasure cruising circuit comprising the Marne, Seine, Canal St-Martin and Canal de l'Ourcq (see Chapter 16). There are several 'branches' on portions of the natural Marne which are bypassed by canal sections used by through traffic. These are described in the text below.

Mention of the River Marne produces two immediate mental images: the production of champagne, mainly in the upper reaches around Épernay, and the engagements of World War I – the Battle of the Marne late in 1914 and the Victory of the Allies from July to November 1918. Many towns and villages were severely damaged and most bridges blown up; there are monuments and memorials. But the Great War does not impose an oppressive atmosphere on the river such as that which is felt on the Meuse in the area of Verdun. This is a gentle and peaceful waterway, flowing past woods and reed-fringed islands with numerous punt-ensconced fishermen. Much of the course features great loops as the Marne makes it way through hard limestone: navigational improvements have considerably reduced the original length with a series of bypass channels. Scenery is finest between Château-Thierry and Meaux, although it is all very pleasant until a different kind of interest intervenes with the approach of the Parisian suburbs. As with the Upper Seine, the people of Paris flock to the Marne for relaxation, the most fortunate among them living in agreeable riverside houses.

Commercial traffic is brisk, especially in the lower reaches, and the locks increase in size from the *péniche* chambers near Épernay to structures 125m in length. Those at the downstream end are mostly worked electrically, with a programme of gradual conversion currently in progress for the others. Some locks are to function automatically without the aid of keepers.

Instructions will be issued to craft on entering the navigation. At present, pleasure craft are normally grouped through manned locks or, where practicable, made to share with commercial traffic. If no other boats arrive within 20 minutes, they will normally be allowed to proceed alone.

While long used for navigation purposes, the Marne was described as 'both slow and dangerous' in the late 17th century, with barges being wrecked 'every day'. Throughout the 18th century a succession of individuals and companies sought to build improved navigation works in return for toll receipts for periods ranging from 30 to 60 years. But it was not until implementation of a government scheme that the river was finally canalized between 1838 and 1865 with 18 weirs, 20 locks, two tunnels and four branches. This created the basic navigation that now exists. The 20th century improvements include a new weir at Meaux (1939), the replacement of the St-Maur lock with other works (1933), and the deepening of the Marne towards its junction with the Seine.

At the head of navigation 5km duplicate the course of the Canal Latéral à la Marne between the **Dizy** junction (see Chapter 14) and **Épernay** and this length is normally known as the Épernay Branch; distances quoted do not therefore include this section. Even if making a through passage along the river and canal, it is worth undertaking this detour for there is plenty of interest in the town, with excellent shopping and mooring facilities. Jetties will be found at the *Port de Plaisance* on the south bank beyond the bridge (fuel available at the north approach to the bridge) with water supplies and slipway. Various wars have stripped the town of almost everything of architectural interest, but fascinating visits can be made to the cellars of several *maisons* of this leading centre of champagne production. Moët et Chandon (18 av. de Champagne) is open between 9.00–12.00h and 14.00–17.30h (not Sat, Sun or public holidays). The 45 minute tour includes part of a system of 28km of underground chambers. Mercier (75 av. de Champagne) welcomes the public every day from April 1–Oct 31, 9.00–12.00h and 14.00–17.30h. In 45 minutes you can travel through galleries on an electric train and see exhibitions devoted to cooperage and grape pressing. Finally, De Castellane (57 rue de Verdun) opens its doors from 9.00–11.00h and 14.00–17.00h (not Sat, Sun, public holidays or in Aug). Their premises include 10km of galleries. Further details of local winemaking will be seen in the Museum of Champagne and Prehistory, housed in a 19th century *château* in the Avenue de

Champagne and once belonging to the firm of Perrier. Opening times are 9.00–12.00h and 14.00–18.00h weekdays and 10.00–12.00h and 14.00–17.00h on Sun and public holidays (closed Tues and throughout Dec, Jan and Feb).

All around, the countryside is devoted to the culture of vines – 24,500 hectares with annual production exceeding 186 million bottles of champagne of which about 54 million are exported. Britain is a leading importer, consuming more than 23 million bottles in 1989. Both black and white grapes are grown, the traditional *grande marque* champagne being blended from 33% white and 66% black.

Dropping downriver past a vista of vineyards, there is a possible mooring on a pontoon above the bridge at **Cumières** (K2.5); elsewhere the water is often shallow at the edges. An artificial cut leads right, to the Écluse de Cumières (K3.2), which together with the next two locks features awkward sloping sides. **Damery** (K5.4) is a charming small town alongside a bridge and benefiting scenically from a backdrop of vineyards. All shops are a short distance from the quay (right bank, above the bridge). Wooded banks lead to the Damery lock cut, Écluse 2 being situated at the far end (K8.2). The next reach contains two possible ports of call: **Reuil** (K11.8) with moorings under the bridge while visiting the grocer or baker and the slightly industrialized **Port-à-Binson** (K14.8), a town of grain silos with a commercial harbour and pleasure boat jetties (suitable for small craft only) on the left, downstream of the bridge. Shopping and eating are good, and there is an official swimming place at a campsite on the upstream, left-hand side of the island. A garage is situated a short walk from the bridge. **Châtillon-sur-Marne**, 2km north, occupies a 148m hilltop rising from the vineyards and in medieval times was an important stronghold. A giant statue of Urbain II, Pope from 1088–99, was erected in 1887 to acknowledge his original name of Eudes de Châtillon. It was he who instigated the first Crusade to Palestine.

Écluse 3, Vandières (K17.7), is built on a short cut (take the right fork to avoid entering the weir stream). At the confluence of the little River Semoigne (K22.3) be careful of silting on the right bank. Moor near the next bridge, Pont de Try, for a visit to **Verneuil**, 1km north. Here there is a lovely 12–13th century church. Beyond, the **Tardenois Plateau** saw fierce actions during the Second Battle of the Marne. **Vincelles** (K24.3), right bank, has few facilities and is anyway best avoided for there is a line of rocks alongside, where the river bends. For shopping, continue a short distance to **Dormans** (K26.3), with a mooring quay, right bank, by a public swimming pool/camping site.

Comprehensive supplies with restaurants are to be found, and an official swimming beach is situated on the right bank about 250m upstream of the bridge. During the religious wars in the 16th century between the Catholics and Henri III, the Catholic leader the Duke de Guise was wounded, resulting in his nickname Le Balafré ('Scarface'). The Chapelle de la Reconnaissance in the grounds of a *château* commemorates both Battles of the Marne. The popular sport of windsurfing is practised in former gravel pits by the waterway beyond **Trélou-sur-Marne** (K28.5, pontoon mooring). Soon afterwards, Écluse 4, **Courcelles** (K30.5) appears ahead, followed by a succession of small villages on each bank, none of which offer much in the way of facilities. One of the most attractive is **Marcilly** (K35.2), a place of rough stone houses in front of a backdrop of vineyards.

Looking upriver from **Jaulgonne** (K37.3), you will be rewarded with a magnificent view of the champagne fields. All shops, fuel and restaurant (with its own quay immediately below the bridge) make the town a useful stopping point. There is a well-marked quay for the use of pleasure craft up to 20m in length. Be sure to stay in the centre of the channel at a place that is silted on each bank where the River Surmelin enters on the left (K39.5). **Mont-St-Pierre** (K41.5), right bank, offers a choice of two mooring piers downstream of the bridge should you require its baker, butcher, grocer or restaurant. Downhill traffic passes to the right of a broad island just above Écluse 5 (K42.5), where there is a quay close to the Château-Thierry district navigation office. Further villages lying well back from the Marne lead to **Brasles** (K48.2), a slightly industrialized suburb of **Château-Thierry** (K50.4). It takes its name from Thierry IV, the 8th century Merovingian king. Rather better known is the author of fables Jean de La Fontaine (1621–95), born here the son of the Director of Waters and Forests. The house of his birth is now a museum devoted to La Fontaine relics and his statue stands near a bridge crossing the northernmost of two river channels. (This route is set aside for navigation, the Fausse Marne being reserved for angling.) In 1814 Napoléon had an engagement with the combined Russian and Prussian forces under the command of Blücher. In the First World War, British troops under General Haig crossed the river at this point in September 1914 and four years later Château-Thierry was the location of the first American offensive. This event is recalled by a vast memorial at the top of Hill 204. Little remains of the *château* in a park above the *Hôtel de Ville* in the main square. Vertical quays provide excellent moorings for shops and restaurants. One eating place is on a *péniche* (left bank, K51).

The valley of the Marne now becomes most agreeable, with thick woodlands alternating with vineyards. Écluse 6, **Azy** (K56.2), is followed by a long reach to **Nogent-l'Artaud** (K63.3), where there are moorings near the bridge, all facilities and an old water mill. The church is partly 12th century. Delightful scenery continues past Écluse 7, **Charly** (K66.6), with mooring and restaurant at the bridge. There is a quay (by a diving board) at K70. Fuel supplies are conveniently close to a quay in the village of **Crouttes** (K73, right bank), while the next town, **Nanteuil-sur-Marne** (K74.2), has moorings by a restaurant at the bridge, a grocer and a baker. A wider variety of shops exists in **Saâcy-sur-Marne** (K76.1), reached from a bridge downstream of Écluse 8, **Méry-sur-Marne**. Without question, this is the finest part of the whole waterway as it flows round a great double loop. An isolated overnight berth will be found on the left bank, where there is a quay about 400m above the railway bridge of Saussoy (K85.8).

Although still countrified, towns and villages become progressively less rural as we come to an area within commuting distance of Paris. Écluse 9, **Courtaron** (K87.1), is in a lonely position on the left bank: keep the same side to avoid a wide shoal shortly below. The Marne increases in size at the junction with the Petit Morin in **La Ferté-sous-Jouarre** (K90.6). It was here that the finest millstones in all France were once quarried. Nothing remains of the one-time island fortress, the riverbanks now being shaded by pleasant walks. Shopping is good; quayside moorings reach a reasonable depth, left bank, downstream of the second bridge, about 100m above a slipway. Alternatively, craft drawing less than 1.20m can use a pontoon behind a small island upstream of the first bridge (K89.9). The British Expeditionary Forces crossed the Marne near here in 1914 using a floating bridge; its site is marked by rectangular stone pylons. Late in 1928, an impressive memorial was unveiled in memory of 3,888 Britons who died during the 1914 battles of the Marne, Aisne, Le Cateau and Mons. South 3km is **Jouarre**, whose 7th century abbey is one of the oldest religious buildings in the country. The public is admitted and Benedictine services are held in French and Gregorian chant.

To state that there is little of interest on the succeeding reaches would be to ignore the fact that surroundings are remarkably pleasant. But features of note are rare. Moorings below the bridge (right bank) in **Ussy-sur-Marne** (K95.2) must be approached with great care (shallow water and rocks): if you do make it safely, you will be rewarded by a baker, butcher, grocer and restaurant. Several hundred metres south of the bridge, at the crossroads, is a fuel station. Downstream, pass to the right of the Île de la Fosse-Tournille (K96), but to the left of another island below the *autoroute* bridge (K97.6). Pleasure boating is much in evidence at the approach to **Changis-sur-Marne** and its twin town **St-Jean-les-Deux-Jumeaux**, either side of a road crossing (K99.4), for there is a yacht club with craning facilities. Shopping is best in St-Jean. Écluse 10 (K100.7) lies a little beyond. Mooring is permitted above the lock. Neither **Armentières-en-Brie** (K104.1) or **Tancrou** (K108.3) are likely to detain one; give them a miss and press on instead to the riverside resort of **Mary-sur-Marne** (K110.7), a favourite objective for townsfolk, with restaurant (in the 18th century riverside *château*), food shops and pedalos for hire. From here for much of the way to the Seine, gravel-winning is an important activity, sand barges becoming a leading user of the waterway. A glance at the map will indicate how the Canal de l'Ourcq (see Chapter 16) now strikes up an intimate association with the Marne, having run from its terminus to the north at La Ferté-Milon. The two navigations share a similar winding course for many kilometres, but there is currently no connection between them.

Seemingly in no hurry to reach the Seine, the Marne twists through one direction and then another round the Montceaux Forest, passing on the way **Îles-les-Meldeuses** and Écluse 11 (K113.1), limited shopping and restaurant, and **Germigny-l'Evêque** (K121.2). Ignoring channels that pass through islands on the right immediately before the bridge, mooring can be attempted on the left, with care because of shallows, just downstream. The village offers a restaurant and slipway. A full range of shops and fuel will be found in **Varreddes**, a town near the Canal de l'Ourcq, about 2km north. Around the next bend, the Canal de l'Ourcq swings in close to the Marne (K123): navigation is to the left of a long island, with the *Port de Plaisance* of **Poincy** at its lower end, right bank (K125). This makes an excellent overnight mooring, with water supplies alongside the sheltered jetties. Modern French waterways history was made at this site, when Pierre Zivy opened the country's first ever hire cruiser base in 1958, Saint Line. A great Anglophile, M. Zivy had been inspired to begin his business after enjoying inland cruising in England. He subsequently moved his craft to Baye on the Canal du Nivernais, but like other pioneers had withdrawn from the industry a little before it had become today's popular and profitable operation.

Trilport (K127) has shops, fuel, restaurants and adequate moorings just below the bridge on the left

Convenient pontoon moorings for visiting craft in Meaux. A busy market and wide range of shops are virtually alongside.

bank: but be warned – the narrow channel past a small island just beyond is obstructed by rocks and navigation marks must be followed exactly. Sadly, few signs now remain of a long-disused twin tank inclined plane connection between the river and the Canal de l'Ourcq on the right bank at K 129. But until quite recently, the site was denoted *Transbordeur* on certain waterways charts. Industrial development has engulfed the approach basin. On the opposite bank is the keeper's house of the vanished Basses-Fermes lock.

Meaux (K 133.5), capital of Brie, spreads around a horseshoe bend of the Marne. It is a city with a long and rich past, with the cathedral of St-Étienne and a charming *jardin* nearby designed by Le Nôtre. The natural river suffers from an overdose of concrete, all through traffic being diverted through the automated Écluse 12 and into 12km of bypass channel, the Canal de Meaux à Chalifert. Best moorings for Meaux are on a pontoon in the town centre (water and electricity: 48hr limit). Excellent shopping is within a short distance: excitingly varied food and clothing market on certain days including Sats. In cutting off a great loop of the Marne the canal avoids several attractive villages including **Trilbardou**, **Charmentray** and **Précy-sur-Marne**: however, these are all served by the Canal de l'Ourcq. In **Condé-Ste-Libaire** (K141) the Grand Morin river flows under the canal to join the Marne, and is shortly succeeded by a lateral canal (now closed). The appealing village has several shops and a restaurant. More extensive supplies can be found on the right bank in **Esbly** (K142.5) with a good quay beyond the bridge (garage and all shops within a short walk). **Coupvray** (K144) was the birthplace of Louis Braille (1809–52), inventor of the blind reading system. A museum has been set up in his parents' house.

Soon after Écluse 13, **Lesches** (K145, bar), the canal passes through the 290m **Chalifert** tunnel, controlled by traffic lights. Écluse 14, Chalifert lies beyond a basin at the far end and immediately before a return to the natural river. Facilities here include a restaurant and boating centre with slipway. 7km of the bypassed Marne may be navigated upstream from here to **Annet-sur-Marne**. Doubtless, small craft will be able to travel even further in the direction of Meaux. One most enjoyable object of this exercise would be to visit the admirable Leisure Park of **Jablines**, where very extensive gravel workings have been expertly landscaped to provide water space for windsurfing, dinghy sailing, rambling and swimming from a large sandy beach. It is a popular attraction for the people of Paris on hot summer afternoons.

The Touring Club de France has a pleasure boat harbour on the left bank (K150.2), offering most aids for civilized cruising such as slipway, water, cranage, mains electricity, restaurant and overnight moorings. With the remainder of the journey progressively becoming more urban, there is much to be said for staying here for a period and visiting Paris by public transport.

Shopping and eating facilities are now to be encountered at frequent intervals: consequently they are not listed here. While towns follow each other in quick succession, several of them retain a distinct identity in spite of the influence of ever-expanding Paris. One such is **Lagny** (K151) where old houses and a fountain of great antiquity are among the sights. Quayside moorings, convenient for shops and restaurants. Écluse 15 (K156) at **Vaires-sur-Marne** marks the start of the

Canal de Chelles bypass channel, with gravel pits, cement works and normally hectic commercial traffic. This continues through **Gournay-sur-Marne** (left bank K161) and **Chelles** (right bank), past **Noisy-le-Grand** (left bank K164) and **Neuilly-sur-Marne** (right bank), with Écluse 16 (K164.8), bringing the navigator back onto the Marne upstream of **Bry-sur-Marne** (K166.5). All is now busy suburbs whose attributes can scarcely compete with the romance of fast-approaching waterside Paris.

Midway between **Le Perreux-sur-Marne** and **Nogent-sur-Marne** is a chandler and slipway (K169.8, opposite the Île d'Amour), while good moorings with water point, slipway and electricity will be found in the *port de plaisance* de Nogent (K170.9, right bank, up a backwater, right side of the lock island). Eventually, 600 craft will be able to lie here. A Metro station is about 1km distant. One final change to the original course of the river is encountered at **Joinville-le-Pont** (K173.4), where a huge loop through **Champigny-sur-Marne**, **La Varenne** and **St-Maur-des-Fosses** is avoided by the 600m St-Maur tunnel, controlled by traffic lights and soon followed by the St-Maur lock (K174.6). It is possible to cruise for a distance up part of the bypassed loop, through **Créteil** lock to a commercial port area at **Bonneuil**. No freight traffic works on the section beyond, and it should be cruised with due caution keeping a careful watch for anglers and oarsmen.

Below St-Maur lock there remains just one more lock, Écluse de St-Maurice (K177.2, 48hr mooring 400m above) downstream of **Maisons-Alfort**. The Seine confluence is at **Alfortville** (K178), about 5km above the Île de la Cité and the heart of Paris (see Chapter 13). The Romans called the Marne *Matrona*, 'The Good Lady', an apt description of her normally placid nature. Although mostly unremarkable, the river provides peaceful and enjoyable cruising.

16 · Paris. Canals St-Martin, St-Denis and de l'Ourcq

Carte Guide: *Les Canaux Parisiens*
Canal St-Martin from the River Seine, Quai Henri IV, upstream of the Île de la Cité, to the Bassin de la Villette (Jaurès Metro station), junction with the Canal

de l'Ourcq. 4.5km with 9 locks.

Canal St-Denis from a junction with the Canal de l'Ourcq near the Bassin de la Villette, to the River Seine downstream of Paris at St-Denis. 6.6km with 7 locks.

Canal de l'Ourcq from a junction with the Canal St-Martin at the Bassin de la Villette to Port-Aux-Perches, terminus. 108.1km with 10 locks.

This group of three waterways is controlled by the City of Paris and consequently is quite unlike other navigations in France. Most easily described as a single canal, the St-Martin and the St-Denis provide an alternative passage to a 30km loop of the Seine, their combined length being little more than one-third of the distance. They offer the possibility of a circular cruise through Paris; this is of very great interest, providing back door views of the city and its western suburbs. At the junction of the two canals, the Canal de l'Ourcq heads eastwards, running parallel with the River Marne for much of its course and often directly alongside it. At Mareuil, the bed of the River Ourcq itself is used and is canalized to the terminus at Port-Aux-Perches, NE of La Ferté-Milon. Once clear of its urban Parisian reaches, the Ourcq is a surprisingly beautiful navigation, running through villages and woods in the Marne valley. Its banks are maintained with immaculate flair, making it an agreeable setting for towpath walking as well as cruising. Each day, Paris uses 380,000m^3 of raw water for cleaning gutters and sewers and for watering parks and flower beds. More than half is supplied by the Canal de l'Ourcq. Water flow is considerable throughout the Ourcq, especially through narrow bridge holes. Thus, an upstream journey is noticeably slower than one in the return direction.

Until 1983 the waterways of Paris were virtually closed to pleasure craft; apart from commercial traffic close to the city, the only boats to use the upper Ourcq were elongated narrow boats (*flûtes*) engaged on maintenance work. Now all that has changed, and the canals have been revitalized with a magnificent marina in the Bassin de l'Arsenal, just off the Seine, and a system of mechanized locks worked with borrowed keys by pleasure boaters navigating the upper part of the Ourcq. Elsewhere, keepers operate locks and swing bridges 9.00–17.00h (6.30–19.30h on the Canal St-Denis).

Operators of hire craft were not slow to establish bases serving the Canal de l'Ourcq, whose dimensions preclude use of boats able to navigate most other French waterways. The lure of the rural Marne valley coupled with a possibility of also reaching the heart of

Paris is appealing. For details of firms consult advertisements in *Fluvial* magazine (see Appendix).

Passenger vessels are in service over various sections during the summer season. These include the *Patache-Eautobus* which makes morning runs from the Quai Anatole France (by the Pont Solferino) up the Seine and along the length of the Canal St-Martin to the Bassin de la Villette, with a return cruise in the opposite direction in the afternoons. Details from Quiztour. Additionally, Canauxrama have a larger boat leaving the Bassin de la Villette for the Port de l'Arsenal, also on the Canal St-Martin (mornings), returning in the afternoon. The same company offers a 10hr voyage along the Canal de l'Ourcq from the Bassin de la Villette towards Meaux and return on several days each week.

Dimensions of the canals are such as to admit 38m long *péniches* (or larger vessels on the Canal St-Martin and Canal St-Denis); however, the majority of the Canal de l'Ourcq is equipped with long but narrow locks and is only suitable for boats whose maximum dimensions do not exceed 58.8m length × 3.2m beam × 0.8m draft × 2.4m air draft. A small charge is made for using the St-Martin and St-Denis though passage of the Canal de l'Ourcq is free. Necessary permits are supplied by lock keepers on arrival.

Consideration has been given to construction of a new lock, or perhaps a 13m boat lift, connecting the Canal de l'Ourcq with the River Marne near Lizy. Preliminary studies were carried out in 1984 when it was widely accepted that such a facility would be very useful, providing the opportunity of making a circular cruise via the canal, Marne and Seine. No further action appears to have since been taken.

Brief history Rising in the Fôret de Nesles SW of Soissons, the upper part of the River Ourcq was originally made navigable in the 16th century: it featured an early form of pound lock, believed to have been designed by Leonardo da Vinci. The enterprise was not a great success and was taken over by the Duc d'Orléans in return for toll proceeds in perpetuity. He rebuilt the line between La Ferté-Milon and the Marne near Lizy, installing 21 locks, and met with considerable prosperity, conveying great quantities of timber for the fires and stoves of Paris in barges known as *demi-Marnois*. In 1676 Riquet, promoter of the Canal du Midi, proposed an extension of the route by constructing a canal into the heart of the capital, with water powered corn mills sited by locks at the final descent towards the Seine. Wars intervened and nothing more was to be achieved until the early 19th century.

A decision was made in 1802 to start work on all three canals, the St-Martin and the St-Denis originally being known under the curious but quite correct name of the Canal de la Seine à la Seine. At the time of its opening it was likened to the Regent's Canal in London, for both waterways brought trade and urban expansion to their respective territories, situated to the north of the leading river navigation. Construction was hardly rapid and although the Bassin de la Villette was finished in 1808, the Canal St-Denis was not ready until 1821, followed the next year by the Canal de l'Ourcq (Paris to Mareuil) and the Canal St-Martin in 1825. Navigation ceased on the Ourcq between Mareuil and the Marne in 1824 and the toll collection rights were removed from the family of the Duc d'Orléans by the City of Paris.

Severe water shortages resulted in long stoppages on the network and pumping stations were subsequently built during the 1860s at Trilbardou and Isles-les-Meldeuses to lift supplies from the Marne into the Canal de l'Ourcq. Also during this period, part of the Canal St-Martin was roofed over to create a boulevard above, resulting in a long tunnel section known as the Voûte Richard Lenoir. Various other modifications followed such as modernization of the Canal St-Denis (1884–92), the covering of the St-Martin's Bassin du Temple to create a further tunnel section (1906–7), and the enlargement of the St-Denis (1923) and the 11km of the Canal de l'Ourcq nearest Paris (1925–34). Locks on the Ourcq are to this day a mere 3.2m wide, able to pass maintenance craft known as *demi-flûtes de l'Ourcq*, and almost certainly the narrowest chambers still in use anywhere in France.

One curiosity was a form of inclined plane linking the Ourcq with the Marne near Meaux. This was described in 1936 as a 'roller staircase' and appears to have consisted of a pair of counter-balanced tanks in which merchandise (but not barges) was transferred from one level to the other. Now, its site is difficult to discover in the growing sprawl of an industrial estate. In 1890, it was claimed that more than a quarter of all water-based traffic entering Paris emanated from the Canal de l'Ourcq. From a pre-World War II annual tonnage of 905,000, all but the western part of the waterway gradually ceased to carry commercial goods and by the early 1980s its sole function was water supply to Paris. The final chapter of its history came in 1983, when it was designated a leisure waterway with the French rarity – boatman-operated locks. In this rôle it seems assured of a bright future. Cruising facilities throughout are excellent, with liberal supplies of mooring bollards and water points. Signboards with distances ensure that you can readily locate your whereabouts.

CANAL ST-MARTIN

One bright morning in early May I journeyed the length of the waterway aboard the trip boat *Patache-Eautobus*. As one who finds passenger craft travel rather tame compared with navigating my own vessel, I was quite captivated by the 3 hour run and can think of no better way of describing this short navigation than to recount the experience. Having obtained tickets many weeks in advance for my companion and myself, we presented ourselves at the Quai Anatole France by the *Chambre des Députés* Métro station and after a little searching among the moored *peniches* and houseboats discovered the *Eautobus* bobbing gently on the Seine swell. It immediately recalled Mr C. J. Aubertin's early 20th century craft featured in *A Caravan Afloat*: a rectangular catamaran hull with upright cabin accom-

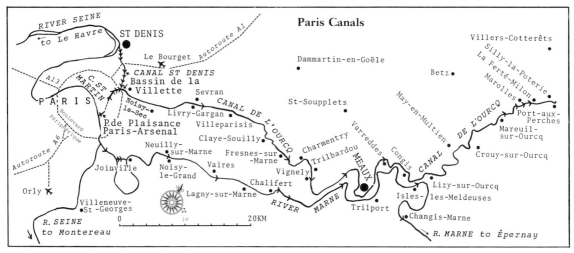

modation amidships, forward steering and boxes of red geraniums on the bow, which the captain proceeded to water by scooping liquid from the turbid river. In all, there were just six adult passengers, suddenly augmented by an invasion of lively school children who were (thankfully) herded within. We took what we considered to be the best position at the front, next to the helmsman. An attractive girl student was present as guide/hostess, but her unamplified voice was hardly strong enough to deliver a commentary to all aboard. She therefore passed the voyage moving between three positions at the extremities of the craft, delivering a well-phrased account of the waterside attractions – in French. Being the only two foreigners, we did not like to insist on the advertised English translation. From time to time, we caught her sneaking a glance at her written notes, keeping roughly one building ahead of the commentary. But, then, it was early in the season.

Opposite the Île de la Cité we were overtaken (at alarmingly close quarters) by a laden 350 tonne *péniche*. We then pulled into a narrow entrance on the northern embankment just below the Pont d'Austerlitz, where a lock could be discerned in the gloom. This was the beginning of the Canal St-Martin. A delay ensued and it appeared that the keeper was not ready for our scheduled arrival. The guide clambered ashore and soon afterwards the gates of Écluse 9, La Bastille, opened to receive us. Beyond is an extended pool, now converted into the most extensive marina in Paris: the *Port de Plaisance* Paris-Arsenal. Inaugurated in February 1983 by the Mayor, it comprises over 160 berths of which some are reserved for visiting boats. The others are occupied by private pleasure craft and residential vessels up to a maximum length of 25m. Typical charges for an 11m cruiser range from 80F to 150F per day (depending on the time of year) with reductions for the first night. Safe from the troublesome wash of the Seine and within walking distance of tourists' Paris, this is easily the most agreeable place to lie. Although there are over 160 moorings, advance booking is strongly advised. (Capitainerie du Port de Plaisance de Paris-Arsenal, 11 Bd de la Bastille, 75012 Paris. tel. (1) 341.39.32.) Annual charges are levied on residential boats with the possibility of negotiating leases up to 30 years. Among facilities are a Harbourmaster's office (and remote control point for Écluse 9) with toilet block, showers, telephone and shops; there are waterside planted areas, a children's play enclosure, restaurant, and lifting arrangements for craft up to 6 tonnes.

At the far end of the basin (K0.9) is the Place de la Bastille and its July Column surmounted by the figure of Liberty. For many years the canal has been enclosed at this point in a series of tunnels, the Voûtes de la Bastille, Richard Lenoir and du Temple, totalling 2,019m. Boulevards are planted with trees and shrubs overhead. While there is no artificial illumination, the vault is dimly lit by shafts from above and the ghostly columns of light produce a highly charged and eerie atmosphere. The children confined to the cabin of the *Eautobus* fell strangely quiet, while the captain repeatedly tried to persuade me to photograph reflections of bushes and lamp standards – a reminder of the normal world outside. Twin towpaths increase the generous proportions of the tunnel, which has a marked bend beyond its halfway point. Comprehensive cleaning operations are carried out every other year: during a recent stoppage, the tunnel produced a bath, four sewing machines, several bicycles, a machine gun, assorted revolvers and the remains of a cow, complete with horns and tail! The Canal St-Martin has long been a popular film location and the passengers exchanged knowing looks when informed that both Vigo's *L'Alalante* and *L'Hotel du Nord* were shot here.

Once clear of the tunnel, the waterway emerges amid the streets and buildings of an old Paris that looks not unlike a film set, with its images familiar from such favourites as *Le Ballon Rouge*. Characteristic features are planes and horse chestnuts, several appealing iron footbridges, the swing bridge de la rue Dieu, and three sets of two-rise locks invariably thronged with bystanders when a boat passes through. The first of these is Écluses 7/8, du Temple (K2.8) which leads to the Bassin des Marais. Commercial wharves receive sand and gravel by barge from the Seine, but most other goods now arrive by road. Écluses 5/6, des Recollets, (K3.3) and 3/4, des Morts (K3.9), are close to the Gare de l'Est. Then follows the Bassin du Combat, named after an infamous cockpit. One more tunnel remains to be negotiated, the 103m Voûte Lafayette: lacking a towpath, horseboats were hauled through on an endless rope of which vestiges can still be seen. Then comes the final staircase, Écluses 1/2, de la Villette (K4.5) and the junction with the Canal de l'Ourcq's Bassin de la Villette. As we disembarked, several *péniches* were waiting to descend to the Seine, evidence that these urban canals still carry respectable quantities of freight. We bade farewell to *Patache-Eautobus* and her friendly crew and made our way to the nearby Jaurès Métro station to return quickly, but more prosaically, to central Paris.

CANAL ST-DENIS
Although lacking the scenic interest of the St-Martin, this route (in common with almost all urban waterways) is certainly worth exploring, especially as part of

La Patache-Eautobus carries passengers through a two-rise lock near the Bassin de la Villette.

a circumnavigation of Paris. Much of the canal, however, is quite straight and being lined with wharves takes on the appearance of an extended dock. Commercial traffic is generally heavy (mainly consisting of astonishingly overladen gravel barges), but as locks are mechanized and duplicated, side by side, no great delays should be anticipated. Good shopping facilities are always close at hand. Having left the *Gare Circulaire* at the Canal de l'Ourcq junction, the St-Denis immediately plunges into a deep lock, Écluse 1, Pont de Flandre, with a railway station of the same name beyond. Alongside is the splendid museum of science and technology, completed in 1985 in a 1960s structure (originally designed as a central abattoir). The site is dominated by a massive silver dome of the Géode cinema, which has a 1000 sq. metre curved screen.

Écluse 2, Quatre Chemins (K1.3); Écluse 3, Pont Tournant (K2.2) and Écluse 4, des Vertus (K3.2) all lie within the suburb of **Aubervilliers**. Just after Écluse 5, Porte de Paris (K4.6, convenient supermarket) is the railway station of **St-Denis**, a town of great historical note before it was absorbed into Greater Paris (see Chapter 13). Écluse 6, de la Gare (K5.7), and Écluse 7, de la Briche (K6.5), are shortly followed by a junction with the River Seine.

CANAL DE L'OURCQ

Extending for 700m with a 70m width, the **Bassin de la Villette** acts as a raw water reservoir for Paris. Entered from the west by the Canal St-Martin, it is well served by shops, restaurants and other urban facilities, with a Métro station, Jaurès. During the late 1980s, extensive improvements were made to provide pleasure craft moorings and bases for hire cruisers and passenger craft. One of the largest open spaces in the capital, it is dominated by an 18th century former tax office – the Rotunda, designed by visionary architect Nicholas Ledoux. At the far end the canal passes beneath a remarkable iron lift bridge, de la rue Crimée (K0.8), dating from 1885. Surmounted by heavy winding wheels, the deck rises horizontally by hydraulic pressure when a boat pauses for several seconds by a sensor (as instructed on a notice board). The waterway still carries freight over its first 9.6km, having been widened to Freycinet gauge and rendered suitable for *péniches*. Given a boat of suitably slender dimensions, a return cruise from Paris to the head of navigation can comfortably be made in four days. At K1.4 the Canal St-Denis forks off towards the Seine, and from this point to a crossing of the Boulevard Périphérique (Paris ring road), the Canal de l'Ourcq runs through the Villette Museum Park. After the considerable commercial activity at **Port Serrurier**, with grain and gravel wharves, we arrive in the **Pantin** district (K2.9), with a large basin, shops, garages, restaurants and Métro station. Very considerable effort has been diverted towards landscaping the canal's surroundings. Virtually throughout, the towpath is admirably surfaced, encouraging use by walkers, joggers, cyclists, sunbathers, fishermen and even long-distance roller skaters. All this presents a highly animated scene, illustrating the newly-developed role of inland waterways in the Age of Leisure. Curiously, however, pleasure boat use is sparse. The way ahead lies through a series of suburbs and railway tracks, always close to essential services. These include: **Bobigny** (K4.5, shops, fuel, restaurants and Métro. Note the explicit, but rather well executed, waterside murals on a long stretch of concrete wall; **Romainville** (K5, shops, fuel, restaurants and the 18th century church of St-Germain-l'Auxerrois); **Noisy-le-Sec** (K6.6, shops and fuel); **Bondy**, by a crossing of the A86 *autoroute* (K8, shops, fuel and restaurants); and **Pavillons-sous-Bois** (K9.6), end of the enlarged part of the canal (local shops).

Livry-Gargan, right bank, and **Aulnay-sous-Bois**, left bank (K11.2), both feature normal suburban facilities with further shops in **Sevran** (K13.5). Here the lock keeper issues cruising permits and appropriate keys to fit paddle gear on the remaining nine locks. A degree of fluency in French is necessary to understand lock working instructions arranged in cartoon form in the *Guide*: if in doubt, request a personal explanation here. Festoons of ivy hang over the parapet of the Pont de la Pouderie (K15.1), brushing the deck of the boat as you pass. The waterway continues quite straight through **Villepinte** (K15.7, shops and fuel 200m from bridge). A curiosity to visit is the dogs' cemetery, on the

road towards **Tremblay-les-Gonesse** (K17.2, shops). Next follow **Villeparisis** (K19.3, shops; Sunday morning market) and **Mitry-Mory** (K19.6) on the boundary of Greater Paris, with shopping and fuel 300m from a bridge.

Onwards from here, the Canal de l'Ourcq increasingly becomes most agreeable with a winding course through hilly country and numerous pleasant villages. In **Clay-Souilly** (K27.3) craft with less than 2.2m headroom will be able to slip beneath a drawbridge without having to open it. Fuel may be obtained within 200m, while there are also shops, water point and a launching ramp. The first boatman-operated lock occurs near **Fresnes** (K32.9, choice of waterside restaurants): like several others, this was constructed with duplicated chambers, only one of which is now available. Although virtually foolproof, these DIY locks are time-consumingly complicated. By inserting the borrowed key (marked 'A') another is released... and so through six operations paddles and gates are worked until a final key, identical to that you arrived with, is detached for use at the next lock. Sensibly, all keys are attached to plastic floats. Our association with the River Marne begins in **Charmentray** (K35.7), a lovely area of thickly wooded banks with a drawbridge. This part of the river, lying well below canal level, is bypassed by the Canal de Meaux à Chalifert (see Chapter 15). **Trilbardou** (K39) is situated between the Canal de l'Ourcq and the now unnavigable Marne, a pleasant little village with lime tree shaded square, basic shopping, an antique dealer and restaurant. This is the site of a pumping station, lifting water into the canal by means of a hydraulic wheel installed in 1864 and a turbine added in 1920. Visits are possible by making advance arrangements with La Section des Dérivations et Canaux, 6 quai de la Seine, 75019 Paris, tel. 607.34.51.

Another lock, Écluse de **Vignely** (K40.2), lies a short distance west of the village where there are shops and a restaurant. Shopping and a café can be reached in **Isles-les-Villenoy**, beyond the next bridge (K42.8). Both the Marne and its navigation canal converge on the Canal de l'Ourcq near **Mareuil-les-Meaux** (no access possible) with several shops and a garage about 500m west of a bridge at **Villenoy** (K46). Farther on the Écluse de Villenoy has a dry dock, used for maintenance of the *flûtes de l'Ourcq* workboats. Staff here were unusually anxious to provide us with a conducted tour. One *flûte* was being restored as a museum exhibit. Our route follows a broad curve around **Meaux** (K48, see Chapter 15): the best approach is from the twin basins each side of a bridge, very close to the centre of the old city. A full range of facilities is at hand.

This is the end of the passenger boat run to Paris.

The next lock, Écluse **St-Lazare** (K54.7), is followed by the remains of the inclined plane (*Transbordeur*) connection with the Marne (K57.4) and a gradual return to agreeable countryside. **Trilport** (reached down the N3 road from a bridge at K58.5) lies beyond the Marne, while **Poincy** (K60.7) is between the two waterways. Each is briefly described in Chapter 15. The canal winds through woodland to a lock near **Varreddes** (K64.7); this is immaculate, with cast iron decorated lamp standards. Shops, restaurants and fuel (500m). Tantalizingly close, the Marne again approaches the canal beyond **Maladrerie** (K66.5) and once more (after the village of **Congis** K70.9, with grocer, restaurants and fuel) near **Îles-les-Meldeuses** (K73). A second pumping station, equipped with a huge Girard hydraulic wheel, installed in 1867, delivers water to the canal at a rate of 420 litres per second. Visits on application to the Authority (address above). The town itself is about 2km SE across the Marne and has adequate shopping and restaurants.

Of various possible locations for a lock or lift connection between canal and river, the confluence of River Ourcq and Marne (K74.7) appears the most likely. If built, the cruising potential of each navigation would be greatly enhanced, although a sizeable and expensive structure will be needed to overcome the 13m difference in levels. For a time the Ourcq runs alongside the canal before eventually becoming absorbed into the navigation at Mareuil. This is a little known valley that boasts several enchanting small towns such as **Lizy-sur-Ourcq** (K76.4, shops, restaurants, fuel and railway station). The 15th century church should be visited to see its ancient stained glass. The waterway played a decisive part in the Battle of the Ourcq in the opening weeks of World War I. Fierce fighting raged from Aug 24 to Sept 13 and the Germans made many early gains until the night of Sept 7, when a fleet of 600 Paris taxis carried 6,000 fresh troops from the capital; the eventual outcome was an Allied victory and the advance on Paris was stopped. **Ocquerre**, east of the canal at K79, is notable for a beautiful Renaissance farmhouse on the road towards Lizy. These upper reaches of the navigation (from east of Meaux to the terminus) must rank as among the most beautiful stretches of canal in the whole of France.

May-en-Multien, NW of the canal at **Marnoue-la-Poterie** (K83.4), offers a broad view over the Ourcq valley from the 15th century church tower: this served as an invaluable lookout point in World War I. There are shops, a restaurant and garage. Close to the Pont de la Ferme de Gesvres is the moated site of a feudal fortress erected by Louis d'Orléans and much

remodelled in the 18th century as the Château des Ducs de Gesvres. Only fragments of the building now remain. **Crouy-sur-Ourcq** lies beyond the river from a basin at K89, and is a useful source of shops with restaurant, garage and railway station. Nearby, discover the remains of the 14th century Château de Houssoy, with four-sided keep tower, now rather decayed and incorporated into farm buildings. Shops and restaurant are to be found in **Varinfroy** (K90.4) with more shops and cafés at **Neufchelles** (K93).

At K94, a right-angled junction signals the start of the 1.2km long **Canal de Clignon**, a fully navigable waterway which appears to have escaped mention in all the reference books. Maximum dimensions are 3.2m beam, 2.9m headroom and 0.8m draft. Boats up to 18m can turn round at the terminus, a very worthwhile objective with the Ancienne Commanderie de Moisy – a suberb collection of fortified buildings, derelict church and impressive gatehouse with spiral staircase. We were especially excited to make this diversion as its existence was totally unexpected!

We finally join the canalized River Ourcq in **Mareuil-sur-Ourcq** (K96.6) with a slipway in the port, shops, restaurant, garage and railway station. The beautiful 13th century church of St-Martin commands a wide view of the valley. Écluse de Mareuil (K97.2) is the first of four with larger chambers, 62m long × 5.2m wide. The next two are Écluse Queue d'Ham (K99.7) and Écluse de **Marolles** (K102.4, no facilities). These enlarged upper locks have sloping sides of either grass or concrete which would be difficult to negotiate had the authorities not installed ingenious mooring 'rafts' which ride up and down on wheels. An idea that should be adopted in similar situations on the Yonne and Marne! About 4km NW in **Autheuil-en-Valois**, a mid-12th century priory church in the Romanesque style has degenerated into a barn.

Perhaps the canal's most interesting town with considerable historical associations is **La Ferté-Milon** (K104.1), site of the uppermost lock. Almost at the head of the waterway, it has sufficient shops, cafés and refuelling points to ensure that there is no sense of anti-climax near the end of the line. Originally standing as one of a chain of medieval fortresses, it features the ruins of an important *château*, started in 1393 by Louis, Duc d'Orléans who assumed the throne and took Queen Isabeau as his mistress when his brother Charles VI was declared insane. Once guarded by 24 towers and four gateways (of which only two of each remain), the great *château* still retains elements of its grandeur. Even though building work was never completed, Louis being assassinated on the orders of the Duc de Bourgogne in 1407 (for the sequel, see Chapter

13) the structure was able to hold out for four years during the Wars of Religion until it was taken by Henry IV in 1588 and its ramparts demolished. The town was birthplace of poet Jean Racine in 1639. Another architectural feature of Le Ferté-Milon is the 12th century church of Notre Dame, largely reconstructed by Catherine de Medici in the 16th century. Much of the exquisite original stained glass was destroyed in bombardments during 1918. One museum is devoted to Racine, while another contains a collection of agricultural machinery.

Deep countryside past **Silly-la-Poterie** characterizes the uppermost 4km of the Canal de l'Ourcq, with portions of artificial cut bypassing three natural river loops. Navigation continues to a terminus in the hamlet of **Port-aux-Perches** (K108.1).

17 · Canal Latéral à l'Oise and River Oise

Carte Guide: *Picardie*

From a junction with the Canal de St-Quentin at Chauny to the canalized River Oise at Janville, 33.8km with 4 locks. Connections with the Canal de l'Oise à l'Aisne at Abbécourt and the Canal du Nord at Pont l'Evêque. The River Oise continues the line from Janville to join the River Seine at Conflans-Ste-Honorine 104.3km with 7 locks. A junction is made with the River Aisne at Choisy-au-Bac, near Compiègne.

A most important freight route between the Seine and the Channel Ports and the Low Countries, the River Oise and its lateral canal have an obvious significance for pleasure craft. Commercial traffic is hectic, in excess of 29,000 craft each year or as many as 100 on a busy day. Barge convoys up to 180m long × 11.4m wide can navigate the river between Janville and the Seine; 91m long × 5.6m wide, Janville to Pont l'Evêque; and from Pont l'Evêque to Chauny locks admit standard 38.5m *péniches* only. Trade has resulted in much industrial development, although the Oise still features some pleasant rural reaches. The lateral canal is wide and tends to be somewhat dull. River locks are duplicated, side by side; as entry channels sometimes divide well before the chambers are reached, binoculars are useful to ascertain from light signals which route to take.

It would be difficult to imagine a better advertisement for the benefits of commercial transport than the Oise; but it does underline a requirement for locks on the grand scale. It is all very far removed from the 25 tonne capacity narrow boat canals of the English Midlands which I mistakenly promoted for freight use (together with many other enthusiastic protagonists) in embarrassingly recent times! This is a 'blue flag' waterway, where commercial vessels display a blue flag or signboard (or flashing white light) to indicate that they are taking the 'wrong' side of the channel.

Rising in the Belgian Ardennes, close to the French border, the Oise flows in a deep valley carved through chalk and fed by springs from fissures. Its gentle slope demands few locks. Apart from public holidays (Easter Sunday, May 1, July 14, Nov 11 and Christmas Day) locks are open all day, throughout the year. Night passage of locks at Boran, Isle-Adam and Pontoise is available to pleasure craft on payment of a substantial fee. Conditions relating to this facility are contained in the appropriate *Carte Guide*.

Rather because of *where* it goes than taking the traveller through outstandingly attractive surroundings, the Oise has often featured in cruise accounts. Robert Louis Stevenson (*An Inland Voyage*, 1878), in spite of driving rain, subsequent boredom and finally being arrested on suspicion of spying, declared himself 'the happiest animal in France' while canoeing down the river below Compiègne. William Moens (*Through France and Belgium by River and Canal in the Steam Yacht 'Ytene'*, 1876) found that the 'river is much like the Upper Thames with its willows, poplars and rushes' but was generally more interested in monuments and buildings ashore. E. P. Warren and C. F. M. Cleverly (*The Wanderings of the 'Beetle'*, 1885) scarcely allude to the Oise itself, finding greater interest in their shore encounters when seeking nightly accommodation. And in his *Small Boat to Luxembourg* (1967) Roger Pilkington takes advantage of flood conditions to miss out the locks and shoot a series of weirs, whose tackle had been raised well clear of the water. An estimated $2-2\frac{1}{2}$ days' run was accomplished in 6 hours, leaving little time to comment on the passing scenery at all! Thus, the Oise has earned an unjustified reputation for anonymity, at least with waterway writers.

And yet, it has to be admitted that this is no dreamy or idyllic stream: just a heavily worked waterway with a number of pleasant ports of call. It could be helpful to remember that the northernmost corner of the French network features various lengths which are infinitely more dreary!

Brief history As a major tributary of the Seine, the Oise has been navigable for many centuries: accounts tell of

Norman raids in *drakkars* to ransack bankside villages. Powers were obtained by the Duc de Guise to extend the waterway upstream of Noyon to La Fére in 1662. The exceptionally winding and difficult course of the Seine resulted in a scheme being launched in 1724 to construct a canal from Paris to the Oise at Méry-sur-Oise, to be the Canal de Bourbon. This would have enabled barges to travel between the two rivers in a single day. Six years later the project was abandoned; the only portion of the line to be built was the short Canal St-Denis (Canal de la Seine à la Seine).

With the opening of the Canal de St-Quentin in 1810 and creation of a direct route between the Oise and the Escaut, traffic increased substantially. A shortening of the journey was achieved by laying out a lateral canal to bypass loops on the upper section of the Oise: the Canal Latéral à l'Oise, on which work started in 1821. Electric haulage by tractors on rails was introduced during World War I. Since World War II locks have been enlarged, enabling the Oise and part of its lateral canal to accept large barges from either the Seine or the Canal du Nord.

Starting at a junction with the Canal de St-Quentin in **Chauny**, the Canal latéral à l'Oise is well served by a down-market shopping district in this manufacturing area. Diesel fuel and water are both available from a chandler on the left bank just below the second bridge. **Abbécourt** (K3), at a junction with the Canal de l'Oise à l'Aisne, is a pleasant little barge village with *péniche* yard and baker. Several old wooden freight craft lie rotting in the reeds and a café/grocer at the lock has closed for business, now that motorized vessels can travel a greater distance each day than did the dumb boats of former times. The countryside is quietly pleasant down to the first of the mechanized and duplicated locks (Écluse 1, St-Hubert, K9). Water point, with butcher in the adjacent village of **Appily**. Cutting a straight line past the very wriggling Oise, the canal is served by a restaurant near a road bridge at **Le Jonquoy** (K15.4), and arrives at Écluse 2, Sempigny (K18) with shopping and eating facilities in **Pont l'Evêque** (water point). A barge repair works with slipway (Rousseau-Debacker) is located in an arm between the locks and the junction with the Canal du Nord which provides access to the Canal de la Somme and waterways of the North.

Several villages are of little interest to the pleasure boater until **Ribecourt-Dreslincourt** (K27), whose shops are within walking distance of a pair of road bridges. Écluse 3, Bellerive (K28.1) is passed a little upstream of **Béthancourt**. There are numerous facilities in the next pound, through **Thourotte** (K32) and **Longueil- Annel** (K33): they range from shops, restaurants and water point to a choice of three barge repair yards and a bankside fuelling depot, on the left side before Écluse 4, **Janville** (K33.9). Beyond, the navigation passes an island (downstream traffic takes the right channel) and from here onwards we are on the canalized Oise, with a reach of about 2km in use by boats above the junction.

Augmented by the waters of the River Aisne (left bank, K38), the Oise increases in size on its approach to **Compiègne**. The Aisne and its lateral canal provide a route via Soissons and the Canal des Ardennes to the Meuse. Even if your intended destination is the Seine, it is well worth turning up the Aisne for 5km and through one mechanized lock to moor at **Le Francport**, within 1km of one of the most historic sites of the 20th century. This is the *Clairière de l'Armistice* (Armistice Clearing), deep in the heart of the Compiègne Forest. Railway lines were laid here during World War I to enable massive guns to be brought under cover of the trees. By November 1918 Germany was facing defeat and representatives of the two sides came by train to this secret rendezvous to discuss terms of surrender. It may well be that the punitive reparations demanded of the enemy by Marshal Foch were in part responsible for the Second World War, but after four years of slaughter France was not feeling generous. So ended the Great War, and the Wagon-Lits dining car where the document was signed was later brought back to its forest lair for permanent exhibition by the landscaped clearing. With more than a sense of history, Hitler performed a reverse ceremony in the same coach in 1940, before it was moved in triumph to Berlin, where it was later destroyed by Allied raids. The Compiègne site was restored at the end of World War II and an identical carriage found, to be equipped in just the same manner as that used by Foch as his mobile office. In spite of frequent swarms of tiny school children far too young to understand what they have been brought to see, and a thriving souvenir shop, the monument with effigy of Foch and dead imperial eagle, symbolic of the vanquished Germany, is all strangely moving. If preferred, the *Clairière* may be reached by walking 6km from Compiègne.

The city stands on the banks of the Oise about 2km downstream of the Aisne. Ample moorings exist on quays among working *péniches* but a small *port de plaisance* close to the centre below a railway bridge appears not to welcome visiting boats. It is an impressive town, surprisingly intact considering the wartime punishment it received: the late 18th century bridge was destroyed in 1914, rebuilt in 1926,

Gothic magnificence in the Hôtel de Ville, *Compiègne*

demolished again in 1940 and re-erected in 1949! Its great treasure is the royal Palace, built on the site of a 14th century *château* by Louis XV and Louis XVI shortly before the Revolution. Third in national importance to Versailles and Fontainebleau, it was improved by Napoléon and enjoyed a glittering if brief period under Napoleon III and his Empress Eugénie in the years that led up to the German invasion of 1870. House parties known as the *Séries de Compiègne* were attended by all the leading personalities of literature, music, art and science. One was expected to arrive complete with personal servant and there are tales of less wealthy guests prevailing on their friends to act as *valets*. But these were far from stuffy occasions and

those present remarked on the informal atmosphere and efforts of their Imperial Highnesses to make their guests feel completely at ease. Open to the public through the year (except Tues and holidays), the Palace contains sumptuous furnishings and a road vehicle museum whose exhibits date back to the middle of the 18th century. There are two statues of Jeanne d'Arc, one by the bridge and another in the square at the magnificent Gothic *Hôtel de Ville*, erected by Louis XII at the start of the 16th century. Alongside, the fascinating Musée de la Figurine Historique contains no fewer than 85,000 model soldiers dressed in uniforms throughout the centuries. Many agreeable walks or cycle rides can be taken in the Forest, a district of hills and lakes with villages and leafy prospects. Stylish shops, numerous convenient restaurants, a main line

81

railway station within a stone's throw of the river and tripping boats (details from the local Syndicat d'Initiative) combine to make Compiègne the highlight of the Oise. Fuel is obtainable from a tanker barge a little upstream of Écluse 1, Venette (K41), where the left chamber, above a weir, is the one generally in use except during flood conditions.

Except for the intrusion of a railway line, the reach that follows is quiet and rural, with little to delay the boatman apart from a restaurant by the suspension bridge of **La Croix-St-Ouen** (K49). Having passed through Écluse 2 (K54, on the right of the lock island) we arrive in the small town of **Verberie** (K55) with quay moorings upstream of the bridge, on the left bank or (with permission) at the nearby water-ski club. Shopping is good on each side of the river and there is the impressive Château d'Aramont. Another rather featureless section leads under the A1 *autoroute* (K58.2) and on to Écluse 3, Sarron (K65, water point), a little upstream of **Pont St-Maxence**, a grimy industrial town producing paper, pottery and metalwork. The best place to lie is on a quay, left bank below the bridge, with shops and fuel stations not far. In such an unlikely setting I discovered a purveyor of *brocante* (collectable junk) who not only objected to his stock being examined but was charging laughably inflated prices. Patches of riverside industry alternate with open country through **Villers-St-Paul** and **Verneuil-en-Halatte** (K75) where there is a slipway by the bridge and food shops in the village (800m).

In spite of first impressions of heavy industry in the twin foundry towns of **Nogent-sur-Oise** and **Creil** (K79), there are several interesting features reached from quay moorings above and below the bridge spanning an island. St Medard's church (13–16th centuries), the Gallé-Juillet Museum with a collection of furniture and *faïence* and the 12–13th century church of Nogent are all worth visiting. There are streets of old houses and remains of ramparts with ample shops and restaurants. Water is available on the quay (opposite the long island, right bank). Écluse 4 is also on the right bank (K81), the alternative channel and former lock being disused.

Now come considerable tracts of heavy industry, railway sidings and a huge power station with four prominent chimneys. The area improves by an elegant suspension bridge at **St-Leu-d'Esserent** (K86), with moorings on a quay upstream of the bridge. All facilities are conveniently close as is the most impressive large church, built of local stone in the 12th century. Troglodyte houses are to be found in the district. 5.5km SE is the *château* and Forest of **Chantilly**, one of the country's leading racecourses and a great centre

for breeding horses. It is possible to mistake the magnificent stables at Chantilly for the *château* itself! Set amid lakes and formal gardens, the Palace occupies the site of a Middle Ages fortress and the present structure was planned between the 16th and 18th centuries. 9km further to the east is **Senlis**, whose history began under the Romans and is well worth an excursion: attractions include the cathedral, Musée de la Vénerie (devoted to hunting relics) and a *château* of the Merovingian and Carolingian kings, ruined since the Revolution.

Gravel pits on the right bank lead to the Pavillon St-Hubert restaurant in the left bank hamlet of **Toutevoie** (K88); there are convenient quay moorings. Next follows the small town of **Précy-sur-Oise** (K90) with suspension bridge and suitable points to tie up either on the quay under the bridge (shallow water: approach carefully) or on grassy banks. Shops, garage and restaurants are within a few hundred metres. **Boran-sur-Oise** (K94) is a noted riverside resort, beloved by speedboat enthusiasts. Below the bridge is an extensive swimming pool/*plage*, while yacht club jetties can doubtless be used by visiting craft. After rather bleak parts of the river this little town is really attractive: moreover, plenty of shops, restaurants and fuel station could result in a productive halt. 4.5km SE, the Abbey of **Royaumont** is open to the public every day in the summer except Tues. Founded by St Louis in the 13th century, it was sold into private ownership in 1791. Below Écluse 5, Boran (K95, water point), the channel divides, the left arm following the river's original course behind a large island to **Noisy-sur-Oise** (K99). Provided they adhere to a 5kph limit, pleasure boats may take this course to discover a *base nautique* and pontoons 600m from the heart of the pleasing stone-built village topped by an exquisite church commanding a wide view of the valley (café and grocer).

On each side of a road bridge, **Persan** is a slightly industrialized satellite of **Beaumont-sur-Oise** (K103). Moor judiciously under the right-hand arch for good shopping and eating (there is even a Chinese restaurant!). On top of old ramparts is a terrace looking down to the river and relics of a feudal *château*, demolished in the early 16th century. More gravel pits and a power station give way to wooded scenery past **Champagne-sur-Oise** (K106.2, poor moorings and almost too far to be of much interest). One-way traffic indicators send boats round each side of the Île de Champagne and ahead are seen the twin lock chambers of Écluse 6, **L'Isle-Adam** (K109, water point). To come ashore, pass **between** a pair of islands by the Cabouillet bridge crossing from Parmain to L'Isle-Adam (K110) and moor to a splendid floating pontoon on the left (water, electricity and rubbish disposal), directly outside a restaurant. The town centre, with all shops, is about 300m distant. Known as *Novigentum* in Roman times, L'Isle-Adam stands on the borders of Île de France and the Valois. It was invaded by Normans in the early 9th century and chosen for the site of a fortified castle by Louis the Pious in 825 (on the Île du Prieure). This was destroyed 61 years later and rebuilt by Robert the Pious in 1014. Adjacent forests covering almost 1,700 hectares were landscaped by Le Nôtre. Honoré de Balzac wrote: 'L'Isle-Adam is now paradise on Earth': it remains a delightful area with 14th century church and *Hôtel de Ville* of 1866 in the Renaissance style. The two swimming pools and riverside beach are claimed to be the largest inland *plage* in France. The complex was officially opened in 1949 by champion swimmer Johnny Weissmuller ('Tarzan').

Restaurant, garage, baker and slipway are found near a road and railway bridge at **Butry-sur-Oise** (K113). Downstream, the long village of **Auvers-sur-Oise** (K116) is scarcely visible from the river, being concealed by trees and a railway line. Mooring is possible near the slipway before reaching the head of the Île de Vaux. (Shops, garages, restaurants and station.) Passage through the bridges of Méry-Auvers and **Chaponval** (K119) is potentially dangerous if pushed barge convoys are approaching: consult diagrams in the *Carte Guide*. Auvers is associated with an important group of 19th century artists attracted by the quality of light on the waters of the Oise; among them were Daubigny, Corot, Cézanne, Pissarro, Gauguin and Daumier. Vincent Van Gogh, while receiving treatment for his mental problems, killed himself, dying in a room of the Café Ravoux (now known as *À Van Gogh*); both he and his grief-stricken brother Théo are buried in the cemetery and there is a monument in the Parc Van Gogh.

The river runs past sandy beaches to the ancient city of **Pontoise** (K123), site of a 10th century fortress and to which the *Parlement* was exiled in 1652, 1720 and 1753. Remains of fortification walls and narrow streets recall some of its historic past close to useful mooring quays (by the town bridge, alongside a swimming pool). All facilities are easily reached from here. Pontoise is expanding rapidly and has a huge new town, **Cergy-Ville-Nouvelle**, in a bend of the river below Écluse 7 (K124, water point). As the Oise begins to curve towards the west, above a railway bridge (K126), there is a *base nautique*, offering moorings, diesel fuel and craneage with restaurant.

We now travel along a giant loop past **Cergy** (K129). Extensive gravel workings have been landscaped as a magnificent water park (no direct access to

pleasure boats: approach by road from the Pont de Cergy) which features waterside walks, riding, sailing, windsurfing and swimming in a huge 'natural' sand-bordered pool. A combined housing/restaurant and mooring development with 150 boat spaces has been created at Cergy-Pontoise. In the remaining distance to the River Seine, **Neuville-sur-Oise** (K134) provides useful shops and there are excellent facilities of all kinds in the junction town and leading barge port of **Conflans-Ste-Honorine** (K138). Waterside fuel, water point and slipway are all located here. Moorings may be difficult to find, amid a veritable mass of freight vessels. (See Chapter 13).

18 · River Aisne and Canal Latéral à l'Aisne

Carte Guide: *Picardie*

The River Aisne is navigable from its junction with the River Oise at Choisy-au-Bac, near Compiègne to a junction with the Canal Latéral à l'Aisne at Condé-sur-Aisne, 57km with 7 locks. The Canal Latéral à l'Aisne continues the line eastwards from Condé-sur-Aisne to a junction with the Canal des Ardennes near Vieux-lès-Asfeld, 51.3km with 8 locks. Connections are made with the Canal de l'Oise à l'Aisne at Bourg-et-Comin and with the Canal de l'Aisne à la Marne at Berry-au-Bac.

The Aisne and its continuation eastwards via the lateral canal forms an important link between the Rivers Oise and Meuse, and consequently provides a connection between Paris and Belgium. With few locks, it offers relaxing cruising past woods and meadows, considerable cargo traffic being generated by gravel pits. Locks on the river section (46m × 7.95m) are rather larger than those of Freycinet proportions on the lateral canal; all are mechanized, with keepers in attendance.

By 1680 the Aisne was fit for boats between the Oise and Pontavert, about 34km beyond the point where the lateral canal now takes over. For more than a century, a scheme was current to create a canal link from Pontavert to the River Bar and so join up with the Meuse: in 1778 this plan was known as the Canal de Champagne. But when the Canal Latéral à l'Aisne became a reality in 1841 it comprised a longer length of artificial channel than once envisaged, much of the higher Aisne being abandoned by craft except for the floating of timber, an activity still practised until the 1930s. The eastern portion of the route, via the Canal des Ardennes, had been finished in 1833 and also consisted almost entirely of a man-made cut. Great quantities of German and Belgian coal were once carried by barge to Paris, but in more recent years commodities have included timber, sugar and sugar beet.

Flowing into the Oise a short distance upstream of Compiègne, the Aisne is agreeably rural, for it forms the northern boundary of the great Forest of Compiègne for a considerable distance. On arriving in **Choisy-au-Bac** (K2.5) the best moorings are to a quay (left bank, below the bridge). Heavy road traffic does not entirely spoil its countrified aspect and all kinds of shops, restaurants and garages are within close range. A short canal cut leads through Écluse 15, Carandeau (K3.3, water point) to the hamlet of **Le Francport** (K5.5) and the Auberge de l'Armistice. Taking care to avoid an underwater shelf beneath the bridge, moor to the right bank to visit the atmosphere-laden *Clairière de l'Armistice*, scene of the German surrender in 1918. It is a walk of about 1km, down a leafy road (see Chapter 17). Still on the edges of the Forest of Compiègne, **Rethondes** (K9) at the next bridge is an agreeable village of stone buildings with gardens tumbling down to the water's edge. It has a restaurant and baker, with mooring possibilities above or below the bridge on the right bank.

Écluse 14, Hérant (K10.4, water point) is followed by a pair of slightly industrial towns: **Breuil** on the right bank and **Berneuil-sur-Aisne**, left bank. Both provide a full range of facilities and can be reached from the **La Motte** bridge (K14.6). One curious architectural feature of this region is a pattern of stepped gable ends seen on many of the stone buildings, especially in **Attichy** (K17.7), after Écluse 13, **Couloisy** (water point). You may tie up to grassy banks near the green bowstring bridge and walk several hundred metres to the shops. Well worth exploring is **Vic-sur-Aisne** (K22.7), approached either from below Écluse 12 (water point) and across a pedestrian bridge over the weir stream, or from the road bridge (moor above, on the left). Near the *Hôtel de Ville* is a very fine moated *château*, with convenient shopping, restaurants and garage. From the river, dominated by huge concrete grain silos, Vic does not appear as the very attractive town it is. Moving upriver in wooded surroundings, the next place of note is **Port-Fontenoy** (K27.8) with a useful landing stage outside the Auberge du Bord de l'Eau. **Fontenoy** itself, about 2km east, can only be reached from here, although it lies but a short distance

from Écluse 11 (K29.8); however, in an emergency it might be useful for its bar, baker and butcher.

The sleepy village of **Osly-Coutil** (K31.3) on the left, downstream of a small island, has a bar, while **Pommiers** (K35.4), surrounded by gravel workings below a bridge, has a few shops and bar. Urban surroundings now start to close in on the river at the approach to the city of **Soissons** (K41.7), the other side of Écluse 10, **Vauxrot** (K40.2, water point and shopping). Soissons derives little aesthetic benefit from the Aisne, imprisoned in a canal-like concrete channel, and it must be admitted that it is not a specially beautiful place, having suffered the misfortunes of war much too frequently. Its history goes back to the days of Belgian Gaul and it was here that Clovis beat the Roman army in AD 486. Its greatest treasure is a 13th century cathedral of St Gervais and St Protais in the Gothic style with fragments of an 11th century abbey nearby, mostly demolished in 1805. Within the cathedral is a Rubens, painted by the artist for the monks in gratitude for the care he received while lying ill. A legend concerns the celebrated Vase of Soissons, one of a number of items plundered by the Franks from the Church. Newly converted to Christianity, the young Clovis sought to recover this treasure and return it to the rightful owner. Such actions did not meet with wholehearted approval from certain of Clovis' warrior followers, one of whom expressed his disgust by smashing the Vase with his sword. Annoyed as he was, Clovis awaited his opportunity to redress the balance: some years afterwards he came upon the same warrior in Paris, during an inspection of troops, and with a mighty stroke of his sword cut the man virtually in two, remarking: 'I do to you what you did to the Vase of Soissons!' The tale is known to every French schoolchild. Or should be....Some years ago an Inspector of Education was making a tour of Soissons: he singled out a boy sitting at the front of his class and asked him: 'Who broke the Vase of Soissons?' The child looked slightly frightened and replied: 'It wasn't me, Monsieur!' At which the teacher anxiously declared: 'Pierre is an honest pupil. If he says he did not break the vase, you may be sure he is telling the truth!' Horrified at this ignorance of history, the Inspector sent a full report on the affair to the Minister: in no time at all a substantial file had grown. Then, there was an election and a change of Government. A new Minister was appointed who determined to bring the Soissons case to a speedy conclusion. 'Does it really matter who broke this vase?' he questioned. 'I'll pay for a replacement out of my own pocket, and that will be an end to the matter!'

Pleasure boats may moor midway between the upper end of the Écluse 10 lock cut and the Pont du

Mail, with easy access to the main shopping street, restaurants and garages. It is even possible to dine aboard a converted *péniche*. The quays are generally busy with working boats. On the eastern outskirts, Écluse 9, **Villeneuve St-Germain** (K44.2, water point) bypasses the Aisne as it flows through **Crouy**. This weirstream is used by members of the local motorboat club, who have a slipway immediately downstream of the lock.

In the final upper reaches of the Aisne there are several small towns with useful facilities: **Venizel** (K49.3) with shops and restaurant near the bridge; **Missy-sur-Aisne** (K53.3) – moor with care near a bridge of two flat arches for basic shops; and **Condé-sur-Aisne** (K56.4), baker and bar. Ahead, the navigation divides: the left branch is all that remains navigable of the waterway that once enabled barges to reach Pontavert. It can be followed for 2km to **Vailly-sur-Aisne**. But there is little object in so doing, for the Canal latéral à l'Aisne, entered on the right, passes through a two-rise lock (Écluses 7/8, **Celles**, K57.2) and runs almost as close to Vailly-sur-Aisne (K60.5). Although marked 'Bar, Restaurant, Épicerie', a building near the locks is not obviously any of those: one lunchtime I watched a series of suited businessmen arrive, ring the doorbell for admittance, and retire within. It seemed that normal passing custom was not sought. Perhaps more in-depth research is called for! The business was advertised for sale in 1989. Right of the bridge at Vailly is a petrol station (no diesel) with bar/restaurant, while a short walk over the river bridge introduces civilization in the form of a large supermarket.

In many ways, it is rather a relief to have left the river with its shortage of safe moorings and to enter a canal that involves itself with towns and villages instead of keeping facilities at a safe distance from the prospect of flooding. For a spell, the canal is, however, as wide as many rivers and even has an official swimming pool. During my last visit the crews of moored *péniches* were happily cooling off, as a steel barge can be an oppressive home in a heatwave. As the waterway enters a long straight at Écluse 6, St-Audebert (K61.6, water point), a bar and bakery may be visited in the bankside hamlet of **Presles-et-Boves** (K63.1). **Cys-la-Commune** (K63.8) is a deeply rural hamlet by Écluse 5, with *café* and odd little asymmetric church in a farmyard. Signs that the canal has outlived a railway at **Pont d'Arcy** (K67.9) are evident from a disused station. A café, Au Petit Train, stands by the canal bridge, with À la Renaissance du Pays restaurant at the river bridge. Écluse 4, la Cendrière (K69.8), is immediately followed by a left-hand junction with the Canal de l'Oise à

l'Aisne and all facilities in **Bourg-et-Comin** (see Chapter 20).

The canal now enters a tract of gravel pits and swamps in the Aisne valley that is wild and by no means unattractive. Just after the second bridge from the junction, **Villiers-en-Prayères** (K69.1) is approached from the water across an extraordinary gravel square surrounded by great barns. Beyond is a small restaurant and grocer. Two succeeding villages offer various services: **Maizy** (K75.7), baker, grocer and restaurant – moor well beyond the bridge to a quay, right: a series of open-fronted half-timbered barns faces the canal, and **Pontavert** (K83.7), baker, grocer, restaurant and garage, all beyond the bridge spanning the once navigable Aisne. Écluse 3 (K89.9, water point) stands at the **Berry-au-Bac** junction with the Canal de l'Aisne à la Marne. It is a veritable boatman's town with *péniches* moored or negotiating the tight 90° turn between each waterway. Waterside diesel pumps supply commercial and pleasure craft alike and right alongside the Aisne à la Marne's top lock is a near-legendary canal shop supplying all needs from fresh fruit and vegetables to rope, oil, fishing tackle and rubber boots. Just like the general stores to be found in the more remote parts of Ireland, this establishment is also a bar. As the years pass, these fascinating shops sadly decrease in number, so all readers are urged to help in the survival of this example by taking on galley stores there. Or so I once thought; but on my most recent arrival, our reception and treatment was so surly that I was forced to conclude that pleasure boat custom was not required! Readers' comments would be welcomed. Nearly opposite, jetties are used by the Champagne Navigation hire cruiser company. Two possibilities for eating ashore present themselves. To the right of the N44 road bridge, La Cote 108 restaurant advertised a 'surprise' menu at 210 francs not including service or drinks! In the early 1980s, this represented a considerable investment and even now is not to be considered cheap for provincial France. With appetites sharpened after a long day's boating, we were informed by a haughty waiter that they were fully booked, a fact that was difficult to credit in view of the totally deserted dining room. This rebuff had fortunate consequences, for we soon discovered superb value and friendly service at the Restaurant de la Mairie in the village itself, with butcher and baker nearby. When I returned later in the summer, I presented myself without hesitation for a second helping of Madame's unpretentious cuisine.

Some mysterious variety of chemical works on the towpath marks the exit from Berry-au-Bac, followed by a wilderness of swamps and trees to **Condé-sur-**

Suippe (K94.5) and Écluse 2 (water point). The village has a restaurant and a weird openwork concrete spire. Away to the left, the Aisne has become a very pleasant stream and attracts many caravans, campers and anglers. Silos and a sugar works give a purposeful air to the small town of **Guignicourt** (K95.4), whose comprehensive shopping centre (with garage) lies immediately north of the river. Next comes the agricultural village of **Pignicourt** (K101.1), providing the Auberge de l'Étang restaurant and a water point at Écluse 1. 300–400m towards the Aisne shops, restaurant and garage will be found in **Neufchâtel-sur-Aisne** (K103). Neither **Brienne-sur-Aisne** or **Evergnicourt** are easily approached from the waterway and the final reach suffers from heavily overgrown banks making mooring difficult. The Canal Latéral à l'Aisne merges with the Canal des Ardennes at the next lock, Écluse de Vieux-lès-Asfeld (K108.3). For a continuation of the route towards the Meuse, see the Canal des Ardennes (next chapter).

19 · Canal des Ardennes

Carte Guide: *Champagne Ardenne*
From Vieux-lès-Asfeld, junction with the Canal Latéral à l'Aisne to a junction with the River Meuse (Canal de l'Est [Branche Nord]) at Pont-à-Bar, 88km with 44 locks. There is one tunnel, St-Aignan, 196m. A branch connects the main line at Semuy with Vouziers (terminus), 12.5km with 4 locks.

As part of a direct link between the Oise and the Meuse, the Canal des Ardennes is a continuation of the River Aisne and Canal Latéral à l'Aisne with no visible difference from one to the other. Something of a misnomer, it does not in fact pass through the Ardennes although it points in that general direction. From Vieux-lès-Asfeld it climbs up the Aisne valley, in effect a lateral canal to the river which follows the Vouziers branch from Semuy. No fewer than 27 locks in 9km then lift the waterway to its Le Chesne summit level and soon afterwards the route strikes up an acquaintance with the River Bar which is never far away until the Meuse. Pleasantly unremarkable at the western end to Attigny, the canal is thereafter remote and of great beauty, ending with rolling cornfields and forests towards Pont-à-Bar. Official km marks run from Vouziers to Vieux-lès-Asfeld and from Pont-à-Bar to Semuy. For simplicity, distances quoted below are continuous from one end of the main line to the other.

Traffic is moderately heavy, reaching about 2,000 craft a year. Locks operate to normal hours, with a half-hour midday break. All locks on the western portion are manual, with keepers, while the flight from Semuy to Le Chesne (Nos 26–1) form an automatic chain with radar beams or projecting poles to activate the mechanism.

Time and again waterways writers have commented on the very Englishness of the Canal des Ardennes, a conclusion with which it would be difficult to find fault.

Brief history There was a plan in the latter part of the 17th century to connect the Aisne and the Meuse, using in part the River Bar; but nothing was to be achieved until work began on the line in 1823, completion coming ten years later. One key to water supplies was creation of the Étangs de Bairon reservoir, whose 5 million m³ capacity was sufficient to maintain levels in the Le Chesne summit except in the driest of summers. Each of the seven locks nearest the Meuse were equipped between World Wars I and II with pumping stations and as a result the waterway is almost always able to cope with *péniches* carrying 250 tonnes. Its original depth of 1.3m was subsequently increased to 1.8m, and it is generally regarded by commercial users as a quicker and more convenient route than the Canal de la Marne au Rhin.

In the 1960s a scheme was advanced to enlarge and improve the Canal des Ardennes, replacing the 27-lock Montgon flight with an inclined plane overcoming the 75m change in levels in a single operation. The summit level so resulting would have been 30km in length and a new St-Aignan tunnel was to be followed by one deep lock falling to the same level as the Meuse. This idea appears to have been rejected and improvements made to date have been the automation of locks 1–26, all others on the waterway being manually operated.

The Canal Latéral à l'Aisne undergoes a metamorphosis into the Canal des Ardennes at a bridge by Écluse 14, **Vieux-lès-Asfeld** (K0). The village itself is a pleasant little place, reached from the following bridge, next to a grain silo (basic shops, restaurant and garage). **Asfeld** (K2.9) lies to the right of the next bridge and is notable for a remarkable late 17th century Baroque church of pinkish brick. The main part of the building is circular with a series of interconnected walkways and galleries; a brick colonnade, forming an extended porch, provides a link with the tower. This most unusual building can be seen to good advantage across a large grassy square, with terraces of little houses in matching brick. The town is at the heart of a flourishing agricultural region and is well served by shops, restaurants and fuel stations. Écluse 13, Asfeld (K4.6), is succeeded by a rural length leading to the English-sounding **Balham**, and **Blanzy-la-Sablonaise** (K9.5) with canalside restaurant and very limited shopping.

Never far from the River Aisne, the waterway continues to Écluse 12, **Pargny** (K12.5). A timber yard and silos by a bridge mark the approach, via a pair of river bridges, to the useful small town of **Château-Porcien**; it is an excellent shopping centre with the *Hôtel de Ville* standing at the base of a chalk cliff. Pleasing wooded scenery now accompanies the route through **Nanteuil-sur-Aisne**, Écluse 11 (K20.2) and Écluse 10 (K22.3). M. Beaudoux in the village of **Acy-Romance** will deliver diesel oil by tanker (but only in substantial quantities). Then comes the important town of **Rethel** (K24.4), north of the Aisne and the only opportunity for really comprehensive shopping on the entire waterway. There are remnants of a 10th century *château* and the imposing church of St Nicholas, comprising two naves side by side. One (12th–13th centuries) was for the use of Benedictine monks and the other (15–16th centuries) intended for people of the parish. Photographs show how extensive was the destruction in 1940, with windows wrecked and the lofty vaulted roof completely smashed. But apart from the modern design of the replacement stained glass, it is difficult to detect where the damage occurred. In the two world wars 85 per cent of Rethel was reduced to rubble and rebuilding has been to an unusually high standard. The river crossing has always been of strategic importance: a plaque on the town bridge records invasions in 1411, 1543, 1650, 1814, 1870, 1914 and 1940.

Note a water point by Écluse 9, **Biermes** (K27.5), some distance before the expanding but still predominantly rural village of **Thugny-Trugny** (K30.3, Écluse 8, bar, petrol pump). The road to **Roux** leads from the lock to a very tranquil tree-bordered reach of the Aisne whose deep and chalky waters are tempting for a swim on a hot summer's day. **Seuil**, near Écluse 7 (K33.9), offers nothing more than a bar/restaurant, with further limited facilities in **Givry** (K39.8, café/baker) and, having negotiated Écluse 6 (K40.8), **Attigny** (K43.1) where shops are found in the centre near a late 19th century bandstand with a restaurant close to the bridge. For fuel, cross the river into **Feubourg du Moulin**. This is virtually the last chance to buy food until Le Chesne, 28 locks, 16km and the best part of a day's journeying away. The canal now becomes

increasingly beautiful. Water supplies are at Écluse 5 (K44).

Beyond **Rilly-sur-Aisne** (K47.9) is a broad basin with an unusual arrangement of two locks side by side. On the left, Écluse 27 continues the through route towards the Meuse and lowers craft into a short navigable reach of the Aisne. Right of it, Écluse 4 provides access to the **Vouziers Branch**, fed by the very twisting river. A single lock house is responsible for both routes and has a good example of a tiny window providing the keeper with a view of approaching traffic. Boats wishing to navigate the branch may do so during normal lock opening hours except on Sundays and public holidays, although there is a possibility of obtaining special permission if you telephone in advance. Facilities in the junction area extend to a riverside restaurant, grocer, baker and water point (all in **Semuy**) and reached from the first bridge after the pair of locks (this applies equally to Vouziers and to Meuse-bound craft). The branch is countrified and remote with little traffic. Locks are encountered at **Voncq** (K4 from the junction), **Vrizy** (K7.3), and just below the head of navigation at **Vouziers** (K11.6). There are grocer and baker in Vrizy and all shops, restaurants and garage at Vouziers (K12.5), where the 16th century church of St-Maurille has an intricately carved triple portal. The town developed into a leading commercial centre when in 1516 François I awarded it a charter for a fair.

Heavy concentrations of locks are moderately rare in France, waterways having normally been engineered to avoid long flights. The eastern ascent to the summit of the Canal des Ardennes is a memorable exception, with all 26 in the series now remotely controlled with radar beams and bars that are physically activated as craft enter or leave chambers. Manned control points are established at Écluse 26, Semuy (K49.5) and Écluse 1, Le Chesne (K57.9). Needless to add, this is hilly country, providing splendid views over fields and woods. Once launched into such an automatic flight, I have doubts about the advisability of stopping for anything unless you are caught at the moment when the power is turned off for the night. But in **Neuville-Day** by Écluse 20 (K52.6) there is a water point if you dare linger long enough to take advantage of it and run the risk of delaying another boat or upsetting the control mechanism. A quick visit to the café/baker is best achieved by a spare crew member despatched by bicycle or on foot. Whether the bridge in **Montgon**, below Écluse 14 (K54.9), is slightly lower than most, I am not certain: but I well remember some worrying moments for an unladen *péniche* as it scraped through with barely the clearance of a matchbox – and that was with wheelhouse dismantled! Respite arrives at Écluse 1, water point, shortly before the highly convenient summit level town of **Le Chesne** (K59.6). Mooring on the right in a small basin by the Pont X, shops, restaurants and garage are within a stone's throw. In hot weather a pleasant excursion might be made from here to the canal's reservoir le Lac de Bairon, a magnificent sheet of water 3km north. Such artificial lakes are often admirably managed in France for leisure use: Bairon is no exception and caters for fishing, bird-watching, sailing, windsurfing and swimming with diving pool and sandy beach.

Now dropping down the valley of the River Bar, we meet the first descending lock, Écluse 1, near **Sauville** (K67.4). Already, scenery is not unlike that of the Meuse, with meadows and patches of woodland. Within a short walk of Écluse 2 (K71.1), where there is a massive concrete blockhouse from World War II, the village of **La Cassine** has an appealing little church beyond a *château* (but no facilities). After a sharp bend to the right, moor by a bridge to visit a splendid village of stone houses and imposing church: this is **Ven-**

With wheelhouse dismantled to clear low bridges, this unladen péniche *is expertly handled by a young couple in the thick of the Montgon locks.*

dresse, where farm buildings are huddled together for protection from invaders. Shops, garage and restaurant (about 2.5km). Écluse 3, **Malmy** (K75.9) marks the beginning of dense woodland, the likely haunt of *sangliers* (wild boar). As the River Bar encircles a further tract of forest, the canal dives into St-Aignan Tunnel (K81.7), 196m long. It operates on a one-way basis and boats should take care not to enter unless the route is clear. Écluses 4 and 5 are situated immediately afterwards, divided by a blind right-angled turn.

Arguably the prettiest village on the waterway is **Hannogne-St-Martin** (K85) whose brown stone church was remodelled in the 18th century with a dome covered in shaped slates like fish scales. We have now moved from a region of tiles to the slateland of the Meuse valley, although more recent buildings do not always respect such local traditions. Several food shops make this a useful stop. Fully in keeping with waterways convention, the junction village of **Pont-à-Bar** (K87.1) is tiny, having nothing of interest to the general public except a bar alongside Écluse 6. Here, note the outside skittles enclosure, with chute for the return of balls. The heart of every boater will, however, be gladdened at the sight of a comprehensive range of boat facilities, including waterside diesel pump, commercial dock, water point and a chandler who adds such necessities as *Carte Guides*, bottled gas and rope to his stock of *péniche* requisites. Our journey ends at Écluse 7 (K88), connecting canal with the River Meuse between Sedan and Charleville-Mézières.

20 · Canal de l'Oise à l'Aisne

Carte Guide: *Picardie*

From a junction with the Canal Latéral à l'Aisne at Bourg-et-Comin to a junction with the Canal Latéral à l'Oise at Abbécourt, 47.8km with 13 locks. Much of the summit level is within the Braye Tunnel, 2,365m.

Remarkably similar to the nearby Canal de l'Aisne à la Marne in terms of age, length, purpose and layout, the Canal de l'Oise à l'Aisne likewise climbs to a summit level on its journey between the two rivers and crosses the watershed via a substantial tunnel. With regard to scenery, the Oise à l'Aisne is infinitely more beautiful, passing through deeply rural countryside throughout and hardly touching a village, let alone a town. At its best in early summer when the banks are ablaze with wild flowers, it may well qualify as the most endearing waterway in northern France.

A glance at the map indicates that the canal is a useful connecting link. Commercial traffic is consequently heavy, amounting to 7,000 or 8,000 boats a year or upwards of 25 boats each day in summer. All locks are mechanized, Nos 10–13 working as an automatic set in conjunction with Braye Tunnel.

Completed as recently as 1890, the canal suffered serious damage during World War I and was not returned to service until complete reconstruction was finished in 1931. Up to 1914, freight had included 2 million tonnes of coal alone, so the required detour of 55km enforced during the long closure was regarded seriously. Water supplies were improved as part of the rebuilding programme. Electric bank traction and an electrically driven towing device suspended from the tunnel roof have now been abandoned, all craft being self-propelled.

Leaving the Canal Latéral à l'Aisne, we enter the Oise à l'Aisne which crosses the River Aisne by means of a small aqueduct, with approach to the village of **Bourg-et-Comin** from a bridge immediately beforehand (K0.3). Here are basic food shops, restaurant and garage. A long straight leads to the first of four locks on the ascent to the summit level, Écluse 13, **Verneuil** (K2.9). All work as an automated series: for operating instructions, consult the *Carte Guide*. Surroundings are hilly with cornfields – on a summer day the epitome of everything you seek in waterway travel. By Écluse 12, **Moussey-Soupir** (K3.8) is a useful grocer/bar. Two further locks lead to a deep cutting and the impressive Tête Aisne portal of **Braye-en-Laonnois** tunnel (K7.1), illuminated inside and out. Entry is controlled by lights with a waiting time up to 1hr. Totally rebuilt in concrete in recent years, the tunnel mouth is equipped with a large circular extraction fan, similar to the engine on a jet aeroplane. A lane to the right provides an approach into Braye village, a lost little farming settlement in a hollow with a succession of cast-iron street pumps (no shops). Beyond the tunnel's far end, known as the Tête Oise, the first bridge leads, right, into a charming small town called **Chevregny** (about 3km). In spite of evidence of former commercial activity, the only remaining shops are a café and baker. There is, however, one compelling reason to pay a visit: a small Departmental Museum of Elementary Education, set up in an old school. Exhibits mainly date from the early 1900s and provide a fascinating insight into that regimented system of learning processes where endless repetition was once intended to produce proficiency. Two examples of pedagogical propaganda that caught my eye were line after line of childish copperplate proclaiming '*L'Ivrogne boit le sang de ses enfants*' (A drunkard drinks his children's blood) – presumably part of a 'project' on alcoholism; and '*Je ris. Je sais lire. Je suis content!*' (I laugh. I can read. I am happy!) Three tramway cars await restoration in a barn alongside and the ancient hand-operated local fire engine is given pride of place in a gravel courtyard. The museum opens on Sundays only.

If waiting overnight for the tunnel on a southward bound journey, stop at Écluse 9, **Pargny-Filain** (K12.7) – but do warn the keeper of your intentions, otherwise the traffic control sequences for the tunnel and locks 10–13 may be reduced to a state of confusion. In addition to bar, grocer, baker, restaurant and water point, the Lac de Monampteuil reservoir adjacent to the waterway has been admirably adapted for various forms of water sport with swimming from a *plage*.

Écluse 9 is the first of the descending locks. The majority have water points. On arrival at a quay with grain silo by Écluse 8, **Chavignon** (K14.1), a bar will be found left of the busy N2 road crossing, with a garage about 1km to the right. A similar distance in the opposite direction brings you to shopping and restaurant in Chavignon village, which can also be reached (3km) from Écluse 7, **Chaillevois** (K16.7). Now comes a long, shaded pound through the Forêt de Pinon to Écluse 6, **Pinon** (K21.7). Stop by the first *road* bridge afterwards to visit the good shopping centre of **Anizy-le-Château** (K22.3) with a garage nearby in the Pinon direction. Further dense woodland with a great feeling of remoteness lines the canal past Écluse 5, **Vauxaillon** (K25.7) and Écluse 4, **Leuilly** (K30.6). Note a bar and garage by the N37 (or D1) road crossing between the waterway and the hamlet of **Béthancourt** (K31.8). A Oise tributary, the Ailette, is never far away to the right for the remainder of the journey.

Écluse 3, **Crécy-au-Mont** (K33.5), is the closest approach to **Coucy-le-Château**, about 3km north, a splendidly defended town within a ring of 28 towers until it was disastrously bombarded in 1917. But enough remains of the *château* to make a visit worthwhile (open May–Sept 9.00–12.00h and 14.00–18.00h, shorter hours in winter; closed on Tues). There is an interesting local history museum in the Porte de Soissons. Another tourist attraction is the exceptionally beautiful small stone church in **Pont St-Mard**, 1.2km south of the bridge before Écluse 2, **Guny** (K36.4). Guny itself, left of the canal, has a café, grocer, butcher and baker.

The final pound runs through the **Arblincourt** woods and past **Bichancourt** (K45.7), close to which is a poignant reminder of the troubled recent past. Six poplars surround a memorial stone in the windswept cornfields with an inscription recalling the secret parachute drops made possible by *Résistance* worker Ernest Pruvost and the people of Marizelle-Bichancourt in the summer of 1943. There is a bar and grocer near a concrete canal bridge, shortly followed by an aqueduct spanning the Oise. Ahead of a basin is the last lock, Écluse 1, **Abbécourt** (K47.6) and a T-junction with the Canal Latéral à l'Oise (see Chapter 17).

21 · Canal de l'Aisne à la Marne

Carte Guide: *Champagne Ardenne*
From a junction with the Canal Latéral à la Marne at Condé-sur-Marne to a junction with the Canal Latéral à l'Aisne at Berry-au-Bac, 58.1km with 24 locks. There is one tunnel at Billy-le-Grand, 2,302m long.

Climbing up to the Billy-le-Grand summit level from the Marne valley and dropping northwards to the valley of the Aisne, this link is a useful connection via the city of Reims. Banks are of concrete virtually throughout and although largely rural and pleasant, it can scarcely be described as a beautiful navigation. The most appealing part is the southern ascent, through a rolling terrain with horizon-reaching views. Being heavily used by *péniches* (especially from Reims to the Aisne), all locks are mechanized, the majority grouped in automatic radar-controlled batches. The northern section passes between 8,000 and 9,000 craft each year (averaging 25 to 30 daily), while the length from Condé-sur-Marne is used by 5,000 to 6,000 craft (averaging 15 to 20 daily). A half-hour lock closure for lunch takes place at 12.00–13.00h depending on traffic. Because of water leakages, it is forbidden to moor in the section from Écluse 24, Condé-sur-Marne, to Écluse 17, Vaudemange, when the canal is closed on public holidays: $3\frac{1}{2}$hr must be reserved for negotiating this flight to avoid becoming 'trapped'.

Opened to boats in 1866, the canal soon became very busy. After World War I electrical traction speeded up traffic considerably and water transport played an important part in revitalizing the seriously damaged industries of Reims. Freight includes sand and potash for the Reims glassworks and supplies for the numerous bankside sugar refineries. There are important commercial docks in Reims. Most recent modernization increases the flow of boats through the locks and the Billy tunnel.

Although equipped with all basic facilities, water point and garage, **Condé-sur-Marne** is a featureless little town. Here the first of eight locks in an automatic series introduces an agreeable climb through isolated woods and cornfields towards the summit level. Most road bridges are of utilitarian steel girders. **Isse** at Écluse 22 (K3.5) is devoid of shops, with an equal lack in **Vaudemanges** some distance west of Écluse 17 (K6.6). A shallow cutting leads to the portal of **Billy-le-Grand** tunnel (K9.3) which operates on a one-way system controlled by lights. A keeper is installed in a modern concrete cabin over the vault: his life seems an

enviable one, watching craft movements on closed-circuit television and exercising his angling skills in the periods between telephone calls. Further lights and an internal telephone system are installed at the far end. This would be an ideal lunchtime or overnight halt with a visit to the Auberge de la Voûte restaurant in the woods (north end of the tunnel), were it not for the difficulties of mooring in the cutting. You might try obtaining permission from the keeper, taking notice of the information he has about on-coming boats.

From here to Reims we share a valley with the River Vesle, a stream that eventually joins the Aisne above Soissons. To the right of the second bridge after the tunnel, the village of **Sept-Saulx** (K14.8) is one of numerous places in the vicinity where champagne is produced. In addition to a barge port (water point),

Catering for the boat families, this general shop sells everything and is at Berry-au-Bac, junction with the Canal Latéral à l'Aisne.

there are good shopping facilities and the Cheval Blanc hotel/restaurant with mini-golf and tennis. Still on the summit pound, **Courmelois** (K17.5, right bank) is a pleasant but expanding village with grocer and bar, and a prominent silo served by *péniches*. The first of the descending locks is Écluse 16, Wez (K18.5), soon followed by **Beaumont-sur-Vesle** (K19.7) at Écluse 15. Within 200m of the large basin are plenty of shops, restaurant and garage. After Écluse 14, l'Espérence (K22.5, large war cemetery), **Sillery** (K24.1) offers good shops and a garage with water at Écluse 13. Beyond, to the right of the canal by the N44 highway, the Fort de la Pompelle is on view as a museum of World War I relics. Constructed in 1880, it safeguarded one approach to Reims and played a decisive part in the two Allied victories on the Marne. It is open throughout the year (8.00–19.00h summer, 10.00–18.00h winter).

Outer suburbs of **Reims** make their presence felt after **Taissy** (grocer and baker with a restaurant near the bridge of St-Léonard, K28.6). From the waterway the city is no beauty, as it is virtually bisected by the A4 *autoroute* and other high-speed roads and encircled by industrial sprawl. A series of three automated locks (Écluse 12, Huon, water; 11, Château d'Eau and 10 Fléchambault, water) lead to pleasure craft moorings near the centre (water, electricity), but the area is unpleasantly noisy. If you can overcome initial unfavourable impressions, Reims will be found to be a place of great interest, notwithstanding the fact that 80 per cent was destroyed during World War I. Founded by a Gaulish tribe, it became the provincial capital Durocortorum under the Romans. The cathedral of Notre-Dame, begun in the early 13th century, is among the finest churches in Western Europe. Exten-

sive restoration was required after the 1914–18 bombardments. Other attractions are a selection of museums, beautifully landscaped city centre and several champagne houses, each with cellars extending for as much as 18km. Full details of visits will be supplied by the Syndicat d'Initiative. Needless to add, shopping and eating facilities are comprehensive. Quays are busy with empty barges, while cargoes are handled in a big basin, the Port Colbert (K37.7) to the NW. Bulk supplies of diesel fuel may be obtained here from M. Lecomte, chandlery.

Many French cities display great charm, especially viewed from the deck of a boat. But Reims is characteristic of a modern and less appealing aspect of the country: the kind of place you are frankly pleased to leave. All shopping requisites will be found either side of the bridge in **La Neuvillette** (K40.5) (including a vast supermarket). I once had occasion to use the skill of Michel Gavatz, whose Electric Service 51 caters for freight *péniches* as well as pleasure craft. He can be contacted at 67 Route National, La Neuvillette, tel. (26) 09.62.58 or on VHF radio channel 13. The final run to the Canal Latéral à l'Aisne is a little dull, with shops and restaurant in **Courcy** (K45.6) and then another series of automated locks, Écluses 9–6 spread through 3km. Garage and restaurant are close to Écluse 7, Fontaines (K48); while No. 6, **Loivre** (K48.7), is within easy reach of basic shops and restaurant (water point).

A huge military cemetery is a prominent feature of the pleasant countryside around the last five locks (automatic sequence) leading to **Berry-au-Bac** junction (K58.1). This lively canal settlement has all boaters' needs, including waterside fuel and a notable *batelier*'s general shop (see Chapter 18).

III·FRANCHE COMTÉ, ALSACE, LORRAINE AND THE ARDENNES

22 · Canal de l'Est (Branche Sud)

Carte Guide: *La Meuse et le Canal de l'Est de Liège à Corre*

From a junction with the canalized River Moselle at Messein, near Neuves-Maisons to a junction with the River Saône at Corre. 121.5km with 93 locks. Junctions are made at Méréville with the Nancy Branch leading to the Canal de la Marne au Rhin at Laneuveville-devant-Nancy (10.2km with 18 locks); and at Golbey with the Épinal Branch, which runs to a terminus in Épinal (3.4km, lockfree).

Sometimes treated as a continuation of the River Meuse and Canal de l'Est (Branche Nord), this waterway has in fact always connected with its northern section by a shared length of the Canal de la Marne au Rhin between Troussey and Toul (see Chapter 27). 25.3km of the Branche Sud's course from Toul to Messein were originally laid out using the River Moselle. But following the canalization of the Moselle to Grade IV standards, completed in 1978, the old Branche Sud works have been replaced and navigation now follows the Moselle Waterway (see Chapter 29).

Rather heavily locked, the Branche Sud climbs up the Moselle valley to a summit level near Épinal, 360.6m above sea level. It then seeks out the River Coney which remains close by until the Saône is reached at Corre. Almost from end to end the canal passes through thickly wooded surroundings of considerable beauty. Several peculiarities of this route should be noted: owners of deep-drafted craft or large vessels such as converted *péniches* will find that there are somewhat shallow sections with a stony bottom and sides. In places, two substantial boats may have difficulty in passing. In recent years, locks have been closed to all traffic on Sundays, giving keepers one day's rest followed by a Monday of traffic jams! It would be wise to check the current position in case changes have been instituted. A speed limit of 6kph (8kph for pleasure craft under 20 tonnes) is strictly enforced throughout the canal with travelling times between the locks carefully noted and compared by telephone. Transgressors are subjected to payment of savage fines! Mobile lock keepers are employed for passage of most locks between Charmes and Corre. Advance instructions are issued before arrival in this section and pleasure boats are grouped together where possible. Elsewhere, a high proportion of the keepers are former boat people. Many locks are equipped with rubbish disposal facilities and drinking water points. Repeatedly, you will notice small open barges with upswept bows: these are ice-breakers.

With few exceptions, French inland waterways seldom provide opportunities for short circular cruises. However, an agreeable circuit demanding perhaps two days of boating may be tackled by navigating the Nancy Branch, (see above) a part of the Canal de la Marne au Rhin and the uppermost reaches of the River Moselle.

Brief history The Roman general Lucius Vetus is said to have made tentative plans to link the Moselle with the Saône along a line similar to that occupied by the present waterway. It is difficult to understand how this might have been achieved at a period many centuries before invention of the pound lock. Towards the end of the Middle Ages the Moselle was certainly used by horse-drawn barges in the Épinal area, and it appears that some form of connection existed between there and the Rhine. During the latter part of the 18th century, a M. de la Galaizière made attempts to join the Moselle and Saône, with the support of the ex-Polish King Stanislas of Nancy. But the loss of German Lorraine to the Prussians after the French defeat of 1870 was to be the incentive for building the Branche Sud, so avoiding passage through hostile territory. Works commenced in 1874 and were finished by 1882. By 1936 annual freight tonnages were not far short of 3 million; this had been reduced to about 400,000 tonnes in the mid-1960s. Towing of unpowered barges by rubber-tyred bank tractors ceased in the early 1960s.

At some stage in the future, according to the Fifth Plan, a new 1,350 tonne barge route is scheduled to replace the Branche Sud (see Chapter 29). If carried out, this will follow the same route from Neuves-Maisons to Charmes and then diverge to the west through Mirecourt before reaching the Saône at Corre. The present course of the Branche Sud will then be taken out of service, except for the portion from Charmes to Épinal, remaining as a *péniche*-sized branch.

After the massive new basin of the Moselle Waterway and its **Neuves-Maisons** steel works at **Messein** – basic shopping, restaurant and garage with waterside diesel (see Chapter 29) – the surviving section of the

Branche Sud begins at Écluse 47. Écluse 46, **Mereville** did no function on Mondays at the time of writing (but check the latest position). Here, the Nancy Branch enters on the left, with a flight of five locks leading up to a 2.7km summit level, the Bief de Partage du Mauvais Lieu, a narrow and rock-lined cutting. Surroundings are moderately rural but ill-kempt, with many of the lock houses now deserted. Two teams of mobile keepers work craft through making use of a well-maintained towpath. Descending locks 1–10 are arranged in a flight 1.9km long. Écluse 11 is situated on its own, followed in due course by the last pair of very deep chambers at the Canal de la Marne au Rhin junction in **Laneuveville-devant-Nancy** (see Chapter 27).

Spanning the un-navigable River Moselle: an impressive aqueduct near Flavigny.

Southwards, the continuation of the main line is past the village of **Richardménil** (K3.5), with the gardens of small houses backing onto the water. Always close at hand between here and Épinal, the shallow course of the Moselle is a profitable source of gravel, with cranes excavating its bed. Plastic storks in lock gardens are a reminder that Alsace lies to the east: the bird is prized as a symbol of fortune and fertility. The N57 road is close to the canal for a long distance: while its intrusion may be regretted, it does encourage facilities such as restaurants and garages. Quietest overnight moorings are often to be found close to locks, where the highway briefly swings away from the waterway. Écluses 45 and 44 are encountered at **Flavigny-sur-Moselle** (K5.7), with a good range of shops and restaurants on the far side of the river. During one passage of Écluse 43 (K7.9) the keeper was attacking a wasps' nest with an aerosol of poison and the air was filled with angry insects. As soon as it was humanly possible, we launched into the impressive 125m aqueduct which spans the Moselle, while an unladen *péniche* hovered at the far end. Shortly before the next bridge is a café/restaurant, left bank; very popular with lorry drivers, a sure sign in France that the food is good.

Progressively, the canal becomes more and more pleasant, with dense shade at the Forêt de Benney at the approach to Écluse 42 (K13.2). **Crevechamps** (K15) has a restaurant by Écluse 41. When you sound the horn, a keeper will pull aside a curious floating bridge set on oil drums at **Neuviller-sur-Moselle** (K18), near Écluse 40. In addition to a church with witch hat spire, a 19th century *château* rises from a lovely complex of ancient fortified farm buildings. If you moor by Écluse 39 (K20.9), all facilities will be found in **Bayon**, about 2km east beyond the river. Alternatively grocer, baker, restaurant and service station are close to the next lock, Écluse 38 in **Roville-devant-Bayon** (K22). Rocky castle remains appear at Écluse 36, **Bainville-aux-Miroirs** (K25.2), where shopping includes a grocer and baker with restaurant and garage: on the river is a charming little bathing *plage* with a sandy bottom. Tall wooded cliffs characterize the next pound to Écluse 35, **Gripport** (K27.7), which has a grocer.

Locks 34–31 lead to **Charmes** (K35.7). Drinking water will be found about 500m downstream of Écluse 31, with most other facilities in this small but rather dull little town; deep quayside moorings are near the bridge. Several times destroyed, most recently by the retreating German army in 1944, Charmes has been extensively rebuilt. The most notable building is its modern *Hôtel de Ville* with roof of multi-coloured glazed Burgundian tiles, water and electricity.

After the village of **Vincey** (K38.5, grocer) give a prolonged blast on the horn as a warning to any traffic that may be approaching round the sharp bend above Écluse 28, **Portieux** (K39.7). A small aqueduct only 6m wide immediately follows Écluse 26, L'Avière (K43.5). To the left lies **Châtel-sur-Moselle**, a small town of red tiled and slated roofs, while **Nomexy** is rather closer on the right with a good mooring just before Écluse 24, La Héronnière (K46.3), suitable for a shopping expedition. Some locks will long remain in the memory; one such is Écluse 22, **Igney** (K48.9). At the time of writing, this is the home of a boatman and his family who retired from their *péniche* ten years ago. For the first time in their lives they have a garden to cultivate and it is filled with a riotous collection of freight craft memorabilia, ranging from flags flying from a mast to pockets of flowers created from discarded nylons, painted barge signal beacons made from portions of washing liquid containers, and naïve boating scenes on wood surrounded by lucky horseshoes. Some were advertised for sale and we were quite unable to resist the temptation to buy. Grocer and chemist are in the village.

Thaon-les-Vosges (K51.4) can be reached from either Écluse 20 or 19; it is slightly industrial but has most shops (800m), with a garage and bankside diesel by the road at Écluse 19. Locks become more frequent towards the summit, especially after No. 15, Côte Olie (K57.3, drinking water and motel/restaurant) where the 3.4km Épinal Branch forks off on the left, shortly to cross the Moselle via a substantial aqueduct. Between here and **Épinal** is a level run by the side of the river, terminating in a drab basin quite close to the city centre. As this is the only sizeable city between Nancy and Chalon-sur-Saône the detour can be recommended; Épinal was founded on the cotton industry. On Maundy Thursday an old tradition, the Fête des Champs-Golots, marks the end of winter. Gutters of the Rue de Général Leclerc and adjoining streets are filled with water along which the children pull illuminated toy boats. Soon afterwards the surrounding woods are ablaze with thousands of wild daffodils. Among the interesting buildings is the Basilica of St Maurice, parts of which date from the 11th century. Many fascinating hours could be spent in the Musée Départemental des Vosges et Musée International de l'Imagerie, situated on the head of an island in the river a short distance upstream of the limit of navigation. Displays range from an outstanding collection of paintings from all parts of Europe to local history and folklore. In France, publication of colourful story books in cartoon form has long been established: many are designed and printed in Épinal.

Lock garden, pénichier *style.* Écluse d'Igney.

Back on the main line, 14 closely spaced locks in slightly squalid scenery lift the canal to its summit at **Pont du Bois l'Abbé** (K60.5). Collectively known as the Montée de Golbey, each is separated by a short broad pound, designed to conserve water supplies. If working astern of another craft, it is best to stay at least one lock away to avoid problems associated with temporary lowering of levels. A café is situated at Écluse 10. Even the most ardent canal devotee is likely to welcome the respite of 10.9km along the winding summit level to the north of a large canal reservoir (de Bouzey). After small villages at **Les Forges** (K63.3) and **Sanchey** (K65.3), we arrive at a most agreeable little place called **Chaumousey** (K67.8), lying well below the level of the embanked waterway. Five tunnels for pedestrians and vehicles pierce the canal at intervals, and provided other traffic can see you a moderate distance away there are good towpath moorings close to the church (its over-zealous clock strikes each hour *twice*). Facilities are unfortunately few, amounting to a very good grocer, baker and restaurant. Another mooring possibility is at the far (western) end of a basin (beware of silting elsewhere) on the side of Chaumousey nearer the Saône descent. The southern section of the summit enters a cutting lined with stone blocks and with little room for two *péniches* to pass.

Between here and the Saône is an almost endless chain of locks, never more than 4km apart and often much closer. The first 13 are worked by a mobile keeper who drives ahead of the boat (fortunately the towpath is maintained in excellent condition). Arrangements for booking his services change from time to time: a schedule of current regulations is supplied to each boat about one day's travelling time from the locks in question. No payment is demanded although it would be a nice gesture to invite the keeper to share your lunch, and cold drinks from time to time will be welcome! Earning on an hourly basis, these peripatetic lockmen can expect to accumulate a better weekly wage than workers based at a single location; those in the latter category earn the same money for passing three boats a day as they would for twenty. Ours was named Étienne, and after enduring our far-from-fluent French for some hours was able to summon up sufficient tact and civility to claim that we spoke the language better than he did! One great disadvantage of the system, however, is that there is almost no opportunity to stop the boat for more than a few minutes: any required shopping must be undertaken by a crew member released from locking duties on foot or bicycle. Should a prolonged halt be imperative, you will not unreasonably be requested to wait there until the following day.

These thirteen locks drop the canal from Écluse 1 (K71.3, grocer, chemist, café and garage) to **Thié-louze** (K79), Nos 5–11 being known as the Descente du Void de Girancourt. Impressive farm buildings at Écluse 5 are based on the walls of an old *château*. Surroundings are exceptionally agreeable near **Méloménil** (K80.8), where there is a restaurant. During the height of the pleasure boating season many of the locks from No. 14 to the Saône are manned by students, who are well compensated for their agreeable task in the sunshine. This arrangement enables regular keepers to take a holiday and overcomes delays that would otherwise be caused where more than one lock is normally in the charge of just one man. A butcher and café will be found near the large basin at Écluse 18, Uzemain (K82.8). An association is struck up with the little River Coney near Écluse 20; it is a delightful stream of sparkling weirs and mill houses among trees that stays with the canal all the way to the Saône. Pretty lock houses punctuate the journey through pine woods and on to a swing bridge by a factory in **La Grande Fosse** (K87.3) between Écluses 23 (restaurant) and 24 (Restaurant Au Saut du Truite). From here a bicycle pilgrimage can be staged to visit the Source of the Saône at **Vioménil** 9km NW along the D44 and D40 through **Thunimont**, **Harsault** and **La Haye**. Close to this point is the Caveau des Fées, rising place of a Moselle tributary the Madon. Waters run in one direction to the North Sea and in the other to the Mediterranean.

Moving onwards through Écluses 25–28 we arrive at Écluse 29, Pont du Coney (K93.7); a locally renowned beauty spot, it has a restaurant, hôtel and group of holiday apartments. 4km east is the spa town of **Bains-les-Bains**, a mid-19th century settlement whose waters range in temperature from 31° to 53°C and are used in the treatment of heart ailments and circulation problems. Further locks, among them the curiously named Écluse 31, Manufacture de Bains (K95.4), lead to a stone-lined cutting with blind corners shortly before **Fontenoy-le-Château** (K99.9), shops and congenial restaurant. This fascinating and ancient place makes an excellent overnight halt, whether you are running north or south. An important fortified town between the 13th and 17th centuries, it declined after an attack by French and Swedish troops in 1635. As it is perhaps the most pleasant town on the entire Branche Sud, there is every reason to explore thoroughly. Recent developments include moorings for craft in transit (water, electricity, showers), a base

M. Pérochon, the canalside baker of Fontenoy-le-Château.

for Blue Line Cruisers and passenger vessel 'relay' stage. You can scramble up a low cliff by the towpath to arrive among vegetable gardens with a bird's eye view of the canal as it passes through Écluse 35 and onwards through the town centre in a narrow depression. The Coney and other streams trickle past old water mills, one with an ancient round tower. Shops are scattered rather than being gathered in one place, some businesses having the appearance of closing their doors to the public at some point prior to World War I. Among a pretty row of cottages flanking the canal is the baker's shop of René Pérochon who will apologize for having no fresh bread until 9.00 am on account of his wood-fired ovens being a little slow. He is quick to assure one that their product is greatly superior and takes little persuasion to let you follow him to the back where logs are piled alongside an object like a giant sized cast-iron kitchen range. Long may this remarkable relic survive in use! I learned from Madame Pérochon that until recent times 'the biggest man in the world lived here, selling postcards. He weighed more than 300kg'. (On checking the accuracy of the claim with Norris McWhirter of the *Guinness Book of Records*, he told me that they generally bothered to list only people in *excess* of 300kg. The giant of Fontenoy was not among them.) In the main street near the Post Office is a well known Museum of Embroidery, and above rooftop level the very fragmented remains of a *château*, now partly used as a graveyard.

The remaining part of the journey is through first-rate scenery, rocky cliffs rising from the Coney with numerous watermills and weirs. Beyond Écluse 37, Gros-Moulin, the splendid Château de Freland hides behind monumental railings and alongside is a disused swing bridge. Take care at an extremely sharp bend in the canal between Écluses 36 and 37. Supermarket, garage and restaurant are within easy reach in **Selles** (K110.8), access to this red-tiled Burgundian village being from the swing bridge (see also Chapter 47), while a pleasant woodland mooring is found with a restaurant at Écluse 42, Village de Selles (K112.7). Nearing the Saône, the woodland that accompanies the canal for most of its course finally gives way to open meadows supporting a rich flora, with carpets of autumn crocus in early September. 3km NW of the bridge at **La Basse Vaivre** (K114.3) in **Passavant-la-Rochere**, the glassblowing works is reputedly the oldest in France (open on Tues, Thurs and Sat 14.30–17.00, May 11–June 29; and every day except Sun, Mon and July 14, from June 30–Sept 30).

Demangevelle (K117.8) near Écluse 44 is notable for several rows of really dreadful barrack-like dwellings, erected just before World War I as accommodation for cotton workers. After Écluse 45, Vougécourt (K120) the grey stone spire of **Corre** church will be seen ahead. Moor either side of the bridge to reach a variety of shops and garage in the pretty, flower-filled little town. About 200m from the canal, the Restaurant du Centre is the hub of Corre's social life. Not only does it offer diners first-rate value, but in the garden at the rear a covered skittle alley kept the younger members of our party amused late into the evening. Extensive Roman remains were discovered during the 19th century, among them a magnificent white marble Venus, beautifully preserved. Objections to her nudity resulted in the statue being broken into a number of fragments and the abdomen was converted into a holy water stoop which can still be seen in the church porch! Other, less precious antiquities were removed to a museum in Besançon. One final lock is situated just upstream of the confluence of the Saône and the Coney (see Chapter 47).

23 · River Meuse (Canal de l'Est – Branche Nord)

Carte Guide: *La Meuse et le Canal de l'Est de Liège à Corre*

From a junction with the Canal de la Marne au Rhin at Troussey to the Franco-Belgian border at Givet,

272.4km with 59 locks. A junction is made with the Canal des Ardennes at Pont-à-Bar, west of Sedan. There are four tunnels: Ham 565m, Revin 224m, Verdun 45m, and Koeur 50m.

It is a marvel of French bureaucracy that one of the country's most attractive river navigations should officially be known as the Canal de l'Est (Branche Nord). Yet except in its uppermost reaches, where the waterway is mainly a lateral canal, it generally follows the course of the River Meuse itself. From its source on the plateau of Langres near Bourbonne-les-Bains, the Meuse makes a 950km journey through France, Belgium and Holland before entering the North Sea as the Maas. In the French Ardennes the river offers some of the finest forest boating to be found in the whole of Europe. Unlike the holiday resorts which characterize its banks in the fashionable southern part of Belgium, the French Meuse is little known to tourists and although it is well supplied with facilities in a succession of towns and villages, pleasure boating is far from being well developed. At the time of writing there are only a few craft hirers (including those at Sedan and Dun-sur-Meuse): this situation would, of course, be quite different if the Meuse enjoyed the Mediterranean climate of the Canal du Midi. But it has to be admitted that weather in the Ardennes is decidedly changeable. In my experience, it is best to visit the region in anticipation of frequent rain: any heatwaves encountered can be regarded as an unexpected bonus!

An inevitable consequence of rain (which repeatedly features in numerous published cruising accounts on the Meuse) is springtime flooding, although this is probably no more likely than on many French rivers. High water levels have been recorded since ancient times but never with such interesting results as in March 1408 when thawing snows inundated much of the Meuse valley, demolishing buildings and wrecking bridges. In appearing before a gathering of stricken farmers, the Devil claimed that he had been responsible for the chaos; he would, however, remove the floodwater, repair all the damage and go so far as to guarantee a total freedom from flooding for the next century. All that he required in return was the souls of any children born between the end of Mass and the beginning of Vespers on the Feast of the Annunciation. When news of the bargain spread there were some who were dismayed, not least those families expecting an increase to their numbers. Eventually an ingenious solution was devised: on the date in question, Mass celebrated throughout the region would be extended to last until it was time for Vespers! Thus the children

The goddess of the Meuse pressed into service to advertise locally brewed beer. An enamel sign, produced in 1905.

pâté de grives (thrush pâté, sometimes in a pastry case), *quenelles de brochet* (mousse of pike), *dragées de Verdun* (sugared almonds) and *madeleines de Commercy* (shell-shaped sponge cakes).

In ancient times the Meuse formed part of a freight and passenger route through the Ardennes: by resorting to an overland portage near the source at Langres, communication was possible via the Saône and Rhône with the Mediterranean. One frequent 8th century traveller was St Hubert. But it was not until the demands of the iron industries around Nancy became considerable during the 19th century that a proper canalization scheme was put in hand. Present locks mostly date from 1875–80. By 1964 the border port of Givet was the 16th busiest in France, with the French Meuse carrying an annual 3.5 million tonnes of goods. From 1908 a steam tripping vessel, the *Givet-Touriste*, ran a regular summer service on the northern reaches, freight traffic then consisting of horse-drawn *péniches* and smaller flat-bottomed barges. One improvement of recent times has been the installation of automatic equipment at locks in the Sedan – Revin section.

born on March 25, 1408 were saved from the clutches of Satan; and, although effectively outwitted, he seems to have stood by the agreement, for no really bad flooding was to engulf the Meuse until 1510.

Through Holland and Belgium the Meuse is of large proportions, locks conforming to at least Class IV dimensions up to the French border. But the French length is effectively to Freycinet *péniches* standards only, even though Écluses 20–58 are both longer and wider than the 38.5m × 5.1m locks between Troussey and Verdun.

It is impossible to travel the Meuse without constantly being reminded of repeated wartime slaughter, culminating in the dreadful Verdun bloodbath of World War I. This border country has been fought over for centuries, towns fortified by Vauban including Givet, Charleville-Mézières, Stenay, Sedan and Verdun. Charleville-Mézières alone was bombarded in 1815, 1870, 1914, 1918, 1940 and 1944, while smaller places were reduced to total oblivion. Around Verdun, no trees remain from before the 1914–18 holocaust. Vast cemeteries adorn the landscape. Time has healed the scars and peace has returned to the valley, but an inevitable sombre quality lingers.

In places, slate and iron industries have long been established, but rarely do they detract from the beauties of this gem among French river navigations.

Food specialities include various freshwater fish, *jambon cru* (raw ham), *pâté de sanglier* (wild boar),

After its junction with the Canal de la Marne au Rhin near the village of **Troussey** (see Chapter 27), the Canal de l'Est (Branche Nord) descends through a series of four locks to the hamlet of **Sorcy-Gare** (K2). Water point, Écluse 1, Troussey. Nearby, the small and reed-fringed River Meuse winds through meadowland and briefly joins the navigation for the first time downstream of Écluse 5, **Euville** (K6.1). Typical of many villages that will be passed, this is an intensely rural settlement with a most elegant classical fountain and a butcher, baker, grocer, garage and small lockside bar/restaurant. Not long afterwards a mobile weir, right, marks the junction with a canal cut leading into **Commercy** (K10.2), a pleasing little town with foundries, hilly narrow streets, various weir streams and an impressive square entered via gateways. All supplies can be obtained within easy reach of the public quay by the main bridge. Its chief claim to fame is as home of *madeleines*, light sponge cakes which when dipped in tea produced the celebrated flood of memories recounted by Marcel Proust in *À la Recherche du Temps Perdu*. The delicacies are reputed to have been first served to ex-Polish King Stanislas, Duke of Lorraine, who was responsible for the 18th century splendours of Nancy.

From time to time the navigation channel follows the true course of the river, but for the majority of the distance downstream to Stenay we shall be travelling along a lateral canal. A succession of villages, all of them worth exploring, is now encountered: **Lerouville** (K16.4, most shops, sloping-sided guard lock), **Vadonville**, by Écluse 7 (K17.5); and **Sampigny** (K20.3) with butcher, baker, grocer and garage. It was here that St Lucy lived with a hermit after travelling from her native England. Avoiding a broad loop of the Meuse, the waterway passes through the 50m **Koeur** tunnel (K22.8) where for the first time tree-covered cliffs provide a hint of dramatic scenery yet to come. Écluses 8 (water point) and 9 lead to the village of **Bislée** (K26.2) and a glorious reach of river upstream of **St-Mihiel** and Écluse 10 (K30.8). Limestone rocks are a picturesque background to this medium-sized town; all facilities and moorings by the boat club. A Benedictine abbey was founded here in the 8th century and during the 16th century it became the centre of a brilliant school of religious art led by the sculptor Ligier Richier. Examples of his work will be found in the churches of St Michel ('The Swooning Virgin') and St Étienne ('The Placing of Jesus in the Tomb'). A celebrated German attack in September 1914 is remembered as Le Saillant de St-Mihiel.

Leaving the river for a long canal section, we next pass **Maizey** (K36.4) and Écluse 11, **Rouvrois-sur-Meuse** (K38.3), with the possibility of mooring near Écluse 12 (water) in **Lacroix-sur-Meuse** (K41.2, baker, grocer, restaurant and garage). In addition to a fine grey stone church with slender slated spire, this village boasts an amazing classical fountain erected in 1836 in celebration of the arrival of a pure water supply. Latin inscriptions adorn a massive arch with human figures and a pair of giant fish. Later wording shows how it was adapted as a village memorial to those who fell in the First and Second World Wars.

Top of the Meuse at Sorcy. The first crop of summer hay is being gathered.

Troyon near Écluse 13 (K46.6) has a baker and restaurant, while **Ambly-sur-Meuse**, Écluse 14 (K49.5), has little beyond a military cemetery, orchards, butcher and what was described by the lock keeper as 'the best baker on the River Meuse'. This claim was fully justified by the quality of the delicious *brioche*, a type of large sweet bun which we often eat warm for breakfast. Further on, **Génicourt-sur-Meuse** (K51.3) should be visited for its remarkable 16th century church with fine stained glass and wood carvings attributed to Ligier Richier. Clogs are still made here. Between river and canal, **Dieue** (K57.7), reached from Écluse 15, is a pretty village of stone houses. The lockside supermarket could hardly be more convenient or the proprietor more willing. Continue to the left bank of the Meuse for a few shops and restaurant in **Ancemont**. First impressions of **Dugny-sur-Meuse**, beyond the river shortly before a crossing of the A4 *autoroute*, are that it is a dirty little quarry town with a military cemetery. But it does possess a rather splendid 12th century Romanesque church.

The large town of **Verdun**, where there is a fully equipped and central mooring pontoon for visiting boats, is entered after negotiating a 45m tunnel through defensive walls, immediately before Écluse 19 (K68). Everything about the city pales into insignificance on learning that no fewer than 800,000 men lost their lives in the most terrible battle of World War I. In spite of savage bombardment, the 12th century cathedral of Notre-Dame remains, as does the extensive Citadel, built during the 1890s to become the strongest fortress in the whole of France. The public are admitted to view a maze of underground galleries and brick-lined dormitories where French troops would rest before returning to the battlefield. It was here, in 1920, that the Unknown Soldier buried in the Arc de Triomphe in Paris was selected. The Town Hall has a War Museum devoted to the city's part in the 1914–18 massacre; there are reminders of nine villages that were totally destroyed and never rebuilt. One of these was the unfortunate **Fleury**. In the surrounding countryside pine forests have covered some of the scars of this tortured landscape. If the imagination should need any prompting, numerous forts, cemeteries and other reminders may be visited. Perhaps the most telling sites are the Trench of the Bayonets, where troops were buried while fighting, and the vast Ossuary of Douaumont, burial place for 100,000 unidentified soldiers. Detailed information is contained in the *Green Michelin Guide to the Vosges* (in French) or in a leaflet (in English) available from the local tourist office, found to the right of the navigation opposite the Porte

Chaussée. World War I has become a major tourist attraction of Verdun and while the subject may lend itself to production of picture postcards and other souvenirs, chocolate shells containing a small detonator seem tasteless in the extreme.

Verdun displays considerable style in its 19th century public buildings, all carefully restored so that it is now almost impossible to imagine its once ruinous state. Shopping and eating ashore are available in great variety close to the central quays, while a tripping vessel enables the car tourist to get afloat. At the height of the season it makes four short journeys each day, working through the lock and tunnel and returning to the city centre. Fuel can be bought from a garage downstream of the Porte Chaussée; the keeper at Écluse 19 will provide water supplies.

Downstream of the city is unpleasantly smelly, so it is advised to press on past the twin towns of **Thierville-sur-Meuse** and **Belleville-sur-Meuse** (K70.5) to the village of **Bras-sur-Meuse** at Écluse 20 (K76.2) where there is water point, grocer, baker, restaurant and garage. **Charny-sur-Meuse**, on the side of the river, is notable for its exceedingly run-down railway station, which would require little adaptation to render it ideal for a film set in the early 20th century. The canal winds considerably in close company with the Meuse as they pass through a shallow dish-shaped valley and on to **Champ**, at Écluse 21 (K84) and its associated village of **Neuville**. Old tractors and waggons clutter the muddy streets, where most buildings are either barns or farmhouses. A sign near Écluse 22 (K88) proclaims '*Ici était Samogneux*'. **Samogneux** did exist until 1916 when it was blown to pieces.

Beyond Écluse 23 at **Brabant-sur-Meuse** (K91.1) we join the Meuse once more and shortly arrive at the most inconvenient lock on the whole river – Écluse 24, **Consenvoye** (K93.4), a sloping sided chamber. The village offers baker, grocer, restaurant and garage. Identical facilities are also to be found in **Sivry-sur-Meuse** (K98.2), as rural a village as you might find anywhere in France and with moorings in a fine basin. **Vilosne**, a flowery village on the river after Écluse 25 (K99.8), has an alarmingly large number of names on its World War I memorial and it would seem that virtually all the young men were killed. Old shells up to 2m high adorn the doorways of cottages in the little farming settlement of **Liny-devant-Dun**, by Écluse 26 (K106.7). At a respectful distance from the centre is a German cemetery, carefully tended but, more than 70 years on, little visited by the families of those that lie there. Willows, weirs and intent fishermen typify these reaches. There is a café close to the lock.

Verdun's defensive walls are pierced by a short tunnel.

The river winds through flat water meadows to arrive in **Dun-sur-Meuse**, Écluse 28 (K110.1). Meuse Nautique cruiser hire. Most shops will be found in the long main street. The oldest quarter and church are clustered on a cliff, high above the water. Shops for fishing tackle and hunting point to the popularity of *la chasse*, although the casual visitor is more likely to encounter stuffed wild cats or boar than the live article! Iron railings of the town's river bridge feature a stars and stripes design, with a plaque recording: 'The Veterans of the Fifth Division of the American Expeditionary Forces have erected this railing to commemorate the crossing of the Meuse River and the establishment of a bridgehead on its eastern bank by their Division during the World War.' Near the church, the ruins of a building destroyed in World War I are all that remains of the house of Étienne IX, who reigned as Pope for a mere eight months in 1057–8. Downstream, former gravel workings have been landscaped into a pleasing water space with a small beach and fishing facilities. If you moor on the river between **Milly** and the stop lock at **Sassey-sur-Meuse** (K114.1), a 3km walk or cycle ride to the west will bring you to the important 11th century church at **Mont-devant-Sassey**; during the 17th century wars it was transformed into a fortress.

Further water parks based on gravel pits are followed by the rural town of **Mouzay**, Écluse 30 (K120.3). Navigation once more passes into the Meuse to arrive at Écluse 31, **Stenay** (K123.6), with moorings in a small port, right bank. Although local industries include a paper works and foundry, this is a lovely old town, fortified by Vauban under Louis XIV. It was held by the Germans throughout much of World War I, and from the *château* the German Crown Prince directed the attack on Verdun for eighteen months. All shops, restaurants and fuel are close at hand. Again a poplar lined canal, the waterway runs through **Martincourt** (K128.5) before returning to the river after Écluse 32, **Inor** (K130.2), an isolated village of massive stone barns with baker, grocer and restaurant. From here onwards much of the journey is along the Meuse itself, by now a sizeable winding river with sparkling weirs, mill houses and reedbeds.

Pouilly-sur-Meuse, Écluse 33 (K134.5) is a particularly charming village. Small and quiet it has a grocer and a public telephone concealed inside a barn. All the time the scenery is becoming more spectacular, and there is every incentive to linger in the coming length that extends to the Belgian border. Écluse 34, **L'Alma** (K141.6), is succeeded by a delightful reach leading to the ancient town of **Mouzon** (K149.3). *Port de Plaisance* in a side channel upstream of the lock

(water, electricity, WCs). This remarkable place dates back to Gaulish times, was a Roman market and was not absorbed into France until 1379, in the reign of Charles V. Several Spanish houses recall an Iberian siege in 1650. Alone among remaining fortifications is a four-storey gateway, the Porte de Bourgogne. The church of Notre-Dame is a most imposing structure, started at the end of the 12th century. Although it is now a very small town, it is impossible not to appreciate the former greatness of the place.

Running downriver through beautiful surroundings past **Autrecourt** and **Villers-devant-Mouzon** (K152.7), Écluse 36, **Remilly** (K159.6), is the first of a series of radar controlled automatic locks extending to Revin. See the *Carte Guide* for operating instructions. Frequent concrete pillboxes line the river, emphasizing the strategic importance of the Meuse. As recently as 1936 the **River Chiers** was listed as navigable for 35km from **La Ferté-sur-Chiers** to the Meuse at **Remilly-Aillicourt**. Its very twisting course had no locks and would appear to offer adventurous exploration at least for small, shallow draft craft. 2km NE of the bridge before Écluse 36 lies the village of **Bazeilles**. A former café here, known as La Maison de la Dernière Cartouche (The House of the Final Cartridge) is a curious museum, containing 5,000 objects from the Sedan battlefields of 1870. **Sedan** itself lies on both sides of a short cut leading to Écluse 37 (K165.4), central control point for the automatic locks. Best overnight moorings are at a camping site with pontoons, water and electricity; this is reached down a side channel from the upper end of the lock cut. All facilities will be found in the town, and a boat repair firm, Grelardon, 2 rue de Metz. The name of Sedan is synonymous with the French defeat of 1870 when Napoléon III surrendered to the Prussians, resulting in turn in the Siege of Paris and the loss of Alsace-Lorraine. A huge fortress, begun in the 13th century and much enlarged in the 15th, towers over the town with 30m high ramparts. Within is the Palace of the Princes of Sedan and a fascinating museum. 17th century houses that escaped destruction during a series of bombardments will be found in the Rue du Ménil, and an enjoyable visit can be made to the Botanical Garden near the river to the south of the *château-fort*.

Villette and Écluse 38 (K169.1) are on a canal cut which avoids a loop of the river and are followed by **Donchery**, Écluse 39 (K172.8), a useful shopping stop. A blind turn under a bridge marks the junction with the Canal des Ardennes at the tiny hamlet of **Pont-à-Bar** (K176.1, see Chapter 19). A diversion through the first two locks brings you to a barge repair yard and chandlery (gas, water, fuel). Hire cruisers also operate from here. Shops, restaurants and fuelling facilities in **Dom-le-Mesnil** or rather closer in **Nouvion-sur-Meuse**, both reached from Écluse 40 (K177.5). The railed enclosure of a former swimming pool in the river 1000m upstream of Nouvion bridge makes an ideal mooring. The very pleasant curving river reaches now lead to Écluse 41, **Roméry** (K188.1). **Charleville-Mézières** (K192.7) is a pair of quite distinct towns that together form the largest urban area on the French Meuse. They spread around two great bends of the river each of which is bypassed

From his plinth in the Place Ducale, Charleville, Charles de Gonzague surveys the town he founded.

by canal cuts with Écluse 42 and 43. Mézières is the older place, with fortifications and ramparts; Charles IX married Elizabeth of Austria in the church of Notre-Dame d'Espérance in 1570. The outstanding attraction is without doubt Charleville's vast **Place Ducale** enclosed by 17th century buildings with covered arcades at street level. It bears comparison with the Place des Vosges in Paris. One most unfortunate decision taken in 1843 was the replacement of the Ducal Palace by the present *Hôtel de Ville*, although fortunately the chosen style blends well with the yellow stone and pink brick façades of the earlier structures. Until a thorough cleaning and restoration in 1982, many of the frontages bore faded but elegant examples

of painted 19th century signwriting. A flourishing market including *brocante* is held in the square and among bargains to be discovered are now popular wood-burning iron stoves cast in this part of the Ardennes.

Charleville was founded as a 'new town' in the 17th century by Charles de Gonzague, Duke of Nevers, Rethel, Montferrat and Mantua, and his statue graces the Place Ducale. He set up factories making carpets, glass, marble and printing, but none were as successful as the nail-making operation he founded which in time grew to manufacture arms and now specializes in mechanical engineering. In spite of such origins, the town is a bright and cheerful place with an excellent pedestrianized shopping street. Best moorings (within a short distance of the Place Ducale) are up the weir-stream on stages by the municipal camping site (water point and other facilities). Nearby is a swimming pool and the much recommended Mont Olympe restaurant (seafood specialities). Opposite, on an island, is the Vieux Moulin (old mill), a monumental four-storey structure which houses an Ardennes folklore exhibition and a display relating to the local poet Arthur Rimbaud (1854–91).

Now begins one of the finest portions of river landscape in Europe. Thickly wooded hills close in, the almost impenetrable foliage serving as excellent cover for wild boar. Though long associated with iron-working, **Nouzonville** (right bank, K199.8) is a pleasant little town with moorings on a quay by the bridge close to all facilities, including a heated swimming pool. Small terraced fields with sheep and orchards cascade down to **Joigny** and Écluse 44 (K202.2). Good moorings on bollards will be found on the left bank above the lock, or downstream of the next road bridge (again on the left). An acute bend leads past **Braux** (K207.3) to Écluse 45, **Levrézy** (K208.6). **Château-Regnault-Bogny** (K209.4) has a public jetty on the right upstream side of the bridge and provides all shopping and eating facilities. Its castle was destroyed by Louis XIV. A little downriver cliffs on the right are known as Le Rocher des Quatre Fils Aymon, their form said to represent the legendary horse Bayard and the Four Sons of Aymon who incurred the displeasure of Charlemagne and were pursued to their mountain hideout above the Meuse by the Emperor's men. On the opposite bank are the lofty Roche aux Sept Villages

and the Roche de Roma: their summits provide spectacular views of the Meuse meanders.

The extremely tortuous and unnavigable River Semoy enters on the right at **Laval-Dieu**: its valley provides pleasant walks through chestnut and fir trees to the Belgian border 20km to the east, near **Les Hautes Rivières**. Magnificently situated at the corner of a tight bend, **Monthermé** (K213.9) lies beneath towering wooded slopes formed by the Longue Roche spur. Brightly painted houses cluster along the water's edge with all facilities for the boater. A popular tourist centre for exploring both Meuse and Semoy, Monthermé has a number of rocky peaks which can be reached on foot, among them the Roche à Sept Heures and the Roc de la Tour. St Léger's church was built between the 12th and 15th centuries and is fortified.

Sliding past immense forests, the navigation channel passes to the right of a long lock island at the approach to Écluse 46, **Deville** (K218.2). In recent years this was the home of a donkey named Tonerre: he helped boats pass through by hauling on their lines! Deville village on the left bank would be useful for basic shopping. One of the most agreeable moorings on the entire Meuse must be close to Écluse 47, Commune (K222.4), opposite the village of **Laifour**. Mooring bollards, right bank, with pedestrian access to the village via the railway bridge (take care!). Sheer-sided cliffs are clothed with a dense variety of trees, ranging from dark-leaved pines and yews to the light green of limes. The valley reverberates with the whine of power saws, while water ripples over a weir alongside the lock.

A considerable distance of the left bank up to and beyond Écluse 48 (K227) is known as Les Dames de Meuse: nowhere are the cliffs more impressive or dramatic. This time, the legend concerns the promiscuous wives of three knights, turned into stone for their infidelity. There must be worse fates than to be immortalized as the centrepiece of such a splendid view! After Écluse 49 (K231.7) a loop of almost 360° is bypassed by a short cut with the 224m **Revin** tunnel (one-way) immediately followed by Écluse 50 (233.3). Moorings for the town should be selected on the river itself, near the road bridge to the left of the lock exit. The old quarter is not without interest, and meets all shopping and eating requirements. Those in search of an idyllic rural mooring will find a stone quay on the left bank at the camping site in the Bois de Fumay, several hundred metres upstream of Écluse 52, K239.4. **Fumay** (K240.2) is a brooding little slate quarry town, useful for shopping, very close to the Belgian border where a narrow strip of France extends north along the river. After Écluse 53, Vanne-Alcorps (K246.7), the town of **Haybes** is seen on the right bank by a road bridge,

Wooded cliffs in the French Ardennes at Revin.

cowering beneath a magnificent craggy hillside. All around is excellent walking country, objectives including viewpoints at **La Platale** and the **Roc de Fépin**, north of Écluse 54 (K257.4).

Vireux-Molhain and **Vireux-Wallerand** (K257.4), either side of a road bridge below Écluse 55, introduce a brief element of industry with their ironworks. Moor on the left bank well above Vireux bridge, but do not attempt to continue down this side of the island and through the bridge arch. Useful shops and restaurants will be found. The Molhain church is built on a 9th or 10th century crypt. The next town down river, beyond Écluse 56 (K259.3), is **Aubrives**, surrounded by rich green meadows with lumber yards. A little distance to the west will be found the ruins of a frontier *château* at **Hierges**, constructed between the 11th and 16th centuries. One final loop of river is avoided by a cut at **Ham-sur-Meuse**, where Écluse 57 (K264) is succeeded by an iron drawbridge and then the 565m Ham Tunnel, cutting under a hill at the neck of the Meuse peninsula.

The journey along the French Meuse ends at **Givet** (K268.4), a place of considerable interest for a border town, with the massive Fortress de Charlemont, ruined and overgrown. Originally planned by Charles V and updated by Vauban, it was heavily bombarded during World War I. Pleasure craft should moor immediately above the road bridge (left bank), where all facilities are within easy reach, including the French Customs office. Alternatively, use floating jetties below the bridge (right bank). Industrial activities, notably metalworking and textiles, are served by an extensive river port alongside a cut leading to the final French lock, Écluse 59, Les Quatre Cheminées (K271.9). 4km east is the Grotte de Nichet, open to the public May–Sept and comprising 12 chambers well encrusted in the approved manner of underground caverns. In former years pleasure boatmen would experience dreadful delays at the hands of the Customs, but lately the procedure for passing into Belgium has become more relaxed. Old postcard views depict officers equipped with special backpacks enabling them to camp out in the forests along this border and so arrest nocturnal would-be smugglers! The Belgian Customs office (left bank) has a convenient quay. A little downstream, the Léonard chandlery supplies water and gas as well as other boating requirements. Cost of diesel fuel is markedly below that in France at the time of writing. Once over the border, the Meuse discards its air of secrecy and assumes a rôle of well-organized gaiety with waterside villas, hotels, tripping launches and much increased activity. All craft venturing onto Belgian waters must fly a *drapeau de navigation* on the bows.

This is intended to indicate to lock keepers and other vessels that your boat is under way. It consists of a red square flag with a smaller white square in the centre.

24 · Canal du Rhône au Rhin

Carte Guide: *Doubs et Canal du Rhône au Rhin* (Vagnon) [Saône-Rhine only]. *Marne au Rhin* [portion of Canal du Rhône au Rhin between Rhinau and Strasbourg]. *Fluviocarte 1, Naviguer en Alsace* includes both Colmar Branch and the Rhinau-Strasbourg section of the Canal du Rhône au Rhin.

From a junction with the River Saône at St-Symphorien-sur-Saône to a junction with the Grand Canal d'Alsace at Niffer, 236.2km with 114 locks and 2 tunnels. An additional part of the original line between Île Napoléon (Mulhouse) and Friesenheim (totalling 64.6km) was taken out of service when duplicated by the Grand Canal d'Alsace. One short portion, however, remains available, so maintaining a connection between the Grand Canal d'Alsace at Neuf-Brisach and the Canal du Rhône au Rhin's Colmar Branch. Neuf-Brisach to Colmar is 23km with 3 locks. A further isolated part of the canal links the Grand Canal d'Alsace at Rhinau/Friesenheim with Strasbourg, junction with the River Ill and the docks (with communication to the River Rhine and Canal de la Marne au Rhin), 35.8km with 14 locks. Other branches are: on the River Doubs at Besançon, 3km, 1 lock; from the main line at Allenjoie to Belfort, 14.9km with 11 locks; and to the Nouveau Bassin in Mulhouse, 1.9km. A portion of the former Huningue Branch (originally extending to Basle) remains available between the current main line and the town of Kembs, 1km, 0 locks.

From the late 1970s until the late 1990s; this outstandingly scenic navigation was due to be rebuilt for large international barges, providing an important heavy tonnage link between the Rhine and the Saône. However, the scheme was dropped because of the unpopularity of the environmental effect of flooding the valley of the Doubs and the high construction costs. Some enlargement has meanwhile been carried out between Mulhouse and the Rhine.

Climbing from the Saône up the Doubs Valley, the canal traverses the rugged Franche-Comté or Jura region, which remained quite independent of France until the 17th century. Almost throughout its association with the Doubs the surroundings are spectacular, with great wooded cliffs and progressively bluer folds of hills receding towards the Swiss/German border.

The two leading towns, Dole and Besançon, enjoy dramatic settings.

Reaching a summit level near Montreux-Château, the waterway drops sharply through many locks towards Mulhouse, with decidedly Swiss and German influences to be seen in architecture and language as the route passes into Alsace. The main line terminates at a junction with the canalized Rhine – the Grand d'Alsace, on the border with Germany only a little downstream of Switzerland. While still (just) remaining in France, boats must pass down the Grand Canal before re-entering a detached portion of the Canal du Rhône au Rhin, leading to the city of Strasbourg where the finest urban mooring in Europe is to be found.

Commercial traffic is currently quite light, only increasing significantly at Mulhouse. Presumably because of the impending modernization scheme, virtually amounting to constructing a totally new waterway, maintenance has not lately been afforded much priority. This is especially true along the Doubs section, and great care is necessary to follow the chart closely and anticipate the sometimes concealed entrances to lock cuts; lack of attention could quite easily result in heading for open and unmarked weirs. The other vital point to remember is that even in wide river reaches rocks and shallows lurk just below the surface should you stray from the correct dredged channel. Again, keep a close watch on the chart and any bankside signs showing exactly where the deep water is to be found. As a general rule, if you stay near the towpath you will be safe unless otherwise indicated.

A noticeable degree of self-sufficiency is practised by the lock keepers: many keep goats, chickens, ducks, geese and rabbits with well cultivated fruit and vegetable gardens. Locks on the section between the summit and Mulhouse are worked by travelling keepers who accompany boats and a passage must be booked in advance the previous day. Equally, many river locks will be operated by mobile keepers, especially outside peak pleasure cruising season. Shore facilities have considerably improved since the mid-19th century and the journey of three Englishmen in a rowing boat from Paris to the Lower Rhine (*Our Cruise in the 'Undine'*, by Edmund Harvey, 1854). One of the earliest published accounts of a Continental pleasure boating expedition, it records the very primitive communal sleeping arrangements experienced in bankside inns along the Canal du Rhône au Rhin, with five-course meals (wine included) available for 7p.

Brief history In Roman times freight is known to have ascended the Rhône and Saône from the Mediterranean and thence via the Doubs to Montbéliard, where

Some vigilance is necessary to avoid being carried onto unmarked and unguarded weirs on the River Doubs.

it was portaged overland to the Upper Rhine. Without the aid of locks these ancient craft must have been of extremely shallow draft. A properly engineered waterway was first proposed by de la Chiche in 1744, but no progress was made until the scheme was taken up by Bertrand and construction begun in 1784. It halted in 1802 and began again under the Restoration with engineer Joseph Liard in charge. By this time it was known as the Canal Napoléon. Stopping again at the fall of the Empire, the waterway was eventually finished (under the name of Canal Monsieur) between 1821 and 1833. Alsace was annexed to Germany in 1871, until the end of World War I. Nevertheless the St-Symphorien – Deluz portion was enlarged to Freycinet gauge in 1882; the Germans similarly upgraded the Mulhouse – Strasbourg length in 1892. But it was not until 1921 that the first 38.50m *péniche*, the *Maréchal-Joffre*, was able to travel from one end of the Rhône au Rhin to the other.

The next major development was the enlargement in 1961 of the Canal de Huningue section between the Grand Canal d'Alsace and Mulhouse for 85m × 12m Rhine barges. About this time some 64.6km of the original canal Mulhouse – Friesenheim was closed to traffic. During the 1970s, radar control was introduced between Friesenheim and Strasbourg.

With the completion of the Rhône and Saône to Class IV standards by the early 1980s, the Canal du Rhône au Rhin is the only sub-standard portion of a 1,350 tonne route via the Rhine between the North Sea and the Mediterranean. Rebuilding the Rhône au Rhin was first projected in 1961 and agreed in 1965. At first the scheme envisaged 22 new locks and 2 inclined planes with associated hydro-electric power stations. It was later modified to 24 locks throughout 229km: 7 between the Rhine and the summit, 17 falling towards the Saône. 140km of the Doubs was to be canalized from Voujeaucourt to Dole with 89km of artificial canal completing the route. Minimum dimensions would have provided a 55m wide channel and 4.5m depth, the locks accommodating 183m convoys comprising two barges and a pusher tug. The Compagnie National du Rhône was awarded the contract in 1979; total cost was then estimated at £900 million.

Environmental protests at the new waterway were particularly vociferous throughout the Doubs valley, which would have been flooded to create a series of lakes. The attitude of town and village residents was easily appreciated. With the exception of a canal bypass at Montbéliard and an upgrading of the line between Mulhouse and the Grand Canal d'Alsace (Rhine), none of these great works were carried out. Unlike its neighbour Germany, France now seems to have lost an appetite for creating upgraded commercial waterways. The exceptional beauty of the canalized Doubs seems likely to remain unchanged.

Important canal junctions are quite often non-places. So it is with **St-Symphorien-sur-Saône**. You could quite easily cruise past the first lock of the Canal du Rhône au Rhin without realizing that this is the beginning of a vital route to Germany and Switzerland. Marked by a large three-storey building the canal joins the Saône some distance upstream of St-Symphorien itself. All facilities are found 4.3km down river at St-Jean-de-Losne (see Chapter 47). Entry to Écluse 75, Saône, can be difficult when the river is in flood. First encounter with the lock gear reveals highly efficient paddle levers which instantly release a solid mass of water into the chamber, with wheels on tripods to work the gates. Between here and the Doubs at Dole navigation is via an artificial canal. Surroundings are pleasant but unremarkable, through woodland, carpeted with cowslips in springtime. At Écluse 73, La Tuilerie (K1.1), a stone mill still grinds flour by water power. Locks 72–70 are electrified, with grocer, restaurant and a baker known for the quality of his bread at **Abergement-la-Ronce** (K6.8). Be sure to replenish water supplies at Écluse 71, La Ronce (K8.3), as the next opportunity does not arise until Écluse 59, 37km ahead. Overhead cranes, commercial boat activity and the brief intrusion of industry discourage lingering near **Tavaux-Cité** (K10.4) with its Solvay chemical

works. For basic shopping moor above Éluse 70.

First meeting with the beautiful River Doubs is at Écluse 68, La Prise d'Eau (K17) downstream of **Dole** (K18.5, a real gem of a town. Moorings on pontoons above Écluse 67, Jardin-Philippe, have the benefit of a magnificent view of the Notre-Dame basilica rising above tiers of brown-tiled houses. Once Capital of Franche-Comté, it was attacked and burned by Louis XI in 1479. The inhabitants lost no time in rebuilding and erecting strong fortifications. The town was placed under siege in 1636 when Richelieu's 20,000 troops and 8,000 horses arrived. After these stirring times, Dole is best remembered as the birthplace of Louis Pasteur, scientist and father of immunology. The house in the Rue des Tanneurs where he saw the light of day in 1822 is now a museum devoted to his research (English commentary). Numerous old buildings from the 15th–18th centuries make this a fascinating place to explore on foot. Shopping and restaurants are excellent.

East of Dole, the canal passes through Écluse 66, Charles-Quint (K19.4), and along a pound shaded by great plane trees, recalling the Canal du Midi. **Brevans** (K21.2) is a waterside village with a veritable jumble of rooftops set at all kinds of angles. Grocer and restaurant in **Baverans**, close to Écluse 65 (K22.1). The canal sections ends after a guard lock at **Rochefort-sur-Nenon** (K25.8) where an ascent (by road) of cliffs offers a rewarding view down to the Doubs and a fortified mill. Good pontoon on the river by a group of trees (grocer, baker and restaurant). Onwards from this point, great care must be taken to follow the chart, thus avoiding rocks and weirs.

Audelange lies by a short cut between Écluse 64 (K27.6) and the guard lock, 64 *bis*, which is followed by another river reach. The alternating pattern of canal and river is typical of much of the Doubs. **Orchamps** (K33.6) is on a canal by guard lock 63 N and makes a useful shopping halt (fuel and restaurant reasonably close). But avoid mooring in the narrow section of cut. Keeping near the left (towpath) bank on the following river reach, enter a short rock-lined cutting with restaurant and bascule bridge near Écluse 62, Moulin des Malades (K37.6). Beyond, the canal, while occupying part of the river bed, is at the highest level of a three-tiered arrangement of channels. The previous lock keeper is responsible for Écluse 61 (K38.6) leading to the canalside village of **Ranchot** (K39.4, mooring stages, baker and restaurant). Beyond, the waterway becomes increasingly attractive: long lines of hills stretch into the distance and numerous heron and kingfisher can be seen.

Weaving from river to lock cut, this lovely navigation passes few villages of much importance: **Dampierre** near Écluse 60 (K40.7) has a grocer; **Fraisans**, between canal and river by guard lock 60 *bis* (K42.3), a grocer, baker and chemist. Moor at **Osselle** (K53.4) for a visit to the Grottes d'Osselle, about 4km by road. This system of caves extends for about 8km and has been visited since the early 16th century. A long loop of the river is bypassed by a 185m tunnel, partly through unlined rock at **Thoraise** (K59.5). The far portal shelters a statue of the Virgin, a wise precaution in view of the blind 90° corner that follows: hoot vigorously! Now comes a very fine reach past rocky cliffs rising to a great height and topped by the ruined tower of the Château de Montferrand. Caution is required when leaving the river to pass into the two-rise Écluses 54/55, **Rancenay** (K63.1), especially if a strong current is flowing. While there is a restaurant below the locks, a better one is found at **Aveney** (K66.1), beyond a 411m one-way section of canal. Both this village (waterside garage) and **Avanne**, reached by a bridge over the Doubs, are pleasantly situated; the latter has a full range of shops.

From here onwards to **Besançon** the natural course of the Doubs is followed, Écluse 53, Gouille (K68.3) and Écluse 52, Velotte (K70), having boulder-strewn weirs directly alongside. Midway between the two is a floating chandlery, right bank, with a fuel station just above No. 52. Besançon's fortifications and Citadel provide an impressive approach to the city, Capital of Franche-Comté. Walls and turrets snake along the skyline, with tree-covered cliffs rising from the river. Having negotiated the mechanized Écluse 51, Tarragnoz (K73.5), central moorings lie directly ahead, right bank. Almost 3km of river encircles the city, with mooring possibilities at Port Battant and Port République. Known as La Boucle du Doubs, this diversion is an excellent introduction to the area. During the summer cruising season, when the channel is marked by buoys, it is possible to navigate 'the long way', through the town and upstream via a D.I.Y. lock (maximum permitted draft is 1.4m). The normal and more direct through route, however, is via the 394m Tunnel de la Citadelle, illuminated by strip-lights and entered at Écluse 50 which is partly underground.

First established in Gallo-Roman times, Besançon's most notable feature is the hilltop *Citadelle*, constructed by Vauban in the 17th century. Reached on foot from the waterway by way of many steps or a steep road, it contains a small zoo and a museum devoted to the Resistance and the Nazi attrocities of World War II. But most visitors make the ascent for the spectacular view down to the Doubs valley. Being a centre of clock-making, Besançon has a museum of horology

Wooded cliffs near Besançon provide memorable scenery for passengers on a hotel barge.

and a remarkable astronomical clock close to St Jean's cathedral. Writer Victor Hugo and the Lumière brothers (pioneers of cinematography) were born here in the 19th century. Emerging from the east end of the tunnel, one sees very dramatic views of wooded cliffs. When passing through electrically operated Écluse 49, La Malate (K76.3), downriver craft should ask the keeper to telephone Écluse 50 and have the tunnel lights turned on.

Chalèze (K82.7) marks the end of a particularly fine river section. After Écluse 48 (with the Restaurant Coursaget offering regional specialities), a canal cut extends to the guard lock at **Roche-Les-Beaupré** (K85.2), with a good mooring before the narrow bridge and convenient for restaurant and shopping. Most facilities (including a railway station) are found in **Novillars** (K87.8), shortly followed by a two-arched bridge connecting **Vaire-le-Petit** with **Vaire-Arcier** (K88.1). There is little advance warning of arrival at a two-rise staircase lock, Écluse 46/47, **Deluz** (K90.4), providing access to a charming little town on a canal cut. In addition to good village shopping, a halt is recommended to enjoy a magnificent selection of summer flowers planted in all kinds of antique artefacts such as farm carts, vintage prams and seed-sowing machines. When the river has once more been rejoined, high cliffs create one of the most dramatic sections of the navigable Doubs. These extend past Écluse 45, Aigremont (K94.7) to **Laissey** (K96.5) whose lock is obstructed along one side by concrete beams, requiring either an agile or a very short keeper.

For a time there is an absence of artificial cuts, locks being placed close to river barrages. One especially lovely reach is encountered above Écluse 43, **Douvot** (K99), with an island, willows and cliffs extending to Écluse 42 at **Ougney-Douvot** (K101.4). Scenery remains consistently fine past **Fourbanne** Écluse 41 (K103.6), and **Esnans**, where there is a 17–18th century *château*. Écluse 40, Baumerousse (K107.1) marks the beginning of a canal section serving the substantial town of **Baume-les-Dames** (K109.6), reached from a bridge beyond guard lock 40 and on the left bank of the Doubs. All shops lie within a moderate walking distance, while essential services are close at hand: water point almost opposite the navigation authority yards, a huge and extremely comprehensive supermarket near the river bank, and a garage on the nearer outskirts of the town centre. The greatest point of interest in Baume to the navigator is that here, on the river, the world's first experimental steamboat was tested in 1776, many years before such craft were generally introduced. With virtually no precedent to guide him and only using the service of a local blacksmith, Marquis Claude-François-Dorothée de Jouffroy d'Abbans constructed his extraordinary vessel. It was 30m long with a beam of 1.95m; a Watt steam engine drove elementary paddles. The boat made a series of successful journeys between Besançon and Montbéliard, but thereafter little seems to be known about its fate and it was left to later engineers to perfect steam propulsion. The Marquis died in 1832 and in 1884 a monument was erected to his memory. Now rather worn and decayed, this stone memorial stands by the Doubs, a splendid collection of nautical devices surmounted by a funnel and paddle wheels.

Rejoining the river, a sharp turn to the left is made at the confluence with the (unnavigable) River Cusancin, soon followed by an equally sudden bend to the right into Écluse 39, Lonot (K111.7) at the beginning of a short cut. Care is necessary to follow the channel closely from Écluse 37, Grand-Crucifix (K116.1), to Écluse 34, the keeper here also being responsible for Écluse 33, Branne (K123.2), beyond the village of **Roche-les-Clerval**. For the first time in a long distance all services are within close range at the pleasing twin towns of **La Vesselotte** and **Clerval** (K126.6), either side of a road bridge. Each features brownish red roof tiles, with a church in Clerval containing relics of St Herminfroy, a 16th century *pieta* and a tower topped with a structure like a harebell, characteristic of the region. The baker's shop in La Vesselotte is built into the side of a rocky cliff. With several restaurants from which to choose, this is an obvious stopping place, although the moorings above the bridge are a little shallow.

Pompierre-sur-Doubs (K130.5) lies left of Écluse 31, alongside a length of artificial channel. There are no shops but clusters of flowers, a pretty church and a café by the railway station are all reasons to make a visit. The next lock, No. 30, Plaine de Pompierre (K132.1), lies in a flat and marshy region, very unlike most of the Doubs valley. In the early 1980s its keeper carried out a thriving business producing rabbit pelts, but was quite unable to provide any information on their eventual destination. As the waterway finally leaves the Doubs at the entrance to a cut at Écluse 27, Papeteries (K139.7), its surroundings are as beautiful as ever. But from here onwards its only function is as a feeder to the lateral canal before eventually swinging away to the south and through a series of magnificent gorges towards its source near **Mouthe**. As its name suggests, **L'Isle-sur-le-Doubs**, left of the canal at Écluse 26 (K140.8), is partly surrounded by water. Pretty houses and shops rise from the banks of backwaters, with ornate balconies and small overhanging rooms whose purpose is evident from the basic plumbing. Busy shops and restaurants are near a square with bandstand. As the canal is narrow, moorings must be chosen with care. The bridge immediately below Écluse 26 is one of the lowest on the route, but if necessary the keeper (who also operates Écluse 27) will arrange for the water levels to be dropped slightly.

Locks now increase in frequency as the canal climbs to its summit level, closely followed by the Doubs as far

Monument to a forgotten genius at Baume-les-Dames, recalling the invention of the world's first steam boat by the Marquis de Jouffroy.

as Voujeaucourt. Several of the villages offer basic resources and are most attractive: a typical example is **Colombier-Châtelot** by Écluse 23 (K147.5), a place bright with flowers, streams once serving water mills, stone houses with huge barns and a grocer and baker. **St Maurice-Échelotte** near Écluse 22 (K149.9) is one of many places on the route with a railway station and hotel. At the time of writing the lock keeper had a veritable menagerie of pigeons, ducks, rabbits, chickens and a pack of assorted hounds used for hunting wild boar, catching more than two dozen each year. Water can be obtained at Écluse 21, **Colombier-Fontaine** (K151.8) with a full range of shops, and garage in the town itself, near a lift bridge. Moorings on a vertical quay just before Écluse 18, **Dampierre**

The tunnel and lock carved from the hillside on which the fortress town of Besançon is built.

(K157.4), are convenient for restaurant and baker. After passing through a guard lock, Écluse 18 *bis* (K159.1), the Doubs is crossed on the level at a four-way junction, potentially dangerous in times of flood. I was once aboard the first boat in two weeks to descend the Doubs after a period of dangerously high water levels. At this point, the stream slammed us violently to one side before use of our total engine power allowed us to gain the safety of the artificial channel beyond. Uphill craft should keep to the right (following the towpath) and will soon reach the safety of Écluse 17, **Voujeaucourt** (K159.9). Tie up above the lock to find shops, garage and restaurants within easy reach.

A further lift bridge after Écluse 16, Courcelles (K162.1), marks the start of the **Montbéliard** conurbation, home of a Peugeot car works (visits possible). Its hilltop was a Roman stronghold. The main historical attraction is an impressive *château* built in the 15th

century by Henriette de Wurtemberg. The interior is open to the public (mornings and afternoons, except Tues and public holidays). Although noisy, there are excellent moorings in a basin before Écluse 14 (K164.8) with water, fuel, electricity and slipway.

Improvement works completed about 1913 resulted in certain locks becoming disused, and the numbering of those now in service up to the summit reveals that three of the original chambers have been dispensed with. Écluse 12, **Exincourt** (K168.2), is a *bureau de contrôle*, where arrangements must be made for keepers to travel with craft during the descent between Montreaux Château and Mulhouse. Several km of totally new waterway with a deep mechanized lock were opened in 1987. The raw earth banks have been planted with 700 semi-mature trees, conveyed by two *péniches* from a nursery near Lyon. After Écluse 10, Marivées (K171.3), the canal makes a 90° turn to the left, passes through Écluse 9, **Allenjoie**, and then crosses the River Allaine via an aqueduct. A large basin at the far end marks the start of the 14.9km branch (left) to Belfort. Originally designed as the Canal de Montbéliard à la Haute-Saône, it was intended to form a link with the Saône, at Conflandey but was never finished - nor is likely to be. Construction began in 1882 and suffered various interruptions, so that opening was not achieved until 1923. A portion of the route west of Belfort was additionally dug, including tunnels of 650m and 1330m, but these 10km were never flooded. Craft wishing to explore its pleasantly shaded reaches should first obtain updated local information, booking a passage at least 8 days in advance by contacting the engineer responsible at Le Subdivisionnaire du Service Navigation, Le Port, Montbéliard, tel. 03 81 91 17 32. Normally there will be no difficulty in negotiating the first two locks to **Châtenois-les-Forges**, a town with all facilities including boatyard. Crews are expected to work their own locks. Further progress through eight locks to **Belfort** is not currently possible, as some of the chambers were infilled in 1992. For many centuries, the city guarded the 'invaders' route' from the east, being situated in a gap between the Vosges and the Jura ranges. Heavily fortified by Vauban under Louis XIV, its 16,000-strong garrison held back 40,000 Germans in 1870 for more than 100 days. This heroic stand is recalled in an 11m high stone Lion of Belfort, carved in 1880. Wide views from the ramparts.

Swiss or German influences in architecture, place names and language itself increase during the final climb to the summit. Navigational instructions appear in German alongside the French, and Alsatian German is widely spoken in the villages – sometimes, it would appear, in preference to French. In the early 1980s there were skilfully executed *graffiti* under the bridge by Écluse 8, Fontenelles (K174.1), depicting canal barges in an appealing naive style. This is followed by a pleasant reach of the River Allaine at its confluence with the Bourbeuse: avoid a weir if there is floodwater. The ascent is completed at Écluse 3, **Montreux-Château** (K185.5), a useful little town with water point, restaurant and most kinds of shopping.

A deep summit level runs past **Montreux-Jeune** and **Montreux Vieux** (both offering limited facilities) before starting the descent towards Mulhouse and the Rhine at Écluse 2, **Valdieu**. Passage through this section will have been booked the previous day at Écluse 12 (for Rhine-bound craft) or at Écluse 41, Mulhouse (for boats heading towards the Saône). These special arrangements are necessary to benefit from the services of teams of mobile keepers who travel from one lock to the next by car. Boats will be grouped together where possible, although single working is practised when traffic is light. The first team is responsible for locks 2–15; the next takes over for 16–27; and the final team will see you through locks 28–39, Mulhouse. Efficient though the arrangement is, it allows no opportunity for mooring throughout the day's locking, except during the keepers' lunch break. However, there is always ample opportunity for crew to take off on their own for sight-seeing or shopping, catching up with the boat one or more locks farther down the canal. Scenery is mostly of a high quality, with broad open fields of cattle or maize, huge barns of brick and half-timbering, and stacks of logs – the winter domestic fuel supply.

Écluses 3–13, from Valdieu to **Retzwiller** (K193.3), are arranged in a dramatic flight with curious keepers' 'lobbies' on the lockside, crowned with heavy red tiled roofs. **Dannemarie** near Écluse 16 (K195.1) has all services, another equally useful town being Illfurth by guard lock 32 (K208.4). Rather than halt by Écluse 38, to patronize the shops of **Brunstatt** (K216.3), it is preferable to continue through Écluse 39 (K217.4) and so benefit from the resources at **Mulhouse**.

A large and bustling place, noted for its industry and university, Mulhouse is not obviously very attractive, but at least its services are highly convenient for the canal traveller. Moorings are easily found along the tree-lined banks, although the best and most secure place, with pontoons and water supply, is the Vieux Bassin, opposite the railway station. An indication that you have temporarily left rural France for the 'amenities' of a large city is provided by numerous 'ladies of the night' seeking custom from car drivers in the waterside boulevards as dusk falls. In addition to shopping and restaurants, Mulhouse has an elaborate 16th century *Hôtel de Ville* with a painted façade, a superb collection of steam locomotives and other relics in the French Railways Museum 2km N of the centre, off the Ave. de Colmar, a Fabrics Museum and some memorable medieval stained glass in the church of St Étienne (Protestant).

Two quite outstanding attractions should on no account be missed: they are both unique in Europe. First, the Car Museum (192 avenue de Colmar) is a remarkable collection of vehicles from earliest times to the 1950s, displayed under cover along 2km of walkways illuminated by a forest of cast iron lamp standards. 500 priceless exhibits include a number of Bugattis (among them one of only six Bugatti Royales ever built). Although definitely not a car enthusiast I consider this to be one of the most thrilling museums I have ever visited. The story of how this extraordinary hoard was seized from its rightful owners is, however, not at all a happy one. Secondly, about 12km north of Mulhouse at Ungersheim, the Alsatian Open Air Museum (*Ecomusée*) has re-erected over 50 traditional rural buildings on a 10 hectare site. Mostly of timber-frame construction, each has been restored complete with appropriate farm animals, nesting storks and other reminders of an otherwise vanished agricultural past. Here are medieval houses, vineyard huts, barns, dovecotes and most remarkable of all, a 12–13th century fortified dwelling tower, discovered during demolition of shops in Mulhouse in 1983. Operated with obvious enthusiasm and mainly run by volunteers, the *Ecomusée* has an admirable traditional restaurant and extensive centre for Alsatian gifts. In several hours you would learn more of bygone Alsace than might be gleaned from weeks of touring through the region! It is almost certainly the leading non-waterway excursion recommended in this book.

For two centuries Mulhouse was a free city, belonged to Switzerland from 1515 until 1648, next became an independent republic until absorbed into France in 1798, and finally came under German control from 1871 to 1918. Not surprisingly, people of the area still regard themselves as Alsatian rather than French. After the Vieux Bassin, a 140m tunnel takes the navigation under a square by the main railway station, with garages on the reach that follows or more convenient fuelling services just beyond Écluse 41 (K220.4) where there is a water point.

Île Napoléon (K223.1) marks the start of a broad-gauge enlarged section of concrete lined channel, capable of taking 85m Rhine barges. If intending to leave France for either Germany or Switzerland, Customs clearance can be carried out here. In my experience

A 12/13th century fortified tower is among more than 50 traditional Alsatian buildings at an Ecomusée *north of Mulhouse.*

these formalities can safely be ignored if you are bound for the international Grand Canal d'Alsace, provided you remain in France by entering the Canal de la Marne au Rhin at Strasbourg. But it would be a wise precaution to have ship's papers and personal documents ready for inspection if challenged. Urgent repairs can doubtless be carried out at a commercial boatyard with drydock at the junction with the now closed continuation of the line towards Strasbourg. Plans were announced in 1994 for the restoration of this disused portion of the Canal du Rhône au Rhin, enabling craft to reach Strasbourg without using the much more demanding Grand Canal d'Alsace route. But for the present, it is necessary to follow what is technically the upgraded Huningue Branch, 13km of waterway through forests joining the Grand Canal d'Alsace at the Écluse de **Kembs-Niffer** (K236.2). The ultra-modern concrete control building was designed by Le Corbusier. A new, larger, lock has, since 1995, lowered craft into the canalized Rhine. Beyond this point the Canal de Huningue is technically closed to traffic, although a portion southwards remains fully navigable for about 1km to **Kembs**. Turn right onto the Grand Canal for the Swiss border and city of Basle; or left for a connection (in due course) with isolated portions of the Canal du Rhône an Rhin – the Colmar Branch and the section leading into Strasbourg. When leaving the Grand Canal, the cut leading to the Écluse de Kembs-Niffer is easily overlooked.

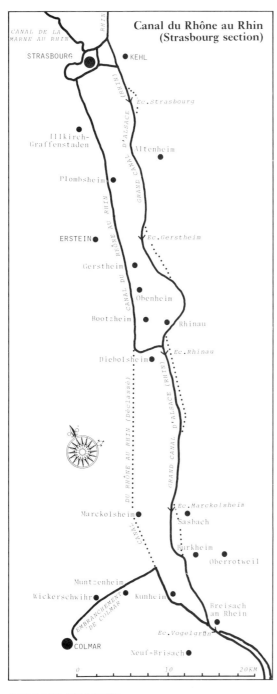

**Canal du Rhône au Rhin
(Strasbourg section)**

the Canal du Rhône au Rhin at **Kunheim**. Pontoon mooring (for shopping) by the junction with the disused canal. A further 3km of waterway through Écluse 63 leads to the start of the branch itself. This was opened to traffic in 1864. For the first 11km it runs very straight and level, scarcely touching the villages of **Muntzenheim**, **Wickerschwihr** and **Bischwihr**; there is little traffic of any kind and few signs of life apart from water birds and anglers. After climbing through the Écluse de l'Ill, it crosses the River Ill and enters a canalized part of the River Lauch. The former commercial port of **Colmar** has been transformed into a fine marina (53 berths) where facilities include showers and laundry. One feature is an ancient blue-painted crane. In spite of being moderately expensive and quite a long walk from the city centre, it is well worth boating this far as Colmar is a place of great interest and beauty which merits three stars and four pages of text in the *Green Michelin Guide Vosges*. One of the great medieval cities of France, it was fortunately saved from the serious damage during World War II. Narrow Streets at the centre are filled with a wealth of carved wooden houses of which the finest are the Maison Pfister and Maison des Têtes. As the Capital of Alsace, food is distinctly Germanic, many forms of sausage taking pride of place. Local wines are celebrated with a Fair in the middle of August and a Fête de la Choucroute in the following autumn. Buildings that might have been imported from a film set line the banks of the Lauch in the Petite Venise quarter. Two world-famous paintings must on no account be missed: Martin Schongauer's 15th century 'Virgin and the Rosebush' in the church of St-Martin and Mathias Grünewald's Issenheim Altarpiece from the early 16th century. Comprising scenes from the New Testament, it has been in Colmar since 1793 and is the great prize of a superb collection in the Musée d'Unterlinden, housed in a 13th century monastery.

RHINAU TO STRASBOURG
Although duplicating the Grand Canal d'Alsace, 35.8km of the northern end of the canal have been retained: they offer pleasure boats a much more peaceful journey than the hectic and rather anonymous canalized Rhine. (Plans have been formulated to restore the southern line of the Canal du Rhône au Rhin, so extending the cruising area available to hire boats – which are not permitted to use the Grand Canal d'Alsace.) Locks are remotely controlled by radar equipment: this appears to function well provided small craft copy the slow-moving *péniches*. Run really gently past the spherical sensors that lurk among reeds

COLMAR BRANCH
A most enjoyable diversion of 23km and just 3 locks can be made by leaving the Grand Canal d'Alsace at K226.5, downstream of Écluse de Vogelgrün (Chapter 25). 5.2km of new channel with 1 lock, Écluse Rhin, links the Grand Canal with a remaining fragment of

each side of the locks: high-speed manoeuvres will be treated with the same disinterest as the passage of a flying swan! With good reason, the canal staff repeatedly call out '*doucement, doucement*'. In the event of equipment failure, lockside telephones or your own VHF radio place you in touch with central control. Be prepared to receive instructions via loudspeakers at a volume designed to inform the entire neighbourhood of any mistake you may have made.

Entry to the line from Grand Canal d'Alsace is at K258, 1km downhill of the Écluses de Rhinau. Here at **Friesenheim** a modern *péniche*-sized lock with gates that slide sideways provides access to 3.4km of link canal, joining the Rhône au Rhin a little south of Écluse 75 (K4.3, distances being measured in this book from the Grand Canal). After the canalized Rhine the friendly intimacy of the waterway is a pleasure to savour. Commercial use is light and bankside facilities are sparse, with little beyond the occasional café. Vines hang over the doorways of lock houses and a crossing of the Ill is made between Écluses 79 and 80 (K16.3). **Plobsheim** (K23) and **Illkirch-Graffenstaden** (K25.9) provide the best possibilities for shopping. Most of the nearby Alsatian villages are well worth investigation. Between Écluses 81 and 82, a boatman's chapel stands in isolation in the meadows (visits possible). Near the edge of **Strasbourg** the navigation

Boat boy and towing team, circa 1905.

passes through a memorable avenue of plane trees. Be sure to fill water tanks at Écluse 85 (K32.9), especially if planning to stay in the River Ill section of the city.

The Ill shortly enters on the left. By turning right you will reach Écluse 86 with boatyards, converted barges and the Bassin d'Austerlitz, an extension of the large dock area of Strasbourg. One of the old electric towing 'mules' has been preserved near the lock. This is the most direct route to the canalized Rhine at Écluse Sud (projected pleasure boat harbour), or to the Canal de la Marne au Rhin and the Rhine at Écluses Nord. To reach the heart of the city and enjoy the delights of the finest urban moorings in Europe, keep straight on, ignoring the Bassin d'Austerlitz, and enter the River Ill, a little known but quite enchanting navigation that passes close to the cathedral and makes a junction with the Marne au Rhin. This route is both shallow (maximum draft below La Petite France is 0.7m) and there is reduced clearance under several bridges. Larger cruisers must therefore reach the city centre via the docks. For a description of the route and of Strasbourg itself, see Chapter 26.

25 · River Rhine and Grand Canal d'Alsace

Carte Guide: *Le Rhin et La Moselle* (Éditions de la Navigation du Rhin) or *Rhein-Handbuch 1 - Basel-Koblenz* (DSV Verlag, text in German). Or *Fluviocarte 1, Naviguer en Alsace* (Rheinfelden-Strasbourg, including Grand Canal and remaining portions of Rhône-Rhine Canal and River Ill).

Part of the upper reaches of the navigable Rhine lies along the border with France and Germany and consequently finds a legitimate place in this book. From the French-Swiss frontier at Huningue to Lauterbourg, where the river starts to flow entirely within Germany, 183.5km with 10 locks. Junctions are made with the main line of the Canal du Rhône au Rhin at Kembs-Niffer (K185.5); the Rhône au Rhin's Colmar Branch, via the Canal de Neuf-Brisach (K226.3); the Strasbourg section of the Canal du Rhône au Rhin near Rhinau (K258); the Strasbourg Docks at Écluse Sud (K291); and the Canal de la Marne au Rhin in Strasbourg, Écluses Nord (K295.5).

Navigating the upper Rhine is rather like eating tripe: interesting for the first few mouthfuls and exceedingly monotonous thereafter. A century and a half of far-reaching works have changed the ambience of the river beyond all recognition. Most of the surroundings alternate from an arid wasteland of gravel pits to endless lengths of concrete lined channel. Interest is of course provided by frequent large-scale commercial traffic and the engineering grandeur of the massive locks. But apart from a limited number of pleasure craft harbours, there is little possibility of mooring in safety, and even lying at lock approaches should only be contemplated with an instant readiness to move smartly should several thousand tonnes of cargo vessel appear.

Management of the Rhine has greatly reduced its flow: nevertheless, moderate currents can be expected in the vicinity of the hydro-electric power stations and on remaining sections of natural river. Having travelled the French Rhine in a hire cruiser of no more than average power (with special permission) I found it presented no great dangers or difficulties (unlike the treacherous German reaches in the Gorge downstream of Bingen). For preference, however, smaller craft might be well advised to time their journeys to avoid being on the waterway overnight. Passage from the Canal du Rhône au Rhin at Kembs-Niffer to the safety of Strasbourg Docks can be accomplished during a single long day, with the opportunity of escaping to safe moorings on the Rhône au Rhin's Colmar Branch, or the Strasbourg section near Rhinau. Being an international waterway, the theory is that Customs must be cleared when entering and leaving the Rhine; but in practice I have found that if you are intent on remaining within France you may be able to avoid the procedure.

Curious effects of wash from commercial traffic will be experienced: sometimes a severe buffeting arrives as much as five minutes after a vessel has passed. Pleasure craft are mainly ignored by the lock keepers if you allow barges to enter first and then quickly take up a position at the back of the chamber. Filling or emptying reaches a vertical rate of about 3m per minute, but floating bollards sliding up and down in cavities in the walls avoid any need to adjust lines. Small craft will need to make fast, bow and stern, to a single bollard, as they are positioned at widely spaced intervals.

Passenger ships offering a considerable degree of luxury operate throughout the Rhine from Holland to Switzerland. Some are truly gigantic, able to cater for 1,200 passengers; halts at main towns and cities allow for some sight-seeing ashore. A journey encompassing the whole river takes four days downstream or five days up. Day trips are also possible from Basle and Strasbourg. Local enquiries will provide the necessary details.

Brief history In use as a navigation for more than 2,000 years, the Rhine is Europe's greatest inland waterway, carrying vastly greater volumes of freight than any other route. Flowing from Switzerland's Lake Constance (the Bodensee), it first receives traffic at Rheinfelden, 145km from the source. A long-term plan envisages modification of this highest length, making it suitable for boats. Passing near the Black Forest with two locks in Switzerland, upstream of Basle, it enters the French territory of Alsace at Huningue, the right bank of the river being in German Baden. Total distance to the North Sea beyond Rotterdam is 1,030km from Constance. The upper waters above Strasbourg, once 3–4km wide with hundreds of islands, were navigated in ancient times by rafts or light craft hauled by men or horses. Initial measures to improve the channel were begun in 1818 by the engineer Gottfried Tulla, who built a series of dams to convert the wide, shallow river into a deep, fully navigable one. This was not completed until 1876, the course being shortened by no less than 82km. Steam tugs had clawed their way to Switzerland against the current since the early 19th century, but as improvements progressed the Rhine ran ever faster and more powerfully, causing severe scouring. Former ports were stranded far from the new waterway, and the scrublands and desert that was left was an ecological catastrophe.

After the return of Alsace to France under the Treaty of Versailles in 1919, it was decided to build the Grand Canal d'Alsace as a lateral canal. The first consideration was creation of a series of hydro-electric power stations with associated navigation locks each capable of passing six 1,500 tonne barges. Work commenced in 1928, with the famous French architect Le Corbusier contributing design schemes for the barrages. Installations at Kembs (1932), Ottmarsheim (1952), Fessenheim (1956) and Vogelgrün (1959) were all built on a canal independent of the Rhine. It was then appreciated that consequential reduced river levels were producing disastrous effects, so the remaining four locks of the Grand Canal were planned on shorter lengths of channel, allowing water to return to the course of the Rhine at regular intervals. The later locks are Marckolsheim (1961), Rhinau (1964), Gerstheim (1967) and Strasbourg (1970). Together, the eight power stations can produce 7,000 million kW hr of electricity a year, roughly equivalent to the consumption of Greater Paris.

This was intended to be the end of Rhine engineering, but it was found that severe scouring below Strasbourg Lock still threatened to leave nearby ports stranded. There was no alternative but to build another lock at Gambsheim (1974), and still one more, in German territory, at Iffezheim (1976). Earlier problems were repeated, and yet more locks are planned farther downstream. Constriction of the river's course has posed a very serious threat from flash floods, which could create monumental inundations in the German cities of Karlsruhe and Mannheim. It is likely that a series of dams will have to be built throughout the upper Rhine, encouraging floodwater to overtop the banks progressively: the habits of the river will thus be similar to the situation that prevailed early in the 19th century, before interference by man.

Falling 140m in its French length, the Rhine is used by more than 25,000 barges annually; 25% of all Swiss freight arrives by water, principally timber, coal, chemicals, grain and oil. In Alsace 65km² of canalside land have been earmarked for industrial development as a result of the excellent transport facilities, and already levels of chemical pollution are massive: 90% of the Rhineside woodlands have been destroyed as a direct consequence of changes to the river during the 20th century. France has achieved a waterway larger than both the Suez and Panama Canals at great cost.

Distances in the following description follow the normal convention of measuring from Lake Constance (Bodensee). **Huningue** (K168.5), a suburb of the flourishing city and port of **Basle**, marks the upstream limit of the French Rhine. The right bank of the river is Swiss, becoming German at K170.

Boats wishing to travel to the highest navigable point of the Rhine at the Swiss town of **Rheinfelden** (K150), should note that the only practical mooring for visitors to Basle is in the Kleinhüningen harbour (K170) at the downstream approach to the city. Here is the Swiss Customs post: you are likely to be subjected to a very thorough investigation, judging by what we experienced with *Avonbay*. Questions asked will relate to the quantities of coffee, cameras, tape recorders and firearms (!) carried on board. Even in summer, water flow is rapid through the city and particularly under the bridges. We managed quite well with our normal 8 knots cruising capacity. Two Swiss locks, **Birsfelden** (K163) and **Augst** (K156, with a chamber of difficult sloping sides), take the navigator to the charming town of Rheinfelden. Here the current is very rapid; motorized craft should not attempt to proceed through the town bridge. A possible mooring is to the uppermost series of piles, west bank *inside* a small island just below the bridge, by arrangement with the Café Graff.

Twin chambers at the giant Marckolsheim lock

Below Basle, a fast current does not deter oarsmen and canoeists, who seem quite relaxed about taking their chances with heavy freight traffic, passenger vessels and private cruisers. Car ferries link one shore with the other. Industrial development, especially on the German bank, with large houses by the water in France, provides plenty of interest. Until about 1961 the Canal de Huningue branch of the Canal du Rhône au Rhin offered an alternative route between here and Kembs. Its course remains largely intact, with drawbridges by several of the disused locks.

Entry to the upper end of the Grand Canal and the Bief de Kembs is at K174. Generally banks are higher than the surrounding countryside, which consists of a wilderness of willow trees and melancholy swamps. Nothing can be seen of various quite pleasant villages such as **Rosenau** (K178), where a military tank has been preserved as a war memorial to events in this much disputed land. In any event, shore attractions must be ignored, for mooring is rarely practicable. The first of the duplicated locks is **Kembs** (K179); each has a fall of around 15m and working is accompanied by an unearthly screeching as the floating bollards slide up or down. Entry to the main line of the Canal du Rhône au Rhin is at K185.5. Beyond, a nature reserve has been established in desolate land at Île du Rhin, soon followed by a growing industrial zone and Port of Mulhouse-Ottmarsheim, downstream of **Ottmarsheim** Locks (K194).

Commercial traffic apart, there is little of interest to **Fessenheim** Locks (K210.5), site of a nuclear power station. **Vogelgrün** Locks (K244.5), where the hydroelectric works are open to the public, mark the point where the Rhine is rejoined and escape is possible from the Grand Canal d'Alsace. At K226.5 is an entry, left bank, to the Colmar Branch (see Chapter 29). Alternatively, cross to the German shore and head upstream to

Strasbourg Docks, a thriving commercial complex off the Rhine.

find a yacht harbour with fuelling facilities and water point (K226). Local pleasure craft frequently penetrate farther up the original river by negotiating a 67m lock situated above the bridge at **Breisach**; it is available daily 7.30–16.30h, but it should be appreciated that this diversion demands Customs clearance.

Each pound of the Grand Canal now alternates with a section of river navigation, with a width up to 1,000m. The journey thus continues down the canalized Rhine between K266 and K234.5 where a left fork leads to **Marckolsheim** Locks (K240). Scenery at last improves, several appealing towns on the German bank having half-timbered houses and vineyards. Once more the navigation divides at K249, the left channel connecting with **Rhinau** Locks (K256) with possible moorings at a yacht club near the entrance to the Strasbourg section of the radar-operated Canal du Rhône au Rhin (Chapter 24). We found that in the long hours of mid-summer daylight (but depending on waiting time for the locks) it is possible to tackle the Kembs-Strasbourg run non-stop via the Grand Canal. However, if in doubt, make advance arrangements to avoid being on the Rhine overnight. Additionally, unless in a great hurry to travel down river, you are much recommended to take the older and much more pleasant 'back door' route to Strasbourg; any initial enjoyment offered by the Grand Canal d'Alsace will doubtless be wearing thin by now. The next fork downstream is at K268.5, upper end of the **Gerstheim** Locks section (K272). Shortly afterwards a vast compensation basin appears on the left: reserved for sailing craft, it may not be entered from the navigation.

Facilities should be available at a yacht club on the German side, above the great Strasbourg barrage (K283.7). A further club lies inside No. 4 dock of the Strasbourg complex, below **Strasbourg** Locks (K287). The city provides many quiet short-stay moorings, with fuelling and other facilities near the Écluse Sud exit from the Rhine (K291, pleasure boat harbour projected) or on the German side of the river by the Strasbourg-Kehl road and railway bridges (K293.8). A map of the port showing its connections with the River Ill, Canal du Rhône au Rhin and Canal de la Marne au Rhin at K295.5, Écluse Nord, is provided, with a brief description of the city, in Chapter 26. Easily the most pleasant and central Strasbourg mooring is to be found on a quay of the Ill (quai des Pêcheurs) opposite a mid-river fountain and the entrance to the Fossé du Faux. See map in the *Carte Guide Marne au Rhin*.

The final section of French/German Rhine, Strasbourg to the German border at Lauterbourg, comprises the river's natural course with locks at **Gambsheim** (K309) and **Iffezheim** (K333.7). There are few facilities for pleasure craft, but short-term mooring should be possible in a selection of commercial harbours lying off the main thorough-fare. One of these is near the French border town of **Lauterbourg** (K349.3), an agreeable place with entrance gateway in red brick and stone.

When bound for Germany via the Rhine, it is no longer necessary to visit French and German Customs. However, you should expect investigation by the German water police. For craft of under 15 tonnes displacement, an RYA International Certificate of Competence (or equivalent) is required. Far more rigorous boat handling qualifications are demanded for larger vessels.

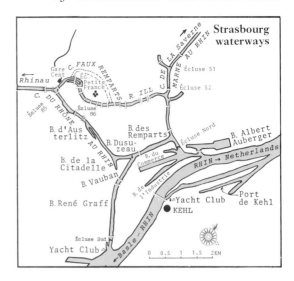

Strasbourg at La Petite France.

Scenically, this part of the Rhine is disappointing, and in no way approaches the grandeur of the Gorges between Bingen and Koblenz.

26 · River Ill

Carte Guide: *Canaux de la Marne au Rhin et Houillères de la Sarre*
From a junction with the Canal du Rhône au Rhin in Strasbourg, near the Port de l'Abattoir, to Nachtweid, near Illkirch-Graffenstaden; approx. 7km with 1 lock. A junction is made with the Strasbourg Branch of the Canal du Rhône au Rhin near its Écluse 85. Former connections were made with the canalized River Bruche and the Canal des Faux-Remparts, but both these routes are now closed.

When navigating from the Canal du Rhône au Rhin at **Strasbourg** (see Chapter 24), ignore the right turn that leads to the Bassin d'Austerlitz; instead, continue ahead and pass through the square arch in the Barrage Vauban, headroom being limited as at certain other bridges on the river; also, note that draft from here to the area near the Cathedral is officially limited to 0.7m. Beyond, the channel divides into three arms. The first watercourses, right, are millstreams passing under the Ponts Couverts. Follow the next opening, which provides access to the heart of the city. (A further channel with derelict lock is the beginning of the disused Canal des Faux-Remparts.) You will shortly arrive in La Petite France, a beautifully preserved district of 16th century gabled half-timbered buildings once housing tanners, fishermen and millers. It gained its name as a place of safety for Huguenots escaping from religious persecution. Several buildings, such as the Tanners' House of 1572, former seat of the Tanners' Corporation, have been turned into restaurants specializing in Alsatian wines, beer and food. At one time a giant plane tree could be climbed via a wooden staircase; drinks were served to seated customers high among the branches. Other notable buildings nearby are the half-timbered lock keeper's residence and, about 500m downriver, the Old Customs House, dating from 1345 and one of the oldest surviving structures in the city. Several attics are quite open to the wind and were used for drying skins during tanning. The traditional bird of Alsace is the stork: efforts are made to encourage pairs to nest on rooftops, now an increasingly rare event;

when chicks are successfully hatched, they are accorded front page newspaper coverage! Quays and buildings are floodlit by night.

Once a thriving port area, with numerous barges carrying all manner of freight, the Ill was also put to a more sinister use, criminals being plunged in cages into the heavily polluted water in order to extract a confession. Murderers were not so fortunate: they were merely cast into the stream in weighted sacks. Perhaps Strasbourg's darkest time was in the mid-14th century when 16,000 citizens were killed by an earthquake, followed in turn by a raging plague. Somehow, the Jewish community was blamed for these misfortunes: their property was seized and no fewer than 1,884 men and women and 900 children were stripped and set alight in a huge fire. Over half the children and a selection of the more attractive women were rescued by a group of appalled citizens. Hysterical acts of penitence followed, the population indulging in an orgy of mass flagellation.

Best moorings are to a stone quay on the right, a little before a swing bridge operated by the keeper of a lock around the next bend. Alternatively, he may allow you to lie between bridge and lock, where you will immediately become a tourist attraction for hoards of visitors to this, the most appealing, area of the city. In such a superb setting, it is at first difficult to believe your good fortune in being permitted to moor here!

Now the largest port on the Upper Rhine (and the fifth biggest in France), Strasbourg attracts international freight and is served by an extensive network of docks off the river. The name of the original Celtic settlement was Argentoratum, but by the 6th century AD it had become Stratisburgum, already an important crossroads. Over the centuries, various rulers have arrived and been deposed, the most recent domination being by the Germans for 47 years until 1918 and again during World War II. Germanic influences are still a powerful force. While Strasbourg is one of the finest cities of France, it has to be admitted (in a sweeping generalization) that people serving in shops and restaurants often lack the caring charm so noticeable in other parts of the country. It seems almost as if, safe in the knowledge that the city has been Capital of Europe since 1949 and boasts so many splendid buildings, sufficient tourists will come regardless! It is hopeless to attempt to list all the sites of interest here. Supreme is the great Gothic cathedral, dating from the 11th to the 15th centuries. The spire, recalling a multi-tiered wedding cake, soars to 142m; among its treasures are many superb stained glass windows and an astronomical clock of 1838 which trundles into fascinating action with moving figures at 12.30h each day (curiously showing a time half an hour later than normal).

The boatless visitor may get afloat in tripping craft that operate from a quay on the Ill near the cathedral. Itineraries include the Ill, La Petite France and the docks and last from $1\frac{1}{2}$ to 3hr. Departure times appear in the *Michelin Guide Vosges* or may be obtained from the Syndicat d'Initiative.

A water depth as little as 0.7m will prevent larger craft from reaching the upper part of the Ill, where a moderately strong current will be experienced. Most pleasure cruisers will have to approach the city centre from a downstream junction with the Canal de la Marne au Rhin, travelling no further upriver than the convenient moorings on the quai des Pêcheurs, opposite a mid-stream decorative fountain. Here, the quay may be congested in mid-season, requiring double-breasting of boats. Agreeable leafy surroundings eventually bring one to a junction with the Canal de la Marne au Rhin, with access right to the Rhine, or left through the Vosges to the Moselle and Northern France. (See Chapter 27.)

27 · Canal de la Marne au Rhin

Carte Guide: *Canaux de la Marne au Rhin et Houillères de la Sarre*

From Strasbourg, junction with the River Rhine to Vitry-le-François, junction with the Canal de la Marne à la Saône and the Canal Latéral à la Marne. Originally 313km, one section of 23.4km between Frouard and Toul has been closed, a through route being provided instead by the canalized River Moselle. There are 152 locks (not including those on the Moselle), an inclined plane boat lift at St-Louis-Arzviller and four tunnels: Arzviller (2,306m), Niderviller (475m), Foug (866m) and Mauvages (4,877m). A branch leaves the main line between the Mauvages Tunnel and Demange-aux-Eaux and terminates at Houdelaincourt, 3.2km. Additional connections with the River Ill in Strasbourg, the Canal des Houillères de la Sarre near Gondrexange, the Nancy Branch of the Canal de l'Est at Laneuveville-devant-Nancy, the River Moselle at Frouard, the River Moselle at Toul and the Canal de l'Est (Branche Nord) at Sorcy.

Given just one day to convert a person to the delights of French canal cruising, I would choose to take them along the 20km of Canal de la Marne au Rhin from Saverne to Niderviller in NW Alsace. We would climb through radar-controlled locks into the steep-sided and thickly wooded valley of the Zorn to Lutzelbourg; marvel at this charming little town in the Vosges; journey onwards to where the St-Louis-Arzviller inclined plane lifts our boat up a cliff face; voyage through the pine trees; and finally dive underground through two tunnels towards the more gentle countryside of Lorraine. It is 20km that contains a microcosm of all that I find irresistible about French waterways.

While this is the highlight of the waterway, almost from one end to the other it is packed with interest, well supplied with waterside restaurants and shopping facilities and with a healthy level of commercial traffic. Post-war modernization ensures a good standard of maintenance and the great majority of locks (except for some at the western end) are mechanized, many being radar-controlled. Surprisingly slow to be discovered by the pleasure boating industry, the canal now has several hire craft bases, including those at Lagarde, Lutzelbourg and Hesse. The automatic locks are negotiated quite easily, with instructions in French and German available on entry to the navigation. In some locations, boat crews are issued with a portable electronic device (similar to a television remote control) which activitates paddles and gates. Bank traction, once a great feature of the waterway, lasted through the Foug Tunnel until 1980; the only survivor of this kind of practice is an electric tug that hauls boats through the Mauvages Tunnel.

Starting in Strasbourg, the route leaves the Rhine and climbs to the valley of the Zorn. Crossing four watersheds, it encounters the valleys of the Sarre, Sânon, Meurthe, Moselle, Ornain and Saulx, but avoids direct contact with them all. Apart from a fairly brief association with heavy industry near Nancy, the course is intensely rural virtually throughout with delightful villages and small towns among the most interesting of NE France.

Brief history Built between 1838 and 1853, the object of the Canal de la Marne au Rhin was to connect Paris and the North with Alsace, the Rhine and Germany. Considerable obstacles had to be overcome in hilly terrain: hence the many locks and several tunnels. In places, construction was facilitated by its exact contemporary, the Paris-Strasbourg railway. Water supplies were assured by reservoirs, notably at Gondrexange and Stock, augmented by pumping in dry seasons. Early in the life of the waterway, Alsace and Lorraine fell to the German Empire, the eastern section passing from French control. As a result, plans were rapidly implemented to create a new line towards the Saône – the Canal de l'Est (Branch Sud) from near Nancy.

Designed with locks to accommodate 35m × 5m *flûtes* with 1.6m draft, the navigation was enlarged to the 38.5m Freycinet standard. Traffic flourished and a period of considerable prosperity followed the return of the lost portion at the end of World War I. During the late 1950s barge use had practically reached saturation point, many of the craft being wooden *bilanders*, lumbering box-like 300 tonne capacity vessels, mainly hauled by the towpath tractors of the Compagnie Générale de Traction sur les Voies Navigables. As early as 1925 financial concessions were offered to operators of *automoteurs* of finer lines and greater speed, there being as many as 7,000 *bilanders* in use throughout France. Yet the last of them were to linger on until the 1960s, forcing all other boats down to their tedious pace. With the end of towpath traction they were eventually outlawed; coupled with important improvements to the waterway itself, the Marne au Rhin was able to achieve a new level of speed and efficiency.

The 1960s saw the replacement of 17 locks in the Zorn valley by the St-Louis-Arzviller inclined plane and the substitution of 6 further locks by a single deep one at Réchicourt. On the 151km Nancy – Strasbourg section the number of lock-kilometres was reduced from 236 to 216 and the barge journey time improved from about 94 hours to 53. Most recent improvements include lock mechanization and the suppression of the Frouard-Toul length by taking advantage of the newly canalized River Moselle between these points. Thus, of *péniche* waterways, the Marne au Rhin is one of the most efficient and up-to-date in the country.

Entry to the waterway from the Rhine is through the Écluses Nord, situated in the NE part of **Strasbourg** by its dock complex. One route towards the city centre is provided by a left turn into the Bassin des Remparts; a more agreeable approach leading to the very centre near the cathedral and the Petite France area is to turn left onto the River Ill (K1.6). This navigation and Strasbourg itself are described in Chapter 26. The first of the canal's mechanized locks, mostly equipped with radar sensors since about 1979, is Écluse 51 (K1.7). The pleasant village of **Souffelweyersheim**, with facilities, lies immediately after Écluse 50. There is also an hôtel/restaurant in the pound 49/48. Further locks lift the canal through clean modern suburbs with at least five waterside restaurants in the section between Strasbourg and Écluse 44 (K22.1). Shopping is equally well catered for in a succession of small towns. One

chain of automatic locks runs from Écluse 46 to 42, with a further set from 41 to 37, inclusive. As passage through one prepares the next in the sequence, stopping midway would seem to be ill advised. **Waltenheim** (K22.1), a deeply agricultural village with Restaurant de l'Ancre, offers a first encounter with the River Zorn, whose steep-sided valley contributes greatly to the attractions of the route. **Hochfelden** (K27), to the right of the D25 road bridge, is a modern town. Lines of distant hills ahead indicate the proximity of the Vosges, with a progressively steeper ascent for the waterway. Écluse 36, shops and restaurant.

Churches with sharply pointed spires dominate each village. At Écluse 34 (K40.8), beyond **Steinbourg**, a notice warns of a strong current: you are advised to tie up securely. A patch of industry at **Monswiller** (K42) is notable for one factory advertising its products in the form of a giant wheelbarrow; the same motif is repeated in its decorative boundary fence. Turning sharply into a large basin, the waterway arrives in **Saverne** (K44), a magnificent Alsatian town of half-timbered houses, some carved and painted. It is a rose-growing region and an important touring centre with many walks into the surrounding hills. Good moorings in the basin (water, electricity, refuse disposal) enjoy a view of the vast Neoclassic summer palace of Cardinal Louis de Rohan. Rather an overpowering structure in red sandstone, it was built in the 1740s and is now somewhat half-heartedly used for various municipal purposes. Saverne has several good restaurants, a busy market and flourishing shops in a pedestrianized main street; it is the last easily approached town with comprehensive facilities for a long distance. Local industries include cut glass and the creation of exquisite Alsatian scenes in marquetry. We placed an order at the *atelier* of M. Straub for a framed view of *Avonbay*, leaving him with a photograph from which to work; some weeks later, the finished product was despatched to England: a remarkably accurate representation with authentic backdrop. Turning sharply at the end of the basin, we find an unusually deep lock, Écluse 30/31, the result of combining two conventional chambers in 1880 and utilizing the principle of the underground side-pond, whereby one third of water consumed on downhill operations is saved for the next uphill passage. Rise and fall is 5.43m.

Almost every crag in the surrounding hills is crowned with a ruined castle. One was reputed to be a finishing school for witches, several centuries ago! Another is the **Château de Haut-Bar**, overlooking the canal and about 5km by road from the town centre. It is well worth an expedition on foot or by bus to visit this famous viewpoint, overlooking the Alsatian Plain and the Zorn Valley; in clear weather the spire of Strasbourg cathedral is visible. The ruins contain a most acceptable restaurant, decorated in a traditional local style with wall paintings and Germanic furniture.

Lumber yards and the whine of power saws are an essential ingredient of the district, with tree trunks arriving by lorry from the nearby forests. This is an area to discover at a leisurely pace, for its great beauty encourages lingering. This is especially true of **Lutzelbourg** (K54), a real gem of a town grouped about Écluse 22 (Drydock). Road, canal, railway and River Zorn are squashed into the narrow valley, with bright green woods and tiny fields providing a backdrop to slate-roofed buildings in pinkish sandstone. A church spire peeps shyly above the top of an extraordinary butcher's shop with stone sphinxes and a Dutch gable overlooking the water. Sadly, this had closed for business by 1989. In the Hôtel des Vosges we discovered an old-established restaurant that can hardly have changed since the 1920s. It took little effort to imagine a jolly Dornford Yates party climbing from their touring Bentley to occupy a table in the large dining room. Among the delicacies on offer were blue trout from the Zorn. A company operates hire cruisers, so take the opportunity to replenish fuel and water supplies.

Four more locks ending with Écluse 18 (K57.2) bring a glimpse of the **St-Louis-Arzviller** inclined plane boat lift, a concrete track up a tree-clad cliff face, opened in 1969. This marvel of waterway engineering replaced Écluses 1 to 17. After considering various existing types of vertical lifts, water slopes and longitudinal lifts (similar to that at Ronquières in Belgium), an international competition was held and a transverse lift was eventually selected as being most suitable for this particular site. It is a single water-filled caisson or tank, able to accommodate a *péniche*, fitted with 32 flanged wheels running on a pair of rail tracks. It travels up or down a 108.65m path angled at a 41% slope. Electrically operated guillotine gates seal the ends of the tank, which weighs 850 tonnes when filled with water. Two sets of 14-wire cables run from the tank, over a pair of winch drums in the building at the top and back to two counterweights on either side of the central spine. Travelling at a maximum speed of 0.6m per second, each boat takes about 25 minutes for the transfer from one level to the other, compared with $8\frac{1}{2}$ hours for working through the locks. During a 13 hour working day no fewer than 39 craft passages can be achieved. The design allowed for installation of a second caisson running side by side with the existing tank, but this has not yet been added. If and when it is, daily capacity will increase to 78 barges. Regarded as a small-scale prototype for 1,350 tonne routes projected between the Rhône and the Rhine, the inclined plane was completed in a little under 5 years at a cost of 60 million francs. 1,209m of new approach channel was excavated at the lower end with 3,308m of new canal dug from the cliff face at the top. Riding up the plane is a thrilling experience, the journey being exceptionally smooth with splendid views over the forests of the Zorn Valley. Boats travel free of charge, while land-based tourists pay an entry fee to the upper complex, with a guided tour, well stocked souvenir shop and café, and the option of excursions in a tripping vessel. This runs daily between March and November. On the bank at the top, a St-Jean-de-Losne registered *péniche* is preserved as a graphic indication of the size of barge able to use the structure. A small canal museum is contained within, where specialist waterways books may be purchased. Tourist excursions around the site are available aboard a little road-based 'train'.

The series of old locks is now closed to traffic: they remain as an awe-inspiring spectacle, each with a keeper's cottage alongside. These are well worth exploration on foot or by bicycle. Although the old canal bed is virtually dry, all lock gear remains intact together with portions of a narrow-gauge railway, once used for hauling barges. At one point, this crosses a pound elevated on a structure of steel girders. Note the former locomotive shed near the top of the flight, with several engines slowly rusting on their tracks. Shortly after a junction with the line leading to the former Écluse 1 (K61) will be seen the control house containing a complicated array of switches governing traffic signals, closed-circuit television, ventilation fans and sodium lighting for the Arzviller and Niderviller Tunnels (2,306m and 475m long). Each is equipped with towpath and narrow-gauge railway track on which the electric towing 'mules' once operated. The bores are separated by an 802m open section where craft can pass. Lights give warning of any oncoming boats, both tunnels being one-way.

Rather more than 33km of summit level between the inclined plane and the next lock at Réchicourt offers a remarkable contrast to the Zorn scenery. The canal winds through rolling hills and pastureland less dramatic but nonetheless very pleasant. **Niderviller** village (K67.6) has the large Bassin d'Altmuhle (moorings, showers, slipway, water, electricity). A huge roofed drydock, which I first noticed in the early 1980s, still lay derelict late in 1989. This seems to be an ideal site for some form of pleasure boating business: I am amazed that it continues to remain deserted. 6km NW, the small town of **Sarrebourg** on the River Sarre has a fortified *château*, a regional museum (14th century ceramics and Gallo-Roman remains) and a World War I

cemetery containing about 13,000 graves. Europe's largest stained glass window, by Marc Chagall, can be seen in the Chapelle des Cordeliers. Villages with exceedingly un-French names include **Schneckenbusch** (K69.5) and **Hesse** (K72.3), the latter with a broad basin where Blue Line Cruisers opened a hire base in 1985. This impressive development incorporates a massive building used for winter boat storage (diesel and water). Arrangements can usually be made for long term mooring of private craft, while I have several times been very satisfied with their standard of repairs and maintenance. Basic shopping and restaurant in the attractive, partly fortified village. The River Sarre is crossed via a 45m aqueduct (de Laforge). Now comes a tree-lined cutting with stone banks, near **Imling**, with a further embanked section providing glimpses of distant towns at the approach to **Xouaxange** (K76.8). Basic facilities are available here, the town being composed of a hilltop cluster of buildings in reddish-brown stone with slate roofs. Several places announce their presence by signs on the canal bridges – a good idea that should be copied elsewhere.

Héming (K80), with prominent cement works, is a useful little town, shortly followed by **Gondrexange** (K82.4, shopping, taxi, restaurants) where a guard lock is fitted to cope with the possibility of any burst on the embankment which divides the waterway from its vital water supplies at the adjacent Étang de Gondrexange reservoir. Widely used for leisure activities such as windsurfing, sailing, caravans and camping, the lake is a recognized holiday area. A lonely junction, right, marks the beginning of the Canal des Houillères de la Sarre (Sarre Coalfields Canal), a surprisingly pleasant route leading to the navigable River Sarre and the German frontier (see Chapter 28).

Engineering features of the Marne au Rhin are notable as the canal begins to fall away from its eastern summit. Considerable changes carried out in the early 1960s have replaced 6 locks by a single deep one at **Réchicourt-le-Château** (K90.5), now known as Écluse 1. First, you pass through the level chamber of the old top lock and ahead the former line of the canal will be seen branching to the right. Instead, take the left fork to arrive at the new structure, whose rise and fall is a massive 16m. It empties by raising the guillotine gate at its lower end, an impressively rapid procedure akin to pulling out a highly efficient bath plug. A keeper is on hand to offer advice and French/German instructions; very necessary floating bollards are a great help.

One of the most exciting waterway structures of post-war France: the St-Louis-Arzviller inclined plane boat lift.

Beyond, the waterway now passes through the centre of the Étang de Réchicourt reservoir – a novel experience – with re-entry to the canal alongside the old Écluse 6, where the stone wall has been partially removed. A combination of wind and water flow can produce a strong current at this point. Following locks are radar-controlled, the first being No. 7 (K93.2); note the long-closed Épicerie-Café-Dépôt-du-Pain whose faded sign probably dates from the early 20th century.

Facilities in a collection of waterside villages now encountered are sparse but most necessities are available, especially if a scout can be sent ahead by bicycle while the boat negotiates locks. One most important stopping place is **Port-St-Marie** (K97.6), a tiny hamlet on the D40 road near **Moussey** and Écluse 10. A garage owned by the proprietor of the Auberge du Port (restaurant) is one of few canalside sellers of boat diesel. The procedure for filling a vessel's tank is fascinating: first the required quantity of fuel is pumped into a drum on a small cart. This is then attached to a motor mower and trundled down to the towpath, where its load is piped aboard by gravity. We supplied the *garagiste* and his assistant with large whiskies in gratitude for their services, which had only just averted real problems! The country lanes near here pass through extensive forests where there is every chance of seeing foxes, while the little River Sânon strikes up a close relationship with the canal that is to last all the way to Dombasle and the River Meurthe.

Lagarde (K103.2), near Écluse 12, is well worth a visit, being intensely rural with exceptionally friendly villagers serving in the baker, grocer, bar and restaurant. The Navig-France cruiser base offers fuel, gas and water. Reeds, corn, sheep and tracts of dark forest characterize the reaches past **Xures** (K107.1), with a section of canal up to 200m wide (possibly a natural lake?) west of **Parroy** (K111.4). A business once extending to butchery and grocer's shop by Écluse 16 (K114.6) has now contracted into a more useful bar and restaurant; as always in France, the wonder is that such village enterprises can remain in business, but being family-run, wage bills are greatly reduced. If you have time, go ashore at **Bauzemont** (K117.9), near Écluse 17: few supplies are to be had, with the exception of eggs and milk from a farm, but the grouping of houses, massive barns, haystacks, tractors and waggons in the main street is most picturesque. **Einville** (K121.9) is one of those small towns that seems to have seen better days; shops appear to open at irregular intervals, if at all. But there is a garage by the bridge and a hôtel/restaurant at the far end, before a basin. Steaming pans are evidence of salt production. Écluse 18 (K122.6) like others in the area, has an elegant cast-

British, German and Swedish holidaymakers share a lock at Foug.

iron name plate. A restaurant is near the bridge. Water supplies, a bar and a canalside diesel pump at Écluse 21 (K131.5).

After the next lock, Écluse 22 (K133.5), begins a rare but extremely interesting industrial area based on the chemical works of **Dombasle-sur-Meurthe** (K134.6). Massive factories line the waterway, with numerous bridges and gantries connecting one bank with the other. This is the Solvay soda enterprise; its products are used in glass, aluminium and plastics. Up to two dozen Solvay *péniches* in their smart livery would, until recently, be encountered, loading and unloading. The fleet numbered nearly 100 craft. The complex is best viewed from the isolation of a boat, and while there are copious shore facilities more travellers will wish to press on. Several locks have been duplicated, side by side, to cope with increased traffic, starting with Écluse 23 (K135.7). Should you pass through one chamber while the other is occupied by a barge, you will experience the curious effect of simultaneous vertical and lateral movement.

Virtually without a break, Dombasle merges into **St-Nicholas-de-Port** (K136.6). This little town on the banks of the Meurthe was the chief industrial centre of Lorraine in the Middle Ages. Its great Gothic basilica, built between 1494 and 1530, attracted many pilgrims and from an earlier church Joan of Arc set off on her

celebrated mission. Long ago, before construction of the canal, shallow draft barges would make their way from the Moselle and up the Meurthe to St Nicholas, an appropriate destination for craft whose owners venerate the Saint as their special patron. This brief incursion into an industrial landscape, recalling something of England's Black Country, ends as suddenly as it began. Although odd patches of factory development are scattered in the fields around **St-Phlin** (K140.6), there is a period of comparative countryside before further urbanization at the outskirts of Nancy. An aqueduct carries the canal over the Meurthe a little before duplicated Écluses 24 with a similar pair of locks in **Laneuveville** (K144). Water supplies are available alongside the right-hand chamber. Immediately beyond, the Nancy branch of the Canal de l'Est enters (closed until c.1993) and offers the most direct route to the Saône. This little town is exactly the kind of place that you would be unlikely to visit except by boat, but it provides convenient shopping and an agreeable atmosphere at the nearby Restaurant de la Marine.

The Canal de la Marne au Rhin now follows the valley of the Meurthe through one more pair of duplicated locks – Écluses 26 at **Jarville** (K146.5) – before entering the conurbation around the great city of **Nancy** (K149.2). Situated in a wooded area by the River Moselle, south of the Lorraine Plateau and the frontier of German Lorraine (1871–1918), it is an important manufacturing region, leading industries including salt and ironworks. Canal transport plays a vital rôle in distribution of goods, with extensive loading basins near the city centre at **Port Ste-Catherine**. Most central mooring is the Bassin Ste Catherine; alternatively try the Port de Malzéville, a little further on (water point and dry dock, with navigation authority workshop). Nancy is much more than an industrial complex: it has many large and stylish shops, several outstanding restaurants (such as the Capucin Gourmand in the rue Gambetta, whose specialities include *coquille St-Jacques à l'anis*, and La Gentilhommière in the rue Maréchaux, noted for *sauté de langoustines à la mousseline d'estragon* – prawns with tarragon) and a Museum of Lorraine History in the former ducal palace. *Art Nouveau* flourished here at the turn of the century: there remain many fine buildings in the style. Devotees should visit *Le Musée de l'École de Nancy*, housed in a villa at 38 rue du Sergent Blandon. In its Place Stanislas, Nancy has perhaps the finest square in France, a magnificent group of 18th century classical buildings with superb iron gateways, gilded lanterns and a huge fountain with wrought-iron screen. These features were introduced by ex-King Stanislas of Poland, who was granted the Dukedom of independent

This elaborate fountain and screen is a feature of the Place Stanislas, Nancy.

Lorraine by his son-in-law Louis XV on the understanding that it would pass to the French Crown on Stanislas' death.

On reaching **Frouard** (K158), an extensive inland port, through navigation is achieved via a lock on a short branch and entering the canalized River Moselle, some distance upstream of Metz. This section of the Class IV waterway was opened to traffic in 1972 and the subsequent extension of the river navigation up to Toul and Neuves Maisons was progressively achieved

in the years that followed. The canal has now been closed to traffic as far as Toul, its course being duplicated by the Moselle (see Chapter 29). Much of the line has been filled in, an impressive 187m aqueduct over the Moselle at **Liverdun** demolished (little more than a decade after it had been enlarged), and the adjacent charming port and approach to the 388m Liverdun Tunnel reduced to an overgrown wasteland. Thus 23km of the canal are now replaced by the Moselle. As an aid to planning travelling times, this distance is counted in the figures quoted in the description here.

Turning off the Moselle at K369.2, shortly before **Toul**, turn right into a new linking branch and pass through the boatman-operated automatic Ecluse 27 *bis* and back into the Marne au Rhin at the Port de Toul. (If bound for the Canal de l'Est (Branche Sud) and the River Saône, it is necessary to remain on the Moselle until K394.) To complicate the situation still further, about 20km of the Canal de l'Est's through route between the Branche Nord and Branche Sud follows the course of the Marne au Rhin up to Sorcy (K201.4). This intricate and confusing layout is explained in the *Carte Guide*.

Toul occupies the pre-historic bed of the Moselle and has long been a frontier city. Massive stone fortification walls originally designed by Vauban are pierced by the waterway as it runs through the city's moat towards the Port de France, a convenient mooring between Écluses 26 and 25 and within easy reach of good shops, a garage and with water point. There are mooring jetties, pleasant landscaping and a preserved towpath-towing-locomotive. Local canal information is available at a waterside navigation authority office. Heavily bombarded in 1940 and 1944, much of the old town went up in flames, but some ancient buildings remain, notably the 13–16th century cathedral of St Étienne which was much restored during the 1980s. The nearby Syndicat d'Initiative is a useful source of information on attractions of the area. Electric locks 24–14, the last with chambers duplicated side by side, lift the canal through pleasant suburbs to **Foug** (K190.9). All facilities lie to the right, the other side of a railway. Ahead, a one-way cutting runs up to the 866m Foug Tunnel which is illuminated and controlled by lights. Until 1980 boats were pulled through by electric mules, but this service is now suspended and craft may

Inside the 866m Foug Tunnel.

proceed under their own power. Vessels approaching from the west end at **Lay-St-Rémy** (K192.8) may be required to wait in a newly constructed basin until the way ahead is clear; information on traffic movements is available from a keeper.

North of the waterway, the Lorraine Regional Park is evidence of tracts of fine countryside that extend to the canal as it winds along a 19km level close to willow-fringed water meadows by the infant River Meuse. The course alternates from grassy cutting to broad cornfields and clumps of woodland. Almost all the villages have great charm: **Pagny-sur-Meuse** (K196.6) has a grocer and baker while **Troussey** (K200.6), by the reedbeds of the river, is a noted fishing centre. A prominent lime works stands near the junction with the Canal de l'Est (Branche Nord) at **Sorcy-St-Martin** (K201.4), the route for the canalized Meuse, Belgium and Holland (see Chapter 23). Modernization resulted in the replacement of an old stone aqueduct over the Meuse by a concrete structure, the Troussey Aqueduct (K202.3). There are magnificent views in this green and wooded valley. Running SW, the canal skirts the splendidly run-down little town of **Void** (K208.7), a place of agricultural equipment suppliers with a massive cast-iron hand-operated water pump and a bridge over the fast-flowing and rock-strewn course of the delightful little Meuse. Grain silos are served by *péniches*, and on the canal bank an obelisk erected in 1969 commemorates Nicholas Joseph Cugnot (1725–1804), to whom is attributed the invention of the automobile. A plaque illustrates the steam-driven vehicle for which he was responsible. Several km south, the small town of **Vaucouleurs** is worth a visit: fragments of a medieval castle still remain to see and strong links with Joan of Arc.

Locks 12 to 1 raise the waterway to another summit level. These are controlled by lights and pleasure craft must be sure to hold back the metal bars when entering and leaving the chambers for 10 seconds, otherwise the mechanism will not function. This is most easily achieved with a mop or boathook, a procedure that can be ignored by *péniches*, whose beam fills the width of the locks exactly. Lock conversion here was completed in 1979 at a cost of about 1 million francs per chamber. One manually-worked paddle remains at each end for use in the event of a breakdown in the electrical equipment. Their situation is superb, through rolling pastures as the hills gradually close in ahead. Limited facilities, including the Café de la Gare, will be found in the most attractive village of **Sauvoy** by Écluse 7 (K214.4).

Some delay is likely at the one-way Mauvages Tunnel, perhaps providing an opportunity to walk

from a bridge into the single street village of **Mauvages** (K220.3) where grey stone farmhouses once drew water supplies from elaborate cast-iron pumps decorated with faces. Narrow-gauge towpath locomotives stand disused in a cutting leading to the 4,877m tunnel, and portal plaques record the original construction in 1841–6 and rebuilding in 1911–14 and 1919–22. Boats must join a convoy behind a venerable electric chain tug, dating from 1912. Similar in design

LEFT *Switchgear at an automatic lock on the ascent to the Mauvages summit level. Working is normally remotely controlled, and activated by sensors.*

BELOW *The ancient chain tug emerges from the 4,877m Mauvages Tunnel.*

to the tunnel tug of Pouilly-en-Auxois on the Canal de Bourgogne, this dinosaur heaves its *rame* (convoy) at the speed of an *escargot*, each tow consisting of up to ten barges with pleasure craft positioned at the back. Making up the tow is a noisy and exciting operation, but once engines have been silenced and boats move off into the darkness (there is lighting at intervals) the passage is surprisingly quiet and relaxing. Adequate fenders are recommended. On my most recent passage of the tunnel, in company with just one other small cruiser, the tug driver allowed us to proceed astern of him unattached and using our own power: he pointed out that steering would be much easier like this. As the tug moves through the vault it trips switches, automatically turning on lighting in the approaching length and turning it off astern. Welcome though this assistance was, we felt that the value for money was limited when asked to make a payment for the tug's services at the next lock! Passage lasts about 90 minutes. There are currently two convoys daily in each direction. Consult nearby locks for details of the timings. At the far end, a 3.2km branch on the left leads to an active commercial basin in the small town of **Houdelaincourt**, with the Auberge du Pere Fours, a garage and some shops. At nearby **Gondrecourt-le-Château** there is a Musée du Cheval, devoted to the part once played by horses in transport and agriculture.

The remainder of the journey is quite heavily locked as a long descent begins through hilly and broken countryside, starting at Écluse 1, Tombois near **Demanage-aux-Eaux** (K228, supermarket, telephone and water point). Closely followed by the D966 road in the valley of the River Ornain, locks 1–17 are mechanized and radar-controlled: it appears likely that 18–70 will be similarly modernized when funds become available. Meanwhile, in 1986, Écluses 18, Longeaux, to 59, Remennecourt, were placed under the control of mobile keepers. Boats should provide details of their intended schedules at Écluse 1, Tombois, or 70, St Étienne. Any changes of plan must be telephoned to the Bar-le-Duc control point. Experimental procedures have been introduced for the automatic Écluses 12, Charmasson, to 17, Menaucourt. Because pleasure boaters often failed to hold back the sensor devices when leaving locks (which were mainly designed for barge use) problems arose with automatic setting of the next lock in the sequence. Craft entering this section are now issued with handheld transmitters which indicate when the detector has functioned.

Never is there a shortage of beautiful villages, all close at hand: St-Joire (K234.2), Tréveray (baker, K237), with water at Écluse 11, **St-Amand-sur-Ornain** (K240) and **Naix-aux-Forges** (supermarket,

K242.2). Here wooded cliffs of chalk rise from the water, remaining through **Menaucourt** (K244.7) and **Givrauval** (K247.4) to the agreeable town of **Ligny-en-Barrois** (K249.9, pontoon mooring with water and electricity). All supplies are available here with elaborate decorated gateways at the main road entries. A garage is close to Écluse 22. Available facilities in this area include drinking water, shopping and restaurant at Écluse 25, **Velaines** (K252.9), and a café and baker in **Tannois** (K258.9).

Locks progressively become the chief preoccupation (there are no fewer than 70 in the 86.6km from Mauvages to Vitry-le-François!). All remaining manually worked locks are fitted with an overhead connecting rod enabling both bottom gates to be opened by operating winding gear on only one side of the chamber – a considerable saving of time and energy for the keepers. Try to make time for a brief glance at **Longeville** (K261.1) whose houses are clustered in all manner of angles. For the first time since Toul, we shortly arrive at a substantial town, **Bar-le-Duc** (K265.5). Although now a flourishing centre for textiles, clock-making, woodwork and engineering, Bar was virtually an independent country from the mid-10th century and in 1354 its counts took the title of dukes. But towards the later 15th century it was absorbed into Lorraine and became fully French in 1776. The sizeable River Ornain is a feature of the centre with numerous 15th century buildings. In World War I it provided the only available route to besieged Verdun, 58km to the north: this road remains un-numbered, being known as the Voie Sacrée. The Marne au Rhin passes quite close to the centre with a pair of bascule bridges; moorings here are somewhat noisy, close to the railway station. In fact, from the water there are few signs that this is both a historic and attractive town. The most convenient shopping is at a supermarket (with garage) on the left shortly before Écluse 38, Marbot.

Note the three-arch aqueduct – one of a large number on this section – by Écluse 40, Chantereines (K268). In the rather urbanized village of **Fains-les-Sources** (K269.7), butcher, baker and grocer are very close to Écluse 42. In its final reaches, the canal is pleasant but unremarkable. The first place of any size is **Sermaize-les-Bains** (K288), slightly industrialized but providing reasonable shopping. Note the disused dry-dock and barge-building works. Now in the valley of the River Saulx, buildings are generally of red brick rather than the previous stone. Eating ashore is possible at a restaurant by Écluse 64 at **Pargny-sur-Saulx** (K293.4); there is also a water point, garage and grocer. After crossing a small aqueduct festooned with highly productive vines, by Écluse 65, **Etrépy** (K296), notable for its traditional *cheminées* (fireplace) factory, stone drinking fountain and *lavoir* (public washhouse), the canal passes vast unfenced fields. Among features in this length are the shallow and winding course of the willow-fringed Saulx and a huge Classical-style château in grey stone near **Bignicourt** (K298.2). Lights control traffic on a tight bend above Écluse 68, **Brusson** (K306).

The last 14km of the waterway comprise two very straight sections, rural but featureless (water point at Écluse 70, St-Étienne, K309.7), leading to **Vitry-le-François** (K313), an important barge town at the junction with the Canal de la Marne à la Saône and the Canal latéral à la Marne. Dozens of *péniches*, some withdrawn from regular service, lie on moorings with a short branch terminating by a disused dry dock. Decline in barge traffic has caused closure of an important chandlery and fuel point, although supplies can be arranged by road tanker. There is a freight exchange here, where boat people are offered cargoes. Vitry, capital of the Perthois, was established by François I in the mid-16th century as a fortified town replacing the medieval settlement of **Vitry-en-Perthois** destroyed in 1544 by the forces of Charles V. The centre lies quite close to the Canal de la Marne à la Saône and although not a place of great beauty, with much municipal housing and a sizeable Turkish population, it is worth visiting the main square, the Place d'Armes, dominated by a 17–18th century church. In the middle, a terracotta fountain of 1842 features the goddess of the River Marne, a paddle firmly clasped in one hand: graphic evidence that we have indeed reached a very different region from the Rhineland where this journey began.

28 · Canal des Houillères de la Sarre and River Sarre

Carte Guide: *Canaux de la Marne au Rhin et Houillères de la Sarre*
From a junction with the Canal de la Marne au Rhin near Gondrexange to the canalized River Sarre at Sarreguemines, 63.4km with 27 locks; 9.3km of navigable River Sarre with 3 locks runs from Sarreguemines to the German frontier beyond Grosbliederstroff.

Translated as 'the Sarre Coalfields Canal', this waterway suffers undeservedly from its gloomy title. With scarcely a hint of mining activity throughout the French portion, it drops steadily from the Marne au Rhin past a succession of lakes in the Lorraine Regional Park. Beyond Sarrable the navigation is along the River Sarre, an important stream comprising the Sarre Rouge and the Sarre Blanche which both rise near the French town of Donon. After Sarreguemines the line is officially known as the Canalized Sarre, and only on reaching the frontier with German Saarland is there any evidence of coal production.

Together with the Rhine and the Moselle, the Sarre (or Saar in German) offers a water route from France to Germany. When improvements are completed on the section across the border (see below) the possibility of a really interesting circular cruise becomes a reality: this will comprise the Houillères de la Sarre, the French and German River Sarre, the German and French River Moselle, and the Canal de la Marne au Rhin. For the present, pleasure boat traffic is very slight for the waterway is a cul-de-sac. A return cruise to the German head of navigation involves 60 locks in the round trip of 145.4km.

Brief history There is evidence of commercial traffic in small boats on the River Sarre during the Middle Ages, but the waterway we have now dates from the 19th century. First projected by Napoléon I, the canal was not finally constructed until 1862–6, shortly prior to the Franco-Prussian War of 1870 and the loss of Lorraine to Germany until 1918. But before these problems arose the French and Germans had agreed to co-operate in making the Sarre navigable from Sarreguemines to Luisenthal (25km with 6 locks), later extended a further 14km with 3 locks to Ensdorf, still a considerable distance from the German Moselle. A German fleet of *péniches* based on the Saar consequently had to make a long detour through France along the Canal des Houillères de la Sarre, the Canal de la Marne au Rhin and the Rhine itself before reaching the main part of the German network. Today, more than 100 barges fall into this category. The French Sarre and its canal handled 1,211,000 tonnes of freight, mainly coal, in 1936, a figure that has since fallen to less than 100,000 tonnes a year.

The Germans published a plan for the canalization of the lower Saar to link with the Moselle near Trier in 1930. Nothing materialized until 1969 when it was proposed to build a completely new 130km waterway, the Saar-Pfalz-Rhine Canal direct from the river to the Rhine. This was to have three inclined planes, an 18m deep lock and three long aqueducts: estimated to cost over £250 million in 1970, the idea was discarded. Three years later creation of a new navigation along the German Saar and suitable for Rhine barges and push-tows was agreed. This includes 6 locks 190cm in length with extensive excavation to lessen the effect of a series of exceptionally tight bends. The new route was completed upstream of the Mosel by 1989, except for a short section near the Franco-German frontier. At the time of writing, the breakthrough was scheduled for the year 2000. Total cost was in the region of £250 million. Smaller duplicate locks are scheduled for the use of *péniches* and pleasure craft.

Branching from the Canal de la Marne au Rhin at a lonely junction near the Étang de **Gondrexange** (see Chapter 27), the Canal des Houillères de la Sarre skirts a thickly wooded area near **Houillons** (K1.9) on the borders of the Lorraine Regional Park. Use of locks is subject to informing the authorities before 16.00h the previous day. This may be done by telephoning various offices (some are also equipped to receive VHF calls on channel 18). Details appear in the *Carte Guide*. Mobile keepers accompany boats. It then runs along the east shore of the extensive Étang de Stock (K5.5), a very attractive lake serving as a canal reservoir and heavily used for leisure activities. In an inlet on the west bank, the appealing village of **Rhodes** has a waterside church and a main street devoted to agricultural matters: it is filled with herds of cattle, hay carts and huge stacks of winter fuel in the form of logs. Écluses 2–12 are in a flight spread over 6.4km between **Albeschaux** and **Angviller-les-Bisping** (K17.4). Now in the 4,500 hectare Forest of Fénétrange, noted for roe deer and wild boar, we pass through part of the Grand Étang de Mittersheim and arrive at Écluse 13 in **Mittersheim** village (K20). This lake is also a reservoir, maintained by the navigation authorities, and is admirably adapted for sailing, small motor cruisers and bathing. A vast congregation of summer chalets and caravans takes advantage of the delightful location. Diesel supply in Mittersheim, opposite the useful pleasure boat harbour. A left fork between Écluses 13 (Restaurant L'Escale) and 14 is the start of the disused **Canal des Salines**. This originally ran about 17km SW to **Dieuze**: closure came in 1939 due to subsidence caused by brine pumping.

7km east of Mittersheim, along the rural D38 and thoroughly meriting a detour on bicycles, lies **Fénétrange** on the banks of the Sarre. Established as a medieval fortified border town, it is entered via a well preserved gateway, La Porte de France, featuring an *oubliette* (secret dungeon) complete with skeleton.

There is a castle and a slightly half-hearted Syndicat d'Initiative housed off an extraordinary curved stone courtyard. Several quite elaborate restaurants indicate the town's popularity with visitors. German appears to be spoken among the locals quite as much as French, the frontier lying about 36km to the north.

At the next bridge, variously known as **Pont-Vert** or **Pont-Neuf** (K22.5), a large restaurant could be useful for a lunchtime or overnight halt. Écluse 16 (K27.1) is mechanized (most locks are not). Good moorings between Écluses 17/18. The navigation becomes absorbed into the River Sarre at **Sarralbe** (K41.1), a thriving little town and the first place of any size on the canal. It is worth going ashore to see the town's 18th century gateway and a working watermill. Fuel is available at Écluse 20. We pass beneath the A34 Metz–Strasbourg *autoroute* just before **Herbitzheim** (K44.9), and after negotiating Écluses 22–26 on a winding section through **Wittring** (K52), a pleasing village of somewhat upright houses clustered around the church spire, and **Remelfing** (K61.1) reach **Sarreguemines** and the final canal lock, Écluse 27 (K63.4, *port de plaisance*). This town has long been associated with the production of *faïence*, pottery and porcelain: a pair of *faïence* ovens can be seen behind the *Hôtel de Ville*. An even more striking build-

The ultimate in French 19th century architecture on the riverbank at Sarreguemines.

ing, on the right bank of the river above the bridge, is the Casino de Faïences, an early 20th century structure covered with coloured tiles. Just downstream is a really amazing gateway in the form of a turreted gazebo with elaborate stone embellishments and all that was considered to be the ultimate in architectural taste when it was erected in 1880. A certain amount of industry, assisted by a substantial Turkish population, does not detract from the utility of excellent shops within a short distance of convenient moorings.

Three locks take the river into Germany, through **Welferding** (K66.4) where the right bank is German and the left French. Only at the twin towns of **Grosbliederstroff** and **Kleinblittersdorf** (71.6) is there at last any evidence of the mining that gives the canal its name, for here overhead cables carry an endless procession of coal buckets. Once across the frontier, spoil tips and power stations are a feature of the **Saarbrücken/Völkingen** conurbation. The river is now the Saar and is used by passenger boats and pleasure cruisers. As it journeys through the wooded hills towards the Moselle (*Mosel*) it extends a promise, soon to be fulfilled, of a memorable voyage down to the vineyards of Trier.

29 · River Moselle

Carte Guide: *Le Rhin et la Moselle* (Editions de la Navigation du Rhin) or *Mosel-Handbuch* (DSV-Verlag). The section Neuves-Maisons to Frouard is featured in **Carte Guides** *Canaux de la Marne au Rhin et Houillères de la Sarre* and *La Meuse et le Canal de l'Est*

From a junction with the Canal de l'Est (Branche Sud) at Neuves-Maisons to the Luxembourg and German borders at Apach (the German Mosel then continues to join the Rhine at Koblenz): 152.2km with 16 locks. Where new canal cuts have been excavated, certain of the former river reaches remain in use by pleasure craft and are noted in the following text. There are extensive dock systems at Thionville, Richemont and Metz, with two branches: the Embranchement d'Hagondange, from K283 to the Port d'Hagondange, 1.5km; and a line serving the Port de Nancy-Frouard, from K346.6, 2km with 1 lock. Additional connections with the Canal de la Marne au Rhin (West Section) at Toul, K369.3; and the Canal de la Marne au Rhin (East Section) off the Nancy-Frouard Branch, near K346.6. Parts of the original Canal de l'Est (Branche Sud) and

Canal de la Marne au Rhin have been absorbed into the course of the newly canalized Moselle which now provides through routes in each case. (See Chapters 22 and 27 respectively.)

Since World War II the Moselle has been totally reshaped to provide a Class IV navigation suitable for 1,500 tonne barges and 3,000 tonne push-tows all the way from Neuves-Maisons to the Rhine at Koblenz. Previously only its central portion was used by *péniches*, although the length from Neuves-Maisons to Toul formed part of the lateral Canal de l'Est (Branche Sud). The far-reaching works that have been carried out are one of the great success stories of modern French waterways.

Pleasure craft should experience little difficulty in sharing the route with heavy commercial traffic provided they adhere to the regulations and apply customary common sense. At various points yacht harbours have been established or are planned, and not infrequently there are side arms or sections of the old river for an escape to wash-free overnight moorings. The barges tend to move between dawn and dusk.

Rarely does the scenery approach the celebrated grandeur of the German Mosel. Rising in the Vosges near Bussan, it is first navigable at Neuves-Maisons, noted for its steelworks. The downstream run to Frouard, near Nancy, is extremely pleasant with hilly tree-covered banks. Industry intervenes here and returns again between Metz and Thionville, with steel production predominating. As the Moselle nears Germany the first vineyards appear and thereafter its course remains spectacular all the way to the Rhine.

It can be important to realize that between 1871 and 1918 the river from Arnaville (upstream of Metz) to the present frontier lay within German Lorraine. This occupation, while detested by the French inhabitants, has left lasting reminders of Prussian influence in architecture, language and food. Passenger vessels operate at Metz and from Thionville to the German border.

Brief history Freight rafts were used on the Moselle by the Romans, and according to Tacitus there was a scheme to link the river with the Saône thus providing a navigation all the way from the Mediterranean, via the Rhône, to the Rhine at Koblenz. But this dream was not to materialize (at least over that particular course) until the mid-20th century. Initial attempts to render the Moselle fit for barges were made in the 17th century by Vauban; but by the end of the 18th century the river was reported to be useless for regular trade. A start was made by Chedeaux in 1816 to deepen the channel and ill-fated trials carried out with a passenger steamer, *Ville de Metz*, in 1839. Lack of draft and problems with the Prussians killed the project. Two years later, four steam-driven paddlewheel *inexplosibles* went into service from Nancy to Metz and Metz to Trier. They had been built on the lower Loire at Nantes and were navigated all of 2,011km to the Moselle via the Loire, Seine, Oise, Meuse, Belgium, Holland and the Rhine. Floods and droughts eventually put paid to the scheme; railways were opening and within seven years the vessels were sold for use on the Rhine.

Renewed efforts to tame the river began in 1867 with a programme of lock and weir construction from Frouard to Metz. The Franco-Prussian War intervened and the section remaining in France (downstream to Pont-à-Mousson) was opened by 1876. Prussian railway interests obstructed further progress and the traffic from French Lorraine was forced to reach the Rhine via the heavily locked and longer Canal de la Marne au Rhin to Strasbourg.

With the 1918 peace, thoughts again turned to Moselle improvements and in 1929 30km with 4 locks was canalized between Metz and Thionville. Known as the Canal de Mines de Fer de la Moselle (CAMIFEMO), this was finished in 1932. Meanwhile Hitler's Third Reich had begun to canalize the German Mosel: work continued until 1944 and the first lock at Koblenz was completed in 1947.

Subsequent history of the river is a prime example of the benefits of European co-operation. A Société Internationale de la Moselle was established between France, Luxembourg and West Germany in 1956 with the object of creating a Class IV waterway. The Thionville – Koblenz section was inaugurated in 1964; an extension to Metz was achieved in 1970; the new inland port of Frouard was ready by 1972; and the final stage Frouard – Neuves-Maisons was ready for traffic late in 1978 (this part alone had cost nearly £40 million). More than 12 million tonnes of freight passes through the Mosel at Koblenz each year, about 9 million of it to France. And as the waterway is in existence, it actively attracts traffic and new industries in addition to those for which it was originally designed.

The story of the Moselle is not yet complete: one further stage was proposed in the mid-1960s under the Fifth Plan. It envisages a totally new navigation between Neuves-Maisons and the Upper Saône at Corre, with a 52km summit level served at each end by 42m and 68m high Class IV inclined plane barge lifts. Thus the Rhine will be linked to the Rhône via the Moselle with 1,350 tonne barge capacity, compared with the 350 tonne *péniches* that currently use the Canal de l'Est (Branche Sud). Construction has yet to begin.

In the description that follows, distances quoted coincide with the kilometre posts which are measured from the Rhine at Koblenz.

Waterways enthusiasts – especially devotees of commercial use – will regard the start of the Moselle at **Messein** (K394) with pleasure. But other travellers may consider the area rather dreadful. As the *péniche*-sized Canal de l'Est (Branche Sud) passes through its Écluse 47 (see Chapter 22) it is instantly transformed into a route for Eurobarges at a big concrete-sided basin. Ahead, alongside a broad reach of new canal, are the ironworks of **Neuves-Maisons**, with an even larger basin at the far end shortly before the first of the massive locks. Flood marks show how the Moselle, a short distance to the left, has at times put the whole complex under more than a metre of water. Note a concrete wall rising from a road by the side of the lock: it is recognizable as part of the chamber of a demolished Canal de l'Est lock. The town is frankly very dreary, with rows of squalid foundry workers' houses; nevertheless, we found the shopping to be most comprehensive even if we did begin to regret having piled the bicycles with laden boxes which then had to be pushed 800m in sweltering heat back to the boat! There is the promise of charming countryside soon to come. 5km of artificial canal leads past the suggestively-named **Sexey-aux-Forges** (K388), a hilly little town set above the river and the fast-decaying remains of the Canal de l'Est.

Telling evidence that for many years Metz was under German occupation. This postcard, offering greetings from the Metz steamers, was sent in 1899.

Having joined the natural river in rural surroundings, **Maron** (K387.2) provides some shore facilities if a suitable mooring can be found near the D92 road bridge. **Nancy** lies about 12km NE on the far side of the Forêt de Haye.

The following reach to the fortified village and citadel of **Villey-le-Sec** (K380.6) is extremely pleasant. Pleasure craft harbours may have been established in basins off the right bank at K381.7 and K380.5, above and below an electric cable crossing. (No facilities other than mooring free from the wash of passing traffic.) If you wish to explore Villey, moorings might be possible with care on the portion of river that leads to a weir (right bank). The Écluse de Villey-le-Sec lies on a short canal to the left. **Pierre-la-Treiche** (K376.1) is followed by **Chaudeney-sur-Moselle** (K374) where a recently constructed concrete road bridge was demolished to allow the passage of barge traffic. Pleasure boats are no longer permitted to use an old *péniche*-sized lock in **Toul**: they must follow the Moselle navigation and pass through a large mechanized lock alongside. The fortified city is a short distance away on the left (see Chapter 27). Several hundred metres downstream of the Pont de Toul, a left turn provides access to a new automatic lock (worked by the boat's crew) leading to the western part of the Canal de la Marne au Rhin in the direction of Vitry-le-François (Chapter 27). Good moorings on the canal at the Port de France between Écluses 25 and 26.

At intervals on the left bank will be seen bridges and lock houses of a closed portion of the Canal de la Marne au Rhin, withdrawn from service between Toul and Liverdun when the Moselle was opened to traffic. Infilling is well advanced, a curious and rather sad situation for a canal that had so recently carried very heavy quantities of freight. From K373 to K361 navigation is through an artificial channel, somewhat isolated from small towns such as **Gondreville** (K365.4) and **Fontenoy-sur-Moselle**, where there is a lock (K364). On reaching **Villey-St-Étienne** (K361), junction with the natural river, it is possible to turn upstream and cruise safely for almost 5km to a weir beyond Gondreville. On the way you will pass Fontenoy once more where upwards of 60 small cruisers lie on moorings by a slipway and petrol point.

Aingeray Lock is situated on a short canal at K356. An agreeable wooded reach now extends to a broad loop at **Liverdun** (K352), site of a demolished two-way Marne au Rhin aqueduct and disused tunnel which pierces the tree-covered hill on which the town is built. The area is ambitiously known as Little Switzerland in Lorraine and has marked waterside cycle routes. One road entry is through a 16th century

gateway. Houses are clustered in layers amid the greenery of a cliff, and the once charming canal basin is now a bleak wasteland overlooked by a boatman's café where a faded sign advertises stabling for barge horses. (See also Chapter 27.)

Industry begins to close in as the valley narrows at the approach to **Frouard** Lock (K348), followed without a break by **Pompey** (K347), a place of ironworks. After a railway bridge there is an important junction: right leads to the Port de Nancy-Frouard, a sizeable commercial harbour reached through the Écluse de Frouard-Clévant. Pleasure boats should aim for the smaller Freycinet chamber on the right: this leads into a large basin with an arm at the top right providing access to the eastern part of the Canal de la Marne au Rhin, direction Strasbourg. Even if travelling further down the Moselle, it would be worth considering making a detour along here in order to visit **Nancy** by water (see Chapter 27). Otherwise, public transport or taxi would serve the same purpose: the distance is only about 8km.

Turn left at Pompey junction to continue down river, with the Moselle's once-navigable tributary the Meurthe reaching its confluence near K345. Although close to the A31 Nancy–Metz *autoroute*, the next section of waterway is pleasant, especially below the Écluse de **Custines** (K343.6) and on to **Belleville** (K341.5). Here a weir across the river marks the start of the short Belleville cut, the Moselle being rejoined at K339.5. Remains of the old *péniche*-sized waterway include a disused but intact lock and canal near K338, with a further length leading out of the new Blénod-Liégeot Dérivation at K334.9 and running as far as **Pont-à-Mousson** (K327.5). This well known foundry town boasts one of the finest waterfronts on the entire Moselle. Moorings will be found either on a vertical quay near the bridge or alongside meadows. Constant bombardments in World War I and in 1944 resulted in serious damage to this gateway to German Lorraine. An encounter between the American forces under General Patton and the Nazis is recalled by a large fountain decorated with lamp standards, presented to the town by the United States. It dominates the remarkable Place Duroc, an almost triangular 'square' surrounded by 16th century stone buildings with arcades at street level and quite equal to the rather similar centre of Louhans, on the River Seille in Burgundy. The Maison des Sept Péchés Capitaux illustrates the Seven Deadly Sins in carvings, while another fine structure is the delightfully named Château d'Amour. East of the river is the Butte de Mousson, a hill surmounted by the ruins of a feudal castle built by the Dukes of Bar. Walk to the top for a magnificent view over the surrounding countryside. Pleasure craft are welcomed at a harbour downstream of the town (K326.8).

Navigation from K325.7 to the Écluse at **Pagny-sur-Moselle** (K318) is by means of a canal, with the village of **Vandières** (K321.6) en route. The years of Prussian occupation up to 1918 are remembered in **Arnaville** (K315) by the Rue des Anciennes Douanes, where there was once a frontier Customs post. Remains of a Roman aqueduct which spanned the river will be seen between **Jouy-aux-Arches** and **Ars-sur-Moselle** (K307): 18m high and about 4m wide, it brought water supplies to the city of **Divodurum-Medio-Matricorum**. In later years it was believed to have been constructed with the help of the Devil! Next comes the Écluse d'Ars (K306.7). At K302.3 (left bank) is the Metz Yacht Club (fuel, chandlery, with supermarket – also selling bottled gas – 600m distant). To reach a very agreeable mooring in the heart of **Metz**, take the channel at K298.5 just upstream of the *porte de garde* de Wadrineau; follow the river on the far side, pass beneath the A31 *autoroute* bridge and emerge in a broad pool by the Esplanade and near the Allée Victor Hugo. Many cruisers are moored here on floating stages. Continue to a quay (right) a little upstream of the Protestant Temple. In 1986, 11km of navigation, which had been closed for more than 20 years, was brought back into use. This duplicates the route of the main waterway between Jouy-aux-Arches (K306) and the centre of Metz. There are two locks on the line: l'Esplanade and la Citadelle.

Metz is a French Army garrison city founded 2,000 years ago. A 13th century *château*-fort, the Deutches Thor or Porte des Allemands, straddles the little River Seille. In later years fortifications were designed by Vauban and these same structures helped the Germans hold out against General Eisenhower for more than two months in 1944. There was dreadful slaughter in this vicinity during the Franco-Prussian War and a great gloom and sadness settled on Metz after 1871, many of the French inhabitants moving away. The great Gothic cathedral of St Étienne is among the finest churches in the country. By climbing to the top of the Tour de Mutte a splendid view is obtained. A famous bell cast in 1605 rang on momentous occasions such as the German defeat at the end of World War II. Other monuments include the long Pont des Morts de Metz, a bridge spanning two arms of the Moselle. Building and maintenance costs were obtained for 500 years from the 13th century by means of a law that required every man dying within the See of Metz to leave his best suit of clothes to be sold for the benefit of a special fund. The church of St Pierre aux Nonnains is the oldest basilica in France, once attached to a 7th century abbey. When the railways arrived, tracks were laid over the site of a huge Roman amphitheatre – an appalling act of vandalism. Shopping facilities are excellent with a large classical market hall. A fascinating sidelight on one-time domestic washing arrangements in Metz is provided by an American, George Waring, whose book *The Bride of the Rhine – Two Hundred Miles in a Mosel Row-Boat* was published in 1878. He discovered that it was possible for residents to order a hot bath to be brought to their homes: a waggon would arrive at the front door bearing two portable tubs, a barrel of water and a stove and boiler to heat it. For payment of 1.20 francs, servants would carry the necessary equipment indoors while the neighbours would be supplied with fullest details of the frequency of one's personal cleansing!

Beyond Metz navigation is along the course of the river, through the Écluses de Metz (K297) and past the entrance to the Nouveau Port de Metz (K294), an area that increasingly attracts industry. The river broadens into an elongated lake (K290–288) fringed by large houses and much used by dinghy sailors. At the far end, turn off into a long canal with a pair of locks at **Talange** (K283.6) followed immediately by a branch serving the Port d'**Hagondange**. After the Écluses de l'Orne at **Richemont** (K277.7) we join the river once more, with further yacht clubs (K276.6 and K275.6). Another canal starts at K273.2 with connections to extensive railway sidings in the Port Public de Thionville-Illange.

Thionville is entered after locks (K269.9) and is seen to good advantage from the waterway. The city marks the end of a succession of steelworks, power stations and refineries, and although containing its fair share of industry is not without considerable interest. Over the centuries it has frequently changed hands. The Merovingians built a castle which was adopted by Charlemagne in the 8th century. By the 13th century the Counts of Luxembourg had raised a huge fortified *château* which in subsequent years was held in turn by the Burgundians, Hapsburgs and the Spanish. Finally, the city was granted to France in 1659 and the ubiquitous Vauban surrounded it with fortifications. While under the Germans from 1870 to 1918, Thionville was provided with additional defensive works and many impressive public buildings reflecting the Prussian taste in architecture. Recent years have seen the creation of a pedestrianized shopping centre. Moorings will be found in the pleasure boat harbour upstream of the lock (chandler, fuel and gas), although the immediate locality is very commercial and unattractive.

Pleasant scenery now follows the valley of the

Moselle past the villages of **Ham** (K262) and **Basse-Ham** (K260) a little before a short cut leading to the Écluse de **Koenigsmacker** (K258.2), with overgrown gravel workings now popular with anglers. **Malling** (K254) is on the riverbank and dominated by the spire of its Gothic church. **Rethel** (K249) has possible moorings on a wall (check depth) and the first terraced vineyards for which the lower Mosel is so famous. Apple orchards and plantations of walnuts are a feature of **Contz-les-Bains** (K247) as the valley narrows through wooded hills.

Sharp bends demand that commercial traffic slows to a tickover as the barges line up for the next reach, leading past a yacht club (K246.3) into the delightful little town of **Sierck-les-Bains** (K245.5). Like other border settlements it suffered a stormy history, and was sacked by the Swedes in the Thirty Years War, with further serious damage towards the end of World War

II. Vines cover the slopes on the opposite shore and a busy little railway divides the main part of the town from its waterfront. Useful shopping with a choice of restaurants are an encouragement to moor up, the best site being on a small concrete jetty directly alongside the K246 marker post or in the *port de plaisance*, just downstream of a camping site (several hundred metres from the town centre). Do not attempt to lie on walls elsewhere: these are obstructed by underwater rocks. Sierck is dominated by the ruins of a very extensive *château-fort*, extending along the skyline. Its intact outer walls look down onto the roofs of houses and provide a splendid view of craft moving along the Moselle. Built in the 11th century on the foundations of a Gallo-Roman fort, it successfully held out against the Duke of Marlborough in 1705, was demolished after the Treaty of Utrecht a few years later and was rebuilt in its present form in 1773. Many roofed por-

Vineyards by the Moselle near the German border.

A large-capacity freight vessel heads downstream towards the German border at Sierck-les-Bains.

tions remain, with vaulted tunnels and staircases leading to circular rooms: it all provides scope for a fascinating tour of discovery. (Public admitted 9.00–12.00h and 13.30–19.00h, May 1–Sept 30.) Seen from the riverbank at night, the *château* is pure magic, the lower parts illuminated by orange lights with the upper towers in white. It floats above a dark band of

rock and trees, with street lamps twinkling in the water far below. Barges move through the gloom, their engines chuffing relentlessly, proving that skippers have intimate knowledge of every metre of the waterway, for only the bridge arches are lit after dusk.

One last lock remains in France, at **Apach** (K242.5), a village of railway sidings and former Customs posts at the frontier with Germany and Luxembourg. Craft are now able to pass downriver unchallenged – one positive benefit of the European Community.

Mr and Mrs George Waring explore the Moselle by rowing boat in the 1870s. Note the practical sunscreen at the stern and the capacious trunk in the bows.

IV·BRITTANY AND THE LOIRE COUNTRY

30 · River Rance

Carte Guide: *Bretagne*
From the Atlantic coast at Dinard and St-Malo to the Marine Lock at Le Châtelier, near Dinan, junction with the Canal d'Ille et Rance: 22.6km with 2 locks.

The Rance in its lower reaches occupies a flooded valley, with steep wooded banks and numerous inlets. For experienced sailors this is most attractive water, but it should be regarded more as a tidal estuary than an inland waterway. An 800m barrage incorporating a tidal power station also provides a road link between **Dinard** and **St-Malo**. Exceptionally high tides make the site very suitable. A 65m long lock on the Dinard side of the barrage operates at all times when there is a depth of at least 4m above and below. Full details of the operation are contained in the *Carte Guide*. Depending on the requirements of the generating station, there can be a strong flow in the impounded estuary upstream, with water levels falling by as much as 1m in 10 minutes. Having calculated the tide times, it is advisable to pass through the Rance without delay and reach real inland water beyond the second lock, **Le Châtelier**. The most favourable time to leave the barrage is about 3hr before high water, having the advantage of the flood tide over the mudbanks at **Mordreuc**, near the upper end of the tideway. Le Châtelier Lock operates between 6.00 and 21.00, but only when there is a level of at least 8.5m in the tidal basin.

Yachtsmen accustomed to the ways of the sea will take these problems in their stride (their real fears only usually begin on entry to shallow still-water canals, with bridges and waterway bottoms threatening the ship from more than one direction). But inland boating enthusiasts, and especially those in hire cruisers, will stay well clear of the tidal Rance. Instead, you can embark on a passenger vessel which completes the journey from St Malo and Dinard to **Dinan** or *vice versa* in about 2½hr (May–Sept). It is possible to leave your cruiser in Dinan, travel down the estuary, enjoy a day at the seaside in either of the two resorts and return

Barrage and tidal power station on the Rance estuary.

by water in the evening. Dinard is a fashionable resort not unlike Torquay, developed since the middle of the 19th century and always popular with the British. By contrast, St-Malo is an ancient fortified port, fully restored after the destruction of World War II, and now a busy sailing centre with moorings for more than 800 craft in two huge basins.

31 · Canal d'Ille et Rance

Carte Guide: *Bretagne*
From the estuary of the River Rance at Le Châtelier Lock, near Dinan, to Rennes, junction with the River Vilaine: 84.8km with 47 locks.

A very verdant waterway through lush pastures and woods and little changed since the days of commercial traffic, the Canal d'Ille et Rance is quite well maintained. Some locks – unusually for France – retain wooden balance beams to open the gates and all are operated by keepers. The towpath is generally fit for cycling or walking. The most notable engineering fea-

ture is a flight of 11 locks at Hédé, normal enough for the habitual canal user but regarded with a degree of horror by the crews of the many small sailing craft using this route between the English Channel and the Bay of Biscay. A large proportion of private craft seem to be owned by Channel Islanders. The canal is rural throughout, one of the most attractive lengths being the section nearest Dinan, along the valley of the Rance. Nowhere in France are the lock gardens so magnificently filled with flowers as on the Ille et Rance. Pleasure boaters assist in the annual judging of the best display by completing a voting form.

Brief history By 1539 the River Vilaine was navigable from the Bay of Biscay to the Brittany Capital, Rennes. It was one of Europe's first waterways to be equipped with pound locks. An obvious further move was to cut a canal from there to connect with the Rance and open a trade route to the Channel coast. Plans were eventually drawn up in 1736, but progress was dreadfully slow: by the time the Revolution had intervened little had been achieved. According to various printed sources, the Canal d'Ille et Rance was eventually inaugurated in 1838, 1839 or 1842. Considered only of secondary importance at the time of the Freycinet Act of 1879, like other Brittany canals it was never enlarged. With no reliable connection to the rest of the French network, any great upturn in trade seemed unlikely.

At the beginning of the 20th century freight craft in use included *Rance chalands*, *gabareaux de Rennes* and *pénettes de Redon*. Most were of wood and horse drawn; some were rigged as sailing barges for estuary work. Motorized barges were introduced in the late 1920s, mostly working near Rennes. Freight boats appear to have lingered on until the early 1960s. For a time thereafter, before the growth in pleasure cruising, there was a strong possibility that this and other Brittany canals might be closed down. Exploitation of the leisure use of the navigation was actively carried out by the Committee for Promoting Tourism on Breton Canals. Maps and guides were published, signboards erected at town and village moorings advertising the facilities, and advice given to prospective hire cruiser companies. As a result, waterways of the area are now among the best managed from a pleasure boating viewpoint.

An electrically operated lock at **Le Châtelier** is effectively the upstream limit of the maritime River

Sailing cruisers on the Canal d'Ille et Rance across Brittany, widely used by such boats.

Rance (see Chapter 30). It is said that high tides can still, on occasion, flow over the weir and affect levels as far as the second canal lock, Pont-Perrin, No.46. Moorings here tend to be somewhat congested with private craft and hire cruisers. There is a slipway and restaurant. Wooded cliffs run down to the water, with a broad pool up to 450m wide. Stakes and buoys mark the navigation channel, which only begins to narrow at the approach to **Dinan** (K7). Still very much in the world of the yachtsman, there are extensive jetty moorings along the right bank packed with sailing craft and cruisers, with a stern uniformed official ever alert to collect a not inconsiderable fee; attempt to tie up on the deserted quays opposite and he instantly becomes highly agitated! (Water, fuel, showers.) But the attractions of the town are such that inland boaters must become resigned to paying for facilities that virtually everywhere else on French rivers and canals are free. Slipway, water, fuel, rubbish disposal and crane for lowering masts are all laid on. Charming old buildings line each side of the port, with a pretty gothic bridge upstream. Diesel powered passenger craft operate a service to Dinard and St-Malo, replacing steamers that worked over the route up to a hundred years ago. Several restaurants and basic shops will supply most needs.

The old town of Dinan stands above the river surrounded by ramparts and fortifications. Its great hero is Bertrand du Guesclin, a peasant warrior who defended the fortress against the English in the 14th century. Steep cobbled streets lined with half-timbered houses (mainly 15th century) lead the visitor from the river up into the town centre. Various craft workshops specialize in weaving, pottery, cane work and glassblowing. One of the finest buildings is the 15th century Governor's House in the Rue du Petit-Fort. Visits should be made to the 14th century castle with its 34m Coëtquen Tower and the slightly later Clock Tower in the Rue de l'Horloge. Splendid views down to the river are obtained from the English Gardens, overlooking a massive stone viaduct carrying the N176 across the deep valley. Shopping is excellent, with many opportunities for buying tasteful souvenirs. Visit also the retail fish market, a curious structure of concrete colonnades. Dinan is one of the best preserved medieval towns in France.

Above the bridge the waterway immediately narrows and follows a winding course through dense woodland. This Rance section is perhaps the most attractive part of the canal. The well surfaced towpath provides an agreeable walk to Écluse 47, **Léhon** (K9), downstream of the partly ruined priory of St Magloire with 12th century church (vaulted roof and tombs) and

17th century cloisters. Moor at a small landing stage above the little stone bridge. Lying in the bottom of a steep-sided valley, Léhon has a few shops and a splendid open-air swimming pool. The possibility of floods has resulted in the prohibition of overnight mooring between Léhon and Écluse 43, La Roche; however, little danger exists in summer and the rule appears not to be enforced.

Past a *château* with slated towers among the trees, Écluse 46, Pont-Perrin (K11) is approached via a channel on the right. (If in doubt, always follow the towpath.) Where the river is regained, at a junction above, is a huge stone quarry with buttercup-filled water meadows, white poplars and alders. One of the most agreeable locks on the entire canal is No.45, **Boutron** (K14) on a short artificial cut. Immediately alongside the chamber (spanned by an iron swing bridge) is a stone watermill with intact wheel; the keeper's house built into a cliff on the right is approached up a double flight of steps, an indication of the likelihood of flooding. Very derelict ivy-clad farm buildings rise from the towpath, above. Several of the locks about here have gates opened and closed by a capstan arrangement. Elsewhere wooden balance beams are used, although these have sometimes been sawn off and a more modern winding device installed. The River Rance finally leaves the navigation at Écluse 43, La Roche (K18). Floods are not the only difficulty to have affected the canal in the past, for a plaque on the lock cottage at **Évran** (K19) records a drought that resulted in total closure from June 1921 to February 1922. Almost all the Brittany waterways were similarly interrupted by the Great Drought of 1976 and towards the end of summer 1989. The small town is dominated by a large church with spire. Convenient shopping; moorings are on a towpath quay, with water point, above the lock.

Repeatedly one is surprised in France that small historic buildings can be allowed to sink into dereliction. It is said that if they have been in a family for many generations, the owners would prefer this state of affairs to making a sale. A good example is seen opposite Écluse 41, des Islots (K23), where a turreted stone building bearing the date 1641 stands empty and unloved. It cries out to be restored, but with flourishing farmhouse alongside it is presumably surplus to requirements. **Tréverien** (K24) has a canalside church with square tower and spire, a wharf and shopping facilities. Écluses 40 and 39 are followed by the pound into **St-Domineuc** (K28), a rather ugly little town strung out along the busy N137, with shops and garage within 800m. By the stone quay a factory makes domestic lamps, with a winding hole (wide part of the canal for turning boats) opposite. Meals are available at

the Auberge des Deux Ponts. Both canal banks have been laid out with a curious 'athletic course': various timber obstacles enable participants to leap from ramps into sandpits and swing from parallel bars as an alternative to jogging. Instruction boards feature pin men at their exercises. Pleasant countryside, with woodland and cornfields, accompanies the canal past locks 38 to 34 before reaching **Tinténiac** (K38), the leading town between Dinan and Rennes, and grouped about a massive 19th century church. Electricity points, refuse disposal and water have been installed by the local authority along a grassy wharf with camping site. All kinds of shops are within easy walking distance, with at least two restaurants: the Auberge d'Halage by the waterway and the Hôtel des Voyageurs in the town. The latter offers an ambitious, but hardly over-priced, menu with toast served in an unusual windmill arrangement. Several *châteaux* in the vicinity are worth an excursion. The nearest, **Montmuran**, is 5km via the road to Les Iffs (open every day June–Sept, weekends for the rest of the year). The oldest portions date from the 12–14th centuries, and Bertrand du Guesclin was knighted here in 1354 after an encounter with the English. Other possibilities are **Combourg**, 13km NE, 11–15th centuries and owned in the 18th century by the Count of Châteaubriand, father of the celebrated writer François-René de Châteaubriand; and **Caradeuc**, 10km along the D20 to Bécherel in a fine park.

Open country leads past Écluse 32, La Moucherie (K40) to the beginning of the 11-lock **Hédé** flight through woodland to the summit level. Most keepers are responsible for two locks each, and assuming slight delays for other boats or chambers not being made ready in advance of your arrival the series should be negotiated in a little under 2hr. With grassy banks and thick foliage, the Hédé Locks are among the most pleasantly situated of any in Brittany. To visit the town, moor in a basin immediately north of Écluse 28, La Madeleine (K43) – but inform a keeper of your intentions. Alternatively continue to the top lock, moor and return by bicycle to the bridge just below Écluse 25, Parfraire. Hédé is about 2km, partly up a steep hill past a crowded cemetery. At the outskirts note the big 19th century Gothic *château* with exceptionally slender towers. This quiet little town has a broad square in front of a Romanesque church (the clock strikes the hours twice, as if to make certain that everyone knows the time). Continue down a lane containing the *Théâtre de Poche* (Pocket Theatre) to arrive at the impressive ivy-covered ruins of an 11th century feudal *château* on the edge of a precipice with distant views over the plain below. Within, are two tarmac sports

Working up the leafy flight of Hédé locks.

pitches and a pile of World War I shell cases that have been removed from the memorial. Most shops and at least two restaurants will be found.

Deep in a shaded cutting, the 7 km summit level is supplied by two reservoirs: the Bassin de **Bazouges** and the Bassin de Partage des Eaux at **La Plousière** (K50). By La Plousière bridge is a stone quay and café/bar. Water supplies are augmented by a 50m circular basin above Lock 20, **Villemorin** (K51), whose duplicated upper gates face in each direction for conservation of water in the event of an accident. The

descent begins to the River Vilaine through the valley of the little River Ille. Some of the locks are worked by keepers responsible for two, and they will charge off down the towpath by motorbike in an attempt to have the next chamber ready before you arrive. Écluse 17, Lengager (K53), has a superb garden, its name carefully spelled out with trimmed perennial shrubs, replanted in 1978. Above is a good stone quay with mooring bollards. Follow the D12 eastwards for 1.5km to the centre of **Montreuil-sur-Ille** (shops and station, with restaurant towards the next lock, Écluse de Haute-Roche, No.16, K54). Winner of the annual lock garden prize for several years, the keeper here has created a wonderland of cascades of pink clematis, sturdy arum lilies and geraniums: finishing touches are a brightly painted Snow White and all Seven Dwarfs with a windmill and lighthouse! The effect is admirable. Water point.

Once I arrived at Écluse 15, Ille (K55), to discover an amazing machine in use near the top gates. Looking not unlike a wood-fired traction engine, this turned out to be a mobile cider still with shining copper and brass pipework. Its proud owner lived in St-Médard-sur-Ille and was licensed to operate in twenty neighbouring parishes. Farmers would bring barrels of the previous year's cider which after distillation flowed in a steady stream from a tap in the form of a throat-burning proof *eau-de-vie*. Although it was breakfast time, I accepted the jolly operator's invitation to sample some. Further practitioners of this craft were later encountered on the Vilaine and the Sèvre-Niortaise.

The Smell is first noticed in the woods at Écluse 14, Dialay, a nerve-shattering place with the constant clatter of a stone crushing works. Subsequent research traced it to a gruesome *abattoir* in the fields beyond St-Germain-sur- Ille. With the wind in certain directions it is quite sickening! After **St-Médard-sur-Ille** (K58, shops, restaurant and garage) the waterway passes through a narrow cutting crossed by three bridges of the Rennes-St-Malo railway with its little red and cream three-coach trains. Honeysuckle, dog roses, hazel, alders and sweet chestnut create a confused tangle on the banks and at times there would be insufficient space to pass another boat. Through Écluse 12, Bouessay, and on to the 11th lock, **St-Germain-sur-Ille** (K61), with a small water authority yard where winter moorings are possible. The local passion for flowery locks is almost carried to excess, with pots actually secured to the gate beams. Moor just below, left bank, for drinking water. On the right, **La Ville-en-Bois** consists of little more than an old quarry gantry and bar/restaurant. Climb a steep hill into St-Germain for most shops. In the post office, a marble plaque sadly records (in translation): 'Here Armandine Mallet, postmistress, was killed by the Germans at the age of 45. August 1, 1944.' Shortly afterwards, this part of France was liberated.

It is appropriate to mention that all canal locks have been equipped with safety ladders and ropes slung along the chamber walls at full and empty levels, a practice that could well be repeated elsewhere.

Écluse 8, Grugedaine (K67), is typical of several that bear a close resemblance to a farmyard. Dogs, goats, chickens and geese take a lively interest in newly arrived boats. Fruit trees and walnuts provide an autumn crop and neatly sawn piles of logs ensure

winter fuel. Add to this the produce of a vegetable garden and certain lock keepers must be approaching self-sufficiency. Water point, and shops in the nearby village of **Chevaigné**.

Between **Betton** (K72) and Rennes the River Ille wanders in and out of the canal, much of its original course being indistinguishable from the navigation. Betton has a quay (right bank, below the bridge) with a good view of the hilltop church beyond a modernistic civic centre, incorporating *Mairie* and post office. Shopping is good here or alternatively on the opposite side of the canal in **La Levée**, where the banks are situated. One recommended restaurant is La Levée, a short distance left of the bridge. A hire cruiser base supplies fuel.

As it approaches Rennes the Canal d'Ille et Rance remains pleasantly rural past Écluses 6, 5 and 4. Even the landscaped housing estates of **St-Grégoire** (K80) are not without interest, with traditional building designs and individual gardens *au style anglais*. Further suburbs and then factories follow the waterway to Écluse 2, St-Martin (K84), a mechanized structure with sinking radial gate at the top end. Écluse 1, Mail (K84.8), works on the same principle and it is essential to wait for a green traffic light before crossing the submerged gate. City centre moorings, with water point, are immediately upstream of lock 1, where seats and shrubbery are a magnet for inebriates. (The city has a shop named Alcoolisme International – an emporium devoted to the requirements of the DIY drink enthusiast.) Should the lock keeper be absent, his house is close by, overlooking the Vilaine. A dark bridge-hole and the voyager finally leaves the canal to join Brittany's chief river.

Rennes, leading city of Brittany, is an important administrative and industrial centre. Much of the medieval town was destroyed in a great fire which burned 1,000 houses in 1720. Some ancient buildings do remain and a long pedestrianized street of shops makes sight-seeing a pleasure. This leads from close to the canal to the magnificent Palais de Justice, the former Houses of Parliament. Domestic shopping for the galley can be attended to in excellent covered and open-air markets (crabs, lobsters, fresh fruit and vegetables, everlasting flowers); alternatively, try the very good food department of a large store facing the river in the Quai Chateaubriand. Special features of Rennes include the Thabor Garden, Museum of Breton Life and Breton Motor Museum (about 3km NE of the centre).

Left: *Sunset at Honfleur harbour, estuary of the River Seine.*

Below: *Boating on the Canal de la Somme at Dreuil-lès-Amiens*

Left: *Moorings on the Canal de l'Ourcq at Villeparisis, outskirts of Greater Paris.*

Right: *In the city of Metz, off the Moselle navigation.*

Below: *Laden péniches on the River Meuse at Givet, on the border with Belgium.*

Right: *Brittany seafood lunch on the River Vilaine.*

Below: *Working through a lock in the Hédé flight, Canal d'Ille et Rance.*

Left: *Lockside building on the Canal de Briare near Rogny.*

Below: *Canal Latéral à la Loire. The world's longest navigation aqueduct at Briare.*

Left: *Late summer colour at a lock cottage on the Canal du Centre near Chalon-sur-Saône.*

Right: *Canal du Nivernais. In the deep summit level cutting near Baye.*

Below: *River Yonne. The Auxerre waterfront.*

Left: *Life-sized angling figures on the Canal de Bourgogne at Vandenesse-en-Auxois.*

Right: *River Saône, Lyon. St Jean's Cathedral and the Basilica of Notre-Dame-de-Fourvière.*

Below: *Canal de Bourgogne. Summer morning mist on the southern descent from the summit level.*

Opposite: *Canal de la Marne à la Saône. A laden péniche runs south near Chaumont.*

Left: *An occasional hazard of boating in February: on the River Saône at Tournus.*

Below: *River Sèvre-Niortaise. In the Marais Poitevin at Coulon.*

Left: *Petit Rhône. Swimming from a 'desert island' at K293.*

Below: *Côtes du Rhône wine country at Tournon.*

Right: *River Rhône. The famous Pont d'Avignon.*

Below: *A particularly fine 'lavoir' (public wash-house) near the Canal Latéral à la Garonne at Valence d'Agen.*

Left: *Canal du Midi. Cruising boats share a typical curved-sided lock chamber, Lalande, near Carcassonne.*

Right: *River Lot. A lock beneath one of the arches of the 14th century Pont Valentré at Cahors.*

Below: *In the Camargue. Flamingoes by the Canal du Rhône à Sète near Frontignan.*

Above: *On the River Baïse at Nérac.*

Left: *Étang de Thau. Sunrise at Marseillan harbour.*

32 · River Vilaine

Carte Guide: *Bretagne*
From St-Méen, 2.7km upstream of Rennes to the Bay
of Biscay at Tréhiguier: 139.7km with 15 locks. Junc-
tions are made with the Canal de l'Ille et Rance in
Rennes and the Canal de Nantes à Brest (Northern
Section) at Redon and (Southern Section) at Rieux.
Distances are measured from the canal junction in
Rennes.

A long river, of variable scenic quality. The finest reaches are past wooded cliffs upstream of Port-de-Roche,
where many locks have pleasing old stone watermills
and sparkling weirs. Flat somewhat featureless meadowland accompanies long stretches of the middle
river, up and downstream of Redon. Then, from
Foleux down to the last lock at the Arzal barrage,
beginning of the tideway, the wooded rocky banks
recall the estuary of the Dart in Devon or even the
lochs of the Caledonian Canal. No fewer than 42km
between Redon and Arzal are lock-free (75km from
Arzal to Mâlon, if the Redon barrage is in its open
position), enabling rapid progress to be made by craft
running between the Channel and Atlantic coasts. This
is excellent sailing water for small cruisers and
dinghies, now much changed in character since construction of the barrage excluded the tide.

The Vilaine suffers from a reputation for shallow-
ness and many yachtsmen tell stories of being grounded. But those who experience trouble tend to be the
owners of deep-keel sailing boats. Provided your draft
is within 1.60m and you pay due attention to navigation marks, no problems should result. Often the channel in the upper river lies close to the towpath, in spite
of the apparent width of the waterway. It will, of
course, take many years before the Great Drought of
1976 is quite forgotten. By late summer the canal
system of Brittany was all but drained and even
shallow-draft cruisers were unable to make progress
over shallows below Guipry. (I arrived for a fortnight's
hire cruiser holiday and exhausted the available possibilities within three days. Consequently, the boat was
used as a floating hotel at La Roche-Bernard and we
passed each day sight-seeing or visiting beaches.)

Winter floods can be ferocious: as in February 1981,
when the locks were completely awash. Perhaps this is
the origin of the river's name – literally, 'nasty' or
'unpleasant'. Or maybe the one-time shallows and
difficult tidal reaches should take the blame. In either
case, the Vilaine no longer merits the slur.

Brittany is famous for its seafood, *crêpes* and cider.
Outstanding dishes to sample in restaurants include
civelles nantaises (deep-fried baby eels), *boguette* (traditional fish soup), *boudin aux pruneaux* (savoury pudding or sausage with prunes), *rillettes de lapin*
(preserved rabbit pâté), and *maingaux* (cream cheese or
whipped cream, served with fruit).

Brief history The Vilaine was the first river of France to
be rendered navigable by using pound locks (as
opposed to 'flash' locks or navigation weirs). Craft were
able to ascend from the sea to Rennes by 1542,
although further improvements were carried out
during the next 40 years. Traffic increased with the
opening of various connecting canals in about 1840 and
it is recorded that 3,787 barge journeys were made in
1886, representing a total freight tonnage of 172,500.
Returns for 1936 show only a slight decrease to
163,000 tonnes, mostly in horse-drawn craft with some
motor barges. Shallows and rocks reduced the size of
loads and all traffic on the lower river was subject to
tides which flowed beyond Redon to the first lock at
Mâlon.

Working boats lingered on, with a pair of sand
barges running between the Loire and Redon until the
long drought of 1976 forced them out of business. In
1980 several sand and gravel boats worked through
three locks between Blossac and Rennes, but this traffic
seemed to have ceased at the time of writing.

Of recent changes, the most far-reaching was the
construction of a barrage and lock near the sea at Arzal,
in 1968–9. This resulted in an expanse of impounded
water between there and Redon, previously tidal.
Rocks were cleared from the channel around Mâlon in
1964 and many facilities for pleasure craft have since
been created, following transfer of most financial
responsibility for the waterway from central to local
government. The future of the Vilaine thus lies entirely
with tourism.

About 300m of the Vilaine in **Rennes** was roofed over
to create a Boulevard car park in 1963. Navigation is
no longer encouraged upstream of the junction with
Canal de l'Ille et Rance. For a description of Rennes,
see Chapter 31. Downstream of the city the river
surroundings are rather urbanized with factories,
electricity pylons, tower blocks and a prominent communications mast. After passing through Écluse 2, du
Comte (K1.8), the waterway dives under a new con-

crete bridge and after a further group of factories emerges in countryside that constitutes some of the loveliest cruising water in Brittany. Although it is possible that gravel barges may have ceased to operate, locks 3, 4 and 5 are equipped with mechanized paddles to speed up traffic. Other signs of commercial activity are steel campshedding on the banks and numerous gravel workings. After passing through Écluse 3, Apigné (K5.5), a slipway will be found up a backwater, reached from the lower end of the poplar-shaded cut (turn upstream, on the right). A powered bascule bridge spans Écluse 4, Cicé (K11). The last of the locks with mechanized paddles is No. 5, Mons (K14.3), from which the small town of **Bruz** can be visited (2km) for all shopping facilities.

Gravel workings line the right bank and past a small group of islands (keep to the left bank) to Écluse 6, **Le Pont Réan** (K17.8), where the skeletal remains of two wooden freight barges are upstream of the chamber. Take care to avoid marked shallows between the lock and a fine old eight-arched stone bridge: the navigation

arch is the third from the left bank (when descending). A small cruiser fleet occupies pontoons on the right bank, but visiting craft should be able to find space on the quay (water point) while visiting shops in the town or taking a meal at the waterside hotel.

Easily the most spectacular section of the Vilaine begins at a railway viaduct upstream of **Le Boël** (K21). Towering cliffs of slate, well covered with undergrowth, tumble down to the water. The area has been designated Parc Naturel de Boël and an easy climb via paths results in a superb view of an open weir with a charming stone millhouse at its centre, the upstream wall being pointed in the form of a cutwater. Rennes inhabitants come here in numbers on summer weekends. One of the river's best restaurants is Le Vieux Moulin de Boël, a creeper-clad building on the lockside shaded by a large horse chestnut tree. It is small, pleasingly decorated and rather expensive (advance booking recommended). If the *carré d'agneau* I selected can be regarded as typical, the presentation of food is outstanding: it arrived on a vast salver, liber-

Crusing downstream at Le Boël.

ally decorated with marguerites, sprigs of fir and fennel. The channel stays near the right, towpath, bank and past some tiny rocky islands to a bridge at **Laillé** (K23.7), close to the Château de Bagatz and other late 19th century mansions. A restaurant, Au Fil de l'Eau stands on the towpath.

The next lock, No. 8, Bouëxière (K26.8) has a stone millhouse of four storeys dated 1885 and well restored, and another restaurant, Le Moulin de Bouëxière, will be found towards the end of the lock cut. **Glanret** (K28.5) is a small village with bridge and restaurant, shortly followed by an exquisite mooring above a weir at the hamlet of **La Courbe** (K30.2). On the far side of a grassy square is a café/bar offering basic food. The town of **Bourg des Comptes** is close by. During normal summer water levels, safe swimming is possible in a pool above the weir, reached by crossing a narrow planked walkway. Écluse 9, Gailieu, is alongside. The river now winds past a series of *châteaux* to Écluse 10, Molière (K33.8), with yet another restored millhouse on an island. Pedalos and rowboats can be hired at a riverbank resort shaded by poplars by the bridge of **Pléchatel** (K35.3). Cliffs in the steep-sided valley extend downriver to **St-Malo-de-Phily** (K39.9), where facilities include butcher, restaurant with mooring pontoon, and rubbish disposal. A much extended millhouse, now a factory, lies on the weir stream by Écluse 11, Macaire (K40.5): keep watch for approaching craft in the narrow high-walled lock cut below.

Recent excavations off the river, left, have produced a marina complex upstream of **Messac** (K47), some pontoons being reserved for Crown Blue Line's Brittany hire fleet, while others are for visitors or private craft. A wide range of boating facilities can be found here (including fuel, crane, slipway and water): the site constitutes one of Brittany's leading boatyards. Services in the twin towns of Messac and **Guipry** are most conveniently reached by stopping on a stone quay below Écluse 12, Guipry (K48), where a bridge spans the waterway. By 1989 both this lock and No. 13 had been automated by installing hydraulic rams for working gates and paddles. The keeper wears a portable transmitter for controlling the various functions. In the 17th century this was an important river town owing to the salt trade. Several shops will be seen alongside, while comprehensive supplies can be obtained in a supermarket several hundred metres towards Guipry town centre. Cross to the Messac side for the railway station and agreeable Hôtel de la Gare restaurant. Near the lock, visit the tiny chapel of Notre Dame de Bon-Port, built in 1644 as a thanks offering by the Lord of Tréguilly whose valuable stores of sea salt were threatened by an unusually high river flood. The

manor house escaped as the waters began to recede and the little chapel is the result. The fête of Notre Dame de Bon-Port is held on the last-but-one Sunday in July.

Various markers and signboards inform boatmen that although the river is wide below Guipry, the deep-water channel lies close to the right, towpath, bank: elsewhere, there are rocky shallows. Écluse 13, **Mâlon** (K52), is now the last change in level before reaching the tideway at Arzal. Its deep chamber is somewhat turbulent for uphill-bound craft. Dense woodland covers both banks at the *Bois de Boeuvre* and *Bois de Baron* with a spectacular seven-arched railway viaduct and tunnel (K56.7), Corbinières. Rocky cliffs are well covered with pines, sweet chestnuts and oaks with cascades of blackberries towards the end of summer. Little fishing punts and hundreds of rickety fishing platforms point to the popularity of angling. Upstream of the bridge at **Port-de-Roche** (K62.2), note a mellow old manor house with extensive outbuildings. Cast iron plaques on the lattice-girder bridge of 1868 bear the initials of Louis Napoléon Bonaparte and his Empress Eugénie. A startling example of the way in which earlier beliefs were Christianized is provided by the legend that 28 ancient menhirs (Cromlech des Demoiselles) are the bodies of a group of young girls, changed into stones by God for dancing one Sunday morning instead of attending Mass! They are south of the station at **Langon**, 3km from Port-de-Roche via the D56.

Scenery remains attractive as far as **Beslé** (K69.2), a pleasant little village upstream of a bridge with moorings on a stone quay. The restaurant of the Hôtel du Port overlooks the water, while a short walk over the level crossing and up a hill brings you to shops and a garage. Moorings are less convenient at **Brain-sur-Vilaine** (K71.6), whose quay is rather broken down; meals are available at the Auberge Les Moulins Neufs. Deserted flat countryside with tumbledown farm buildings and numerous fishing punts bearing names like *Mon Repos* and *La Disette* (*The Shortage*) accompanies the river until the outskirts of **Redon** (K89.2), crossroads of the Brittany waterways. The Canal de Nantes à Brest crosses the Vilaine at right angles near the town centre with entrance locks on each side of the river. Neither are now in regular use: if you wish to travel towards Nantes, continue for 7km downstream to another entrance at Écluse de Bellions. This involves passing beneath the central guillotine of Le Grand Vannage, a prominent barrage with three sluice gates which marked the start of the Vilaine tideway until construction of the Arzal barrage at the mouth of the estuary. Except in times of flood, there is a free passage. Should the barrier be closed it will be neces-

The Corbinières viaduct.

sary to turn sharp right, into the first lock of the Canal de Nantes à Brest, Écluse de l'Oust; straight on is the route for Josselin and Pontivy, while a left turn into the Écluse du Grand Bassin provides access to the extensive *port de plaisance*, with facilities ranging from moorings to hire cruisers, water, fuel and crane. This is the best place to lie while visiting the town. An exit to the Vilaine will be seen at the far end.

Dating from the 9th century, Redon is now rather an ordinary place devoted to prosaic matters such as manufacture of cigarette lighters and plastic imitation leather. But there are 17th and 18th century shipwrights' houses with cast-iron balconies and the former abbey church of St Sauveur with an important Romanesque 12th century tower. The lively open-air market is bisected by a railway. As recently as the early 20th century, all traders bound for the market would be stopped by Agents d'Octrois, officials who levied a tax on all produce from a basket of apples to a cartload of pigs.

Now that the strong tidal flow has been banished from the Vilaine, the reach between Redon and the sea is an ever-widening stretch of water with a succession of small 'drowned' creeks. Surroundings are unremarkable at first, past a modern concrete bridge at Cran (K101.9) with opening span for large craft and sailing vessels (cruisers can pass beneath). Foleux (K114.9), right bank, has a small harbour with jetties, slipway, fuel and water point. From here on the pine-covered rocky shores recall the lochs of the Scottish Highlands and among boats you can expect to meet are occasional coasters, passenger tripping launches and many large sea-going yachts. Gradually, the world of the inland waterways is superseded by a more marine atmosphere. The first intimation of **La Roche-Bernard** (K122) is a magnificent suspension bridge spanning the Vilaine at a height of 50m. In the 17th century this was an important ship-building town. Now, there are extensive pleasure craft moorings on the river, with more to be found after turning left around a massive rock outcrop up the St-Antoine Creek. Most boat facilities including fuel, water, showers and repairs. Dozens of delightful stone buildings of great antiquity will be found alongside the port and up steep passages leading through the Old Quarter into the town centre. Boating enthusiasts have 'discovered' La Roche-Bernard in the decade since the mid-1970s, so it is a bustling and thriving place in summer. Various restaurants and *crêperies* attract customers: personal experience leads me to recommend the Restaurant des Deux Magots. Livestock of all varieties can be inspected in a street market, together with excellent dairy produce and locally made clogs. A visit should be made to the Musée de la Vilaine (see 'Waterways Museums'). Just 9km of non-tidal water remains downriver to the barrage of **Arzal** (K131), where a full range of boating facilities and moorings caters more for the deep-water sailor than the riverman. If moorings are congested on the right shore, it is worth trying the jetties of a hire cruiser base, opposite. Access to the sea via the last 6km of river is through a lock spanned by lifting road bridge. Boats can pass through every day, on the hour, between 7.00 and 20.00 provided it is daylight. Among recent developments are a restaurant, shopping centre, tripping boat office, boatyards and boat sales, fuel, water, cranes and slipways. At present the area around Arzal is modern, bleak and dominated by concrete. Inland boaters will prefer the more agreeable upper reaches of the Vilaine.

Enquiries in La Roche-Bernard will produce details of bus services for excursions to the coast and several towns of great interest. However, there is so much to attract the tourist that it would be worth keeping several days in hand for a tour by car. Among the highlights are the following (with distances measured from La Roche-Bernard): the beach at **Plage de la Mine d'Or** (13km) near **Pénistin**; plenty of other sandy beaches are found all along the coast and one popular with naturists is **Pen Bron** (35km), south of **La Turballe**; to the NW the city of **Vannes** (39km) has ramparts, beautiful moat gardens and fashionable shops on the shores of the Golfe du Morbihan: this could be combined with a visit to the unique Ménac Lines of no fewer than 1,009 ancient standing stones at **Carnac** (68km), a place of huge fascination, especially in early morning or late evening, when deserted. Although there are no opportunities for getting afloat, a 57km road circuit can be made through the **Grande Brière** (18km), an atmospheric region of marshes, peat bogs and pastures, long ago the delta of both Vilaine and Loire. Covering 6,000 hectares, it is intersected by many tiny canals on which the inhabitants use flat-bottomed craft called *blins* for transporting thatching reeds, bog oak and hay. It is a great wildfowling and fishing centre, now preserved from development as a regional park. In contrast to the dark Celts of much of Brittany, the people of the Grande Brière are often fair-haired and are said to be the descendants of ship-wrecked Saxon pirates; they are very insular and much inter-married. A suggested road tour is detailed in the *Green Michelin Guide to Brittany*.

33 · Canal de Nantes à Brest

Once a tidal estuary at La Roche Bernard, this part of the Vilaine offers excellent waters for sailing.

Carte Guide: *Bretagne* Alternatively, *Canaux Bretons et Loire* (Vagnon), which additionally includes coverage of the Canal de Nantes à Brest Branche Finistèrienne.

From a junction with the River Loire and the Sévre-Nantaise at Nantes to Pontivy, junction with the Canal du Blavet. The through route is interrupted here. 207km with 107 locks. Junctions are made with the Upper River Erdre near Nort-sur-Erdre; the River Vilaine at Écluse des Bellions, near Redon; and the River Aff near Écluse 19, above Redon. A further, now detached, portion of the original waterway is available between the Écluse de Goariva near Carhaix-Plouguer and the Bay of Brest at Landévennec: this is sometimes known as the Aulne et Hyères Canalisées or the Branche Finistèrienne du Canal de Nantes à Brest. 106km with 45 locks.

This long waterway offers as much variety as any navigation in France. Almost always, the scenery through the Breton interior is very beautiful, taking the boater to places rarely visited by the tourist. Combining sections of canalized river with artificial cuts, it is heavily locked in places, but for those with plenty of time it offers a fascinating passage between the south coast of Brittany and (via the River Blavet, see Chapter 34) the

west coast at Lorient. Leaving Nantes, the course is first through the broad lakes of the River Erdre; then follows a canal and the River Isac to the Vilaine at Redon; from here to Rohan the waterway largely consists of the River Oust; the journey continues by canal with numerous locks to Pontivy, junction with the Blavet. A portion of the Nantes à Brest is out of service until navigation resumes once more beyond the Guerlédan reservoir. It then continues with a length of canal leading to the navigable courses of first the River Hyères and then the River Aulne.

With an absence of commercial traffic, none of the Canal de Nantes à Brest is particularly heavily used by pleasure craft. There are small numbers of private cruisers and a growing fleet of hire boats, especially on the Redon-Josselin length. While cruisers can be rented on the isolated Finistère portion, it is still possible to spend a week on these deserted waters, meeting a mere handful of other boats. The lakes of the Erdre are much frequented by small cruisers and sailing craft, with luxury passenger vessels providing a service from Nantes that is only equalled in France by the bateaux-mouches of Paris. Some of these craft are ultra-modern and equipped with superb restaurants for public trips and private functions. Unusually, they even operate to a restricted winter service with central heating. Lock keepers are employed throughout the eastern part of the canal (with the exception of a series of locks between Nantes and Redon) but not on the Finistère section, where boat crews work unassisted.

Brief history Some of the river sections – notably the Erdre – have been navigable for many centuries. Among famous visitors were the Queen of Navarre in 1437, René Descartes in 1617, Madame de Sévigné in 1680 and the Duchess of Berry in 1828. But it was not until Napoléon's time that serious consideration was given to a barge route between Nantes and Brest to ensure carriage of freight, safe from the threat of the British fleet off the Atlantic coast. Work began at Port-Launay near Châteaulin in 1811. But Napoléon was soon to meet his Waterloo and the period of unrest and financial stringency that followed was not favourable to expensive public works. Construction recommenced in 1822 with the establishment of a Canal Company of Brittany. By 1836, 385km of waterway with 238 locks providing a change in levels of 555m was opened from coast to coast. Improvements such as deepening the channel continued until 1875. While Napoléon was never to see his great work, his nephew Napoléon III declared open a sea lock on the Aulne at Guilly-Glas, below Châteaulin, during his Breton tour of 1858. Financially, the new route was not a great success and freight receipts were disappointing. From less than 10,000 tonnes of goods in 1860, traffic gradually increased to an annual 40,000 tonnes. One great mistake of the early 1860s was the construction of a fleet of 62 iron barges, each with a capacity of 140 tonnes: but the water depth allowed them to load only 70–80 tonnes. Leading traffics were Welsh coal and Spanish iron ore.

By 1870 freight tonnage had fallen back to its 1850 level. Horses replaced bow-hauliers and the journey time between Châteaulin and Redon was cut from 25 to 15 days. For a brief golden age between 1890 and 1914 the canal carried 35,000 tonnes a year: one important commodity was fertilizer which transformed agriculture along the banks. World War I growth of road transport and opening of the Carhaix–Châteaulin–Camaret railway in 1911 all contributed to a slump in barge traffic. Finally, a hydro-electric scheme and barrage at Guerlédan, finished in 1928, divided the waterway into two separate halves. There was talk at first of building a barge lift round the obstacle, but nothing ever came of the plan. Most of the barge operators elected to stay on the eastern section, where traffic had always been more flourishing. 1936 freight returns for the whole canal make the surprising claim that over 300,000 tonnes was transported with 4,080 barge journeys. The last barge passed through Châteaulin Lock in 1942 and elsewhere lingered on until the 1976 drought forced the remaining Nantes–Redon gravel craft into retirement. Now the working boats are just a memory: some had highly evocative names such as *Berceau-du-Marin* (*Boatman's Cradle*), *Brise-des-Nuits* (*Night Breeze*) and *Fleur-de-Mai* (*Mayflower*).

From the mid-1960s the main section has been progressively improved for tourism. Meanwhile the western Hyères and Aulne navigation fell into disuse after World War II and was officially closed in 1957. The story of its repair and rebirth under the Département of Finistère is one of the successes of modern French waterway history. Transferred to the local authority in 1966, 73km and 33 locks were reopened in 1975. A further 8km through 11 locks, Kergoat to Goariva, was brought back into use in 1983, thus completing restoration of the entire length in Finistère. With a total cost of about 10 million francs to date, efforts must now be made to attract more than the present tiny number of craft.

At its junction with the tidal waters of the River Loire very close to the centre of **Nantes**, the Canal de Nantes à Brest enters Écluse 1, St-Félix, electrically operated. Craft can pass between tideway and canal 2hr before Nantes HW until 3hr afterwards. A keeper is on duty 6.30–19.30h (summer) and 7.30–17.30h (winter). On Sundays, Nov–March inclusive and certain public holidays, the lock is not available. Nantes is a city of many attractions: for a description, see under River Loire (Chapter 35). From 1929 onwards parts of the waterway near the cathedral were roofed over creating the 800m St-Félix Tunnel; passage is controlled by lights. At the far end moorings in the Bassin Ceineray (K1.4) are conveniently close to the city centre. Most of the River Erdre section of the waterway, between Nantes and the second lock at Quiheix, is exceptionally wide, giving the impression of a series of beautiful lakes. This arrangement results from a dam constructed in the 6th century by St Félix, Bishop of Nantes, who was anxious to 'drown' unhealthy marshland upstream of the city. It is one of the most beautiful rivers in the whole of France, with more than a dozen outstanding *chateaux* visible from the water. Tripping boats depart from the Quai de Versailles, left bank (K2), with moorings, repair facilities, hire craft, slipway, water and fuel. Large numbers of powered and sailing boats point to the great popularity of the Erdre with the Nantaises. Cruising, wildfowling, coarse fishing, boardsailing and water ski-ing are all practised in an area more like the Norfolk Broads than a French river.

Bankside moorings are sometimes few and far

between: if in doubt about water depths, it is safer to drop the anchor and go ashore by dinghy. The first time the British Army used inland water transport in France during World War I was when a depot for sick horses was established at a *château* at **La Chapelle-sur-Erdre** (K5.4). The problem of conveying fodder from supply ships in the Loire was solved by using barges between Nantes and the Erdre, unloading them at a wooden wharf in the *château* grounds. The village now has a waterside restaurant. The next town of note is **Sucé** (K15.1), at a narrows crossed by a road bridge. Sandy beaches, slipway and moorings are all found here, with friendly shops and restaurants. Above the bridge the navigation broadens once more into the huge Lac de Mazerolles, 5km long with a width up to 500m. Its banks are fringed with willows and the sandy bottom is ideal for swimming. Trailed boats can be launched from the end of a lane leading from the D69 in the middle of the west shore: even if you only have a few hours to spare, it would be difficult to imagine anywhere more pleasant for an afternoon's boating. At the far end of the lake the river narrows and Écluse 2, Quiheix (K21.7), will be seen on the left: this is the route for Redon and points beyond. But a pleasant diversion can be made by staying on the Erdre for a further 6km to the terminus at the Pont St-Georges in **Nort-sur-Erdre**. There is a small port with showers, shops and restaurants. The adventurous can continue still further by dinghy, up a winding stream fringed with alders.

By 1989, seven of the locks between Nantes and Redon had been adapted for working by boat crews unassisted. Modifications include reduction of paddles to one per set of gates, with sliding locking bars preventing gates from being opened while paddles are raised. The system, which is fairly foolproof, is rather slower than normal; similar adaptation of further locks is likely. Returning to the canal, there are few facilities as you climb through locks 3–7, spread out over 6km. This is the summit level, with a descent towards the Vilaine beginning at Écluse 8. By the N137 bridge, **Glanet** (K38.3), a halt can be made for the restaurant. Fuel is available from a garage. Dense forests surround the town of **Blain** (K50.2), beyond Écluses 8–11. Moor below the imposing *château*. There is an excellent restaurant and range of shops, with water point at the port. Most of the waterway's course is now along the canalized River Isac, a very winding stream. Parts are especially lovely, particularly the loop that passes the mid-17th century Château de Carheil-en-Plessé in its wooded 200 hectare park (K69). Moorings are available on both banks by the Pont St-Clair, with all facilities in the town of **Guenrouet** (K72.8). The

church has some exquisite stained glass, erected 1944–51, with background colours mainly in tones of deep blue. Shortly before the canal leaves the Isac, there is a sandy river beach and restaurant at **Le Cougou** (K79) with the Château de Bogdelin in the edge of the Forest of St Gildas. This level stretch of canal is very peaceful, offering 23km of lock-free cruising.

At the second bridge after the river junction, Pont-Miny (K83.3), it is about 3km by road into **Fégréac**, once a Gallo-Roman settlement. Old houses and a 15th century Calvary – an ecclesiastical speciality of Brittany – are among the attractions. There are also shops. Soon after, a junction is made with the Vilaine at Écluse des Bellions, No. 17, with the small town of **Rieux** on the far bank of the river. All craft must take this route, as 6km of the Canal de Nantes à Brest from here to the **Redon** crossroads (K94.9) is closed to traffic as a through route, although northwards access remains possible to the village of St Nicholas-de-Redon. Therefore, if bound either for Redon and the canal to the NW or for the waterway to Rennes, proceed up the Vilaine for 7km. The canal's through route is reached by forking left into the Grand Bassin, working through a lock at the far end with bascule bridge and then turning left. (For information on the town, see Chapter 32.) This diversion from the original course adds little in distance and presents an identical number of locks.

The River Oust provides a navigation route for the canal for most of the way between Redon and Rohan: however, the first 7km out of Redon are via an artificial channel. If wished, about 10km of the Oust can be navigated between the Vilaine (downstream of Redon) and a barrage, running parallel with the Canal de Nantes à Brest; but there is no link between the two at the upper end. Leaving Redon by means of a rock-lined cut, the Oust is joined above a weir (K101.7). This is without doubt the finest portion of the river, with a width of between 200m and 300m and pine-covered cliffs rising to 45m. There are plenty of pleasant moorings and enough space to sail a dinghy. The channel lies near the left, towpath, bank and bears away into a section of canal cut at Écluse 19, La Maclais (K105.3) alongside **L'Île aux Pies** (Magpie Island).

Before taking this route, it is strongly recommended to make one of the most interesting short diversions on the whole of the French network: up the mysterious **River Aff** for 9km to La Gacilly. Continue straight ahead into a wide pool edged with reeds and water crowfoot. Almost immediately the atmosphere undergoes a complete change: there are fishing boat stakes projecting from the marked channel and a sense of utter desertion. If you wish to visit the village of

Glénac, carry on to a wooden landing stage and walk a short distance to discover a restaurant, baker and grocer's shop. To enter the Aff itself, turn right into the middle of a vast reedbed up to 1km wide. Recalling the least used of the Norfolk Broads, this is an extraordinary marshland and a tricky place to suffer an engine breakdown, as there is no possibility of locating solid land to get ashore. In spite of the assurances of the chart, you feel that you must have taken a wrong turning. After a road bridge near **Sourdéac** the river narrows between high banks overhung by oak trees whose branches brush the deck. But for stone bank protection at a second bridge, it is difficult to believe that commercial traffic ever penetrated this *African Queen* waterway, let alone as recently as 1965. Boulder strewn cliffs and pines finally lead to a modern three-arched bridge with weir and elaborate municipal washhouse in 1930s concrete, decorated with pots of geraniums. To the left is a small quay. You have arrived in **La Gacilly**, at the head of navigation.

In the hilly streets of old stone houses are shops, restaurants and a garage. The town is also something of a craftsmen's colony, with workers in iron, glass, leather and semi-precious stones (fine tables and lamps in onyx). A stone mason sculpts granite into fire surrounds, plaques and sundials; he will proudly inform you that he has carried out restoration on Nantes cathedral. Much older relics are to be found in the shape of a dolmen, the Tablette de Cournon, and a 5m high *menhir*, the Roche Piquée, hidden in a sweet chestnut grove. It takes abut 70 minutes' cruising to return to the Oust and to the more prosaic straight canal which leads via a set of flood gates, Écluse de Limure (K109.8), back into the river with drifts of water lilies. Moor by the Pont d'Oust (K112.5) for **Peillac** (all facilities within 2km).

After Écluse 21, Le Guesclin (K116.6), a bridge of eight square arches appears, with two restaurants and basic shops in the waterside village of **St-Martin-sur-Oust** (K117.9). 9km SW by the D777 lies the famous *ville fleurie* of **Rochefort-en-Terre**, surely one of Brittany's most delightful towns. For an old-fashioned French provincial restaurant it would be difficult to better the Hostellerie Lion d'Or, which serves a mouthwatering pudding called *Île Flottante* – caramelized poached egg white with almonds, floating in a sea of vanilla custard. Beyond Écluse 22, Rieux, **St-Congard** appears on the left bank by a bridge (K123.7). I discovered a mobile wood-fired distillery here, built by Charles Coyac of Nantes in 1927. It is worth going ashore for several shops, but do not bother to walk 800m to a disappointing antique shop cluttered with over-priced 19th century furniture. Woods give

way to open cultivated fields: the ugly factory by Écluse 24, Foveno (K129.6), pours effluent into the river and makes butter and cheese.

Malestroit (K132.2) is an important small town with a lively atmosphere. Originally fortified, it is situated by an island with many Gothic and Renaissance houses. The church of St Gilles was built in the 12th and 16th centuries. Half-timbered buildings are decorated with humorous painted carvings showing a man in a nightgown beating his wife, a hare with Breton bagpipes (*biniou*) and a pig spinning. Every other Thursday an open-air market is held. Shopping is good. Many waterway holiday makers begin their cruise here at a British-owned hire base (slipway, water and fuel). Flash floods in summer can cause sudden rises in water level on the Oust with a strong current, in contrast to upper parts of the canal which sometimes run rather short of water. Most locks have keepers, frequently women, and the low-geared paddles are somewhat tedious to wind: the accepted practice for closing is to wind them fully open, remove the pawl, and swing the fixed windlass (*manivelle*) causing the mechanism to drop under its own weight. (This method may well be forbidden elsewhere.) Many of the locks are like small farms with cattle sheds, rabbits, chickens and goats, and although there are vegetable gardens few keepers seem to bother to sell produce, ice cream or postcards to passing boaters as happens on more heavily used canals. Cottages are in traditional Breton style, often single storey with dormer windows in the roof and granite door and window surrounds.

Leaving Malestroit and Écluse 25 via a straight cut lined with poplars and acacias, the waterway is really lovely in early summer: the meadows are ablaze with buttercups while yellow iris fringes the banks. The river is rejoined after Écluse 27, Lanée (K135.4, stop lock normally open at each end), and winds past farmhouses to **Le Roc St-André** (K141). The eleven-arch bridge with a cross at the centre was built in 1760 and carries the N166 road between Ploërmel and Vannes. Use the sole navigation arch, third from the left. High on a cliff alongside, the church has an ornate open spire; there is also a grotto and altar by the towpath. Excellent menus, with a choice of seafood, will be found at the Val de l'Oust restaurant; shops are convenient. In the reach that follows, the towers of the Château Crevy appear among trees on the right bank. Its park was landscaped by Le Nôtre and it now houses a costume museum.

Derelict-seeming houses will be found in **Montertelot** (K143.7), with an elegant waterside church and moorings to a quay above Écluse 29. Facilities are limited to a café, grocer and baker. Dense woods and hills lead up to Écluse 31, **Guillac**, and if you want to visit the sizeable town of **Ploërmel**, 7km distant, moor at the preceding bridge (K147.9). Once the seat of the Dukes of Brittany, it contains a number of fascinating old buildings. A little to the east is the extensive **Forêt de Paimpont**, none other than the ancient Forest of Brocéliande where, according to the Arthurian legend, Merlin the Wizard was beguiled by the sensuous Lady Vyvyan. Writing in 1927, yachtsman Capt. Leslie Richardson (*Brittany and the Loire*) comments: 'Wolves, boars and deer, woodmen and charcoal burners were the only inhabitants of the great forests. Today one may still meet with all of them, though the wolves are almost if not quite extinct ... *Wolf Hunting in Lower Brittany* is unfortunately out of print in English, though a capital French translation can be obtained in Paris.'

Écluses 32–34 intervene in a nearly deserted landscape filled with summer flowers – dog roses, yellow broom, red campion and foxgloves – until we arrive at the architectural *pièce de résistance* of the Canal de Nantes à Brest, the magnificent Château de **Josselin** (K157.5). Posters or brochure photographs of Josselin's trio of massive stone towers rising sheer from the river have persuaded many cruiser hirers to choose the Brittany waterways: the reality of the castle is in no way a disappointment. Home of the Rohan family since the 14th century, it was seized by François II, Duke of Brittany, in 1488 and dismantled. His daughter, Anne of Brittany, on becoming Queen of France, compensated the Rohans and in rebuilding the *château*. Jean II de Rohan showed his gratitude by decorating the structure with ornamented initial As. The Rohan motto *Roi ne puis, Prince ne daigne, Rohan suis* (I cannot be King, I scorn to be a Prince, I am a Rohan) illustrates their proud outlook. In 1629 Henri de Rohan, leader of the Huguenots, suffered partial demolition of the castle; five of the nine towers were destroyed by Richelieu. Boastfully, the Cardinal cried: 'Monsieur le Duc, I have just sent a ball into your ninepins!' Josselin fell into ruin 200 years later and was restored in the early 20th century. There is a fine view from the terrace down onto the river and lock, but although open to the public the interior is less fascinating than might be expected, especially if you have difficulty in understanding the learned remarks of the French guide.

During the Middle Ages consumption of meat was strictly forbidden in Lent, much to the delight of the Josselin fishmongers. However, their greatly enhanced earnings were subject to a special tax, and on Low Sunday those who would not pay were forced to remove all clothing but their shirts and jump into the river, to the ribald comments of the townsfolk. A basilica Notre Dame du Roncier (Our Lady of the Bramblebush) dates from the 11th century and commemorates the finding of a statue of the Virgin by a peasant in about AD 800. He carried it home only to discover repeatedly that it reappeared in the fields, where a church was subsequently erected. An important *pardon* (a Christianized form of the Druid ritual, consisting of prayer and feasting) is held there on the second Sunday of September. A legend tells of Our Lady, disguised as a beggar, seeking alms of washerwomen on the banks of the Oust. When they refused, they and their descendants were condemned to bark like dogs. As would be expected of a town that sees many tourists, there are several restaurants and useful shops. Hire cruisers, water and fuel (not waterside). Note a series of charming gazebos in the gardens of waterside houses above the bridge.

Locks now increase in frequency as the waterway climbs into the hills. Restaurant and mooring by Écluse 38, Rouvray. Between Nos. 39 and 40 there is a restaurant by the Pont de **Bocneuf-la-Rivière** (K164.7). Écluse 42, La Tertraie (K167.2), is a guard lock, normally open, with shops in **Les Forges** 3km NE of Écluse 43, Cadoret. At **Penhouët** (K175.4) a bar/*crêperie* lies 100m west of Écluse 48. Close to Écluse 50, **Timadeuc** (K178.4), Trappist monks founded an abbey in 1841. The monastic buildings are closed to the public, although a slide show with commentary is available at the gatehouse. Sung Mass with Gregorian chant can be heard from Easter to mid–Sept at 11.15h (10.45h on Sundays and holidays).

The last opportunity for shopping in a real town before many locks are negotiated is found in **Rohan** (K181.5), a pleasantly uncommercialized place with a large mooring basin. The town takes its name from a 12th century *château* built on the *Roc'Han* by Alain de Porhoët. One of the most famous families of France, the Rohans, originated here.

In wild country with very few facilities, the canal now embarks on one of the greatest concentrations of locks in France. These are obviously well worth tackling if it is your intention to continue down the beautiful River Blavet from Pontivy. Traffic is currently light and normal draft, Rohan to Pontivy, is reduced to 0.8m. Between Écluse 53, St- Samson, beyond Rohan and Écluse 107, Ponteau, in Pontivy, there are no fewer than 55 chambers in 22km, representing an extremely full day's work!

Having once begun this arduous task, there will be little temptation to halt for sight-seeing: indeed it is preferable to press on, your arrival anticipated by the lock keepers. A final parting with the River Oust comes between Écluses 54, Le Guer, and 55, Coëtprat

(K185.8). Between **Gueltas** (186.8) and **St-Gonnery** (K191.3, butcher, baker, grocer) 23 locks intervene; by now at a height of 129.59m above sea level, a 5km summit pound follows. Descent begins with Écluse 79, Kéroret (K196.3, restaurant) and some crew members may wish to leave the boat to go shopping in **St-Gérand**, a walk or cycle ride of just under 4km if you rejoin the boat at a bridge below Écluse 87 (K197.3). Locks 88–89 (K201.3) are arranged in a flight; the final 8 are more widely spaced. If craft and personnel are still intact, you will arrive in **Pontivy** (K204.5) in a state of near exhaustion, full of misgivings about the conventional meaning of the word 'holiday'! There should be a great sense of achievement. One plan that considerably speeds up the operation is to send a crew member ahead, down the towpath, by bicycle (or even motorcycle) to alert the next keeper and help prepare the lock with a great saving in time.

Pontivy lies at the junction with the canalized River Blavet (see Chapter 34) and provides most urban facilities and cruiser hire. This meeting of the waters is dominated by a brooding *château*, with ramparts, 20m high walls and moat. Erected by the seemingly insatiable castle builder Jean II de Rohan in the 1480s, it later attracted the attention of Napoléon: he chose the town as a military base, laid out new streets and buildings on a formal grid, and ordered construction of the Canal de Nantes à Brest as a freight route safe from the English fleet. For a time it was even called Napoléonville, then reverted to its original name, changed once more under the Second Empire and has been Pontivy thereafter. Bustling shopping streets are within 200m of the waterfront, with a selection of 15th and 16th century houses in the Rue de Pont, Rue du Fil and Place du Martray. In front of the castle a restaurant barge offers cheap to medium priced menus. Capt. Leslie Richardson (*Brittany and the Loire*, 1927) noted with pleasure: 'The *Ouest Éclair* came out with a most flattering account of *Sylvabelle II* and her crew. This is a capital litle paper produced in Rennes.' Not everything in Pontivy was, however, to his liking: 'Our departure was hastened by the arrival of a boatload of drunken coal-heavers, who jumped overboard, dived off the bridge in their clothes, and carried out other manoeuvres.'

Pontivy, at the junction with the River Blavet.

At the time of writing, plans to reinstate the 20km of canal with 12 locks between Pontivy and the **Guerlédan** dam have not been scheduled, but this section is likely to be rehabilitated in due course. The authorities state that a project to construct some form of boat lift at the site of the dam may well be carried out, but not in the near future. Reopening of the through route to Brest is a most attractive proposition, although it will be extremely expensive. Waterway enthusiasts will rightly resent the existence of the Guerlédan Lake: it is nevertheless a beautiful expanse of water about 10km long with thickly wooded banks, and offers dinghy sailing, passenger boats and small waterside 'beaches'.

BRANCHE FINISTÈRIENNE

After a long break, caused by the Guerlédan reservoir and dam, navigation begins once more at the border between the Côtes du Nord and Finistère Départements. Distances and lock numbers are calculated from Nantes. Apart from the sea lock at Guily-Glas, there are no keepers and boat crews must work unassisted – a situation that on most French waterways would result in serious trouble if a boatman so much as dared to operate a lock without supervision from its keeper! A windlass must be hired from the navigation office at 1 Rue du Stade, Châteauneuf-du-Faou. Keep 5–10m from the towpath bank, as elsewhere depth may be limited. All locks must be left empty, and paddles wound down rather than being dropped.

Since 1983 navigation has been possible downhill of Écluse 192, Goariva (K279), 52km beyond Guerlédan. For 8km the waterway takes the form of an artificial canal, before entering the River Hyères below Écluse 203, Kergoat (K289). 3km from the bridge spanning the pound between Écluses 197 and 198 (K284) lies the ancient town of **Carhaix-Plouguer**: in Roman times it stood at the junction of seven roads. The local hero is Théophile-Malo Corret, known as La Tour d'Auvergne (1743–1800). A student of the Breton tongue, he sought to prove that this was the language of Adam and Eve! Also a highly respected soldier, he was killed in the Rhine campaign. A church is dedicated to St Trémeur, whose father heard a prediction that he would be killed by a son. Accordingly, the Count of Comorre murdered each of his first four wives when they became pregnant. The fifth wife managed to place her baby in the safe-keeping of some monks before she too was put to death. Years passed and when by chance Comorre met Trémeur he immediately recognized a resemblance to his mother and had him beheaded. Wasting little time, the boy picked up his own head and made for his father's castle, which he reduced to ruins by throwing a handful of earth against the walls. Comorre was buried alive and St Trémeur was ever afterwards depicted carrying his head in his hands. This bloodthirsty legend dates back to the 6th century. Facilities at **Port de Carhaix** (K286) include restaurant, grocer and mechanic.

With lush woodlands and very few boats, this part of the Canal de Nantes à Brest is a magical waterway. There is a restaurant by Écluse 204, Coz-Castel (K288). Within 1.5km of Écluse 206, Stervallen, the village of **St Hernin** offers a grocer and restaurant, with parish close (*enclos paroissial*) at the church. Alternatively, walk uphill for about 2km from Écluse 207, Le Ster (K295), to reach the small town of **Cléden-Poher** with grocer and restaurant and huge neglected church with exquisite ossuary/chapel outside, held together with steel cables and used as a bicycle store. The churchyard has a fine Calvary; a *pardon* is held on August 15. Navigation leaves the Hyères and joins the River Aulne at **Pont-Triffen** (K298) with grocer, café, water and mechanic close by; within 2km at **Landeleau** there is fuel, restaurant, butcher and baker. Several more locks intervene with a rocky slate scree cascading into the river 1km before Écluse 217, Boudrac'h. To the south lies **St-Goazac**, on the edge of the Montagnes Noires. Such lost and isolated villages have changed little since Mrs Lewis Chase described them in *A Vagabond Voyage through Brittany* (1915): 'Small children clung to their mothers' skirts when meeting us on the road, bigger ones, less afraid, jeered at us and one old woman crossed herself. We were apparently agents of the devil because we came from the outside world.' At this time country folk and Breton lock keepers regularly wore their traditional costume.

Several broad loops eventually lead to the quay at **Châteauneuf-du-Faou** (K317), a charming little place with waterside Auberge Le Chaland and ancient ivy-covered bridge. A launching ramp is suitable for small trailed craft. The centre of town is well above the river, with all facilities; water is available at a camp site. Of special interest in the main square is the Bar-Musée, a café filled with antique Breton furniture and presided over by an elderly lady adorned with Breton *coiffe* and dress. Framed press photographs indicate that she is something of a celebrity. Another café is also an antique shop. A *pardon* is held on the penultimate Sunday of August. Châteauneuf is perhaps the most appealing part of the Aulne Valley and is noted for its salmon and pike fishing. Most of the locks are equipped with special salmon weirs, enabling the fish to run upstream to their spawning grounds.

While many locks retain their original keepers' cottages, they have all been sold into private ownership and are elaborately extended as weekend retreats. Some lock sites are remote and the towpath is maintained in excellent condition from end to end, allowing riparian owners car access. Further expense has been lavished on buoys to mark the approach of the open weirs, a feature often lacking elsewhere. Small restaurants will be found at **Pont-ty-glas** (K 324) and **Ty-men** Bridge (K 331.5). Throughout, the river is thickly wooded and there is never a hint of commercial development. When you reach **Pont Coblant** (K 338) (most shops, restaurant, hire craft, fuel and water) it is worth taking to bicycles for a 6km ride into **Pleyben**. Its parish close is full of treasures, including the largest Calvary in the whole of Brittany (16–17th centuries), two belfries, one a magnificent Renaissance tower, and a 15th century ossuary. The church interior is a remarkable display of painted baroque.

As the Aulne approaches the sizeable town of **Châteaulin** (K 360), it describes a series of six giant loops, increasing the straight-line distance several times. Making the most of its river situation, the town has tree-shaded quays with a colourful market. One old legend tells of the Duke's park being surrounded by a high wall 30km long and built in a single night by the Devil in return for his soul. Between February and July anglers arrive from far and wide for the celebrated salmon: the fish features on the town's coat of arms and somewhat irreverently the locals are called *Pen Eog* (Breton for 'salmon heads'). After passing through Écluse 236, Châteaulin, with its massive viaduct, the river arrives in the maritime world of **Port-Launay**

Sizeable craft can penetrate the waterway from the sea and reach Port-Launay.

(K364), whose once flourishing quays now offer moorings for substantial sea-going pleasure craft. Shops, garage, supermarket and restaurants are all nearby. Although upstream of the sea lock, this reach is sometimes affected by high tides. One final lock, **Guily-Glas** (K367), provides access to the tideway: its 40m × 10m chamber is considerably bigger than those upriver. The keeper will be pleased to provide information on the 27km of estuary that extend from here to the sea at **Landévennec**. It is an outstandingly beautiful run past pine-clad rocky hills and under a great suspension bridge, the Pont de Térénez.

34 · Canal du Blavet

Carte Guide: *Bretagne*
From Pontivy, junction with the Canal de Nantes à Brest to a junction with the Blavet Maritime below Hennebont, 59.8km with 28 locks.

Why the Blavet should officially be described as a 'canal' is a mystery, as in all respects it is a normal navigable river. Forming the western part of a through route from central Brittany to the Atlantic coast, it is an exceptionally attractive waterway, well maintained and passing through heavily wooded countryside. Pleasure boat use is very light, amounting to a mere 100 craft a year in 1982. During a cruise down the Blavet you are likely to get closer to the true heart of Brittany than on any other route. Most of the locks have keepers; those without will be operated by the guardian of the adjacent lock. Abiding memories will be of rural isolation and lively weirs.

Conceived by Napoléon as a military necessity for the shipment of goods free from the coastal interference of the British, the Blavet was not finally opened to traffic until 1825. Further information is oddly difficult to find. For the next century a certain level of success was achieved, leading cargoes during the 1930s being pit props from the Armorican uplands of Brittany for export to Wales with return loads of coal for the steel works at Lochrist, near Hennebont. Barges were pulled by horses or tractors and made 2,709 individual journeys in 1936, with a total tonnage of 163,000. After World War II freight movements declined rapidly, what remained being carried in motor barges. By 1966 all the working boats had gone.

From its **Pontivy** junction with the Canal de Nantes à Brest (see Chapter 33 for details of the town), the route is briefly slightly industrial. But by the time Écluse 2, Lestitut (K2.4), is reached, wooded and hilly banks, so characteristic of the Blavet, are there to enjoy. Throughout the non-tidal section the navigation channel lies near the left, towpath, side; elsewhere, rocky shallows may cause grounding. For the uppermost 34km a railway closely follows the river, but is rarely intrusive. Écluse 5, Divit (K9.6, water point), epitomizes the very best qualities of a rural French river: a lock cottage with customary small farm, tumbling weir comprising semi-circular waterfalls and footway, and clusters of mature trees. Where fields are under cultivation they appear extremely fertile. Occasional glimpses of stone farmhouses are often the only sign of civilization. From Écluse 7, Kerblesquer (K13.9), a steep hill leads through woodland for about 3km to the amazingly ornate and impressive **Chapelle St Nicodème**, a 16th century Gothic church with superb carved stone details. Repeatedly in Brittany it appears that there are almost too many ecclesiastical monuments of the very highest quality for many of them to be maintained much beyond a level that verges on dereliction. So it is with St Nicodème, situated by a cluster of farm buildings. Ask for the key at the house alongside, to see the interior or climb the massive tower. It is almost deserted except during its *pardon*,

An unusual type of weir, formed from a series of semi-circular waterfalls, at Écluse 7, Kerblesquer.

held on the first Sunday of August. An alternative, closer, approach from the river is up a track that leads from the towpath some distance upstream of Écluse 8, Guern (K15.8).

With very few waterside villages, most boaters will wish to stop at **St-Nicholas-des-Eaux** (K17.8), a settlement of thatched houses in a deep valley by two loops of river that each turn almost completely back on themselves. Ice creams, Breton clogs and postcards are sold by the lock keeper, while good food is available at the nearby Hôtel de la Vallée. Shopping. High above the navigation on the D1 road to **Castennac** you will discover a lookout point with a superb view down onto the Blavet. This is close to the ancient Site de Castennac, with a prehistoric burial chamber (in a small caravan site). Reminders of ancient religions are never far beneath the surface of Christianized monuments in Brittany. On the Montagne de Castennac is a holy well where a stone image of Isis dates from Roman times. The goddess gradually became known as Nôtre Dame de la Couarde (Couarde being a local sorceress) and the idol was said to cure the sick of various complaints. When in 1661 the Jesuits had the statue cast into the Blavet in an attempt to stamp out non-Christian beliefs, the villagers were irate and blamed the following winter's floods on this action. Accordingly, they dredged the stone from the riverbed, only to have it thrown back once more by Count Claude de Lannion. The local population expressed little surprise when the Count was unseated from his horse and remained unconscious for 24 hours. There persists a strong belief along the Blavet valley in the equivalent of Ireland's 'little people'. Most powerful are the *poulpicans* (fairies' husbands) who like to dance round dolmens or menhirs. They will exact savage penalties from permissive young girls, wickedly embrace maidens who stay too long at fairs, ring bells to mislead shepherdesses or goatherds, and issue dreadful cries on dark winter nights. Within living memory, mothers would leave a jar of honey outside at night to prevent the *poulpicans* removing babies from their cots and substituting a fairy child. Beliefs like these seem almost possible when you moor up in the woods by the curious little chapel of St Gildas on the right bank below a railway bridge that follows Écluse 10, La Couarde (K19.6). Built like a stone barn into the base of a bare rocky cliff, this was once a holy place of the Druids. Gildas appears to have travelled widely in the Celtic world of Cornwall, Wales, Ireland and Scotland. He arrived in Brittany in about AD 540 and is said to have preached Christianity to the people from a rough pulpit, now contained within the chapel.

The surrounding countryside is noted for astonishingly rustic farming villages, little changed in many centuries. A typical example to visit is **Bieuzy**, about 2km from the river to the right of Écluse 11, Camblen (K21.1). After an uphill walk you will enter a jumble of old stone houses, each with a decorated stone well and cattle looking out of barns in the main street. Several shops and a restaurant, and fuel may be obtained (there are few easily accessible garages on the upper Blavet).

At a similar distance from the navigation at Écluse 13, Boternau (K25), the village of **St-Rivalain** has a restaurant, baker and grocer. Several of the Blavet weirs drive small hydro-electric power stations, dating from the 1930s: an admirable way of using 'free' energy. These include Écluses 16, 17 and 23 and prove that even rivers with a gentle gradient can drive generators. Moor on the bank immediately upstream of Écluse 16, **St-Adrien** (K30.9) to explore the village of great charm and tranquillity (bar, grocer and baker). A rare small boatyard with hire craft and fuel will be found in a basin at **Pont-Augan**, just above Écluse 18, St-Barbe (K36.4). Water and electricity are laid on. (Grocer, baker and restaurant.) Downstream of the bridge and a junction with the River Evel, avoid the remains of a bridge support in the middle of the waterway. Up to Écluse 19, Minazen (K39.4), weirs and lock chambers have been immediately alongside each other: but here there is a real lock island, with short canal. Ice creams are sold at a small bar/café.

In the pound between Écluses 20 and 21 the Restaurant Au Vallée Verte by the D102 bridge, Pont Neuf (K46.5), would be convenient for an overnight stop. Further delightful river scenery with several more locks leads to the slightly industrialized little town of **Lochrist** (K54.6). This is the last chance for shopping or a visit to a *crêperie* before the tideway at Écluse 28, Polhuern (K57.3). There is little except the lock to mark transition from a peaceful waterway to the upper reaches of an estuary that virtually dries out at low water, to reveal a rock-strewn channel. Inland craft would perhaps be advised to travel no farther. However, if bound for the coast, boats should aim to leave the lock about 1hr after high water and moor to a pontoon immediately above the first of two bridges in **Hennebont** (K59.8) until there is enough headroom to pass beneath. Travelling in the opposite direction, leave the coast at **Lorient** 2hr after low water, so having sufficient depth to clear the shoals while still being able to get under the bridges. Hennebont is an interesting fortified town dating back to the 11th century. It was under siege in 1341, during the War of Succession, and was relieved when the English fleet sailed up the Blavet. All facilities are within easy reach of the mooring pontoons. 13km downstream at the river mouth, the modern town of Lorient provides safe pleasure boat moorings in the Bassin à Flot, whose tidal lock operates from 1½hr before high water until 1hr afterwards. In all, there are three marinas as well as the submarine pens of World War II fame. Most facilities including slipway and cranes may be used. The appropriate marine chart is No. 544, published by Editions Grafocarte.

35 · River Loire

Carte Guide: *Les Rivières des Pays de la Loire*
From Nantes, junction with the Loire Maritime to Bouchemaine, junction with the River Maine (for the Rivers Mayenne, Oudon and Sarthe): 83km with 0 locks. The river from Nantes to the coast at St-Nazaire (52.5km) is really a seaway, accepts shipping drawing about 9m at any state of the tide, and is beyond the scope of this book. Junctions are made with the River Erdre section of the Canal de Nantes à Brest and the Sèvre Nantaise (leading to the Petite Maine), both in Nantes. One short isolated length of the River Loire, 1.2km, links the Canal Latéral à Loire with the Canal du Nivernais at Decize (see Chapter 41).

The Loire is the fourth longest river in Western Europe and the longest in France, extending about 1,000km from its source in the Massif Central, a mere 160km north of the Mediterranean and 48km from the Rhône at Valence. But it chooses to flow northwards through gorges towards Nevers and Orléans and then west past Tours, Angers and Nantes to the Atlantic. Once navigable for 825km and officially described thus in highly optimistic terms as recently as 1936, the waterway is a shadow of its former self. Now, no fewer than 685km are virtually abandoned by commercial traffic, with the exception of very local and limited use by gravel barges. What does remain is lock-free, tidal and slightly difficult, a narrow channel wandering between vast expanses of shingle and sand. In spite of a reputation of being lined with great *châteaux*, these are to be found in the middle reaches which are not available to boats. Determined canoeists *might* contrive to journey downstream from Orléans, making portages over obstructions during low summer water levels or taking a severe risk at times of spring flooding. The scenic attractions from a small boat are rather limited as the wasteland of willows and sandbanks soon becomes monotonous; the majority of towns and villages sensibly lie well back behind high flood walls.

Both J. L. Molloy (in *Our Autumn Holiday on French Rivers*, 1874) and C. S. Forester (*The Voyage of the Annie Marble*, 1929) brought little boats down the stream from Orléans to Nantes and wrote glowing accounts. Forester considered it 'the loveliest river in Europe' and was so enraptured with the final length that he abandoned all attempts to make notes and shamefully dismisses this part in a single page! Molloy was equally impressed by 'the noblest of French rivers'. Perhaps the scope open to very light-draft craft is greater than that available to medium sized motor cruisers. While there are few navigational problems for pleasure boats downriver of Bouchemaine, I find the surroundings often far from exciting. The channel is clearly marked with buoys and no difficulty should be had in picking a way through the various branches provided you carefully follow the *Carte Guide*. Facilities, and especially safe moorings, are adequate but not extensive. For many, therefore, the Loire is a useful approach from the coast to a network of much more pleasing river navigations controlled by locks and allowing access to such towns as Segré, Laval and Le Mans. Some commercial traffic remains to Bouchemaine and the various tributaries are well served by hire cruisers. But the whole area is generally remote

St Gildas' chapel, on the riverbank below Écluse 10, Blavet.

and under-used: it is perhaps the region of French waterways where navigation most seems like a genuine voyage of discovery.

There are numerous ramps for launching small trailed craft from the tops of stone flood banks, but care must always be taken in approaching former commercial quays which now rise from rocky shallows. If in doubt stay in deep water, lower the anchor and come ashore by dinghy. Drinking water and other boating supplies are not plentiful, so top up as the opportunity arises. Where it is cultivated, the flood plain of the lower Loire is very fertile, producing cheap but most acceptable wines. Nearer the coast the most famous is Muscadet, a fresh, dry white that normally accompanies seafood. Further upstream you will discover the Coteaux d'Ancenis, an area of white, rosé and red. Among food specialities are several noted forms of duck and pork near Nantes; elsewhere, try *brême farcie* (stuffed bream), *alose à l'oseille* or *beurre blanc* (shad flavoured with sorrel or a sauce made with butter, shallots and Muscadet), *tanche au four* (baked tench), *quenelle de brochet* (pike dumpling), *friture* (freshwater 'whitebait'), *andouilles* (tripe sausages), *chevreuil* (venison) and all kinds of game.

Brief history The story of freight and passenger transport along the Loire is utterly absorbing, as it was one of the great highways of France for well over 2,000 years until its collapse with the introduction of railways during the 19th century. Better documented than most river navigations in the country, it was used by the Romans upstream to Roanne (Rodumna). Even earlier, the Phoenicians and the Greeks had regularly taken goods up the Rhône to Lyon, where a great market was established. From there, it was a fairly short overland journey with packhorses to reach the Loire and access to the Atlantic. Much later, there are records of the city of Tours being besieged by the Vikings, who had arrived in longships.

River traffic reached its height in the 17–19th centuries, although a toll system was widely used in medieval times. Various payments were exacted by feudal landlords such as the Count of Nevers, Duke of Bourbonnais, Count of Gien, Count of Touraine and the Duke of Brittany. Additional costs to freight transport came from town tolls (at such places as Gien, Tours, Decize and La Charité); church tolls; and 'special' tolls, levied on pilgrims, Jews and corpses. Exemptions applied to the clergy, merchants bound for fairs and arms makers. Collection points were established where boats could most easily be boarded, for example when passing through the arches of bridges.

For a long period attempts were made to keep open a navigable channel with wooden embankments and dredging. During the 17th century Colbert undertook a programme of stone training walls and quays from Roanne to Nantes which helped make the river more reliable. It was nevertheless frequently stopped through flood and drought, and as late as 1860 the Loire was only passable for 129 days from Orléans to Tours by craft drawing up to 0.5m and for 149 days in the section Briare to Orléans. As boatmen were generally paid for a journey rather than for the time taken, there was every incentive to travel on floods, with wrecks being predictably frequent. In 1707 Loire floods were said to have drowned 50,000 people; during their height, the water rose more than 3m in two hours at Orléans!

Many different kinds of craft were used, with timber hulls universal until the early 19th century. Until about 1760 the most common vessels were *chalands* (sometimes called *sapines*), 25–30m long on a beam of 3–4m. *Toues* were similar in construction but smaller, and both drew under 0.5m. Later versions were *sentines* or *vergées*, the latter equipped with mast and sails. All were built of pine planking on oak frames. *Cabanes* and *coches d'eau* (water coaches) capable of loading 50 tonnes were rowed. Typical passenger timetables for Orléans to Nantes allowed eight days for the trip and upwards of 14 days for the reverse direction against the stream. The more affluent traveller would have his coach placed on board for a modicum of home comfort. Madame de Sevigné made such journeys on the Loire in 1675 and 1680. Rather later, the English writer Arthur Young commented in his *Journeys in France* that there was a service of passenger boats between Nantes and Orléans. Aboard one, he had six fellow travellers who each paid a golden Louis for the privilege of sleeping on the ground at night during the $4\frac{1}{2}$ day voyage. They feasted off lampreys, salmon and shad and were regaled with fine wines which abounded throughout the valley. Where craft were not rowed or sailed they were hauled by horses (sometimes up to their necks in water) or oxen, a form of traction that survived on several navigations including the Rivers Adour and Dordogne until the 1930s. Bow-hauling by teams of men was also practised.

A further sort of boat was the *Roannaise*, a big barge of pine with oak sheathing built for one-way downriver trips from Roanne. On arrival they were dismantled and the timber sold, certain fittings being retained for future use. The master boatmen were a hardy race and an important section of the population in every river port. In cold weather they sustained themselves with mulled wine, well sweetened and taken with slices of toast. One traditional dish was *matelote*, a fish stew which modern travellers may like to prepare, perhaps adapting the recipe to suit the galley of a pleasure cruiser: take a large copper cauldron and hang it over an open wood fire on a tripod of tree branches. Slice an assortment of fish such as eel, tench, pike and barbel, removing the heads, and cover with red wine, adding plenty of salt, pepper and garlic. Cook for 15 to 20 minutes. Then mix a liberal quantity of butter with a little flour and some of the hot wine; add this to the fish and boil briefly. The wine should have a high alcohol content, enabling the stew to be flambéed for a few moments. The *matelote* is now ready to serve.

While the boat people's patron, at least from the time of the Troubadours, was St Nicholas, on the Loire he competed with St Arigle, a Bishop of Nevers. His final wish was that his body should be placed on a boat and left to the mercy of the river current. Great was the surprise of the spectators when the vessel began to travel upstream, eventually coming to rest at Decize!

Sometimes owning several craft, the Loire mariners were a proud band of men, wearing loose pantaloons and a blouse or smock of canvas or blue serge, fixed at the waist with a silver pin. A bright red scarf (known as a *tabac*, for it was a useful place in which to keep pipe tobacco), wide-brimmed black hat and wooden shoes of poplar or willow completed the outfit. Relics of the life are preserved in an excellent small museum, the Musée de la Marine de la Loire at Châteauneuf between Orléans and Gien. Displays are devoted to photographs, paintings, documents, boat models, clothing, cabin furniture and barge equipment.

Steam-driven craft appeared on the Loire shortly after the beginning of the 19th century and for the first time it was possible to work upstream with a degree of reliability. These vessels were almost exclusively used for passengers, with scheduled services operating between Nantes and Orléans by 1829. Six years later lighter, faster boats were introduced, known as *hirondelles* (swallows). But there were several dramatic and costly accidents caused by over-taxed boilers, notably an 1837 disaster between Angers and Nantes. The publicity resulted in a reduction of clients and so the *inexplosibles* appeared in 1838–9, gradually spreading throughout the Loire and its tributary the Allier. Speeds of 10kph upstream and 16–18kph downstream were achieved. At this time freight steamers or *remorqueurs* also appeared, carrying 15,000 tonnes in 1843. Foreign imports such as leather, salted fish, Spanish oranges, English metals and Welsh steam coal arrived in Nantes by coaster, while a whole range of commodities came downstream from the French interior. Many of the barges acted as floating shops, selling pro-

duce to towns en route. Also in 1843, the Upper Loire carried 37,440 passengers; the Lower River 69,504 people.

The boom was not to last long. From the 1840s passenger traffic moved to the newly constructed railways and the four regular steamboat lines were eventually forced out of business in spite of their smaller charges. Canals serving the higher portions of the river (such as the Loire Latéral, Berry and Orléans) kept their freight, but with the exception of rafts of pine logs (used until 1895) trade on the Loire died above Bouchemaine.

There remained some advocates of river transport, and in 1900 the Société de la Loire Navigable proposed building a fully usable waterway between Nantes and Briare: 24km was actually completed from Angers to Montjean. However, traffic upstream of Nantes declined still further, reaching a mere 12,000 tonnes by 1923. Thereafter any works were restricted to making training walls and dredging in the Nantes-Angers length. What had been the greatest waterway in France was now virtually dead. From time to time grandiose schemes are suggested that would give the Loire transport status commensurate with the Seine or Rhône. The latest, advanced in 1962, envisaged making the Loire fully navigable to near Saumur, junction with the River Cher. The route would then pass through the valleys of the Cher and Yèvre to Bourges, along the line of the disused Canal du Berry to Beffes, and finally join up with the Canal latéral à la Loire to gain access to the Saône at Chalon via the Canal du Centre. Although General de Gaulle was said to personally support the idea, it is now largely forgotten.

Little needs to be said of the broad estuary of the Loire from where it leaves the Atlantic at the port of **St-Nazaire** to run for 52.5km to Nantes. The lower portion is in every sense a seaway, accessible to large ships and covered by Service Hydrographique chart 5456. St-Nazaire was a harbour as far back as Roman times and achieved some importance under the Duke of Brittany. But in 1850 the population was a mere 4,000; since that time the port has expanded greatly as a shipbuilding centre and harbour for Nantes, itself inaccessible to modern ocean-going vessels. No difficulty should be experienced in working upriver on a rising tide, keeping to the marked deep-water channel. En route, anchorages can be used at the entrances to the now disused Canal Maritime (south shore) in **Paimboeuf** and **La Martinière**. Surroundings vary from salt flats on the coast to commercial wharfs and oil refineries, with muddy banks and willows growing just

Long-vanished traffic on the upper Loire near Tours, depicted by Turner in the early 19th century.

above the high water mark. If mooring in St-Nazaire, several agreeable southern Brittany sea beaches are within quite easy reach, notably a craggy cove with fine sand at **Chémoulin**, between **St-Marc** and **Ste-Marguerite** about 9km SW of the city centre.

More than most French rivers, the Loire is subject to considerable fluctuations in height: under normal conditions a tide will be experienced from Nantes only as far upstream as Ancenis. It is strongly advised to follow the *Carte Guide* regarding the depths that can be expected in the river at any given time. Built at the confluence of the Loire, Erdre and Sèvre Nantaise, **Nantes** is a thriving modern city with considerable evidence of its one-time greatness as Capital of Brittany. It lost its independence under the Dukes of Brittany in 1491 when Anne de Bretagne, daughter of Duke François II, was married to King Charles VIII. A quarter of a century before, the huge Château des Ducs, whose towering walls are the city's showpiece, had been begun. Now open to the public (not Tues), the most interesting sections are a Maritime Museum, with some exhibits relating to Loire navigation, and

displays of traditional Breton folk art and furniture. Visitors should also see the Gothic cathedral of St Pierre and St Paul, started in 1434 and not finished until the late 19th century. Long one of the leading ports of France, Nantes was eclipsed for a time from the middle of the last century by St-Nazaire, but recently improvements to the river channel have brought about a resurgence in trade. Until the 1930s it was the main importer of Welsh steam coal, while rather earlier slave ships (*negriers*) called there from Africa before sailing to the West Indies and America. In the troubled times of 1793, prisoners (mostly royalists) crowded the gaols and the revolutionary Carrier solved the problem with a drastic solution: 4,000 men, women and children were herded into river barges which were then flooded with water or scuttled. The victims became known as the *Noyades*: within months Carrier was tried, found guilty and guillotined.

Various pleasure boat facilities will be found on the river, but in many ways it is more convenient to lock out of the Loire and into the Canal de Nantes à Brest, on the left bank upstream of Pont Aristide-Briand immediately before a prominent football stadium. Moorings will be found here in the Bassin Malakoff or beyond the 800m St-Félix Tunnel in the *port de plaisance* (see Chapter 33).

Nantes spills onto a large island, both river channels being navigable. If you take the right-hand course, you will pass a junction just beyond the first (railway) bridge with the **River Sèvre Nantaise**, open to boats for 21.5km. When making this detour along the little known and seldom frequented waterway, it is best to leave the Loire about 1hr before high water: 45 minutes on a rising tide should be sufficient to reach the only Sèvre lock, Écluse de Vertou (available seven days a week except public holidays, 6.30–19.30h). Thereafter draft is restricted to about 1.2m. A winding course passes through deserted countryside and Muscadet vineyards. Good shopping is available at **Vertou** (K6.5 from the Loire), with a series of *châteaux* (de la Frémoire, de Rochefort at **La Haie Fouassière**, and du Briel) all close to the river banks. At K10.5, beyond **Portillon**, the **Petite Maine** enters on the right and can be followed for 4km to **Château-Thébaud**. Depth is generally only 1m or even slightly less. Craft are able to reach the head of navigation on the Sèvre at Port Domino in the little town of **Monnières**, surrounded by vineyards.

Leaving Nantes to head up the Loire, the great river soon assumes its characteristic form: a wide expanse of sandbanks, substantial islands and willow-overhung backwaters. Boats much larger than dinghies are firmly advised to keep within the buoyed channel. During hot summer weather this can be a wonderful setting for idle cruising: stopping to swim or make barbeques from driftwood fires on isolated sandy beaches. Admittedly there are long stretches with few land-based facilities, and where stopping points are suggested here this must not be taken to imply that proper bankside moorings exist, unless specifically stated. Shortly upstream of the first bridge after Nantes is a restaurant in **Belle-Vue** (K6 above Nantes). Soon after, the channel divides (K8): take the right fork and pass upriver to a bridge connecting **Le Haut-Village** (K10.5, right bank, restaurant) with **Thouaré-sur-Loire** (all shopping). Dramatic tree-covered rocks rise high from the river on the left for a long distance.

Village restaurants are situated in **La Chebuette** (K12.5, right bank) and **Mauves-sur-Loire** (K16.5, left bank and reached from the bridge). One of many launching ramps for small craft is on the left, immediately downstream of **Vandel** (K21.5). There are few really good Loire pleasure boat harbours and none better than that near the mouth of the little River Hâvre at **Oudon** (K25, left bank). It is quite a relief to leave the Loire briefly for a hint of civilization and the *port de plaisance* features pontoon moorings, slipway and a garage 200m uphill to the left. Moreover, there are two restaurants overlooking the water with butcher,

baker and grocer in the village. The tower of a medieval keep (open in midsummer) rises alongside the port, its roof providing broad valley views.

We are now on the edge of Anjou, a great wine-producing region: one of the most popular varieties is *rosé*. **Champtoceaux** (K26.8, right bank), however, specializes in white. Unfortunately, moorings are not convenient, so the town and its fair range of facilities are perhaps best avoided unless you continue past the tail of the Île Neuve, tie up on the right bank and walk back downstream. Seated on a great rock, Champtoceaux features a lookout point or *belvédère* near the church. The next place of note is **Ancenis** (K34, left bank), with a fine suspension bridge and the possibility of mooring along a stone quay (approach carefully to avoid loose boulders). On the border between Brittany and Anjou, it has an impressive *château* begun in the 16th century and now a school (visits possible, afternoons during school summer holidays). Much of the town's charm lies in its hilly streets of old houses. Originally a busy port and centre of sailmaking, leading industries are now a pig market, Muscadet wine and the *rosé* Gamay. Among the leading *caves* is that of Bossard (retail sales) in **St-Géréon**, 3km NW. Plenty of shops, restaurants and other facilities are close to the bridge, where there is also a small slipway and a monument to members of the *Résistance* who fell in the defence of 1944. Tidal flow is scarcely a consideration above this point.

Buoys in the long reach that follows are changed according to the scours created as the channel alters; there is little worthy of comment in these 11km until we reach the hamlet of **Marillais** (K45) at a confluence with the small River Evre. There are few signs that here Charlemagne had built what is variously described as a great church or a royal palace in the 9th century. Legend tells that he arrived at a lake then by the river and struck a rock thrice with his gold and silver sword decorated with diamonds: the rock shattered and he flung his sword towards the water, saying: 'Where this sword falls shall be erected the church of Notre Dame!' The resulting edifice was a structure of great magnificence, progressively enriched by succeeding Carolingian monarchs. Its 45kg bell of solid gold was hauled from the Loire by fishermen in the 11th century. In later years the building was repeatedly plundered and little remains today.

Upstream, **St-Florent-le-Vieil** (K47) stands on the right bank at a bridge crossing: it occupies a most attractive situation on a rocky outcrop, crowned by an early 18th century church in the Classical style. The town features in an exquisite series of 61 steel engravings, *The Seine and the Loire*, produced from paintings made by English artist J. M. W. Turner and originally published in 1833–5. Throughout, the pictures show extensive barge traffic. In his *Our Autumn Holiday on French Rivers* (1874), J. L. Molloy describes St-Florent as 'the loveliest spot we had yet seen either on Seine or Loire'; the travellers spent several days there and recorded the 'beginning and the end of the great Vendéan insurrection. In 1793, the inhabitants of La Vendée rose to a man against the Revolution, and declared themselves for the King, the priests and the nobles. It commenced at this little village on the 10th of March, and the first movement had for its chiefs two men of the people – Cathelineau, a *voiturier*, and Stofflet, a gamekeeper. Then came Rochejacquelein and Bonchamps-Charette, Marigny, and the rest. For a time they had a vein of brilliant success. They took Thouars in May, Saumur in June, and followed up by driving the garrison out of Angers.

'But the same month they went down to Nantes – were defeated, and lost Cathelineau. Thenceforth everything went against them. They had neither science nor organization, and what guns they possessed they had taken in battle. The army of Mayence, under Kleber, followed them, and in October routed them mortally. They fled in confusion, and at night eighty thousand people, soldiers, old men, women and children, found themselves once more at St-Florent, with no alternative but to abandon La Vendée and cross the Loire. There were 4,000 Republican prisoners shut up in the church, and the Vendéans, to avenge their disaster at Cholet, were pointing their cannon upon it when Bonchamps, who was mortally wounded, begged for their lives with his dying breath.' In the classical early 18th century church is the tomb of Bonchamps, the work of the great sculptor David d'Angers. Today St-Florent is a popular riverside resort with plenty of shops and several restaurants (advance booking is advised). Moorings on the most obvious quay above the bridge should be approached with great caution. If in doubt, lie off and anchor. Moving on, the next place is **Ingrandes** (K 56), a long, grey town overlooking vast sandbanks crossed by an exceptionally wide 19th century multi-span suspension bridge. Moor judiciously

Safe and peaceful moorings for small craft off the main river at Oudon.

on a sloping quay, left bank just above the bridge. Close by is a slipway. Shops are highly convenient and the restaurant of the Hôtel du Lion d'Or is greatly recommended, both for its appetizing seafood and reasonable prices. Two or three hundred years ago there were notorious battles between Customs officers and salt smugglers, but it is now difficult to visualize the former extensive port. Further memories of vanished industrial activity are provided by realization that in the 19th century extensive coal pits were worked in this region and downstream to **Montrelais**, some of the seams reaching under the Loire itself.

Following a well established pattern of all facilities and potential moorings being placed near bridge crossings, little of note intervenes until the right bank town of **Montjean-sur-Loire** (K60.3). Here, the most impressive features are a six-arched suspension bridge, massive stone quays with iron mooring rings and vast quantities of granite setts and training walls: all evidence of the totally disused infrastructure of the commercial waterway. Craft should stem a strong flow and pass through the second bridge arch from the right, any possible moorings being a little downstream. Facilities include a slipway, garage (300m uphill) and most types of shopping with a choice of nearby restaurants. 3km NW of the bridge are the ruins of the *château* of **Champtocé-sur-Loire**, whose one-time owner Gilles de Rais was the inspiration of Charles Perrault's infamous Bluebeard. Devotees of the macabre may care to visit the setting for his magic rites which demanded a regular supply of children's blood. Forty skeletons were subsequently discovered here, and twice as many at Bluebeard's other residence, the Château de Machecoul.

Soon the Loire divides, the navigable part flowing to the right of a large island, the Grande Île de Chalonnes. Exploration by dinghy of a tree-hung backwater is worthwhile to reach a pretty hamlet, **La Maison Blanche** (K63) – a cluster of peaceful stone cottages, fishing punts, car ferry and in the hilly hinterland expanses of vineyards. **Chalonnes-sur-Loire** (K69) stands on the right bank by a series of bridges that cross no fewer than four Loire channels, close to a junction with the River Layon. The church, founded in the 6th century by St Maurille, was once so popular that open-air services were held to accommodate the crowds; a balcony still encircles the bell tower as a form of pulpit. Flax for sailcloth was once a main crop; today its place has been taken by tobacco. Numerous pleasure cruisers will be found here, for there are good moorings to a gently sloping quay just above the suspension bridge. Slipway, water point at the camping site, garage, marine mechanic, shops and restaurants combine to

make this a welcoming town. Across the river, 7km north at **St-Georges-sur-Loire**, is the superb moated Château de Serrant from the 16–18th centuries. From 1749 it was home of several generations of Irishmen named Walsh who had supported the Stuart cause by conveying Bonnie Prince Charlie to Moidart. Within the great building are magnificent furnishings. The public are admitted between Palm Sunday and Oct 31 (9.00–12.00h and 14.00–18.00h; closed on Tues except in July and Aug).

Towards the upstream limit of the Île de Chalonnes is an intensely rural little village called **La Tete de l'Île** (K70). Cows and chickens spill into a narrow waterside lane by stone farm buildings with clusters of climbing roses and Madonna lilies. Here can be found one of the professional Loire fishermen, whose signboard advertises 'bulk and small supplies'. Unusually noisy frogs croak in the surrounding marshland. Various streams unite once more below a railway bridge, and beyond the tracks is the small town of **La Possonière** (K74.6) where it is possible to tie to a causeway provided the river levels are not unduly low. Water at a camping site and there is a slipway, most food shops and a garage. The narrow streets make a pleasant shore excursion.

Now we leave the main stream of the Loire and pass up a narrower channel to the north of the Île de Béhuard. Although the mooring is rocky, if you can manage to stop by the first bridge, Pont de la Guillemette (K78.3), a restaurant will be found down the road on the south section of the river. **Savennières**, 2km north, may be visited for a moderate selection of shops and a famous vineyard, *La Coulée de Serrant*. Perhaps the most appealing village on the entire navigable Loire is **Béhuard** (K79), an extraordinary island settlement of buildings rising from rocky outcrops. Its 15th century church, with one wall of living rock, was built by Louis XI as a thanks offering following his near-drowning. There is also an unusual chapel consisting of altar backed by a stained glass window and otherwise open to the sky; services are regularly held. Facilities include several restaurants and a grocer. For once moorings, though not easy to locate, are quite good: on the south bank of the navigation channel look out for a tiny sandy beach, approached from the village down an avenue of willows and ash trees. Run the bows ashore gently to avoid touching loose rocks.

Two final stopping places are available before the upper navigation limit of the waterway: on the left bank at **Chantourteau** (K82), where fishing punts will be found on the ends of dykes (limited shopping) and to a quay on the left, just inside the mouth of the River Maine (K83.5), which may be used by pleasure craft provided it is not needed by petrol barges. Here ends

Loire boating for any but the shallowest draft craft. But much remains to be explored by following the Maine to Angers (Chapter 36) from which there is access to the Mayenne, Oudon and Sarthe.

36 · Rivers Maine and Mayenne

Carte Guide: *Les Rivières des Pays de la Loire or Guide 10, Pays de la Loire*
From a junction with the River Loire at Bouchemaine to Mayenne, 129.5km with 46 locks. A restoration programme was carried out during the 1980s, repairing twenty disused locks between Laval and Mayenne. Junctions are made with the River Sarthe upstream of Angers and with the river Oudon above Grez-Neuville.

This truly exquisite river rises in the Orne Département in Southern Normandy. The navigable portion winds through a steep-sided valley, often remote from towns or even main roads. Locks are all fairly small at 31m x 5.2m (the lowest eight are 33m). At the time of writing lock hours are 9.00–12.30h and 14.00–20.00h, April–Sept, with a closing time of 17.30h for the rest of the year. All recently recommissioned locks upstream of Laval are worked by boats' crews without the aid of keepers. Lasting memories will be of agreeable rural villages, numerous watermills (some converted into splendid houses, while a few continue their original function) and secretive reaches past shady meadows.

Technically the lowest 12km, from the confluence with the Sarthe at Angers to the Loire, are known as the River Maine, but for convenience both waterways are usually regarded as one.

Brief history One authority writes of the Mayenne as being used by barges as early as 1492; but it is unlikely that much trade was possible until after the inhabitants of Laval had petitioned the King to render the route suitable for large craft in 1536. This achieved, there were interminable disputes relating to freight taxes. During the mid-17th century Cardinal Mazarin

undertook the work of advancing the waterway from Laval to Mayenne. Locks then in use were time and water consuming navigation weirs or flash locks (*portes marinières*) of which 22 existed in the 36km between Château-Gontier and Laval by about 1724.

The present appearance of the river results from canalization of 1859–64, most of the locks being designed with weirs directly alongside. Already railway competition had arrived, but a steady traffic in chalk, stone, wood, coal, grain, fruit and vegetables built up, using 130 tonne barges. In 1899 there were 1,244 movements through Écluse 34, Château-Gontier, alone, and steam-driven passenger craft operated in the summer. By 1936 annual tonnage was 218,000, the leading cargo slate from the great quarries near Angers. Thereafter traffic died away and locks began to decay in the middle and upper reaches. Just in time, pleasure cruising saved the waterway from closure, and several hire firms were established by the early 1980s.

Leaving the Loire, we enter a broad reach of the River Maine and soon arrive at **Bouchemaine** (K2, left bank) where small craft can approach a sandy beach by the camping site below a suspension bridge. Alternatively anchor above a bridge, within easy reach of a restaurant and several food shops. Wide flood meadows accompany the river up to the city of **Angers** (K8). Shortly before the Pont de l'Atlantique, a new lock, Écluse du Seuil en Maine, ensures a more reliable water depth than was previously available. Long ago there were strong connections between Angers and England, resulting first from the marriage in 1129 of Geoffroi, son of the Comte d'Anjou, to Matilda, grand-daughter of William the Conqueror. Geoffroi's habit of wearing a sprig of broom (*genét*) gave rise to the name Plantagenet. The son of this union married Eleanor of Aquitaine in 1152 and soon afterwards was proclaimed Henry II of England. Angers is now a large town, noisy with motor traffic and looking down on to a busy waterfront. Sometimes known as 'Black Angers' on account of the slate roofs produced in an 800-year-old quarry at **Trélazé**, 8km east, and responsible for more than half the slates mined in France, the city is dominated by 17 round towers of a huge *château* erected by St Louis in the early 13th century. Among the treasures most worth seeing is a collection of tapestries, including the famous 14th century Apocalypse Tapestry 168m in length. Converted *péniches* and cruisers on moorings in a small basin opposite the *château* indicate the best place for visitors to lie, but take care to avoid the tripping boat berth.

One good mooring is the CVA Yacht Club. Slipway and water point are both on the right bank opposite the Hôpital St-Jean; other boating facilities are supplied by hire cruiser operators, including diesel.

Above Angers we enter a region of flat marshes frequently under water in times of flood. Immediately beyond a railway bridge the River Sarthe makes a junction with the Maine and Mayenne (K11.2). We turn left into the Mayenne, passing the west side of the huge Île St-Aubin which can only be reached by ferry from the 'mainland'. (Restaurant on the right bank.) One further junction (K14.4) at the NW corner of this island is with a channel known as La Vieille Maine, offering an alternative approach from the Mayenne to the Sarthe at Écouflant. The first village on these somewhat bleak lowest reaches of the river is **Cantenay-Épinard** (K16), a pleasing settlement with baker, butcher, grocer, garage and restaurant. Once above the next lock, Écluse 45, **Montreuil-Belfroy** (K18.1), the river assumes its beautiful character. Take advantage of the water hose by the lock. 1km of uphill walking from here brings you to the town centre (all services and restaurant). A quay on the left side above a road bridge at **Juigné-Béné** (K20.6) is convenient for restaurant and garage; 5.5km NW lies a magnificent *château* at **Plessis-Macé**, begun in the 11th century and enlarged in the 15th. (Guided tours available 10.00–12.00h and 14.00–18.30h, July–Sept. Out of season hours are 13.30–17.30h, no visits on Tues or Dec 1–Feb 28.)

On the right side of a bend in the river, grandly named **Port-Albert** (K23.3) consists of a pair of cottages fronting a grassy meadow with mooring rings. Several shops, restaurant and garage are 1.5km NE at **Feneu**. When the Roman legions set up a camp in this area in the winter of 57–56 BC they discovered a riverside tribe and their temple dedicated to various Celtic gods. Écluse 44, **Saultré** (K24.4), is situated in woodland upstream, alongside a broad weir and mill. Another charming millhouse has been converted into a private residence at Écluse 43, **La Roussière** (K26.4) with splendid cruising above and below. There is a *château* among trees just before the lock.

Bankside moorings at the site of a disused ferry crossing enable a visit to be made to **Pruillé** (K27.4), an ancient village high above the waterway (left bank) where butcher, baker and restaurant are only 400m distant. Slipway. **Grez-Neuville** (K30.8) spreads over both banks by a road bridge below Écluse 42. This is a lovely collection of mainly 17th and 18th century houses in grey stone with a 12th century church, lily-filled backwaters and mill. Drinking water and slipway at the Anjou Plaisance hire cruiser base,

meals in Le Cheval Blanc restaurant occupying a pretty Classical stone building (all near the lock). Basic food shops are on the right bank and petrol at a garage in **Crieul** 1.5km SW. A lock cut now leads to the junction with the River Oudon along which a diversion can profitably be made for 2km to **Le Lion d'Angers** for all facilities including a quay with drinking water (see Chapter 37).

Montreuil-sur-Maine (K36.8) is a small hilly village with rowing boats for hire at Écluse 41, grass bank moorings near a noisy church clock that strikes the quarters but mercifully stays silent after 21.00h, and convenient pontoons downstream of the lock whose right wall is flanked by a substantial watermill erected in 1858. (Grocer.) Avoiding the broad curve of a weir, Écluse 40, La Roche Chambellay (K40.1) is entered on the left bank (slipway) and not far beyond the bridge of **Chambellay** comes into sight (K41.6). Children may welcome a fluvial swimming pool, right bank by the football field, where there is also a water point. Pontoon moorings have recently been built above the bridge, left bank, close to slipway. The village offers grocer, baker and restaurant. As a reminder that an idyllic calm has not always prevailed, there is a crucifix near a cross-roads east of the Mayenne erected 'In memory of the Liberation of Chambellay and Chenillé-Changé, 8 August 1944'.

Isolated from **Chenillé-Changé** (K43.2), Écluse 39 is on the left bank. The attractive brown stone village is one of the most pleasant on the entire river: perhaps this impression is partly due to water power

Water power is still used to grind corn at the mill in Chenillé-Changé.

still being used to grind corn at the crenellated mill, built in the 19th century in a style remarkably similar to those on southern Ireland's Barrow Navigation. Jetties cater for visitors with fuel and restaurant close to the moorings. Maine Anjou Rivières have a cruiser base. (No shops.) Showing no signs of decreasing in width, the river continues past tree-covered slopes to **La Jaille-Yvon** (K45.6), perched high above the water. Jetty moorings and slipway are reasonably convenient to the grocer and baker, although a more direct approach is from Écluse 38 which is accompanied by yet another massive water mill. During the 19th century river views from the hilltops attracted the wealthy to construct *châteaux* throughout the valley. One such is on the right bank at **Le Port-Joulain** (K47.6). Now comes the small town of **Daon** (K49.9), a busy inland resort with water ski-ing, slipway, vertical stone quays each side of the road bridge, a camping site, grocer, baker, restaurant and garage. Rowing boats and pedalos may be hired. Numerous *châteaux* are in the vicinity, the most outstanding being the 16th century Manoir de l'Escoublère whose ancient turrets are surrounded by a moat. The owner will grant permission to walk round the exterior. From Daon, take the road towards St-Michel-de-Feins and turn left down a long avenue (about 3km).

Long and beautiful reaches extend either side of Écluse 37, Fourmusson (K50.9), and on to **Ménil** (K54.8), a useful overnight halt with pontoon just downstream of a car ferry recently withdrawn from service (slipway) and quay shortly above. This backwater of a village offers grocer's shop and reasonably priced meals in its *crêperie* restaurant Au Blé d'Or. Écluse 36 is on the left by a pair of wide weirs with well

L'Escoublère, near Daon, a 16th century manor.

restored millhouse. On the outskirts of Château-Gontier a slipway, mooring pontoon and water point have been installed in **Azé** (K61.5, right bank) 300m downstream of a railway bridge and close to café and baker. At the heart of the *Chouan* country, home of Royalists during the Vendéen War of 1793, **Château-Gontier** (K63.2) was once a leading river port and is now the busiest veal market in France, selling up to 5,000 calves each Thursday. Facilities are comprehensive with excellent quayside moorings and water point above the older of two bridges near the Nautical Club office and hire cruiser base. Should you need a more rural overnight stop, continue to Écluse 33, **Mirwault** (K64.9) with old and new mills in contrasting styles each side of the weir and a pleasant restaurant.

Take care to avoid water skiers in the following stretch leading to Écluse 32, La Roche-de-Maine (K66.9). Having negotiated Écluse 31, Neuville (K70.9, pontoon moorings) note the impressive Château de la Rongère on the left bank upstream of Écluse 30, La Rongère (K73.9). Towns and villages are now generally remote from the waterway and it may be necessary to moor immediately below the Pont de la Valette (K74.9) and walk almost 2km uphill into **Houssay** (food shops, garage and restaurant). Curving past wooded slopes, the Mayenne climbs through Écluses 29, **La Fosse** (K79.9); 28, **La Bénâtre** (K81.9, pontoon and water supplies); 27, **Briassé** (K83.9) and 26, Persigand (K87.9) and finally arrives at a bridge in **Port-Rhinegeard** (K89.7) where there is a mooring pontoon on the right at the foot of a vertical weir alongside Écluse 25 (most of the Mayenne weirs are sloping). Close by is the Trappist Abbey of Port du Salut, founded in the 13th century. The monks made and marketed a well known variety of *St-Paulin* cheese here until they sold their licence to a commercial company in 1959; it operates a factory nearby. Visits to the abbey are possible every day, 9.00–18.00h.

Now close to Laval, the river maintains its quality of secrecy through Écluse 24, Bonne (K90.9) with good moorings and slipway in the old village of **St-Pierre-le-Potier** (K94.4). Écluse 23, Cumont (K94.9), provides access to the outskirts of the city of **Laval** (K98), with Écluse 22 in **Avesnières** (K97.9) and No. 21, opposite the ramparts of the severe 11th century *château*. Built by the Counts of Laval, but seized at the time of the Revolution, the Nouveau Château has been extended to act as Law Courts. Visits to the interior of the vast Vieux Château are possible 9.00–12.00h and 14.00–18.00h (not Tues). In the Old Town are many beautiful 16th century houses with overhanging upper storeys. Waterways enthusiasts will be fascinated by a pair of well restored *bateaux-lavoirs* (laundry boats),

once a feature of most large French towns. One houses a Nautical Club and tripping boat office, while the other, *St Julien*, is a museum – almost certainly the only one of its type in the country. Opening hours as for the Vieux Château. Believed to have been introduced to the Mayenne about 1850, within 20 years there were no fewer than 25 *bateaux-lavoirs*; by 1925 numbers had fallen to 13, with 5 in 1960. Several designs were to be seen, mostly built on hulls in Angers. *St Julien* dates from 1904, features two decks, accommodation for the proprietor and his family, and a series of coal-fired boilers to heat cauldrons of river water. Professional washerwomen would collect laundry from private houses, wheel it to the boat in barrows and work up to 12 hours a day in reasonably

Mill and Lock 43, La Roussière, near Grez-Neuville, River Mayenne.

unpleasant conditions. Artefacts preserved include old photographs and an archaic electrically-driven spin-drier of massive proportions. In spite of the advent of domestic washing machines, *St Julien* remained in service until 1970, being presented to Laval by its owner the following year. On the day of my visit an enthusiastic student provided me with a guided tour, often corrected by her grandmother, a former *laveuse*.

Laval has recently begun to make good use of her waterway, providing central moorings, slipways, a tripping boat converted from a *péniche* and a hire cruiser fleet, Brilhault Plaisance. The latter operates jolly little canvas-sided camping motorboats available by the day, weekend, 'mini' week or week. Numerous shops and restaurants are within easy range of the water.

Uppermost reaches of the river, only lately returned to navigation, are frequently punctuated by boat crew-worked locks. There are few shopping or other facilities and the waterway is frequently virtually deserted by craft. Villages are mostly little more than a cluster of houses. Twenty locks intervene in the 30km to the town of Mayenne. Mooring is possible (take care to avoid stones) at a quay in **St-Jean-sur-Mayenne** (K109, shopping). Restaurants close to the waterway will be found downstream of Écluse 16, Ame (K113) and by Écluse 14, La Fourmondière (K115.6).

Mayenne (K129) has long been of strategic importance and suffered widespread destruction during World War II. Its feudal *château*, dating from the 11th century, remains largely intact.

37 · River Oudon

Carte Guide: *Les Rivières des Pays de la Loire*

From a junction with the River Mayenne above Grez-Neuville to Segré, the terminus, 18km with 3 locks.

What the Oudon lacks in length is more than compensated for by scenery with excellent facilities in the two leading towns, Le-Lion-d'Angers and Segré. Surroundings are similar to those on the nearby Mayenne (see Chapter 36).

Painstaking research has totally failed to provide any information about the origins of this little navigation: seemingly it is too insignificant to feature in any of the standard reference works. It would appear likely that development followed similar lines to the River Mayenne, with the few locks constructed in the mid-19th century. As recently as 1968 the Segré head of navigation was visited by no fewer than 416 commercial craft, carrying a total of 15,449 tonnes of freight. The Oudon is now the preserve of pleasure boats alone.

Beginning at a confluence with the Mayenne upstream of Grez-Neuville, the Oudon passes through the same kind of pastoral scenery and shortly arrives in **Le-Lion-d'Angers** (K2) where landscaped moorings and water point are immediately above the bridge on the

left. It is known best for its horse stud (Haras Nationaux de l'Isle Briand) in 160 hectares between the two rivers. Visits are possible by advance arrangement (tel. 91.82.46). A Romanesque church begun in the 11th century contains a series of ancient and faded murals discovered during restoration work in 1852. Facilities of interest to the boater include numerous shops, a slipway and garage near the bridge. While eating ashore is one of the frequent delights of cruising in France, there are two possible pitfalls: Sundays are traditionally an occasion for local families to dine out, meaning that advance booking is advised. In order to recover from this, the busiest day of the week, many of the smaller establishments close on Mondays. Consequently the itinerant boater may well be faced with two days of self-catering. The impressive-seeming Hôtel des Voyageurs opposite the moorings in Le-Lion-d'Angers bore a cluster of enamel plate recommendations, including one from the Automobile Association. Monday or not, I judged them to be open for business, made a gesture towards respectability by recovering socks and trousers from the nose of my inflatable and after a moment's consideration decided that I stood a good chance of being admitted to the restaurant without a tie. Appetite sharpened, I discovered that the only fare advertised was 'Workman's Dinner (at a bargain price), Wine Included'. Main dining room closed, I entered the bar, approached a formidable but efficient Madame and requested a table: the place was half filled with blue-denimed lorry drivers. She eyed me briefly and bluntly declared: 'It's Monday. We're closed!' 'But the Workman's Dinner', I protested, realizing that perhaps the socks had been a mistake. She studied me once more and decided that I might *just* qualify. Five minutes later, when I was well into my 'inclusive' carafe of red wine, she loudly declared to the assembled company that more expensive meals were unexpectedly available after all, but not the Gourmet's Menu at the top of the range. In the event I consumed the equivalent of a Super Workman's Dinner for which the bill was trifling, wine, coffee, and service *compris*. It was the best French meal I had enjoyed for many days. On leaving, I stole a glimpse into the proper Tuesday-to-Sunday 'posh' restaurant and decided, on balance, that an evening in the company of lorry drivers and Algerians had been more interesting.

With a gentle breeze rustling the trees, the upstream run is sheer magic, scarcely a house in sight until arrival at Écluse 3, **Himbeaudière** (K8). 2.5km across the fields to the NE, is a fine old stone mansion, Le Logis

Boat club moorings at the head of navigation in Segré.

du Coudray, run as a cultural centre with concerts and exhibitions. Signs of civilization are few and far between: if the need is great, it may be necessary to make an overland foray from the Port aux Anglais bridge (K9.2) 2km west to **Andigné**, passing an isolated *crêperie* en route. The hilltop village provides no more than a tiny grocer and garage.

Écluse 2 is located at the lower end of a short cut in **La Chapelle-sur-Oudon** (K14.2). A water hose is available at the lock where there is a fine converted mill and a broad pool. 150m up a hilly lane from the top end of the cut brings you to the heart of the village, a sleepy place with much atmosphere and a delightful church with typical 'harebell' spire. Baker and grocer with garage on the N163 crossroads. An incongruous feature of the burial ground is the grave of a local count, protected by a metal-frame greenhouse! 3km NW lies the classical 18th century Château de la Lorie (open July 1–Sept 15, 15.00–18.00h, not Tues). A slightly quicker approach is from a riverside lane midway between La Chapelle-sur-Oudon and Écluse 1, Maingué (K17).

The journey ends with a flourish in **Segré** (K18), Capital of the Segréen, an area of wooded farmland. Shortly below a junction with the River Verzée, the local boating club has excellent pontoon moorings for two dozen smallish cruisers with bar/clubhouse, slipway, 4 tonne crane and water point: a perfect example of the facilities that should be available at every head of navigation. The town spreads on both sides of the deepening valley of the Oudon, with waterside walks, a domed church (like a scaled-down version of the Sacré Cœur in Paris) and a wide choice of shops and restaurants. Road and rail transport provides communication with such places as Angers, Nantes and Sablé, making for easy car recovery if cruising one-way with a trailed boat. Upstream, the Oudon is canoeable for a further 16km to **Châtelais**.

38 · River Sarthe

Carte Guide: *Les Rivières des Pays le la Loire*

From a junction with the Rivers Maine and Mayenne above Angers to Le Mans, terminus. 131.6km with 20 locks.

Rising on the south side of the *Fôret d'Ecouves* upstream of Alençon, the Sarthe is in many ways similar to its neighbour the Mayenne, meandering through woodland and meadow in the district known as the Angevin Maine. Farmed for cereals and vegetables with extensive orchards towards Angers, the countryside is gently pastoral, its greatest interest being supplied by the many small bankside towns. Most of the 30m × 5m locks have associated water mills and long weirs, generally protected with buoys at the upper level. The peaceful valley encouraged building of numerous *châteaux* and large country houses.

Rapid decline of commercial traffic resulted in some of the uppermost locks falling into disrepair after World War II, but with the introduction of small numbers of hire cruisers in the late 1970s and early 1980s the whole line is now quite well maintained up to Le Mans.

Brief history Earliest development of the Sarthe took place in the 14th century and there was a sizeable fleet of *gabarres* working in the 17th century, many launched in Juvardeil. Later conditions deteriorated so much that demands were made to *restore* the waterway in 1744 and again in 1751. A tributary, the Huisne, was rendered suitable to float timber from the Fôret de Bonnetable to Le Mans in 1750. By 1778 craft were able to work through 3.7m wide flash locks upstream as far as Malicorn-sur-Sarthe, 40km below Le Mans. At this time there was even a plan to extend the barge route up to Alençon, dig a section of canal from there to the headwaters of the River Orne and so create a communication between Brittany and the Normandy coast via Caen. The present locks and lengths of canal were constructed in the middle of the 19th century.

Sarthe and Mayenne converge at the southern tip of the great Île St-Aubin a short distance up the Maine from Angers. Almost immediately we are into the Sarthe there is a hazard in the form of a low ferry cable that must wearily be wound below water level while a cruiser hovers in the considerable current. The river's first 18km are lock-free at the time of writing, formerly giving rise to winter floods and shallows in late summer. The situation has improved greatly with construction of a lock on the Maine below Angers. These lowest reaches do not constitute particularly fascinating boating, with little of interest until the village of **Écouflant** (K4.6) opposite a junction with the Vieille Maine (which provides an alternative route into the Mayenne). Here you can stop (on sometimes muddy banks) and walk 500m up the Rue du Bac into the village centre for shopping, garage and restaurant.

2km away is a commendable leisure park, Les Sablières, created from worked-out gravel pits. Very popular with people from a wide area, it provides sandy beaches, pine trees, pleasant waterside walks and all distractions necessary to amuse children on a hot day. Although of great length, having risen west of Chartres, the Loir River entering on the right (K9.7) is not navigable. (Le Loir is quite independent of its larger neighbour La Loire.) Cherry, apple and pear orchards abound. **Briollay** (K11.7) on the right bank is the Celtic Briara-Ledus; selecting moorings with a degree of care, it provides a wide range of shops, water point, garage and a choice of restaurants, one combining the functions of *crêperie* and antiques/*brocante*.

After passing the right-bank village of **Verigné**, continue for about 1km to a point where the navigation channel swings over to starboard. By mooring on the left bank, just downstream of a rocky obstruction, you can walk or cycle 4km along lanes to visit an outstanding *château* at **Le Plessis-Bourré**, approached by a causeway bridge over its broad moat. This exquisite white building with slate roof was erected in the 15th century by Jean Bourré, Financial Secretary to Louis XI. A guided tour of the interior is thoroughly recommended (April 1–Sept 30, 10.00–12.00h and 14.00–19.00h; closed 17.00h outside the season and totally from Nov 15–Dec 15. Also shut on Weds except in July and Aug).

With the first lock, Écluse 20, **Cheffes** (K18.3), river scenery greatly improves. Although smaller boats can approach the town on its downstream side, where scores of fishing punts lie in an island backwater, it is preferable to work through the lock and moor there to a pontoon or on the bank below the road bridge (water point). Shops and restaurants are within easy reach near the church. The three-star Hotel du Château de Teildras boasts an excellent reputation. **Tiercé** (K21.2) on the right lies beyond an unnavigable backwater out of boaters' reach. However, **Juvardeil** (K25.8) extends along the left bank, with moorings at

Fishing punts at Cheffes are an indication that angling is the most popular outdoor activity in France.

the upstream end beyond shallows. Adequate food shops and restaurant are near the 14th century church, together with a garage. It was here that the Royalist leader Bonchamps was born (see Chapter 35).

Châteauneuf-sur-Sarthe (K28.3) has almost everything you could wish for in a riverside town: several stylish restaurants, ample shops within a few steps, excellent moorings with water and fuel, a slipway and a base for hire cruisers of the Maine Anjou-Rivières fleet. Écluse 19 is shortly upstream. In the reach that follows, take care to avoid the submerged remains of an old weir about halfway to **Brissarthe** (K34.3), and another on the right just below the town. Moorings with bollards are in a grassy square downstream of an island. Many of the houses are fine examples of Anjou architecture and there is adequate shopping and restaurants. In 886 Robert le Fort, sent by Carolingian King Charles the Bald to fight the Normans, was killed in front of the church. Once through Écluse 18, Villechien (K38.2, water point) an almost straight reach leads to the market town of **Morannes** (K41.1) with good moorings upstream of the bridge on each bank. Slipway, shops, fuel and restaurants. Rowing and fishing punts may be hired and for those wishing to make a stay in the area (perhaps while exploring the river by day boat or car) inexpensive self-catering apartments can be rented in a *gîte rural*, established in the impressive waterside Château des Roches, 2km towards Précigné. **Chemiré-sur-Sarthe**, left of the bridge, also has a fine 19th century *château* and a range of shopping facilities, but is considerably farther from the river than Morannes.

Écluse 17, **le Pendu** (K44.3) is on a short cut left of an island with millhouse (water point), while **Pincé**, on the right bank downstream of Écluse 16, **Beffes** (K50.3), is a delightfully sleepy riverside hamlet where vegetable gardens extend to the edge of the Sarthe and there is a restaurant and slipway. Sites of former weirs (both on the right) will be seen at islands near **La Cognière** (K55.5) and **La Bouvrerie** (K57.1), before reaching the important town of **Sablé-sur-Sarthe** at Écluse 15 (K58.5). A former sand barge port on the right bank provides excellent moorings close to a network of narrow streets of shops and restaurants. Various boating facilities are available at the busy France Anjou Navigation hire cruiser base, with a modern tripping vessel the *Sablésien* providing excursions to such places as Solesmes. Opposite on the left bank, a huge early 18th century *château* was constructed by Colbert de Torcy, nephew of Colbert, the Minister of Louis XIV. It is now used by the National Library. The Sarthe is very much a feature of this manufacturing town, with flower beds and attractive walks.

Nearby, black marble veined with white was once quarried to be used in such buildings as Versailles. Beyond the bridge the River Erve flows in from the NW.

Écluse 14 (K61.6) and its lock cut introduce **Solesmes** and the towering granite mass of the Benedictine abbey of St Pierre. Founded in the early 11th century, most of the buildings were erected at the end of the 19th in a Romanesque-Gothic style. You do not need to be a Roman Catholic or even particularly religious to appreciate celebration of the Latin Mass, sung in Gregorian chant. From June 24–Sept 14, Mass may be attended daily at 10.00h and Vespers at 17.30h (16.00 Thurs, May–Sept). At other times of the year Mass is at 9.45h with Vespers at 17.00h. Shopping in Solesmes is fairly basic with additional possibilities across the river in **Le Port de Juigné**. But, in common with most sites of Catholic pilgrimage, there is a first-rate hotel, the Grand. After days of the simple river life it can be good for morale to be pampered. For a very reasonable price, I dined here magnificently (two half-bottles of wine and coffee included) on *hors d'oeuvre*; wild salmon in thin slices with *vinaigrette* sauce and lettuce, served with toast; wood pigeon in pastry with truffles and mushrooms; green salad, local cheeses and fresh strawberries. This pilgrim's feast was value indeed!

Near Écluse 13 (K63) is the little harbour of **Juigné-sur-Sarthe**, a place of 16–17th century houses and a good view of the abbey in Solesmes. The rough stone tower of its Romanesque church would be more in keeping with a medieval fort. Good shopping facilities. Quiet reaches lead to Écluse 12, Courtigné (K68.6) and on past **Avoise** (K71.1) with grocer, 15th century manor house La Perrine de Cry and moorings to a quay on the upstream side. Restaurant and garage (no diesel). **Parcé-sur-Sarthe** (K73.6) is a medieval hilltop village with many 16–17th century stone buildings: possibly the most pleasing spot on the entire waterway. Best access is through Écluse 11, up to the head of the lock island and back a little way down the weirstream to a quay with bollards. A swimming enclosure is sited just downstream of the weir itself. All shops, garage and restaurant. Not far beyond is Écluse 10, by the *Moulin d'Ignères* (K76.6), followed by a long lock-free section (restaurant in the right-bank hamlet of **Dureil**, K84.4) running into the sizeable town of **Malicorne** (K85). First-rate moorings have been created on a quay by the mill: these are reached by negotiating Écluse 9 and turning downstream from the upper end of the lock cut, through the bridge and stopping immediately before a weir (water point). A lovely 17th century moated *château*, frequently visited by Mme de Sévigné, is very pleasing. Shops, restaurants

St Pierre's abbey at Solesmes.

and several *faïence* potters' workshops make this an interesting place to linger.

Moving upstream and past the Château de Rivesarthe, Écluse 8, **Noyen** (K90.6, water point), is followed by a long cut with substantial railway viaduct spanning the river beyond. Moor alongside the town, left bank, where there is a quay and slipway 200–300m from shops and restaurants. Houses, mill, weir and gardens together create a pleasing prospect. The next village upriver is **Fercé-sur-Sarthe** (K99.1), at a bridge crossing past Écluse 7. A peaceful little place rising above waterside trees, it has a grocer and restaurant. Turning to the east, the river now heads for Écluse 6 and **La-Suze-sur-Sarthe** (K105.1), with bollard moorings, shops on each bank, garage and several res-

taurants. The 15th century *château* was built on the site of a 12th century fort. Small craft can be launched at a ramp below the bridge in **Roëzé-sur-Sarthe** (K108.6); moorings on a grassy bank 75m from the church square (shops and restaurants). Market day is Weds a.m. Écluse 5, Roëzé (K109.6), marks the beginning of a long cut bypassing the town of **Guecélard**; protected by a guard lock at the upper end, it is united with the Sarthe once more at **Fillé** (K114.6), a village that is both charming and convenient, having fuel, shopping and restaurant facilities.

A further tree-shaded lock cut begins at Écluse 4, **Spay** (K116.6). Stop by the lower bridge for a grocer and restaurant in **Prélandon**. Alternatively, follow this same bridge to the left, cross the unnavigable river and within about 1km a variety of shops, restaurant and garage will be found at Spay. Rather than establish a headquarters in Le Mans, the Club Nautique Maine-Marine have created an agreeable boating centre just beyond the Spay lock cut at **Le Noyer**, an easy taxi journey from the city. Visitors are welcome to use the clubhouse, moorings, water and electricity points, slipway and 6 tonne crane. Moving upstream, the outer suburbs of Le Mans increasingly become evident and the river gradually starts to lose the rural freshness so characteristic of earlier reaches. After passing an island, **Arnage** (K118.8) will be seen on the right bank: a useful halt for shops, restaurants and fuel station. Between Écluse 3, Chahoué (K125.6) and Écluse 2, Raterie (K126.6), each built with a short lock cut, Gallo-Roman remains from a local archaeological site will be found on exhibition in the town hall of **Allonnes**, reached from a road bridge. Restaurants, fuel and shopping.

The final lock, Écluse 1 (K129.5), is in urban surroundings a little above the mouth of the River Huisne. First impressions of **Le Mans** are not entirely favourable, for the river is overlooked on each side by tall blocks of modern flats. Nevertheless there are central moorings on somewhat high stone quays, very convenient for food shopping. Hire cruisers are operated by Sarthe Plaisance. Now a large provincial city, Le Mans was the birthplace of Henry II of England; today, it is better known for its associations with motor cars, the Bollée's 12-seater road steamer of 1873 having reached speeds in excess of 40kph. Since 1923 the Le Mans 24-Hour Race has attracted car enthusiasts from many countries. Renault established a factory here in 1936 and there is a Motor Museum with more than 150 exhibits. Substantial portions of the medieval town remain within the massive ramparts of Gallo-Roman fortification walls, rising sheer from the Sarthe. Detailed information on ancient houses, a selection of museums and the magnificent Gothic cathedral of St Julien will be found (in English) in the *Green Michelin Guide, Châteaux of the Loire*. Restaurant specialities to try include Loire Valley *rillettes* (diced pork, preserved in jars); *chapons* (capons cooked with cider); and *poulardes dodues* (roast chicken).

Unloading a small barge with wheelbarrows, shortly before World War I. Le Mans.

V·BURGUNDY AND BOURBONNAIS

39 · Canal du Loing

Carte Guide: *Les Canaux du Centre*
From a junction with the River Seine at St-Mammès to a junction with the Canal de Briare at Buges, near Montargis: 49.4km with 19 locks.

Forming part of the 'Bourbonnais' route between the Seine and the Saône (see Chapter 48), the Canal du Loing is a really pleasant waterway in its own right. Apart from two sections where the course of the River Loing is put to use, the navigation is a lateral canal along the river valley with a total fall of about 37m. Popular with motor yachts in transit between Northern France and the Mediterranean, the Canal du Loing is still used by commercial *péniches*, although there are far fewer than would have been encountered twenty or thirty years ago. Almost from end to end, surroundings are of woodland with a succession of pretty villages, convenient for shopping and eating ashore. Some of the lock keepers will sell produce from their gardens. The Loing has a reputation for teeming with coarse fish: anglers will be seen in large numbers on the canal, and seated in little black or dark green punts in the secretive and shaded pools of the river. It is always appropriate to read of the experiences of other waterway travellers: two contrasting accounts are C. S. Forester's delightful *The Voyage of the 'Annie Marble'* (1929) recording a journey by motorized camping dinghy along the Seine, Loing, Canal d'Orléans (now being restored) and Loire; and *Isabel and the Sea* by George Millar (1949, reprinted 1983), which recounts the progress of an auxiliary ketch from the Channel to the Mediterranean via the Bourbonnais route.

Brief history Construction of the Canal de Briare, completed in 1642, provided a water route between the valleys of the Loire and the Seine. Dry summers or contrary winds on the Loire between Briare and Orléans prompted Louis XIV's brother the Duke of Orléans to create an alternative and more reliable navigation from Orléans to the Briare near Montargis: construction began in 1682, the 79km line with 28 locks was finished 10 years later. Now attention was turned to that part of the Loire-Seine route which used the River Loing from Montargis to the Seine. Hampered by 26 inconvenient locks (navigation weirs), it was subject to frequent flooding, while boatmen were forced to bargain with numerous mill owners to 'buy' water supplies and be able to pass these obstacles. Sometimes the journey over this section would take 5–6 weeks rather than 2–3 days. At the end of a downstream journey towards Paris barge proprietors would frequently have to sell off their craft at rock-bottom prices, the ascent of the Loing being too difficult and time-consuming. Inspired by the success of his first canal and anxious to better its trading prospects, the Duke of Orléans sought letters patent to build a Loing lateral canal. Engineered by the Régemortes (father and son), it was begun in 1720 and finished remarkably quickly by 1723. Many of the locks had sloping earth-sided chambers and at two points, near Nemours and approaching the Seine junction, the original bed of the Loing was used, these lengths being known as *râcles*. Consignments bound for Paris included large quantities of firewood and timber. The Canal du Loing obviously prospered for 3,815 loaded barges passed through in 1752 alone. In its early days the Capital was connected with Montargis and Briare by a passenger-carrying *coche d'eau* service, taking precedence over freight vessels and achieving a Briare–Paris journey time of 5 days.

The canal was purchased by the State in 1863 and extensive modernization was put in hand over the following 30 years, enlarging capacity of the locks and improving the channel. By 1936 the Loing and Briare Canals together carried an annual 1,524,000 tonnes with 9.675 barge journeys. George Millar states that conditions had deteriorated badly immediately after World War II, poor depth and heavy weed impeding the few motorized barges. Most traffic then was in horse or tractor hauled wooden barges, including the painfully slow, small-capacity *berrichons*. Now, the great majority of craft are intent on pleasure and many towns and villages have enthusiastically provided convenient overnight moorings.

There could scarcely be a greater contrast between the wide and busy waters of the Seine and the intimate nature of the Loing at **St-Mammès**, shops, restaurants, water, fuel, barge works (see Chapter 13). Écluse 20, near the junction, has been redundant for some years and is a useful mooring place, opposite several small barge repair yards. After a large railway viaduct comes Écluse 19, **Moret-sur-Loing** (K1.7), a real highlight of the journey. (All urban facilities.) The superb town was fortified with gateways and has many royal connections going back to the time of Louis VII (1137–80). Its bridge is one of the most ancient in the whole of the Île de France. Old buildings stand in a ravishing waterside setting with willows. Saturday evenings between June 20 and Sept 5 are devoted to a summer festival, with *son et lumière* on the banks of the Loing recalling the town's history over 900 years. The English-born Impressionist painter Alfred Sisley (1839–99), totally unrecognized during his lifetime, lived and worked here for many years; his studio is 19 Rue Montmartre. The river is claimed locally to be better supplied with fish than any other watercourse in France. Many find their way to the tables of Moret restaurants together with a wide variety of edible fungi, as much appreciated here as they are neglected in England. You can buy a speciality in a timber building near the church of Notre Dame: *sucre d'orge*, a caramellized barley-sugar once made by the nuns. An excursion can be made to the Palace of Fontainebleau (see Chapter 13).

Skirting the SE edges of the Fontainbleau Forest, the Loing soon reaches the village of **Bourgogne** (K2.5). Beyond Écluse 18 is the thatched house of Michel Clemenceau (1873–1964), La Grange Batelière, open to the public during weekend and public holiday afternoons with commentary by Mme. Clemenceau. Moving on, we pass old gravel workings landscaped with poplars. **Écuelles** (K4.2), left bank before Écluse 17, has a grocer, while **Épisy** (K8.4), near Écluse 16, offers grocer and restaurant. A full range of shops can be found at **Montigny-sur-Loing** within 2km of the canal from the road bridge beyond Écluse 15, Belleville (K10.7). This, and the village of **Grez-sur-Loing** (approached from the bridge after Écluse 14, Bordes), are both pretty riverside settlements. The English composer Frederick Delius (1862–1934) lived in Grez. Note at the locks the keepers' little huts with heavy tiled roofs and a stove for winter warmth.

Montcourt-Fromonville (K14.5), a straggling village on the left, has grocer and restaurant and is followed by guard lock 13, Fromonville (K16.8), leading into a broad section of the River Loing, a tempting place for a swim on a hot day. Left of the junction a lane meets the towpath with the Restaurant Au Chaland qui Passe close by. This green peace is momentarily shattered by a high-level bridge carrying the A6 *autoroute* over the river. Take care at the right-angled junction just before the next bridge, where the navigation again becomes a canal, with Écluse 12, Buttes (K19.3), concealed on the right (water point). One possible mooring for the city of **Nemours** is in a park by the River Loing immediately above this junction. Apart from all normal facilities, there is a 12th century castle, the 12th century church of St John the Baptist erected to house relics of the saint brought back from the Second Crusade, and a park containing an array of curiously formed rocks, the Rochers Gréau.

In a book such as this there is a danger in making specific references to restaurants where a good meal has been enjoyed: as time passes standards may fall or the ownership change altogether. But the family-run Auberge au Fil de l'Eau by Écluse 11, **Chaintréauville** (K22), was so unusual when I ate dinner there in 1979 that it demands inclusion. As we approached, a flock of white ornamental doves scattered. The main door was obstructed by two cockatoos and a mynah bird perched on top of their cages. As we took our places at table, a woolly half-blind dog of uncertain breed, a small alsatian and a whippet grouped themselves expectantly. Tropical fish swam in a tank the length of the bar. During the meal doves would fly through the open window in search of crumbs. Furnishings were equally bizarre: well-worn easy chairs and sofas with Far Eastern antiques, paintings and ecclesiastical items that might once have graced the village church. When he had finished in the kitchen, the proprietor came to drink with us in a grubby white apron, all the time giving kisses to the cockatoo that perched on his shoulder. The food was palatable and inexpensive and, judging by the clientele of anglers and the lock keeper, visitors from the outside world were probably rare.

The canal winds on through avenues of planes, with the Loing flowing through woodland close by on the right. Shopping is good in **Bagneaux-sur-Loing** near Écluse 10 (K23.7) and quite sophisticated in the small town of **Souppes-sur-Loing** (access from the third bridge, after Écluse 9, Beaumoulin K28.2), where there is a fine fish shop. Close to Écluse 8, Égreville (K32.5) are baker, grocer and restaurant, while a small aqueduct spans the water lily-filled River Fusain beyond Écluse 7, **Néronville** (K33.5, restaurant).

Nargis (K39.1) is approached along a magnificent avenue of planes, growing at curious angles up to Écluse 6, Brisebarre. The little town has most shops and a restaurant near Écluse 5, its church surmounted by a bulbous slated spire like an upturned tulip. Beyond the river, to the right, the Forest of Montargis introduces a deeply rural character to the waterway, most noticeable between Écluse 3, Montabon (K43.5, restaurant on the towpath) and Écluse 2, des Vallées (K44.3). In the mid-1970s I complimented the keeper on his lovely lock house with its speckled brown roof standing against a backdrop of trees, as he cut me a supply of spring lettuce from his productive garden. He agreed wholeheartedly, adding that after spending 30 years there he was convinced that there was no finer place on earth.

Lights control passage through a narrow, concrete-lined section by the bridge in **Cépoy** (K48.3, all normal shore facilities). The Canal du Loing ends at a junction with the Canal de Briare at Écluse 36, Buges (K49.4), the disused **Canal d'Orléans** entering on the right. 79km in length with just 27 locks, rising to a summit at Le Gué-des-Cens and then falling towards a junction with the Loire, it was abandoned as recently as 1954, the locks never having been enlarged to Fréycinet standards for *péniches*. When last in use, maximum craft dimensions were: length: 30.18m; beam: 5.0m; draft: 1.3m; air draft: 3.35m. By the time all traffic had forsaken the upper Loire in the 19th century it passed only sparse rural communities and the city of Orléans itself. Principal places served include St-Maurice-sur-Fessard, Chailly-en-Gauhais, Fay-aux-Loges and Combleux. C. S. Forester had little to find in its favour when he passed through in 1928, describing it as 'utterly filthy and swarming with mosquitoes'. His impressions were doubtless soured by breaking a propeller near Lorris and having to wait impatiently for a replacement to be brought out from England. In 1936 a mere 439 animal-hauled barge journeys were made. It remains remarkably intact, upper lock gates being replaced by concrete weirs.

Complete restoration started in the latter 1980s, with renewal of lock gates and paddles. Impetus for a return to navigation appeared to have slowed by 1999, in spite of extensive works having by then been completed. However, in France canal reopening can occur with surprising rapidity: make local enquiries as to whether it is yet possible to penetrate this very worthwhile diversion.

40 · Canal de Briare

Carte Guide: *Les Canaux du Centre*

From a junction with the Canal du Loing at Buges, near Montargis, to a junction with the Canal Latéral à Loire at Belleau, near Briare: 54.1km with 32 locks. 2.6km and 3 locks of the original route between Belleau and the River Loire in Briare were reopened to navigation in 1988.

An agreeable and well established waterway, now well over 300 years old and consequently very much a part of the towns and villages along its course. Shore facilities are quite numerous. The Canal de Briare climbs from Montargis to a summit level between Dammarie-sur-Loing and Rogny and then falls towards the River Loire. Relics of the original 17th century navigation works are of particular interest to canal enthusiasts.

Brief history Planned as the first watershed canal in Europe, the Briare was conceived by Henry IV and the Duc de Sully in 1604. Its object was to provide communication between the valleys of the Loire and Seine. Taking Italian and Belgian experience as a model, the engineer Hughes Cosnier started work on the line in 1605, using up to 6,000 men. Navvies' wages were paid in the form of tokens, exchanged in establishments set up by the proprietors on the work sites. Each coin carried the wording *Via Ligeris in Sequanam* ('the Way from the Loire to the Seine'): those for meat were marked *Necessitas supplementu*; for drink, *Recreatio laboris*; and for bread, *Laboris fulcimentum*. Changes of policy on the King's assassination in 1610 brought building to a halt when 35 of the locks were substantially complete. This brought financial ruin to those supporting the scheme. Nothing more happened until 1638, when Jacques Guyon and Guillaume Bouteroue were granted permission by Cardinal Richlieu to recommence works. All was ready to receive traffic by 1642. Although supplied from carefully designed reservoirs the canal suffered from water shortages at first, reducing the draft of the barges to 2–3 *pieds* (about 0.6–0.9m), though this was no worse than allowed by the depth of the adjoining River Loire. Locks were built at 24 sites: examples of double, triple, quadruple and at Rogny septuple staircases resulted in a total of 41 chambers. Craft were able to negotiate each chamber in about 6 minutes.

As late as 1778 all hauling was done by men, generally two to a boat or log raft, typical cargoes including wines from the Mâcon, Beaujolais, Charollais, Sancerre and Languedoc regions; firewood, timber, coal and iron; *faïence* from Nevers and fruit from the Auvergne. Most was destined for the Paris area and attracted heavy tolls. By the mid-18th century more than 500 wine barges were in regular use. Disadvantages of this route were canal stoppages and Loire water shortages which often brought closures of 2–3 months each year. Together with the Canal d'Orléans, the Briare was purchased by the State in 1863 and all locks enlarged to *péniche* standards by 1893, the multiple chambers being replaced by single locks on new sites. At Briare, a steam (later electric) pumping station was built in 1895 and the Bourdon reservoir constructed in 1904. Today the waterway carries a moderate amount of commercial traffic with an ever-increasing number of pleasure craft.

From its junction with the Canal du Loing just north of Écluse 36, **Buges**, the Briare follows the valley of the River Loing as far as Rogny. The union of the two waterways is an agreeable place, with a substantial lock

Écluse de la Marolle, Montargis.

house and the weed-filled Canal d'Orléans entering on the right (see Chapter 39). It is now a short distance through Écluse 35, Langlée (K1.8), to **Montargis** (K4), capital of the Gâtinais area. A system of picturesque side canals branch off the navigation in a plane-shaded reach below Écluse 33, de la Marolle, giving the town its slightly fanciful title 'Venise Briade'. Not available to craft larger than punts, these streams are lined with ancient houses, the water lapping at their back doors and *lavoirs* (washing posts). A charming municipal notion is to anchor dinghies filled with petunias and other flowers at strategic points. In the town centre the canal is crossed by a steel footbridge. There is a busy open-air market and wide choice of eating places. In the time of Louis XIII, the chef of the Duc de Plessis-Praslin invented a recipe for a confection made from roasted almonds covered with knobbly sugar. They became known as *praslines* or *pralines* and first went on public sale in a shop opposite the Church de la Madeleine. We once spent the night at the Grand Hotel de la Poste when returning home after a hire cruiser holiday. Suitably impressed at our arrival in an elderly (but much admired) Bentley, the Manager showed us to his best table, where a brass plaque

recorded the visit of the 'Prince of French Gastro-nomes'! In such a challenging situation we had no choice but to order from the most expensive and lavish menu. Water is available at the lock Bureau de Contrôle and a fuel tanker will deliver diesel on request.

Écluse 32, La Tuilerie (K8.7), has a nearby restaurant. A reminder of horse-drawn barge traffic, which only finally disappeared towards the end of the 1960s, is a wheel and pulley arrangement for passing towlines under the bridge by Écluse 29, Moulin de Tours (K13.1). The pound between Écluses 28 and 27 features another ingenious device: a curve obstructs vision to the next lock, so black or red panels are displayed, remotely changed by wires, a simple form of traffic signal. **Montcresson** offers shopping and a restaurant. The remains of an ancient amphitheatre can be seen on the right shortly before **Montbuoy** (K22.4, shops and restaurant). Écluse 26, here, is unusually deep: nearby are signs of the original canal with locks. Steel bascule bridges will be encountered at various locks: the first at Écluse 25, Lépinoy (K24.7). Their purpose is somewhat obscure as it is rarely necessary to raise them more than slightly to allow a boat to pass. Many French locksides feature gravel where you might expect to see lawns; and nowhere more so than on the Bourbonnais route. Sometimes, it is painstakingly raked into intricate patterns, so beware walking across it.

Châtillon-Coligny (K27.8) was already old when the canal arrived in its centre. During the summer you may visit the exterior of a 12th century *château*, reconstructed in the 16th century by Admiral Gaspard de Coligny and much damaged at the time of the Revolution. In early September, reputedly at 7-year intervals, the little town holds a great fair 'in honour of Agriculture': buildings are lavishly adorned with festoons of paper flowers and sheaves of corn. Car and tractor salesmen demonstrate their wares and an illuminated marquee dance hall throbs far into the night. By the main bridge, the Auberge de la Marine serves good food where boat horses were once stabled. All shops are conveniently close. Regularly spaced locks lead to **Dammarie-sur-Loing** (K33.4) with several shops, restaurant and the remains of an old lock staircase.

Six locks at **Rogny** (K38.1) are separated by short pounds. This was not always so, for here is one of the great achievements of French waterways history: the famous seven-rise staircase, preserved as an ancient monument and floodlit by night. Providing a change in levels of 34m, they became redundant in 1887, having seen 245 years of use. Water point and most shops at the bottom of the modern flight. Cruiser hire, *port de plaisance*. A 4.6km summit level follows, constructed much deeper than normal to preserve water, with no

Although now gateless, the seven-chambered staircase of locks at Rogny is preserved as an Ancient Monument.

fewer than 15 reservoirs in the vicinity with a capacity of 18 million m^3. A descent towards the Loire begins at Écluse 12, Gazonne (K44.3) with further disused locks and old cottages by Écluses 10 and 9. Shopping and fuel from a garage can be obtained in the slightly industrial town of **Ouzouer-sur-Trézée** (K48.5), where caravans and tents are clustered around the river banks. At a V-junction (K53.6) the original line of the Canal de Briare descends through three small-capacity locks to join the Loire in the town of **Briare**. Long derelict, this section was reopened in 1988, so that the town could benefit from the boom in pleasure boating. A well-planned *port de plaisance* provides water, electricity and showers. Should you not wish to divert down this line, the huge church decorated with mosaics and a very busy narrow main street are within walking distance of the through route of the Canal Latéral à la Loire by the 'New Port' and Briare Aqueduct. (See also Chapter 41.)

41 · Canal Latéral à la Loire

Carte Guide: *Les Canaux du Centre*
From a junction with the Canal de Briare at Belleau, near Briare, to a junction with the Canal du Centre at

Digoin, 196.1km with 38 locks. There are several navigable branches as follows, locks into the River Loire not normally being in use. (1) From St-Satur to the Loire at St-Thibault, 0.7km. (2) From Givry to Fourchambault, 2.4km with 1 lock. (3) From Sermoise-sur-Loire to Nevers, 2.9km with 2 locks. (4) From St-Maurice to the River Loire at Decize and via the river to the Canal du Nivernais at St-Léger-des-Vignes, 1.8km with 2 locks (for convenience, the navigable section of the Loire is included here rather than under the entry for the river). (5) From Abbaye de Sept-Fons to a basin at Dompierre-sur-Besbre, 2.7km. A junction is made with the Canal de Roanne à Digoin at Chassenard, near Digoin.

Yachtsmen passing non-stop through the waterway often complain that it lacks interest; this view is only justified in part, for if you bother to explore nearby towns and navigate the short branches you will discover many fascinating places. A perennial difficulty is that the waterway's name suggests a continual prospect of Loire *châteaux*. These, however, lie much farther downstream, beyond Orléans. From one end of the canal to the other the Loire is never far away, but it is really rather a dull river of great shingle banks and willow trees, navigable for small craft only on a very localized basis. The Canal Latéral à la Loire enjoys the advantage of three important aqueducts, the Briare being quite outstanding, and there are few locks in proportion to its length. It serves a leading wine production region around Sancerre. Travelling from north to south, the waterway climbs throughout, the descent to the Saône beginning much later as the Canal du Centre heads SE.

Brief history By the late 18th century and completion of the Canal du Centre, the Bourbonnais route from Seine to Saône was substantially in its present form except for a length of navigable River Loire between Briare and Digoin. Beset with problems arising from winter floods and summer droughts, widespread dredging works and introduction of steam haulage failed to produce reliability similar to that offered by the canals. Accordingly the Canal de Grande Jonction (or Canal Latéral à la Loire) was constructed between 1827 and 1838, traffic largely ceasing on the Loire after that date. Aqueducts were designed to cross the River Allier at Le Guétin and the River Loire in Digoin. Surprisingly, a similar method of crossing the Loire at Briare was not adopted, mainly because of the river's extreme width. Instead, the new canal was excavated

along the river bank upstream of Briare and locked into the river to make a crossing on the level near Châtillon-sur-Loire. This procedure brought obvious disadvantages.

An opportunity to rectify this deficiency came during the latter part of the 19th century, when the whole of the Bourbonnais route was improved with larger capacity locks. Some 13.5km of new canal was built from Belleau to L'Étang and a steel trough aqueduct erected over the river upstream of Briare. At 662.69m, the Briare Aqueduct is still almost certainly the longest such structure in the world. It was opened to navigation in September 1896, the whole of the new line being put into service in October of the following year.

Having left the Canal de Briare at a junction with the old route down to the Loire, the Canal Latéral à la Loire arrives at a commercial basin shortly before the Briare Aqueduct (K2.9). Here are moorings within a short walk of all facilities in the centre of **Briare** (Chapter 40), with pleasant footpaths along the banks of the Loire and a restaurant at the eastern approach to the aqueduct. Two features merit special mention: the yard of a *brocante* merchant selling a fascinating array of jumble and antiques where in 1979 I purchased a delightfully ornate Petit Godin wood stove in cast-iron and brown enamel for one-tenth of its current market value; and a Motor Museum on the N7 towards Cosne-sur-Loire (walking distance) that contains over 80 examples of early road vehicles whose rarity value is only matched by a frequently poor state of preservation. The great aqueduct is most impressive, particularly when illuminated by dozens of original electric lamp standards. Carried on a series of 15 masonry supports at 40m intervals, it was constructed by the Société des Établissements Eiffel (of Tower fame) at a cost of about 35 million francs (1964 value). Twin towpaths are sufficiently wide to admit small cars, while it is not unknown for *péniche* skippers to walk alongside, leaving the barge to steer itself. Architectural detail is very fine, especially on the entrance columns, bearing the arms of Nevers, Roanne, Montargis and Paris, together with the names of many towns that can be reached by water. One arch was blown up by the French *Résistance* in 1940 and repaired; four years later a flying bomb made a hole in the trough. Pairs of stop gates enable the structure to be drained for maintenance via eight sluices.

Having traversed the Loire, the canal continues to **Châtillon-sur-Loire** (K8.6), a useful shopping halt with bathing 'beach' on the river. Soon the line of the original canal is seen on the left, at a lower level. It was reopened to navigation in 1998. Permission to navigate is available by ringing the tel. number signposted.Old and new lines unite at **L'Étang** (K13.5), with further shopping and restaurant in **Beaulieu** (K15.5). Good mooring with a flourishing market. Now comes a stretch with widely spaced locks at **Maimbray** (K17.8) Écluse 38 (grocer, restaurant), Belleville (K20.6) Écluse 37 (restaurant, baker, grocer and moorings with water, electricity, showers), Sury-Près-Léré (garage, baker, restaurant), Léré (K24.8) (shops restaurant, moorings with fuel, electricity, showers), Houards (K26.6) Ecluse 36 (grocer), and Écluse 35 Peseau (K30.5). By mooring at the bridge in **Les Fouchards** (K32.1) a visit can be made to **Cosne-sur-Loire** 2.5km distant on the far side of the river. This former river port was an important centre for casting cannon and anchors until 1872 when the factory was closed, its fortunes reduced by the extinction of the Loire traffic.

The next length includes a restaurant in the village of **Bussy** (K32.9) and a canalside garage with basic shops and restaurant at Bannay (K34.5), Écluse 34. We now reach the most worthwhile part of the whole canal, where you should aim to spend one or two days if possible. I once met a party in a hired cruiser from Marseilles-lès-Aubigny who were quite content to have travelled a mere 34km through 7 locks in order to pass most of their fortnight's holiday moored up here, by the three towns of Sancerre, St-Thibault and St-Satur. **St-Satur** (K40.6), opposite a junction with a branch that leads to the Loire, appears a little dull and grubby at first, but improves on inspection, with narrow streets of stone houses. Situated on an impressive hilltop west of the waterway, **Sancerre** thrives on its famous dry white wine made from Sauvignon grapes, and red and *rosé* from the Pinot Noir. Views of the immense vineyards are obtained from the Promenade de la Porte César on the ascent to this town of shady alleys. During the 16th century, the *château* was a Protestant Huguenot fortress: nothing remains of it but the Tour des Fiefs whose top provides a superb panorama of the Loire Valley. A notable local product from nearby **Chavignol** are small round goat cheeses bearing the curious name of *crottins* or 'goat droppings'. Best moorings in the area are down the short branch canal ahead of a lock (not in general use) by the river bank. Fuel, water and drydock at a boatyard. This is the village of **St-Thibault**, once a Loire boatmen's settlement, with a charming row of stone cottages overlooking a sandy river `beach' and swimming area roped off from the sometimes rapid flow of the former navigation. St Roch, patron of the local barge-

men, is recalled in the name of the church and in a floating restaurant based on the steel-sheathed hulls of two *berrichons* (sadly condemned on health grounds in 1998). Freshwater fish specialities are served, such as *matelote d'anguille* (eels stewed in wine). St Roch's feast day is celebrated with a water carnival on Aug 16. Aspiring motor cruiser captains receive tuition at a 'boating school', using the scarcely navigable waters of the Loire: doubtless a high level of proficiency results from coping with strong currents and avoiding willow-clad sandbanks. The public open-air swimming pool is modern and inviting, but remains in use only until the end of Aug. Once a busy wine port, the last barge came up the Loire in 1903; now the only sizeable river craft (sand dredgers apart) is a tripping vessel operating during summer weekends. Supermarket by the main line, 700m after the branch.

Ménétréol (K43.1) is convenient for food shops and service station, while **Ste-Bouize** (K47.5) at the second bridge after Écluse 33 has shops and a restaurant. As elsewhere on the rural canals of France, wild flowers are abundant with numerous lizards (some bright green examples are surprisingly large), butterflies and jumping beetles. Scenic interest is somewhat lacking past Écluses 32, La Grange (K50) and 31, La Prée (K55). Food shops, restaurant and water point are available in the village of **Herry**, Écluse 30 (K58). Unless in a great hurry, you will want to stop in the basin at **La Chapelle Montlinard** (K63.1, dry dock) and go by foot or bicycle to **La Charité-sur-Loire**, about 3km away on the far side of the Loire. This is a delightful old town with a 16th century stone bridge of many arches. Converted to Christianity in the 8th century, La Charité had by the 11th century become a great place of pilgrimage to the Benedictine priory and basilica of Notre-Dame: at one time this was the greatest church in France, after Cluny. 12th century fortifications provide a memorable view of the wide reaches of the Loire, site of a great port until its decline towards the middle of the 12th century. While held by the Burgundians in 1429, La Charité was unsuccessfully placed under siege by Joan of Arc: this lack of divine aid was a material factor in determining her eventual fate. Agreeable shops and restaurants enhance a visit to the town.

Butcher, baker and restaurant are located near Écluse 28 at **Argenvières** (K67), with similar facilities in **Beffes**, Écluse 27 (K71.7). The sort of place where the locals prefer to eat is a little restaurant on the waterside near a cement works (K73.6): called the Papillon Rose, it offers no choice of menu and represents good value. Now follows the once important canal port **Marseilles-lès-Aubigny** (K74.5), with Écluses 26 and 25 at its centre close to the island-filled River Loire. So thoroughly has the romantic narrow beam **Canal de Berry** been obliterated, that it is quite difficult to find its junction, on the right between the upper lock and the *port de plaisance*. Complete restoration will undoubtedly be achieved one day. (see Chapter 43A). 8km down the old line towards **Fontblisse** you can find an intact lock with single gates at **Patinges**. Meanwhile, a pastiche of a Berry bascule bridge stands at the centre of a traffic roundabout in Marseilles-lès-Aubigny.

Cours-les-Barres (K80.1, *halte nautique* service stations, grocer and baker) is followed by a short branch with Écluse 24 *bis*, Grille, down to the Loire at **Givry**. Then comes an agreeable wooded section through Écluse 24, Laurbray (K84.1), to a junction beyond the village of **Cuffy** (baker, butcher, restaurant). Ahead is a 3km disused branch which formerly provided a connection with a Loire tributary, the Allier. This is well worth investigating by foot or bicycle to visit the remarkable circular **Écluse des Lorraines**, where three sets of gates gave access to the river on two levels, above and below a weir. The structure is overlooked by a very fine canal engineer's house. Back on the main line, bear left for a two-rise lock staircase (Écluse 21/22, Guétin K89.7), followed immediately by a fine 18-arch aqueduct that is 343.06m long, spanning the Allier. This arrangement is a notorious bottleneck, for in the case of a southbound *péniche* the narrow cross-section of the trough prevents refilling the locks until the vesssel has completed its river crossing. A grocer, baker, butcher and restaurant serve this popular tourist location; there is a pleasant walk down the river to its confluence with the Loire.

From **Plagny** (K97.5, butcher, baker, grocer) the city of **Nevers** can be seen in the distance. Well worth a detour through locks and down the 2.9km branch (mechanized locks). A final lock into the Loire has been obliterated by a multi-tiered municipal swimming pool complex. Good moorings in a large basin, above. Nevers, reached by walking across the river bridge, is the Capital of the Nivernais and has a long history. The Duchy of Nevers passed to the Gonzaga family from Mantua in 1565; this explains a strong Italian influence in the Ducal Palace. A famous *faïence* industry was introduced from Italy at the same time; the handpainted enamelled earthenware is widely sold and makes pretty souvenirs. Tours of the oldest pottery, Bout-du-Monde, are conducted at 14.50h every Wed from the firm's

shop near the Porte-du-Croux, a magnificent 14th century gateway. The uncorrupted body of St Bernadette of Lourdes can be seen in a glass casket in the chapel of the Convent of St Gildard, Boulevard Victor-Hugo. She died here in 1879 and was canonized in 1933. No visit is complete without seeing the great cathedral of St Cyr and Ste Julitte, a huge structure combining architectural styles from the 10th to 16th centuries.

Back on the canal's main line, pleasant farming country takes the boater through a succession of little villages: **Chevenon** (K106.7) – *château*, baker, grocer; Écluse 20, Jaugenay (K110.4); **Uxeloup** with the 13th century fortress of Château de Rosemont and Écluse 19 (K114.3); **Fleury-sur-Loire**, Écluse 18 (K119.4) – baker, grocer; and **Avril-sur-Loire** (K123.3) – quay, Ecomusée. An important junction occurs at **St Maurice** (K131.7, water point) with a two-lock branch leading through a former gravel barge basin into the Loire. Crown Blue Line hire base, with supermarket nearby. By navigating 1.75km downstream the entrance to the beautiful Canal du Nivernais is reached at **St-Léger-des-Vignes** (see Chapter 45). Until the demise of horse-drawn traffic a chain tug hauled dumb craft between the two canals and as recently as the mid-1970s a fee was demanded of all motorized vessels for this unrequired and (by then) unperformed service. Another casualty of the 70s was a pair of donkeys used for pulling sand barges on the river: they were trained to walk in a circle round a lockside bollard, thus halting the boat unaided. In addition to the two canals and the Loire, the Vieille Loire and the River Aron all meet here, **Decize** being situated on an island between the two Loire branches. Most conveniently visited

Berrichon life, circa 1905. Less fortunate examples were pulled by the boat people themselves.

by mooring near the river bridge, it is an agreeable hilly little town with a wide variety of shops and some gigantic plane trees in the Promenade des Halles. Should you wish to remain on the Canal Latéral à la Loire, Decize is about 2km walk from the N478 bridge west of the junction.

Unremarkable country takes the canal through **Les Feuillats** (K135.7, restaurant). Butcher, baker, restaurant and garage lie 1km from the waterway (Écluse 12, Vanneaux, hire base K147.4) in **Gannay-sur-Loire**, where the remains of an ancient tree are protected by a shingled roof. 900m beyond Écluse 10, Rosière (K154.7), is a useful garage, with all services in **Garnat-sur-Engièvre** (K159.7). **Beaulon**, close to Écluse 8 (K162.5), similarly has a range of shops with *crêperie*, a distinctly odd 19th century Gothic church in red brick and pebble-dash, and a Musée Rural de la Sologne Bourbonnais, open June–Oct, Sun and holidays, 15.00–19.00h. Although the Trappist **Abbaye de Sept-Fons** (K170.1) is closed to the public, a slide show on the 18th century building is presented on Sun and holidays (17.30h June–Aug, 16.30h the rest of the year). This is situated near the beginning of a short branch line in good condition leading to **Dompierre-sur-Besbre**. Hire craft base. In addition to the usual facilities not far from the terminal basin, there are public showers and a swimming pool (about 5 minutes' walk). The canal now crosses the River Besbre via a four-arched aqueduct at Écluse 6 (K171). **Diou** (K174.7) has several food stores, service station and hotel, while the charming little town of **Pierrefitte-sur-Loire** (K180.9) with its 19th century *château* offers most supplies. Mooring basin and restaurant. **Coulanges** (K185.8) lies beyond Écluse 3 (aqueduct over the Loddes) with baker and fuel station. Near Écluse 2, at **Coulanges**, are a *halte nautique*, shops and restaurant. On the right bank (K194) a T-junction marks the beginning of the Canal de Roanne à Digoin (see Chapter 42).

With memories of vineyards reaching to the horizon around Sancerre, fields ablaze with the yellow flowers of rapeseed in early summer and the broad, deserted reaches of the great river, this efficient, well engineered but sometimes slightly dull canal is now nearing its end. One burst of magnificence remains: the eleven-arched **Digoin** Aqueduct (K195.2) whose 241.57m provides a last view of the Loire. The town flourishes on a trade of ceramics and *faïence*. Ahead is the Canal du Centre, last link in the chain of waterways between the Seine and the Saône.

42 · Canal de Roanne à Digoin

Carte Guide: *Canaux des Centre*
From a junction with the Canal Latéral à la Loire near Digoin to a terminus in Roanne, 55.6km with 10 locks.

Until recent times the canal was little used by commercial or pleasure traffic and consideration was seriously given to its closure in 1971. Best regarded as a continuation of the Canal Latéral à la Loire, the navigation climbs up the Loire valley to Roanne, where a junction lock once provided a link into the river. Although its windings along the contours provide tranquil cruising of a kind now undreamed of in England and rarely encountered in France, it is conspicuously lacking in the sort of features likely to encourage anyone off the through route to make the necessary double journey down to the Roanne terminus and back. In 1982, after some years of doubt about its future, an Association was formed under the presidency of the Mayor of Roanne to seek its preservation and development: this has the support of the Loire, Loiret, Saône and Allier *départementales* authorities. But they can scarcely expect the sort of success that has brought tourism on a major scale to the neighbouring Canal du Nivernais, whose situation was equally desperate in the early 1960s. Some regular traffic is now generated by hire cruiser bases.

Designed for barges carrying between 100 and 150 tonnes, the canal was built by the Franco-Suisse Co. and opened to traffic in 1838. In its original form there were 13 locks, reduced to the present 10 during major improvement works (1898–1905) which made the line available to 38m Freycinet *péniches*. 549,000 tonnes of freight was carried in 1936, 300,000 tonnes in 1962 and a mere 19,500 in 1976. By that time barges rarely exceeded two or three each week. Most of the traffic was to the steel, cotton and textile mills of Roanne, with coal and other cargoes coming in from the nearby Canal du Centre. For the current lock opening times, consult the *Carte Guide*.

Following the junction near **Digoin** (see Chapter 41), the waterway rises through Écluses 10–8, not far from the village of **Chassenard** (K3.6, grocer, restaurant). Lock 10 has a water point, and the mobile keeper is based at No. 9, Beugnets. Then follows a 25.7km level past **Bonant** (K13.1, restaurant) and **Avrilly** (K15.2, grocer) to Écluse 7, **Bourg-le-Comte** (K19, grocer, baker, restaurant). Frequently the Loire is within easy reach, as for example in the village of **Chambilly** (K22.5), where shops include baker, grocer and butcher together with nearby garage and restaurant. The keeper is based at the middle of the group of Écluses 6, 5 and 4. Beyond the river, 3km east, **Marcigny** lies at the foot of the Brionne hills and offers all services in addition to a selection of ancient half-timbered buildings, a 12th century church and the splendid 15th century Tour du Moulin containing a local history museum and selection of Nevers *faïence*.

The next pound of 18.2km serves **Artaix** (K26.5, grocer), **Melay-sur-Loire** (K29.5, grocer, baker, butcher, restaurant and garage) and the old riverport of **Iguerande** (K3 4.4), useful for a full range of urban amenities and reached from a bridge near an isolated restaurant. Shortly before Écluse 3 (water point), further basic food shopping, garage and restaurant will be found in **Briennon** (K40.9), with all the services of a moderate sized town at **Pouilly-sous-Charlieu**, 4km east. Écluse 2, **Cornillon** (K46.4), has a restaurant alongside and after a short branch at **Oudan** (K53 .5) we arrive at the final lock, providing access to the terminal basin by the Loire in the centre of **Roanne** (K55.6). Historically the town was regarded as the highest navigable point on the river, for the gorges above – although sometimes passed on downstream journeys – were hazardous in the extreme. The town grew considerably after the arrival of its canal and is now a bright and modern place with local boating on the Loire. Reputedly one of the best eight restaurants in France will be found at the Hôtel des Frères Troisgros, awarded three rosettes by *Michelin*, meriting the comment: 'Superb food, the epitome of French cooking. Fine wines, faultless service, elegant surroundings... One will pay accordingly.' With such a recommendation, there would seem to be every incentive to make the round trip by water of 111km. Roanne-Plaisance have established a cruiser base and a pair of previously disused drydocks are back in working order. The admirably-equipped Pleasure-boat Port has a reputation for providing winter moorings at very reasonable rates.

43 · Canal du Centre

Carte Guide: *Canaux des Centre*
From a junction with the Canal Latéral à la Loire at Digoin to the River Saône at Chalon-sur-Saône, 112.1km with 61 locks.

For much of its life the Canal du Centre derived a substantial proportion of commercial traffic from the coal mines at Montceau-les-Mines. Industry hardly makes its presence felt, however, and the abiding impression is of a very winding, thickly wooded waterway, parts of which are exceptionally beautiful. From Digoin, it takes a NE direction along the valley of the Bourbince, climbing to a summit level at Montchanin. Then comes a rapid descent down the valley of the Dheune, before turning SE towards the River Saône. The great majority of locks onwards from Montchanin are mechanized with sensors preparing chambers by remote control. Situated throughout in Burgundy, local restaurant cuisine reaches high standards. One unusual feature of the canal is that its towpath serves as a public road almost from end to end. Although this arrangement inevitably creates a degree of intrusion from road vehicles, it is of great use if sending crew ahead by bicycle or motorbike to set the next lock. The dangers of the system to the barge horses which remained until the late 1960s will be obvious.

Brief history Originally known as the Canal du Charollais, this communication was first suggested during the 16th century, under François I, with a detailed plan prepared by Adam de Craponne in the time of Henry II. But no positive action was taken until the Chief Engineer of Burgundy, Émiland Gauthey, obtained building powers in 1783. His scheme relied on selecting a route which climbed the chain of hills dividing the valleys of the Loire and Saône with the provision of adequate water supplies at the summit. The first stone was laid by the Prince de Condé in 1784; in spite of the intervention of the Revolution, the works were completed in 1792. 80 individual locks were built to climb 77.64m from the Loire, followed by a 130.9m descent to the Saône. Extensive works at the summit comprised no fewer than 20 reservoirs. Exceptional floods on the Loire in 1790 totally wrecked a new port in Digoin and put back completion by many months.

The canal brought new life to the Charollais and within 20 years of its opening many villages had sprung up along the banks. Writing in 1822, Huerne de Pommeuse looked forward to completion of the Canal Latéral à la Loire, commenting that this development would triple the toll income of the Canal du Centre (*Des Canaux Navigables*). In 1867–9 a feeder to the River Arroux near Digoin was made navigable for *berrichon*-sized barges, and between 1880 and 1900 the whole line was enlarged to Freycinet standards by rebuilding all locks (which were reduced in number) and deepening the channel. Wooden lock gates were replaced by metal ones. During 1936 some 1,622,000 tonnes was carried in 9,825 barge journeys and Montceau-les-Mines became one of 10 inland ports in France to handle over 1 million tonnes, most of it coal.

At the end of the 1950s about 5km of canal with 3 locks through the centre of Chalon was replaced by a new cut to the Saône upstream of the town with a single 10.76m deep lock. Mechanization of most locks on the Saône side of the summit has since been carried out, with photo-electric cells detecting arrivals. Pleasure craft should remember that the lock sensors were designed for slow-moving *péniches* and they must be passed very sedately if they are to function correctly.

Leaving **Digoin** (see Chapter 41), a fixed bascule bridge marks the start of a now unnavigable 14km narrow-beam feeder from the Arroux with 2 *berrichon*-sized locks. Distinctive lock-operating gear on the Centre comprises massive spoked iron wheels connected to the gates by chain-driven rods. Écluses 26–24 intervene before **Paray-le-Monial** (k12.8) whose magnificent triple-towered Romanesque basilica was built by St Hughes, Bishop of Cluny in 1090–

1109. During the late 17th century Marguerite-Marie Alacoque witnessed a succession of visions, but it was not until the 19th century that the devotion of the Sacred Heart made Paray-le-Monial a town of national pilgrimage. Sister Marguerite-Marie was canonized in 1920 and hotels now cater for an influx of religious tourists. The Bourbince waterfront is particularly memorable. Paray offers excellent shopping and restaurants, while splendid central moorings are available over a long distance. There is a convenient supermarket on the northern outskirts.

Near the canal at **Digoine** (K26) is an elegant 18th century *château* (not open to the public) on the site of ancient fortifications. All facilities are to be found in the small town of **Palinges** (K29.2). On the bank beyond Écluse 17, **Montet** (K31.6), is a waterside bar. Most shops in **Génelard** (K32.6), with houses grouped around a wide basin (moorings) and Le Chaland café. Another pretty village is **Ciry-le-Noble** (K38.6), with shops, restaurant and waterside garage. It is immediately obvious that Écluse 13, Azy (K40.3), is in the charge of a former boatman, connections with the batellerie including

The basilica at Paray-le-Monial on the edge of the Bourbince.

a steel dinghy filled with flowers, flags and clusters of plastic blooms. Restaurants are in Galuzot (K45.4) and by Écluse 11, Vernois (K46.5). Le Pont des Vernes restaurant is recommended. This chamber is the first mechanized one at the time of writing: others will be converted in due course. Really delightful hilly pastureland with a wealth of pleasing farm buildings now begins to give way to the industry of **Montceau-les-Mines** (K50.2), a town dominated by a power station, pit-head winding gear, railway sidings and an impressive coal washing plant served by a huge basin. Coal traffic by *péniche* is a shadow of its former greatness, but the site continues to illustrate the advantages of bulk carriage by water. Montceau is a surprisingly pleasant town, its main square lined with plane trees near a canal basin (partly infilled to provide car parking). Both the swing bridge and an exceptionally robust steel bascule bridge have been adapted to open automatically for canal traffic. Large *port de plaisance*, immediately beyond. The area is well remembered by a friend whose large motor yacht was trapped by an emergency canal stoppage in the mid-1970s. With an important *rendez-vous* to collect guests elsewhere, he secured the services of a crane and low-loader to take his vessel round the obstruction. The crane collapsed and the yachtsman was involved in a complicated lawsuit.

To the north, the industrial **Creusot Basin** thrives on coal, steel works, brickfields and potteries. In the middle of the 19th century a navigable branch line, with 1,267m tunnel, served the area via Torcy. A chain of mechanized locks extends from **Blanzy** (K54.9), a not unattractive place with shops and the Restaurant-Hôtel du Centre, one of a number of most convenient eating places to be found close to the waterway. Écluse 1, Océan (K62), with a large basin and nearby reservoir, marks the beginning of the short summit level, a deep tree-shaded cutting passing near the iron and tile-making town of **Montchanin** (all services). Locks are renumbered from Écluse 1, Méditerranée (K66), the first group of four still known as Les Sept Écluses, a situation changed a century ago. No. 3 has a garage, there is a general shop in the pound between 3 and 4, a butcher at 4 and a café by 5 (K67.6). Multi-coloured Burgundian roof tiles of local manufacture decorate houses in the village of **Écuisses** (K68.4), with butcher, baker and restaurant. The canal now runs in company with the River Dheune past **St-Julien-sur-Dheune** (K69.8): the reach between Écluses 8 and 14 is exceedingly pleasant through rolling scenery and poplar trees. (Restaurants at Écluse 8, in the pound between 9 and 10, at 15 and by 17, **St-Bérain-sur-Dheune**, K77.3.) Given unlimited time,

the opportunities for eating ashore are numerous. Good shopping in **St-Léger-sur-Dheune**, (mooring basin) where the bridge reduces headroom to 3.42m compared with 3.50m elsewhere. Surroundings become more populated, with shops and garage at **Dennevy** (K83.8) and a restaurant in **St-Gilles** (K85.9). After Écluse 23 a welcome 11km pound commences, with shops and garage at **Cheilly-les-Marange** (K88.1).

Now on the southern edge of the famous vineyards of the Côte d'Or, **Santenay** (K89.7) produces wine and lithia mineral waters. A visit can be made to the little church of St Jean, standing in isolation at the foot of a semi-circular cliff. **Chagny** (K94.9), a gloomy industrial town, has useful facilities and a modern concrete aqueduct over a railway. Remains of the old stone aqueduct, basin and canal approaches can be seen. 12 more locks in the final 15.9km are generally without facilities, as the canal drops downhill on the edges of the Forest of Chagny. Note a charcoal kiln in a timberyard at the approach to **Le Gauchard** (K103). A choice of restaurants, each side of the bridge. The Canal du Centre passes under the A6 *autoroute* and skirts **Chalon-sur-Saône** (see Chapter 47). Pleasure craft are not permitted to enter the truncated remnants of the former canal into the town centre (St-Gobain Branch). Supermarket, left, 3 bridges before the final lock. Écluse 35, a cavernous concrete chamber with a drop of 10.76m, lowers boats to river level just upstream of the *port fluvial* with extensive bargebuilding yards. Moorings and all requirements for cruisers are to be found at a marina on the Saône, opposite the town.

43A • River Cher & Canal de Berry

Carte Guide: *Pays de la Loire et Le Cher Navigable* (Vagnon)

The Cher is currently navigable from Vallet, (some distance upstream of its former junction with a canal branch to the Loire at Tours) and Noyers-sur-Cher, junction with a restored portion of the Canal de Berry: 40.2km with 11 locks. Note that normal draft is only 0.7m. Further restoration is planned downstream to Tours.

A reopened portion of the Canal de Berry extends from a junction with the Cher at Noyers-sur-Cher to Selles-sur-Cher: 11.9km with 6 locks, passing craft of up to 2.7m in beam. Permitted draft is 0.8m.

At present isolated from the main waterways network, these navigations were restored from complete dereliction in the mid-1990s. British-built narrow boats are available for hire. The available length is sufficient for a leisurely week's exploration, out and back. The rural surroundings are very agreeable, while passage through the arches of the magnificent Château de Chenonceaux is an experience unique in the whole of France. Apart from those at each end of the Chenonceaux pound, Cher locks are electrified and like several bascule bridges on the Canal de Berry are activated by magnetic cards. Bed and breakfast is offered at several of the lock cottages.

Brief history Once *flottable* (for example by rafts of timber) in its upper reaches from the Moulin d'Enchaume to Vierzon (131km), this unlocked part of the Cher was abandoned by commerce after duplication by the Canal de Berry in 1834. A further 70km of Cher with several flash locks between Vierzon and Noyers was described in 1888 as "rarely used" by light-drafted barges. 62km, with 18 locks, from Noyers to Tours, canalised from 1840-50, was navigated by 65-tonne capacity sailing barges known as *gabares* until the early part of the 20th century. The route was abandoned in 1933.

The Canal de Berry was formerly an extensive Y-shaped network, providing a connection between the Canal Latéral à la Loire at Marseilles-les-Aubigny and the Cher at Noyers. A further branch ran southwards along the valley of the Upper Cher from St-Amand to a terminus at Montluçon. These lines totalled 261km and were served by 96 narrow beam locks, 2.7m wide. Constructed 1822-40, the Berry resembles the smaller canals of the English Midlands. Special barges, known as *berrichons*, were used. Hauled variously by donkeys, mules and even the boatmen themselves, they were built in timber, 27.5m long x 2.62m beam, and generally had a central stable. In later years, several were constructed in iron and motorised. A handful still exist, converted into houseboats, for pleasure use or as museum exhibits. One especially attractive example works as a fuelling boat in Paris. A leading traffic was in cast iron from the forges at Montluçon, with coal, pit props, cement, lime, building sand, wines and spirits, slates and tiles.

Enlargement to the Freycinet standard in the 1880s was considered too costly in terms of likely benefits. In spite of growing railway competition, problems with water supply that eventually necessitated decreasing available draft and the smaller-than-normal payloads possible – up to a maximum of 80 tonnes – the Canal de Berry achieved its best-ever traffic figures in 1905. By 1936, tonnages had slumped to less than 400,000, representing about 5,000 boat journeys. Then followed a gradual decline, resulting in total abandonment in 1955.

While several km from the Marseilles-les-Aubigny junction have been completely infilled, the great majority of the Canal de Berry remains intact, although former swing bridges are fixed and lock gates frequently replaced by weirs. Much local clearance and restoration has taken place in recent years and most of the system remains in water. Considerable sums of money have been spent by the Societé des Amis du Canal de Berry on restoration of a 17km length with 2 locks and an aqueduct between St-Amand and Ainey-le-Vieil, while a small canal museum at Reugny near Montluçon exhibits two *berrichons*, various artefacts, documents and photographs. It is open Sat. and Suns., July to September, or for parties by arrangement with René Chambareau, an enthusiast for all European waterways (who speaks English): Les Vignauds, 18, Rue des Godignons, 03190 Reugny. Among many fine engineering features is the 96m-long Tranchasse aqueduct, near St-Amand. Situated mainly in a deeply rural region, bordering the mysterious lakeland wilderness of the Sologne, setting of Alain Fournier's compelling novel *Le Grand Meaulnes*, this is one waterway that definitely deserves to be restored.

River Cher
Navigation currently begins above **Vallet** lock (K0). Travelling upstream, all facilities are available in **Bléré** (K3.7), a pleasant market town with lock and ancient buildings in the main square. Écluse de **Civray** and Écluse de **Chisseaux** (K11.3) have both been rebuilt as 19th century replicas, with wooden gates and balance beams and manually-worked paddles, in recognition of the environmental importance of the intervening pound. A mobile keeper supervises passage through each. One curious stipulation of the restoration scheme was that up to a maximum four boats at a time would be allowed to enter this section, where no mooring is permitted, presumably because large numbers of pleasure craft would detract from the delights of the **Château de Chenonceaux** (K9), which spans the river.

Of all French *châteaux*, Chenonceaux is perhaps the most memorable, being built on a series of stone arches across the Cher. The great white edifice dates from the early 16th century and on the death of its owners was appropriated by François I, in settlement of debts. Henry II presented it to his mistress Diane de Poitiers in 1547 and subsequently it passed to Catherine de Medici. It was the setting for lavish festivals, where arriving guests were welcomed by mermaids emerging from moats alongside the approach avenue while groups of nymphs appeared in the undergrowth. Naval battles were re-enacted on the river, with grand firework displays. Restored in the 19th century, it is now the property of the Menier family. Open to the public throughout the year. Boat trips are available.

Chissaux (K10.8) is a riverside resort (most facilities), with moorings, and water point, left, upstream of the lock. A charming manor house occupies the site of a fortified mill on an island. Once through the **Écluse de Chissay-en-Touraine** (K14.3), it is possible to moor at **Le Port** and cross a bridge into the little town (most facilities, including supermarket) where the 15/16th century *château* is flanked by a series of round towers.

After working through a lock (K18), it is well worth halting by a trip boat landing stage (left bank, water and electricity) to explore the small town of **Montrichard** (most facilities). Sites include a medieval castle keep (visits) and the Caves Monmousseau, 15km of wine cellars housed in former quarries. Guided tours of the wine-making museum with tasting throughout the summer. Take care to follow the correct channel past several islands above and below Écluse de **Vallagon** (K20.9). Further locks, **Vineuil** (K23.4) and **Mazelles** (K27.3) are situated in prosperous farming country, renowned for its goat cheese, mushrooms cultivated in caves, asparagus, fruit and vegetables.

A quay, left, downstream of the bridge, is convenient for investigation of the impressive Roman remains (each side of the Cher) at **Thésée** (K29), shops and restaurants. Troglodyte dwellings in tufa chalk cliffs. Midway between Écluses **Talufiau** (K31.2) and **de la Méchinière** (K34.2), there is a useful overnight quay mooring at a camp site, opposite the wine-producing village of **Mareuil-sur-Cher** (access difficult).

St-Aignan (K38) is an exceptionally pretty little town of pale grey stone buildings, rising above the waterway. The lock is built into an arch of the road bridge, with good moorings (water and electricity) upstream, right. Not far beyond, the unnavigable Cher continues, right, while a channel leads through flood gates to the beginning of the Canal de Berry at **Noyers-sur-Cher**, there are adequate facilities (K40), with its small port where charter narrow boats are based.

Canal de Berry

An operational fragment that is more than enough to whet the appetite for the eventual restoration of this fascinating miniature canal network. It features narrow-beam locks and several automated bascule bridges. It closely follows the unnavigable River Cher from **Noyers-sur-Cher**, lock 1 (K0), and after further locks, **de la Limonière** (K1.6), the delightfully named **Trompe-souris** ('Trick-the-Mouse', K2.4) and **des Roches** (K3.4), emerges into a 7.1km pound, spanned by lifting bridges at **Les Martinières, La Rue, Trevety** and **Châtillon-sur-Cher** (shopping and restaurants).

A stone aqueduct carries the canal over the River Sauldre, shortly before reaching **Val de Sauldre** lock (K10.5). The final lock, Écluse **de La Thizardière** (K11.3), is shortly followed by **Port de Selles** (K11.9) with moorings and a turning basin at the current head of navigation. It is worth walking along the banks of the unrestored canal and over the Cher into **Selles-sur-Cher** to visit the abbey church of St-Eusice (local history/folklore museum in the cloisters) and the *château*, part 13th century fortress, part Renaissance mansion.

44 • River Yonne

Carte Guide: *Yonne or Bourgogne Voies Navigables Tome 1.* Also *The Yonne and the Nivernais* by Tony Paris. (Enterprise Guides.)
From a junction with the River Seine at Montereau-faut-Yonne to a junction with the Canal du Nivernais at Auxerre, 108km with 26 locks. There is a connection with the Canal du Bourgogne at Laroche Migennes.

Navigation on this splendid river with its succession of wide, sparkling weirs is considerably longer than suggested by the data above. For it continues to quite a distance upstream of Auxerre, where it forms part of the Canal du Nivernais. The only problem is a number of locks with awkwardly sloping sides. Scenery is consistently good with several towns of outstanding interest and a mass of pleasing villages. Commercial traffic is generally quite modest (especially in the upper lengths), except during late summer and autumn when barges are loaded with grain. Locks are worked manually with most efficient gate-mounted paddle levers that require movement through 180° to open them fully.

Brief history Canal promoter the Duc d'Orléans commented in 1740 that there was no river more risky to navigation than the Yonne, cluttered with rocks and suffering much of the time from a depth of only 30cm. By the late 18th century the section from Auxerre to Montereau was obstructed by 13 sluices built mainly for milling purposes rather than as an aid to traffic. Freight, chiefly log rafts from the Morvan, could manage downstream journeys with great difficulty. Conventional barges were able to take only a third of their designed load, the contents of three boats being transferred into one identical craft when they arrived at the Seine.

Frequent early attempts to improve the navigation resulted in works being washed away in floods and it was only when the Canal du Nivernais and Canal de Bourgogne were fully operational that a rectification of the Yonne was considered imperative. Canalization started in 1840 when a series of artificial cuts were dug and huge locks built, often with one or both sides of the chamber of sloping stone blocks. Further improvements were carried out late in the 19th century following the Freycinet scheme for nationwide waterway enlargement. Few changes have been made in the present century, except where alarmingly decayed structures were rebuilt or substantially repaired after World War II. Commercial traffic (only 104,000 tonnes in 1936) is now light except in the lowest reaches, while pleasure craft increase in numbers every year with much improved facilities for hire cruisers and private motor yachts. In common with many French rivers, the Yonne is prone to flooding in Spring and care is advised when approaching locks situated directly alongside weirs.

Intense barge activity on the Seine and around its Yonne junction in **Montereau** may result in difficulty in locating suitable moorings near the town (see Chapter 13). There is normally bankside space near the first bridge, the Pont de Moscou (K1.2), with cheap shopping close by. Street market, Saturday mornings. Soon comes an introduction to the river's far from convenient design of locks: **Cannes**, Écluse 17 (K3.3) where both sides of the chamber are composed of sloping and slippery sides. Twin-screw craft are the most vulnerable, especially when descending. Techniques are to lie alongside a *péniche*, where space permits; to hold station under power in the centre of the chamber (often expressly forbidden by the keeper); or to lie close to the short vertical section near top or bottom gates, taking

care to avoid being lowered onto the sill. One would expect all locks to have been built to a similar design, but they vary considerably in both length and width, while the walls range from vertical, to sloping one side and vertical the other, or sloping on both sides. Water and restaurant will be found at the lock itself, shopping in **Cannes-Écluses** on the right by the next bridge. Initial reaches of the Yonne are a little dull, past gravel workings and large open meadows.

Écluse 16, **La Brosse** (K7.3), has two sloping sides, as has Écluse 15, **Barbey** (K11.8). If you can select a suitable mooring on the left bank downstream of a road bridge, **Misy-sur-Yonne** (K13.6) is a useful and delightfully situated village halt, with grocer, butcher, baker and restaurant. Up to now locks have been located directly alongside their foaming weirs, with potentially hazardous approaches when the river is in flood (a not infrequent situation). Écluse 14, Port-Renard (K16.2) marks entry to the first portion of artificial channel, bypassing several loops. Known as the Dérivation de Courlon, it has another lock in the middle, Écluse 13, **Vinneuf** (K17.8, both sides sloping). Deep-draft craft should keep strictly to the centre of the channel when returning the original river after a guard lock at **Courlon-sur-Yonne** (K20.9). A bridge dated 1868 pinpoints the year when this cut was excavated. The village is agreeable with restaurant and basic shopping. Scenery has by now started to improve greatly.

A long reach runs past groups of islands and the hamlet of **Serbonnes** (K25.9) to Écluse 12, Champfleury (K27.8). A new bridge replaces the original crossing at **Pont-sur-Yonne** (K29.6) of which an Avignon-like portion remains. Shown intact on early 20th century postcards, it was demolished in 1952 to facilitate passage of barges. There is good shopping and a variety of restaurants. Waterside houses are clustered around an attractive 13th century church. Moorings with bollards are found on the right bank downstream of the new bridge and on the opposite shore is a garage. The popularity of the riverside is evident from a huge caravan park although local pleasure boating – fishing punts and hired pedaloes apart – is still surprisingly limited. Further locks intervene: **Villeperrot**, 11 (K33.5, sloping sides) and **St-Martin**, 10 (K38.4, water point). Repairs and moorings at Evans Marine.

The broadening of the river by a large island (follow the left channel) marks the approach to **Sens** (K41.2), an ancient city named after a Gallic tribe, the Senons. 20th century industrial expansion, waterside grain silos and traffic-filled streets should not be allowed to detract from the many sights of Sens. Most important is the great Gothic cathedral of St-Étienne, started in the 12th century; among its treasures are vestments of

Thomas à Becket, St Thomas of Canterbury. The roof is partly covered with coloured tiles. Architectural brilliance of another age is seen in a 19th century cast-iron market hall, and the Musée Municipal contains a very fine collection of Gallo-Roman antiquities and other objects, among them the hat worn by Napoléon at Waterloo. Good moorings will be found on a vertical quay a little downstream of the bridge and not far from the main shopping centre. A privately-run pleasure craft harbour with range of services is established on the upstream head of the island. Écluse 9, St-Bond (K41.7, sloping sides) is on the city's edge. Then comes Écluse 8, **Rosoy** (K47.4, sloping sides), where a small village, upstream on the left bank, provides restaurant and grocer assuming your draft allows access for mooring. Restaurant, grocer, baker and butcher can be reached in Étigny (K51), right bank below a concrete road bridge. Écluse 7 (K51.9, sloping sides) shortly appears upstream.

Typically, **Villeneuve-sur-Yonne** (K57.9) is now anything but new. It was created by Louis VII, husband of Eleanor of Aquitaine, in the 12th century. Entry by road is through one of two magnificent gateways, the Porte de Sens or the Porte de Joigny. Further remains of fortifications include a red brick tower at the river's edge, with moorings alongside, at a quay below the bridge, or by arrangement at a hire cruiser base on the right bank (water point). Quiet, now that it is bypassed by the N6, Villeneuve is a most pleasant little town of red-roofed buildings, compact and with convenient shops and eating establishments. Moving upstream once more, we pass through Écluse 5, **Armeau** (K63, sloping sides), where basic shops, restaurant and garage can be found (left bank, shortly above). A bridge connects **Villevallier** (K66.1) with **St-Julien-du-Sault**. The former is useful for food shopping, restaurant and garage, while St-Julien has a full range of facilities about 500m beyond a railway. Legend tells of St Julien's horse making a remarkable leap here to escape his enemies. Fine stained glass windows of the 13th century decorate its church, and there is a magnificent view onto the river and up to the next lock, Écluse 4, Villevallier (K67.6). Hereabouts is perhaps the most lovely part of the navigable Yonne. Moor near **Villecien** (K71.6, left bank) where there are two restaurants; alternatively, continue a short distance to the start of the Dérivation de Joigny and select a suitable stopping place at Écluse 3; **St-Aubin** (K72.6, sloping sides), where there is a grocer and restaurant. 1.5km SW lies **Cézy**, a charming small town providing all shops and restaurant.

Reaching a cutting depth of 20m in places, the acacia lined canal rejoins the Yonne by the Épizy guard lock (K75.3) with a Ponts et Chaussées drydock on the right bank. Ahead lies the lovely town of **Joigny** (K76.6) whose medieval street pattern and numerous 15–16th century timber-framed houses arranged round small squares, passages and courtyards are a delight to explore. Rising sharply from the river banks, the heart of Joigny is reached via a pedestrian shopping street where quality goods range from practical supplies for the galley to appealing souvenirs. St Jean's church crowns a sea of brown-tiled roofs. Quays provide central moorings, just downstream of an 18th century bridge with nearby garage. Water can be obtained from Locaboat Plaisance on the opposite bank. Garden vegetables were available from the keeper at Écluse 2, Pêchoir (K79.3), during my last visit. In the following reach two small islands mark the site of a former lock and weir with keeper's house. Launching small craft is possible at a slipway near the hamlet of **St-Cydroine**, on the left bank a little downstream of Écluse 1, Épineau (K83.1).

Laroche-St-Cydroine (K84.2) signals the approach to the start of the Canal de Bourgogne (see Chapter 46). Depending on their overall dimensions, Saône-bound craft have a choice of turning off here or carrying on to Auxerre, the equally attractive Canal du Nivernais and finally the Canal du Centre. Shopping is easier at the Pont de Laroche railway bridge than in **Mignennes** (unless you are taking the Bourgogne route or need to buy fuel from a waterwise diesel pump in the basin above the first canal lock). Numbering of Yonne locks now changes, presumably because the nine uppermost ones were in service first as a link between the Bourgogne and the Nivernais. Thus Écluse 9, La Gravière (K86.8), appears on the right bank shortly beyond a confluence with the River Armençon, along whose valley the Bourgogne was dug. Next feature is a road bridge connecting the villages of **Bonnard** and **Bassou** (K90.1, grocer, butcher, baker and restaurant). Shortly afterwards the River Serain enters on the left with Écluse 8, Bassou (K90.9), directly ahead. Keep to the left bank to enter the Gurgy canal cut at Écluse 7, Raveuse (K92.6). Much of the canal near Écluse 6, Néron (K94.1), is bordered by security fencing and watchtowers belonging not to a prison camp but to a military training centre. Eating ashore is possible at an isolated restaurant on the right bank a little beyond the next bridge. 4km SW lies **Appoigny**, a town with all facilities but probably too far to be of use except in an emergency. The long canal section ends with a guard lock in the village of **Gurgy** (K97.9), a halt that is both useful and attractive. Boating facilities, including slipway and water point, are supplied by hire cruiser firm Navitour. Although still primarily a farming centre, Gurgy is gradually developing as a residential village easily reached from Auxerre. Its very tumbledown church incongruously has a small fire station attached to one end. There are basic shops and a restaurant.

Agreeable countryside leads to a bridge of the A6 Paris-Lyon *autoroute* (K99.1), with Écluse 5 (K100.4) on the outskirts of **Montéteau**. All traffic follows a channel on the left of the river, past an island above the lock and up to a bowed girder bridge. All shops, supermarket and garage within close range; an excellent restaurant, Le Lido, has moorings virtually alongside. Three further locks, Éluse 4, Boisseaux (K102.1); Écluse 3, Dumonts (K103.7) and Écluse 2, l'Île Brûlée (K105.5) bring the navigator to the edge of the beautiful city of **Auxerre** (locally pronounced 'Ossaire') and junction with the Canal du Nivernais (K108). Having passed the final lock, Écluse la Chainette (water point), the flying buttresses of St Étienne's Gothic cathedral come into view with a superb waterfront of elegant buildings lining lower ground on the right bank of the Yonne. Extensive deep moorings can be found here along the Quai de la Marine, or on the left shore in the *port de plaisance*. Hire cruisers operate from this point, a most convenient location for slipway, water, electricity, diesel fuel, showers and mechanical repairs. Auxerre was the first major French city I arrived at by water, during a cruise in 1968. Since then it has become firmly established as one of the country's most pleasant ports of all and every keen inland navigator will eventually moor here to admire the memorable view. Recent years have seen much progress in revealing and restoring scores of wonderful timber-framed buildings. The city centre is reached by a series of sharply-rising streets leading to pedestrian shopping areas whose outstanding feature is a 15th century tower embellished with a richly decorated 17th century clock. Little remains of fortification walls begun in the 12th century and replaced in the 18th and 19th by tree-planted *boulevards*. Auxerre's position close to the A6 *autoroute* makes it an ideal overnight stop for British car drivers heading for the south and one hotel providing a constant welcome is the Normandie in the Boulevard Vauban, with a restaurant almost next door. Headache sufferers will note with interest that a long road leading to the Hospital is known as the Rue des Migraines! Statues of St Nicholas are not infrequent by French waterways, for he is the boat peoples' patron: none is finer than the painted stone effigy on the wall of a building in a small square upstream of the Pont Jean Moreau.

Auxerre ought to be as good a place as any to sample Burgundian cuisine and the products of the nearby

St Nicholas, patron of the barge people, in a small square overlooking the Yonne at Auxerre.

Chablis vineyards. Perhaps the best choice is Le Maxime, on the Quai de la Marine, although it is pricey. Specialities include chocolate *escargots* and real ones cooked in wine, *matelotes* (freshwater fish stews), crayfish in wine, and (originally from Joigny) saddle of veal.

45 · Canal du Nivernais

Carte Guide: *Canal du Nivernais*   Also *The Yonne and the Nivernais* by Tony Paris. (Enterprise Guides.)
From a junction with the River Yonne at Auxerre to a junction with the Loire at St-Léger-des-Vignes, providing a connection with the Canal Latéral à la Loire at Decize: 174.1km with 110 locks and 3 tunnels. There is a 3.9km branch with 2 locks between the waterway near Écluse 70, St-Aignan and Vermenton.

One of the loveliest canals in the whole of France, the waterway climbs to a watershed between the Loire and the Yonne, passing through the thickly wooded area of the Morvan. Quite heavily locked and with a central section admitting craft smaller than those of the Freycinet navigations, it is almost unused by commercial traffic but has seen a dramatic increase in pleasure boats since the mid-1970s. There are few large towns but numerous delightful villages, thus sustaining an interest difficult to match elsewhere. North of the summit level at Baye its course lies in the valley of the Yonne, the river serving as a navigation channel for most of the 60km between Auxerre and Clamecy. Having crossed the divide, it descends to the Loire down the valley of the Aron.

While not the quickest of the four routes between Paris and the Saône, the Nivernais is certainly the most charming. The French network features rather few circular routes which can be cruised within a reasonably short time: but that comprising the Yonne, Nivernais, Latéral à la Loire, Briare, Loing and a short part of the Seine can be tackled in an energetic fortnight, requiring about 116 cruising hours. Because my first French cruise followed this course, starting and finishing on the Nivernais in the autumnal mists of 1968, I have a special affection for the area. In the early 1990s, some alarm was being expressed at the low level of maintenance, for much of the waterway has been transferred from national to local control. In 1998, I passed through the allegedly shallowest sections (south of the summit level) with a 1.3m draft, seldom touching the bottom.

Peculiarities of the Nivernais include a tradition of planting the banks with different kinds of fruit and nut trees, the crop once helping to defray running expenses, with produce from seven trees each side of the locks belonging to the keepers. Lock gate and paddle gear is of extraordinary variety: wooden balance beams in one place with iron rods elsewhere; paddles that must be wound up to be closed; it is claimed that the tireless efforts of the *Résistance* during World War II to sabotage equipment and so frustrate transport resulted in this curious mixture. While a number of the lock keepers are elderly (with a preponderance of ladies), younger people have been attracted by the advantages of the agreeable rural life in recent years. Almost without exception they are friendly and helpful, often augmenting their income by selling vegetables, eggs and other local produce. I did once meet an exception: a sour old woman who could barely cope with gates and paddles but vigorously refused any help. Another keeper told us of two narrow-beam cruisers that had recently passed through the lock of this ogress; when one of the pair of bottom gates had been opened, they slipped out into the pound beyond, only to be called back and made to wait until *both* gates were

wound back and they could complete the procedure in strict accordance with the regulations!

Passing through western Burgundy one expects a degree of gastronomy on the Nivernais. Specialities of the Morvan include *cul de veau à la Clameçyoise* (cold chump end of veal with vegetables), *jambon à la Morvandelle* (ham braised in wine and served with cream sauce); *potée Morvandelle* (a thick meat and vegetable soup); *fricassée Morvandelle* (stew of liver, ox tripe and blood), *galettes* (open pastry tarts, both sweet and savoury), and *macarons*.

Brief history The idea of connecting the Loire and Yonne across the Nivernais was first proposed in 1708 with the Canal de Cosne, following the valleys of the Nohain and the Druyes, with a junction at Surgy near Coulanges-sur-Yonne. There was prolonged opposition from the Duc d'Orléans, proprietor of the Canal du Loing, and the scheme eventually foundered. Jean du Gert's early 17th century plan under Louis XIII had envisaged a link up the valley of the Aron from the Loire at Decize to the Beuvron and thence the Yonne at Clemecy. In modified form, this was the chosen line of Mennassier on which construction started in 1785. From the beginning it was considered inferior to the Bourbonnais route via the Briare and Loing, on account of the very winding and shallow navigation of the Yonne, the large number of locks, and the cost and inconvenience of the tunnels and cuttings at La Collancelle summit. The canal was built during an exceptionally long period, not being open throughout until 1842.

A traditional traffic was in pit props to the coalfields of the North, together with timber and firewood to Paris. *Flottage*, a system of floating logs from the Morvan forests down various streams and into the Yonne where they were assembled into giant rafts, had been practised since the 16th century. However, the trade was outlawed in 1881 on account of disruption to other traffic, all timber thereafter being required to be carried aboard barges. The last free-floating logs (as opposed to those formed into rafts) nevertheless were not to leave Clamecy until 1927. 58km of the canal between Sardy and Cercy-la-Tour remained with 30m locks instead of the general Freycinet 38.5m standard, with a consequential decline in through traffic. By 1936 there were only 1,932 barge journeys with a total of 208,000 tonnes. Fewer than 50 craft of all types a year made a passage in the early 1960s and the threat of closure was very real.

Entire credit for saving the Canal du Nivernais goes to waterways enthusiast Pierre-Paul Zivy, an Anglophile who had cruised rivers and canals in England and established the first inland hire cruiser fleet in France on the River Marne. Obtaining assurances that neglected maintenance would be tackled by the authorities, he set up the Saint-Line Cruiser base at Baye in the mid-1960s and campaigned for the threatened section to be transferred to the local Département. There are now many holiday boat firms and hotel barges operating on the waterway and any notion of it being shut is quite unthinkable.

Once you can tear yourself away from the delights of **Auxerre** (see Chapter 44), your association with the River Yonne is by no means finished, as the Canal du Nivernais uses its course for many km. The navigation undergoes its name change above the Pont Paul-Bert and shortly enters the first lock, Écluse 81, Batardeau (K0.4, water point). Rudimentary weirs built of clusters of 'needles' were designed to be dismantled for the passage of timber rafts. **Augy** (K5.5) lies to the left of a lock cut (Écluse 79) and offers baker and grocer. Fishing punts, summer houses by the water and a concrete bridge of lattice construction are features of the small town of **Vaux** (K6.2), a waterside resort beyond Écluse 78, with slipway, grocer and À la Petite Auberge restaurant. On the lock island (Écluse 77, Toussac, K7.9) is another restaurant; **Champs-sur-Yonne**, left bank, offers all shopping.

From the Middle Ages onwards, the wines of Auxerre were widely appreciated. During the 19th century vines were all but wiped out by phylloxera, but have since recovered. The champagne-type Gremant de Bourgogne can be purchased at cellars in **Bailly** (K10.6), beyond Écluse 75, also a good point from which to visit **St-Bris-le-Vineux**, 5km. Here a great network of medieval cellars extends under the town (visits possible); red, white and *rosé* wines are produced. Half-timbered and stone buildings, many centuries old, date from when this was an important fortified market centre. At the lock is a small hydro-electric station, a sculptor's studio and a keeper specializing in domestic stained glass. **Vincelles** (K13.5, shopping and fuel) and **Vincelottes** face each other across the river between Écluses 74 and 73. The latter has a splendid 13th century cellar (now a discotheque) where wine was once loaded onto barges for the journey to Paris. Another delightful Burgundian wine village is **Irancy**, 4.5km NE, surrounded by vines and fruit trees.

Rocky ridges cultivated with vineyards rise to the left of the valley at the approach to **Cravant** (K18.4), with a basin, restaurant and garage. This was the site of

a battle between the victorious Anglo-Burgundian forces and the King of France in 1423. The next lock upriver, Écluse 71, du Maunoir (K19.7), stands by a lovely old house in stone with red tiled roof. 3.9km of navigable branch line leads via 2 locks to **Accolay** (shops, restaurants and hire cruiser base) and **Vermenton**, an ancient settlement on the Roman route between Rome and Boulogne (shopping and restaurants). Wines of the locality are remembered in the old saying with its built-in pun on the town's name: '*Chablis, Cravant, St-Bris, Irancy, Vermenton vous font la trogne rouge et non pas vert menton*', or '... Vermenton may give you a red and boozy face, but they won't leave you with a green chin'.

Almost every village in the green and peaceful river landscape is worth exploration and most have at least basic shops. Some care is required to locate lock cut entrances (which are poorly indicated) and there are several opportunities for taking a wrong turn into un-navigable weir streams. **Mailly-la-Ville** (K28.7) has shops, water point and restaurant.

This is a convenient point from which to travel 8km east to the valley of the River Cure, a fast-flowing stream once used in the *flottage* of timber and now a favourite of canoeists. A system of underground caverns, La Grand Grotte d'Arcy-sur-Cure, contains a subterranean lake and fantastic geological formations. Visits throughout the summer. The canal describes a huge horseshoe bend beneath the heights of **Mailly-**

As a barge thunders out of the Écluse de Ravereau, a pleasure cruiser maintains a position of safety close to the bank.

le-Château (K32.4). Near the bridge in the lower town is a restaurant, while a steep ascent by road or an even steeper climb up a rocky path with steps leads to a terrace by the 19th century *château* with a superb view down to the bosky valley of the Yonne (shopping). Upstream lies the most impressive section of the entire river: the cliffs of **Le Saussois** above guard lock 59b (K36.2). Formed from hard chalk, they reach a height of 50m and are a popular training area for mountaineers. A track provides a less energetic method of reaching the top. Refreshment can be obtained at a riverbank bar/restaurant. **Merry-sur-Yonne** is best approached via the bridge at Écluse 59b.

The first indication of **Châtel-Censoir** (K41.5) is its small country railway station. Elegant stone houses are clustered on a hill by the fascinating 15th century church of St Potentian. Boating services are supplied by a small marina with a full range of shops. By now much of the navigation channel is artificial, although the Yonne continues to act as a feeder for a long dis-

tance. During the early 1980s Écluse 56, **La Place** (K43.9), was notable for its immaculate gardens, featuring flower pots on the gates, doves and a peacock. On my suggesting to the keeper that it was the prettiest of all Nivernais locks, he assumed an air of mock offence and claimed that there was none better in the whole of France! Earlier open reaches come to an end as surroundings become more intimate at **Lucy-sur-Yonne** (K48 small restaurant), notable for the Renaissance Château de Faulin whose rôle is now little more than an unusually splendid farmhouse. At Écluse 55, Lucy, we once spotted a sign '*Défence à ramasser les escargots*' (collecting snails is forbidden); not withstanding, several characters with plastic bags were busily beating the undergrowth with sticks in a search for these prized constituents of Burgundian cuisine,

Le Saussois, where the canal enters the River Yonne in the shadow of towering cliffs.

doubtless destined for the local restaurant. Baker and grocer also in the village.

From **Coulanges-sur-Yonne** (K51.3), where garage and all shops and restaurants are within easy reach of Écluse 52, it is about 20km to **Vézelay**, an historic hilltop town in the Cure valley. Ste Madeleine's great basilica is all that remains of a monastic foundation of the 9th century; allowed to decay after the Revolution, it was restored by Viollet-le-Duc between 1840 and 1859. Coulanges has excellent moorings, well restored canal banks, shower/WC block and a very welcoming bar/restaurant, La Grange Batellerie. Liberty line opened a hire cruiser base in 1991. Nearby are remains of Gallo-Roman baths at **Fouilles des Fontaines Salées**, with traces of even earlier occupation at a Mesolithic camp dating from 10,000–3,000 BC, where 19 wooden dug-out boats have been discovered.

Further chalk cliffs are passed beyond **Surgy** (K53, restaurants and shopping) with guard lock 51, Basseville, leading to a level crossing of the Yonne with a weir on the right. Ahead, craft immediately pass out of the river into Écluse 50, Basseville (K55.6), a manoeuvre where horse-drawn craft required winches in times of flood. At the approach to **Clamecy** (K59.7), Écluse 48 and 47b and a 1.5km length of canal cut are no longer in use, boats instead making a sharp turn to the left and into the Yonne. Although the town basin has recently been enlarged, moorings are sometimes crowded. This is the only substantial town on the waterway between Auxerre and Decize and makes an agreeable mooring with a full range of facilities, including water point by Écluse 47, Les Jeux. Two restaurants particularly recommended for excellent food at reasonable prices are La Boule d'Or and the Hostellerie de la Poste. Narrow hilly streets are lined with ancient buildings. For five centuries the exiled Bishops of Bethlehem lived here. A bronze statue by the river commemorates Jean Rouvet, who founded the local *flottage* industry in 1549. Logs from the Morvan forests were floated down streams and rivers to be assembled into 72m long rafts for transport via the Yonne and Seine to Paris. Clamecy was the leading centre for this activity, which reached a peak in the early 19th century when an annual 70,000 tonnes of timber took about nine days to reach the capital. The traffic continued until 1927, the river being filled with logs from bank to bank and causing serious delays to normal barge movements. The history and lore of *flottage* is fully recorded in several publications on sale in the town and a fascinating collection of associated relics and ephemera is preserved in a museum in the former Hôtel de Bellegard. At the centre of the Pont de Bethléem a stone image of a

Statue of a flotteur *on the bridge at Clamecy.*

flotteur with *picot* (hooked shaft for dragging logs) is another reminder of this activity. Timber trades continue to flourish in the district and charcoal burners will be discovered in woodland glades.

From here onwards, the narrowing River Yonne adopts a subservient rôle as feeder to the canal with several disused locks indicating one-time connections. Upstream of Clamecy, the Canal du Nivernais is bordered by a cliff covered with huge beech trees. **Chevroches** (K64.2), a hilltop village rising above the woods between Écluses 45, Armes and 44, Chantenot, is followed by lines of old fruit trees laden with mistletoe. Beware very variable water levels in the Chevroches pound, where the canal bed suffers from chronic leaks; moored boats may be grounded overnight. This is unfortunate in view of the recently constructed quay which otherwise offers a pretty halt. A selection of drawbridges, operated by the nearest lock keeper, are a characteristic of the next 23km. **Villiers-sur-Yonne** (K69.5), a jumbled village, right, with baker, is a suitable mooring for visiting the hamlet of **Sur-Yonne**, left bank, site of a Merovingian burial place where tools, jewels and arms are on show. The bridge below Écluse 40 (K72) leads into **Brèves**, a pleasant village on the banks of the Yonne. **Tannay**, 2km west of a two-rise lock (Nos. 39/38), is a good shopping centre with an opportunity for sampling local white wines. Beyond the Yonne, left, **Cuzy** (K78.3) is quite convenient for fuel; canalside water taps and the restaurant of the Hôtel du Morvan are found near the old port. Lying beyond the Yonne, **Monceaux-le-Comte** (K83.5) is a little market town with the ruins of a 13th century *château* built by the Comtes de Nevers – shops, restaurant and fuel. Two more bascule bridges are encountered at the farming settlement of **Dirol** (K84.7), a place of vegetable gardens, walnut trees and stone buildings with brown speckled roofs. Restaurant and garage are on the other side of the river from the road bridge below Écluse 34.

Comments on a cruise made in 1979 were provided by eight-year-old Diana, who drew up two columns in her exercise book, headed *Good* and *Bad*. The first contained no entries, while the second listed youthful reasons for anxiety: 'Burst in canal bank; Mummy broke a cup: Weather is awful'. Baker and grocer are located in **Marigny-sur-Yonne**, 300m from Écluse 31, Gravier (K89.5). A drawbridge guards the approach to a wide basin at **Chitry-les-Mines** (K92.3), where silver was discovered several centuries ago. An impressive *château* with four towers was a centre of *Résistance* activity during World War II. Ted Johnson, based here, is an expert in most types of British-built marine engines (especially Leyland). Water point and grocer. At the top of the two-rise Écluses 26/25, Eugny (K94.3) the N77 road leads 3km to **Corbigny**, a once fortified town well known for its cattle market and leading shopping place for this part of the Morvan. A narrow one-way section of canal runs to Écluse 24, Yonne (K96.5) with a hire cruiser base.

Locks sharply increase in number as the canal climbs through delightful woodland to its summit: Nos. 22–1 occur within the space of 6km, an obvious situation for sending at least one person ahead by bicycle to help prepare the flight. The long wooden building with verandah by Écluse 22, Surpaillis (K97.5) housed German refugees in the First World War and French refugees in the Second. Avoid mooring near the noisy and dusty neighbourhood of Écluse 21, Picampoix, dominated by a porphyry rock crushing works; not surprisingly, the lock cottage is untenanted. Features of this length include a lovely 15th century *château* in **Marcilly** (beyond the river from the road bridge between Écluses 22 and 21); grocer in **Sardy-les-Épiry**, left of Écluse 16, with water point; and a water point by Écluse 1, Port-Brûlé. Be sure to inform the keeper here whether you intend to moor on the summit level or wish to pass directly through the tunnels to the first downhill lock at Baye (K108.2), for most of the length is subject to one-way traffic controlled by lights.

Water supplies for the northern descent of the canal towards the Yonne are brought from a reservoir to the east: the **Lac de Pannesière-Chaumard**, with more than 20km of feeder channel and an impressisve aqueduct over the Yonne at **Montreuillon**. It is uncertain if the authorities would approve, but I know of one enthusiast who came downstream on the *rigole* in a dinghy only a little narrower than the channel at a speed of between 2 and 6kph. The miniature waterway is equipped with tunnels and many small aqueducts

and passes through exciting rocky terrain. The canal proper passes through three tunnels near the village of **La Collancelle**: des Breuilles (212m), de Mouas (268m) and La Collancelle (758m). The approaches are through deep, stone-lined cuttings running with waterfalls. At certain points the passage is so narrow and tortuous that barges approaching the maximum dimensions of the locks can get through only with difficulty. At the far end you enter a broad pool with a hire cruiser base, right, providing slipway, fuel, water and electricity at a basin. Ahead, the Étang de **Baye**, covering 100 hectares, is connected with the canal via a guard lock. A channel on the east side is available to cruisers wishing to visit a yacht club, although most of the lake is preserved for sailing and fishing. Northwards, the Étang de Vaux (198 hectares), brings additional supplies to the southern part of the navigation. Attractive moorings are found all along a stone dyke that divides the Baye lake from the canal. Restaurant and water point close to Écluse 1, Baye, start of the descent towards the Loire.

One of the last remaining 'short' wooden motor barges able to navigate the central part of the canal is *Aster*; working as a local authority passenger vessel, she is likely to be encountered near here. **Chavance** (K114.7) features a three-rise staircase (Écluses 4/5/6), a basin and then a two-rise (Écluses 7/8). It is customary to fill the chambers without closing the intermediate pairs of gates, causing impressive turbulence. The same remarks apply to another two-rise at **Marré**, Écluses 9/10 (K116). Once, when locking through here, I helped the keeper remove the bloated corpse of a large fish from the lock chamber. 'Can you eat that fish, monsieur?' I asked him. Horror-struck, he replied that the fish had been dead for weeks! 'Non, monsieur', I explained. 'Can you eat that variety of fish?' He gave me a withering look and then added gravely: 'In France, we eat *all* fish!' On another occasion, a friend found himself in identical circumstances. Indicating a rotting fish (and purely in the interest of polite conversation), he observed to the keeper: '*La pollution, monsieur?*' '*Non, monsieur*', came the answer. '*C'est un poisson!*'

Several locks intervene before **Châtillon-en-Bazois** (K123), an atmospheric little town (shops, restaurants) where the best moorings are to the towpath opposite the towers of a *château*, illuminated by night. Vestiges of ancient stonework suggest that the canal occupies the site of its moat. Shopping, while comprehensive, is of rather poor quality. Total lack of visibility at a right-angled turn by the bridge (garage nearby) makes use of a horn imperative. Beyond, there is water on the quay, right, and then a pair of locks,

Écluses 14 and 15, at each end of a long basin. In closely following the course of the River Aron the canal winds very considerably for the next 15km. Take care to keep close to the towpath and so avoid shallows in a river section above guard lock, 16 Cœuillon (K125). A bridge in the middle of the pound between Écluse 18, Meulot and Écluse 19, Villard (*Relais de Plaisance*) provides access to **Biches** (K132.2) – restaurant, baker, grocer and garage. **Brienne** (K135.8), with restaurant, lies midway between Écluse 20, Brienne and Écluse 21, Fleury, the latter lock being a base for the Flot-Home cruiser fleet.

After Écluse 24, Anizy the Aron is entered once more. Shortly before guard lock 25 in **Panneçot** (K147.5), turn left by a small island for a *port de plaisance* with facilities by a camping site. Water is also supplied by the lock. This makes a really tranquil overnight halt, but facilities consist of nothing more than a village bar. A full range of shops will be found in **Moulins-Engilbert**, 5km NE where there are remains of a *château* built by the Comtes de Nevers. An excursion well worth undertaking is to travel 4km NE, either from the Pont des Hâtes de Scia (K148.1) or Écluse 27, Moulin d'Isenay (K150.5). You will arrive in the little town of **Vandenesse** (basic shopping) and discover a really huge *château* with many towers dating from 1475. The next point of interest is **Cercy-la-Tour** (K158.2), a charming town rising above a length of navigable river on which a 'beach' has been established. The shopping is good, and a large church square provides a view down to the navigation. Little remains of one-time fortifications, but it is said that an underground passage climbs from the river to the Café de la Tour, (now closed) built as a hotel in 1786 and now mostly divided into apartments. Here we were once served coffee in cups decorated with lurid

Passing a bascule bridge near Chitry-les-Mines.

fruit designs, sufficiently unusual to demand comment. 'We have had them these last 30 years', replied Madame, adding with barely a hint of menace: 'And not a single one has ever been broken!' A white statue of the Madonna, considerably bigger than lifesize, is lit up by night. The Rivers Alène and Canne add their waters to that of the Aron. Moorings are above the lock, or below, on a pair of pontoons. Boat sales, moorings, repairs and chandlery. Try the charming Hôtel Val d'Aron for sophisticated cuisine and swimming pool. Cercy provides the best railway service on this part of the waterway, with connections to Nevers, Paris and Dijon. The town also hosts regular and spectacular fishing competitions where boaters may not be welcomed other than with flying maggots and abuse!

Several interesting features are passed as the canal nears its end: a pair of old towers on the towpath at **Le Chantelier** (K163.6); the village of **Verneuil** (restaurant, garage, 12th century Romanesque church with wall paintings and 15th century château) lies 2km NW of a bridge at K164.2; and a small aqueduct over the River Andarge above Écluse 32, de Roche (K165.9). **Champvert** (K170.5), beyond Écluse 33, perfectly epitomises the idyllic scenery in this agreeable valley. It has a church with a twisted spire, several shops and a garage. Le Port de la Copine (K171.1), right bank, now serves as a cruiser yard with facilities. Approaching the outskirts of **St-Léger-des-Vignes** a useful stop can be made below Écluse 34, Vauzelles (K172.2) to visit garage or supermarket on the left bank. Dry dock near Écluse 35. The town of St-Léger (K174) extends along the right bank above a junction with the navigable River Loire. Good shops, fuel and water are conveniently obtained. Supermarket between the final two locks. Due north, the curiously named town of **La Machine** (suggesting all kinds of possibilities) is disappointingly nothing more exciting than a coal mining district. For details of the Loire passage past **Decize** (all facilities) and into the Canal Latéral à la Loire, see Chapter 41.

46 · Canal de Bourgogne

Carte Guide: *Canal de Bourgogne* or *Bourgogne Voies Navigables Tome 1*. Also *The Canal de Bourgogne* by Tony Paris (Enterprise Guides.)
From Laroche Migennes, junction with the River Yonne, to St-Jean-de-Losne, junction with the River

A cutting in the one-way section at the three tunnels of La Collancelle.

Saône: 242km with 190 locks. A 3,350m summit level tunnel at Pouilly-en-Auxois operates to a one-way timetable.

Judging by the number of hire cruisers and hotel boats using this route, it is probably among the three most popular pleasure boating waterways in France; others are the Canal du Nivernais and the Canal du Midi. Of four available ways of navigating between Paris and the Mediterranean, it is the shortest, but rather more heavily locked than the Bourbonnais route via the Canal de Briare; generally, the latter series of canals will provide

Stone distance marker by a lock on the Canal du Nivernais.

a quicker journey if needed. But for scenery, historical interest, gastronomy and all that is best in French waterway cruising, the Bourgogne is difficult to better. The 50km in the Ouche valley from the summit to Dijon is quite outstanding.

Running SE from the Yonne, it follows the windings of the River Armançon up to the Pouilly-en-Auxois summit level, flanked by the Langres Plateau to the east and the Morvan Regional Park to the SW. Having crossed the watershed, the navigation seeks out the valley of the River Ouche (adding a considerable distance in the process) and beyond Dijon carves out a straight and less interesting course towards the Saône.

At the heartland of France, one immediately obvious feature is the excellence of Burgundian food and wine. There are numerous regional specialities, ranging from delicious varieties of Dijon mustard, blended with herbs and spices, to *jambon persillé* (cold ham in a white wine jelly, pressed with parsley); fungus in profusion, such as *girolle* (chanterelle), *mousseron* (the St-George's mushroom) and *cèpe* (boletus); many types of cheese, made from both cow and goat milk; Dijon gingerbread and *cassis* liqueur; and classic dishes like *boeuf bourguignon* (beef in red wine with mushrooms and onions). Nowhere are *escargots* hunted and devoured with greater fervour and it is a common sight to encounter drab figures beating the undergrowth with sticks after a rainfall. And in Burgundy it is scarcely necessary to draw attention to the range of local wines.

Almost all locks are manually worked by resident keepers with the exception of a handful on the Saône side of the descent from the summit at Pouilly. These are operated by pleasure craft crews who are given instructions (in French or English) at the preceding locks. Most paddle gear is efficient; one variety of 'ground' sluice has indicator dials marked 'O' and 'F' (*ouvert* or *fermé*). The normal gate-opening mechanism is an iron scissor-like device – a cranked version of the balance beams widespread on English canals. The waterway is closed to all pleasure craft from 11 November – 27 March; also on various public holidays when navigation is, however, possible on payment of a special locking fee. Craft longer than 20m must be accompanied at the various DIY locks. Detailed explanations and opening times appear in the *Carte Guide*.

Brief history First contemplated in the early 16th century under François I, and seriously considered by the Midi's celebrated engineer Riquet in 1676, the Canal de Bourgogne was not eventually started until 1775, at almost exactly the same time as the Canal du Centre and the Canal du Nivernais. Three gangs totalling 600

Large ground paddles and an unusual scissor-like device to operate gates are characteristic of the Bourgogne's locks.

navvies were put to work on the northern section between Laroche and Tonnerre. Eight years later the Burgundy States was granted permission to commence the Dijon-Saône section: progress was slow, greatly hampered by the Revolution and its accompanying turmoil. It is claimed that English prisoners of the Napoléonic Wars were used in the construction of the great Pouilly Tunnel: sealed inside the workings, food was lowered to them via shafts with the promise of release when the task was completed. Few are said to have survived and the corpses of many were buried behind the stone lining. By 1808 the first barges reached Dijon from the Saône. Little more was achieved until 1822 when a scheme to attract private capital was launched with the aim of connecting the finished portions. Late in 1832 a barge left Paris, navigated the tunnel and arrived in Dijon on January 3, 1833: the canal was finally an operational through route. Further necessary work involved construction of five reservoirs near the summit, ensuring adequate water through the driest of summers.

Railway competition now presented a threat, with much of the route duplicated by a new line running between Paris and Lyon in 1851. Waterborne traffic immediately declined. Something of the atmosphere of these times is contained in two published cruising accounts written by Englishmen travelling through the Canal de Bourgogne by rowing boat in 1854. Edmund Harvey in *Our Cruise in the 'Undine'* comments: 'In towing barges, &c., along the canal, horses are seldom, if ever, used. The method generally adopted is this: when (as is frequently the case) they are one family travelling with the barge, the mother on one side of the canal and son on the other, with a rope each, haul the barge along, necessarily at a very slow pace (say a mile and a half in the hour), while the father stays on board, smokes his pipe, and steers the barge.' And near Tonnerre: 'We here learnt that the Emperor was to pass along this canal in a few days, and the good people supposed that we were the engineers appointed to conduct his small steamer for him. Some opined that ours was the boat in which he was to travel; while others said it was only the convoy.' Beginning his 1854 French voyage in Dijon, Robert Mansfield (*The Log of the 'Water Lily'*) had to contend with a raging cholera epidemic in Burgundy: 'The three principal directions given by the French physicians in the printed notices about the cholera were, that everybody should avoid fruit, and never expose himself to night air, and check the first début of colic: consequently we ate all the ripe fruit we could get, always slept with our windows open, and therefore never had occasion to observe the third rule.'

Mechanical bank haulage was introduced to the Bourgogne in 1873, such a practice then being quite novel in France. It lasted until 1968 on the reaches nearest to Saône where dumb craft regularly carried sand and gravel to Dijon. Horse-drawn traffic continued to navigate the whole waterway until well after World War II, but all long-distance boats are now *automoteurs*. Such freight movements are restricted to each end of the canal only, with no regular traffic passing over the summit. Gradual decline in commercial carrying very nearly resulted in parts of the canal being converted into roadways near Dijon during the 1960s. Since that time, undreamed-of changes have taken place and the Canal de Bourgogne is firmly established as one of the country's leading pleasure cruising routes.

The Canal de Bourgogne begins inauspiciously, leaving the River Yonne at the twin towns of **Laroche** and **Migennes**, a bustling railway junction with few attractions other than the broad basin of the waterway, entered via an unusually deep lock with large spoked iron wheels to open its gates. Water and bankside diesel fuel are on hand, together with drydock and full range of shops and eating places. Locks are more or less constant throughout the route, increasing in frequency on each side of the summit. After the second lock, Écluse 113 (K1.7), the canal runs quite straight to **Brienon** (K9.2), a slightly industrialized small town with useful shops and a fine 18th century *lavoir* (washhouse) with oval basin. In the pound below Écluse 110 a railway bridge carries the magnificent TGV.

Excellent moorings with water point will be found in the basin following Écluse 108 (K18.6), where the delightful River Armançon flows under an aqueduct at

St-Florentin with prospects of a lively weir far below the heights of the town, which is topped by an outstanding 14–17th century church with superb 16th century stained glass. Once heavily fortified, St-Florentin contains a wealth of ancient stone buildings and is a popular tourist magnet with quality shopping and restaurants. A camping site enjoys a riverside situation beyond the basin with safe swimming for children just two minutes from the canal. Well known cheeses, St-Florentin and Soumaintrain, are made locally, and a bloodless bullfight is staged each year on July 1.

The next place of note is the double lock of **Germigny** (bottom chamber alone in use), Nos. 106/7 (K21.8) with baker, grocer, butcher and restaurant. **Percey** (K27.5) midway between Écluses 104 and 103 provides baker, grocer, restaurant and garage. This area provides some classic Burgundian countryside. Then comes **Flogny**, Écluse 100 (K30.9), with comprehensive shopping, water supplies and garage. Restaurant and garage are close by a bridge at **Tronchoy** (K37.9), a collection of jumbled waterside buildings in stone, with another restaurant and butcher reached from the next lock, Écluse 98, **Cheney** (K39.1). A further pleasant village with grocer, baker and restaurant is **Dannemoine** by Écluse 97 (K40.3), where there is a water point.

We shortly arrive in the sizeable town of **Tonnerre** (K44.2) whose basin between Écluses 96 and 95 is home to the Heron Cruisers hire fleet. Boat services include water, gas and diesel. Situated where the Armançon divides into several channels, Tonnerre is the Roman Tornodorum and 2,000 years ago its chief source of drinking water came from the Fosse Dionne (Divine ditch), now a pool containing greenish-blue spring water. The huddled collection of ancient houses is absolutely typical of Burgundy, each capped by a rusty-red roof of tiles and many covered in thin layers of stone, *laves* a speciality of the district. Notre-Dame des Fontenilles is a hospital founded in 1293 by Marguerite de Bourgogne, sister-in-law of St Louis. The great 80m ward with carved wooden ceiling and the chapel containing a 15th century *pieta* are open to the public (June 1–Sept 30, 10.00–11.30h and 14.00–17.30, closed Tues). One peculiar – indeed notorious – son of Tonnerre is still remembered: Charles Geneviève Louis Auguste César Andrée Timothée Déon de Beaumont (1728–1810) who appears to have spent much of his life alternating between male and female – and with a brilliant success. Among his exploits was a journey to Russia as a lady secret agent, followed by a period in London as male secretary to the French Ambassador. He was created

Chevalier d'Eon by Marie Antoinette, spent part of his declining years in England and died near Tonnerre, well known as a woman of huge appetite. D'Eon had been a source of curiosity for much of his life and it was only after his corpse was examined that he was conclusively declared a man.

The long ascent continues up the Armançon valley to **Tanlay** (K52.2) between Écluses 90 and 81. Surroundings are particularly fine, with rolling hills, white Charollais cattle and poplars festooned with mistletoe. Of all Burgundian *châteaux*, that at Tanlay is generally acknowledged as the finest. There are in fact two buildings, the *petit* and the *grand*, the larger approached via a bridge over a moat. Mainly 16th century, it has remained in the ownership of one family since 1704 and can be visited (Palm Sunday to Nov 2,

9.15–11.30h and 14.15–17.15, closed Tues). Shops, restaurants, water point and garage all close to the basin. The canal continues to wind along the course of the Armançon with plenty of shore facilities: grocer and baker at **St-Vinnemer** (K56.4) by Écluse 88; restaurant and grocer in **Argentenay**, Écluse 87 (K59.6) and **Ancy- le-Libre**, Écluse 86 (K61.4); all services, water, restaurant and garage near Écluse 85, **Lézinnes** (K63.3); and baker, grocer, restaurant and butcher in **Argenteuil-sur-Armançon**, between Écluses 82 (K69.7) and 81. Écluse 84, Batilley, was converted to automatic working in 1984. Fifteen more are planned, including the series of locks at Marigny (K125).

Remnants of fortifications are evident among the buildings that cluster around St-Florentin's church.

A useful halt can be made by the bridge connecting **Cusy** with **Ancy-le-Franc** (K73.7) shortly before Écluse 80, with water point, shopping and restaurants. Ancy has a magnificent Renaissance *château* – a great square structure in grey stone with massive towers and a suitably grand front door, painted in pink. Interior decoration is rich beyond description. Notables who stayed there include Henry IV, Louis XIII, Louis XIV and Mme de Sévigné. Public opening times: Easter–All Saints' Day, 10.00–12.00h and 14.00–18.00h. Écluse 79, **Chassignelles** (K75.4), provides basic shopping and a restaurant in the hilly street of grey stone with a full range of facilities in the pleasant town of **Ravières** (K82.6), midway between Écluses 76 and 75. An age-old conflict between spiritual and bodily needs is summed up in a sign of 1701 in the church, stating that 'a solemn Mass with Benediction is held each evening for three days before Ash Wednesday in atonement for the excesses of the pre-Lenten Carnival'. Water may be taken on at Écluse 73, **Cry** (K87.2), with grocer and restaurant in the nearby village of ancient stone houses. Alternatively, continue to the second bridge after Écluse 71, **Aisy** (K92.4), to find fuel, grocer, butcher, baker and restaurant. Scenery continues to be extremely pleasant. Throughout the 1980s, an industrial site, **La Grande Forge** (K94.5), has been undergoing restoration. Much remains of the elegant 18th century ironworks founded by Buffon (see below). Open summer afternoons (not Tues). Small restaurants occur frequently: at **Buffon** (K95.5); **St-Remy** and **Blaisy** (K98.7) before Écluse 67; and by Écluse 66, Fontenay (K100.6).

Montbard (K102.2) is a small industrial town whose prosperity was due to the Comte de Buffon (1707–88), a leading 18th century ironmaster. He established himself on the site of a fortress built by the Dukes of Bourgogne (only two towers now remain) and there compiled his important *Histoire Naturelle*, published volume by volume during a 40-year period. His park and workroom are on public view. Canal travellers may perhaps show equal interest in the large covered market whence galley provender can be carried back to the boat. Mechanical repairs, water and other services are available at a hire cruiser base in the town basin, with further water points at Écluses 64, Montbard, 61, **Courcelles** (K108.2), and 57, **Granges** (K112.8). Useful quay mooring (water) 100m before the lock.

Now follows a feature of the Canal de Bourgogne which is regarded with dread by most coast-bound yachtsmen, and genuine interest (or even enjoyment) by those travelling the waterway for its own sake: a chain of no fewer than 56 locks in the 30km that remain to the Pouilly summit. Arranged in two groups with a 10km break, their negotiation tends to take precedence over every other activity. It pays here to have at least one member of the crew working ahead by bicycle. A good place to lie for the night in contemplation of the next day's task would be **Venarey-les-Laumes** (K115.6), between Écluses 56 and 55. Baker, butcher, grocer, water point and garage are all moderately close. Good, deep, mooring on a quay with bollards (telephone). Supermarket, 1km, near Les Laumes station. Should you wish to further postpone the fateful time when the real work begins, halt near the bridge (K116.3) in the pound Écluses 55/54 and travel 4km east to **Alise-Sainte-Reine**, site of the fortress of Alesia where Caesar besieged Vercingetorix in 52 BC and Gaul finally fell to the Roman Empire. During the 1860s, excavations discovered many relics now in two museums. The hillside is crowned by a massive bronze statue of the Gallic hero, visible from a long distance.

And so, eventually, to the locks. They are in a succession of flights: Mussey (53, 52); Pouillenay (51–37); Chassey (36–31); Marigny (30–18) and Charigny (17, 16). Then follow three widely spaced from Braux to Pont-Royal with a 10km level pound. A final 12 chambers go to the watershed. Set in magnificent gently rolling cornfields, amid terrain well known to all A6 *autoroute* travellers, they offer a possibility of overnight stranding far from village amenities. There are water points at Écluses 48/9, 45 and 27. If time allows, moor up in **Pouillenay**, Écluse 46 (K119.6, basic shopping, restaurant, garage and water), and take a taxi 10km west to **Semur-en-Auxois**, a perfect example of a small medieval Burgundian city. Set in a hollow of the Armançon valley, four circular 14th century towers soar from a mound of pink granite and one is slightly fearful of the structural cracks that run from top to bottom. The Tour de l'Orle d'Or houses a small museum, quite fascinating for its amateur dreadfulness. Elsewhere are ancient stone gateways, precipitous views onto riverside vegetable gardens and restrained tourist development. Notre-Dame de Semur is probably the most beautiful Gothic church in Burgundy.

Back on the canal, we plunge into the thick of the locks. By Marigny-le-Cahouet at Écluse 26 (K125.8), another pause may be called for. Facilities extend no further than bread, water and groceries. Within walking distance, La Ferme de la Cure is a highly recommended restaurant where clients share the same large table. The building has been owned by one family since the 16th century. Cost of dinner when I visited was reasonable. A plaque at Écluse 23 records it as the birthplace of Bernard Roy, who overcame his humble origins to become Governor General of Tunisia. The 13 locks in the Marigny flight are to be converted to automatic operation. A restaurant can be reached in **Villeneuve-sous-Charigny**, west of Écluse 16 K129.9). By this point, the pace is more relaxed and some form of celebration may be required. Grandly-named **Pont-Royal** just before Écluse 13 (K137.5) has a friendly bar and water point. The broad quayside no longer witnesses any freight barges and it seems as if a planned greatness has quite passed the village by. 1,130m of narrow cutting at **Creusot** is followed by a bridge providing access to **St-Thibault** (K140), whose 13th century church was erected to shelter the saint's remains. Having learned of the richly decorated Gothic doorway and columbarium suspended over the high altar, worked by a series of chains and pulleys for displaying the Blessed Sacrament, I persuaded half the ship's crew to venture across the dew-laden meadows to attend Mass one August Sunday morning. From previous close association with such matters, I calculated that a service would begin at 8.00h. To our consternation, the great building was locked; as we retired to the nearby *boulangerie* for

During the long climb to the Pouilly-en-Auxois summit, the boater is rewarded by wide views over the well wooded Burgundian countryside.

freshly-baked breakfast *croissants*, we learned that M. le Curé was absent. 'Why, even the good Lord must take his summer holiday', exclaimed Madame. Thus thwarted, we returned crestfallen to the boat, where the heathen members of the family were still in bed. As in other French villages, the grocer and restaurant of St-Thibault are similarly threatened by August closure during the *congé annuel*.

The *autoroute* swings close to the canal at Écluse 12, **Gissey** (K147.9), a steady roar of traffic making the next 7km slightly disagreeable. Doubtless, when the waterway was dug close to a lovely old fortified *château-ferme* on the right bank at **Éguilly**, the intrusion was considered barely tolerable. Now it is subjected also to the thunder of motorway wheels and for some years after 1973 it stood forlorn and deserted. An astonishing plan to create a medieval service station proved abortive and in 1983 it was bought by Roger and Françoise Aubry who continue with the huge task of restoration virtually singlehanded. On request, an English-speaking tour can be arranged; it is suggested that visitors make a suitably generous donation towards the cost of works which have received no form of Government grant. The Château is undoubtedly one of the canal's highlights, not least for its admirable recent recovery. Once through the remaining locks we

arrive in a sizeable basin, the port of **Pouilly-en-Auxois** (K154.7). Situated a little outside town, this area has experienced great changes in the last decade for it has been developed as a thriving boat harbour with hire fleet, slipway, dry dock, electricity points, water, showers and restaurant. Navig France operates hire cruisers from a pretty little building newly designed in the 'traditional rustic' style often associated with French leisure planning. Hotel barges may well be moored up (there are possibly more on the Bourgogne than any other canal). When the harvest is in full swing, an endless procession of grain lorries heads for the Co-operative silos on the right bank. Pouilly is a large and flourishing town, centre of a mainly agricultural region but more and more catering for tourism. In 1974 I enjoyed a truly breathtaking exercise in four-star gastronomy at one of its restaurants: the highlight was a small bird presented in a fragile 'nest' woven from deep-fried potato. But on returning the following year with suitably prepared appetite, we found the food and service to be extremely mediocre – hence no recommendation by name! There are several restaurants for the canal traveller to make his own selection. Pouilly's best known feature is, of course, the 3,350m tunnel. Headroom is somewhat less than at most other French tunnels: 3.1m in the centre, reducing to 2.2m at the sides. If in doubt, it is safer to obtain precise details in advance. Long ago, the problem of empty *péniches* being unable to pass beneath the vault was solved by a simple but elegant method. A rudimentary vessel known as the *bac* or ferry is fitted with sluices like lock paddles: the *péniche* is floated on board and by releasing some of the water, a 0.6m reduction in height is achieved. This service is also available to pleasure boats, provided they are moderately flat-bottomed and draw no more than 0.8m; application should be made to Écluse 1, Pouilly, at least 24 hours before; the 1983 charge was 300F. Commercial craft, now a great rarity, are drawn through by electric chain tug, taking power from a perilously close overhead live wire. Pleasure boats may proceed under their own power when they have obtained authority from the nearest lock keeper. The former towing charge (whether the tug was required or not) has been abolished for cruisers.

Tunnel safely tackled, one can now relish the pleasure of one of the loveliest portions of navigable waterway in all France. From here down the course of the Vandenesse and later the valley of the Ouche to Dijon is a succession of delights. After emerging from the stone-lined tunnel cutting, the canal arrives at an expansive basin in the hamlet of **La Lochère** (K160.1). The only facility in this intensely rural place is a drydock, although a restaurant, butcher and grocer are to be found in **Créancey** 2km north. Closely spaced locks lower the canal from the summit, and in 1983 a new arrangement whereby pleasure craft up to 20m long were expected to work themselves through Nos 1–13 was introduced. Instructions in French or English are issued on arrival. Boats over 20m are accompanied by a mobile keeper. Feeders from several reservoirs bring water supplies to the navigable channel in this area.

Another mooring basin appears after Écluse 8, **Vandenesse-en-Auxois** (K163.1), a useful halt with garage, grocer and restaurant. Ahead on the left is the first view of the most romantic and fascinating village on the entire canal: **Châteauneuf**, occupying a prominent hilltop a little under 2km east of a bridge in the middle of the pound between Écluses 10 (K163.9) and 11, **La Rèpe**. Like a miniature version of Carcassonne on the Canal du Midi, but devoid of both commercialism and hoards of tourists, Châteauneuf is an amazingly intact and original 12th century survival comprising a gaunt turreted castle begun by Guy de Chaudenay and further extended and fortified during the following 300 years. Now belonging to the State, it is open throughout the year (10.00–12.00h and 14.00–18.00; 17.00h Oct–March inclusive; closed on Tues and main public holidays). Views from the heights, across the glinting ribbon of the Canal de Bourgogne and to the far-off woodlands of the Morvan, are among the finest in Burgundy. *Château* apart, the village within its encirling walls is fascinating, containing a variety of elegant houses built for rich Dijon merchants in the 14–17th centuries. Except for an antique shop, a ceramic craftsman and a goat cheese specialist, there is no commercialism; indeed, in 1990 a number of magnificent stone buildings were for sale and cattle still occupied ancient barns with massive roof timbers. A visit is further enhanced by a meal at the Hostellerie du Château in the shadow of the feudal castle. I enjoyed a truly gastronomic experience when I dined there, my chosen meal including a *vol-au-vent* filled with salmon and frogs' legs; slices of duck in *cassis* with blackcurrants and lightly cooked fresh vegetables; peaches in white wine; and a selection of prime local cheeses. With coffee and wine the charge was around 200F. Presentation of the food and the atmosphere of the establishment (which is also a small hotel) made this perhaps the best value I have ever encountered in France. Although an uphill walk from the waterway, lunch or dinner in Châteauneuf would be a highlight of any cruise (tel. (80) 49.22.00).

Cruising southwards down the canal, repeated views of the *château* appear beyond the towpath poplars, although the A6 *autoroute* is uncomfortably close from

Écluse 12, Revin (K165.1), to Pont-d'Ouche (K173.1): if possible, overnight mooring is best avoided in this reach, well known to motorists roaring along between Paris and Lyon. Each change in level is punctuated by delightful little lock houses whose continued working existence was so recently threatened by closure of the waterway. **Crugey** at Écluse 16 (K169.2) has a cheap fixed-price restaurant, and shortly facilities begin to proliferate as we approach the very beautiful section within easy driving distance of Dijon. Écluse 17, quarry and very sharp bend; Écluse 18, thickly wooded with high cliffs on the right. In keeping close company with the River Ouche the navigation, having run SE since Pouilly, swings sharply to the NE at **Pont-d'Ouche** (K172.6) between Écluses 19 and 20. Here there is a basin and hire cruiser centre, water point, garage and English-run restaurant, with a low two-arched aqueduct. The A6 sweeps across the valley on a great concrete viaduct. Progress is being made to restore an extremely early narrow-gauge railway between Pont-d'Ouche and **Bligny-sur-Ouche**, 9km south. Conceived as a connection from Épinac to the canal, it was opened in 1837 with oxen and horses pulling trucks on level sections, stationary engines being used for the inclines. Gradually replaced by larger railways and road traffic, portions remained in use for freight and Sunday fishermen until total closure in 1968. Ten years later, 3km was reopened from Bligny to **Oucherotte**, with further rehabilitation planned as time and funds permit. Steam-hauled passenger trains operate May 1–Oct 1, Sat and Sun with

Clog-wearing canal boatman with his donkey team. Early 20th century.

diesel runs on weekdays. One locomotive, *La Burgonde*, dates from 1910 and saw service during World War I.

There now follow a succession of riverside villages scattered along the steep-sided valley, each with a backdrop of dense forest. **Veuvey-sur-Ouche** (K175.7) midway between Écluses 22 and 23 (restaurant), with camping site on the canal banks and an attractive pointed spire church. **La Forge**, Écluse 25 (K179.1) comes next (grocer, baker) with **La Bussière-sur-Ouche** on the opposite, left, side below Écluse 26 (K179.6, grocer). Visits can be made every day except Tues, 14.30–18.30h, to a restored 13th century Cistercian abbey. **St-Victor-sur-Ouche**, after Écluse 29 (K182.5), consists of a jumble of well restored stone cottages by a disused railway station with café/restaurant. The special character of this length of canal owes much to rows of poplars planted on each bank, to the fine Burgundian architecture and to the hillyness of the terrain. Most canal bridges lead to much older crossings of the Ouche as in **Gissey-sur-Ouche** (K186.5), after Écluse 32 (restaurants and grocer and day boats for hire). Descending rapidly down the narrow valley, we shortly arrive at **Ste-Marie-sur-Ouche**, Écluse 36 (K190.5), a picture postcard village set around an ancient stone bridge (baker). One of the best seasons for a cruise through this Dijonnaise countryside is in autumn, when the trees become a blaze of red and yellow. Now never far from the busy N5 Montbard–Dijon highway, the canal nevertheless retains a tranquil identity of its own with restaurants, baker and garage in **Pont de Pany**, Écluse 38 (K193.5); all basic shops, restaurant and garage are to be found at **Fleurey-sur-Ouche** (K196.7) between Écluses 41 and 42.

Shopping and eating ashore is similarly possible in **Velars-sur-Ouche**, Écluse 45 (K201.7). 6km south, the 600m high **Mont Afrique** provides outstanding views to nearby Dijon and the plains of the Sâone far beyond: in the clearest weather it is sometimes possible to see Mont Blanc. A series of lock gardens and cottages is among the most pleasing to be found anywhere, but gradually real countryside changes to suburbs as Dijon approaches. Note the little tourist railway on the canal's left bank from Écluses 46–48. **Plombières-les-Dijon** not far from Écluse 50 (K207) is a good halt for all shops, garage and restaurant. Children might enjoy an expedition to the splendid leisure lake extending from Écluse 51 to 52. Best access from the canal is to walk through a small railway arch. Formed by damming the Ouche, it takes on the appearance of a Mediterranean beach during hot summer days, activities including swimming, windsurfing and dinghy sailing.

Locks 52–54 lead to the centre of **Dijon** (K212.2) where a landscaped basin is reserved for pleasure craft (water, electricity and mechanic). This facility dates only from the early 1980s and it is an ideal mooring within 1,200m of the main shopping area. Note the obelisk marking completion of the waterway in 1833. For a time in the 14–15th centuries Dijon was capital of Burgundy, which then extended as far north as Flanders. Parliament building and Ducal Palace, the 13th century cathedral of St Bénigne, museums devoted to fine art, sculpture and Burgundian life and folklore: the choice of attractions is numerous. Some roofs are covered with riotous patterns of coloured glazed tiles, a widespread form of decoration in this part of France. No stay would be complete without a visit to an old established mustard merchant, whose shop is filled with antique *faïence* jars. Replicas can be bought containing many varieties of the condiment. The recipe for the most popular type dates from the 4th century AD. 300 quarts was consumed during a feast laid on by the Duke of Burgundy for Philip de Valois in 1336. Although a modern and expanding city, Dijon retains much from its brilliant past and several pleasant hours could be spent in exploring the maze of narrow streets around the Quartier Ancien.

Leaving the city on its southern side, there is every opportunity to appreciate Dijon's commercial and industrial expansion in the latter 20th century. Gone are the earlier windings of the Ouche valley: the waterway strikes out across a great plain in an utterly straight line for the remaining 30km to the Sâone. It is not exciting cruising. However, freight traffic, now quite absent from most of the Bourgogne, becomes brisk onwards from Dijon's commercial port between Écluse 56, Colombières (K214.9) and Écluse 57, Romelet. A further attribute is the succession of charming lock houses, little stone bungalows each with an ornate circular attic window overlooking the chamber. After **Longvic** (K216.7, comprehensive shopping) and its banks of airport lights, we enter open country once more. Villages within easy reach are mostly farming settlements whose buildings are grouped tightly together for protection from marauders of long ago. **Thorey-en-Plaine**, Écluse 67 (K226.3), has a restaurant, while **Longecourt-en-Plaine**, Écluse 69 (K228.2), offers most shops in addition and a beautiful *château* almost on the canal bank.

Écluse 71, **Aiserey** (K231.8), is notable for a big sugar processing works. In the town 1km west will be found good shopping. Alternatively, travel a similar distance east to **Echigey** for a village restaurant. **Brazey-en-Plaine**, Écluse 74 (K236.9), provides all shops including a supermarket 300m west of the bridge after the lock. Those in search of an ecclesiastical excursion can take a taxi for 12km to the **Abbey de Citeaux**, established in 1098 as the first Cistercian house. Only fragmented ruins remain of the original buildings, but members of St Bernard's order set up a new community here in the 19th century. 14km west of Citeaux will be found **Nuits-St-Georges** at the centre of the world-famous Burgundian vineyards.

The Canal de Bourgogne finally joins the Sâone at **St-Jean-de-Losne** (K242), a town devoted to inland waterway traffic, commercial and pleasure. Every possible boating need is supplied from drydock to diesel pump, chandlery to yards that will convert a *péniche* (see Chapter 47). The locals are now quite used to the sight of holiday cruisers, but it was a very different story when Edmund Harvey and his companions arrived there as recounted in *Our Cruise in the 'Undine'* (1854). As they carried their rowing boat to the courtyard of the Hotel du Commerce for the night, it was with difficulty that they prevented enthusiastic inhabitants from trampling it underfoot! Half the town began to assemble at 3.00 a.m. in readiness for their planned departure up the Sâone some six hours later, and the Englishmen took delight in encouraging all manner of exaggerated rumours about the purpose of their voyage.

47 · River Saône

Carte Guide: *Saône*

From a junction with the Canal de l'Est (Branche Sud) at Corre, to Lyon, junction with the River Rhône: 363km and 24 locks and 2 tunnels. Additional junctions are made with the Canal de la Marne à la Saône at Heuilley; the Canal du Rhône au Rhin at St-Symphorien; the Canal de Bourgogne at St-Jean-de-Losne; the Canal du Centre at Chalon-sur-Saône; the River Seille at La Truchère, and the Canal de Pont de Vaux at Fleurville, 3.5km with 1 lock.

The Saône ranks as one of the most important navigable rivers in France where pleasure craft are concerned: all or part of the route will be followed by boats cruising to or from the Mediterranean. Equally, the gentle scenery of Burgundy and the Bourbonnais, at the very heart of the country, is well worth exploration for its own sake. Almost totally rural surroundings with numerous attractive towns and villages have encouraged establishment of a range of hire cruiser bases: general facilities for pleasure boats are thus better than in many parts of France.

The uppermost reaches, between Corre and Port-sur-Saône, are often little wider than a *péniche* canal, with numerous artificial lock cuts which bypass some of the more twisting sections of the natural river. As far downstream as Auxonne, locks are restricted to the 38.50m length of the Freycinet gauge; but from there to Lyon, far-reaching modernization has recently resulted in locks 185m long, enabling 5,000 tonne push-tows to operate. It is thus a river of considerable contrasts. Commercial traffic is only moderate in the upper reaches, becoming progressively busier farther downstream. Now that the scheme for enlargement of the Canal du Rhône au Rhin has been shelved, any resulting increase in freight activity between Lyon and St-Symphorien seems unlikely.

The Saône has a very gentle gradient, falling a mere 59m over its total navigable length: consequently the current is normally slight. Conversely, serious flooding is not infrequent in the winter and craft are directed over some of the upstream weirs, the adjacent locks being taken out of service. But during the cruising season the river is placid, with unusually clear water. There are excellent opportunities for swimming from tiny sandy beaches.

Typical Saône features are long avenues of bankside poplars, broad meadows where white Charollais cattle graze, multi-coloured glazed Burgundian roof tiles and waterside villages in grey stone. Rarely spectacular, the scenery is at times monotonous – rather less so when illuminated by a summer sun that already promises more than a hint of the south.

Although much of the river is within easy reach of the famous Burgundian vineyards, they are rarely in evidence from the water. Excellent local wine is of course readily available; the food is as would be expected of this richly productive part of France. Lyon proudly claims to be the world centre of gastonomy and the reputation for first-class cuisine extends far beyond the city limits. In addition to the wines of Chalon, Mâcon and Burgundy, the outstanding dish of the Saône is *pôchouse*, freshwater fish such as eel, bream and burbot, stewed in white wine with garlic: Verdun-sur-le-Doubs claims the credit for the recipe, but it will be found on the menus of restaurants throughout a wide area.

Brief history Together with the Rhône, the Saône has formed a vital transport corridor through France since prehistoric times. A major trade route during the centuries of Roman domination, there are also records of the river being navigable downstream of Auxonne in the times of the Crusades. But a lack of weirs or other navigation works, resulting in frequent low water levels, hindered traffic until a management plan was adopted in 1837. This determined to provide a minimum water depth of 1.60m, similar to that of the newly completed Canal de Bourgogne. In the upper reaches, from Port-sur-Saône to Verdun-sur-le-Doubs, it was considered possible to manage without locks, improving the depth by dredging and building submerged training walls. This work was mainly carried out between 1842 and 1855. The programme was only partly successful and in 1864 legal measures' were adopted for the installation of a series of weirs with locks: 15 from Corre to Gray; 9 between Gray and Verdun-sur-le-Doubs; and a further 6 between there and Lyon. The French defeat of 1871, and consequent loss of territory to the east, had prompted building of the Canal de l'Est northwards from Corre (completed by 1882). The Saône thus formed an important north–south navigation and remained substantially unchanged until the 1970s.

Up to the beginning of the 19th century, barges and boats using the river were of very shallow draft: various regional types were to be found, including *savoyardes*, *seysselandes*, *penelles*, *sapines*, *cadoles*, *flûtes* and rafts. Passenger craft (*coches d'eau*) worked with sails and oars or were hauled by men and horses. Great improvements were made with the introduction of steam tugs from about 1835, with a tradition for construction of iron-hulled barges being established in Chalon in 1839. Passenger-carrying paddle steamers first went into service on the Chalon–Lyon section in 1826; there were 17 by 1850 and 449,736 people travelled aboard them.

The river supported a wide range of trades of great commercial importance to the region. Floating mills and other types of mobile water-powered factories were common in the early 19th century. Professional fishermen, floating washhouses and sand and gravel dredgers all derived a living from the Saône. So did pilots, whose detailed local knowledge of shallows was invaluable to the barge operators. Even in recent times it has been suggested that owners of large pleasure craft are well advised to take on a pilot for the lower sections of the Saône, where the submerged training walls present a hazard. In my experience, this is no longer necessary, provided due attention is paid to navigation marks and the chart.

Pleasure boating came earlier to the Saône than to many other French waterways. A rowing regatta was established in Mâcon in 1873, while steam launches were in use by 1886, according to Philip Hamerton's *The Saône* which records in great detail a summer voyage between Corre and Lyon. Hamerton hired a donkey-hauled *berrichon* to travel the upper reaches, using his own sailing catamaran downstream of Chalon. He noted that this part of the Saône was 'the best river to sail on in Europe, and probably the world', having a slow current in summer and 'good exposure of the surface of the water to the action of different winds'. Regularly used throughout the 20th century by yachts on passage through France, the river only became popular as a cruising ground in its own right after the arrival of a number of hire craft companies during the 1970s.

The Saône's latest stage of development has been carried out from the mid-1970s, with very sizeable engineering works to upgrade the lower section from Auxonne to Lyon. Practically completed by 1982, these measures brought the waterway to international standards as part of the projected North Sea–Mediterranean Waterway. All locks have been replaced or eliminated; the huge new concrete chambers measuring 185m × 12m with a normal depth over the sill of 4m. This work involved digging several new lock cuts and the removal of former weirs. Some of the old locks remain intact, their approaches creating useful moorings for commercial and pleasure craft.

Little has changed in the upper reaches, except that six of the locks are now equipped for automatic working, without the need for keepers. They are Ormoy, Cendrecourt, Port-sur-Saône, Chemilly, Scey-sur-Saône and Charentenay. Pleasure craft are issued with a leaflet at the final manned locks up or downstream of the series giving instructions on how to activate the gear.

Although the Saône's navigable length has been reduced to 363km at the time of writing, the kilometre posts on the banks continue to take account of many natural bends, since bypassed: the distance from Corre to Lyon might thus appear to be increased to 407km. As an aid to identifying where you are on the river, the post distances are used in the following description, so following the pattern established by the navigation charts.

A three-way junction between the unnavigable Saône, the little River Coney and the Canal de l'Est (Branche Sud) marks the start of the waterway on the outskirts of the small town of Corre (see Chapter 22). As the Coney is the larger of the two streams, it would appear to have a greater claim to the name 'Saône'. In former times boats were built on its banks at **Selles** and floated down to Corre on the winter floods.

These uppermost sections of the river are moderately wooded in quite hilly surroundings, unlike the wide open meadows so characteristic of much of the downstream Saône. Shortly after K405 is the first of many lengths of artificial cut, leading past the village of **Ormoy** (baker and grocer with piled mooring) to a lock, one of a series converted to automatic operation in 1980. Many of the weir-streams resulting from these 19th century improvements may be explored (with care) in small craft; indeed some of them provide the only practicable access to villages that have long been bypassed. A guard lock at the top end of the cut can be closed to prevent flood water passing into the canal.

The second lock is similarly approached by a long cut near the village of **Cendrecourt** (K392), a charming place of grey stone farmhouses, red roofs and basic shopping. The nearest mooring is at the lock, although it would be safer to lie downstream of the D46 road-bridge. Shops and restaurants in **Jussey**, about 2.3km. At K386 an extremely sinuous part of the river has been avoided by a short length of canal, the **Coupure de la Hang**. This is soon followed, left, by the village of **Montureux-les-Baulay** (K385.5), a collection of houses strung out along the bank and featuring a charming church with zig-zag patterns of coloured tiles. Access is difficult and facilities few. Another lock with short cut follows at K383.

Baulay (K380) has a reasonable mooring immediately downstream of the road bridge and lies within easy walking distance. Here are all basic shops, including supermarket, butcher, baker and post office, together with a restaurant. It is a pretty little place, filled with flowers. Cut wood lies in giant stacks as a source of winter fuel. A little upstream, on the opposite bank, is **Fouchecourt**, situated on a ridge above flood level.

There is little to delay the navigator at the road bridge of **Port d'Atelier** (K376) and pleasant countryside continues to Conflandey Lock, which has no cut: merely a foaming weir alongside the stone chamber. The barrage is made of numerous small 'needles', which can be removed to allow surplus water to escape. The keeper is wound over the torrent in a cradle from a gantry, to do this. In times of real flood, passage of the lock becomes unnecessary and craft merely pass over the weir, rather like boats negotiated flash locks that remained on the Thames above Oxford until the 1930s. Take care just below the lock, where a stream on the left can produce a strong current across the navigation channel. Below, a large island marks the approach to **Conflandey** (K372): downstream traffic takes the right channel, upstream boats the left. Although there is a sizeable wire mill opposite the village, it is otherwise a forgotten little place. An old fortified mill stands on the island, connected to each bank via a footbridge. The best (but rather shallow) mooring is on the village shore, opposite the tail of the island, where a faded sign advertises the long-closed Café de la Marine. The supermarket is good, but apart from a bar by the church the local people rely on mobile shops (the baker calls at midday).

That **Port-sur-Saône** (K 366) was once a town of some importance is suggested by the availability of a substantial history book in the stationer's. The single main street boasts a good range of basic shops and restaurants. I have several times eaten at the Restaurant de la Pomme d'Or (across the Saône bridge) and recommend it wholeheartedly. Good moorings are found a little below the bridge by the Service de la Navigation offices, where there is also a water point. A marina is established, opposite, in a basin: services offered include hire cruisers, repairs and fuel. This is a specially lovely part of the river, with woods and fields leading to the short cut and lock at **Chemilly** (K 360). A wide weir bars the entrance to the stream on which the village is situated, but it can be approached by boat from the lower end, mooring near the impressive towers of a beautifully restored fortified *château*.

Although now bypassed by the through navigation, **Scey-sur-Saône** (K 356) is worth a detour, following the natural course of the river from the upstream end of Scey lock cut. Ski-ing and other water sports are popular here. A convenient jetty mooring is within 500m of the shops and restaurant, but lies immediately above a weir and so should not be approached if there is a strong current. One surprise here is the vast supermarket, concealed behind a narrow frontage. Halfway down the lock channel is the Restaurant des Deux Ports, opposite a large but silted basin. The 689m St Albin tunnel (K 353) approach channel lies not long after Scey lock: it is, of course, rather unusual to encounter tunnels on river navigations, this example being made necessary when bypassing a huge loop of the Saône through the village of **Traves**. An approach by water can be made by navigating the old river channel upstream for 5km from the Écluse de Rupt (shops and café). The tunnel and its approaches are worked on a one-way system extending to the bridges above and below. Craft must wait for traffic lights before proceeding: they are operated by the lock keeper at Rupt, and downstream craft are required to hoot on entering the tunnel cutting. A microphone relays the sound to the lock, more than 2km away.

Rupt-sur-Saône (K 343) demands a visit: visible across the fields from the lock, it is dominated by its *château* with a tall round stone tower rising above the treetops. Village tradition claims that the tower once had a roof as tall as itself. Moor by the Pont de Chantes and walk a short distance up the D27. At the turn of the 18th and 19th centuries, the *château* was the property of the Comte d'Orsay, who was born in Paris and died here. An elaborate tomb in the churchyard is directly visible from his former home. The higher parts of the village provide good views of the river. This is an exceptionally sleepy place, offering few facilities beyond butcher's shop and bar. The public washing place is enhanced by a large 19th century lion in bronze. Another quiet village worth walking to is **Ovanches**, situated in the centre of the island formed by the river and the Rupt lock cut; it is approached from the road bridge at the downstream end of the tunnel.

A broad weir marks the beginning of the cut leading to **Chantes** lock (K 340). This is followed at K 338 by a guard lock (normally open) on a cut near **Cubry-les-Soing**. The landscape here is open and very appealing. Yet another canal section avoids a broad loop of the river, preventing craft from directly visiting the village of **Soing** (K 333.5). As mooring is prohibited in the narrow cut, it is probably wise to reject any idea of walking there over the otherwise convenient river bridge. Through Soing lock, the Saône is soon regained. At K 328, a right-angled bend leads to **Charentenay**, at the upper end of a lock cut. Still on the natural river, a little downstream of this junction, is a *relais nautique* with pontoon moorings at a camping site. Fuel and water supplies are available (diesel oil is otherwise rare on the upper Saône): these facilities are under the same ownership as the Auberge de Paris, a useful restaurant by the lock cut bridge where steaks are prepared over an open wood fire. The village is served by a mobile butcher and baker. A fine wooded reach of canal leads to Ray lock (K 324), below which is one of the finest views on the entire French waterways system.

After turning right up the natural course of the river, the village of **Ray-sur-Saône** rises from clusters of willow trees. Buildings of creamy stone with brown-tiled roofs are topped by a church, dated 1768, whose tower is covered with a 4-sided bell-shaped structure riotously decorated with glazed tiles in a zig-zag pattern. (A particularly fine early 16th century 'Entombment' is within.) Still higher are the crenellated towers, massive walls and park of the *château* of Ray, now the property of Comte Hubert de Salverte, a descendant of the Duc de Marmier. He began extensive restoration work in 1941. Parts of the structure go back to medieval times. It was reduced to ruins during the Ten Years War (17th century) and rebuilt and extended in the 18th century. The strategic site was a stronghold in Roman times. The *château* is open to the public (Sun and holiday afternoons, Easter–Oct 1) and the park is open throughout the year. It is claimed that a passage carved from the rock connects the *château* with the river. Although technically not navigable, the river is sufficiently deep to allow craft to approach the village, mooring bow-on to a grassy bank. All basic facilities including supermarket in Ray. There is also an impressive washhouse with an oval basin and roof.

A guard lock on a long artificial cut at **Ferrières-lès-Ray**, although normally open at each end, presented problems for deep-laden barges. In 1978 I watched a somewhat underpowered *péniche* being winched over the sill. Now navigation is possible (draft up to 1.5m) along the natural river at this point, so avoiding the cut. **Recologne** (K319), at the tail of the cut, offers no facilities but is a pleasant little village with flowers and cattle sheds among the houses.

At K315 begins another long and narrow cut with the 643m **Savoyeux Tunnel**. Downstream boats should hoot to alert the keeper at Savoyeux lock and wait for a green light before proceeding. The very extensive basin of the Port de Savoyeux, 1km upstream of the tunnel, was developed as a marina and hire craft base in 1981 (moorings, water, fuel, slipway etc). Pleasant but unremarkable scenery takes the navigation through **Véreux** lock cut (K298–296) and on to **Prantigny** (K294), where mooring is possible downstream of the bridge on the left bank. Apart from a pleasing cluster of stone barns and houses, there is little reason for exploration ashore. Rigny lock cut (K289) is unusually treeless. **Rigny**, 10 minutes' walk from the middle of the cut and over a river bridge, offers a baker, restaurant and supermarket. Otherwise it can be reached by water by turning up the river from the lower end of

The château *of Ray-sur-Saône and church tower decorated with coloured Burgundian tiles, alongside a navigable backwater.*

the lock channel. (Draft reduces to 0.5m). From this point, the river opens out and the hilly surrounds of its uppermost reaches are left behind. For the first time a series of black and white buoys (K286) warn of rock in the riverbed: keep well in to the right bank. Similar navigation markers will be observed frequently during the journey down to Lyon.

In keeping with its growing proportions, the Saône now meets its first real town – **Gray** (K280). Initial impressions are of considerable industry, for this is an important agricultural centre with waterside grain silos and rail connections. Occupying a hilltop with the church of Notre Dame (prominent onion-shaped spire and begun in the 15th century), it is a first-rate shopping centre. Water point, showers and other facilities are available to pleasure craft immediately upstream of the bridge, thanks to the local Syndicat d'Initiative. Some care is required in approaching the lock on the right bank because of a nearby wide weir. The chamber itself is spanned by the road bridge. We noticed that the lock keeper took his midday meal at a small restaurant to the right of the bridge, and having moored at the convenient stepped quay below followed his example. Crowded with workmen, this establishment provided us with a meal of excellent value. There are lovely views over the river from the flag-decorated bridge, with formal gardens. A magnificent honey-coloured stone Town Hall in Renaissance style dates from 1568; its roof of coloured glazed tiles is one of the best in all Burgundy. The 18th century *château* houses the Baron Martin Museum, whose 20 rooms contain a fine collection of European paintings from the 16–20th centuries. It is interesting to recall that Gray and the lands of Franche Comté were lost by France as recently as 1688: the Saône had long been a natural frontier and Hamerton notes that in 1886 the bargemen continued to refer to the left bank as the *Empire* and the right bank the *Royaume*. The right bank at K281 has a waterside restaurant with mooring possible to an old diving platform.

Quite one of the loveliest moorings on the Saône is reached at **Mantoche** (K276), where a grassy quay, draft about 0.7m, extends along the river frontage of a real gem of a small *château*, reputedly a former royal hunting lodge. On one occasion the lady living there accepted an invitation to come aboard our hired cruiser and we were sorry that pressure of time prevented us from looking round her exquisite home the next morning (it is not normally open to the public.) Another *château* is concealed among thick trees nearby, with the coloured tiles of a tower peeping through the foliage. Narrow lanes lead into the village centre, where there are basic shops and a café. The placid Saône here seems more like an ornamental lake than a river.

The approach to the upper end of the **Apremont** lock cut (K275), once dangerously close to a weir and presenting a blind corner, was improved by excavating a new channel in July 1983. Apremont lock is rather wider than the *péniche*-sized chambers upstream and, like some of the disused locks lower down, was designed to accommodate craft side by side. Dense woods with evidence of summertime fishing and waterside caravans characterize the 11km reach to the next lock cut at **Heuilley** (K257). Small craft may be launched at a former ferry crossing on the right bank (K260). We pass from the Haute-Saône *département* into the Côte d'Or at K268. Heuilley lies conveniently close to the canal (moor at the bridge) and offers a general shop, restaurant/bar and blacksmith. The main activity here is farming and market gardening: local enquiry should result in the purchase of fresh vegetables. Traffic signals control the junction with the Canal de la Marne à la Saône, immediately before Heuilley lock.

Large meadows, low banks and grazing cattle establish a type of scenery that will last for much of the journey to Lyon. **Pontailler** (K251), a pleasant little town with fine architecture in its domestic buildings and large Italianate church, offers convenient moorings with rubbish disposal and water (downstream of the bridge, right bank). The riverside Restaurant des Marronniers is pleasantly situated and all shops are within easy reach together with garage and obliging taxi service. For those with yearning for slight adventure, the town may be circumnavigated by small boat using the course of the Vieille Saône. This sometimes narrow waterway, likely to be congested with fishing punts in places, joins the main navigation a little upstream of the road bridge over the Saône. A very convenient *halte nautique*, used in part by a hire cruiser company, offers pontoon moorings and water supplies for boats in transit. Draft beyond this basin may be limited to little more than 1m and a speed limit of 6kph is imposed. The 2km course of the Vieille Saône passes a public park (moorings possible) before finally returning to the Saône at K249.5, a much more convenient approach to the detour. Pontailler was virtually destroyed by Général Mercey in August 1636: a mere 22 people and 5 houses escaped. It was here that Philip Hamerton was made prisoner by the police aboard his *berrichon* in 1886, his sketching activities having been mistaken for spying (the Franco-Prussian War was still a fresh memory). Negotiations at a high level secured his

Mantoche, one of the loveliest moorings on the whole of the Saône.

release. Modern travellers are probably safe from massacre or arrest in Pontailler, though it would be unwise to test the present extent of official complacency by mooring on a forbidden section of bank from K249.5–247. The trees conceal a national gunpowder works: punted fishermen can be noted lying here in considerable numbers (waiting for stunned fish in the event of an explosion?).

And so on to **Lamarche-sur-Saône** (K246), a little town with basic facilities and moorings on the far bank, downstream of the bridge. Launching slipway 300m downriver (town side). 3km on, the canal cut and lock of **Poncey** are reached, followed at K234 by the sizeable town of **Auxonne**, former Capital of a small state independent of both the Duchy of Burgundy and the Kingdom of France. Sailing, windsurfing and water-skiing are popular here. Very central moorings will be found on a pair of pontoons just upstream of the bridge. Napoléon spent a year in the town barracks in 1788, his stay being commemorated by a collection of relics in the Musée Bonaparte (open May–end Oct). Turreted fortifications remain on the river bank. The shops are old-fashioned and offer little to tempt the passing tourist, but several fine timbered buildings remain in the town centre. Trees line the long straight cut leading to Auxonne lock (K230), the last of the 'small' unmodernized chambers of the Saône.

In anticipation of enlargement of the Canal du Rhône au Rhin, a large barge port was projected for the Saône at **Maillys** (K224), serving the Burgundy Region.

The next place of note is the junction with the Canal du Rhône au Rhin (K219) upstream of the small village of **St Symphorien**. Little exists here except a lock and keeper's house, and the yard of barge conversion specialists Bourgogne Marine.

St-Jean-de-Losne (K215) is the first real commercial port yet encountered on the river. True, there may have been some *péniches* on passage through the top reaches; perhaps several loading or unloading in Gray or Auxonne. Numerous barges and push-tows laden with sand and gravel will have provided interest. But here we come to a town devoted to water transport. Something of a showplace for waterways enthusiasts, St-Jean-de-Losne has grown on account of its situation at one terminus of the Canal de Bourgogne, route for Dijon and the River Yonne. Through the canal's lock 76 lies an expansive basin with wharves, a drydock generally busy with *péniche* repairs or conversions to barge yachts, and gravel unloading points. Alongside, at river level, is a huge grass-banked basin, the *gare d'eau* (barge dock) with two islands at its centre. Originally a safe place to lie out of reach of Saône floods, or where freight tows could be assembled, it is still used by working boats awaiting cargoes. But a newer function annually increases in size: moorings for pleasure craft. M. Joël Blanquart, a former barge captain, presides, with a floating chandlery. All possible boat needs are catered for, from water to gas, diesel and rope. On the far side the British-owned Crown Blue Line Cruisers have one of their many French hire cruiser bases, with floating pontoons and a most ingenious drydock adapted from a large barge. This company came to France in 1969 to become the second hire boat firm on the network and now owns considerably more craft than any of its rivals. Many British waterways enthusiasts leave their boats on convenient pontoon moorings in the care of Charles Gérard's H²O company. All services are available including repairs and barge conversions. Since its formation in the latter 1980s, H²O has achieved a reputation as one of the leading brokers of cruising barges and motor yachts in France. Fluent English is spoken. Back on the main channel of the river, *péniches* are often moored two or three abreast; an annual *gymkhana* or rally is held for the boat people, with barges travelling long distances to be present.

St-Jean-de-Losne was a leading river port long before arrival of the canal. Little remains of the original fortifications from its glorious history. In 1273 the lords of Franche-Comté attacked with 500 men dressed as women: the townsfolk discovered the deception and killed them all. Then in 1636, when Pontailler was decimated at the start of the Thirty Years' War, 80,000 troops of the Holy Roman Empire arrived, including Hungarians, Croatians and Spaniards under the command of Général Gallas. Believing St-Jean to be the gateway to Burgundy and the city of Dijon, he laid siege to it, expecting little resistance from the 400 arms-bearing citizens and 150 soldiers. The town held out for a week and the situation was so desperate that plans were made to burn the houses and wreck the river bridge if the walls should be breached. Only just in time, reinforcements arrived from Auxonne. The Imperialists, having lost 800 men, retreated: against huge odds, St-Jean-de-Losne was saved. Ever since it has proudly carried the suffix La Belle Défense. A German advance was similarly repulsed in 1870. These brave deeds are commemorated by a stone monument between the bridge and the church. Shopping facilities are excellent, (with a good supermarket almost alongside the *gare d'eau*) and of several restaurants a personal favourite is the Auberge de la Marine on the east side of the bridge.

Recent 'improvements' to the navigation course have reduced the waterway from 20km to 10km by means of a straight canal running from K208, some distance below the former lock of St-Jean-de-Losne to **Seurre** (K187). From a scenic viewpoint these developments are a disaster: much of the new channel is steel-piled or concrete lined with high banks making for tedious cruising in a small underpowered boat. Sections of the former through route remain navigable: notably 11km between Seurre and the disused **Le Chatelet** lock, available from the downstream end only, but these possibilities are only likely to be of interest to local boaters.

After the depressing surrounds of the Seurre lock cut it is agreeable to emerge on the river once more:

there are lines of horse chestnuts, numerous little fishing punts and a row of brick and stone buildings fronting a quay upstream of the bridge. The best mooring may be occupied by *péniches* loading from lorries (although transport of one cargo, maize, is doubtless seasonal). But Seurre more than merits a halt, both for its shops and for the restaurants. One of these, facing the river, offers a number of freshwater specialities, including *friture* (tiny fried fish), frogs' legs, snails, trout and river crayfish. The huge 17th century building (partly converted into private houses) has at various times been a salt warehouse, a hospital and a bridge toll house. Reputedly, it was visited by Napoléon. Remains of the demolished weir can be seen on each side of the channel by the infilled former cut of Seurre lock (K184).

Chazelles (K181.5) lies on the left bank at the border between the Côte d'Or *département* and Saône et Loire. Several long barns in stone with red roofs

Loading a péniche *at Seurre.*

overlook the water. There is also a restaurant and a sloping quay with moorings rings. **Charnay-les-Chalon** (K178) has now been bypassed by the new cut and lock of Écuelles. To approach too closely would bring a boat dangerously near the weir. However, it is worth mooring somewhat upstream and walking along the riverbank to visit one of the Saône's prettier settlements. It was here, during the 19th century, that the mayor hated the schoolmaster so much that he set fire to all but one of the thatched houses, accused the teacher of arson and brought about his transportation. The mayor made a death-bed confession years later, and his former enemy was pardoned; but he remained so bitter that he rejected any idea of returning home.

Water and telephone are at Écuelles lock, a large mechanized chamber of few attractions. By contrast, the village of **Écuelles** (K174), right bank, is almost Italian in appearance, intensely rural and worth exploring. Moorings are moderately good on a grassy bank in front of the church. Among the facilities are a baker, bar and grocer.

Now follows a very fine reach, with wooded cliffs on the right, leading to a camping site (left) on the outskirts of **Verdun-sur-le-Doubs** (K167). The last of the river's 19th century locks remained in service here until 1986. Now there is no change in water levels. To reach Verdun it is necessary to turn into the mouth of the **Doubs**, the same river that forms much of the course of the Canal du Rhône au Rhin. This section of the Doubs is navigable, with care, for about 8km past the villages of **Saunières**, (restaurant), and **Sermesse** to **Pontoux** to the railway bridge at **Navilly**. Maximum draft 1.80m. Keep a careful lookout for gravel barges which may be dredging from this length and avoid their mooring hawsers. The trip is mildly adventurous, past overhanging willows, and you are unlikely to meet many other pleasure craft.

Verdun has perhaps the finest waterfront of any Saône town: a jumble of irregular stone buildings rising sheer from the river. Excellent shops of all kinds surround a small square. *Pôchouse*, a fish stew with wine and onions, is the local speciality. For this and other good value cuisine, try the Restaurant des Trois Maures, facing the moorings. An alternative route back to the Saône for boats drawing up to 1m is offered by the Petit Doubs. (Technically, this is only available to unpowered craft.) A French-owned hire cruiser company operates here.

Chauvort (K165) offers a restaurant by a stepped quay near the site of a former suspension bridge. Few ancient bridges remain on the Saône, for it has experienced too many invasions over the centuries. The fol-

lowing reach is wide open, with tiny sandy beaches ideal for swimming on a hot day. Upstream of the Pont de **Gergy** (K159) are several fine country houses, one decorated with a Burgundian tiled roof which somehow avoids looking gaudy in the green surroundings. The village of **Verjux**, a short distance from the river on the left, was home to a poor young laundress in the middle of the 19th century. She travelled to Paris and married a shopkeeper who soon died, leaving her his business. The shop prospered, becoming a leading store of the capital – *Bon Marché*. Never forgetting her origins, Madame Boucicaut dispensed a sizeable fortune to charity, and in 1886 provided the considerable sum of £20,000 for construction of a new bridge over the Saône at Verjux.

Little of note is passed on a long straight reach past the village of **Alleriot** (K150), whose restaurants are of use only to craft of shallow draft. In such circumstances, it is perfectly possible to lie at anchor, however, and go ashore in a dinghy, a procedure I have sometimes adopted when cruising in a large motor yacht. Alleriot faces the river square-on, seemingly deriving pleasure from its situation, unlike many other Saône settlements that shrink away from the waterside, probably fearing winter floods.

Now follows one of the major cities of the valley **Chalon-sur-Saône** (K142). Open country gradually gives way to houses and just downstream of K145 is the new entrance channel of the Canal du Centre, one of four possible routes to the Seine, Paris and the English Channel. This is shortly followed on the right bank by extensive barge works capable of handling the largest vessels trading on the river. In the 19th and early 20th century, there was a great shipbuilding enterprise here, Schneider de Chalon: production included 81 torpedo boats for various navies between 1889 and 1906; destroyers, submarines and all kinds of steam tugs and other inland vessels. The problem of transporting large sea-going craft to the Mediterranean via the Saône and Rhône, whose depth was clearly insufficient, was cleverly solved by building a shallow draft ship carrier, the *Porteur*, hauled by a pair of steam tugs.

An important town in pre-Roman times, Cabillonum was chosen by Julius Caesar as a food store during the Gallic Wars. Little remains of Roman fortifications or architecture other than several museum relics. In the summers of 1982–3 remains of a 3,000 year old Bronze Age village were discovered in the river, under 5m of water. Working from a specially adapted *péniche* named *Praehistoria*, archaeologists recovered an amazing collection of objects including bronze vases, swords, over 350 ceramic pots and a 15th century boat loaded with pottery artefacts. All are destined for preservation in the Musée Denon. Under the Romans, the city marked the head of navigation with its own river superintendent (*praefectus navium araricarum*). About the 6th century Chalon was the capital of an extensive Kingdom of Burgundy, extending north–south from Sens to Avignon, and east–west from Lake Geneva to the Loire. Under the Duchy of Burgundy, in the 15–16th centuries, it was a stylish city with fortified bridge, walls and towers. A few timber-framed buildings remain from this period. Although owing everything to its position on the Saône, Chalon has many times suffered from winter floods: as in the early part of 1982 when all communications with Mâcon were cut for several days, with the exception of the A6 *autoroute*. Throughout that summer debris caught in the trees remained as a reminder of the height of the waters.

Excellent visitors' moorings are found on the Bras de la Génise to the left of the Île St Laurent, peaceful yet fairly convenient for the shops and main attractions. The long upstream jetty is reputedly available without charge. Moorings on the sloping town quays are not convenient for small craft. Supermarket 300m. Overlooking the main channel, the 15th century Tour du Doyenné (Deanery Tower) was dismantled on its original site near the cathedral and rebuilt on the island in 1928 (open for public visits). Close by, the Hospital of 1528 displays fine carved wood, early stained glass and a collection of *faïence* jars. On the right bank is the main part of the town: several streets have been pedestrianized. Leading attractions are the cathedral of St Vincent, founded in the 5th century and mainly 12th and 15th centuries with 19th century towers; the Musée Denon, an Empire-style former convent whose collections include examples of Gallo-Roman sculpture and the history of Saône navigation (open daily except Tues); and the splendid stone river quay, decorated with flower containers: it was built by the local engineer Émiland Gauthey who was also responsible for the Canal du Centre and parts of the Canal du Rhône au Rhin. In late February and late June, Chalon stages *foires aux sauvagines* (wildfowl fairs) which originated in medieval times.

Even the briefest halt should allow time to pay homage to Chalon's greatest celebrity, Nicéphore Niépce, the father of photography. Born in 1765 in the rue de l'Oratoire, he contrived to preserve a photographic image produced with a *camera obscura* in 1822. Among other achievements was the design for an internal combustion engine. His statue, on the quay, was inaugurated in the later part of the 19th century with a day of celebrations that included brass bands, speeches, a banquet and fireworks. 150 years after the world's first

photograph, Chalon set up the Musée Nicéphore Niépce in a splendid 18th century hotel overlooking the river at 28 Quai des Messageries (open daily except Tues). Not only does this excellent display commemorate Niépce with examples of his original equipment, but it brings the history of photography up to modern times. One extraordinary exhibit is M. Givaudan's photo-sculpture machine of 1922–4, one of whose sitters was the movie film pioneer Louis Lumière.

Chalon makes a good centre for visiting Burgundy and the vineyards: the famous wine town of Beaune lies 33km distant.

The New Port of Chalon, in a huge basin south of the town at K137, increases the river's width almost to 1km. There would appear to be ample scope for greater use of its facilities. A hint of the approaching South, in the form of Provençal red pantiles, is noted at **Port d'Ouroux**, a small village by a bridge at K131 (restaurant). Overnight moorings are possible on a vertical quay at the mouth of the River Grosne (right bank, K128.5); this small waterway is navigable for light craft for a short distance to the village of **Marnay**. Long unchanging vistas take the navigator by the former **Gigny** lock (K123, moorings). **Ormes**, on the left bank (K120.5), is notable for a most attractive small *château* with Burgundian tiled roof, cottage and gazebo. Then comes the giant Ormes lock, completed in 1979. If water levels are high, craft are directed instead over the weir, a phenomenon I once experienced in mid-June.

One of the most pleasing towns on the entire river is

The proprietor of the Boulangerie Robert proudly displays his young son's baking craftsmanship. Tournus.

Tournus (K112) with moorings on a quay close to the modern bridge. All facilities (including fuel within a short walk to the N6) are at hand. The abbey church of St Philibert shelters the remains of St Valerian, who was martyred in the 2nd century. This unique Romanesque church dates mainly from the 11th and 12th centuries, although the crypt is 6th century. Surprisingly, the recorded choral music played for the benefit of pilgrims actually enhances the experience of a visit, as does the modern abstract stained glass. Tasteful souvenirs available in the town include reproduction stone carvings and basketwork. There is an over-priced antique shop in another 11th century church and a collection of antique dealers installed in an equally historic building where the traders have the effrontery to charge a not insubstantial entry fee!

6km below Tournus, the Saône is joined by its sole navigable tributary (discounting the Doubs, which is a locked waterway in its middle reaches only). This is the beautiful River Seille (K106, see Chapter 49). A sloping quay offers mooring outside an isolated restaurant where the road from **St-Oyen** runs down to the waterside (K100.5).

On the left bank by the bridge of **Fleurville** (K97.5), the short **Canal de Pont-de-Vaux** runs for about 3.5km (1 DIY lock) to the town of that name. It was restored in 1993 for F10 million and is navigable for craft up to 1.3m draft. Effectively a lateral canal to the River Reyssouze, there are good moorings and urban facilities at the terminus (hire boats and convenient supermarket). Restaurants exist on each side of the Saône, with the best mooring on a pontoon at the canal entrance. Most shopping facilities are available in Fleurville, 1km away on the N6. The navigation channel lies to the right of the long wooded Île de Brouard (K96). In clear weather it is sometimes possible to see the snow-covered heights of Mont Blanc which rises to 4,807m, 160km SE. From here to Mâcon the busy N6 is often close to the right bank, and beyond it the A6. Waterside restaurants occur at **Asnières** (K90), **St-Martin-Belle-Roche** (K89) and near **Vesines** (K87.5), where there is a pontoon with water supplies. Upstream-bound craft have a fine view of the *château* at **St-Jean-Le-Priche** (K87).

High-rise buildings are the first indication of **Mâcon** (K81), now bypassed by a large new canal, running between K83.5 and K79 and enabling large commercial craft to avoid the city's Pont St-Laurent with its restricted clearance. Smaller vessels and pleasure boats are able to follow the natural course of the waterway through the town centre. At K83, right bank, is the excellent Port de Plaisance de

Mâcon, with all services including fuel, water, 3000kg crane and slipway; it is, however, rather far from the town to serve as a convenient mooring when sightseeing. The Quay Lamartine (water point) has a vertical section (elsewhere, the stone banks are sloping) and is close to all shops and the market: its name recalls Alphonse Prat de Lamartine, the poet and politician (1790–1869) who was born here. Although the fortifications of the Middle Ages have now vanished, the eight-arched Pont St-Laurent dates from the 14th century and was reconstructed in the 19th. It is thus a Saône rarity, other ancient bridges having been destroyed in the frequent battles that have raged in this border country. A statue of St Nicholas, patron saint of barge people as well as children, occupies a niche between the second and third arches on the right, upstream, side: quite correctly, he is visible only to river travellers. Little more than two octagonal towers remain of St Vincent's cathedral, mostly destroyed in the French Revolution. The Mâconnais vineyards, extending from Beaujolais in the south to Tournus, may be visited from here, the celebrated villages of **Pouilly** and **Fuissé** being about 8km distant. Mâcon is a sunny town of red pantiles presenting a distinctly southern air. Worth visiting are the Préfecture in the French Renaissance style and the Hôtel-Dieu with its collection of apothecaries' jars. Opposite the junction with the river and the new bypass channel is the commercial barge port (K79), with a much larger Nouveau Port, right bank (K77).

Downstream of the Île d'Amprun (K75) is a viaduct carrying the exciting new high speed trains (TGV). In 1990, one of these on the Loire Valley Atlantic Line broke the world record with a speed of 479kph (298mph). **Arciat** (K73) is notable for excellent deep moorings, right bank, downstream of the bridge, where there is a restaurant with water point and slipway. Fuel supplies and basic shopping may be obtained at **St-Romain-des-Iles** (K66) which lies between the A6 and the Saône: moor at the small marina. **Thoissey** (K63) lies 1km east of the navigation, with several restaurants, camping site and sandy beach by the bridge. Another of the new locks is the Écluse de Dracé (K62), right bank: strong eddy when the chamber is filling. The reach that follows provides good views of hills to the right, with a château on the left bank. Changes in the river levels resulting from rearranged navigation works have produced the effect of a 'drowned valley' in reverse: from here for the next 10–15km it has the appearance of a tideway at low water. There is ample depth in the channel, but many former quays now rise from sandbanks and mooring for all but the smallest boats is difficult. In time, these lengths of exposed foreshore will be covered with vegetation. Typical of the towns with mediocre access is **Belleville** (K55), a sizeable place 1km beyond the A6; two good restaurants and a grocer are near the bridge, right bank. Avoid tying up at the quay, reserved for sand barges. Medium sized cruisers may be able to lie bow-on on a shoal above the bridge.

Below a pair of islands, **Montmerle** (K52) in part occupies a hill, left bank, surmounted by its church and is a good shopping centre. The vertical quay offers a water depth at least 1m less than originally and should therefore be treated with caution. Similar problems affect moorings at **Port Rivière** (K48.5) where there are several restaurants. These towns would do well to install floating stages to attract passing custom. Crane, fuel and slipway at the Velu boatyard (K43, restaurant), much the best stopping point for **Beauregard**, less than 1km downstream. Elaborate menus are provided at the Auberge Bressane, whose terrace overlooks the suspension bridge. A convenient (but rather commercialized) mooring lies downstream, right bank, at the port of **Villefranche-sur-Saône**. The town itself is 2km to the west and dominated by tower blocks. **Jassans Riottier** (K40), by the Pont de Frans has good marina moorings with town facilities close at hand. Increasing leisure use of the river is now evident, with numerous camping and caravan sites, small swimming beaches and widespread weekend use of little motor cruisers.

Thickly wooded surroundings past the village of **St-Bernard** (K35) are popular with sunbathers throughout the summer: Many people doubtless come from **Trévoux** (K30.5), the onetime Capital of the Principality of Dombes and not incorporated into France until the middle of the 18th century. Built over a hill on the left bank, the town is one of the most attractive on the whole river. Good quay moorings by the remains of a suspension bridge may be occupied by barges; if so, a boat club upstream of a new road bridge, right bank, will doubtless welcome visitors. A sour note is introduced by the activities of small high-speed motorboats that race through the town, creating a wash far more dangerous to little cruisers than that produced by 1,500 ton freight craft. Frantic gestures to prevent these thoughtless maniacs swamping my inflatable dinghy were of no avail. A serious accident will eventually be caused and perhaps the authorities will feel obliged to enforce the speed limits. Such behaviour on the Upper Thames would bring instant prosecution with heavy fines or even imprisonment. The centre of Trévoux

consists of a terrace high above the river, with the church on one side and the late 17th century Palais du Parlement (superb painted beams) on another. Italianate turrets and pantiles in the steep and narrow streets are very southern in feeling, especially in the delightfully named, precipitous Rue Casse-Cou (Broken Neck Street). A very sharp incline leads to a feudal 10–13th century *château* at the top of the town with walks along the battlements, ruined towers and a magnificent view along the Saône valley and across to the Beaujolais hills. Philip Hamerton described this panorama as 'the fairest landscapes on the Saône, perhaps the fairest scene in France', a claim that is not greatly exaggerated. A market is held on Saturday mornings. Slipway on the east bank, below the bridge.

No longer is the Saône the quiet river of its upper reaches: the closeness of Lyon has brought much development to the valley and this rather enhances the pleasure of cruising, with more sights and people to watch. There remain sandy beaches like that in a grove of white poplars at K24. Ahead, are the wooded slopes of Mont d'Or (625m), with good moorings at les Chantiers Naval yard (K23 fuel, water and 2.5 tonne crane) on the right bank some distance outside **St-Germain-au-Mont-d'Or**.

Villevert and **Neuville-sur-Saône** are either side of a bridge (K21) with good shops close by and reasonably convenient moorings. Garage on the left bank. Écluse de Couzon (K17) is the final Saône lock downstream of a spectacular reach with wooded cliffs. At this end of the 45km pound that extends all the way from the Écluse de Dracé, water levels have been raised 'drowning' numerous trees whose dead remains rise direct from the river. In 1983 an old steel *péniche* the

Waterside campsite for the author during an inflatable dinghy cruise on the Saône. Near Mont d'Or, upstream of Lyon.

Parfait Amour, was inaugurated as an inland water-ways information centre. Hauled onto the lockside and raised on piles, it provides an excellent opportunity of appreciating how large these 38m craft really are. Floating jetty, K17, outside is reserved for trip boats. Close to the bridge of **Couzon-au-Mont-d'Or** (K16.5), the Château de Rochetaillée houses a motor museum with over 180 vehicles. River traffic follows a one-way course round each side of the Île Roy (K14), as the Saône narrows through a shallow wooded gorge. Take the left-hand channel going downstream. Several grand houses perched on the slopes were the 19th century residences of Lyon merchants. Among the most famous restaurants in France is that of Paul Bocuse, upstream of a railway bridge at **Collonges** (K12). This superb, but very expensive establishment, which attracts lunchtime custom from as far away as Paris, is served by a landing stage.

One of the most perfectly situated homes on a French river rises from a rocky outcrop at the head of the **Île Barbe** (Wild Island, K10): 600m long and up to 130m wide, this place was occupied by a leading Lyonnaise abbey for a thousand years, from the 5th century. Eventually the monks became so rich and powerful that they were submerged in turpitude and vice. With disarming honesty, they petitioned the King to be disestablished; the request was passed to Pope Paul III, who duly granted them their wish in 1549. A suspension bridge now connects the lower end of the island to each bank of the mainland. There is a public park, a fine restaurant Auberge de l'Île, several houses and the crumbling remnants of the ecclesiastical past.

To arrive by water in any great city is a fascinating experience. **Lyon** (K7 onwards) is no exception for this is the second city of France, the self-proclaimed gastronomic capital of the world, and a place so full of attractions that several days could easily be passed in exploration. I came here for my first foreign holiday as a fourteen-year-old and subsequent visits never fail to recall the adventure of wandering through the streets alone, always a little uncertain that I would safely find my way back to my apartment off the Rue de la République. It would be impossible to describe all the sights, which are more than adequately covered in the green *Michelin Guide Vallée du Rhône*. Although large (pop. 1,200,000), the most historic quarter is fairly compact. Important Roman remains include two well preserved amphitheatres and the remnants of an aqueduct. There are broad quays along the banks of the Saône and the blue-green glacier-fed Rhône. The famed silk industry, dating from the 16th century, is commemorated in a sumptuous fabric museum. Fashionable stores are located along the pedestrianized Rue de la République. Contributions of the latter 20th century include a sparkling new *Metro* system that serves a splendidly revamped railway station, Gare de Perrache: a bus terminal is incorporated into this complex of glass and orange plastic, with escalators and brightly lit shops under cover. Come here to view the record-beating *TGV* trains. Limited research indicates that the best value in restaurant food is near the station, although *Michelin* lists an array of establishments offering superb fare.

Navigation through the central part of the city is arranged on a one-way basis in times of flood, at 2½hr intervals. Consult the indicator boards for the appropriate times. Façades of tall Renaissance Italian buildings by the Pont de l'Homme de la Roche are succeeded by several bridges to the city centre. Best recommended mooring is at the old Port de Plaisance, a rather scruffy quay with no facilities facing the Gothic cathedral of St Jean (left bank, between Pont Marechal-Juin and Pont Bonaparte). As in any large town, the security of a boat cannot be guaranteed and it is wise to ask the skipper of a nearby vessel to keep an eye open if you plan to be away for a short time. Although situated in a rather noisy area by railway tracks, moorings, left bank, are combined with hire cruiser base, fuel and chandlery (K0.2). From the Gare St-Jean, take the funicular railway to the huge 19th century Basilica of Notre-Dame-de-Fourvière: at this height, there are views down over the rooftops to the two rivers. The Roman theatres are close by.

Best of all, try to reserve time to wander at will, savouring the sights, the open-air flower and fruit market by the Saône, the clusters of barges, and absorbing the colourful Lyonnaise atmosphere. Many holidaymakers will have seen a little of the city from the main north-south *autoroute*, which dives through tunnels and along the Rhône quays: but there is much more to discover in this wonderful place, where tradition says there are *three* rivers – the Saône, the Rhône and the wine!

The river finally empties into the Rhône below the Pont de la Mulatière. A former lock now provides moorings for pleasure craft: if a long stay is contemplated this could be the place to try. Water and fuel may be obtained from the Société Decarpentrie *péniche* on the Saône's Quai Rambaud, left bank just above the final bridge.

48 · Canal de la Marne à la Saône

Carte Guide: *Champagne Ardenne*
From a junction with the Canal de la Marne au Rhin and the Canal Latéral à la Marne at Vitry-le-François to the River Saône at Heuilley-sur-Saône: 224km and 114 locks. There are two tunnels: Condes (308m) near Chaumont and Balesmes (4,820m) near Langres. Craft proceed through under their own power.

Of four possible direct routes between Paris and the Mediterranean, the Canal de la Marne à la Saône is the longest; but having almost the same number of locks as the 77km shorter Bourbonnais route, it is well worth consideration. And for craft crossing France from Belgium or Holland, it is an obvious first choice.

The northern part of the waterway is, in effect, a canal lateral to the River Marne which it follows closely to a point near the river's source on the Plateau de Langres, 71 locks on from Vitry-le-François. After passing through the Balesmes summit level tunnel, the route falls sharply via 43 locks in the valley of the River Vingeanne to join the Saône upstream of Pontailler-sur-Saône. Only one sizeable town, St-Dizier, lies directly on the canal and a degree of careful planning is required to ensure that adequate food and fuel supplies are taken when needed. Drinking water points were very infrequent: here, we found that information supplied by lock keepers was more accurate than reference to the *Carte Guide*.

Rural almost from end to end, the waterway is a little straight and dull through gravel-bearing land from Vitry-le-François to St-Dizier. Thereafter the scenery is consistently fine, past wooded cliffs, riverbank watermills and an amazing variety of trees, many planted in avenues along the canal sides. These include Scots pines and larches.

Most locks are manually operated with a high proportion of lady keepers. Paddle and gate-opening gear is heavy but efficient. A substantial quantity of locks on the Saône side of the summit level have been automated. Of a great number of bascule, swing and vertical lifting bridges, many have been converted for automatic operation with radar beams activated by the passage of craft; instruction leaflets are issued on entry. Canal architecture and engineering is often most interesting, from the lock houses whose date plaques enable the traveller to trace the progress of construction during the latter 19th century to a large number of small aqueducts, frequently situated at the upstream ends of locks. Locks are currently closed on Sundays, and the one-way working of the Balesmes Tunnel could result in a delay of as much as 10 hours. It is thus a good notion to plan a stop where some shore facilities are available.

Brief history Conceived as a continuation of the Canal Latéral à la Marne, opened in 1845, and originally known as the Canal de la Haute Marne, the waterway ran for 73km from Vitry-le-Francois. Construction was carried out between 1863 and 1879. Soon afterwards, the far-reaching Freycinet Plan for French waterways development was introduced, resulting in enlargement of the newly built locks to their present *péniche* dimensions and the extension of the line southwards to join the Saône. All was ready by 1907 and the canal was renamed.

Four large reservoirs near the Langres summit (La Liez, La Mouche, Charmes and La Vingeanne) ensure excellent water supplies and closures through drought have been rare. Two exceptions were for 42 days in Sept–Oct 1954 and 43 days in Nov–Dec 1964. A pumping station was erected at the Charmes reservoir in 1956 for use in exceptionally dry conditions.

Chiefly designed as a linking waterway, with few ports en route, Canal de la Marne à la Saône mainly carried pit-props, building stone, pig-iron and coal up to World War II, totalling 849,000 tonnes in 1936. By 1963 the figure had increased to 935,000 tonnes. 23km of branch line with 8 locks once served the metallurgical district of Wassy-Brousseval, south of St-Dizier, but has been closed for many years.

The feature of **Vitry-le-François** of greatest likely interest to the modern boatman is availability of waterside diesel fuel (delivered by tanker), by no means widespread in this region.

Best approach to the town is from any point between the second bridge and Écluse 71, Désert (K1.1), where water can be obtained. Waterside supermarket, right, a short way into the canal. (For details of Vitry-le-François, see Chapter 27.) Lock operating gear (especially at Écluse 71) is very heavy. Scenery in the early reaches is not particularly inspiring, being through fields of maize with avenues of pines and periodic gravel pits.

Orconte, an expanding village by Écluse 66 (K13.5), is a useful port of call with picturesque half-timbered buildings recalling those of the Normandy orchards. Within 400m are butcher, baker, telephone and two small restaurants/bars. That nearest the canal provides a magnificent simple meal of many courses (no choice) at a remarkably low price, in the tradition of French village eating places: half an hour's notice of your intention to dine should be sufficient. A small range of groceries is available; entertainment is supplied by a bar football table. From here, a long straight leads all the way to St-Dizier, with a restaurant on the N4 between Écluses 64 and 63; the village of **Perthes** (K20.2) at Écluse 63 has basic shopping and a garage. Garage and restaurant (also on the N4) are reached from Écluse 61, **Hallignicourt** (K24.1), the most suitable point from which to travel 4km north to **Villiers-en-Lieu**, home of the French Car Museum where 150 vehicles are on show. (Open most days, 14.00–18.00h, closing 19.00h Sun and public holidays.)

To the south is **St-Dizier** airport, with a *port de plaisance* offering moorings and craneage in a short branch immediately before Écluse 59, La Noue (K29.6). Though now an industrial town based on iron and steel working, St-Dizier was an important 16th century stronghold and in 1544 earned the gratitude of François I when 2,500 citizens repulsed 100,000 soldiers under Charles V. As the only really convenient large town between here and the Saône, its shopping centre 500m right of Écluse 58 is both attractive and comprehensive. Close to the left-hand side of the canal is a main line railway station. There are impressive urban mansions and magnificent public gardens in the Place Winston Churchill. Suburbs lead to a railway swing bridge and a road bascule shortly before Écluse 57, **Marnaval** (K34.1), with baker in the village.

From now onwards scenery steadily becomes much prettier and surroundings remain consistently agreeable all the way to the Saône. This is partly accounted for by the canal clinging to the windings of the River Marne, with regular views of stone watermills. Some care is demanded at a very acute bend by the railway bridge by Écluse 56, **Guë** (K36.3); a plaque records building of the lock in 1865 and its lengthening in 1880. The Café du Port will be seen at the next bridge. A good range of shops, all very close, is found in **Chamouilley** (K38.9): moor at the concrete bridge before Écluse 55. An extensive wood-processing yard, once an important user of canal transport, now receives goods by road. Here the design of paddle gear changes; from now on, locks are fitted with four massive and highly efficient ground paddles that require few turns to open fully. Thick woods and a twisting channel lead to **Eurville** and Écluse 54 (K40.7) where instructional leaflets are issued to southbound craft explaining the working of radar-controlled opening bridges scattered throughout the next 50km. The chief point to remember is to avoid mooring within 500m of either side: this can result in bridges staying open longer than necessary, to the frustration of motorists. The village, a short distance from the lock, is a charming place, with small restaurant, butcher, baker and grocer.

In addition to a succession of radar bridges, this part of the canal is notable for alder-filled swamps and shady pools by the edge of the Marne, with several small aqueducts. **Bayard** at Écluse 52 (K45.9) offers restaurant and grocer, while grocer and baker will be found in **Gourzon** (K47.2) by a lift bridge some distance before Écluse 51, **Fontaines-sur-Marne** (K48.2). This lock garden is like a miniature farm, with pigsty and fattened rabbits in high-rise hutches. Only the closeness of the railway breaks the illusion of remoteness. Écluse 50 (K50.6) has a restaurant offering a good choice of reasonably priced meals, with all shopping about 2km east in the small town of **Chevillon**. Three bascule bridges in succession are encountered after Écluse 48, **Curel** (K54.6) and butcher, baker, post office and restaurant are all to be found in the stone-built hilly village. The waterway swings around the base of a wooded cliff at Écluse 47, **Autigny** (K57.1), and after passing through Écluse 46, **Bussy** (K59.3), we arrive at **Thonnance-lès-Joinville** (K61.1) where restaurant and most shops can be reached from a mooring near the bridge.

Joinville (K62.5), on the right bank beyond Écluse 45, stands in the shadow of a hill once dominated by a feudal *château*, birthplace of the Ducs de Guise. The site is now occupied by the 16th century Château du Grand Jardin, open to the public and containing a fine collection of exotic trees. The Marne flows through the town centre and features waterside walks with displays of flowers. Shopping is good. Barely providing sufficient space for two *péniches* to pass each other, a narrow stone-lined cutting takes the canal southwards, past **St-Urbain-sur-Marne** (baker, grocer and butcher) 1km from Écluse 42 (K67.6). The river water at Écluse 41, **Mussey-sur-Marne** (K70.4), seen from a fine triple-arched aqueduct, is crystal clear. Several shops in the village, also restaurant and garage. By now, there is a distinct feeling of ascending into higher terrain, through fields of maize and corn punctuated with patches of dense woodland. **Rouvroy** by Écluse 40

(K73.2) sees the Marne flow under the canal once more. Facilities amount to little more than a grocer. Écluse 39, **Gudmont** (K76) is not only noisy from trains crossing a bridge, but a pall of dust caused by a stone-crushing works hangs everywhere. Rural peace returns, and after a sweeping bend by Écluse 37, Provenchères (K81.2), the waterway arrives in the little town of **Froncles** (K84.2) where most types of shop are scattered along the banks of the Marne.

Almost at any time during the summer, the great variety of greens displayed by trees along the Canal de la Marne à la Saône is particularly notable. This is especially so in the reaches that now follow. **Vouécourt**, Écluse 34 (K89.7), provides a grocer and restaurant; 4km NW lies **Vignory**, situated in a hollow where there is a ruined *château* and a perfect example of a mid-11th century Romanesque church, St Étienne. The pound between Écluses 33 and 32 features a radar-operated bridge at **Viéville** (K93.2), with a shallow, stone-lined cutting above Écluse 32. All facilities can be found in **Bologne**, beyond the river at Écluse 30 (K97.4), with an aqueduct over the Marne soon afterwards. In a meadow on the banks of the River Marne, left, shortly before Écluse 29, Riaucourt, a stone cross inside a fenced enclosure, is a memorial to some children drowned in the 19th century. The tragedy had a considerable impact on the local community which organized a collection to pay for the monument. **Brethenay** (grocer) has the most pleasingly situated lock on the whole canal, No. 27 (K104.6). Just below is an old drawbridge, with the river and a ruined mill alongside; high above on the right the N67 runs along the edge of a cliff. After a further lock we encounter the exceptionally wide **Condes** Tunnel, 308m long (K105.6); passage of this and the drawbridge beyond an aqueduct on the south side is controlled by the keeper at Écluse 26. Craft travelling north pass through a radar beam before they reach the bridge. Numbers displayed at locks between here and the Langres summit do not always correspond to those printed in the *Carte Guide*.

The waterway winds past the east side of the large city of **Chaumont**, whose commercial port is seen on the left bank after Écluse 25, **Reclancourt** (K108.9). Good supermarket about 400m. Closest approach to the town is from the bridge in the pound that follows and up a steep and winding road for a little over 2km. It is thus probably rather too far for a shopping trip, even with bicycles. There is a choice of two restaurants close to the canal, one selling petrol. Water may be obtained from a canal authority depot; request details from your travelling lock keeper. From its lofty setting on a ridge between the Rivers Marne and Suize, Chaumont was a

stronghold of the Counts of Champagne in the 13th and 14th centuries: fortified ramparts remain from this era. Other features are the Basilica of St Jean Baptiste, the Square Philippe-Lebon, and an outstanding 600m railway viaduct with 50 arches on three levels spanning the Suize valley. Écluse 24, Val-des-Choux (K110.4), is succeeded by Écluse 23, **Choignes** (K111.9), an alternative place from which to reach Chaumont. Clusters of pines on a rocky cliff overlook a stone-lined canal cutting, with a watermill on the river. By this point lock houses bear the date 1884. There are numerous grassy bank moorings and quite lovely scenery. In this area the cast-iron lock paddles are of a very interesting pattern, with a dial and pointer indicating whether the aperture is open or closed.

Shopping for bread and groceries can be done in **Luzy-sur-Marne**, at Écluse 19 (K120.5). However, if you wait until **Foulain** (K124.3), with excellent moorings by a meadow in the reach between Écluses 17 and 16, you can walk across a railway level crossing and into the flourishing village to find a baker, grocer, butcher, restaurant and garage all within 350m of the waterway. The final series of locks to the summit level provides an assortment of limited facilities: Écluse 10, Prées (K136.5), was able to replenish our dwindling water supplies (but only through the kindness of the keeper, who was not obliged to assist); the bridge shortly before Écluse 9, **Rolampont** (K139.2, convenient moorings), is a good point for visiting all types of shop, garage and restaurant, the village being one of few on this route which spreads along the canal bank. Upstream of Écluse 8, St-Menge (K140.4), is a bridge carrying the new A31 Langres–Toul *autoroute*. Three of the canal's important supply reservoirs are quite close by. **Humes**, at Écluse 5 (K144.4), where there is a somewhat scruffy commercial port, is convenient for baker, grocer, garage and restaurant. A manually worked swing bridge mounted on an 'island' in the centre of the canal is the main feature of **Jorquenay** (K145.9), while at Écluse 3, Moulin-Rouge (K148.1), will be seen a substantial timberyard, complete with proprietor's ornate 19th century house and outbuildings which include an extensive washhouse with cistern. Rising in the distance beyond are the ramparts of Langres.

In spite of the 3km (uphill) journey from the canal at Écluse 2, Moulin-Chapeau (K149.8), **Langres** is well worth a journey, both for sight-seeing and more practical shopping purposes. Although the author once narrowly escaped death on this road when flung from the pillion of the boat's motorcycle, subsequent visits confirmed his initial impression that the city has much to offer. Set on a high point overlooking the Langres Plateau and close to the source of the Marne, it was one of the three capitals of Gaulish Burgundy. In addition to the Cathedral of St Mammès, every visitor should make a circuit on foot of the fortified ramparts punctuated at intervals by towers and gateways. The views are superb. A passenger car on a short length of track has been preserved from a former rack railway that once rumbled along a steep incline below the city walls. Shops are good. At this 'Gateway to Burgundy' one of the most agreeable restaurants is at the Hotel d'Europe.

Updated information on passage times for the one-way Balesmes Tunnel (4,820m) can be obtained from the keeper of Écluse 1, Batailles (K152.5). While equipped with lighting, this seemed poorly maintained

in 1990 and was not functioning. As always, it is much recommended that all craft carry a powerful headlamp. At the far end, a stonelined cutting leads to a not insignificant village – **Heuilley-Cotton** (K161.6), with moorings at several points including a 'port' on the left before the first of two bridges. Pleasant though this deeply rural settlement is, it sadly suffers from a complete lack of facilities. But at least there is a public telephone by the church enabling a taxi to be called out from Langres should north-bound boats have tunnel waiting time to kill (or worse still, you have been caught

Southern approach to the 4,820m Balesmes Tunnel, near Langres.

224

by the Sunday lock closure). A much better Sunday halting place (and still within taxi distance of Langres) would be **Villegusien** (K167.1), just uphill of Écluse 9 in a series of closely-spaced deep locks descending towards the Saône. Restaurant, good butcher and baker, and an amazing general emporium selling everything from summer dresses to infra-red lamps for raising chicks. The first twelve locks descending from the summit towards the Saône are mechanized; a further eight were to be similarly automated by 1991. Staff from a control centre at Écluse 1 may be relied on to assist if the gear is reluctant to function correctly.

Consistently pretty surroundings accompany the waterway as it follows the valley of the River Vingeanne and past the delightful village of **Piépape** (baker, grocer), just before Écluse 12 (K169.5). Bankside facilities now become very sparse for a while, with little available until **Courchamp**, Écluse 24 (K185.6), where there is a restaurant. The next village, set well back from the navigation, is **St-Maurice-sur-Vingeanne**, reached from Écluse 26 (K189), with grocer and baker. **Fontaine-Française**, about 5km west of the canal at **Pouilly-sur-Vingeanne**, supplies all urban needs. Nearby, in 1595 Henri IV with a mere 510 horsemen beat a 15,000-strong army composed of troops from Spain and the Ligue. The *château* is open to the public. **St-Seine-sur-Vingeanne**, 2km east of the canal at Écluse 29 (K196.7), is notable for its Burgundian Romanesque church. On the left-hand side beyond Écluse 32 **Fontenelle** (K199.5) is an impressive fortified farmhouse, while the Château de Rosières 3km NE of Écluse 33, **Licey** (K201.8), dating from the 15–17th centuries, merits investigation. Licey-sur-Vingeanne (right bank, between Écluses 33 and 34) has a restaurant.

The bridge north of Écluse 34, **Dampierre** (K204.3), is the best point from which to walk or cycle 2km into **Beaumont-sur-Vingeanne** for glimpses of the exterior of a delightful 18th century *château* (not open to the public). It is of quite small proportions and features a fine roof of coloured Burgundian tiles. Baker and restaurant can be found in **Champagne-sur-Vingeanne** (K206.6), east of the bridge in the middle of the pound between Écluses 35 and 36. River and canal are crossed by a huge concrete railway viaduct a little before Écluse 38, **Oisilly** (K210.5). The first convenient town with a full range of facilities to be found in a long while is **Renève**, at Écluse 39 (K214.2).

With the Saône junction now quite close, the last point of great interest is the small town of **Talmay**, 3km NE of the bridge (K221.1) in the middle of the pound between Écluses 41 and 42. Here is a notable

château, open to the public July 1–Sept 15 (15.00–16.30h, not Mon). The oldest portion is a 46m high 13th century keep to which is attached a classical mid-18th century mansion in cream stone under a roof of coloured glazed tiles. At Écluse 42, **Maxilly-sur-Saône** (K222.7), taxis may be hired from the Café de l'Écluse for a 5km journey into **Pontailler-sur-Saône** (see Chapter 47). One more lock, Écluse 43, Chemin de Fer (K223), now intervenes before the approach to the Saône's **Heuilley-sur-Saône** lock cut where the right-angled junction is controlled by traffic lights. Water is available from the Saône lock keeper.

49 · River Seille

Carte Guide: *Saône*
From a junction with the River Saône (K106) near La Truchère, to Louhans, the terminus: 39km and 4 locks.

An enchanting – almost enchanted – waterway, little known and generally ignored by yachtsmen making for the Mediterranean or hurrying to home ports in the north. For many years its only traffic was a handful of sand barges: these have now ceased to trade. Hardly touched by main roads, the Seille winds through a charming landscape of fields and trees, with agreeable grassbank moorings possible almost throughout. Of moderate width, it was almost deserted in the early 1980s, and even now is generally a peaceful backwater. One is reluctant to provide any form of publicity, as it would be preferable for the Seille to remain just as it is – totally unspoiled; yet regular pleasure craft justify lock maintenance. Navigation from end to end can easily be achieved in a single day, although there will always be a temptation to linger much longer.

It is recorded that rock salt was transported from the Jura to Louhans by waggon and small boats about AD 1000, then transferred to larger craft and moved down the Seille by the monks of Tournus. The present navigation dates from Napoléonic times and was engineered by Emiland-Marie Gauthey.

Urgent remedial work was carried out on the locks in 1981 to cater for a growth in pleasure boat traffic. No special problems will now be expected and there is good water depth throughout.

Lacking any form of signboard, the entrance from the

Water mill by the Seille at Branges.

River Saône at K106 is not immediately obvious. Ignore the large upstream channel (which is a weir outfall), turning instead into a little arm, just above a wood; avoid a shoal on the right of the entrance. This soon leads to La Truchère lock, with landing steps each side of the tail wall. A keeper lives in a cottage alongside an upper chamber marking the site of a former lock. **La Truchère** (K0.5) lies on the left bank, a collection of small houses facing the water in narrow winding streets (Auberge de la Grenouillère, *dépôt de pain*). A restored watermill stands by the weir. **Pont-Seille** (K3) is a three-arched concrete bridge with a small restaurant. Trees and meadows, very reminiscent of the Yorkshire Derwent, lead to **Ratenelle** (K8), with mooring possible by the bridge against a wall on the right. Basic facilities include grocer (bread) and a hotel/bar. An unusually plain church with spire stands near the water's edge. Gallo-Roman relics have been recovered from the river bed.

The five tall, slated turrets of the Château de Montrepost among the trees announce the presence of the small town of **Cuisery** (K13). A channel on the right leads to the lock, where the keeper lives in a building the size of a farmhouse. An ancient and huge *glycine* (wisteria) covers much of the far end and is festooned with masses of pale blue flowers in early summer. Iron spoked wheels are used to open and close the gates. The lock cut leads to a broad reach at the head of a weirstream, just below the N75 bridge (the main road between Tournus and Louhans); pontoon moorings with water and electricity just above. A steep walk into Cuisery provides reasonable shopping; fuel is obtainable in the other direction on the N75. Market day is Tuesday, with a fair on the first one of each month. There are several restaurants of which the most ambitious is the Hostellerie Bressane, with a plaque of recommendation from the Gastronomes of Switzerland (Zurich?). The only fault of the town and an overnight mooring near the bridge is the noise of almost constant lorries and croaking frogs.

Lush meadows, with frequent potential mooring places, accompany the river as it winds towards **Loisy** (K17), with a magnificent stone watermill at the head of the weirstream, left. Access to the village is not very easy: small boats can approach the bank in this stream. Otherwise take the lock cut and cross the lock island from the abutments of a former bridge (this, however, leads over private property). Supplies are limited to baker and petrol. Loisy lock (K18) is unmanned and its cottage falling into ruin. Boat crews operate the lock unaided, a rare event in France. Well above the flood meadows beyond the lock is a sizeable *château* with a large derelict tower and imposing horse chestnut trees; it commands a fine view of the Seille.

Occasional farmhouses and riverside cottages are the only features in a totally rural landscape of trees and meadows as the Seille winds this way and that; midsummer brings carpets of *fritillaires* (snake's head lilies) and glow-worms in the intense silence of night. Craft drawing little water can penetrate a long backwater, left, to reach the old port of **Branges** (K35), which has butcher, baker, grocer and chemist. Hire cruisers commenced operation here in 1983. A stone ramp (former ferry?) would serve as launching slip for small trailed boats. Another substantial mill overlooks a weedy pool. It is necessary to retrace the route to enter the tree-lined cut to Branges lock, No. 4, whose chamber appears to have been lengthened at some stage. Distant hills to the east are a reminder that the Swiss border is a mere 80km away.

The first evidence of **Louhans** (K39) is the superb spire and roof of the church of St Pierre, richly decorated with lozenge patterns in yellow, green, brown and rust-coloured tiles. (Packs of wolves that once roamed the area – *loups* – are the reputed origin of the place name.) Every waterway terminus benefits from having a worthwhile cruising objective, and this little town makes a fitting end to the journey. Centre of the highly productive farming region known as Bresse, it holds a big market every Monday, and fairs on the first and third one of each month. Pontoon moorings near the junction with the River Solnan are convenient for shops and station (trains connect with Seurre, St-Jean-de-Losne and Verdun-sur-le-Doubs). Water point.

Louhans was first recorded in the 5th century. Its leading attraction must be the Grande Rue, where shopfronts are enhanced by 15–17th century timber and stone arcades, providing coolness in summer and shelter from the winter rain. All manner of culinary delicacies are available including the celebrated *poulet de Bresse*, free-range chicken fattened on buckwheat and maize. The Hôtel Dieu contains an outstanding collection of apothecaries' jars: apply to view at the regional hospital.

VI·THE ATLANTIC COAST

50 · River Sèvre-Niortaise

No Carte Guide currently available.
From Niort to the Atlantic at Charron, 72km with 8 locks. Junctions are made with several marshland waterways, the most important being an extensive complex of tiny canals at Coulon and together totalling a huge distance; the Canal de la Vielle Autise between La Barbée and Courdault, 10km with 1 lock; the Canal du Mignon from Bazoin to Mauzé, 17km with 4 locks; La Jeune Autise from Maillé to a weir at Château Vert, 8km with 1 lock; and the Canal Maritime de Marans au Brault, 6km with 1 lock.

While a significant network in its own right, the Sèvre-Niortaise has no connections with the rest of the French system. As a result it is little known outside its immediate region and is used only by local craft. The uppermost reaches are really delightful and well worth exploring by trailed boat or inflatable, with the possibility of cruising the 54km between Niort and Marans during one long summer day. The amazingly complicated and quite fascinating series of little canals west and south of Coulon known as La Venise Verte (Green Venice) is best entered aboard one of the passenger punts (*barques*) available for hire by the hour with a knowledgeable boatman in attendance. If travelling by car, it is easily worth diverting to the area, to enjoy an experience unique in France and justly famous. Other trips into this maze of channels, known also as the *Marais Poitevin*, operate from the following towns: La Garette, Arçais, St-Hilaire-La-Palud, Le Mazeau and Maillezais. In previous years a passenger launch has been in service during the summer between Niort and Marans, and it would be worth enquiring about such trips in either town.

Farming, architecture and the whole way of life of this river is very special. Admittedly the lower reaches across drained marshland are somewhat bleak; but if you like the English Fenlands you will find a similar

compelling fascination. All locks have keepers, but it is advised to give a little advance warning of a passage, by first contacting the authority's office in Niort. Although no cruising guide is available, the Direction Départementale de l'Équipement des Deux Sèvres, Subdivision de Niort, Cale du Port, 79000 Niort publishes a small free map showing the main navigable routes with maximum dimensions. To obtain the fullest enjoyment from a journey, excellent large-scale maps are worth buying: they show every tiny water channel through the marshes on a scale of 1:25,000. The appropriate sheets of this *Carte Topographique* are 1528 Est, 1528 Ouest, 1428 Est, and 1428 Ouest, published by the Institut Géographique National, 107 rue La Boétie, 75008 Paris.

Brief history Two thousand years ago, the Atlantic coastline extended to Coulon and Niort was served by the estuary of the Sèvre. A collection of islands was scattered throughout the bay that as a result of silting and drainage works has become the *Marais Poitevin*, and the sea has retreated more than 40km. From the 11th century, five important abbeys created drainage channels, fisheries, dykes and weirs. These canals filled with silt through neglect during the Hundred Years War, but a comprehensive new plan to win back land from the marshes was proposed by Henry IV in 1599 and put into effect in the early 17th century by a Dutchman, Humphroy Bradley de Berg op Zom, who was granted the title 'Engineer in Chief of Dykes of the Kingdom'. Today, some 55,000 hectares have been drained: 40,000 nearer the coast are highly productive farmland, while the remaining 15,000 are the wetlands of La Venise Verte. In 1808, Napoléon ordered modern navigation works to be undertaken on the Sèvre: these were not fully completed until several decades later. Nothing came of a 1751 plan for a navigable canal from Vivonne on the River Clain downstream of Poitiers to the sea via Niort and Marans. Connecting with the Rivers Vienne and Loire, this would have provided water communication with Paris: the cost was to be defrayed by a lottery!

Most of the freight craft used were very small open

River Sèvre Niortaise

punts: an 1882 census discovered no fewer than 8,902 in use and even today there are thought to be about 3,000. The first steam vessel arrived on the Sèvre in 1840. Otherwise, long trains of poplar logs were floated to the sawmills. The waterways continue to be used for transport of agricultural goods and animals, especially in parts of the *Marais* where there is no road access. The area was declared a Natural Regional Park in 1978.

Rising at Fonbedoire, the River Sèvre-Niortaise becomes navigable in the city of **Niort**, known by the Romans as Novum Ritum (New Ford). At the end of the 12th century there was a busy river port with rudimentary barges and rafts used to transport goods to and from the coast. Throughout the Middle Ages a great market and fair was held here, with salt, fish, corn and wool being exported to the Low Countries and Spain. The leading import was furs from Northern Europe and later Canada. An extensive leather industry became established and glove-making continues today. At the time of the Revolution there were 30 fulling mills in operation. The city's most notable building is the severe stonebuilt Donjon, a fortified 12–13th century *château* believed to have been started by Henry II of England and completed by Richard the Lion Heart. In its original form there were 700m of encircling wall; a pair of massive crenellated square towers are joined by 15th century additions. Used as a prison under the Bourbons, it now houses a regional folklore museum, the collection including a reconstructed peasant house interior and a number of Niortaise headdresses or *coiffes*, known as *grisettes*. Rising from the riverbank, it is a most impressive structure and provides good views from the ramparts. Other highlights are a former town hall built in 1535 on a triangular plan and now the

Musée du Pilori, the Musée des Beaux Arts, and a series of old buildings in the area around the Rue St-Jean, among which is the late 16th century Governor's House, with delicate sculpted decorations. One Françoise d'Aubigné was born in the city: widowed at 25, she secretly married Louis XIV and exerted a considerable influence on the monarch. She is better known as Madame de Maintenon. A marble plaque on the former Hôtel de la Boule in the Avenue de Paris records Napoléon's last stay on French soil, before his exile in 1815.

Niort is noted for a number of culinary specialities, especially angelica, the candied stem of a herb; during the 18th century production reached an annual 10 tonnes. It is the basis of *sève d'angélique* (a liqueur) and used also for cake decoration, *les oeufs angélique* and *soufflé glacé à l'angélique*, an iced soufflé. When he visited Niort in 1852, Louis Napoléon Bonaparte was presented with an imperial eagle made entirely of angelica. Other regional dishes are *poulet sauté à la Niortaise* (chicken with fried onions and potatoes), *porcelet Niortaise* (sucking pig with onions and potatoes), *jonchée* (a goat's milk cheese) and *tourteau fromagé* (a delicious goat cheesecake).

The river divides into a series of millstreams during its passage of the city, the uppermost limit for most craft being Le Port, where the navigation office is situated. Shops, restaurants and a slipway for launching, Écluse I, Comporte (K1), is on the edge of town, with cottages and allotment gardens. The upper gates are conventional mitre doors, with a guillotine at the bottom. The Sèvre soon enters a broad reach past the *base nautique*, with rowing boats, a small number of cruisers and water-skiing. Even in early June this section is inclined to be very weedy: later in the summer you can expect to experience problems with choked propellers for up to 2km. Low banks provide views of cattle in meadows among numerous white poplars. Elsewhere there are fine houses, indicating that this is one of the more exclusive residential zones of Niort. Take care to avoid the chains of two pedestrian ferry punts near the village of **St-Liguaire** (K6). Where several little lanes run down to the water, left bank, trailed craft could be launched. As always, when the channel divides keep to the towpath side to pass island and weirstreams. Summertime chalets bear jokey names like *Mon Rêve* (My Dream) and *Mieux que Rien* (Better than Nothing), just as if this were the Upper Thames.

Navigation markers are well maintained, so there is little excuse in heading for a low three-arched bridge instead of turning sharply to the left to enter Lock 2, **La Roussille** (K7). Like the first lock, this has an irregularly-shaped chamber; its top gate is an electrically-operated guillotine. The lock cottage is dated 1808 and faces the Auberge/Restaurant du Roussille: this grouping of riverside buildings is most pleasing and judging from the numbers of towpath joggers, strollers and fishermen is a popular retreat on hot summer days. Lock 3, **La Tiffardière** (K8), has conventional gates but a chamber with sloping sides: the only lock on the river without a keeper, it is worked by boat crews, the windlass being concealed in a hedge by the former lock house. Beyond a railway bridge the waterway becomes quite narrow before arriving in the large village of **Magné** (K11), slipway on the left bank. A double-leaved bascule bridge at Le Grand Port is flanked by a wood-fired pottery kiln, a Romanesque church and delightful cottages. Everywhere are little wooden boats, mostly black and green, or sometimes blue or red. The upper gate of Lock 4, **Marais-Pin** (K14), is an electrically driven sinking guillotine, with retracting footbridge over the chamber.

Boat people's houses line the banks of the river through the village of **Coulon** (K16), a place animated by numerous small passenger punts (*barques*) offering excursions into La Venise Verte. Holding up to six people, they are propelled with a long pole (*pigouille*) or single paddle (*pelle*). Negotiate with a boatman for tours of an hour or longer through the maze of nearby waterways. A vast grid of navigable channels, all named with signposts, extends north and south of the river: the total length is several hundred km. Some are very shallow and should not be entered by cruisers. In any case there is a powered boat prohibition on certain routes and during weekends and public holidays. The marshland waterways of Le Marais Poitevin are classified according to size and ownership. First are the tiny *fossés*, little larger than a flooded field ditch and pri-

vately controlled; then the *conches*, between 2m and 6m wide and maintained by the local community; the *caneaux*, state-controlled and providing links with many villages such as the old boatmen's hamlet of **La Garette** and **Le Vanneau**; and the *rigoles*, over 6m wide and under the responsibility of the Syndicat des Marais. It would be possible to spend a week by punt or canoe, penetrating this beguiling area where white poplars, willows, ash and alder edge tiny fields of intensely green grass. Ash is used for binding the banks and cropping for firewood, and poplar is felled for the sawmills, one important use being matchsticks. Life abounds in the clear water and among species that find their way to market and restaurant table are pike, stickleback, zander, minnow, bleak, perch, chub, loach, roach, eel, tench, crayfish and frogs. In the shade of the tree canopies many varieties of wild plant will be found, such as arrowheads, water lilies, water hornwort, floating moss (*azolla*) and duckweed. One fascinating highlight is the Village des Rouches (Rush Village) on the edge of the Canal de la Garette, near Coulon. This is a re-creation of a typical marshland settlement where hut-dwellers (*huttiers*) would have lived until 1829. Although local people now inhabit conventional stone and timber houses, many continue to derive a living from the marsh, grazing creamy cattle and goats, fishing and in the winter wildfowling for duck, plover, snipe and heron. With very limited road access, everything must be conveyed in the small *barques*: animals, tractors, churns of milk and timber. Until very recent times, marriage and funeral processions were often seen on the water. Where fields have been drained, and especially on the former marsh towards the coast, fertile market gardens raise artichokes, onions, melons, courgettes, broad beans, garlic and a delicious pulse bean (*mojette*).

Coulon has a slipway, shops, restaurants and an open-air market on Sundays. Greatly recommended is the quayside Restaurant au Marais, where local dishes are served; such as *mouclade* (sea mussels in white wine and cream with a dash of curry) and *bouilliture* of stewed baby eels. From here almost to the sea small farmhouses stand on the river banks – long low structures with cattle sheds and barns under a single roof. **La Sotterie** (K19, literally The Place of Fools) is a tiny village opposite a hamlet named **Le Paradis**, on the edge of Le Marais de la Princesse. Here, Écluse 5 is fitted with two pairs of mitre gates and meals may be obtained at L'Auberge de l'Écluse. And everywhere, named side channels branch off into the marshes. **Irleau** lies 1.2km south of the Sèvre at **Le Pont d'Irleau** (K21.2, restaurant) and is served by its own small waterway, the Rigole de la Garette. Like its neighbour

Le Vanneau, it is a popular local fishing centre.

One curious mystery concerns the great number of small *barques*: like the ubiquitous fishing dinghies of almost every French river, they appear to have been professionally built. But it is rare indeed to encounter a boatyard dedicated to their production. In recent years plastic replicas have begun to appear, but the majority are still of either steel or timber. One of the most charming villages of Le Marais is **Arçais**, 1.5km south of the river and approached from the navigation at K25.2 via the Bief Minet (suitable only for small craft).

Deep in the heart of the maze of small watercourses known as La Venise Verte, approached from the river at Coulon.

An old *château* overlooks the tiny port. 300m before Lock 6, **Les Bourdettes** (K29), a bar/restaurant stands in a group of cottages, with a lift bridge by the lock itself. **Damvix** (K30), with a tall grey church spire, is a small town with most facilities, including garage. Pedalos can be hired with access to La Venise Verte. By a junction with the Nouveau Béjou Canal, take the right fork through **La Barbée** and bear left at a junction with the **Canal de la Vieille Autise** (K32). This navigation may, however, be followed to its terminus at **Courdault**.

Three weirs control water levels at a three-way junction at **Bazoin**, Lock 7 (K34). Another diversion from the through route is possible by negotiating the first of four locks on the **Canal du Mignon** which runs SE

via **La-Grève-sur-Mignon** to a dead end at **Mauzé-sur-le-Mignon**. Soon after Bazoin lock, Le Vieux Batelier Restaurant will be seen on an island, with bridge providing access to the shore. Although the scenic interest in these lower, rather treeless reaches is limited to the many little farmhouses, there is widespread boating at weekends.

La Jeune Autise is navigable from **Fosse du Loup** (K37) by turning right and into the town of **Maillé**, returning if wished by an alternative route down the Contour de Maillé. Impressive waterside ruins of the 11th century abbey of St-Pierre are at **Maillezais**. A similar circular cruise of about 2km is offered by the Contour des Combrands and the Canal de Sablon (K41). While considerably shorter, the Canal de Pomère is uncompromisingly straight (K46) and the original course of the river via the Contour de Pomère is much prettier. The landscape is decidedly Dutch in character and many of the waterside buildings could have been imported direct from Friesland. At the outskirts of **Marans** (K51) fork left; shortly the town appears, with pleasure craft moored on a reach lined with buildings. While shops and other facilities are plentiful, there is a disappointing lack of restaurants. It is well known for its dairy produce and pottery and at first sight is rather a drab place. The atmosphere improves as you enter the port which has a positive maritime flavour, shipyards and extensive moorings. Craft up to 1,500 tonnes capacity can penetrate this far from the sea. Several junctions are now reached: first, with the **Canal de La Rochelle à Marans**, 26km long and no longer available to boats; ahead, the route divides (K54): the left fork is the start of the **Canal de Marans à la Mer**. It is utterly straight and joins the tideway of the Sèvre below a sea lock at **Brault** (K61). Alternatively, take the right channel at Marans, pass through the Écluse des Enfreneaux, No. 8, and follow the tidal windings of the Sèvre Maritime to the coast.

For those in small inland boats, Marans will normally be the end of the journey. From here a regular bus service back to Niort will reunite you with your car (trains also run but are infrequent). Car or bus excursions can be made to the historic port and Protestant citadel of **La Rochelle**, 25km SW; and one of the most beautiful beaches on this coast is on a pine-covered peninsula, **Pointe d'Arçay**, south of **La Faute-sur-Mer** (43km by road from Marans via the N137, D25 and D746 across drained marshland).

51 · River Charente

Carte Guide *Charente*
From Angoulême to the Atlantic Coast at Rochefort, 147km with 21 locks. Subject to the restrictions mentioned later in this chapter, there are connections with two additional lengths of waterway: the River Boutonne, between the Charente at Carillon and St-Jean d'Angely, 31km with 4 locks and an opening tidal barrage; and the Canal de la Charente à la Seudre, from the Charente between Tonnay-Charente and Rochefort (Écluse de Biard) and Beaugeay, 16km with 1 lock.

The Charente is fortunate in that Henry IV (1589–1610) described it as the 'most beautiful river in my kingdom', a testimonial with which it is easy to agree today. In the virtually deserted upper reaches, the wood-fringed meadows, old watermills, stonebuilt hamlets and luxuriant wildlife are far removed from the 20th century. At present you can expect to meet a mere handful of boats in the 119km of non-tidal water: two hotel craft, a tripping vessel and a small number of hire cruisers. Traffic will inevitably increase, for this is a waterway wonderland that is now only just starting to be discovered by the tourist.

Rising near Rochechouart in Limousin, the river flows gently in summer, although the current can be quite fierce early in the season. From Angoulême to Saintes much of the landscape is devoted to vineyards producing grapes for the world-famous Cognac, once exported by river barge.

Apart from two nearest the sea, all locks are operated, unsupervised, by boats' crews. Such a practice in France results from a long period of dereliction from which the river has only recently been rescued. Exceptionally robust lock paddle gear, requiring almost super-human strength, has now been replaced by low-geared rack and pinion sluices.

In spite of its present lack of use, the Charente offers a variety of possibilities for getting afloat. Hire cruisers from St-Simeux or St-Brice; hotel barges which take a leisurely week between Angoulême and St-Savinien; and day trips on the lower river from Jarnac to the coast (details from the Syndicats d'Initiative in St-Savinien, Saintes, Cognac or the Régie Départementale des Passages d'Eau, BP102, 17009 La Rochelle). Private craft may, of course, enter from the sea. Trailed boats are well suited to the Charente and there are several launch and recovery sites. At least three days should be devoted to a one-way exploration of the non-tidal river; there is ample interest for a week's cruise.

Brief history Although commercial traffic long ago vanished from the Charente, the story of many centuries of successful navigation is better recorded than on many French waterways. Starting from limited use of the lowest reaches in Gallo-Roman times, there is evidence of vessels trading to Cognac in the 10th century. By the 12th century, wines of the region were regularly exported by water to England, Denmark and the Low Countries. King Louis IX took steps to improve the waterway in the 13th century and a port was authorized at Angoulême by Philippe the Bold in 1280. Marguerite, grandmother of Francis I, ordered various works to be carried out, but by 1590 local merchants were complaining that the river was in ruins. Under Henry IV conditions became much better, but only at the expense of excessively high tolls. New traffic was generated by the creation of a military port at Rochefort, near the mouth of the river, in 1666. Thirty years later came the first of several schemes to provide a navigable link with the Loire and the Vienne, for which three pound locks and no fewer than 70 flash locks (*portes mariniers*) were required on the upper Charente alone, between Angoulême and Civry. Barges were certainly using this section in 1777, albeit with difficulty.

Tolls were virtually abolished in 1737. Another scheme that foundered was suggested in 1760: this would have resulted in a network of waterways from the Charente to the Garonne, via the Dronne. Many of the present locks were provided from 1767 onwards, at last ridding the river of inefficient flash locks that caused endless disputes between boatmen and millers. There were then about 66 barges in service, taking up to two weeks for a round trip between Angoulême and Rochefort.

Several different types of craft were used: the *galiot* was a barge loading about 10 tonnes; the *galion* a small sailing barge; the *allège* loading 30–40 tonnes; and the ubiquitous *gabare*, a sailing barge between 20m and 35m in length with a single 12–15m mast and loading 80–200 tonnes. Normal cargoes included paper and stone blocks from Angoulême, cannon and munitions from Ruelle, brandy from Jarnac and Cognac; corn, linen and meat. Upstream-bound goods ranged from coal and salt to fish and wood. On the tideway, it was not unknown for 30 pairs of oxen or 200–400 men to bow-haul a single vessel. Upriver, 15 or 20 men would suffice, the work also being undertaken by women and oxen. Steam arrived in the form of a vessel named *L'Hirondelle* in 1822: her machinery was built in Liverpool. By 1840 three return trips weekly were offered by steamer between Saintes and Angoulême, with an annual 40,000 passengers in the 1850s. Four locks were rebuilt and others repaired in 1842: trade flourished.

Then came the railway in 1867: no immediate effect was detected as far as freight traffic was concerned, indeed, 1892 was a record year, with 7,600,000 tonnes carried. Reclassification of the waterways in 1879 had resulted in the Charente being treated as a major navigation.

As the 20th century advanced, goods progressively moved to rail and road transport. During the Great War 4 horses to each *gabare* replaced steam tugs. Thereafter the decline was dramatic and the section from Montignac (24km above Angoulême) to Cognac was officially closed to traffic (*déclassé*) in 1926. The next 7km to Port du Lys were similarly treated in 1927. In spite of the attempts of riverside traders to revise navigation, the last barge sailed from Jarnac in 1930 and remaining traffic between Cognac and the tideway had disappeared by 1944. Some of the last barges were requisitioned by the Germans in World War II and destroyed in British bombing raids on St-Nazaire.

The Charente appeared to have come to the end of its life as a navigation when it was struck off the official list of waterways in 1957. Attempts were made to put a *péniche* into service in 1967, with only limited success. Passenger traffic was restored in 1969 and has since flourished. During the late 1970s dredging work and lock repairs reopened the river between the sea and Angoulême, and a fleet of British hire cruisers was established at St-Simeux in 1980. The resulting publicity has brought tourists to this lovely waterway. Management of the Angoulême-Cognac length is in the charge of the Charente Département, while responsibility for the lower reaches comes under Charente Maritime. For the present, the Charente is one of the loveliest but least used long-distance navigations in Western Europe: how long it stays relatively deserted remains to be seen.

Although once navigable for a considerable distance upstream of **Angoulême**, the city is now considered to be the highest point to which normal craft can ascend. Exploration beyond should be possible by dinghy, taking care to avoid any obstructions. 1km farther up is a junction with the River Touvre, originally used over 7km by barges bring cannon from the foundry at **Ruelle**. Angoulême is an important industrial and commercial centre, built on a fortified hilltop high above the river. Founded by the Romans and later the Capital of the former province of Angoumois, it has been famous since the Middle Ages for papermaking. Completely surrounded by ramparts, from which there are impressive views over the surrounding countryside, it has a first-class pedestrianized shopping centre. St

Pierre's Cathedral dates from the 12th century and features a remarkable sculpted façade. **L'Houmeau** is the name given to the riverport area, where there is a restaurant aboard the converted *péniche Bernard Palissy*. Gastronomes should sample the regional speciality *tripes à mode d'Angoulême* (ox tripe and trotters in white wine with tomatoes and garlic). Lock 1, St-Cybard, is upstream of the port.

Soon leaving the city behind, the Charente rapidly assumes a totally rural character, flowing through a green and peaceful valley. Lock 2, Touérat (K4.6), is followed by the village of **Fléac** (K6.5), surrounded by vineyards and orchards with many walnut trees. Twisting once more towards Angoulême, the Écluse 3, Basseau, is reached (K7.8), with No. 4, Fleurac (K10.3), shortly before **Trois-Palis** (K12.8) where there is a church with spire covered with reddish tiles. Lock 5, La Motte (K13.3) is at the head of a reach that extends to **Sireuil** (K20.3), where the 6th lock is situated. Locks 7, La Liège (K22) and 8 lead to the village of **St-Simeux** (K24), a charming stone-built hamlet with bridge and watermill.

A sheltered climate and pellucid water make the river ideal for swimming, while temporary moorings in total peace abound. Avoiding weirs on the millstream, left, enter a shady cut leading to Écluse 9, Malleville (K24.7), with a pantiled stone cottage long since deserted by its keeper. Willows and alders lead past an island (Les Peyronnets) to **Châteauneuf-sur-Charente** (K27.7) with launching ramp shortly before No. 10, left bank. Access to the former lock house was once via a swing bridge over the chamber; this has been removed and it is necessary to enter the private garden to operate the gate-opening mechanism. In common with several other locks, an absence of landing stages produces problems in getting back on board. (Such facilities have recently been improved throughout the river). Moor near the modern concrete road bridge (pontoon) to visit the town, a remarkably pleasant little place with convenient shops, restaurants, swimming pool and garage. Having a railway station on the Cognac–Angoulême line, this could be a useful point from which to recover a car when cruising by trailed boat. Little remains of a stone *château* built to guard what was then the only river crossing between Angoulême and Cognac: it replaced a wooden structure burned down in the 11th century.

Take a right-hand fork (K30.7) and after passing some islands turn sharp left under a single-arched stone bridge and into the cut of Écluse 11, **Vibrac** (K33.2). Silting is likely at this junction with the weir-stream, so any approach by water to Vibrac village is not advised. Walk from the bridge, 1km for grocer and restaurant. Sloping stone walls are a feature of the exceptionally wide lock chamber; there is a section of vertical wall on the downhill, left, side where craft should moor. But be wary of a concrete shelf near the empty water level: a descending boat could easily become trapped. (This curious design dates from the rebuilding programme in 1842.) Although there are occasional unmarked shallows in the river channel, it is not these that produce small whirlpools, but the emergence of subterranean springs.

St-Simon (K35.2) is one of the Charente's most attractive villages: clusters of ancient little stone houses with narrow streets overlook a quay with pollarded horse chestnuts. At weekends and on public holidays water-skiers are entitled to use this reach, with a 45kph speed limit – a surprising and potentially dangerous concession but which is quite normal on French rivers. During the 19th century this was a leading barge-building centre, 1½–2 years being taken to complete each vessel. Towards the turn of the century a barge laden with cannon and munitions sank here and was not raised for several weeks. Pass under the four-arched stone bridge of **Juac** (avoid underwater abutments) and take the left fork to Lock 12 (K36.2) with the ruins of an old keeper's cottage opposite a more recent structure protected by an ugly security fence. Draft at the village quay is only 0.7m.

A lovely reach of dense woodland, the Bois Charente, leads to the lock cut of Écluse 13, **Saintonge** (K39.2) on the right. The chamber appears to date only from 1913, when considerable works were carried out. Hidden among trees on the left is an earlier sloping-sided lock in ruins with a pretty stone cottage, bearing the date 1837. Follow a woodland path for a view of Saintonge village and its rocky weir. **Bassac** is reached from the next bridge, *Pont de Vinade*, a walk of about 1.5km (restaurant and garage). Bassac Abbey, built about AD1000, suffered in the Hundred Years War and again during the Wars of Religion. Disestablished during the Revolution, it has been a house of the Missionary Brothers of St Theresa of the Infant Jesus since 1947. The public are admitted. **Vinade**, left of the bridge, has a small distillery open to visitors; another is a little upstream at **Graves**.

Vineyards are much in evidence, growing grapes for the brandy industry; others are used in the local aperitif *pineau des Charentes*, a blend of fresh grape juice and Cognac. **Gondeville** (K43.4), where there is a restaurant (water point), may be approached from below Lock 14; alternatively, with care, down the weirstream from above. The short cut, grandly known as the Canal de Gondeville, was dug in 1776–7. Its associated weir, like most others on the river, is in the form of a rocky waterfall, covered with aquatic plants. On the outskirts of **Jarnac** (K46), a delightful *château* on the right bank is approached via its own private backwater. Further desirable residences are scattered throughout woods as the river narrows and passes under the shade of a grove of white poplars. Several mills point to the industrial activity in the town. Lock 15 was lengthened to 80m early in the 20th century and is the largest on the navigation. Alongside, pleasing stone houses rise from the weirpool, where canoe slalom is a popular sport below the millraces. Second only to Cognac for the production of brandy, Jarnac is a busy little town with shops, garages and restaurants and an extensive open-air swimming pool in the weirstream. Founded in Gallo-Roman times, the town is best remembered for a duel between François de Vivonne and Guy Chabot, Count of Jarnac, which took place in 1547 in the presence of Henry II and his court: de Vivonne died of his wounds. Another encounter is recalled by a monument to the Prince de Condé, killed in the Battle of Jarnac in 1559 during the Wars of Religion. Drinking water can be obtained from a boatyard on the left, downstream of the five-arched bridge. Among the famous distilleries are those of Cognac Bisquit and Courvoisier (visits possible). Note the extremely fine 19th century administrative buildings in the style of *châteaux*.

For the first time, the Charente broadens into the width of a real river. Keep to the right bank, past a newly built weir, to enter Lock 16, **Bourg-Charente** (K50). In the village of grey stone buildings with red pantiles, left bank, are shops and a restaurant with moorings. Now comes a superb wooded reach of 3km.

Château de St-Brice, upstream of Cognac.

Opposite an island, stop at the right-bank hamlet of **La Maurie** (K53.6) to walk about 2km to the *dolmen* of **Garde-Epée**, near the D157 (signposted). Past the Château du Perron (left bank), Écluse 17, **St-Brice** (K54.7) is easily seen on the port side. A small hire cruiser firm operates from here. Catherine de Medici, Queen of Henry II, visited the magnificent Renaissance Château de St-Brice, a creamy stone building with slate roof and turrets on the riverbank. Well-cared-for gardens feature topiary and a larger than life-sized stag hunting scene in bronze. After the three stone arches of a bridge at **La Trache**, the edge of **Cognac** appears, left. Note, by the bridge at **Châtenay**, an old building marked 'Bureau d'Octroi', a tollhouse. Skirting the borders of the Parc François I, left, the river becomes almost completely rural again. Apart from racing craft from a boat club, the Charente is virtually unused here, a situation impossible to imagine at a tourist town of similar importance in Britain. Avoiding an open weir, right, there is a waterside restaurant with landing stage, port side: this is good, if slightly expensive. Entry to Écluse 18, Cognac, is via a channel on the right (K61.7). At present there is an almost total lack of navigation markers, resulting in a tendency to mistakenly enter backwaters and weirstreams. A plaque on the lock cottage gives its number incorrectly as 16.

Remains of old fortifications and the 15–16th century castle overlooking the river below Cognac bridge have been a distillery since 1795. The Duke of Angoulême was born and raised near here: he was later to become King François I and is commemorated by a fine equestrian statue in the town. This was cast in Paris and carried down the Seine and by sea to Cognac in 1864. When ascending the Charente, exceptionally low water levels left the barge stranded and a great team of oxen was required to pull it clear. Brandy was first produced in large quantities in the early 17th century: the 'burnt' or distilled wine was called *brandewijn* by the Dutch. Huge consignments were carried down river in *gabares* for trans-shipment and export: many of the leading merchants are British in origin. About 80% of production is exported, notably to Britain and the USA. Some notion of the size of the industry is provided by the startling fact that the 2% of the stored spirit lost to evaporation each year is the equivalent of 20 million bottles!. This is amusingly described as 'the Angels' share'. The white wine is distilled twice in copper pot-stills, then aged in oak casks from the Limousin forests. Among the oldest of the firms are Martell, founded by a Jersey family in 1715, and the Irish Hennessy company which started in 1765. Brandies more than 100 years old are blended with new spirit, although some of the most sought-after and expensive type offered by Hennessy are truly Napoléonic, being laid down at the time of Waterloo. Details of visits to the distilleries are available from the local Syndicat d'Initiative: the most interesting are perhaps Otard, in the former *château*, and Martell which preserves the original premises of 1715. Cognac has good shops, many of them in a long pedestrianized street. A slipway is 500m below the bridge, right bank, suitable for launching sizeable trailed craft. There is a water point at the boatyard of Charente Plaisance.

Lock 19, **Crouin** (K66), was practically destroyed by the floods of February 1980; now re-gated, it is the last to be operated solely by boats' crews. Beyond here the Charente undergoes a character change, with rather muddy banks and ancient fallen willows. The slipway of a water-ski club on the right bank at **Chez Landart** (K71) could doubtless be used for launching. The river now makes a broad loop before running past the base of a grassy hill topped by the ruins of an old castle, and a restaurant with landing stage. **Dompierre-sur-Charente** (K79, limited shops) stands a little above the river, a cluster of rooftops with mottled tiles. Take care to avoid the hand-operated chain ferry for cars. (It may be possible to launch trailed boats.)

Just before a road and rail crossing, the village of **Orlac** (K81.6) advertises a restaurant. Having now passed from the jurisdiction of Charente to Charente Maritime, navigation signs make a welcome appearance, beginning with an arrow pointing to the cut above **La Baine**, Lock 20 (K85). It is a strange experience to be under the orders of a lock keeper with overnight and lunchtime closures. (Available 8.00–12.00h and 14.00–18.00h May–Oct; otherwise by advance notice to Rochefort.) Sheltered by a giant pair of plane trees, the lock house stands in a green meadow, backing onto a broad pool below a stone watermill. It really is an idyllic spot. Here, I witnessed the biggest bow wave I have ever seen on an inland waterway, as the tripping boat *Bernard Pallisy* rushed into the lock chamber moments after I had left it. Her wash continued for a good 5 minutes afterwards. To be fair, the skipper was no more anticipating meeting another craft than I was, but as pleasure traffic increases such behaviour will have to be curbed.

Further launching possibilities by another ferry and a waterside restaurant with shops are found in **Chaniers** (K86), with one more slipway at the site of a former ferry at **Port-Hublé** (K90). Coming into the city of **Saintes** (K97), the Charente skirts the base of a wooded cliff with a proliferation of small fishing punts and trim market gardens. Saintes, Capital of the former province of Saintonge, was thriving before Caesar's

invasion of Gaul in 58 BC. Survivals from the Roman occupation include the impressive Arch of Germanicus, re-erected in a garden setting on the right bank of the river in 1842. More relics are shown in the archaeological museum nearby. There is much to see in this large and busy city: the Cathedral of St Pierre, the Abbaye aux Dames, and remains of a 1st century arena only a little smaller than that at Nîmes. Extensive quays were constructed towards the end of the 18th century and by 1839 industry was responsible for no fewer than 31 wind and water mills. Severe floods swamped the lower parts of the town in 1904 and again late in 1982, even the massive flood wall being unable to save the streets. In 1960 the river was described as being one great lake all the way from Châteauneuf to Saintes. Shops are conveniently close to a footbridge near the Cathedral and a marine engineer is available.

Taking time to recover from the urbanization of Saintes, the Charente has regained its rural charm by the village of **Narcejac** (K103.5), with a fine stone manor house in its miniature walled park. The succession of large country houses, while rarely of the proportions of Loire *châteaux*, does bring a special interest to this waterway. A little upstream of Narcejac is the tiny Middle Ages hamlet of **Port-Berteau** (right bank), where Gustave Courbet the artist set up a studio in 1862. A crossing of the A10 *autoroute* comes shortly before **Taillebourg** (K109), once a small port. Little remains of the feudal *château*, where Louis IX defeated Henry III of England in 1242. 18th century gardens with a terrace offer a broad view over the river; there are shops and most other facilities. Water meadows with grazing cattle suggest a widening of the valley as it approaches the tideway. Many villages are set well back from possible flooding. However, **Port d'Envaux** (K112) is strung along the left bank, with quay, hotel/restaurant, shops, garage and slipway. Tranquil country houses overlooking the river make this one of the most appealing villages on the Charente. **Crazannes** (K116) acknowledges an increasing interest in boating with a small *port de plaisance* (fuel and slipway, with dayboats for hire).

Quite extensive pleasure craft moorings on a pontoon are the first indication of **St-Savinien** (K119). The navigation channel forks to the left for the last lock before the tideway: straight on leads into the centre of town, past the gardens of some delightful houses, many of them once occupied by barge masters. Building of freight craft was a major activity, the last being launched in 1859. Moorings can be found in the centre of St-Savinien on quays near the bridge, with all shops and a selection of restaurants within a very short distance. On a river with several outstanding small towns, this is perhaps the most agreeable. Pleasing details include an ornate 19th century cast-iron water pump surmounted by an urn, by the bridge, and clusters of tiny daisies sprouting from crevices in the river walls. Slightly tidal conditions will be experienced here, although most of the water is held back by a weir and Lock 21 (open 8.00–12.00h and 14.00–18.00h). Above is the *port de plaisance* with cruisers for hire.

If this is to be the limit of a cruise, a railway station provides a rather infrequent train service with connections to Saintes, Cognac, Châteauneuf and Angoulême. In the seawards direction, it is possible to take a train to Rochefort and the coast at **Chataillon-Plage**, south of **La Rochelle**, and so enjoy the attractions of the seaside.

After St-Savinien, the atmosphere of the Charente totally changes. The tideway passes through a marshland world of glutinous mudbanks, frequent fishing nets suspended on cranes and typical Saintonge farmhouses with red pantiled roofs. At **Port-la-Pierre** (K133) is a junction with the **River Boutonne**. Rising at **Chef-Boutonne** 94km above the confluence, its lower 31km are navigable through **Tonnay-Boutonne** to **St-Jean d'Angely**, with 4 locks evenly spaced out on its course (Écluses de Bel-Ebat, de l'Houmée, de Voissay and de Bernouet). Though closed in 1935, a programme of lock restoration had made the route possible once more from summer 1984. The first 500m is subject to Charente tides as far as an opening barrage (de Carillon). A basic chart showing lock approaches is available from Direction Départementale de l'Équipement de la Charente-Maritime, BP 125, 17306 Rochefort-sur-Mer. Back on the Charente, fishing boats are clustered on mudberths in **Tonnay-Charente** (K141), with a 204m suspension bridge erected in 1885. All services and marine engine repairs. A little below, the 39km **Canal de la Seudre à la Charente**, built about 1812 with 4 locks, once provided a connection with the coast to the south via **St-Agnant** and the oyster beds at **Marennes**. Small craft with a draft not exceeding 1m and a headroom sufficiently low to pass beneath several former swing bridges (no longer operable), may cruise 16km from Écluse de Biard, junction with the Charente, to Écluse de Beaugeay, provided 48 hours' advance notice is given to the Biard lock keeper (tel. (46) 99-63-95).

In the Place Colbert at **Rochefort** (K147) the final arrival of the river at the coast is celebrated in a massive stone fountain, on top of which classical figures represent the marriage of Charente and Ocean. All boating facilities in the *port de plaisance*, entered via a lock. Fortified towers and walls are a reminder that it was

here that Colbert established a sheltered naval base in the mid 17th century to protect the Atlantic coast from the English; from 1690 to 1800 some 300 ships were launched. Rochefort ceased to be a military port in 1921. Downstream the estuary gradually widens, eventually meeting the Atlantic opposite the **Île d'Oléron**, the second largest island off the French coast after Corsica. A 3,027m toll bridge has connected it with the mainland at Marennes since 1966. This popular holiday centre has some magnificent sandy beaches, including the vast Grande Plage on the SW shore.

52 · River Dordogne

No Carte Guide available.
From Bec d'Ambès, junction with the River Gironde (26km downriver of Bordeaux) to Flaujagues, 87km with no locks. A junction is made with the River Isle at Libourne.

Mention the name Dordogne and you instantly have a mental impression of deep limestone gorges with thickly wooded shores. This applies only to the higher reaches of the river, well beyond the navigable limit for normal craft. Accessible only to canoeists and downstream drifters in inflatables, these idyllic waters for 173km below Argentat are really outside the scope of this book: but their very special appeal demands that they receive a mention, however brief. Almost all the length available to large craft is tidal and frankly lacks interest in the first 34km up to Vayres. In common with many tidal navigations, a journey up the Dordogne is likely to be slightly adventurous rather than relaxing.

Once clear of the broad expanses of the river near its confluence with the Gironde, the Dordogne was always considered the most difficult and dangerous navigation in southwestern France. For many centuries flat-bottomed sailing barges would descend with the current from as far up as Argentat, 311km from the Gironde. Known as *gabares* or *argentats*, they carried passengers and goods, especially oak for making barrels, to Bordeaux and were broken up for timber on arrival. Towards the end of the 18th century a series of 10 locks upstream of Bergerac improved conditions to Limeuil, junction with the River Vézère, about 175km beyond Bec d'Ambès. These locks were regarded as workable (subject to fluctuating water levels) as late as 1888. By 1936, traffic reached only as far as Bergerac, with horses and oxen in regular use on the towpath. The useful section of river has contracted still more since then.

The lower part of the Dordogne, from the Gironde to Libourne, appears on Maritime Chart 6140, published by the Service Hydrographique. These 43km are easy to navigate for those with experience of tideways, with a buoyed channel and no obstructions other than the nets of lamprey fishermen. Moorings are few and far between: at **Bourg** (K4) arrangements may be made to lie alongside a ferry which takes workers to the extensive oil refineries on the far shore, rather more than 1km away. The town is situated on a cliff, reached from the port by flights of steps. There are excellent views over the river from the top and the terrace of the Château de la Citadelle, the former residence of the Archbishops of Bordeaux. Upstream, the scenery is dull to **Vayres** (K34), where the grounds of the *château* come down to the river bank: gardens in the style of Louis XIII were laid out as recently as 1938. The river is subject to a tidal bore – the *Mascaret* – sometimes reaching a height of 1.5m. Its effect is greatest at Vayres. Predicted bore times are available from the local tourist office. Shipping regularly navigates the river as far as the port of **Libourne** (K43), junction with the **River Isle**. The most comfortable overnight moorings are to quays on the Isle, which is tidal for the 31km that remain available to craft up to the first, disused lock at **Sablons-de-Guitres**. As recently as 1936 it was considered navigable for another 113km through 40 locks to the town of **Périgueux**. Libourne is the most convenient place from which to visit the extraordinary town of **St-Emilion**, 10km by bus. It occupies a series of small limestone hills in a famous region of vineyards: these have been excavated to create many caves, one of which was turned into the underground monolithic church between the 9th and 12th centuries.

Few problems affect navigation upriver to **Castillon-la-Bataille** (K78). Here the English were defeated in the final battle of the Hundred Years War, when the Earl of Shrewsbury was killed in 1453. Another 9km of waterway is available for sizeable boats to **Flaujagues** (K87), although exploration should be possible in small craft at least to **St-Pierre-d'Eyraud** (K117), and depending on water levels as far as **Bergerac** (K131).

Exploration of the outstandingly beautiful Dordogne Valley above Bergerac should be undertaken by

car. Excellent intineries appear in the *Green Michelin Guide Périgord*. Hydro-electric barrages obstruct the river upstream of **Argentat**, but a length of 173km from there to **Lalinde** provides water for one of the finest canoe journeys in Europe, and without any undue hazards. The best time to go is normally in July and August, when the current is reduced. Various types of boat may be hired, with arrangements for recovery at the downstream end. Such a holiday is the ultimate in back-to-nature waterway cruising. The route passes numerous towns and villages, restaurants and ancient *châteaux*. Notable excursions are to the **Padirac Chasm**, 5km south of the river near Castelnau (lifts take you down 75m to an underground cave 99m across, with a subterraean river running for 2,000 – partly negotiated by boat); and to the **Grottes de Lacave**, close to the Dordogne between St-Sozy and Souillac, a network of caves reached by small railway and lift.

53 · Canal Transaquitain

No Carte Guide available.
From the Étang de Cazaux et de Sanguinet to the Étang de Biscarrosse on the Atlantic Coast near Biscarrosse, 5km with 1 lock.

Even in a country as waterway-minded as France, there are bound to be failures. One of these is the Canal Transaquitain, an ambitious scheme of the early 1970s which was stopped soon after construction began on financial and ecological grounds. The original plan was to link a chain of lakes by lengths of artificial canal, thus creating a vast pleasure boating and leisure facility a little inland from the Atlantic through the pine forests and sand dunes of **Les Landes**. When adopted in 1970, the concept envisaged a waterway extending for about 196km from the estuary of the Gironde to the River Adour downstream of Dax, not far from the Spanish frontier. Although only a tiny part was completed, the region offers considerable scope for trailed craft, which can be launched in several reaches of protected water. One of the most compelling reasons for visiting Les Landes is the outstandingly beautiful Atlantic coastline, the **Côte d'Argent**. This is a magnificent 230km long, continuous beach of fine sand: unlike the Mediterranean, it is subject to considerable tides and sizeable breakers, suitable for surfing. As a barrier between coast and interior a belt of sand dunes runs along the seashore: one dune, **Pilat**, south of the **Bassin d'Arcachon**, may be climbed via a footway and flight of 190 steps. 114m in height, it is the biggest dune in Europe and presents a spectacular view over the ocean and the forest.

The most important lakes, all of which are available for boating with ample launching sites and other facilities, are as follows, running north to south: **Lac de Hourtin-Carcans**, 19km long and 3–4km wide; the **Étang de Lacanau**, 8km long; the Bassin d'Arcachon, a huge inland sea connected with the coast at **Cap Ferrat**, much of it dry at low tide; and the **Étang de Cazaux**, inland of **Biscarrosse-Plage**, 10km long by up to 11km wide. Northwards, this is connected with the Bassin d'Arcachon via a little tree-shaded waterway known as the **Canal de Cazeaux à la Teste**, 15km long and suitable for the small motorboats widely used here. Launching sites around Cazeaux include one at a popular sandy beach **Dune**

des Places, with another by a 200-boat harbour at **Ispe**. The entire lake is bordered by attractive sandy beaches, surrounded by pine forests planted in the 19th century. The water is well used by all kinds of aquatic sportsmen and numerous holiday chalets are scattered through the waterside trees, many with small craft on private moorings. The only completed section of the Canal Transaquitain leaves Cazeaux at **Navarrosse** (hotel/bar/restaurant) and heads south for 5km through one lock with a rise and fall of about 0.6m. The chamber measures about 18m × 3m wide and has single gates at each end. Operation is by boat crews, who must insert a coin in a slot to activate gates and paddles. After passing close to the pleasant little town of **Biscarrosse** (all facilities), the canal emerges into the **Étang de Biscarrosse**, 9km by up to 8km wide. These waters are all easy to navigate in a small boat.

Equipped with a car and trailed dinghy or cruiser, the lakeland waterways of Les Landes would make an ideal holiday location for several days. As the coast is always within easy driving distance, the magnificent beaches should not be ignored; they are so extensive that overcrowding is never a problem, even at peak season. Outside the immediate confines of the small resort towns, nudism has become an accepted and popular practice, especially on the north beach at Biscarrosse, north and south of **Mimizan-Plage** and south of **Contis-Plage**. Compared with the much praised Mediterranean, this lovely coast is well worth exploring. Plenty of excellent camping sites have been sanctioned by the Aquitaine Coast Development Commission, which everywhere has ensured that the natural beauty of the region remains unspoiled for all to enjoy.

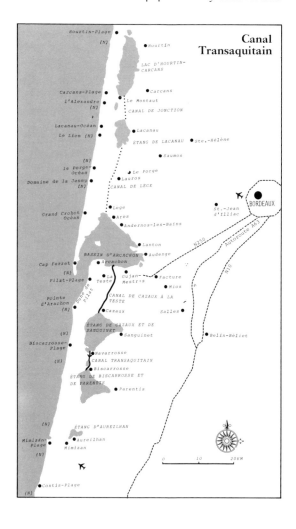

Canal Transaquitain

Fringed by pine woods: a completed section of the Canal Transaquitain at Navarrosse.

54 · River Adour and Adjoining Waterways

No Carte Guide available.

From the Atlantic Coast near the Spanish border at Tarnos to Port de Pouy, upstream of Dax: 76km and mainly tidal (there are no locks). As it has no connections with the rest of the French waterways network and hardly qualifies as an inland waterway in the context of this book, it is only mentioned in the interests of presenting a complete record. Shortly before World War II, 2,808 barge journeys were made on the river each year, vessels being pulled by horses and oxen. The head of navigation was then **St-Sever**, 131.7km from the coast. The leading towns are **Dax** (K6) and **Bayonne** (K66).

In downstream order, navigable branches exist as follows:

Gaves Réunis, 9.4km from Peyrehorade to the Adour at Bec du Gave (K40). Tidal.

River Bidouze, 14.9km from a junction with the River Lihoury (which is navigable for 1.5km) to the Adour near Sames (K43). Tidal.

River Aran (or Joyeuse), 6.2km from Larroque to the Adour near St-Laurent-de-Gosse (K50). Tidal.

River Ardanavy (or Ardanabia), 2.3km from a railway bridge to the Adour below St-Barthélemy (K55). Tidal.

River Nive, 12.3km from Haïtze to the Adour at Bayonne (K66). Tidal.

A short distance along the coast in the direction of Spain are two further tidal rivers: the **Nivelle**, 7km from Ascain to the sea at St-Jean-de-Luz; and the **Bidassoa**, 9km from Bordarrupia to the sea at Hendaye. Throughout, it marks the Franco-Spanish border.

VII·THE RHÔNE VALLEY, GASCONY AND LANGUEDOC

55 · River Rhône

Carte Guide *Rhône*

From a junction with the River Saône in Lyon to the Mediterranean at Port St-Louis, 310km with 12 locks. Additional junctions are made with the Petit Rhône near Arles (for the Canal du Rhône à Sète); and the Liaison Rhône-Fos near Salin de Giraud. (Forbidden to pleasure craft. The Canal d'Arles à Fos from Arles is no longer a through route.) About 30km of the Higher Rhône (with a connection to the Lac du Bourget and Aix-les-Bains) is available to pleasure craft: there is 1 lock and a boat transporter.

Several decades ago, the guide book of the Canoe Club de France said of the Rhône: `Strictly speaking, it is not a river: it is a great torrent'. Far-reaching navigation works, now completed, have changed all that and this essential link between the Mediterranean and the majority of waterways in France is available to all but the most under-powered pleasure craft. In places, the current can still run quite swiftly, depending on how much water is being released by the hydro-electric power stations incorporated into each of the first 11 barrages. The flow is considerably reduced when the demand for electricity falls, that is, during weekends and at night.

The Higher Rhône, between Lake Geneva and Lyon, was originally navigable with difficulty by light-draft vessels. Some of this length is still used by canoeists and members of the Outboard Club of the Rhône. At the time of writing, it is strictly only for those with updated local knowledge.

Below Lyon the rocks, whirlpools, rapids, shallows and debris-strewn shingle banks of waterway mythology have gone. Canalization has greatly improved the look of the Rhône, although in its emasculated form canoeists will regret the passing of one of France's leading long-distance assault courses. Long sections of artificial canal lead to new locks, one of which is the deepest in Europe. Bankside signs indicate safe canoe portages for those who wish to travel over parts of the original course no longer used for normal navigation.

It is now safe to stop and moor at many points and enjoy the sights, instead of having to apply total concentration to steering a safe course. One hazard to be mentioned, however, is the fierce *Mistral* wind that funnels down the Rhône valley, sometimes for days on end. This can create a sizeable chop on the river and make life difficult in a small cruiser. Some exposed moorings can be dangerous, with waves reaching 2m in height.

Scenically, the 40km below Lyon are the most attractive, with green hills and welcoming banks. Surroundings become ever more rugged and parched as you progress downstream. By way of compensation, there are numerous ruins and fortifications towards the seaward end.

Falling 164m from Lyon, the Rhône locks are awe-inspiring but not difficult to negotiate. Keepers' instructions are conveyed by traffic lights and loudspeakers. Here, as on other of the larger French navigations, use of the boat's VHF radio telephone is invaluable in advising keepers of your approach and so saving considerable waiting time on arrival. VHF channel numbers are published in the *Carte Guide*. Craft are able to make fast to floating bollards as they change levels. Locks function between 5.00h and 21.00h. Forming part of the projected Mediterranean–North Sea Waterway via the Rhine, the Rhône is currently not very busy with commercial traffic (about 3.5–4 million tonnes of cargo a year). Those without their own vessel can make the journey from Lyon to Avignon or *vice versa* by passenger craft, taking two days.

For much of the river, bank protection is of loose rock. Before setting out on a day's cruise, it is advisable to check exactly where you plan to moor before nightfall. Some safe and recommended overnight halts include: Lyon, on Saône upstream of Pont Bonaparte; Givors, quay, K18.4; Condrieu, marina K40.8; Tournon, harbour, K90.9; Valence, marina, K112; Le Pouzin, quay, K133; Viviers, quay, K166 on old river; Avignon, marina, just upstream of Pont St Bénezet; Arles, pontoon, K282. 7; Port St Louis, in harbour, K323.

Brief history When the first barge passed through Vaugris Lock in 1980 and the modernization of the once wild River Rhône was completed, the skipper of *Citerna 18* was presented with a selection of gifts, carrying on a tradition which had been performed at the inauguration of all previous locks on the waterway. These presents included a bottle of Côtes du Rhône, a *saucisson de Vienne*, some walnuts and a terracotta oil lamp. One of Europe's most far-reaching waterway schemes was thus brought to a conclusion.

The Rhône had been in use as a highway since the times of the Greeks and Romans: but it was an uncertain navigation, suffering from fierce currents, shallows, floods as the winter ice melted and frequent droughts in late summer. There are many reminders of more than 20 centuries of navigation in the form of ancient towns and fortifications. Until the early 19th century, passengers travelled in *coches d'eau* (water coaches), drawn by men, horses or propelled by sail. Such a journey was dangerous in times of high wind or floods. Trade on the upper river was carried out in *barques du Rhône*, 75 tonne capacity sailing barges 30m × 3.5m and fitted with a huge rudder and long tiller. Most travelled bearing a painted cross covered with religious symbols as protection against the hazards of the journey. As many as 50 to 80 horses were employed to haul trains of 5 to 7 craft upstream. Goods would be transhipped at Arles into 23m sailing barges known as *allèges d'Arles* for the final run down to the Mediterranean. 30m log rafts brought additional freight down the tributaries, where navigation was equally uncertain (the Isère, Durance, Ardèche, Ouvèze, Arve and the Saône and Higher Rhône). Upstream progress was often out of the question and the craft were broken up when they arrived at their destination.

The first experimental steamboat was built at Lyon by Jouffroy d'Abbans in 1783, but regular steam haulage was not introduced until 1829: it was to last until 1952. Steam passenger vessels 80–100m long made up to 20 kph and were able to do the downstream run from Lyon to Arles in a day. Among the 19th century steam freight craft were *bateaux-anguilles*, giant cargo boats 157m × 6.35m with paddle wheels amidships; *bateaux crabes*, where paddle wheels were supplemented by a huge toothed 'claw' wheel 6.5m across, designed to grip the river bed in the shallows: acting as tugs, they could haul over 500 tonnes; *bateaux à deux culs* (double backside boats); and a range of single and twin-funnelled steam tugs developing up to 1800hp.

In the 20th century powerful motor barges were introduced, such as the *Citerna* fleet, 80 × 8.6m beam, propelled by diesel engines and with a capacity of 1,500 tonnes. Some continue in service, together with push-tow convoys 180m long with 5,000 tonnes capacity and the ubiquitous 38.5m *péniches*.

At various times there have been schemes for construction of a lateral canal down the Rhône valley fed by the river but independent of it. In 1933 the Compagnie Nationale du Rhône was established to tame the waterway with a series of locked barrages and canal cuts, with the triple aim of improving navigation and irrigation and generating electricity. (About one-thirteenth of France's total electricity supply is now provided by the Rhône power stations.) Some progress was made in deepening the navigation channel and constructing scouring walls, before World War II brought work to a halt. It began again in 1948 and continued for 32 years, completion dates of the locks and barrages being: Donzère-Mondragon, 1952; Montélimar, 1957; Baix-Le-Logis-Neuf, 1960; Beauchastel, 1963; Pierre-Bénite, 1966; Bourg-lès-Valence, 1968; Vallabrègues, 1970; St-Vallier, 1971; Avignon, 1973; Caderousse, 1975; Péage-de-Roussillon, 1977; and Vaugris, 1980. Although its initial task is finished, the Company remains in being and has been charged with the responsibility for building the planned new waterway along the course of the **Canal du Rhône au Rhin**.

Hydro-electric works on the Higher Rhône, upstream of Lyon, are currently changing the river's character. Given local knowledge, there is scope for boating on these reaches and current users include canoeists, members of the Outboard Club of the Rhône and passenger vessels. Probably the most useful length is a stretch of about 30km comprising the **Canal de Savières** (from the north end of the **Lac du Bourget** on which is situated the elegant resort town of **Aix-les-Bains**) to the Rhône at Écluse de Savières. This lock admits boats up to 18m × 5.25m with 2.5m draft. Passage then follows an artificial relief channel, the Dérivation de Belley, and through the Lac du Lit au Roi before arriving at the **Brens** power station where there is an 18m drop. Instead of using a conventional lock, boats of up to 5 tonnes are loaded onto a wheeled transporter to gain access to the waterway below. Size limits are 9m long × 3.4m beam. Similar devices are planned for other Higher Rhône sites, so there is a prospect of being able to continue all the way to Lyon in spite of further projected power stations. At present (1990) the area provides about 130km of navigable water.

While the length of the navigation is now 310km, kilometre posts on the waterway's banks continue to record the former distance of 323km and are thus used as a reference in the following description.

Lyon. (K0) For a description of the city at the confluence of the Rhône and Saône, see Chapter 47. Adequate pleasure craft facilities will be found at the Maison d'Eau, left bank (K3.5), before the first lock. The river is here wide and lively, with considerable commercial traffic bound for the many industrial works and fuel depots. The A7 *autoroute* leaves Lyon on the right bank, veering away shortly before arrival at the entrance to the large freight **Port Eduoard-Herriot** (K3, left bank). Ahead, appears the first of the hydro-electric barrages, with a short cut leading to Pierre-Bénite lock (fall 9.25m) on the left. Looking back there is a dramatic distant view of Lyon, rising to the hilltop site of Notre Dame de Fourvière. 11km of artificial rock-sided channel, with little scenic interest, take the navigation beneath the *autoroute* and back into the real Rhône at K15. Now surroundings greatly improve past willow-fringed banks, with sand and gravel works.

Good moorings with nearby shops will be found on the right bank (K18) near the mouth of the River

Uppermost of the Rhone's huge locks: Pierre-Bénite, downstream of Lyon.

Gier in **Givors**, a manufacturing town specializing in glassmaking and heavy castings. The motorway returns near **Loire-sur-Rhône** (K22), also industrial with a commercial harbour. Fuel/gas, right bank, K22.5. Craft wishing to use the quay (K26.5) on the right bank just upstream of an *autoroute* viaduct should approach from *below* the bridge. The Rhône makes a broad sweep through **Vienne** (K29), a Gallo-Roman provincial capital grouped around a junction with the River Gère. Although the A7 is uncomfortably evident all the way along the waterfront, the city is well worth a visit for its historical and gastronomic interest. The best moorings are along a quay with bollards at the start of a public park, below the second bridge, pontoon.

Supposedly founded by the Celtic King Allobrox, allegedly a descendant of Hercules, Vienne was at one time governed by Pontius Pilate. From the 4th century AD until 1922 the city's 131m diameter Roman theatre was buried: now fully excavated, it can be seen in a wonderful state of preservation. Equally fine is the much restored Temple of Augustus. Half an hour's walk leads from the town to Le Mont Pipet with a superb view down to the river. Red wines of the Côte Rôtie are produced in vineyards that extend a long distance down the waterway. Dating in part from the

13th century is the little waterside church of Notre Dame de l'Île (K32), once an important objective for river pilgrims who travelled from Lyon to throw flowers into the Rhône in memory of early Christians martyred here in AD 177. A further A7 viaduct is followed by **Vaugris** lock (fall 6.7m) at K34, the only one on the waterway designed without approach canals. Downstream is a slipway, east bank.

This area is an important centre of fruit production, with trees smothered in blossom in spring. **Ampuis** (K35.5) mostly lies beyond a railway line, and is not-able for its waterside Renaissance *château* and sandy beach, a popular swimming place for local children. Newly raised water levels have resulted in numerous trees being flooded along a very lovely reach that extends to **Condrieu** (K41). Craft from the Saône with limited time would do well to consider this point as their objective if wishing to explore just a little of the Rhône. Condrieu, right bank, and **Les-Roches-de-Condrieu**, opposite, are surrounded by vineyards. The main waterfront, with the ancient houses of Rhône boatmen, is well worth a halt. An excellent marina with pontoons is situated in a basin near the bridge (water and electricity). Hire cruisers are based here. Shopping and restaurants.

Extensive chemical works line the left bank at **St-Clair-du-Rhône** (K43). Several towns now follow in hilly surroundings that extend virtually without a break to Valence. Access is sometimes rather difficult. **Chavenay** (K47) offers moorings, but the pretty vil-lage of **St-Pierre-de-Boeuf** (K51) has been bypassed by the navigation and can no longer be approached by water on account of a barrage at the upper end of the natural course of the river and a sill across the channel below Serrières. Between K51 and K63 craft follow the Péage de Roussillon Canal; mooring is possible on vertical piling in the cut at K56. By travelling on to **Sablons** lock (K61, fall 14.5m) you can seek permis-sion to moor and walk back to **Serrières**, which has shops and an excellent museum of Rhône life in the 12–14th century chapel of St Sornin; exhibits include the highly decorated crosses once carried by vessels as protection from the perils of the river. Slipway in the lower end of the Sablons lock cut, east bank, K62.5.

Between K64 and K69, take care to avoid numerous groynes that extend a considerable distance from each bank towards the centre of the river. A strange stone pillar on the right bank near the village of **Champagne** (K65.5) supported the cable of a former ferry boat. Best moorings in **Andance** (K69) are above and below the suspension bridge, with shops and restaur-ants close by. Very good slipway, west bank, 100m below the bridge. The smaller town of **Andancette**

lies on the opposite side. Scenery in this reach is very fine, resulting in considerable use by local motor cruisers and sailing dinghies.

St-Vallier (K76) has moorings on its sloping quays, convenient for good shops and a railway station. Slip-way below the bridge, west bank. Diana of Poitiers spent part of her childhood at the *château*. If in doubt about coming alongside on the quay at the junction with the River Galaure, it would be wise to continue for another 2km to the concrete and steel quay (K78), where there is also a slipway. The town is within easy cycling distance: circumstances such as this make car-rying at least one bicycle essential, with repeated savings of time and energy.

Splendid views of the St-Vallier Gorge open up ahead, with frequent reminders of the feudal impor-tance of this part of the valley. At the tiny village of **Serves** (K82), the *château* faces a ruined round tower at **Arras** on the opposite shore. Houses with pantiled roofs cluster at the base of cliffs. Moorings are poor, on a rocky bank. Next comes the Canal de St-Vallier lead-ing to **Gervans** lock (K86, fall 10.75m); note the Romanesque 11–12th century church on the right bank, where the lock channel rejoins the river. The King's Table is a menacing rock, marked by buoys at K89, on which St Louis (King Louis IX) is said to have taken a meal when bound for the Crusades in 1248. Its historical significance has saved it from being blasted away during the Rhône improvements.

Now follows an important wine-production region, famous for Hermitage (red), Larnage and Chante-Alouette (white) at the approach to **Tournon** (K91). Steep-sided vineyard terraces recall the Rhine Gorge. Names of the growers are prominently displayed on stone walls that divide one small field from another. Tournon is one of the most interesting towns in the entire course of the river and offers the facilities of an excellent pleasure boat harbour (right bank) upstream of the first of two bridges. Enter with due regard to the current. Water, diesel, petrol and slipway are available. Apart from very convenient shops and restaurants, the 15–16th century *château* offers wide views from its terraces high above the Rhône and across to **Tain l'Hermitage**. Open to the public (March 1–Nov 30 except Tues) the interior houses a museum; exhibits include material on the engineer Marc Seguin, builder of the first Rhône suspension bridge, constructed in 1825 and removed 140 years later. The attractions of the town and its situation provide every encourage-

Vineyards on the Rhône at Condrieu.

ment to linger. Train enthusiasts can travel on the narrow-gauge Vivarais steam railway which passes through a rugged, winding course between Tournon and **Lamastre** along the Doux Valley. Built between 1886 and 1891, this line boasts 9 steam locomotives and 7 diesel units, attracting over 60,000 passengers each year. The journey takes two hours each way, so most of a day should be set aside for the excursion, especially if you wish to spend some time in the gastronomic centre of Lamastre. (Trains run April 1–Oct 30 on weekends and holidays, every day from June 1–Sept 15.)

Limited moorings are available for clients of the Auberge de Frais Matin (K95.5, left bank). If time allows, it is worth visiting the remote village of **La Roche de Glun** (K98.5) at the head of an island formed by the Rhône and Bourg-les-Valence lock cut; there are several restaurants. Once a stronghold of river pirates, it was successfully raided by Louis IX. After a long course from the French Alps and through Grenoble, the River Isère joins the navigation at K102, sometimes causing turbulence in the lock cut. There is a possible mooring on wooden campshedding, west bank, above the confluence. **Bourg-les-Valence** lock (K106, fall 11.7m) is followed by the important city of **Valence** (K109), overnight halt for the Rhône passenger vessels. This is a bustling modern place, with a broad tree-lined *boulevard* at its centre where there are many good shops and restaurants. A water point will be found near the bridge, and pleasure craft are warned to avoid mooring on that part of the quay painted red and white (reserved for commercial vessels). The Rhône current can flow swiftly here: a pair of laden breasted-up *péniches* were noted barely able to make headway upstream. Safest moorings, with a planned 350 berths, are to be found at the Port de l'Epervière (K112), offering all the usual boating services but unfortunately rather remote from the city centre. Shopping can, however, be done at a huge supermarket within 0.5km. The port's clubhouse incorporates a popular restaurant; there is a chandlery and facility for boat repairs. A useful location where boats may be left quite safely between cruises at much less cost than in Mediterranean marinas.

After a very ruined leaning tower (K116), a broad reach of river leads to Beauchastel lock cut (right bank, alongside a weir). A small port (K120) is convenient for the village of **Charmes**. **Beauchastel** (K124) lies close to the lock (fall 12.65m), where water may be taken on the right of the chamber.

Once more back on the original river, **La Voulte** (K128) appears on the right bank. Limited moorings are downstream of the road bridge. Amid a mass of

rusty brown pantiles is the 15/16th century *château*, much damaged by German troops in 1944, and an Italianate church. South of the town, an elegant pre-stressed concrete railway viaduct sweeps over the river: it is the longest structure of its type in France. After a confluence with the River Drôme (K131), **Le Pouzin** (K133) appears at a junction with the River Ouvèze. Moorings are just possible near a garage and restaurant, although the vertical quay is rather too high for convenience. A further disadvantage is the disturbance created by the railway. Intense cultivation is a feature of the rocky, terraced hillside, for the town occupies a cleft between hills. Mountainous surroundings continue into the Logis-Neuf lock cut which runs parallel to 7km of navigable Rhône, accessible from the downstream end only, thus enabling a visit to be made to the village of **Baix**. **Logis-Neuf** lock (K143, fall 13m) is located near the lower end of its canal. A little beyond, at K145, is a most useful harbour, where the sloping quay is well shaded. Not far away is **Cruas**, with basic shops: were it not for a mantle of white dust from a cement works, this ancient abbey town, dating back to a Benedictine foundation in 804, would be even more agreeable. The Romanesque church, in a style similar to that at Tournus on the Saône, is partly 11th century; many of the houses are medieval. Farther downstream is the Cruas nuclear power station, one of several on the Rhône: four huge cooling towers dominate the landscape. A concrete quay opposite offers moorings while a commercial boatyard is on the left bank, sheltered by a reedy island.

The river has become extremely wide and in 1982 an L-shaped harbour (K152) was constructed, projecting far into the main channel. Once more the navigation divides (K153), the left fork leading to the **Montélimar** cut. Now a modern manufacturing city best known for its nougat industry (started in the 16th century), Montélimar lies too far to the east to be of much interest to boaters. **Ancone** (K154) has useful moorings and a few shops. High on a hillside to the west, the 13–16th century Château de **Rochemaure** incorporates a medieval village within its ramparts. Totally inaccessible to boats, the River Roubion flows across the canal at right-angles (K158), followed by the Port de Montélimar (K159.5), useful only as a stopping point for there are no town facilities within reach.

The vastness of Rhône locks is well demonstrated by that at **Châteauneuf** (K164, fall 17.1m), where there is ample space for a 3,000 tonne coal barge, a sizeable passenger vessel and a large twin-engined motor yacht – all at the same time. Buffers prevent craft accidentally hitting the gates at speed. Beyond lies one of the Rhône's most dramatic reaches: the **Donzère** Gorge,

Pont d'Arc, a natural bridge of stone on the River Ardèche.

whose cliffs rise impressively to a height of about 100m over a length of 3km. At its head is the fascinating town of **Viviers** (K166), where a congested public quay and rather shallow pleasure craft harbour do not make shore excursions particularly easy. Be prepared to anchor and go ashore by dinghy. This has been a seat of bishops since the 5th century, St Vincent's cathedral dates from the 12th century and there are remains of ancient fortifications. Narrow cobbled streets and timber-framed buildings together produce a compelling air of mystery: it is not a place to be missed! Should you have grown a little weary of the starkness of concrete or rock-sided canal cuts, it makes a pleasant change to divert along the old course of the Rhône, navigable for about 4km past reedy banks to **Lafarge**.

A prominent statue of St Michael overlooks the upper end of the Donzère Gorge, the last to be seen of the natural Rhône for almost 30km, for navigation passes through the Donzère-Mondragon Canal for this distance. Among the sites thus bypassed is the famous crossing-point town of **Pont-St-Esprit**; the 1,000m long bridge with 25 arches was built in 1595 and fortified in the 17th century by Vauban. Suitable only for canoes and inflatable craft, and so beyond the scope of this book, the outstandingly beautiful **River Ardèche** flows through limestone cliffs and under impressive Pont d'Arc (a natural stone 'bridge' 34m high). It enters the Rhône above Pont-St-Esprit. Organized canoe holidays take participants down 30km of the finest natural river scenery in Europe, with overnight camping halts and opportunities for bathing from sandy beaches. Complete novices are given an initial training, enabling them to tackle the 30 rapids. Alternatively, day trips in small boats are possible from **Vallon-Pont-d'Arc** (Easter to end Oct) with transport back to the start.

Sets of radial gates are installed at the upper end of the canal (K171) to protect the channel from river floods. Information boards 2–3km above and below the cut entrances show whether through navigation is possible: closure during the summer is unlikely. Steel piling could provide a useful mooring. Scenic interest is somewhat lacking on the rather straight course of the canal, the most notable features being an Atomic Energy Centre (K183) and a nuclear power station (K184.5). A short distance east of the D204 road bridge (K185) lies the abandoned hilltop village of **Barry**, where cave dwellings were occupied from Neolithic times until the end of the 19th century. The site provides an excellent view of **Bollène** (Donzère-Mondragon) lock (K188) and its adjacent André Blondel hydro-electric power station. With a fall of up to 26m, passage of this lock is a memorable experience, not least for the speed with which the chamber fills or empties in a mere 7 minutes.

As the first of the Rhône locks, Bollène, completed in 1952, has an architectural style that is now slightly dated, with a hint of *Art Deco*.

By now the river has definitely reached the south, and you instinctively know that Provence and the Mediterranean are at last within easy reach. Coming out of the Donzère-Mondragon Canal (K200.5), note the *château de* **Mornas** to the east, beyond the A7 *autoroute*. Seized by Catholics in the 16th century, the

An awe-inspiring rise and fall of 26m in the chamber of Bollène lock.

houses were decorated for the feast of Corpus Christi with the skins of Protestants who had been displaced: in reprisal, a Huguenot force was despatched from Arles and the Catholics driven over the precipitous cliffs on which Mornas stands. The sun-bleached village of **St-Étienne-des-Sorts** (K204, right bank) was originally a Rhône boatmen's settlement. The quay offers convenient moorings with bollards, handy for basic shops, small restaurant, slipway and garage. Two great chimneys belong to the **Marcoule** Atomic Energy Centre (K210), in service since 1973 for research and the production of power. Public visits are possible, with wide views from a terrace. Next feature is the beginning of the **Caderousse** lock cut (K212.5): the concrete at the lock (K216, fall 9m) and in the approach channel is uncompromisingly severe and a sideways-sliding top gate is an unusual feature. On leaving the canal it is possible to turn back up the old course of the river, running for 4km to **L'Ardoise**, where a marina offers comprehensive services.

After passing beneath the A9 river bridge (K222) a good view of the rocky fortress of La Tour de l'Hers (K225) appears on the left bank. Opposite is a *château* and the town of **Roquemaure**, with moorings on a vertical quay and slipway. This can be a very dangerous place to lie when the *Mistral* is blowing, for the reach is open for several km in each direction. Waves up to 2m are possible. **Châteauneuf-du-Pape**, lies a short distance to the east.

A multiplicity of channels at the approach to **Avignon** results from recent navigation works. The through route is via the Villeneuve Canal, in part asphalt-lined and leading to Avignon lock (K234, fall 10.5m). Glimpses of the city appear through trees on the left and a detour must be made to get there. **Villeneuve** (K242) was developed as the Cardinals' City, during the period when Avignon was the City of Popes. There were no fewer than 15 cardinals' palaces in the town. Various fortifications were constructed by the Kings of France in opposition to structures of the Holy Roman Empire on the Avignon side of the river. Rising sheer from the water's edge is the Tower of Philip-le-Bel (14th century and earlier), a defence of the west end of Avignon's bridge. The top is reached by climbing 176 steps on a spiral staircase. St André's Fort similarly provides a magnificent view: it remains one of the leading examples of medieval fortification and was constructed by Philip the Fair, John the Good and Charles V, in the 14th century. But even greater interest and better mooring facilities will encourage pleasure craft to halt instead in Avignon, reached by heading downriver to the railway viaduct (K244) and then turning upstream along the Bras d'Avignon, the former

through navigation. Pass beneath two bridges, with the totally walled city on your right-hand side. Four remaining arches of the celebrated Pont d'Avignon now appear directly ahead. Just beyond, immediately beneath the city walls and within a short distance of the leading attractions is a marina on floating pontoons. Beware a sometimes fierce current, even in mid-summer. Approaching craft are often met in mid-stream by the harbourmaster's launch and directed to suitable moorings. Here also is the Rhône passenger vessel embarkation point.

First impressions of Avignon are of its very considerable extent: 100,000 people live there in a maze of narrow streets, behind the protection of a massive wall pierced at intervals by gateways. Avignon's golden age began in 1309 when the pope set up court. The huge fortified Palace was constructed by Benedict XII (1334–42) and Clement VI (1342–52). A masterpiece of medieval architecture, its white stone walls and towers rise more than 45m. The exterior is the best feature; within, there is a lack of furnishings and the hour-long guided tour is not everyone's taste. Gregory XI, last of the true French popes, returned Church rule to Rome in 1377: his successor was so unpopular that a series of anti-popes ruled from Avignon until 1403.

The tourists' centre of the city is the Place de l'Horloge, a tree-shaded traffic-free square with numerous restaurants, street musicians and a very animated atmosphere which continues far into the warm summer nights. The Rhône is also busy, with many *péniches* converted into houseboats and other pleasure craft. The old bridge is of course Avignon's greatest claim to fame: a mere four arches survive of the original 22 which together spanned a length of 900m, across an island and over to the far shore at Villeneuve. Legend says that in 1177 a shepherd boy, Bénézet, had a vision commanding him to build a bridge (previous crossings of the lower Rhône had been by ferry). When he miraculously lifted a great block of stone singlehanded, all doubts vanished and funds poured in to complete the task in eleven years. With its chapel of St Nicholas, the bridge has been in its present incomplete state since the 17th century. Visitors may walk over the remaining arches on payment of a fee, and those with few inhibitions may feel inclined to hold hands in a circle, singing '*Sous le Pont d'Avignon on y danse tous en rond*'.

Restaurant delicacies associated with the city include *alose à l'Avignonnaise* (shad braised with sorrel and lemon) and *truffes blanches* (white truffles). A favourite eating place is the courtyard restaurant of the splendid Hôtel d'Europe.

While in Avignon, a most enjoyable excursion might be made by hiring a car and driving to the 2000-year-old Pont du Gard, a Roman aqueduct designed to convey water supplies to the city of **Nîmes**. Restored to its present excellent condition under Napoléon III, the three-tiered bridge rises 40m above the river with an uppermost row of 35 arches 275m long. The bravest of visitors can walk over the top.

At K261, left bank, **Vallabrègues**, is a mooring on floating stages: the approach can be difficult in windy conditions. Adequate shopping.

The speed of the Rhône current is now generally reduced: so is the scenic interest, for long reaches have little except reed and willow-fringed banks. One final lock must be negotiated – the Écluse de Vallabrègues (K265, fall 12.15m), whose entrance canal is situated on the left (K262.5) opposite the confluence with the River Gard. Emerging from the Vallabrègues lock, the twin towns of **Beaucaire** and **Tarascon** (K267.5) will be seen ahead, linked by a road bridge. Most unfortunately, there really is little prospect of mooring to explore the superb *châteaux* in each place. Since changing the Rhône water levels in the early 1970s a former connection with the Canal du Rhône à Sète at Beaucaire has been severed: this point may, however, be reached by boat via the Camargue and the Canal du Rhône à Sète. The huge feudal castle of Tarascon, its legendary beast and the sights of Beaucaire are described in Chapter 61, Canal du Rhône à Sète.

Deserted marshland with irrigation canals accompanies the river to a junction with the Petit Rhône (K279.5), the inland route for the Canal du Midi, Canal du Rhône à Sète and the Languedoc Coast

Tarascon's fortified château, seen from the bridge over the Rhône from Beaucaire.

(see Chapter 56). The Rhône has one further treasure to offer: the incomparable city of **Arles** (K282), a gateway to the Camargue and one of the chief towns of Provence. Established as a river port by Greeks from Marseilles in the 6th century BC, its usefulness was enhanced when the Romans cut a navigation canal linking it with the Mediterranean at the Golfe de Fos, so avoiding the silted complex of the Rhône Delta. Roman relics include a huge open-air amphitheatre capable of seating 21,000 people. During the Middle Ages it was converted into a circular 'village' of 200 houses and only restored to its present state in the early 19th century. Various public events are now held there.

The two great names of Arles are those of painter Vincent Van Gogh, who immortalized the region with over 200 pictures in 1888–9; and the Provençal poet Frédéric Mistral (1830–1914). After the coming of the railway in the 19th century, Rhône traffic declined and with it the importance of Arles. Today it flourishes again thanks to the Camargue rice industry, and as a tourist centre making full use of regional traditions.

Central moorings are on a floating pontoon, opposite the town; shops and restaurants are excellent. The local tourist office will advise on public transport to places of interest nearby; car hire is another possibility. Objectives for day excursions include the Camargue marshes and nature reserves (Chapter 62); **Stes-Maries-de-la-Mer**, with its fortified church where the Camargue meets the sea (most interesting during the gipsy celebrations and pilgrimages, held on May 24–5, the weekend nearest Oct 22 and the first Sunday of Dec); and the fascinating rock village of **Les Baux de-Provence**, 19km NE. All are fully described in English in the *Michelin Tourist Guide to Provence*.

The Roman amphitheatre at Arles.

At the downstream end of Arles, left bank K283.5, the basin of the **Canal d'Arles à Fos** may be reached via a lock. Repairs will be undertaken by a boatyard and long-term safe moorings can be negotiated. About 4km outside Arles the famous double-leaved Pont de Van Gogh drawbridge spans a lock: the wooden structure of the paintings was replaced by a replica in the 1930s. Opened in 1834, the waterway subsequently formed part of a chain of safe navigations extending to **Marseille**, so avoiding the problematical Rhône Delta and the coast. 32km remains available for pleasure craft, with 2 further locks. Scenery is similar to the Camargue marshlands, with no shade. The present terminus is at **Le Relai**. Available only mid-June to mid-September (see the *Carte Guide*). Further east, the **Canal de Marseille au Rhône** between **Marignane** and Marseille has been closed since the collapse of the vast Rove Tunnel in 1963. 7,120m long with a width of 22m and height of 11.4m, it admitted large ships and was among the biggest structures of its type anywhere. Construction was carried out between 1911 and 1927.

The remainder of the Rhône's course is atmospheric, if featureless, as it follows a wide path along the eastern edge of the Camargue. **Salin-de-Giraud** (K316.5) on the left bank is a small plane-shaded centre of chemical manufacture, connected to the opposite bank by busy car ferries (the lowest Rhône bridge is at Arles). Were it not for a lack of suitable moorings, this would be an ideal place to leave a boat and cycle about 5km past mountains of evaporated sea salt (a sizeable industry) and alongside brackish lakes to one of the finest beaches on France's Mediterranean coast. This is the **Plage de Faraman**, an immense tract of pale sand and dunes a little west of the point where the Rhône finally reaches the sea. Its isolation has prevented any form of development apart from a friendly restaurant in a shack. Vehicles may drive over the firm sand and hundreds of people use the beach as an unofficial camp site in summer. Following widely adopted practice elsewhere in France, nude bathing has become quite acceptable.

A choice of routes now exists between Salin de Giraud and the Mediterranean. Since its completion in 1982, the **Liaison Rhône-Fos** (entrance at K316.5) has offered a 7km canal connection to the new **Port de Fos** and its extensive industrial zone. There is 1 lock, near the Rhône end. Intended for use by 5,000 tonne push-tows, it is not available to pleasure craft, who must reach the Mediterranean via Port St Louis.

The above course would, in any event, offer little advantage to boats bound for ports on the Languedoc Coast and destinations to the west. They should continue down the tree-lined Rhône to **Port-St-Louis-du-Rhône** (K323), making a broad sweep into the Maritime Lock (left bank), above which is a large basin. The little town has shops and restaurants, fuel and water points, repair facilities and a Customs office. From here, the blue Mediterranean is a mere 3km away, down the **Canal St Louis**. Most pleasure craft that have successfully descended the Rhône will be adequately equipped for a sea passage: but it must be emphasized that the Mediterranean can be extremely rough and is certainly no fit place for river cruisers, except for short trips in ideal conditions. The last 6km of the Rhône, between Port-St-Louis and the sea, are silted and not suited to navigation.

56 · Petit Rhône

Carte Guide: *Canaux du Midi* or *Le Rhône*
From a junction with the (Grand) Rhône at K279.5, above Arles, to the Mediterranean at Grau d'Orgon, west of Stes-Maries-de-la-Mer: 57km with no locks. A junction is made at K299.5 with the short St-Gilles Canal, providing access to the Canal du Rhône à Sète. The lower 37km from there to the sea are little used, except by small fishing boats and cruisers; maximum permitted draft on this section is only about 1m, with an air draft of 2.7m.

Following closure of the Beaucaire connection between the Rhône and the Canal du Rhône à Sète, the first

20km of the Petit Rhône have been greatly improved from its former shallow condition. It now provides the normal through route for craft between the Rhône and the Canal du Rhône à Sète. The channel, while reasonably narrow and winding, is practicable for large vessels and the St-Gilles lock on the short connecting canal is built to the same dimensions as those on the Rhône. Thick belts of trees and reeds line each bank for the whole distance, with no villages or even houses to be seen. The lower 37km to the sea are similarly desolate, although the tree cover decreases nearer the Mediterranean.

Distances along the river are a continuation of the measurements from Lyon: the junction with the Grand Rhône above Arles is K279.5 and the entry to the sea K336.5. Detailed description of the Petit Rhône is not necessary. In the whole course there are a mere 5 bridges and one ferry crossing; scarcely a hamlet; and in the first 20km not a house to be seen from the water. The sense of isolation is intense and at times it is difficult to be sure where you are. Numerous drainage channels accompany the waterway through the marshes of the Camargue, although little of this fascinating world is evident from a boat. There are no shopping facilities directly on the route. While taking suitable precautions for a slight rise and fall in water levels, there are numerous possible moorings. None is more appealing than a 'desert island' of white sand and tamarisk bushes at K293.3, with swimming beaches offering both deep and shallow water. The nearest contact with civilization is the Pont de St-Gilles (K297) from which **St-Gilles** is within easy walking distance (see Chapter 62). Just before K300 the **Canal de St-Gilles** with its large lock appears on the right. Virtually all craft will wish to pass this way, shortly joining the Canal du Rhône à Sète.

While there is a clearly marked channel from the Grand Rhône to St Gilles lock, there are no navigation markers from St Gilles to the Mediterranean. Consequently this must be cruised with great care to avoid sandbanks. It is, however, a very worthwhile excursion with a good enclosed harbour at **Stes. Maries-de-la-Mer**, reached after a short eastwards coastal passage. This is a lively little seaside resort, noted for huge gipsy gatherings on May 24 and 25, the penultimate Sunday of October and the first Sunday of December.

57 · River Garonne

Carte Guide: *Canaux du Midi*
From Bordeaux to a junction with the River Baïse, near Buzet, providing a 5km-long connection with the Canal Latéral à la Garonne (Baïse Branch). 132km and 0 locks. Entry to the River Dordogne and its tributary the River Isle is from the River Gironde (the name of the estuary of the Garonne) at Bec d'Ambès, 26km downstream of Bordeaux. A further junction is made with the Canal Latéral à la Garonne at Castets-en-Dorthe, 54km upriver from Bordeaux. Most traffic uses the Canal Latéral à la Garonne between Castets and Buzet.

The Garonne rises in the Pyrenees, across the Spanish border. Being tidal throughout its navigable length, it demands more careful use than most inland waterways. The portion below Bordeaux is in effect a seaway and beyond the scope of this book. Forming the western section of the 505km route from Bordeaux to the Mediterranean, the Garonne is a somewhat difficult river and should only be attempted in correctly equipped craft and by people with some experience of tidal waterways. If entering from the Atlantic, use Service Hydrographique marine charts 6141, 6139 and 6140. After Bordeaux there are few possibilities for mooring and it is best to make a passage from there to the canal at Castets (or *vice versa*) on one tide. Rocks will have to be avoided in places, and allowance must be made for a tidal bore which reaches a height of about 1m for some distance above Bordeaux.

Although there is very considerable interest in the villages of many famous Bordeaux vineyards such as Graves, Sauternes and Barsac, they are rarely in evidence from a boat and for much of the time the river banks are lined with a thick belt of trees. Having once made the journey with a flotilla of seven canal cruisers between Bordeaux and Castets, my firm advice is not to to stop en route, except in an emergency.

Brief history As recently as 1936, the Garonne was technically considered navigable for 463km from the Atlantic (including the Gironde from the coast to Bec d'Ambès). But even then, only the section to Castets carried any traffic. In early times craft had been able to reach Toulouse with some difficulty: indeed, this was the route taken by boats between the Atlantic and the Mediterranean after opening of the Canal du Midi in 1681. Boats and rafts brought stone and lime to Toulouse, all the way from Boussens, about 70km upstream of the city. Passengers aboard the Midi 'water coaches' risked grounding in the river and even the prospect of shipwreck. The poor state of the upper Garonne can be judged from the necessity to transfer the contents of a single Midi barge into no fewer than 20 light-draft vessels for the run downriver of Toulouse. Such problems were finally overcome by completion of the Canal Latéral à la Garonne between Castets and Toulouse in 1856. Thereafter, upper Garonne traffic declined and attempts to keep the route dredged were abandoned.

In 1886 it was calculated that there were 1,752km of navigable rivers in the Garonne basin, consisting of 25 waterways (excluding artificial canals): these were regularly used by 30,952 vessels. Among these lost navigations were the Tarn, from above Albi to the Garonne near Moissac (147km with 31 locks); the Lot (256km with 76 locks); and the Dropt, on which there were 21 locks. All have since returned, more or less, to their natural states, although the remains of locks can be found. An isolated 64km portion of the River Lot, upstream of Luzech, was re-opened to navigation in 1990, while a substantial locked portion of the Lower Lot is currently (1999) being returned to service. (See Chapter 59.)

Although 98km from the sea, **Bordeaux** is a sizeable and busy port, capable of receiving large ships drawing up to 8.5m. Moorings may be found out of the tideway in the Floating Basin, reached through a huge lock on the right bank between the Pont d'Aquitaine (suspension) and the Pont de Pierre with its 17 arches. Alternatively, there are two marinas on the river itself: Port du Point du Jour, right bank by the Pont d'Aquitaine; and the Port Fluvial

Ring nets worked from small cranes are a notable feature of the tidal Garonne.

(fuel), between the 17-arched Pont de Pierre and the Pont St-Jean. A most ambitious cruising restaurant aboard the 43m vessel *Aliénor* was put into service in the centre of Bordeaux in 1983. Seating up to 250 diners, it makes journeys on the Garonne, Gironde and Dordogne. Cost of the venture was about £500,000. The most convenient shops are found near the Porte de Bourgogne, close to the Pont de Pierre. Water the colour of cocoa, a fierce tide and violent wash from passing traffic are all factors that discourage a long stay, unless you elect to lock out of the river into the docks.

For two centuries Bordeaux and a sizeable chunk of SW France was under English rule. Eleanor, daughter of the Duke of Aquitaine, married Louis VII of France in 1137, but this union was annulled. Keeping her French lands, Eleanor then married Henry II of England, so providing an eventual cause of the Hundred Years War. Former capital of Aquitaine, the great city is the sixth largest in France. After the fall of Paris it was the seat of Government in 1870 and again in 1914 and 1940; many of the most noble buildings, like the Grand Théâtre, date from the 18th century. Perhaps Bordeaux's greatest claim to fame is as centre of the claret industry. Suggested tours of the vineyards and *châteaux* of the region are listed in the green *Michelin Guide Côte de l'Atlantique*, under *Vallée de la Garonne*.

While the river channel lies mostly in the centre, great care should be taken to follow the chart, avoiding sandbanks and other hazards. Running with the tide, leave 4–5hr before high water; usually it will be possible to follow a freight barge (considerable power is required to keep pace with them). Otherwise pilots are available through the Service de Navigation in Bordeaux. About 6hr is necessary for the journey upriver to Castets.

Kilometre posts are numbered from a point upstream of Castets, which is at K17.5. Should you need moorings en route, there are possibilities at the following places: pontoon by Ile de la Lande (K59); **Cambes** (K56, where a pontoon is in service June–Oct); **Langoiran** (K49, pontoon); **Podensac** (K40, public quay); **Cadillac** (K35.5, pontoon, June–Oct); **Preignac** (K30, short stay only); and **Langon** (K25, pleasure craft harbour projected). All these towns are provided with good shopping facilities. If you decide to explore ashore, Cadillac is possibly the most interesting port of call with fortifications and the Château des Ducs d'Épernon (early 17th century and open throughout the year except on Tues). The town's water gate (la Porte de Mer) has a flood marker which provides dramatic evidence of the wayward nature of the Garonne. In April 1770 the river rose 12.5m above normal, and only a metre less in the flood of 1930.

Atlantic weather brings fogs in the lower part of the Garonne. Other local characteristics are large 'ring' nets, suspended from cranes on the muddy banks: they may be lowered to catch whatever species of fish swims by. Widely advertised specialities include *aloses*, a migratory sea fish known in English as shad and here grilled over vine shoots or stuffed with sorrel; and *lamproies* (lampreys), an eel cooked *à la bordelaise* sliced with leeks, red wine and garlic. Remember that Henry I paid a heavy price for eating too much of this dish.

When arriving at the junction with the Canal Latéral à la Garonne at **Castets** (K17.5), approach via the right-hand arch of the road bridge, on the same side as the locks. Should the lock be ready, enter straight away; otherwise anchor in midstream below the bridge or bring up on a bankside mooring, 200m downstream of the bridge. Hoot for the keeper, who is on duty between 5.00 and 23.00h. The chamber is worked electrically with another manual lock alongside. Craft leaving the canal for Bordeaux and the Atlantic should time their departure to coincide with high water at Castets.

58 · Canal Latéral à la Garonne

Carte Guide: *Canaux du Midi*
From the River Garonne at Castets to a junction with the Canal du Midi in Toulouse: 193.6km with 53 locks; 5 of these locks are duplicated by a 'water slope' at Montech which is not available for use by pleasure craft. Junctions are made at Buzet-sur-Baïse with the River Baïse (two-rise lock) at Moissac (two-rise staircase leading to an attractive reservoir section of the River Tarn); and with the Montauban Branch at Montech (10.8km with 9 locks), now closed to boats.

The approach to the first canal lock at Castets. Care should be taken to select the left-hand bridge opening, for the river is obstructed by rocks elsewhere.

It would be preferable to travel from Bordeaux to the Mediterranean and not *vice versa*. For although the Canal Latéral à la Garonne is very pleasant in parts and passes through a number of places of interest, it would come as a considerable anticlimax to navigate the Latéral *after* the Midi. This is not to imply that the canal is not very fine: the only section that is tediously dull is the final length of about 40km before Toulouse. As a work of the mid-19th century, the Latéral features many long straights, compared to its curvaceous 17th century neighbour. You cannot fail, however, to admire the boldness of its engineering. For much of the journey between Agen and Toulouse the railway is close by – sometimes aggressively so. Bridges are utilitarian rather than pretty, many being concrete bowstring structures. On the credit side, the banks of yellow iris provide a remarkable blaze of colour in early summer. Agen is in one of the most productive fruit growing regions of France, raising every variety from strawberries and cherries to apples, pears, plums and peaches. Vineyards are less in evidence, although wine is a leading industry in the Bordeaux district.

All locks were lengthened in the 1970s to admit 38m *péniches* and the great majority have been mechanized for operation by keepers or automated for working by boat crews. Controlled by a traffic light system, gates and paddles are set in action by turning a pole (*tirette*) suspended over the water about 300m either side of the locks. Further buttons must be pressed when craft are in the chamber. The system appears to be relatively trouble-free. Instructions are displayed in French, German and English. One unfortunate design fault of the locks is the overflow weirs which enable water supplies to run from pound to pound. The inlets and outflows are situated very close to the lock gates, making steering light pleasure boats somewhat difficult.

Brief history It is said that Pierre Paul Riquet, builder of the Canal du Midi, envisaged an artificial waterway to replace the very uncertain navigation of the Garonne downstream of Toulouse. But work on its construction was not to commence for over 150 years after the Midi was inaugurated. Planned under de Baudré, the Divisional Inspector of the *Ponts et Chaussées*, work started in 1838. By 1843 it was sufficiently advanced for a regular passenger boat service to begin between Montauban and Toulouse. The line was in use to Agen in 1850 and extended to its junction with the River Garonne at Castets in 1856. Unfortunately, this was the very year in which the Midi Railway Company completed its connection between Bordeaux and Toulouse. The rival transport concern negotiated a lease (expiring in 1898) for both the Latéral and the Midi and a deliberate policy of canal neglect was adopted. When he cruised between the two seas in his steam yacht *Miranda* (25.9m × 3.35m × 1.42m draft) in 1881, Lord Clarence Paget commented that the railway 'has almost entirely absorbed the traffic'. State control from 1898 brought a change in fortunes. By the end of the 1930s all but a few horseboats had been replaced by motorized *péniches* and steel lock gates were standard through the whole route.

In February 1939 preliminary Government consent was obtained to construct a ship canal for ocean-going vessels between Bordeaux and the Mediterranean at La Nouvelle. The War intervened and nothing more has come of the proposal. Instead, all locks have been lengthened for Freycinet 38m *péniches*, with most chambers mechanized or equipped for automatic operation. Expected increase in freight tonnages is unlikely to materialize now that the planned lock enlargement throughout the Canal du Midi has been suspended. Chief among cargoes still carried are cereals and petroleum products. Meanwhile, where 15 barges a day passed through the Latéral in the mid-1970s, the number has fallen to about 8 per week. Perhaps the most notable innovation was to build a water-slope for *péniches* in place of 5 locks at Montech. Unique in the world for a decade from 1973, it has now been joined by a similar structure on the Canal du Midi at Béziers.

Spectacular Garonne floods prompted building this Castets lock house with a front door at second floor level and approached by steps from the back.

To arrive in the still waters of the canal at **Castets-en-Dorthe** (K0, see Chapter 57), is rather a relief after the turmoil of the tidal Garonne. Not that this waterside settlement is totally safe from the bad-tempered river. Flood marks on the side of the lock house reach up to the *second* storey: at this level the front door is situated, with a magnificent iron stairway sweeping round each side of the building to higher ground at the back. The lock consists of a two-rise arrangement, but only the lower chamber seems normally to be used. Consult the keeper for tidal information if preparing to run down to Bordeaux. Castets village hides away up a hillside, where most supplies can be obtained. A *Halte Nautique* with barbeque facilities has been created at Castets and there is a good restaurant within 200m.

Many villages lie on the course of the canal and are agreeably agricultural. The majority have basic shops, e.g. **Fontet** (K11) or **Hure** (K14), where there is an extremely old church, garage and restaurant. Shortly after passing from the Gironde *département* to Lot-et-Garonne, we reach a real gem – **Meilhan** (K23). At a point where the Garonne swings in towards the wooded escarpment to the right of its valley, the canal passes beneath a cliff on top of which is a restaurant, public terrace and telescope for admiring the view. To reach this lookout is an easy uphill walk of perhaps 10 minutes. Moor on the far, towpath side and cross under the canal via a tunnel thoughtfully provided for fishermen and others to reach the riverbank. Meilhan offers a rare opportunity to appreciate the Garonne landscape from a high level. Thick woods are mixed with arable farming and through the middle of the prospect the sandbank-strewn river flows towards the distant sea: it is difficult to believe that his was once the only water communication with Toulouse.

Black-painted wooden barns with open slatted sides will be seen in the fields: they are used for drying tobacco. The sizeable town of **Marmande** is about 5km from the canal at **Pont des Sables** (K29), a former river port that specializes in fruit growing (especially tomatoes) and tobacco. Pont des Sables has a restaurant and (maybe a little unwise) a rowing club: keep a careful lookout for racing craft training on the canal. One sad accident is recalled by a stone monument on the side of the waterway near **Fourques** (K32). In 1908 all five men aboard the steam barge *Le Gascon* were killed when the boiler exploded; it was said that the captain was drunk. Grocer, butcher and post office in the village. **Caumont** (K33) lies near a basin with easy access to the shops and restaurant of this small one-street town. At **Mas d'Argenais** (K38) a long suspension bridge spans both canal and the Garonne. There is a waterside garage and a good selection of shops within 500m. Houses tumble down a hillside to the water and the site was occupied in Roman times. Among many relics excavated here is the Venus of Mas, now housed in a museum at Agen. There is a Rembrandt Crucifixion in the ancient church of St-Vincent. Crown Blue Line base, with facilities. A church on a high mound and a stream by lock 42, La Gaule, will be found in the very rural hamlet of **St-Christophe** (K46). **Damazan** (K54) is a town of moderate size on the canal bank, devoted mainly to fruit growing.

Craft are encouraged to stop at the *Halte Nautique* in **Buzet-sur-Baïse** (K57), where again all shopping facilities are available. Les Caves Cooperatives de Buzet provide an opportunity for replenishing the ship's wine stores and welcome visitors with a slide show and tour (commentary in English, if desired). It is a friendly little town, with restaurants and a market every Friday. Shortly, there is a connection, via a 2-rise lock, with the recently restored River Baïse (see Chapter 63).

Nearby at Nicole, is a former junction with the River Lot Navigation, once 297km in length. A 65km isolation section above and below Cahors was reopened to boats in 1990. The lowest section with four locks was being prepared in 1999 for a return to navigation. See Chapter 59.

Beyond lock 39, Baïse, the canal crosses the River Baïse (K61), soon to arrive in **Feugarolles** (K64), with several shops and a barge quay. For the first time the

Gravel barges on the Garonne at its junction with the Baïse, St-Leger.

A61 Narbonne-Bourdeaux is noticeable to the right. **Port-Ste-Marie** lies about 4km NE, on the banks of the Garonne. Apart from lock 38, Auvignon, near the village of **Bruch** (K68) and **Sérignac-sur-Garonne** (K77, a gem of a village, grocer, restaurant and post office), there is little of note until the outskirts of the city of Agen. Locks 34–37 raise the canal 12.4m, followed by a magnificent stone aqueduct carrying it for 539m over the Garonne. Here a short branch descends through two locks to the river and is now closed to navigation.

Agen (K86) is the self-styled 'capital of prunes', for of all the fruit grown in the area none is better known than the luscious dried plums to be obtained at various shops in the town, including the Maison des Pruneaux, established 1835. To the left of an extended basin a wooded hillside is dotted with elegant villas. Opposite are moorings at a *Halte de Tourisme* with showers and a clubhouse. Local boating enthusiasts are exceptionally welcoming and are pleased to supervise private craft left here for a period. It is certainly the best and most convenient long-term mooring west of Toulouse and even has a main line railway station adjacent. (Water point, and fuel on request.) By crossing the tracks via a pedestrian bridge, the town centre is quickly reached. With 40,000 inhabitants, there are of course many restaurants. For appetising food at remarkably low costs, I recommend the Jasmin-Terminus opposite the station. St Caprasius 11th century cathedral is disappointingly gloomy: a far more interesting visit is to the Museum, housed in a series of Renaissance mansions. Exhibits include Gallo-Roman remains, among them the superb 2nd century marble Venus from Le Mas d'Argenais, furniture, ceramics and paintings by Goya and Sisley.

Possible excursions from Agen are north to the Lot Valley (Villeneuve-sur-Lot is 27km via the N21); and to **Nérac**, 29km on the D656: local historians make the dubious claim that Shakespeare stayed here and indeed the King's Bathing Pavilion on the banks of the River Baïse is said to be the setting for *Love's Labour Lost*.

The waterway that now follows is pleasant but unremarkable. Never far from the banks of the Garonne, it runs straight for considerable distances sometimes bordered by great fields of maize, elsewhere secluded under a canopy of huge plane trees selected for their ability to counteract erosion. Facilities in the nearby towns and villages are as follows: **St-Nicholas de la Balerme** (K100), grocer,

Lamagistère (K107), all services; **Golfech** (K108), grocer, butcher, baker, post office. Here there is an aqueduct over the River Barguelonne, and downstream of a dammed section of the Garonne, a hydro-electric power station.

An excellent *port de plaisance* (no charge) in **Valence d'Agen** (K112) is close to most facilities. The splendid public washhouse is an example of that peculiarly French 19th century facility where architectural styles are often of Classical proportions. Their use has declined with the spread of domestic washing machines, but it is by no means unusual to see women attending to the family laundry, especially in *lavoirs* fed direct by the murky waters of the canal. Slow right down when passing, to avoid flooding occupants with *your* wash! Through **Pommevic** (K116), grocer and baker and **Malause** (K120), grocer, baker and butcher, the canal is again joined by the Garonne, now much increased in width by conversion into a huge reservoir up and downstream of the junction with the Tarn. It may be entered by boat from the Tarn Branch canal in Moissac.

Easily the most interesting and agreeable town on the Latéral is Moissac (K129). Shortly after Écluse 26, Espagnette is a convenient roadside garage. Approaching the town centre, it is obvious that the canal has been built down the middle of a wide street with brick retaining walls. After the Pont St-Jacques swing bridge (sound horn) there is a delightful garden gazebo attached to a conservatory: the epitome of 19th century French domestic architecture, it has a slender cone of slates for its roof and an ornate cast-iron balcony. Soon the canal leaves this narrow cutting for a broad basin with plenty of mooring space and a drinking water supply. Moissac's great treasure is its ancient abbey, founded in the 7th century and preserved in spite of repeated attacks by Arabs, Normans, Hungarians, the English in the Hundred Years War, and during the French Revolution. Having survived thus far, it might be considered safe; but no - there was a quite determined proposal to demolish the structure to make space for the mid-19th century Bordeaux-Sète railway (the same infamous railway that presented a threat to the Midi canals). Fortunately, the great building was spared. Partly Romanesque and partly Gothic, the abbey church of St Pierre has a wonderful carved south doorway from the early 12th century, depicting the Vision of the Apocalypse according to St John. The intricacies of this Romanesque stonework are remarkable. Completed towards the end of the 11th century, the abbey cloisters are probably the most outstanding in France, the capitals of each arch dec-

Magnificent stonework around the doorway of the abbey at Moissac.

orated with a variety of animal and plant motifs. It seems offensive that a substantial admission charge is made.

Agen is associated with prunes: Moissac has its delicious golden dessert grapes. Shortly before Écluse 25, a branch, right, leads through a two-rise staircase to the **River Tarn**. Sadly, little now remains of the 147km navigation and its 31 locks, once navigable to a point upstream of Albi. But here at least it is possible to join the river and cruise for a distance on the broadened reservoir section, seen earlier from the canal. 400 hectares of water are available with a yacht club and swimming pool. Silting below the locks may reduce available draft to 1m. There is a plan to restore navigation on the Tarn at least between Moissac and Montauban. Note the remains of a lock on the downstream end of the Promenade du Moulin, with a gateless diamond-shaped chamber.

The canal now ascends through locks 23–25 on the edge of the town, where trees and grassy banks make a popular waterside walk for local people. Lock 23, Cacor (K131), is a delightful haven of peace, the gravel forecourt of the cottage being beautifully maintained for *boules*. Magnificent clusters of white arum lilies line the canalside. The Cacor keeper has several times won the prize awarded for the best kept lock on the entire Midi canals

route. Now follows the second of the Latéral's great stone aqueducts, spanning the River Tarn for 356m with thirteen arches. An extraordinary period in its history followed the great flood of March 1930, during which the nearby main line railway viaduct was washed away. The aqueduct's towpath was widened sufficiently to enable a single track to be laid along it, and within six weeks of the disaster trains and barges shared the same crossing. This arrangement continued for two years until the opening of the present new railway viaduct. Leakage on the embankment that follows has resulted in the canal bed being lined with asphalt.

Locks 22–19 now intervene before **Castelsarrasin** (K137), a rather dull little town whose full range of facilities includes an excellent fish shop. Baths and showers near the basin. Two more locks, before and after the village of **St-Porquier** (K144), bring the navigator to one of the most fascinating examples of modern waterway engineering in France, the **Montech Water Slope** (K148). In its original form, the canal passes through a chain of five locks (Nos. 15–11) spread over 2km. Pleasure craft work through these, while barge traffic takes a parallel new route leading to a 443m concrete 'flume' or trough; a wedge of water, in which the barge floats, is pushed up or down the 3% gradient ahead of a shield propelled by a pair of locomotives. Popularly known as a 'push-puddle' lock, this ingenious concept is best suited to sites with substantial changes in level: here it is about 14m. The Montech slope began operating in 1973 and was joined by the world's second water slope at Béziers on the Canal du Midi in 1983. All this modern technology is far removed from the remains of an old wooden Midi barge, decaying in a small dock between locks 11 and 12.

Montech town centre lies about 500m away from a basin beyond the top lock (the obvious mooring place is silted). Most shops and an agreeable restaurant (medium price) are near the crossroads.

The 11km **Montauban Branch**, with 9 locks, has been closed for a number of years. However, there is a plan to restore navigation both here and on the River Tarn, at least between Montauban and Moissac. Scenery is pleasant with an A61 *autoroute* bridge near the village of **Lacourt St-Pierre**. The Branch reaches a terminus in a basin quite close to the middle of **Montauban**: originally a two-rise staircase lock provided a link with the Tarn Navigation. This cut is heavily silted and, local oarsmen apart, craft no longer use the river. No devotee of inland waterways can fail to be stirred by the sight of a ruined lock chamber on this once thriving waterway. The ferocity of the well-remembered great flood of 1930 is dramatically recalled by a bust on the riverbank promenade of a young man named Adolphe Poult. While water swirled through the streets, he saved the lives of no fewer than 317 people before himself being drowned. This is a pleasant city, mainly of pink brick with an early 14th century bridge, a 17th century Archbishop's Palace (now the Ingres Museum), and fine brick arcades surrounding the Place Nationale where a flower market is held in the mornings.

Shortly after Montech the railway returns to the canal bank and remains as a constant and noisy companion all the way to Toulouse. Villages have expanded as a consequence and there are plenty of opportunities for shopping. Surroundings are deeply rural to begin with, through extensive orchards. **Dieupentale** (K162) and **Grisolles** (K167) are both well supplied with shops and restaurants. **Castelnau d'Estrétefonds** (K174) is best approached from Écluse 8. Situated on a ridge with a red brick church and large pedimented *château*, it offers basic facilities. Lock 7 is followed

by an aqueduct about 120m long over the River Hers. The last easily approached shopping village before the Toulouse conurbation in **St-Jory** (K178), within 200m of Lock 6. The neighbourhood of the canal now becomes increasingly industrial as five final locks are negotiated before arrival in Toulouse (K193), junction with the Canal du Midi at the Port de l'Embouchure. (See Chapter 60.)

The world's first water slope for barges at Montech. (Photograph courtesy David Edwards-May.)

59. River Lot

Carte Guide: *Le Lot* (Éditions Grafocarte) or *Le Lot*, (Éditions du Breil). From Luzech to Crégols. 64.3km with 14 locks. Additionally, the lowest section of the river from a junction with the Baïse at Nicole to point upstream of Villeneuve-sur-Lot, was being prepared for reopening in 1999. 40km with 4 locks.

Set in a region rather less known than the neighbouring Dordogne, but displaying equal attractions, the River Lot represents an extraordinary success story in the annals of French waterway restoration. Reopened to sizeable boats in May 1990, it is, for the time being, isolated from the main network. However, it offers ample scope for a week's cruise by hire boat; there are three firms supplying craft. Alternatively, there are sufficient slipways for the use of trailed vessels.

From end to end, surroundings are thickly wooded limestone gorges, placing the Lot among the most exciting river navigations in France. Virtually all bankside towns and villages will repay exploration; many are based on ancient fortified sites. Little affected by 20th century industrialization or tourism, this is a deeply rural area. Remnants of ancient troglodyte castles can be found along the valley. These are the *châteaux des Anglais*, well guarded refuges of English invaders who were active during the Middle Ages.

Like many rivers, the Lot is prone to flooding in winter and spring; care must then be taken in the vicinity of weirs, especially where there are no lock cuts. In these conditions, when navigating upstream, chamber entrances may be obstructed by a strong outfall across the channel. Equally, in a downstream boat, it can be difficult to detect a weir and the adjoining lock entrance until the last minute. Such problems are fortunately rare during the main cruising season. But at all times due attention must be paid to the *Carte Guide*. A series of floating buoys or red/green poles shows where the channel lies. These must be strictly adhered to. Elsewhere, there are shallow patches of mud, solid rock or even submerged remains of former weirs. For all that, the Lot is not difficult cruising and was navigated by scores of novice hirers during its first year in operation.

Landing stages are installed above and below many locks, all of which are worked unassisted by boats' crews. With the exception of one totally new concrete structure, all other locks use the original 19th century stone chambers. Restoration has been carried out to a high standard with agreeable cobblestones on the walkways and well-placed mooring bollards. For

reasons described as *sécurité*, it is impossible to work the gate-operating capstans unless both gate paddles at that end of the lock are fully wound open (there are fixed windlasses). If the paddles are not correctly adjusted, the gate-opening mechanisms infuriatingly become disengaged! Low-geared paddle machinery requires about 100 turns, but is not heavy to operate.

Provided you have road transport, there are numerous excursions to be made in the locality, including the clifftop pilgrimage city of Rocamadour, the valley of the River Célé (good canoeing), and prehistoric cave dwellings (Grotte du pech-Merle).

Eating local produce is a major preoccupation. Goose, duck, *pâté de foie gras*, many varieties of fungus, all kinds of game, freshwater fish (including crayfish), walnuts in salads, crushed for cooking oil or fermented as a sweet *digestif*. Expanses of vineyards around Cahors give us a famous dark red (sometimes almost purple) wine - a favourite with the Russian Tzars.

It is not possible here to include a description of the newly rebuilt lower river, as it had not been returned to service as this edition went to press. A former 10 locks have been reduced to just 4, two of which are adjacent to massive hydro-electric barrages. All (like those on the Baïse) are operated by means of 'smart' cards. The engineering works required were impressive. Towns en route include **Aiguillon, Clairac, Castelmoron** and **Villeneuve**. While lacking the grandeur of the gorges around Cahors, scenery is splendid throughout. It is expected that this section will be united with the higher reaches in due course. For full details, consult the latest *Carte Guides*.

Brief history Although used with difficulty by small, shallow draft craft in the 13th century, the Lot was first improved under Colbert in the 17th century and by 1776 was said to be equipped with twelve pound locks; these would have replaced some of the earlier unreliable navigation weirs, but only partially reduced the Lot's dangerous reputation. Wreckings were frequent in times of drought and, worse still, during floods.

A complete remanagement scheme commenced in 1835, with some 297km being tamed from Le Moulin d'Olt at Entraygues, to a confluence with the Garonne at Nicole near Aiguillon. By now, there were 76 locks (of which three were 2-rise staircases), numerous artificial lock cuts and four tunnels varying in length from 139m to 364m: these cut through high ground at some of the most acute bends in the natural river. A sizeable barge fleet comprised flat-bottomed *sapines* and *gabares* and little swim-ended wooden punts known as *naus*.

Typical loads were cheese from the Auvergne, Decazeville coal and a wide range of agricultural products, chief of which was red wine from Cahors. Greatest tonnage was downstream, destined for Bordeaux, although a substantial quantity of foodstuffs and minerals made upriver voyages. During twelve months in 1851/2, nearly 73,000 tonnes of freight was recorded, including 20,000 tonnes of wine. Railway competition began to exact a savage toll and by 1923 freight figures on the upper and middle river had plummeted to a mere 11,635 tonnes. Late in 1926, the Lot navigation was officially abandoned, all dredging and maintenance on locks and weirs coming to an end. For more than 60 years lock cuts gradually disappeared beneath a tangle of undergrowth and the only boats to be seen were fishing punts and long-distance canoes.

The region suffered economic decline throughout much of the 20th century and with hopes of boosting tourism, M. Ricard, *Préfet* du Lot, prepared an initial scheme for revitalization of the river in 1970. Little was to come of this. Meanwhile, pleasure boating was increasing rapidly elsewhere in south-west France. A report was commissioned from British waterways expert David Edwards-May. Assisted by Blue Line's chief manager, John Riddel, this identified nearly 65km of the most scenic portion of the route which could be restored at a cost of 24 million francs. Financial support was sought from the European Parliament and reconstruction work started at an unusually rapid speed. All was ready to welcome me as the first boat hirer when I made a return journey by water with two friends between Luzech and St Cirq-Lapopie in late May 1990.

In addition to the three cruiser hire companies, there are currently three passenger vessels operating. Looking to the future, problems exist where certain old lock sites are obstructed by hydro-electric installations. One at Galessie was successfully avoided by building a brand new lock on the opposite side of the river. A much larger power station at Luzech prevents downstream restoration – although (expense apart) it would not be impossible to excavate a substantial length of new bypass lateral canal. Thus, if use of the Lot reaches expectations, it is by no means inconceivable that this beautiful waterway will one day be relinked to the Garonne and thus form a part of the interconnected system of France. In the short term, it is hoped to extend navigation upstream to Carjarc, so providing a total of 93km of cruising water. This will involve circumventing a 6m high power station weir either with a 2-rise lock or some form of boat lift. On the lower river there are fewer obstacles: 30km around Villeneuve was navigated by a passenger *péniche* in 1989.

Navigation currently begins upstream of a hydro-electricity barrage immediately north of the small town of **Luzech** (K0). Old postcard views show that a 200m canal with 2-rise lock staircase once cut through the town centre, bypassing a huge loop of the Lot that nearly describes a complete circle. Most signs of the infilled waterway have vanished, although the street which replaces it is unusually wide. There is excellent shopping and other facilities with indications of Luzech's former importance as a centre of the barge trade. Rock-strewn reedy shallows and a disused lock chamber clearly illustrate the dereliction affecting the unrestored waterway. Nearby are remains of the prehistoric **Impernal** settlement, later a Roman city. A severe 13th century keep tower dominates the view from a boat. Now follows a level reach of over 12km, fringed by dense woodland and patches of vineyard. On the left (K0.2), the base of Locaboat hire cruisers was installed in 1990. A waterside holiday centre will be seen on the left at **Caïx** (K0.8) (watch out for canoes, swimmers and sailing dinghies) followed by the four towers of a 17th century *château*, now a summer residence of Queen Margaret II of Denmark (K2.9).

Mooring is possible at many places; first, carefully check water depths. If in doubt, head for sites identified on the *Carte Guides*. One such is the outside wall of the former lock just downstream of the delightful, but seemingly deserted, riverside Château de Langle (K5.6). Due west, **Parnac** lies at the heart of a tract of vineyards, walnut groves and fields of tobacco.

Bishop Raimond de Cornil inhabited the Château de Laroque, perched on a cliff (K11.5) in the 13th century. He was responsible for an early scheme to improve navigation on the river. Beyond a camping site (right) and elegant brick railway bridge of the former Cahors-Fumel line, will be seen the disused chamber of **Douelle** lock (K11.8). Shortly after, Douelle appears in the distance, beyond a rocky weir. A direct approach to Cessac lock (K12.4) is not possible, owing to shallows on the right; these are marked by three floating white buoys. The small town was once a leading barge port and one reminder of this vanished activity is a votive offering in the form of a boat, suspended from the rafters of the church. Most facilities are available, including restaurants. We greatly enjoyed the atmosphere of the cellar-like *Aux Vieux Douelle*, with steaks grilled over a log fire. Crown Blue Line have established a cruiser base (right) below the bridge, with a newly constructed maintenance yard opposite.

Dense tree cover and sheer cliffs characterize the Lot past the 19th century Château de Carriol (K15) and a somewhat tricky approach to the Écluse de **Mercuès** (K19.2). First, rocky shallows (right, K17.9) are marked by floating plastic containers; then, several hundred metres of red and green stakes show where the channel lies. In normal conditions, all should be straightforward. During my cruise, remains of a recent flood cascaded from the weir, pouring over the lock cut bank and resulting in a fierce current immediately below the bottom gates. Mercuès village (left bank, named after a Roman temple to Mercury) is not easily approached from the water. Most practicable mooring appears to be on the same side, upstream of the weir. High above, towers of the 15th century Château de Mercuès command a magnificent view along the valley. Formerly a residence of the counts-bishops of Cahors, it was restored in the 19th century and is now a luxury hotel with splendidly palatial furnishings, a

range of opulent bedrooms, swimming pool and well-manicured terrace gardens. Arriving from a boat would entail a very long uphill walk: we delayed a visit until reunited with our car at the end of the cruise, arriving for lunch via a vineyard road. The *château* produces and sells excellent wines. Rarely in France have I more enjoyed a meal, served in the central courtyard which was protected by a remarkable wall-to-wall 'umbrella' in the shape of an inverted cone and designed to conduct any rainwater into a stone well in the middle of the restaurant. In 1990, the 240F per person all-inclusive

The magnificent Pont Valentré at Cahors.

bill represented very fair value. We voted this meal one of our highlights of the Lot.

Pradines (right bank, K21.2) faces the river with a jumble of small clifftop houses rising from the remains of earlier fortifications. Unfortunately, there is no safe mooring point at present. The lower approach to the Écluse de Labéraudie (K24.5) presents no problem. However, when leaving the upper end it is essential to remain close to the right bank to avoid rocks of a submerged weir. Shortly, we enter a huge loop within which the city of **Cahors** is bordered by water on three sides. Although now a bright and thriving town (there are few better places to buy regional food specialities), its time of greatest glory was many centuries ago. Divona-Cadurcorum in Roman times, it was to become one of the most important commercial cities in France by the 13th century. Today, its greatest jewel is the superb Pont Valentré (K26.7), probably the finest 14th century fortified bridge in Western Europe. Guarded by three massive stone towers and still carrying road traffic, it overlooks a broad weir. Under the righthand arch a diamond-shaped lock draws crowds of spectators gazing over the parapets above, when a boat works through. At one time there were three similar bridges in Cahors; astonishingly, one was demolished as recently as 1906. A good mooring is found just beyond, outside an elegant stone-built pumping station. This is convenient for visits to the city: a little tourist train operates from the left bank, taking in many of the sights. Cruising upriver, sufficient is left of ancient walls and towers to provide a clear impression of how the city must have looked when it was an intact fortress. A day might easily be reserved for full exploration – the most important features are well described in the ECM *Carte Guide*.

Écluse de Coty (K28.6), like many others on the Lot, has an old water mill, one of several in Cahors. Note the impressive stone bollard at the lower entrance to the lock cut. Marker buoys indicate which arch to use at the next bridge, Pont de Cabessut. Elsewhere are rocky shoals.

A further lock, Écluse de Lacombe (K32.6), is followed by remnants of an underwater weir, marked by red floats. Beyond, a very pleasant mooring will be found at a small quay in **Laroque-des-Arcs** (K33.5). This friendly small town takes its name from a series of Roman aqueduct arches. Parts of an old *château*, seated on a waterside rocky outcrop, continue as a private residence. Alongside is a water mill. Nearby, a *château des Anglais* occupies a cleft in a tall cliff. A sharply sloping footpath leads to the tiny chapel of St Roch on top. Here, we spoke to the local mayor who, rather than expressing fears at a possible stream of waterborne

tourists in the wake of the river's restoration, assured us that reopening of the Lot was 'the most exciting event round here for many years'.

Moorings with showers and slipway are located on the outskirts of **Lamagelaine** (K35.6, most facilities). Then comes the Écluse d'**Arcambal**, with narrow lock cut. For the village, tie up by a slipway (K38), opposite **Savanac**. Both places have impressive 14th century *châteaux*. Currently the upper river's only completely new lock, **Galessie** (K39.3), lies on the left bank at a constricted site bordered by a road excavated from cliffs. *Caution*: flow from the weir could make entry from below slightly difficult. An infamous hazard, the Rocher de Tustal, immediately beyond, left, was in the past regarded with anxiety by Lot bargemen. Traces remain of a capstan erected to control craft during their passage.

The most impressive gorge scenery, so far encountered, appears in the reach leading past **Le Couzol** (K41.4). Surroundings are equally fine to the Écluse de **Vers** (K43.1) at the confluence of a small river. Good facilities, including restaurant, remains of a Roman aqueduct, *château des Anglais* and 14th century castle. Wild and rugged landscape continues through the Écluse de Planiols (K45.3), above which avoid vestiges of an old weir by keeping within a buoyed channel on the right. 50m below the outfall of a hydro-electricity station (K47.9), there is a rocky obstruction in midriver (hopefully marked!). Now comes a sharp turn in the lee of cliffs to the Écluse de **St Géry** (K48.2), succeeded by a long cut, providing good views of the weirstream beyond. For the village, moor to a stone wall halfway along the cut, which, curiously, has a tiny island in the centre. One of the most potentially difficult sections is encountered as we pass the disused Écluse de Masseries (K51.5). Much of its former weir obstructs the river, meaning that boats must keep well over to the left bank. Green markers should make the situation clear. All this is immediately below a brick and stone railway bridge.

Bouziès-Bas (K54.8) and the Écluse de Bouziès (K55.5, ruined lock house) introduce what are perhaps the most spectacular reaches now available to boats, with sheer cliffs rising directly from the water in a narrow defile. Beyond a suspension road bridge, **Bouziès** (K56.6) has recently become a well-patronized waterside resort, with hotel, restaurant, passenger vessel and hire cruisers, directly opposite yet another *château des Anglais* halfway up a cliff, where a winding road dives through a series of tunnels. Moor here for the village which contains medieval buildings.

Almost certainly unique on a European inland waterway, 700m of towpath has been carved from the cliff-face at the approach to the Écluse de Ganil (K57.9). Best likened to an open-sided tunnel with unsupported roof, this is one of the strangest examples of river navigation engineering in existence. Admirable shelter would have been provided for towpath horses during heavy rain! The lock is followed by a long and narrow cut whose stone banks are piled high with dredgings ablaze with red poppies in early summer. Opposite is a junction with the little River Célé, popular with canoeists but unnavigable by larger craft. Places to visit on foot or by taxi are the prehistoric cave dwellings of **Pech-Merle** (4km) – 1,200m of grotto with 600 ancient wall paintings – and the Eco-Musée de **Cuzals** (9km), an open air museum with reconstructions of 19th century agricultural life and crafts.

St Cirq-Lapopie (K60.4), self-proclaimed 'prettiest village in France', is certainly unusually special. Perched high over the river, it comprises a series of tiny pedestrianized streets, houses where the roof of one is on the level of its neighbour's front door, open timber balconies, inevitable craft shops and a riot of flowers. Historically, the local trade was that of cauldron-making and wood turning. There are wonderful views down to the Lot, especially from the uppermost tiers by the Gardette *château* and fortified church. Several restaurants are located here. Access from the navigation is best attempted from the lock (K60.7), although there are additional moorings just beyond the upper end of the lock cut.

Cruising must end (for the time being) below a weir at **Crégols** (K64.3), upstream of a ruined lock almost concealed in a tangle of undergrowth. Hopefully, in the

Part of the 700m length of towpath carved from a cliff-face below the Écluse de Ganil.

not too distant future, further exploration will be possible as new lengths of the Lot are returned to navigation.

60 · Canal du Midi

Carte Guide: *Canaux du Midi*
From the junction with the Canal Latéral à la Garonne in Toulouse to the Étang de Thau, an extensive salt lake providing access to the Mediterranean at Sète and to the Canal du Rhône à Sète: 240km and 101 locks. (Some confusion is likely over the exact number of lock chambers, as there are numerous two, three and four-rise staircases, which are generally counted as one single lock; further, enlargement of certain chambers has resulted in some cases in pairs of locks being converted into a single deep chamber.) 1 tunnel. Junctions are made with La Nouvelle Branch at Cesse: this runs for 37km with 14 locks to join the Mediterranean at La Nouvelle; with the River Hérault Branch at the Round Lock, Agde (for the River Hérault and the Mediterranean at Le Grau d'Agde), 5.2km and with the Upper River Hérault in Agde, 6.8km to Bessan.

Easily the most popular pleasure boat waterway in France, the Midi forms part of the route from the

This plaque of Riquet was erected at St-Férréol in 1981, the canal's tercentenary year.

An ornamental fountain fed by gravity from the reservoir at St-Férréol.

Atlantic to the Mediterranean. The reasons for its heavy use are easy to understand. For owners of sea-going yachts, it provides a rapid and convenient way from the west coast of France to the Mediterranean or *vice versa*, avoiding a long passage via Gibraltar. But even more important is the very considerable use by hire craft from a number of bases on the canal itself. Almost throughout, the Languedoc scenery is superb, with numerous historical towns and facilities catering for holidaymakers. Sunshine, while not guaranteed, is almost constant throughout the summer: the heat is often such that one is grateful for the lines of giant plane trees that protect much of the route. A holiday on the Midi combines canal cruising with visits to the seaside, for at its eastern end there are many opportunities for discovering excellent Mediterranean beaches within walking or cycling distance. Development of the Languedoc coast for leisure purposes is one of the most far-reaching plans of postwar France.

Then there is the grandeur and beauty of the canal itself, with its impressively fine locks, buildings and aqueducts, scarcely changed from their completion over 300 years ago. Commercial traffic declined sharply throughout the 1980s and finally disappeared during the drought closure of 1989. Most of all, this is a languid region: a place for lazing in the sun with no incentive to hurry. It is possible to run between Atlantic and Mediterranean in a bare week – but preferable to spend much longer.

Although falling short of the gastronomic quality of some other parts of France, the food and wine of the Midi are reason enough for a holiday there. Much of the agriculture is devoted to vineyards, with opportunities of buying *Minervois* and *Corbières* wines direct from the growers. Castelnaudary's speciality is *cassoulet*, a stew of haricot beans with various meats – preserved goose, pork and sausage. Nearer the Mediterranean, seafood is supreme, with a wide range of fish, shellfish and oysters from the Étang de Thau.

Brief history The story of the Canal du Midi is better documented than that of any other waterway in France. The best modern account in English, is the late L. T. C. Rolt's masterly *From Sea to Sea* (1973). See also Jean-Denis Bergasse's 4- volume illustrated history *Canal du Midi* (J-D Bergasse, Cessenon, 1982–5).

A canal link between Atlantic and Mediterranean had been a concept considered as long ago as Roman times. Over the centuries repeated efforts were made to devise a plan, schemes being suggested under Charlemagne (8th century); François I, who had discussions with the celebrated canal designer Leonardo da Vinci in 1516; later in the same century Charles IX and Henry IV; and in 1633, Louis XIII. But no actual construction work was begun. An unusually stable political climate during the long reign of Louis XIV (1643–1715) coupled with the successful building of the world's first substantial summit level canal, the Briare, linking the Loire and the Seine by 1642, were factors that at last made the Canal du Midi a practicable proposition. Pierre Paul Riquet (1604–80) was the extraordinary man who achieved this aim.

Riquet was born in Béziers, married into money at the age of 19, and purchased the *château* and estate of Bonrepos 19km east of Toulouse. He was appointed a collector of the Languedoc salt tax in 1630, a position which demanded extensive travelling throughout the region, and thus gained much detailed knowledge of local topography. A military contracting business brought, in time, a sizeable fortune. Having noticed that water at what was selected as the canal's summit at Naurouze flowed both towards the Atlantic and the Mediterranean, he devised an admirable system of feeders: the ultimate key to success in driving a navigation through this arid terrain. François Andreossy (1633–88), lately returned from a tour of Italian canals, was adopted as Riquet's hydraulic expert and engineer. Remains still exist of a model canal, complete with locks, feeder channels and a tunnel, built as a prototype on the Bonrepos estate. Archbishop de Boulement of Toulouse inspected these works and the site of the reservoir system in the Montagne Noire, and was so impressed that he engaged the interest of the King's minister Jean-Baptiste Colbert (1619–83). After protracted investigations and surveys, Louis XIV proclaimed an edict in October 1666 enabling construction to begin. The chosen design relied on the unlocked course of the River Garonne between Bordeaux and Toulouse, with an artificial canal between there and the western shore of the Étang de Thau near Agde. Six months before canal building commenced, work was inaugurated on the creation of the port of Cette (now Sète) where the Étang was linked with the Mediterranean.

Finance was provided from three sources: Central Government, the Languedoc local authorities and Riquet himself, the undertaker being entitled to profits from canal tolls. Work began on the complicated feeder system and reservoir of St-Ferréol, which was so cleverly engineered that until 1989 the Canal du Midi could remain open to boats even under the most strin-

gent drought conditions (admittedly, an additional Lampy Reservoir was added between 1777 and 1781). For much of 1989 and 1990 a long portion between Toulouse and near Carcassonne was shut through chronic lack of water. Plans are currently in progress to correct this deficiency by the mid-1990s. About 60km of feeder channels brought water from the Montagne Noire and the addition of 14 locks enabled these to be used for the transport of stone, necessary in the construction of the main navigation. Small barges continued to trade on the feeders until 1725. At the same time, work progressed on the canal running eastwards from Toulouse: after the early failure of a rectangular lock, chambers were constructed with oval sides, a characteristic feature of the waterway today. With a few exceptions, spill weirs were not provided, surplus water cascading instead over the wooden gates.

A lofty steering position on a horse barge in Toulouse, early 20th century.

Men and women unload a barge at Aygues-Vives, near Toulouse. Circa 1906.

265

Intended as a navigation for sea-going craft, the locks were of generous proportions by 17th century standards and admitted two Rhône barges (*çaponts*) in one operation. All proceeded well, an inaugural flotilla of three boats travelling from Toulouse to the summit in 1672.

The design of Le Canal Royal, as it was first known, was intended to bring everlasting credit to the reign of Louis XIV, every effort being made to create a grandiose monument to the power of the Roi Soleil. This is evident in the high quality of locks, aqueducts and buildings, all of which display a supreme architectural confidence. With such a novel and extensive enterprise there were innumerable difficulties to overcome: when work had been in progress for 11 years, criticism of escalating costs was widespread. Legend claims (probably wrongly) that Riquet silenced his detractors by completing the 160m Malpas Tunnel in a mere six days. It was 1677: he was an old and tired man. When he died in October 1680 the great work was finished all but for one league between Adge and the Étang de Thau. Pierre Paul Riquet, Baron de Bonrepos, was buried in Toulouse Cathedral and is celebrated as a hero in Languedoc even now. His waterway transformed the economy of this part of France: over three centuries later it still benefits tourism and makes a very real contribution to local income.

All was complete for a ceremonial opening of the navigation when a procession of 25 vessels carrying freight and dignitaries departed from Toulouse on May 15, 1681, reaching the Étang de Thau on May 25. In spite of its success the canal failed to provide the Riquet family with a return on their investment until 1724. They lost their rights to proceeds under the Revolution, and when the railway from Bordeaux to Sète was opened in 1857 a period of joint control was established until the lease expired in 1898. Thereafter the Canal du Midi passed into State ownership. Although never used as a ship canal as originally intended, much of the freight it carried in barges would doubtless have otherwise travelled by sea. Matters were not helped by the indifferent state of the upper reaches of the River Garonne, a problem not finally solved until opening of the Canal Latéral à la Garonne from Castets to Toulouse in 1856.

Initially, the canal appears to have been mainly navigated by small sailing barges with easily lowered masts, bow-hauled by gangs of men. By the middle of the 18th century horse towing had largely taken over. Early in the 19th century the capacity of vessels was increased to 100–120 tonnes: they were about 27m × 5.3m and able to raise a sail for crossing the Étang to Sète; slightly larger boats carrying 145–170 tonnes and

known as *sapines* were also used, built of timber with an upswept swim-headed bow. Steam tugs to haul trains of craft across the Étang came in 1834 and the use of sailing barges declined. By 1838 there were 273 vessels regularly working on the Canal du Midi. Smaller 'fast boats' known as *sapinettes* with a load of 50–60 tons carried passengers and perishable goods. Packet boats for mail and passengers were fish-shaped in plan with a large cabin and achieved an average speed of 11kph. Initially they avoided working through the thickest congregations of locks, as at Castelnaudary and Béziers, the people taking to the towpath with their luggage to board another vessel. This was eventually considered inconvenient and the same boat would be used for a complete journey, working through all locks and taking 4 days for the run between Toulouse and Sète. Sleeping accommodation ashore was provided at Castelnaudary, Carcassonne and Le Somail. In the interests of increased speed, day and night working was finally adopted, with a non-stop journey time of just 36 hours. With the opening of the railway in 1857 the era of the passenger boats came to an end.

Freight tolls were abolished with State control in 1898, and the first motorized barge came into service in 1925. About this time there were several horse boats in use which towed a strange box-like 'tender' acting as overnight stabling for the horse. The changeover to diesel power was completed by 1935, although horses returned during the fuel shortages of World War II. Some of the old wooden motorized ex-horse boats lasted in operation until the early 1970s after which all freight vessels were purpose-built steel *automoteurs*. Up to the mid-1960s, goods traffic was slightly greater

than it had been during the early 19th century. Thereafter, it rapidly declined; by late 1988, there were only two regular barges left. A year later both these had ceased to trade.

During its more than 300 years of working life the Canal du Midi has experienced remarkably few modifications. Lock gates are now of steel rather than timber; a fine aqueduct was constructed in 1857 to carry the waterway over the River Orb at Béziers, thus avoiding the inconvenient crossing of the river on the level; the city of Narbonne was connected with the main line and an alternative route on the Mediterranean opened up in 1776. Perhaps the greatest change of all commenced in 1978, when a programme of lock lengthening was started to allow 38.5m *péniches* to operate instead of 30m Midi barges. One end of each original oval-sided lock was modified with a new section of parallel-sided concrete chamber. Two and three-rise staircases were replaced by single, much deeper locks. Inevitably there is some loss of historic character, especially where 17th century arched bridges are replaced by concrete spans. The most exciting development was the building of a 'water slope' (1982–3) enabling boats to avoid the six-rise staircase at Béziers: an early failure of the machinery and the resulting enquiry left the water slope disused for the first five years of its life. It was returned to service in 1989, although the adjacent locks remained workable. A 1979 estimate of the cost of the modifications was

The bas-relief erected at Les Ponts Jumeaux, Toulouse, to celebrate the great achievement of the Canal du Midi.

about £35 million. For the present, improvement of the central part of the waterway has been suspended; it seems unlikely that it will be resumed.

One of the most important events in the Canal du Midi's recent history occurred on May 30, 1969, when a flotilla of 7 cruisers arrived in convoy in Toulouse amid publicity that included nationwide television coverage. This was the birth of Blue Line Cruisers (France), then one of only two hire boat companies on the entire network. This British enterprise flourished (it now has two bases on the waterway at Castelnaudary and Port Cassafières, with other centres elsewhere in France) and many more firms have followed Blue Line's example. The hundreds of holiday boats now available on the Midi have transformed the economy of bankside towns and villages. In the early days of the fleet, we were offered a chicken by one of the lock keepers. Noting the bird to be fully feathered and alert, we declined, for under these circumstances our meal might have been a somewhat sad affair. Two years later, the same keeper again asked whether we required a chicken for the galley. Laughingly, we reminded him of our previous encounter. With a flourish he pushed open the door of his cottage to reveal a shining new deep-freeze, filled with oven-ready fowl from the local supermarket! Times had changed. By the early 1980s other changes were not so much to our liking: notably, a reluctance of many keepers to operate locks until at least two cruisers were ready to work through together. Officially, water shortages were blamed, a story difficult to credit while cascades poured over the gates. Quite simply, the staff who used to be delighted to meet a pleasure boat are now conserving their energies. With frequent delays of up to half an hour, it is almost impossible to cruise to any kind of schedule. Perhaps the situation only applies to the peak holiday season.

Seventh largest town in France, **Toulouse** is known as the 'Rose City' on account of the pinkish brick used for many of the buildings. A large octagonal basin, the Port de l'Embouchure, provides long-term pleasure craft moorings (over 21 days). Until the pleasant and tree-shaded banks of the basin were overtaken by road improvements in the early 1970s, a navigable connection, with a two-rise lock, provided access to the River Garonne: this had been the only coast-to-coast route until opening of the Canal Latéral à la Garonne in 1856. A further link with the upper Garonne, above a river dam, was created with construction of the short **Canal de Brienne** in 1776; although no longer used by boats, this channel continues to bring water supplies from the river to the basin. The Brienne's junction bridge and the first bridge over the Canal du Midi are known as Les Ponts Jumeaux (The Twin Bridges). The brick wall between them is occupied by a large and magnificent bas-relief in white marble on which classical deities represent the Atlantic and the Mediterranean and canal-building cherubs are busy with picks and shovels. The monument was designed by François Lucas in 1775. A third bridge has since been added, that of the Canal Latéral à la Garonne (Chapter 58). As it skirts the city centre the waterway is subjected to the full impact of noisy roads on each bank, for traffic is exceptionally fierce. The canal's amenity value is most noticeable, its borders being planted with trees, shrubs, flowers and lawns. By 1984 mechanization was well advanced on the first 9 locks of the waterway, most of them having also been lengthened. Écluse 4, Matabiau has been removed completely, its change in level being incorporated into Écluse 5, Bayard (K3.5, fall 6.2m), a little beyond the very convenient main line railway station. Visiting boats are requested to moor in the Port St Sauveur (water point, repair facilities), where there is a colourful collection of converted barges and pleasure craft. From here to the city centre is a short distance. The rich history and leading tourist attractions of Toulouse are well described in the green *Michelin Guide Pyrénées* (from Castelnaudary to the Mediterranean, use *Michelin Causses*). Even the briefest stay should provide time to visit the excellent shops and the magnificent Cathedral of St Étienne, an extraordinary asymmetrical building of mixed brick and stone, combining the Gothic styles of the Midi and the North. At the base of a pillar near the high altar, a black marble tablet marks Riquet's tomb and honours the man who brought prosperity to Languedoc.

Excursions from Toulouse are available in variety. The Syndicat d'Initiative will advise. Coach tours run to Albi with its great cathedral and Cathar associations (Musée Toulouse-Lautrec, with many examples of the artist's paintings and posters); Montségur, where the Catholic Church finally defeated the Cathar heretics in the 13th century; and to the Montagne Noire and Bassin de St Férréol to view the Canal du Midi's elaborate water supply system. Canal enthusiasts may also wish to visit the Riquet *château* of Bonrepos, set in a 150 hectares park at the village of **Verfeil**, on the N112 east of the city.

For the first 64km of the canal between Toulouse and Castelnaudary scenery is agreeably green and pastoral, but not in any way typical of the Midi country which lies nearest the Mediterranean. At the outskirts of Toulouse, **Port-Sud** (K12) is a newly-developed hire cruiser base with all boating facilities and shops

1km distant at **Ramonville**. The only remaining example in this area of four mills fed by a spillway from the canal can be seen at Écluse 6, Castanet (K14.8). On the right is the A61 Autoroute des Deux-Mers, never far from the waterway between Toulouse and Carcassonne. Fortunately thick tree cover protects the canal from this intruder, although the constant drone of traffic can disturb an otherwise idyllic overnight mooring. The small town of **Castanet-Tolozan** lies equidistant from Écluses 6 and 7, Vic (K17.4), and provides good shops within walking range. The restaurant situated behind a garage forecourt is wholeheartedly recommended. Scattered houses with the occasional factory finally mark the departure of Greater Toulouse, and pleasing wooded countryside with green meadows and hills accompanies the waterway along the valley of the River Hers.

Écluse 8, **Montgiscard** (K24.9), was recently converted to a single, lengthened chamber from a two-rise pair. The village is worth a visit, both for its basic shops and the old church offering a good view from the bell tower. **Aygues-Vives**, Écluse 9 (K28.1), is currently the last of the modernized locks at this end of the waterway (two chambers being replaced by one) with a pleasant watermill alongside. The town of **Baziège**, left, is useful for supplies. An attractive hill leads to the charmingly situated Écluse 10, Sanglier (K29.6), which is a two-rise staircase.

Montesquieu Lauragais (K30.1) is notable for its bridge of narrow red bricks dating from the earliest days of the canal: although not the most constricted of the waterway's crossings, it is nevertheless difficult to visualize an unladen *péniche* being able to pass through. (Butcher, baker and grocer nearby.) By Écluse 11, Négra (K33.2), a miniscule chapel is occasionally used for services. Old inn and stables are further reminders that this was a stage-post for the passenger craft of long ago. Restaurant and shops will be found in **Gardouch**, between Écluse 12, two-rise, Laval and Écluse 13 (K38.9). Shore facilities are now rather limited until Castelnaudary, so every advantage should be taken of **Villefranche de Lauragais** (K43), the largest town since Toulouse and lying 1.5km to the left. The values of canalside property in this part of France may be judged from the fact that in 1982 a lovely house and barn were for sale at Écluse 16, Emborrel, for a mere 24,000F (£2,400). From here, the village of **Avignonet-Lauragais** is within reach (grocer, butcher, baker and restaurant).

Deep countryside now follows, with a remarkable discovery just before a motorway bridge (K50.5). This is **Port Lauragais**, right bank, where a harbour has been created as an integral part of an *autoroute* service station. Facilities shared by road and water transport include fuel, water, shop and restaurant, all at an acceptable distance from the motorway itself. Those in cars may use waterside picnic tables and ponder on which is the more agreeable way to travel. In spring 1983 the Centre Pierre Paul Riquet was opened here as a museum devoted to the canal and its builder. The final lock on the ascent from the Atlantic is Écluse 17, Océan (K51.6), where there is a long-closed café/restaurant and a truly gigantic plane tree. One would assume that many of the planes of the Canal du Midi date from the 17th century: this appears not to be so, for in the early 19th century the canal's four tree nurseries contained 475,000 young plants and seedlings of oak, poplar, larch and ash – but no planes.

The most convenient approach to inspect this end of the canal's support system is from Écluse 17. Within 500m a fast-flowing feeder will be discovered, having brought water from the far-off Montagne Noire. Every devotee of Riquet (and it is impossible to travel his waterway without becoming an admirer) will wish to visit the octagonal basin set amid pine trees and the mysterious stones of **Naurouze**. Legend tells of a prehistoric giant who was stumbling through the area with a heavy pile of rocks: he slipped and let them fall, whereupon they shattered into many pieces. The stones had been destined to build the city of Toulouse, hence its construction in brick instead. These lone boulders have been the subject of much wonderment ever since (Nostradamus predicted the imminent end of the world, if the stones should ever be found joined together). The site was purchased by Riquet's descendants early in the 19th century and on the mound of stones they built an impressive obelisk as a memorial to the canal's builder. The monument rises from a group of walnut trees within a walled enclosure and surrounded on the outside by a circle of cedars. (The local canal lengthsman should be asked for a key to the gate.) Leaving the lock, the canal turns through a sharp bend and within about 300m, left bank, the feeder can be seen pouring into the navigation. Frankly, it lacks the grandeur that might be expected. Two metal plaques record the significance of the place. One lists the lengths of the feeder canals: 65,242m from a catchment point at Alzau; 52,552m from Lampy Reservoir; 34,436m from the St Férréol Reservoir, and 38,121m from the River Sor. The second plaque was recently erected by British waterways enthusiasts, and reads (in translation): 'Homage to Pierre Paul Riquet and all those involved in the construction of the Languedoc Canal, opened May 15, 1681. This plaque is provided by the Inland Waterways Association of Great Britain in recognition of its deep admiration.

May 15, 1981.' It was unveiled by a direct descendant, Mlle Evelyne de Riquet de Caraman.

With the *autoroute* only 200m away from the short summit level, an overnight mooring must be selected with some care. **Le Ségala** (K53.8) is a modest canalside village (water point, baker, butcher and grocer). Beyond a canopy of plane trees are lush fields and orchards (the cherries are ripe by late May). This watershed is 189m above sea level and the long descent begins with Écluse 18, Méditerranée (K56.6). Within 50m is an old pottery, producing local terra-cotta items with a wood-fired kiln: it is well worth a look. The canal now winds from shallow cutting to embankment, heavily shaded by trees until it eventually arrives at the quays of **Castelnaudary** (K64.6). Ahead, a humpbacked bridge close to the base of an old windmill leads to Le Grand Bassin, a sheet of water whose size is at first concealed by a wooded island. Easiest access to the many shops, railway station and restaurants is from this point. Soon the dimensions of the great basin are revealed: totally artificial and acting as a reservoir for the staircase of 4 locks that follow, it is more than 1km in circumference. A jumble of houses on the far shore rises towards the hilltop town: there is nothing equal to it on any canal in Europe. Crown Blue Line have a base on the right-hand side, with fuel, water and drydocks. Noted for its *cassoulet*, Castelnaudary is the ideal place from which to drive to the canal's **Bassin de St Férréol** (take the N624 and D622 to **Revel**). Covering 70 hectares, the great reservoir is surrounded by tree-covered rocky hills; its 800m earth-filled stone dam 30m high is the largest structure of its kind anywhere.

Le Grand Bassin, Castelnaudary.

Sailing dinghies and tripping launches use the lake, and below the dam itself is a network of landscaped footpaths. A constant flow of water emerges from the dam to feed the distant navigation. St Férréol is quite rightly a popular tourist attraction with several fine restaurants. At least two hours should be reserved for a visit from Castelnaudary, whre cars may be hired.

Onwards from this point, the Midi carries the greatest concentration of holiday cruisers. Many of the lock keepers sell groceries such as ice cream, local honey, wine, fruit and vegetables. The multiple staircase Écluse 23, St Roch, is now an electrically worked four-rise complex (K65.5). Then follows Écluse 24, Gay, a two-rise (K67) and the three-rise Écluse 25, Vivier (K68.7).

In common with virtually all French seaside areas, the Canal du Midi has accepted the cult of toplessness. Female fashions that would start a riot on the Leeds & Liverpool Canal are no longer a cause for comment in the hot South.

Some of the lock keepers are great individualists. In 1982 the couple at Écluse 29, La Peyruque (K71.6), had festooned their domain with polite notices in French and English to 'respect the plants and flowers' and to be careful of the 'dangerous dog'. Écluse 30, La Criminelle (K72.1), was the centre of an unashamed campaign for Free Languedoc, with a model of the Toulouse-built Concorde aircraft, a portrait of Riquet, a flag of the region and some tasteful examples of patri-

Fairytale city of Carcassonne, the most impressive relic of its kind in Western Europe. The river in the foreground has never been navigable, though it is shown with barges in several 19th century engravings.

otic graffiti. **Villepinte** (K75.9) has a range of shops quite close to the bridge in the middle of the pound between Écluses 31 and 32. **Bram** (K80.3) lies some distance from a tidy stone quay but does possess a good selection of shops. Almost all of these Midi villages are charming little places of faded stone houses, mostly remaining quite unconscious of their attraction. Nowhere is this more true than at **Villesèquelande** (K89.2), where a grassy quay makes an admirable mooring; 500m across a vineyard lies the ancient church and its cluster of buildings. Facilities are restricted to a minute tobacconist/newsagent and old-fashioned grocery. Exceptionally sharp bends along this section of canal necessitated the erection of towline guides on the most acute angles of the towpath.

Distant views of the Montagne d'Alaric beyond Carcassonne are obtained from the top of Écluse 37, **Lalande** (K98.2), a two-rise. After two further locks the canal enters a deep stone-sided cutting before emerging in a broad basin by **Carcassonne** railway station (K105.2). Mooring here is virtually obligatory, for no one should miss a visit to the unique walled 'old' city. In its original form Riquet's waterway avoided Carcassonne altogether, its citizens being unwilling to produce the finance necessary to construct a more costly line. Later they bitterly regretted their decision, but it was not until 1810 that the present 5.6km deviation was opened to traffic, with a new aqueduct over the diverted River Fresquel.

Shops and restaurants are close to the Carcassonne basin. A longish uphill walk, crossing the River Aude, leads to La Cité. Occupied by the Romans and the Visigoths (5th century), the hilltop site was developed

in the 13th century as Europe's finest fortress. The scale of this splendid town is breath-taking: a double ring of walls with dozens of turreted towers encircles large numbers of houses where there are now 380 inhabitants. It all looks unreal and like the film set it has frequently been. Some critics complain at the thorough restoration carried out by Viollet-le-Duc from 1844, but without his efforts Carcassonne would probably now be little more than a ruinous pile of stones. Inevit-

Viollet le Duc, an energetic restorer of ancient structures during the 19th century. But for him, Carcassonne and numerous other buildings would now probably lie in ruins.

A well-designed Pénichette *hire cruiser in the triple lock staircase at Trèbes.*

ably, the narrow cobbled streets are largely devoted to tourist shops which, in the main, offer good value – as do the restaurants. In 1971 I was moored in the basin on July 14; being a public holiday the locks were closed, providing an opportunity for exploring La Cité at leisure. Water sports on the canal included greasy pole contests and a slightly barbaric game in which young men attempted to swim after live ducks. At dusk, we climbed to high ground beyond the railway station to see the fortress brilliantly illuminated, and the most lavish firework display I have ever witnessed.

The canal runs through the heart of Cathar country and for those prepared to seek there are numerous reminders of the fierce religious wars of 700 years ago. In essence, the Cathars preached a doctrine of reincarnation and rejected the Old Testament and the deity of Christ. Ignored at first by the Catholic Church, the movement spread rapidly throughout Languedoc. Eventually, Pope Innocent III took steps to curb the power of the heretics, but when his Legate was assassinated in Provence a Crusade was declared in 1208. The following year the infamous massacre of Béziers took place. In support of the Church, Simon de Montfort

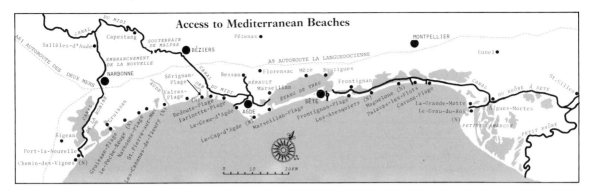

seized Cathar castles one by one and was finally killed in the siege of Toulouse in 1218. Later came the Inquisition and Languedoc was annexed to France. By 1244, the last stronghold of Cathar resistance, **Montségur**, had fallen after a prolonged siege; and a famous treasure was lost, never to be recovered. This briefest account of a stormy period of history is best remembered today in the numerous relics of *châteaux* scattered throughout Aude. One of them, in the village of **Rennes-le-Château** about 35km south of Carcassonne, is the centre of an extraordinary mystery of modern times, which has attracted a sizeable cult following. Somewhat involved research points to the existence of knowledge that could undermine the most basic beliefs of the Church. This could explain in part how the impoverished parish priest of Rennes-le-

A highly atmospheric village is the medieval fortified settlement of Argens-Minervois, near the western end of Le Grand Bief.

Château came by a very sizeable fortune enabling him to make lavish improvements to the area. The arguments are contained in *The Holy Blood and the Holy Grail* by Michael Baigent, Richard Leigh and Henry Lincoln (Cape, 1982).

But back to the canal. A very fine avenue of cypress trees lines each bank for 300m after Écluse 41, St-Jean (K108). Then comes the early 19th century aqueduct over the River Fresquel, shortly followed by an unusual arrangement of locks Nos. 42/43. There are, in fact, three chambers: the first pair are arranged as a two-rise and empty into a large oval-sided basin succeeded immediately by another single lock. Gates and paddles are mechanized and operated by a keeper in a tall steel box planted in the middle of the complex. 150m after Écluse de l'Évêque (K111.6) there is an opportunity for buying wine direct from the producer (right-hand, towpath side). As designed by Riquet, the waterway crossed the River Orbeil on the outskirts of Trèbes on the level (K116.7). This proved unsatisfactory, as much silt was consequently carried into the canal. Maréchal Sébastien Vauban accordingly built the present aqueduct in 1686–7; it consists of three arches, each with a span of about 11m. A suitable mooring will be found on the left, immediately before the busy N610 road bridge, in the centre of the pleasant little town of **Trèbes** (K117.3). A wide selection of small shops is hidden away in a maze of narrow streets. Round the next bend are situated the three-rise Écluses de Trèbes. In 1988, we enjoyed a rapidly served lunch of good value at the Auberge du Moulin, next to the top chamber.

Stop near the third bridge after the locks and you will discover a pleasant settlement of stone buildings, where further local wine may be obtained. This is a very agreeable winding pound, terminating at **Marseillette** (K126.2) with good moorings, most shops and other facilities. All the time the scenery is improving as it assumes the true character of the Midi, with cypress trees and distant views over vineyards and rocky hills. Locks occur at Marseillette (K127.2); Fonfile, triple (K130.6); St-Martin, double (K131.6); and Aiguille, double (K133.4). **Puicheric** (K136) is a medium-sized village dominated by the square tower of its church (most facilities). Here is a further two-rise lock, whose keeper allowed cruisers travelling in different directions to actually pass each other in the chambers the last time I came through.

La Redorte (K140.5) has a useful quay, capable of taking several craft attracted by refuse disposal facilities and two restaurants. Within easy walking distance are all kinds of shops. It was here that we carefully removed a strange fruit on a branch overhanging a garden wall: on dissection it proved to be a pomegranate, just one of the exotic plants that flourish in this warm climate. Two hire cruiser firms operate from the wharf in **Homps** (K145.4), where there are good moorings, a take-away food establishment, restaurant and most types of shop. After the single lock of Homps is the two-rise Écluse d'Ognon (K147), followed by a small aqueduct over the Ognon River built in 1826–7 to replace a troublesome level crossing. On the canal bank is an inexpensive restaurant.

Pechlaurier Lock (K149.8) is a two-rise staircase which was the scene of amazing chaos when I last passed through. While the upper chamber was packed with five descending cruisers, two uphill boats entered the bottom chamber, unknown to the lock keeper. When the operation was half completed the keeper noticed the mistake and ordered paddles to be closed, and requested that the offending craft back out. It was a case of too many keen helpers anxious to do something. No sooner had the lower gates been reopened than someone stupidly raised a paddle on the intermediate set of gates, rapidly washing the two boats into the path of a converted *péniche* laden with children whose cheers turned to shrieks of terror at the prospect of impending collision. Somehow, a catastrophe was averted and we became convinced that lock working should be carried out strictly on the instructions of the resident keeper.

In my opinion, the most beautiful village on the Canal du Midi is **Argens-Minervois** (K155.1). Others have obviously come to the same conclusion in recent years with a resultant rash of new (and not particularly appropriate) houses near the waterside. Situated a short distance from the water on the left this hilltop settlement nevertheless typifies the timelessness of Languedoc. Dominated by the almost windowless towers of an ancient *château*, Argens had until the 1980s changed little in many hundreds of years: certainly the residents of the late 17th century would have looked down from the same houses we see today and

Cruising in the shade of umbrella pines.

watched Riquet's men cutting the navigation. Moor opposite the public washing place (where local children swim) and take the opportunity of filling tanks from the towpath water point. A short walk brings you to the cobbled heart of the village, where it appears there is a single shop; here an enquiry for postcards directed us to the opposite side of the street, where there were certainly no shops in view. But on knocking at the door of a private house, we were led into a front room sparsely furnished with tinned goods – and monochrome postcards. The annual turnover must be minimal. Argens is the sort of place that is seldom visited by tourists. Lizards bask on hot stones and cats laze in the shadows. Doubtless it was once flourishing. We were told that the *château* was reduced to two habitable rooms. Across a courtyard near the main gate we made a remarkable discovery: a terrace of five deserted cottages, built on the edge of a rocky precipice. Probably they had once housed the castle servants. Although structurally sound, they bore every sign of having been empty for at least half a century. Each consisted of two or three irregularly shaped rooms with tiled floors, stone fireplaces and a slate sink draining directly down the cliff face. Quite lacking any concession to modern living, they were utterly medieval in design: a fascinating survival.

But the whole of this portion of the canal is rich in similar little villages, each of them making a rewarding visit. Écluse 56, Argens (K152.3), marks the beginning of Le Grand Bief, a lock-free pound 54km long with some astonishing windings along the contours. It is the longest canal level in France. **Roubia** (K154.8) is suffi-

Narbonne's Roman bridge and Archbishops' Palace.

ciently canal-conscious to have erected some waterside picnic tables and a sign advertising its few shops. Umbrella pines and palm trees border the grounds of a *château* on the outskirts of **Paraza** (K156.1), where there are basic shops and a direct-sell wine producer. The 11m span of a single-arched aqueduct carrying the canal over the River Répudre (K158.8) is believed to be the oldest in the world designed for navigation. **Ventenac d'Aude** (K160.9) is notable for its huge waterside wine cave, where Minervois may be tasted and purchased. Views from the upper windows of this seemingly ecclesiastical building are of vineyards extending to the distant horizon. Moor near the bridge for grocer, baker and butcher.

Among the former overnight halts for the passenger craft and port for the city of Narbonne (before it was provided with its direct canal connection) is **Le Somail** (K165.9), one of the Midi's prettiest villages, around an original stone arched bridge. Although only served by travelling shops that call most mornings, my personal interest in collecting old canal books and postcards was considerably aroused by the extensive antiquarian bookshop. Here, I once purchased a splendid leather-bound copy of the fascinating and extremely rare *Des Canaux de Navigation et Spécialement du*

Canal de Languedoc by de la Lande (1778); an autographed example of Bichambis' *Narbonne* (1922), containing much on the history of La Nouvelle Branch; and a charming 1936 edition of Alphonse Daudet's *La Belle-Nivernaise*, the story of a 19th century canal boat with nostalgic illustrations. My inability to inspect their stock at regular intervals prompts me to reveal the existence of this treasure house. The village has two restaurants, neither of which I would choose to revisit.

Riquet's solution to the challenge of passing the River Cesse was to construct a level crossing with a 205m dam; this was soon found to be a source of silting and flooding, and was replaced by Vauban's present three-arched aqueduct of 1686. Immediately beyond, is the basin of the **Port de la Robine** where diesel fuel and water may be obtained at a hire cruiser base, and the **La Nouvelle Branch** providing access to the Mediterranean via Narbonne. Completed in 1776, this comprises the 5.1km Canal de Jonction; a 657m navigable section of the River Aude; and 31.5km of the Canal de la Robine, between the Aude and the sea. All 14 locks have been modified to admit craft up to 38m long. Even if pleasure boaters have no intention of reaching the sea, a return voyage to Narbonne makes a pleasant detour for which two days is sufficient. Magnificent umbrella pines line the canal at its junction. Five locks lower the Branch to **Sallèles d'Aude** (K3);

here, the 6th lock was until recently a two–rise staircase, the lower chamber serving also as a drydock for barges. Modernization has destroyed this curiosity, resulting in a single chamber with a fall of 5.4m. (A similar arrangement in Béziers has also vanished.) The town offers all facilities. Écluse de Gailhousty is followed by a drydock (permission for use from the canal inspector in Sallèles).

Navigation shortly enters the willow-fringed River Aude; leaving the canal, remain on the right bank and head upriver to a point marked by a cable. Cross to the opposite side of the river and run downstream, keeping about 4.5m from the bank. Deep drafted boats should cross the Aude with extreme care. In 1988, we grounded twice on hard rock with our draft of 1.3m. Drop through a railway bridge and the first lock of the Canal de la Robine, Moussoulens, will be seen ahead. Keep well clear of the weir which crosses the river at this point. After negotiating Écluse du Raonel (K9.9) and the Écluse du Gua (K14.3), the outskirts of **Narbonne** will be reached. Narbonne lock (K15.4) is automated: consult the instructions displayed on the lockside or in the appropriate *Carte Guide*. Best moorings will be found beyond the 'Roman Bridge', a picturesque structure supporting houses, but with limited headroom of about 3.3m; craft with large superstructures may be unable to pass and should therefore select Agde or Sète as their route to or from the Mediterranean. There are mooring rings along the quay, lined with yellow mimosas; avoid tying too close to the public lavatories if you wish to avoid disturbance. An obvious water point of the quayside here features a tap with tedious push-top. A normal one will be found at ground level at the foot of the balustrade above the WCs.

Narbonne was founded by the Romans in 118 BC and soon replaced Marseille as the leading seaport between Spain and Italy; among its governors was the celebrated Marcus Antonius. The Mediterranean has since retreated. The city is now the centre of a wine producing area, Corbières. Its leading attractions are the great slab-sided Archbishop's Palace, 12–14th centuries, and the uncompleted Cathedral of St Just; extensive ramparts were demolished in the 1870s. Excellent shopping is close at hand, with a spectacular 19th century indoor market building. Museums include one devoted to paintings and ceramics and another of Gallo-Roman remains.

The remainder of the journey to the sea is along a canal that passes through salt lakes and marshes recalling the Camargue; you are likely to see flocks of flamingoes. An African Game Reserve has been established on the west shore of the Étang de Sigean. Two final locks must be negotiated: Mandirac (K24.2) and Sainte-Lucie (K34.4); drinking water available at each. There is evil smelling black mud below the final chamber; from here onwards allowance must be made for a slight rise and fall of tide. **Port La Nouvelle** (K37) is a busy place with cargo ships and fishing vessels. Best moorings are on the left of the canal immediately before a right-angled turn into the upper harbour. Elsewhere, most suitable quays or piles are invariably the preserve of local fishing boats, pleasure craft or large cargo vessels which regularly call in. Opposite the canal entrance, the Restaurant du Port is a welcoming family-run concern, noted for its seafood and good value. Fuel and water may be obtained, and cranes for stepping masts. Although the town boasts few tourist attractions, there are several seaside resorts and beaches to be visited by canal holidaymakers.

The entire 180km coastline of Languedoc-Roussillon, between Spain and the Rhône Delta, has been imaginatively developed for half a million tourists since the 1960s: in effect it is a single continuous sandy beach. While there are several exceptionally well-designed new holiday towns, more than a dozen marinas and numerous camping sites on the dunes, substantial portions remain remote and uncommercialized. Many people find the area more to their taste (and better value) than the sophisticated Riviera, farther along the Mediterranean coast. Beaches within easy reach of the Canal du Midi and Canal du Rhône à Sète are shown on the map of the Mediterranean coastline. Toplessness has become universal (but not aggressively obligatory) while nudity is widespread in certain locations, thanks to a relaxed official attitude that began in the late 1970s. These areas can, or course, be avoided if you prefer, and in any event the majority of naturist beaches are 'mixed', so newcomers to this form of relaxation have nothing to fear. If the seaside is to your liking, when hiring a cruiser on the canal it is well worth considering reserving a day or two moored at the base: this generally involves availability of your car and freedom to explore coastal or inland places remote from the waterway. However, it is the intention in this book to mention only those beaches which are within walking, cycling, bus or in-expensive taxi reach of the canal: the choice is considerable.

A good sandy beach lies a short distance SW of Port La Nouvelle. Continue for less than 1km to reach the official nudist section of **Les Montilles**. **Narbonne Plage** (clothed) lies about 12km from the city centre, via the D168.

Back on the main line of the canal at Port La Robine, there is a brief but unfortunate industrial estate; followed at K171.5 by the pleasant little town of

A wine barge descends the Béziers staircase, early in the 20th century. These locks are now duplicated by a water slope.

Argeliers, a little to the east of a long hairpin bend: all shops will be found here after a short walk through vineyards. Of all places in Europe that the celebrated inland waterway author Dr Roger Pilkington might have chosen for his retirement home, he has selected Montouliers, a short distance to the north; this says much for the attractions of the area. Often the waterway is slightly raised on an embankment, providing good views through the plane trees to a fertile region once covered by a series of shallow lakes drained at different times up to the 19th century. The canal makes an extraordinary series of loops before the approach to **Capestang** (K188.3), heading through all points of the compass. I was once moored for the evening several km before the town at a point where the D11 is almost alongside. Wishing to telephone, I cycled down the main road and having no lights decided to return in darkness via the towpath. More than an hour later I had still not reached the boat, although the outward trip had taken barely ten minutes. It was intensely dark under the canopy of foliage with only the incessant sound of the cicadas (*cigales*). One part of the canal looked just like another and I seriously entertained thoughts that I must somehow have set off in the wrong direction. Eventually, I saw the lights of the boat in the distance with considerable relief: ever since, I have had good reason to remember the sinuous course of the waterway. Capestang is notable for one of the lowest and most awkward bridges on the Midi. Large wide-beam motor yachts may have to resort to flooding their bilges or taking on board up to 30 bystanders in order to pass beneath. Beyond is a long quay suitable for mooring while walking the short distance into the town for shopping. This is a popular halt and will be congested in peak season. Above a sea of pantiled roofs, the 14th century church of St Étienne soars upwards, topped by a cluster of bells and loudspeakers for broadcasting public information and sounds of jollification when the town is *en fête*. In November 1766 42m of canal bank collapsed after heavy rain and snow had flooded the channel: 10,000 workmen toiled in dreadful freezing conditions to repair the breach, completing the task within three months. Automatic siphon sluices were subsequently installed here and at Ventenac, to drain off flood water before it can overflow the bank. When the level has dropped sufficiently, air is admitted to the pipe and the flow ceases. Riquet's position of collector of the Languedoc salt tax is recalled by an old salt store beside the former lake of Capestang.

Closure of locks in the evening normally prevents night navigation on the Midi. It is banned by the operators of hire craft, and no one cruising for real *pleasure* in his own boat is likely to want to bash on through the dark, oblivious to all but the faint shapes of the plane trees. But it was different for the working boats and every conscientious *batelier* tried to arrange his journey to arrive on the Long Pound shortly before the locks close. With his knowledge of every bend he could keep moving most of the night. I was once moored under the canopy of trees near Capestang when a furious storm erupted several hours before dawn. It was hopeless to sleep with rain hammering on the cabin roof, so we sat up to enjoy the spectacle as the canal would briefly shine in the brightest green, illuminated by repeated flashes of lightning. Suddenly, the headlight of an oncoming *péniche* could be seen and moments later it was as brilliantly lit as by daylight. The experience was both thrilling and theatrical. And doubtless he was sliding into his first lock before we had cleared away our breakfast.

Poilhes (K194.2) offers water and an electricity point for large craft in a shallow cutting with stone retaining walls. The local authority has gone to commendable lengths to make boating visitors welcome: the tap is fitted with a hose and there are public showers and dustbins. Several shops and a gastronomic restaurant complete the facilities. Beyond, there is a superb view of distant hills. Another disaster occurred near here in January 1744, when 300m of the waterway was blocked by a landslide. A retaining wall was built and navigation restored within 14 days.

Malpas Tunnel (K198.8), although a mere 160m long, is both wide and high. It has the distinction of

Béziers Water Slope in service during 1989. The lifting gate in the foreground is pushed up or down the incline, thus raising or lowering the wedge-shaped pool of water in which the boats travel.

276

being the world's first section of underground navigation canal. Cut through friable sandstone, the western end is badly weathered and much of the inside is lined with stone vaulting. For its date, it is a most impressive structure (one-way working). If you walk NW along the D62 from the far end of the tunnel you will ascend the hill of Ensérune and arrive at the site of **Oppidum d'Ensérune**, an Iberian-Greek city founded in the 6th century BC. Depopulated by the 1st century AD, it has been fully excavated and the pre-Roman archaeological museum is open to the public. Nearby is the curious Lake of Montady, drained for agriculture in the 13th century by monks working for the Archbishop of Narbonne, and displaying an amazing circular pattern of drainage channels radiating from its centre like the spokes of a giant wheel. **Colombiers** (K200.5) is a charming village set around an ancient stone bridge with *lavoir*. Useful shops and a recommended restaurant at Le Château, with tables on a gravelled terrace overlooking the waterway. Just round the corner, a large marina (Navig France hire cruisers) was excavated in 1987. In this area – but also at many other locations throughout the Canal du Midi – we discovered prolific clusters of pheasant's-eye narcissus and the snowdrop-like spring snowflake; an unexpected bonus during a cruise in late March.

Now comes what is perhaps the best-known engineering feature of Riquet's canal: the eight-lock staircase of **Fonserannes** (K206.5). As originally designed, a descent was made to the level of the River Orb in Béziers, the navigation channel following the river for 900m until it turned into an artificial canal on the far bank. As might have been expected, floods and silting were constant problems and over the years there were proposals for various designs of aqueduct and even a tunnel *underneath* the river bed. Nothing was achieved, however, until the opening of the present aqueduct in 1856. This new channel is linked with the lock staircase at chamber 7, meaning that boats pass through 6 locks (and not 7 as is generally stated) with a total rise and fall of 13.6m. The staircase was mechanized some years ago. To the right, a 'water slope' was built in 1982/3 for 38m barges, rather than adapt the shorter, historical locks of the staircase. Based on the pattern of that at Montech (Canal Latéral à la Garonne) it consists of a concrete flume on a 5° slope. Boats are introduced into a wedge-shaped pool of water which is pushed up or down by an electric traction unit. Inauguration was in autumn 1983 and allowed 38m craft to navigate from the Rhône to Narbonne, via the Canal du Midi. The cost was estimated at about £3 million. An early failure led to the structure remaining derelict for some years before eventually being returned to service in 1989.

The slope is now in use on certain days; otherwise craft are directed to the original lock staircase. Both are popular tourist attractions.

The handsome colonnaded aqueduct designed by Magues provides an excellent view of hilltop **Béziers** (K207.6), surmounted by the 13–14th century Cathedral of St Nazaire. The city was established about 36 BC and is best known for the Massacre of 1209, for it was here that the first atrocity of the Albigensian Crusade was perpetrated in the name of Pope Innocent III. Between 15,000 and 20,000 townspeople were slaughtered, and as it was difficult to distinguish between heretic and Catholic the victims included many members of the Church of Rome. Béziers' other claims to fame are being the birthplace of Riquet – his statue stands in the middle of a plane-shaded *boulevard* – and it is now the capital of the Languedoc wine industry. Écluses 57 and 58 follow the aqueduct and are mechanized; they lead to a substantial basin built, like the aqueduct, in the 19th century. The town lies some distance uphill from these moorings. Remember that Écluses 59 and 60, **Villeneuve** (K213.8), close 40 minutes earlier than the others. Essential food supplies are much more easily obtained in Villeneuve than in Béziers.

From now onwards, the Mediterranean is never far away. **Valras Plage** and **Serignan Plage** are 10km and 8km: follow the D37 from Villeneuve. A naturist beach lies between the two. The closeness of the coast is evident in a change of scenery. Gone are the rocky outcrops of earlier reaches, to be replaced by reed banks and marshes. A large basin has been excavated at **Port Cassafières** (K221.6), with hire fleet, fuel, water and restaurant. Moor here or at the nearby bridge for a visit to the sea at **Redoute-Plage** (2km). Everywhere vineyards are planted on the sandy soil, producing the *vins des sables*. If you fancy a little gentle riding, Camargue style, stables near the Port Cassafières bridge have a selection of amiable horses for hire. Short conducted treks through the sand dunes are suitable for all abilities.

Where the **River Libron** flows across the canal on its journey to the sea (K225.2) is a curiosity of waterway engineering that is probably unique. When the river is in spate quantities of silt would be poured into the navigation. To prevent this happening, a special barge with high ramps at each end was originally sunk across the river between stone abutments, isolating the canal on each side; when the flood subsided, the barge was raised and navigation allowed to continue. The present arrangement is an improvement in that traffic is not interrupted. A series of chambers is fitted with guillotine gates: the flooding river is allowed to flow first ahead of a boat, and then, as the subsequent chamber is entered, astern of it. Thus both craft and canal are protected. The structure is normally open throughout. The flat nature of the terrain precluded building a conventional aqueduct. **Farinette-Plage** may be reached from here by following a minor road to the sea.

A succession of moored craft along the towpath bank point to the popularity and interest of **Agde** (K231.4). Additional space to lie is provided in a newly excavated basin, opposite. Note the large and elegant building of the canal authority immediately before the Round Lock. This lock is equipped with three pairs of gates; those at 6 o'clock and 12 o'clock are used when working down the waterway from Béziers to the Étang de Thau. The 3 o'clock pair provide access via a short length of slightly tidal canal into the River Hérault, the fishing

The Libron barrage, enabling canal traffic to continue when the river is in spate.

boat quays of Agde and eventually the Mediterranean. It is unfortunate, but unavoidable, that the lock enlargement programme has spoiled the symmetry of the chamber with the addition of a new section. Railway links with Sète and Toulouse are provided from the nearby main line station, a most useful facility if a car is to be collected from the starting point of a one-way cruise such as offered by Crown Blue Line, between Castelnaudary and Port Cassafières. Regular bus services also run from here to Marseillan and the important seaside resort of Cap d'Agde.

Agde itself lies mainly on the far side of the River Hérault. Founded about the 6th century BC by the Phocaeans of Marseille, it has a network of hilly narrow streets rising from the waterfront quays and the grim façade of the fortified 12th century Cathedral of St Étienne, built of volcanic rock. It is a lively and flourishing town, with shops and boutiques ranging from the trendy to the *chic*, numerous bars and nightclubs, and a sizeable open-air market. Hire cruisers are generally forbidden to enter the Hérault at this point, but a

very pleasant walk of about 5km can be made by following the quayside with its brightly painted fishing boats and craft used for jousting contests, downriver to the sea at **La Grau-d'Agde**. Lovely sandy beaches, **La Tamarissière** and **La Guirandette**, are on either side of the estuary mouth. By 1989, access to the lower Hérault and the Mediterranean (for privately-owned craft) was only available twice daily: for current times, ask the keeper of the Round Lock. Moorings will be found on the short branch linking canal and river. Suitable stopping places on quays in Agde itself are difficult to find as the water is generally shallow near the banks. Beware of becoming stranded on the bottom when the tide falls. There is, however, ample depth in the centre of the channel at all times.

A little further to the east is the splendid new resort of **Cap d'Agde**, constructed since 1969 on a promontory formed by lava flow from the extinct Mont St-Loup volcano. Most of the hotels, shops and self-catering accommodation are designed in a low-rise

Plan and cross-section of the unusual Round Lock, providing a link with the River Hérault in Agde. An engraving from Canaux de Navigation *by de la Lande (1778).*

Provençal style, with arcades and red pantiles. More than 70,000 holidaymakers can stay here and 2,000 boats are berthed in a series of harbours. The 500 business premises include more than 100 cafés, restaurants and nightclubs, with cars segregated from the pedestrianized areas. The sandy beaches are excellent, and widespread planting of sweet-scented shrubs and trees has brought about a surprisingly established atmosphere for so new a city. On the eastern side is Europe's largest naturist resort, where hotels, apartments and camping sites have been built for 20,000 people. Day visitors are welcomed on payment of a small entry fee. Nudity is found not only on the beach but in the supermarkets, boutiques and banks: what would seem incongruous in northern climates soon takes on an air of normality under the hot Mediterranean sun. Among the attractions is windsurfing tuition. Cap d'Agde's naturist tradition began in 1940, when German troops came to use the beach alongside the vineyards of the Oltra family. When the war was over the Germans gradually began to return for nudist camping holidays. Realizing the commercial potential, the French Government capitalized on this tradition when development began on the Languedoc coast in the late

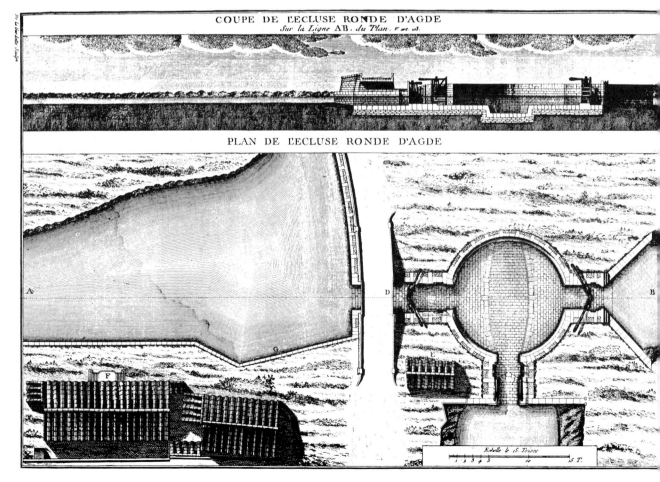

COUPE DE L'ECLUSE RONDE D'AGDE
Sur la Ligne AB. du Plan. r et s3.

PLAN DE L'ECLUSE RONDE D'AGDE

Head of navigation on the River Hérault is at a fortified mill near Bessan.

1960s. René and Paul Oltra have advanced from the life of the peasant farmer to that of the millionaire in a single generation.

After Agde's Round Lock, the canal enters a narrow tree-line stretch to emerge in the **River Hérault** upstream of the town weir. Through navigation of the Canal du Midi is up the Hérault for 1km and into the Prades Flood Lock (generally open at each end) on the opposite shore. If wished, a further 5km of the river is available to boats, as far as the ruins of a mill on the outskirts of **Bessan**. There are no facilities whatsoever on this excitingly Amazonian passage, past tree-covered banks inhabited by buzzards.

In its final stages the canal undergoes a change, passing through marshland and the Étang de Bagnas, location of the last lock (K235.3). Moor by the final road bridge for a visit to **Marseillan-Plage** (2km by road), a very pleasant beach town with shops. 30 minutes' walking along the seashore brings you into Cap d'Agde. The Canal du Midi ends abruptly at **Les Onglous** Lighthouse, entry to the huge expanse of the Étang de Thau.

61 · Étang de Thau

Carte Guide: *Canaux du Midi*

The vast salt-water lagoon extends from the terminus of the Canal du Midi at Les Onglous to the start of the Canal du Rhône à Sète near Frontignan, a distance of 17.5km. A connection is made with the Mediterranean (with no change in levels) in Sète.

Once an inlet of the sea, the lagoon was long ago separated from the Mediterranean by a sandbar – Le Toc. The 8,000 hectares of water are exceptionally salty and intensively farmed for oysters and mussels. A succession of small towns with harbours offer attractive cruising quite unlike that normally to be found on inland waterways. For much of the summer the water is placid, but when the prevailing strong wind – *Le Mistral* – is blowing from the mussel and oyster beds along the NW shore to the sea, very sizeable waves can develop and craft run the risk of damage or of being blown on to the sandbanks of Le Toc. The *Mistral* can raise heavy seas surprisingly quickly, out of a fine blue sky. Navigation was simplicity itself during my first four visits, but in September 1982 the Étang was in a furious mood when we made a passage from Frontignan to Marseillan in a hire cruiser. After waiting overnight for the wind to drop, we attempted the crossing at dawn only to find visibility reduced to nothing by clouds of spray. Setting out once more in the afternoon, after taking local advice, we experienced a very bumpy crossing which literally caused the glass of the saloon windows to burst from the frames. The navigation authority forbids certain of the Canal du Midi hire cruisers (especially narrowboats imported from Britain) to enter the Étang. Much of the time, however, it is difficult to believe that special precautions must be taken.

Use of Maritime Chart 5729, while not essential, is recommended. It shows a navigation channel virtually across the centre of the Étang, for a direct passage between the Canal du Midi and the Canal du Rhône à Sète. From **Les Onglous** (Canal du Midi) to **Marseillan** is about 2km, running directly between the lighthouses at each end. Since establishment of a secondary hire base by Blue Line Cruisers in 1970, the little port of Marseillan has become very popular. Space for visiting craft in the rectangular harbour is often limited, but moorings are always available in the new port to the left of the twin lighthouses. (Be sure to enter via the northern side of the stone breakwater.) Recent years have seen a growing trend to make a substantial charge for overnight stays in the more popular harbours. During 1989, 24 hours in Marseillan cost 90F for a 12m cruiser. Fuel, water and the use of a 2.5 tonne crane. As well as shellfish, Marseillan is devoted to the manufacture of Noilly Prat, a blend of Languedocian white wines and 40 secret herbs. Much of the five-year process takes place in the town, before completion at the firm's bottling plant in Marseille, and visitors are welcomed at the quayside cellars. Here also is the Château du Port, the elegant stone mansion of a wine grower, restored since 1965 to create a friendly hotel and restaurant catering for boating families. The nearby town centre is well equipped with shops and open market. Most convenient is the supermarket just beyond the top of the harbour. From Marseillan it is possible to make a car excursion to the fascinating region of the **Upper River Hérault** (about 36km to **Clermont l'Hérault**). Among places on the itinerary are **Le Lac de Salagou**, a beautiful reservoir with beaches and water sports; **La Grotte de Clamouse**, a series of caves with extraordinary formations and deposits, discovered in 1945 and opened to the public in 1964; the **Cirque de Mourèze**, an ancient rock village with a vast jumble of boulders in a variety of strange shapes; **St-Guilhem-le-Désert**, the finest Romanesque village in Languedoc; and the **Gorges of the Hérault**, between St-Guilhem and **La Grotte des Demoiselles**. Full details of all these appear in the green *Michelin Guide Causses*.

The next port along the western shore of the Étang is **Mèze**, similar to Marseillan but even more lively and colourful. Arrive in mid-August and you may find the town *en fête*, with noisy jousting contests in the harbour and the streets filled with fairground rides. Celebrations will continue until well after midnight. Moorings are reserved for visiting craft at the right of the entrance to the little harbour, congested with private pleasure craft and small fishing boats. Excellent fish restaurants are close by, and there is even a small sandy beach (*plagette*) though the presence of big jellyfish is rather a deterrent to bathing. Quite different in character is **Bouzigues** at the NW corner of the lagoon, a sleepy village of whitewashed stone houses. The small recently created harbour should not be entered in windy conditions. It is also rather shallow – little more than 1.3m draft should be relied on. It is related that when a band of English landed at Sète in

1710, a single shot was enough to make the inhabitants of Bouzigues run off in terror.

In a somewhat forbidding industrial zone, the Canal du Rhône à Sète (Chapter 62) begins its journey across the Camargue at the NE corner of the Étang. It is a short run from here to **Sète** itself, situated at the foot of Mont St-Clair, long ago a Mediterranean island. Little existed here until the site was selected as a port for the Canal du Midi in 1666. It has grown into a French Salt Lake City: the seventh biggest seaport in the country. There is a temptation to liken the elegant stone façades of buildings lining the main canal to Venice: but Sète does have its own quite distinct character. A friend returned from a visit to the fish market, excitedly exclaiming 'It's just like the Bible down there!' Certainly, for sardines, tunny and a wide range of seafood this is the centre of the industry in Languedoc. The locals are noisy and Latin in temperament, speaking their own version of French with a strong, almost Spanish, accent. This is no place to improve your facility with the language if you wish to create a good impression in Paris. At various times throughout the summer grandstands appear along the banks of the Canal de Sète for a performance of the chief sporting activity: jousting from galley-shaped rowing boats. Such celebrations were known elsewhere in medieval times, and major contests usually honour an event or person. For examples, a series of tournaments was staged in 1548–50 in Lyon to mark the accession of Henry II and Catherine de Medici; and the foundation of Sète is remembered each July 27. Distinct regional styles still to be found include Lyonnaise (Rhône and Loire); Nordist (Merville, Arras, Ors, Étreux and Lille); Parisienne; Isle-sur-Sorgue; Strasbourgeoise; and Languedocienne (from Agde to Grau du Roi). But no one does it with more panache than the Sètoises. The craft are elaborately decorated with painted swags and tassels and carry a small band of Moorish trumpets and drums to encourage the jousters, who attempt to knock their opponent off his platform as the boats are rowed furiously at each other. The eventual victor makes a triumphant lap of honour in a speedboat.

Entrance to the town from the Étang is through a pair of opening bridges, lifted in the morning and afternoon to provide access for a mêlée of craft. Most hire cruisers will just be able to pass under at any time. Potential moorings all seem to belong to someone or other and the most likely free space will be found by turning left to the quay near the railway station. A Canal Maritime, with two further swing bridges, is the route to follow for the sea, with water, fuel, crane and restaurant at the Société Nautique in the Vieux Bassin where hundreds of pleasure boats and fishing vessels are moored. Passenger ships cross to Tangier. Fine sandy beaches will be found bordering the N108, which runs for 15km along the SE shore of the Étang de Thau and is known as the Plage de la Corniche. In my experience, Sète is an uncomfortable town to stay in for any length of time, the quays being lashed by constant wash from commercial craft or outboard-powered fishing punts that totally ignore any notion of a speed limit. After one night, we could scarcely wait to return to the Étang and lie peacefully at anchor far offshore.

62 · Canal du Rhône à Sète

Carte Guide: *Canaux du Midi*
From the Étang de Thau near Sète to Beaucaire on the Rhône (connection with the main Rhône navigation now closed): 98km with 1 lock. Junctions are made with the Mediterranean at Frontignan (closed to pleasure craft); Palavas-Les-Flots, via the Grau de Palavas Branch (headroom limited; via the River Lez to Port Ariane, on the edge of Lattes, 6km, 1 lock; at Carnon (headroom limited); and at Le Grau-du-Roi via the River Vidourle or the Maritime Channel from Aigues-Mortes; and with the Petit Rhône via the Canal de St-Gilles (Chapter 56).
Some people may consider this waterway to be rather dull, for throughout it penetrates flat marshland on the borders of Western Europe's most important wilderness area, the Camargue. Its course from Sète to

One of several small ports on the shores of the Étang is Mèze.

A jousting contest in the middle of Sète.

Aigues-Mortes lies through the centre of vast salt lakes, a short distance inland from the coast. The navigation channel is provided with stone banks and a towpath. After Aigues-Mortes it heads inland along the northern side of the Camargue with tree-lined reaches through St-Gilles, ultimately arriving at its terminus in Beaucaire, on the shores of the Rhône. Features to be long remembered are sunsets over the *étangs*, teeming with fish; the little wooden houses of fishermen who stretch nets from one side of the canal to the other; a very rich animal and plant life including flamingoes, wild white horses and black bulls; and the traditional life-style of the Camargue cowboys, *les gardians*. Virtually lock-free, long distances can be cruised in a day if necessary. The greatest interest centres on the Sète – Aigues-Mortes section, with easy access to the beaches at a number of points. The final 49km is somewhat featureless but for St-Gilles and the twin towns of Beaucaire and Tarascon are of interest.

Brief history While the Canal du Midi was under construction in the late 17th century, the States of Languedoc began creating a link from the Étang de Thau towards the Rhône by improving medieval channels through the salt lakes to Aigues-Mortes. The navigation was known as the Canal des Étangs. More than a century of vacillation intervened before a plan was adopted in 1777 to build the Canal de Beaucaire as a link between Aigues-Mortes and the Rhône. Work ceased during the Revolution but eventually reached its successful conclusion in 1808. The whole route is now known as the Canal du Rhône à Sète.

Commercial traffic declined from 250,000 tonnes in 1974 to 22,000 tonnes by 1978. Various improvements saw an increase to 77,500 in 1981, and at the time of writing a three-phase plan has been started to enlarge the waterway to 4,500 tonne push-tow capacity, at a cost of about £66 million. Work commenced in 1983 and includes construction of bypasses at Frontignan (now completed) and Aigues-Mortes (1994), widespread channel dredging and bridge raising, and the removal of a number of tight bends.

Entry to the waterway from the Étang de Thau is at a somewhat desolate spot, with distant views of Sète's industrial zone and a boatyard to the left of the groynes of loose rocks. Arriving from the lagoon, home in on a series of silvery storage tanks. Moorings are possible just before the D20 road bridge. The proprietor of a ramshackle bar/restaurant kindly allowed me to use his telephone, and we were prompted to book a table for lunch, in anticipation of an experience rather than *haute cuisine*. When we returned the place was packed with workmen. As so often happens in France, the meal was one of the best of the holiday: including quantities of red wine, the final cost was a fraction of what we had been paying elsewhere. Just before the N108 road bridge there is a junction with the **Canal de la Peyrade** (K96: distances are measured from Beaucaire) which once offered a route into Sète, avoiding the Étang: it is no longer open to boats. While you are likely to pass flocks of magnificent pink flamingoes in a lake on the right, the ecologists appear not to have been very active. and one pool is being filled with wrecked cars.

Extensive refineries provide a dominant first impression of **Frontignan** (K92.2), but the town has much more to offer. Life for boaters centres on the vertical lift bridge which is opened at certain times in mornings and afternoons (consult the adjacent notice for details). Good quayside moorings on the left bank each side of this obstacle may be used while waiting. Shops are close at hand as well as supplies of the famous Muscat wine, a sweet brownish liquid for which it is possible to acquire a distinct liking. Worth a visit is the church of St Paul, rebuilt in Gothic style in the 14th century, and the small town museum nearby. **Frontignan-Plage**, the local beach, is a short cycle ride of about 3km away. Mainly of fine sand, it is divided into a series of small bays of breakwaters.

Take care to avoid becoming ensnared in fishing nets which stretch from one side of the canal to the other; controlled by a pair of winding drums and a dinghy, they will be removed for the passage of craft. One regular place where they are used is on the outskirts of Frontignan, where the stone-sided waterway passes through the centre of the Étang d'Ingril. Although there are occasional cuts linking the canal with the lagoons, they are shallow and for use by small fishing craft only. A new large channel on the right serves as a bypass for Frontignan and connects with the Mediter-

ranean near Sète. Use is for commercial vessels only. At **Les-Aresquiers** (K86.6) it is possible to moor under a new concrete bridge and walk to a beach about 400m away. While the seashore restaurant here appears to be attractive, I have several times found it closed in the evening; possibly it only serves lunch. A more interesting overnight halt involves continuing across the Étang de Vic and Étang de Pierre Blanche, tying up on the right near the point where a prominent stone gateway is seen on the right. This is **Maguelone** (K78), an ancient settlement on a pine-clad hill by the sea, dating back to the 2nd century AD. A cathedral was erected in the 6th century and was finally disestablished on the orders of Richelieu in 1622. Some restoration was carried out in the 19th century and this important but forlorn structure is open to the public (9.30–11.30h and 15.00–18.00h daily). Little remains of the city but this great church surrounded by trees and vineyards. The entire coastline between Les-Aresquiers and Palavas-les-Flots is undeveloped apart from a few bungalows and camping sites in the dunes and offers some of the best beaches in Languedoc. Although isolated, they are popular during the summer with holidaymakers who drive the rough, sandy track that leads from Palavas. Many nudists gather here, especially SW of Maguelone. To approach from the canal, cycle or walk around the southern boundary of the cathedral grounds for about 800m. A floating pedestrian bridge with opening section powered by outboard motor, enables tourists to cross the waterway. During the season, a comic little train makes regular runs to the beach.

After crossing the Étang de l'Arnel (left) and the Étang du Prévost (right), the resort town of **Palavas-les-Flots** appears (K75.2). The River Lez flows across the navigation and down to the sea at a four-way junction controlled by lights. Watch out for the strong current which follows heavy rain. Large boats should moor at the Ponts et Chaussées depot on the canal, but craft with a headroom of less than 2.40m may pass under a bridge into the Lez and use excellent jetty moorings provided for visitors on the left. A large marina, opposite, is for the use of resident cruisers only. Established as a Customs fort and fishing village in the late 18th century, Palavas grew rapidly as a holiday town when a railway link was provided with the nearby city of **Montpelier** in 1872. Expansion has continued in recent times under the Languedoc-Roussillon Development Scheme. It is a lively and attractive town, very convenient for canal boaters, with fuelling facilities and numerous bars, restaurants and souvenir shops lining the banks of the river. Every imaginable variety of seafood is available. 300m below

Sunset over the salty lagoons near Palavas-les-Flots. Rich in fish life, these waters are sometimes fringed by clusters of nets.

a swing bridge, the river is spanned by a Transcanal 'Le Mickey', a chairlift (surely the only example of this form of waterway crossing in France?). Broad sandy beaches offer safe bathing. Fishing boats and picturesque Mediterranean dories throng the quays. Entertainment includes a large funfair and periodic waterborne jousting contests. Severe flooding inundated the town in the late autumn of 1982.

Lately it has been possible to turn left out of the canal to ascend the River Lez to **Port Ariane**, a marina surrounded by a modern housing development, on the outskirts of **Lattes**. One lock, La Troisième, is passed en route. After crossing the Étang de Pérols, a four-way junction leads, left, to a hire boat base and marina in the **Canal du Hangar** (K70.6). This is the recommended mooring for the nearby resort of **Carnon**. A route to an alternative pleasure boat harbour and the sea via the **Canal du Grau de Carnon** is restricted to small craft under 1.20m headroom. The much expanded town has extensive beaches. To the left is the vast Étang de Mauguio, on whose shores you will see lines of conical fishing nets. Towards the sea, the skyline is dominated by the aggressively modern pyramid-shaped apartment blocks of **La Grande Motte**, a thriving and surprisingly well established 'new' resort. To visit, moor by the transformer station (K64.6) and walk or cycle about 3km.

Pairs of guillotine gates with traffic lights prevent the **River Vidoule** from flooding into the canal (K55). Boats with a headroom of about 2m can make a circular diversion by turning under the towpath bridge, right, and following the Vidoule through two *étangs* to the fishing port of **Le Grau-du-Roi**, once more joining the Canal du Rhône à Sète via the Maritime Channel to Aigues-Mortes. This excursion is safe for boats drawing up to 1m. Pontoon moorings are provided for visiting boats. Privately-owned cruisers can continue through Le Grau-du-Roi, past numerous quayside seafood restaurants and through a swing road bridge (opened at intervals throughout the day) to join the Mediterranean. Good sandy beaches are to be found in the town or eastwards (for nudists) at **Les Baronnets**, beyond the Espiguette lighthouse. A short sea passage to the east leads to the admirable aquatic town of Port-Camargue where there are berths for 4,000 craft, waterside holiday homes, shops and restaurants. Although confirmed inland boaters, we thoroughly enjoyed our brief stay here. **Aigues-Mortes** (K50.8) is one of the most exciting towns in Southern France. Established in 1240 by King Louis IX (St Louis), it provided him with a Mediterranean seaport from which to lead a Crusade to Palestine. His fleet of 38 ships set sail in August 1248, the King being accompanied by his Queen, two brothers, the Counts of Arles and Anjou, the Cardinal Legate and a large retinue. A second crusade was launched in May 1270. Louis was never again to see France, for he died of the plague in Tunis. Aigues-Mortes is built in the form of a square and surrounded by stone ramparts about 10m high with a perimeter of 1,750m. There are 10 gates and 14 towers including the massive Tour de Constance, 33m in height with 7m thick walls. From the top are excellent views over the pantiled rooftops to the canals and marshes below. An eight-year-old Protestant girl, Marie Durand, was imprisoned here for 38 years (1730–68). Although now much frequented by tourists (it was nearly deserted in the early 1970s), Aigues-Mortes contrives to retain the atmosphere of a medieval fortified city rather better than Carcassonne. The bustling shops mostly serve the community that still lives there. St Louis is remembered by a statue in the main square, where the tourist office is housed in a pleasing stone-roomed building. Good moorings (payment demanded) have been provided on the Maritime Channel, the length of the western wall, with the prospect of sailing barges and other craft opposite. If passing through in the direction of the Rhône you should hoot for a railway swing bridge to be opened at the canal junction. Further short-term moorings will be found in the basin beyond, with fuel available from a nearby garage. A canal bypass was opened in 1994.

An expedition to the heart of the **Camargue** can be arranged from here. Our party of eight once hired the local taxi: we brought a picnic lunch and the driver supplied the wine from his own vineyard. (The taxi doubled as an ambulance, but we were assured that no one would fall ill while we spent the day enjoying ourselves.) This method offers the benefit of acquiring an expert local guide who will take you to the best locations for sighting flamingoes, black bulls and wild horses. Covering about 480km² west of the Rhône Delta, this land of lakes and marshes is one of the most important wetland habitats in Europe. Introduction of fresh water for cultivation of rice in paddy fields and chemical pollution present a threat to the unique wild-

Aigues-Mortes and the Tour de Constance. This fortified town was built by Louis IX and is completely encircled by walls.

life. But thanks to the work of conservationists, like Swiss industrialist Dr Luc Hoffman who founded the Tour de Valat biological research station in 1954, the area is protected from the worst effects of the late 20th century. Perhaps you will get closest to the spirit of the Camargue from the saddle: horses can be hired from numerous ranches. Do not be surprised to encounter cowboys more real than their American counterparts; or specimens of the bright green preying mantis; or great heaps of salt, evaporated from the brackish water. The Camargue is a strange, desolate and utterly captivating world. For further suggestions on places to visit, consult the green *Michelin Guide Provence* (in English). Aigues-Mortes lies 8km inland via the Maritime Channel. Looking across the lagoons and salt pans, it is easy to understand its name of 'Dead Waters'. Another industry in evidence is the Lunel wine firm. The sea is reached at the charming fishing port of **Le Grau-du-Roi** (see above).

East of Aigues-Mortes, note on the right the entrance lock to the **Canal du Bourgidou**, one of a complicated network of navigable channels intersecting the Camargue but not available to the public. The Canal du Rhône à Sète now heads inland. From the level of a cruiser it seems rather dull, straight and reedy. But stand on the roof or moor up and you will be rewarded by views of rice fields and the foothills of the Cevennes. Looking back from the bridge at **Gallician** (K39.2, small marina), Aigues-Mortes' Tour de Constance can be seen in the far distance. Among the shops in this village is a wine retailer and the much extended restaurant Chez Colette.

Craft bound for the Rhône must take a right-hand fork (K29.8) into the **Canal de St-Gilles** (see Chapter 56). Long ago **St-Gilles** (K24) was a seaport, served by the Petit Rhône and visited by ships from all parts of the Mediterranean. Now that the canal no longer connects with the Rhône at Beaucaire, commercial traffic is virtually extinct. There are substantial numbers of hire cruisers based here and at the terminus. One of several self-styled 'Gateways to the Carmargue', St-Gilles has modern wine-processing plants (that look more like a petrol refinery) opposite a broad quay from which hire craft operate.

A paving, planting and lighting scheme carried out in 1987 transformed the waterfront. Although never likely to achieve the chicness of St Tropez, this canalscape presents an animated scene when the locals arrive for their evening stroll in mid-summer. In 1990, it was decided to double mooring capacity by installing pontoons for 60 boats on the opposite bank, where another promenade will be built. A pedestrian bridge is to connect the two developments. Now there is talk of excavating a 500 boat-capacity basin on the site of the present distillery. This scheme will include waterside housing in the style of Port Camargue and cost an estimated 70 million francs. St-Gilles seems set to become one of the leading inland ports of France! I spent two weeks carrying out boat maintenance in the town during 1989, eating at the splendid Hotel du Cours (near the main crossroads). A bullfight was staged one afternoon in the arena behind the Blue Line yard: as proof that French versions of this barbaric activity can be quite as repulsive as the Spanish variety, a storm drain entering the canal alongside my mooring was soon bright red with blood!

Restaurants serve a local speciality, *Boeuf à la Gardiane*, beef casserole with onions, olives, garlic, tomatoes and red wine: the variety we sampled was unappetizing and we dubbed it 'cowboy stew'. The town is said to owe its origins to St-Giles, who arrived during the 8th century in Provence from his native Greece aboard a raft. Living as a forest hermit, he struck up a relationship with an albino deer which one day was chased by a large hunting party led by the Visigoth King. Giles intervened and was himself shot in the leg. The King was greatly impressed by this holy man and finally persuaded him that an abbey should be built on the site of his dwelling. Giles travelled to Rome to obtain papal recognition of his foundation and was provided with a parting gift of two doors for the new church. These he cast into the Tiber and they duly made their way to the Rhône Delta, timing their arrival to exactly coincide with Giles' return in France! In 1209, the papal legate was assassinated at the very doors of the abbey, resulting in the atrocities of the Albigensian Crusade. The abbey that now stands in St-Gilles dates from the 12th century and has been extensively rebuilt. Its west front features three doorways with Romanesque arches and some wonderful stone carvings depicting the Life of Christ, completed between 1180 and 1240. St Giles' tomb is in an ancient 12th century crypt.

The canal continues in a somewhat featureless but not unattractive way to **Bellegarde** (K13.2), where there is a woodland snackbar by the Pont d'Arles. All shops in the town about 1km distant. **Nourriguier lock** (K7.7) is a large chamber, mechanized and operated by boats' crews by pushing just two buttons in the control cabin. You are requested to write down details of your passage. **Beaucaire** (K0.7) is entered through a briefly industrial area, but it soon becomes evident that this likeable town is worth making a diversion from the through navigation. Good moorings in a broad basin, where a hire fleet is established. At the far end the canal turns sharply to the right before arriving at its terminus by the disused Beaucaire lock. A junction with the Rhône has been out of service since the mid-1970s when river levels were altered. Plans have been published to reinstate a link with the Rhône, but this is unlikely to be of use to boats wishing to navigate more than a short length of the river. From the 13th century until the coming of the railway in the 19th, Beaucaire held one of Europe's greatest fairs each July: 300,000 crowded into the town, while ships brought goods from throughout the Mediterranean and the Atlantic Coast. All manner of sideshows and performers provided entertainment. These vibrant times are recalled in a Museum of Old Beaucaire in the Rue Barbès. We discovered a rather smaller but busy open-air market on Ascension Day. The old and narrow streets are a delight, with stone archways and a wealth of cast-iron embellishment. The castle ruins, surrounded by an 11th century wall, feature a Triangle Tower providing a magnificent view over the Rhône to the mighty fortress of **Tarascon**. Guarding the eastern border of Provence, Tarascon is without doubt one of the finest medieval, *châteaux* in France and the tour is a fascinating experience. Enlarged to its present state by Good King René in the 15th century, the castle rises sheer from the rocky bank of the Rhône. Although unfurnished, the beautifully proproportioned rooms give a good impression of the royal lifestyle 500 years ago. Much later, it was used as a prison; English captives were held there during the Seven Years' War and under Napoléon. Carved stone inscriptions vividly recall these times: for example that by a London River lighterman taken from the sloop Zephyr and incarcerated for 16 months from August 1778. Open throughout the year, the castle tours start daily at 10.00, 11.00, 14.00, 15.00, 16.00 and 17.00 with a 9.00 visit in summer. It is closed on Tues, May 1 and Dec 25.

Beaucaire is a convenient centre from which to take a bus to Arles and Avignon. Further excursions are listed under those towns, in Chapter 55.

63 • River Baïse

Carte Guides: *Midi* (Éditions Grafocarte) or *Midi Camargue Aquitaine* (Éditions du Breil)

From the River Garonne at St-Léger to the present terminus at Valence-sur-Baïse: 63km with 21 locks, one of which is a 2-rise staircase. Navigation originally continued for a further 21km with another 9 locks to a terminus at Saint-Jean-Poutge. Normal entry to the waterway is via the short branch (2-rise staircase lock) off the Canal Latéral à la Garonne at Buzet.

A deliciously attractive little river navigation, restored from complete dereliction between 1988 and 1997. The middle reaches pass through the Albret region, with the town of Nérac at its centre. It is justly popular with hire cruisers. Some of the artificial lock cuts are very narrow and with little solid bank protection. Until this is remedied, there will be a tendency for the channel to silt up, especially after flooding. Upstream to Lavardac, draft is officially quoted as 1.50m (optimistic at several lock entrances); beyond there, it is only 1.00m. This could be reduced in a dry season. Most locks are electrically self-operated by boaters who must insert a 'smart card' in the chamber-side console. Such cards are available from the staircase lock at Buzet Junction. This state-of-the-art system is fairly reliable, although a telephone link at each lock will pro

duce an engineer, should the apparatus fail. With its succession of delightful and historic towns and villages, a return trip up the Baïse can easily be stretched into a relaxing week.

History Rudimentary navigation using small flat-bottomed craft on the lower part of the river as far as Lavardac dates from the 13th century. Under Henri IV, five wooden flash locks with associated weirs (Buzet, Vianne, Lavardac, Bapaume and Nérac) improved matters, (1598-1600), although beyond Lavardac the waterway was extremely shallow for four or five months of each year. Several schemes to extend navigation in the late 18th century came to nothing. Conditions were described in 1830 as 'archaic'.

Between 1835 and 1839, new locks were installed to enable craft to reach Condom. In order to increase freight capacity to the river's leading port at Lavardac, locks were enlarged there and at Vianne to 31.40m x 5.20m. A further extension to the Saint-Jean-Poutge head of navigation had been achieved by 1877. In 1852, construction was completed of the short branch to the new Canal Latéral à la Garonne at Buzet. The final improvement, in 1881, was a junction lock at St Léger, where the Baïse empties into the Garonne.

By the middle of the 19th century, it was commonplace to see up to 90 barges loading or unloading in Lavardac, in addition to those that were passing through. At its peak, the river carried around 130,000 tons of freight each year. Payloads of 150 tonnes could reach Vianne; with 100 tonnes to Lavardac. Beyond that point, smaller locks and a draft reduced to 1.00m restricted barges to just 75 tonnes. In 1878, the two leading barge companies on the Baïse employed about 200 people between them. All traffic was hauled by horses or mules until the introduction of steam power (paddles or propellers) in 1881.

1905 saw the end of flour milling on the waterway and thereafter tonnages declined. By 1930, all horse-drawn craft had been replaced by motor barges, which in 1932 conveyed about 40,000 tonnes, including wine, timber, cereals, gravel, sand and flour. The last load on the upper river, a consignment of gravel aboard M. René Larrose's boat *St Jacques* reached Condom from St Léger in January 1952. The following month, an unprecedented flood destroyed lock gates throughout the waterway, resulting in abandonment of the navigation above Lavardac.

Utter dereliction over the next 35 years saw lock cuts increasingly choked by silt and vegetation, and several lock chambers were obstructed by small hydro-electric plants. Restoration has not yet reached the uppermost 9 locks between Valence-sur-Baïse and Saint-Jean-Poutge. It is doubtful if they will be returned to service, as there are few obvious attractions for pleasure craft in these deserted reaches.

A lock marks the junction of the Baïse and the River Garonne at **St-Léger**. Most craft using this lowest part of the Baïse will be doing so to reach the Lower Lot, where restoration and lock building was well advanced in 1999. The Lot/Garonne junction lies a short distance downstream at Nicole/Aiguillon. Lock 2 on the Baïse, **Buzet-sur-Baïse** (K4.7) is situated alongside a grim cellulose factory. Moor beyond the lock, right bank for access to the town (see under Canal Latéral à la Garonne). Soon after, on the right, a short branch with 2-rise locks, provides a connection with the Canal. If ascending, hoot to alert the keeper who is responsible for supplying 'swipe cards', required for working most locks on the Baïse. 7km of lonely river winds through a steep-sided valley, past dense tree growth. Debris caught in branches shows how flooding can raise levels 1-2m. The Baïse passes beneath an aqueduct carrying the Canal Latéral à la Garonne close to its locks 39 and 40. Suitable moorings for the attractive little 'Bastide' town of **Vianne** (K15.2) are found by a ruined mill, right, below the weir or, more conveniently, on a quay (water and electricity) upstream of the lock. One of two gateways through fortification walls provides access to a large central square with ample shopping facilities (Friday evening market). A glassworks, situated on the upstream outskirts, sells lamps, vases etc, many items in a distinctive Art Nouveau style.

Lavardac (K17.9) lies on the left bank beyond Lock 4 and a substantial road bridge. Good vertical mooring quay, which a century ago would have been packed with dozens of barges. Among the full range of facilities are restaurants and an excellent fish shop where fresh oysters may be obtained at a bargain price. Note the stone carving (1838) of a sailing barge outside the old town hall. Extensive street market on Wednesdays. Not far beyond, is the confluence with the **River Gélise** (no longer navigable) on which is situated **Barbaste**, notable for its Roman bridge and massive 12/13th century fortified mill. A visit on foot from Lavardac (about 30 mins) is recommended. Friday morning market.

Throughout the Baïse, restoration works have been careful to retain as many bankside trees as possible, resulting in a dense leaf canopy over the narrow lock cuts, where great care is required to pass other boats. Waiting laybys are provided at several points. La Chaumière d'Albret restaurant beyond the very fine **Pont de Bordes** railway viaduct (K18.5), offers moorings and a good selection of menus.

Écluse **St-Crabary** (K20.6) is the first lock with a width reduced to 4.15m. Its keeper's cottage is a *gîte rural*. Most such buildings on the river have

12/13th century fortified mill on the River Gélise at Barbaste, a short distance from the junction with the River Baïse.

long been in private ownership and considerable opposition was voiced by their occupants when restoration plans were announced. Boaters should respect their privacy and moor only where invited (see the *Carte Guide*). Views are restricted by dense forest throughout the lower waterway, although several large *châteaux*, in varying stages of dereliction, will be glimpsed in this area.

Locks appear at **Sorbet**, No 6 (K22.4), with a cluster of stone houses, hydro-electricity plant in the mill and caves; and **Bapaume**, No 7, (K26). Soon after, we reach the jewel of the Baïse–**Nérac** (K27.4), capital of the Albret and famous for its association with Henri IV, whose *château*, high above the river, has a notable long balcony (local history museum). The waterfront, comprising many restored half-timbered buildings is really charming. Moorings on both banks between the two bridges. Excursions are available on a replica barge. A maze of narrow streets awaits exploration. Facilities are good, with a thriving street market on Saturday mornings. Beyond the town is the riverside Parc de la Garenne, containing a pretty gazebo and a grotto sheltering the Fleurette fountain, a memorial to a young girl who allegedly drowned herself when forced to end a liaison with King Henri.

Écluse 9, **Nazareth** (K29.3) is a magical place with dense vegetation, a cottage built into a cliff and a nearby ruined *château*. Well-groomed goats perch on the bollards. Note the disused iron/timber capstans, originally installed for working the lock gates. Hardly a hamlet will be passed in the deep countryside that now follows past Écluse 10, **La Saubole** (K32), 11, **Recaillau** (K33.7), 12 **Pacheron** (K37.2), 13, **Lapierre** (K39.4) and 14, **Vialères** (K42.5). After Recaillau, the wooded scenery characteristic of the Baïse since Buzet, is gradually replaced by open fields.

It is well worth mooring at the bridge-side quay, (water and electricity) a little beyond lock 15 (K44.6), to walk uphill into the enigmatic small town of **Moncrabeau**, on the border between the Tarn-et-Garonne and Gers *départements*. As recently as 1995, the lock chamber was completely obstructed by a small electricity-generating plant. At least since the 18th century, Moncrabeau has been the self-proclaimed World Capital of Liars. The tradition continues with the annual crowning of the Liar King, (first Sunday of August), a position hotly contested as inhabitants vie with each other to invent increasingly fanciful versions of local history. Unfortunately, some aspects of these tales could

quite possibly be true: the visitor will have great difficulty in sorting fact from fiction. Roadside information boards guide you through the streets where barges used to moor before river levels fell 50m. Seek the look-out point, from which, on a clear day, it is possible to see the Straits of Gibraltar. Canal museum, swimming pool and important collection of Impressionist paintings (apply at the Hôtel de Ville).

Further locks, 16, **Autiège** (K49.3), 17, **Beauregard** (K49.3) and 19, **Peyroutéou** (K53.8), lead to the sizable town of **Condom**. Once a leading river port, Condom remains a centre of Armagnac production (museum). It is an agreeable town, with good shopping facilities and restaurants. The cathedral merits investigation. Plenty of mooring space at quays on both banks in the centre. Tripping boat and small craft for hire. Public parkland extends to Lock 19, **Gauge** (K54.6), where the former mill house is now an agreeable restaurant. Paddles (80 turns to lift halfway) and gates are manually worked by boat crews. The narrow cut beyond is shaded by a 'tunnel' of mature alders.

Unusually for a river navigation, Lock 20, **Graziac** (K58) comprises a 2-rise staircase, where the stonework of chambers and bridge has been beautifully restored. As it is manually operated, requiring a degree of heavy labour, it is perhaps fortunate that the authorities do not trust pleasure boaters to work through unaided: a team of keepers is on hand.

Shortly before reaching the present head of navigation, a halt should be made at a bridge-side quay to visit the well-preserved **Abbaye de Flaran**, an important 12th century Cistercian foundation. The monks have departed, but the complex is open to the public. Among the sights is a herb garden and a large Gallo-Roman mosaic floor.

Every waterway ending in a terminus benefits from having some form of objective: the Baïse is well served in this respect by the little cliff-top Bastide town of **Valence-sur-Baïse** (K62), founded by the Cistercians in the 13th century. Good moorings with water and electricity immediately before a road bridge. There are ramparts, a Spanish gate and a central square with arcaded buildings. Navigation beyond this point should not be attempted, as the unrestored river is cluttered with shoals and fallen trees. Exploration by bicycle along farm tracks (travel quickly to avoid angry Alsatians) will bring you to the first derelict lock, whose chamber has been blocked by an ugly little concrete power station.

APPENDICES

Guides and Maps

Carte Guides, which are published by Éditions Grafocarte unless otherwise stated, are essential for exploration of French waterways, providing detailed maps, tourist information and all facilities required by the boater. These, and other waterways publications may be obtained at waterside chandleries in France or by mail order from Imray, Laurie, Norie & Wilson Ltd., Wych House, The Broadway, St. Ives, Huntingdon, Cambs., PE17 4BT, England. Tel. 01480 462114. Fax 01480 496109.

Cruising enjoyment is enhanced by the *Michelin Atlas Routier*, containing maps of the whole of France on a scale of 1:200,000. These do not, however, mark locks, for which larger scale maps are necessary. The best type is the *Carte Topographique* (1:25,000), published by Institut Géographique National (IGN), 107, rue de la Boetie, 75008 Paris.

A number of books listed here are long out of print, but it is well worth trying to find secondhand copies. One firm, specialising in such waterways publications, with regular catalogues and a mail order service, is M & M Baldwin, 24, High Street, Cleobury Mortimer, Kidderminster, West Midlands, DY14 8BY. Tel. & Fax 01299 270110.

Carte Guides de Navigation Fluvials (Éditions Grafocarte, 125, rue Jean-Jacques Rousseau, BP 40, F-92132, Issy-les-Moulineaux Cedex, France.) All carry text in French and English, sometimes additionally German and Dutch. Regularly updated.
1. *La Seine Paris to the Sea.*
2. *La Seine Paris to Marcilly.*
3. *La Marne* Paris to Vitry-le-François via Marne Lat. Canal.
4. *L'Yonne*
6. *Canaux du Centre* Loing, Briare, Loire Lat., Centre.
7. *Canal du Nivernais.*
8. *Champagne-Ardenne* Lower Meuse from Namur, Canal des Ardennes, Canal de l'Aisne à la Marne, Canal Lat. à la Marne, Canal de la Marne à la Saône.
10. *La Saône et la Seille*
11. *Canal du Midi* Atlantic to the Mediterranean.
12. *Bretagne*
13. *Pays de la Loire*
14. *Nord-Pas-de-Calais* Dunquerque-Valenciennes, C. du Nord, C. de Calais etc.
16. *Le Rhône* Including Petit Rhône.
17. *Canal de la Marne au Rhin* Including C. des Houillères de la Sarre, C. du Rhône au Rhin (North Branch).
18. *Bourgogne Tome 1* Yonne, Nivernais & C. de Bourgogne.
21. *Carte de France* All French waterways.
24. *Picardie* Somme, C. du Nord, Sensée, St. Quentin, Oise, Lat. à l'Oise, Aisne, Lat. à l'Aisne, Sambre, de la Sambre à l'Oise.
25. *La Charente*
27. *Le Lot* (central isolated portion).
31. *Canal de Bourgogne*
32. *Canal du Rhône au Rhin*

Paris (Ourcq, St-Martin, St-Denis Canals)

Carte Guides Vagnon (Les Editions du Plaisancier, BP 27, 100, avenue Général Leclerc, 69641 Caluire Cedex, France). Text in French, English and German (sometimes additionally in Dutch).
1. *Midi Atlas* All French waterways.
2. *Doubs* Canal du Rhône au Rhin.
3. *Bourgogne-Centre-Nivernais*
5. *Rhône*
6. *Saône et Seille*
7. *Canaux du Midi* Atlantic to Mediterranean (includes lower Baïse).
8. *Meuse/Canal de l'Est*
10. *Bretagne et Loire Atlantique*
11. *Pays de la Loire et le Cher Navigable*
12. *Lorraine Est*
13. *Lorraine Ouest*

Carte Guides Crown Blue Line (Crown Blue Line, Le Grand Bassin, 11400 Castelnaudary, France).

Text in French, English, German.
Midi Camargue Aquitaine
Bourgogne, Franche-Comté
Loire/Nivernais
Bretagne
Alsace/Lorraine
Lot

Carte Guides Fluviaux EDB (Editions du Breil, Fitou/Le Breil, 11400 Castelnaudary, France). Text in French, English. German.
1. *Bretagne*
2. *Loire/Nivernais*
3. *Bourgogne/Franche-Comté*
4. *Alsace/Lorraine*
5. *Lot*
6. *Charente*
7. *Midi/Camargue/Aquitaine*. Includes all the Baïse.
8. *Champagne*
9. *Canal du Rhône au Rhin*.
10. *Pays de la Loire*.

Fluviocartes (Fluvial, Service Librarie, 64, rue J.J.Rousseau, 21000 Dijon, France). Text in French and German.
1. *Naviguer en Alsace*. The only *Carte Guide* to the canalised Rhine, Strasbourg to Rheinfelden (Switzerland), with the Colmar and North C. Rhône-Rhin Branches.

Enterprise Guides by Tony Paris. (Available from Imray Ltd). English text and especially useful for detailed restaurant reports.
1. *The Canals of the Midi*. Canal du Midi; Canal du Rhône à Sète.
2. *The Yonne and the Nivernais*.
3. *The Canal de Bourgogne* (Out of print).
4. *The Charente*.
5. *The Bourbonnais Route*. Seine to the Saône via C. Lat. à la Loire etc.

General Reading

There are many good guides (not specifically navigational) to regions through which waterways pass. Perhaps the most detailed are the *Green Michelin Guides*, covering the entire country. All appear in French; some are translated into English. Otherwise, titles should be selected from the stock of a bookshop with a good travel section.

No English-speaking visitor should consider travelling in France without *The A-Z Gastronomique: A Dictionary of French Food and Wine* by Fay Sharman, Brian Chadwick and Klaus Boehm (Macmillan). I have used this dozens of times to translate French restaurant menus and (astonishingly) have never once been able to fault it. As it appears to spend long periods out of print, it may be necessary to hunt down a secondhand copy.

Periodicals

Regular articles on French waterways and cruising appear in the following English-language monthly publications: *Motor Boats Monthly, Motor Boat & Yachting, Waterways World*. Also in the French-language *Fluvial* and *Navigation Intérieure* (alternate months).

Bibliography

Limits of space allow only for a selection of titles here. References to various out-of-print (but highly interesting and desirable) books are additionally made throughout the text.

Calvert, Roger. *Inland Waterways of Europe*. Flare Books, London 1975. 316pp, Illus. Outdated, but useful.

Chater, Melville. *Two Canoe Gipsies. Being an account of an 800 mile canal journey through Belgium, Brittany, Touraine, Gascony and Languedoc*. Bodley Head, London 1933. 230pp, Illus. This trip was undertaken for the *National Geographic Magazine*, hence the boat's name, *Nageoma*.

Clavel, Bernard. *Lord of the River*. Collins, London 1973. 255pp. Originally published in French in 1972 as *Le Seigneur du Fleuve*; a powerful novel of barge life on the Rhône in the 1840s.

Cooper, Bill & Laurel. *Watersteps Through France*. Adlard Coles Nautical, London, 1996. 238pp, Illus. Travelogue by converted barge.

Davis, Tony. *Cruising Through France with Bermuda II*. Pentland Press, Durham, 1995. 245pp, Illus. Travelogue by motor yacht.

Edwards-May, David. *Inland Waterways of France*. Imray, St Ives 1991. Illus. A new edition of the guide by E. E. Benest, totally updated and with maps of each waterway, distance tables etc.

Forester, C. S. *The Voyage of the Annie Marble*. John Lane, London 1929. 277pp, Illus. A really charming account of a cruise up the Seine and through the Loing and Orléans Canals to the Loire at Nantes.

Gibbings, Robert. *Coming Down the Seine*. Dent, London 1953. 217pp, Illus. A gentle journey from source to sea by rowing boat and cargo vessel. Notable for the fine woodcuts.

Goodwin, Richard. *Leontyne: by Barge from London to Vienna*. Collins, 1989. 219pp + colour illus. Includes Paris, Bourgogne and Doubs.

Harper, Mike. *Through France to the Med*. Cadogan, London 1983. 224pp, Illus. Practical guide to the French waterways, resulting from a trip in a Zulu fishing boat.

Lawson, Lyle (ed.). *Insight Guides, Waterways of Europe Special*. APA Publications, London, 1989. 450pp, Illus. Includes the most popular regions of France.

Liley, John. *France – the Quiet Way*. Stanford Maritime, London 1983. 159pp, Illus. A wryly amusing and thoughtful description of the French waterways, many photos illustrate the character of different regions.

Marchant, Vernon. *Notes on French Inland Waterways*. Cruising Association, Ivory House, St Katherine Dock, London, E1 9AT. 40pp. Basic information on routes and regulations.

Martin, Marian. *The RYA Book of EuroRegs for Inland Waterways*. Adlard Coles Nautical, London, 1998. 24pp. Illus. A pleasure boater's guide to CEVNI rules, navigation markers etc. *The European Waterways*. Adlard Coles Nautical, London, 1997. 175pp, Illus. A manual for first time users.

Massey, Hart. *Travels with Lionel: A Small Barge in France*. Gollancz, London, 1988. 192pp. Cruising throughout France. Entertaining.

McKnight, Hugh. *The Guinness Guide to Waterways of Western Europe*. Guinness Superlatives, London 1978. 240pp, Illus. The 44 page French section contains many colour photographs. *Slow Boat Through France*. Available from the author, 1991. *Avonbay's* first four years of French travels. 208pp Illus. colour and monochrome.

Millar, George. *Isabel and the Sea*. Century, London 1983. 408pp. First pub. 1948 and partly consisting of a voyage from England to the Mediterranean via the Seine, Canal du Loing, Canal de Briare, Canal Latéral à la Loire, Saône and Rhône. Excellent descriptions of the horse-drawn canal boats, which then worked in large numbers.

Morgan-Grenville, Gerard. *Barging into Burgundy*. David & Charles, 1975. 176pp, Illus. *Barging into France*. D & C, 1972. 215pp, Illus. *Barging into Southern France*. D & C, 1972. 239pp. Illus. Rather 'exciting' tales of the author's explorations aboard converted barge *Virginia-Anne*.

Murrell, T. & D. *Barging About in France*. Murrell/Dutch Barge Association, 1997. Useful guide to cruising with a barge.

Pilkington, Roger. *Small Boat in Southern France*. Macmillan, London 1965. 219pp, Illus. From the Saône to Bordeaux via the Midi. *Small Boat on the Meuse*. Macmillan, 1967. 214pp, Illus. From Belgium to the Marne. *Small Boat on the Upper Rhine*. Macmillan, 1971. 210pp, Illus. Includes all the French Rhine. *Small Boat Through France*. Macmillan, 1964. 211pp, Illus. Meuse, Marne, Seine, Yonne, Nivernais, Loire Latéral, Centre and Saône. *Small Boat to Alsace*. Macmillan, 1961. 214pp, Illus. Belgium to Strasbourg and Colmar, via Meuse, Marne-Rhine Canal and Rhône-Rhine Canal. *Small Boat to Luxembourg*. Macmillan, 1967. 230pp, Illus. From Belgium to the Moselle, via Sambre, Aisne Latéral, Ardennes and Meuse. *Small Boat in the Midi*. Pearson, Burton-on-Trent, 1989. 216pp + colour illus. *Waterways in Europe*. John Murray, London 1972; Tandem paperback 1974. 279pp, Illus. excellent survey with much information on places and moorings.

Rolt, L. T. C. *From Sea to Sea: The Canal du Midi*. Euromapping, 38170 Seyssinet, France, 1994. 237pp. Illus. Very competent history and guide by one of Britain's leading waterways writers.

de Roquette-Buisson, Odile. *The Canal du Midi*. Thames & Hudson, London 1983. 136pp, Illus. Lavish pictorial study translated from French, with much superb colour photography.

Rosenblum, Mort. *The Secret Life of the Seine*. Robson Books, London, 1994. 304pp. Living on a Boat in Paris.

Scarry, Huck. *Travels on a Barge*. Collins, London 1982. 69pp, Illus. Unusual study of barge life on French (and briefly some other) waterways, copious line drawings.

Srevenson, Robert Louis. *An Inland Voyage*. Chatto & Windus, 1878 and subsequent editions. 234pp. (1908 ed. Illus.) A canoe journey through Northern France, including the Sambre and Oise.

Taylor, Arthur R. *Spring on the Somme*. Constable, London, 1995. 212pp, Illus. Exploration of the whole river by rowing boat.

Vine, P. A. L. *Pleasure Boating in the Victorian Era*. Phillimore, Chichester 1983. 159pp. Illus. Survey of boating pioneers, including French navigations.

IN FRENCH

Aïn, Simone. *Toulouse-Cette (Sète) au Fil de l'Eau au Fil des Ans*. Printed by Imprimerie Technic Offset, 34680 St-Georges d'Orques. 1981. 72pp, Illus. A pictorial album (with historical material) to commemorate the tercentenary of the death of Riquet. Describes his Canal du Midi.

Beaudouin, François. *Bateaux des Fleuves de France*. Éditions de l'Éstran, Douarnenez, 1985. 238pp. Magnificent historical survey of all types of barges. Illus. drawings and photos.

Bonnamour, Louis. *La Saône, une Rivière, des Hommes*. Christine Bonneton, 21 bd Maréchal-Fayolle, 43000 Le Puy. 1981. 126pp, Illus. Historical survey of commercial carrying on the Saône; many old photographs and drawings.

Boudellal, M. and Poulet, S. *Gens de l'Eau. Rose et Georges Larrose, Couple de Bateliers des Canaux du Midi en Pays d'Oc*. Editions Garnier, 1980. 128pp, Illus. The story of one boat family on the Canal du Midi, fully illustrated with historical material.

Chabrol, Jean-Pierre. *La Fluviale*. Denoël, Paris, 1986. Colour photo album of commercial craft.

Clavel, Bernard. *Le Rhône*. Hachette, Paris 1979. 125pp, Illus. Erudite study with memorable colour pictures.

Davot, Monique. *Claire et Pascal, Enfants de Mariniers*. Flammarion, 1981. 32pp, Illus. Delightful picture story book in full colour about life on board a French *péniche*. Intended for children, but of compelling interest to all waterway enthusiasts.

Descombes, René. *Canaux et Batellerie en Alsace*. Le Verger, Strasbourg Illkirch, 1988. 192pp. Fully illus. colour and monochrome.

Didier, Louise (et al.) *Dictionnaire Marinier*. Bief Edition, St-Jean-de-Losne, France, 1998. 156pp, Illus. 2,400 French waterway terms explained.

Guide de la Navigation Intérieure. Éditions Berger-Levrault, Paris 1965. Vol. I, 617pp; Vol. II, 311pp. The vital book. Vol. I contains distance tables, lock dimensions, etc but the main interest is in Vol. II where all the waterways are indicated on detailed strip maps. Out of print and hence rare.

Guillet, Jacques. *La Batellerie Bretonne*. Éditions de l'Éstran, Douarnenez, 1989. 366pp. Massive illus. history of commercial barge traffic in Brittany.

Kroemer, Müller-Marein, Oplatka, Andrens and Weber. *La Seine et la Loire*. La Bibliothèque des Arts, Lausanne-Paris 1982. 224pp, Illus. Translated from German. Lavish pictorial with extensive text.

Henry, Marianne and Bernard. *Voyageurs aux Long Jours*. Arthaud, Paris 1982. 216pp, Illus. Lavish picure book with much colour. Mainly on French waterways with strong commercial traffic bias.

Lemare, Jacques. *Le Fleuve Charente de la Galiote au Day-Cruiser*. La Saintonage Littéraire, pont-l'Abbé, 17250 par Saint-Porchaire. 1977. 176pp, Illus. History, navigation and tourism on the River Charente.

Le Sueur, Bernard. *Batelleries et Bateliers de France*. Éditions Horvath, c. 1985. 208pp. Contains many historical illus. of working boats.

La Grande Batellerie, 150 Ans d'Histoire de la Compagnie Générale de Navigation – XIX et XXé Siècles. 168pp. Illus. Barge company history.

Lorenzo, Annie. *Professional? Marinier*. Massin, Paris, 1985. 96pp. Lives of the barge families. Colour illus.

Navigation Intérieure (Vol. 14, Encyclopedie Practique du Bateau). Éditions Maritimes et d'Outre Mer, 17 rue Jacob, 75006 Paris. 1979. 318pp, Illus. Rather patchy coverage by a number of waterway experts of the subject of inland boating in France.

Paon, Roger. *Marine de Rivière: Images de la Batellerie*. Éditions du Cabri. 208pp. Illus. history of French barges.

Pinchedez, Annette. *Le Logement du Marinier*. Musée de la Batellerie, Conflans-Sainte-Honorine, 1994. 40pp, Illus. Life on board a péniche.

Prudent, J. and Kühn, L. *Guide Fluvial, Questions et Résponses à l'Examen du Permis Fluvial*. Éditions Maritimes et d'Outre Mer, Paris 1981. 96pp, Illus. Practical handbook on boat handling, traffic signals, lock working etc.

Rolin, Jean. *Chemins d'Eau. Une Promenade sur les Canaux et les Rivières de France*. Éditions Maritimes et d'Outre-Mer, Paris 1980. 282pp. 2,000km of waterways explored on foot, bicycle and by barge.

Semet, Roger. *Le Temps des Canalous*. Éditions Calmann Lévy, 1972. Illus. Historical account of French boat families.

Le Tourism Fluviale en France. Ministère des Transports, Direction Générale des Transports Intérieures, Sous-Direction des Voies Navigables, 244 Boulevard St-Germain, Paris 7e, 1981. 28pp. Useful for regulations, addresses etc.

Tracol, Michel-André. *Quand le Rhône était un Fleuve*. Pub. by the author, available from MAT, 69 Ave. Gabriel-Péri, 26600 Tain-l'Hermitage. 1980. 144pp, Illus. Life and traffic on the Rhône before canalization. Many historical pictures.

Un Canal...Des Canaux. Picard, Paris, 1986. 416pp. Magnificent volume published in connection with the Paris Canals Exhibition of 1986. Colour illus.

Vagnon, Henri. *Code Vagnon Fluvial. Rivières et Lacs*. Les Éditions du Plaisancier, BP27, 69641 Caluire. 146pp, Illus. Practical guide to boat handling, traffic signals, lock working etc.

Vincelot, Henri. *Les Canaux de Bourgogne*. Rivages, Marseille, 1984. 128pp. Many colour illus.

Voies Navigables de France. Service de Propagande Édition, Information, Paris 1967. 480pp, Illus. All aspects of French waterways with emphasis on commercial trade. Useful for details of modernization then completed or planned.

Glossary of Waterways Terms

allège, Charente barge

amarrer, to moor

amont, upstream

anneau, mooring ring

argentat, extinct Dordogne sailing barge

ascenseur, vertical boat lift

automoteur, motorized freight barge

autoroute, motorway

aval, downstream

bâbord, port; left side

bac, ferry

bâche, small barge, mainly used for carrying sand, e.g. on the River Saône

bajoyer, bank, or side of a lock

balise, navigation marker

barque, small punt, e.g. as used in the marshland canals off the River Sèvre Niortaise

barrage, weir

barre, steering wheel

bassin de virement, winding hole, a widening of a canal where long craft can be turned

bateau-mouche, Paris passenger boat

batelier, commercial boatman

batellerie, the commercial boating fraternity

bief (originally *biez*), pound; a reach of any length between canal locks

bief de partage, summit level of a canal

bilander, type of dumb barge (see Chapter 27)

bitte, bollard

blin, small punt used in the marshes of the Brière, near Nantes

boulard, bollard

bouée, buoy or lifebelt

boussole, compass

brocante, bric-à-brac or antiques

busc, sill (of a lock)

cabane, extinct passenger barge (see Chapter 35)

cadole, former variety of Saône barge

cale, slipway

canot, boat's dinghy

chaland, barge

chemin de halage, towpath

chômage, stoppage; closure of locks or other part of a waterway for repairs

coche d'eau, water coach, an extinct passenger vessel

congé annuel, French habit of closing shops, restaurants etc for a month's holiday and usually coinciding with the height of the tourist season when maximum trade might have been expected.

conche, small marshland canal of the *Marais Poitevin* (see Chapter 50)

cornet, small flat-bottomed punt with upturned bows, used in the *Hortillonnages* at Amiens

crêperie, restaurant specializing in savoury and sweet pancakes (mainly Brittany)

cric, lock paddle

darse, dock

déclassé, describing a navigation closed to traffic but still preserved as a watercourse

dérivation, canal section on a river navigation; usually also a lock cut

deversoire, spillway, or side weir at a canal lock

digue, embankment or dike

ducs d' Alba, mooring piles, generally at the approach to a lock

écluse, lock

éclusier(e), lock keeper

écoutilles, hatch covers

écran radar, radar screen

flottage, system of floating logs (see Chapter 45)

flûte, type of barge of smaller dimensions than a *péniche*

fossé, small marshland canal of the *Marais Poitevin* (see Chapter 50)

Freycinet, the standard *péniche* gauge

gabare, lighter (barge)

galion, small extinct Charente sailing barge (see Chapter 51)

galiot, 19th cent. passenger boat, e.g. on River Seine

gardian, Camargue 'cowboy'

gouvernail, rudder

grau, channel linking salt lake with the sea, e.g. on the Canal du Rhône à Sète

gribanne, 19th cent. Somme barge

grue, crane

haut parleur, loudspeaker

hélice, propeller

hirondelle, fast passenger steamer on the River Loire (see Chapter 35)

Hortillonnages, market gardens at Amiens, intersected by a network of small waterways

inexplosible, 19th cent. steam passenger craft introduced to allay fears resulting from several spectacular boiler explosions

largeur, beam (width) of a boat

lavoir, public washhouse, often on the banks of rivers or canals

longeur, length of a boat

macaron, steering wheel (N France)

manivelle, windlass, or handle to open lock paddles or gates *marinier*, boatman, especially on a river

Le Mascaret, tidal bore on the Lower Seine

mât, mast

noued, knot

pardon, religious celebration and procession (Brittàny)

passerelle, footbridge

péniche, standard 38.5m barge of the Freycinet type

pente d'eau, water-slope, or device for overcoming changes in canal levels. Used instead of locks, e.g. Montech and Béziers

pigouille, punt pole (see Chapter 50)

piquet, mooring spike

plage, *plagette*, bathing 'beach', applied equally to river and coastal situations

plaisancier, pleasure boatman

plan incliné, inclined plane boat lift

point kilométrique, distance marker

port de plaisance, pleasure boat harbour or marina

portes, lock gates

portes marinières, navigation weir or flash lock

poupée, bollard or bitts, on a barge

pousseur, push tug boat

râcle, section of river forming a link between two portions of canal

radié, describing an abandoned navigation

rame, a tow (e.g. of barges being hauled through a tunnel)

relais nautique, pleasure craft mooring with facilities such as fuel and restaurant

remorqueur, tug boat

rigole, canal feeder or waterway in the *Marais Poitevin* (see Chapter 50)

Roannaise, Loire barge (see Chapter 35)

robinet, water tap

rove, steering wheel (Midi)

sablonnier, sand barge

sapine, old type of wooden barge

sapinette, former variety of small wooden barge

sas, chamber of a lock

sauterelle, small crane on a barge enabling crew to disembark when it is not possible to moor directly alongside the bank

savoyarde, former variety of Saône barge

sentine, extinct Loire barge (see Chapter 35)

seuil, sill of a lock

seysselande, former variety of Saône barge

sondeur, echo-sounder

Syndicat d'Initiative, tourist office

timonerie, wheelhouse

tirant d'air, height above water level of a boat; air draft

tirant d'eau, draft of a boat; depth below waterline

tirette, pole suspended over a navigation, which, when turned, activates a lock

toue, Loire barge (see Chapter 35)

trématage, overtaking of another boat

treuil, anchor winch

tribord, starboard; right side

tuyau, water hose

vanne, lock paddle

vedette, passenger launch

ventelle, lock paddle

vergée, extinct sailing barge of Loire region

Voies Navigables de France (VNF), official body responsible for most waterways

Saône steam tugs, from an early 20th century postcard. Note the pet fox on the Lynx.

Index